Frommer's®

Panama

3rd Edition

by Jisel Perilla

WILEY

Wiley Publishing, Inc.

Published by:

WILEY PUBLISHING, INC.

111 River St.

Hoboken, NJ 07030-5774

ISBN 978-0-470-89073-8 (cloth); ISBN 978-1-118-00110-3 (ebk); ISBN 978-1-118-00111-0 (ebk); ISBN 978-1-118-00112-7 (ebk)

Editor: Myka Carroll, with Kathleen Warnock
Production Editor: Jana M. Stefanciosa
Cartographer: Andrew Murphy
Photo Editor: Richard Fox
Production by Wiley Indianapolis Composition Services
Front cover photo: Couple snorkelling, Chapera island (Contadora), Las Perlas archipelago, Panama. ©Sergio Pitamitz / Robert Harding Picture Library / Masterfile
Back cover photo: Waterfall at Chiriqui Viejo River, Chiriqui, Panama ©Alfredo Maiquez / Lonely Planet Images

For information on our other products and services or to obtain technical support, please contact our Customer Care Department within the U.S. at 877/762-2974, outside the U.S. at 317/572-3993 or fax 317/572-4002.

Wiley also publishes its books in a variety of electronic formats. Some content that appears in print may not be available in electronic formats.

Manufactured in the United States of America

5 4 3 2 1

CONTENTS

List of Maps vi

1 THE BEST OF PANAMA 1

The Best of Natural Panama 1

The Best Beaches 3

The Best Adventures 4

The Best Day Hikes
& Nature Walks 6

The Best Bird-Watching 7

The Best Destinations
for Families 8

The Best Luxury Hotels
& Resorts 10

The Best Ecolodges & Wilderness
Resorts 11

The Best Small Hotels & B&Bs 13

The Best Restaurants 14

2 PANAMA IN DEPTH 16

Panama Today 17

Looking Back at Panama 18

A FEAST OF LANGUAGES 22

The Lay of the Land 23

TIPS FOR SEEING WILDLIFE 25

Panama in Popular Culture: Books,
Music & Films 25

Eating & Drinking in Panama 27

3 PLANNING YOUR TRIP TO PANAMA 30

When to Go 31

*PANAMA CALENDAR OF EVENTS
& FESTIVALS* 32

Entry Requirements 33

Getting There & Getting Around 35

Money & Costs 37

Health 38

Safety 42

Specialized Travel Resources 42

Responsible Tourism 44

Staying Connected 45

Tips on Accommodations 47

4 SUGGESTED PANAMA ITINERARIES 49

The Regions in Brief 49

PANAMA IN 1 WEEK 52

PANAMA IN 2 WEEKS 54

PANAMA FOR FAMILIES IN 10 DAYS 55

A HIGH-OCTANE WEEK OF ADVENTURES 56

PANAMA CITY IN 3 DAYS 58

5 THE ACTIVE VACATION PLANNER 59

Organized Adventure Trips 60
Activities A to Z 64
Panama's Top Parks & Reserves 74

Tips on Etiquette & Safety
in the Wilderness 77
Ecologically Oriented Volunteer
& Study Programs 78

6 PANAMA CITY 79

Orientation 80
NEIGHBORHOODS IN BRIEF 85
Getting Around 86
TIPS FOR DRIVERS IN PANAMA CITY 87
FAST FACTS: PANAMA CITY 88
Where to Stay 90
Where to Dine 101
SPANISH-LANGUAGE PROGRAMS 112

What to See & Do 112
WALKING TOUR: HISTORIC CASCO VIEJO 116
Spectator Sports & Recreation 125
Shopping 126
WILDLIFE CONTRABAND: DON'T DESTROY
WHAT YOU'VE COME SEEKING 127
Panama After Dark 130

7 AROUND PANAMA CITY 135

The Panama Canal 136
Gamboa & the Canal Zone 139
LEARN ABOUT THE RAINFOREST WITH
THE SMITHSONIAN INSTITUTE 146
Colón 149

Portobelo 154
Isla Grande 159
Isla Taboga 162
Archipiélago de las Perlas 164
East of Panama City 171

8 CENTRAL PANAMA 172

Pacific Beaches 173
ROADSIDE GASTRONOMY 174
Altos de Campana
National Park 183
El Valle de Antón 184
Western Coclé Province
& Penonomé 194

La Península de Azuero 197
FESTIVALS & EVENTS IN THE
AZUERO PENINSULA 198
PARTY ON! CARNAVAL IN THE
AZUERO PENINSULA 204

9 THE WESTERN HIGHLANDS & THE GULF OF CHIRIQUÍ 212

David 214
Volcán 219
Bambito, Cerro Punta &
Guadalupe 224
West of Volcán Barú: Boquete 229

Parque Nacional Marino Golfo de
Chiriquí & Islas Secas 248
Isla Coiba 252
Santa Catalina 254

10 BOCAS DEL TORO ARCHIPELAGO 258

A WORD ABOUT WATER 260
Isla Colón: Bocas Town 260
FAST FACTS: BOCAS TOWN 264
NEXT VACATION: PICK UP A SKILL 269
Isla Carenero (Careening Cay) 278

Isla Bastimentos 280
Isla Solarte 285
Isla Cristóbal & Laguna
  Bocatorito 286

11 COMARCA KUNA YALA 287

El Porvenir & Western Comarca
  Kuna Yala 290
SPECIAL CONSIDERATIONS IN THE
  SAN BLAS 291
ADVENTURE-TOUR OUTFITTERS &
  ACTIVITIES 292

THE KUNA REVOLUTION 295
THE KUNA SOCIETY 296
Eastern Comarca Kuna Yala 297

12 THE DARIEN PROVINCE 300

Western Darién 301
Punta Patiño 303
Darién National Park & Cana Field
  Station 304

Bahía Piñas & the Tropic Star
  Lodge 306

13 FAST FACTS: PANAMA 308

Fast Facts 308

Toll-Free Numbers & Websites 311

14 GLOSSARY OF SPANISH TERMS & PHRASES 314

Some Typical Panamanian
  Words & Phrases 316

Menu Terms 317

15 PANAMANIAN WILDLIFE 319

Fauna 319

Flora 328

Index 331

Accommodations Index 339

Restaurants Index 341

LIST OF MAPS

Panama at a Glance 51

Panama's National Parks & Protected
  Areas 61

Panama City 82

Walking Tour: Historic Casco Viejo 117

The Canal Zone 141

Central Panama 173

The Western Highlands & the Gulf
  of Chiriquí 213

Boquete 231

Bocas del Toro 259

Bocas Town 261

Comarca Kuna Yala 289

Darién 301

ABOUT THE AUTHOR

Jisel Perilla has written about, lived in, and traveled throughout much of Latin America, where she makes her living as a freelance writer. She currently resides in Bogotá, Colombia, and writes about Latin America for www.latinworld.com and other publications. You can read her personal travel blog at www.anomadlife.wordpress.com. Jisel also is the author of the Colombia chapter in *Frommer's South America*.

HOW TO CONTACT US

In researching this book, we discovered many wonderful places—hotels, restaurants, shops, and more. We're sure you'll find others. Please tell us about them, so we can share the information with your fellow travelers in upcoming editions. If you were disappointed with a recommendation, we'd love to know that, too. Please write to:

Frommer's Panama, 3rd Edition
Wiley Publishing, Inc. • 111 River St. • Hoboken, NJ 07030-5774
frommersfeedback@wiley.com

AN ADDITIONAL NOTE

Please be advised that travel information is subject to change at any time—and this is especially true of prices. We therefore suggest that you write or call ahead for confirmation when making your travel plans. The authors, editors, and publisher cannot be held responsible for the experiences of readers while traveling. Your safety is important to us, however, so we encourage you to stay alert and be aware of your surroundings. Keep a close eye on cameras, purses, and wallets, all favorite targets of thieves and pickpockets.

FROMMER'S STAR RATINGS, ICONS & ABBREVIATIONS

Every hotel, restaurant, and attraction listing in this guide has been ranked for quality, value, service, amenities, and special features using a star-rating system. In country, state, and regional guides, we also rate towns and regions to help you narrow down your choices and budget your time accordingly. Hotels and restaurants are rated on a scale of zero (recommended) to three stars (exceptional). Attractions, shopping, nightlife, towns, and regions are rated according to the following scale: zero stars (recommended), one star (highly recommended), two stars (very highly recommended), and three stars (must-see).

In addition to the star-rating system, we also use seven feature icons that point you to the great deals, in-the-know advice, and unique experiences that separate travelers from tourists. Throughout the book, look for:

special finds—those places only insiders know about

fun facts—details that make travelers more informed and their trips more fun

kids—best bets for kids and advice for the whole family

special moments—those experiences that memories are made of

overrated—places or experiences not worth your time or money

insider tips—great ways to save time and money

great values—where to get the best deals

The following abbreviations are used for credit cards:

AE	American Express	DISC	Discover	V	Visa
DC	Diners Club	MC	MasterCard		

TRAVEL RESOURCES AT FROMMERS.COM

Frommer's travel resources don't end with this guide. Frommer's website, www.frommers.com, has travel information on more than 4,000 destinations. We update features regularly, giving you access to the most current trip-planning information and the best airfare, lodging, and car-rental bargains. You can also listen to podcasts, connect with other Frommers.com members through our active-reader forums, share your travel photos, read blogs from guidebook editors and fellow travelers, and much more.

THE BEST OF PANAMA

For such a thin squiggle of land, Panama offers travelers a surprisingly diverse selection of landscapes, cultures, and experiences. In Panama City alone, modern skyscrapers contrast with 18th-century architecture, and a 10-minute cab ride from downtown puts you deep in rainforest teeming with wildlife. From the cool, fertile highlands in the Chiriquí region to the thick lowland jungle and white-sand beaches of Panama's tropical islands, this tiny nation allows you to pack a lot of fun and adventure into a short period of time. Also, Panama boasts a rich history and a melting pot of cultures, including seven indigenous groups, many of whom maintain their customs today. Best of all, the country is gloriously free of tourists— but get here soon because Panama is far too attractive to stay a secret for long.

The following is a list of the best that Panama has to offer, including hotels, natural areas, adventures, restaurants, and more.

THE best OF NATURAL PANAMA

- **Natural Metropolitan Park** (Panama City): Panama City is the only metropolis that boasts a tropical rainforest within its city limits. Travelers with ample time will want to visit national parks like Soberanía, but if you're just sticking to Panama City, this park is well worth the 10-minute cab ride. Visitors will encounter steamy jungle teeming with wildlife. See p. 121.
- **Soberanía National Park** (near Panama City): This national park is very accessible from Panama City—just 40 minutes by car—yet it feels worlds away. The undulating, pristine rainforest that defines Soberanía is protected in part because it acts as a watershed that provides the water to keep the canal in operation. What's unique about

the park is that wildlife species from North and South America and migratory birds meet here, creating a hyper-diverse natural wonderland. A series of nature trails here include the historic Camino de Cruces, which links the two coasts, as well as the famous Pipeline Road, a trail revered by bird-watchers for the more than 500 species of birds that live in the area. For bird-watchers, Parque Soberanía is a must see. See p. 142.

o **Volcán Barú National Park** (Chiriquí Highlands): The rugged, 3,505m (11,500-ft.) Barú volcano, the highest point in the country, is this national park's centerpiece and a "bioclimatic island." It's home to a wild, dense rainforest packed with bamboo gardens and towering trees dripping with vines and sprouting bromeliads and orchids from their trunks and branches. In higher reaches, an intermittent cloud forest evokes an eerie, prehistoric ambience. The park is very popular with bird-watchers, who come to glimpse the famous resplendent quetzal. One of the most enjoyable full-day hikes in Panama is here along the Quetzal Trail, which links the towns of Guadalupe/Cerro Punta with Boquete, and the crystalline rivers that descend from the volcano provide thrilling white-water rafting. On a clear day, hikers can see both oceans from the summit of the volcano. See p. 233.

o **La Amistad International Park** (Chiriquí Highlands): Like Isla Coiba, UNESCO rated this park a World Heritage Site because it is one of the most biodiverse regions in the Americas. The park is "international" because half of it is in Costa Rica, and it's managed by both nations. Characterized by virgin forests, La Amistad's rugged Talamanca Range is home to more than 400 species of birds and 100 species of mammals, many of them endangered. The park is mostly inaccessible, except near Cerro Punta, where there are several outstanding walking trails suitable for all ability levels, and enjoyable rain or shine. If you go to just one park in Panama, make it this one. See p. 225.

o **The Darién Wilderness** (Darién Province): This tremendous swath of forest and swampland is considered to be one of the last untouched wilderness regions in the Americas. Even the Darién National Park is largely inaccessible, and the surrounding wilderness is so thick that the "missing link" of the Pan American Highway, known as the Darién Gap, is here. If you like your nature ruggedly wild and remote, this is your place. The Darién is rated as a world-class bird-watching site for its flocks of colorful macaws, among other showcase species, but you'll need to join a tour and grab a chartered flight to the Cana Field Station. See p. 304.

o **Isla Coiba National Park** (Chiriquí Gulf): Formerly the site of an infamous penal colony for Panama's worst criminals, Isla Coiba is now an untouched paradise for divers, snorkelers, and nature lovers. The national park and UNESCO World Heritage Site protects 38 pristine islands and marine waters so rich in diversity that the area is commonly referred to as the Galápagos Islands of Panama. Isla Coiba boasts the second-largest coral reef in the eastern Pacific, and its waters teem with huge schools of colorful fish, hammerhead and nurse sharks, dolphins, manta rays, tuna, turtles, whales, and other gigantic marine species—even saltwater crocodiles. As impressive as Isla Coiba is, it's not the easiest place to get to and it definitely doesn't come cheap. See p. 252.

o **The Kuna Yala Comarca:** This tropical island paradise, with more than 350 idyllic islands and islets ringed in white sand, coral gardens, and mangrove swamps, is often populated with not much more than slender coconut palms and a few thatch-roofed huts of the Kuna indigenous community. Given the lack of modern development in the region, the views here are not marred by towering hotels and resorts, allowing the natural beauty of the comarca to shine through. Along the coast, some of Panama's wildest jungle can be explored on hikes arranged by local tour guides, but most visitors come just to soak in the warm breeze and cool turquoise waters. See p. 287.

THE best BEACHES

In spite of the hundreds of kilometers of coastline on both the Caribbean Sea and Pacific Ocean, Panama's beaches are less than noteworthy. There are a few exceptions, but to find glorious tropical beaches, you'll need to visit Panama's islands. There are more than 1,000 on the Pacific Side and a little more than half that number on the Caribbean, so you have a lot to choose from. *A word of caution:* Panama is renowned for its riptides. No matter how refreshing the water looks, analyze conditions, stay out of choppy water, or head to a beach known for calm water.

- **Comarca Kuna Yala:** This is *the* premier beach destination in Panama, with over 350 islands scattered off the Caribbean coast that offer picture-postcard beaches with powdery white sand, coral reef, piercing turquoise water, and clusters of swaying palm trees. The colorful Kuna indigenous population administers this province, and their fascinating culture is part of the reason to visit the region, too. The glitch is that scuba diving is prohibited, and lodging is mostly Robinson Crusoe rustic, but all you'll want to do here anyway is swim, sun, and swing in a hammock. See p. 294.

- **Isla Bastimentos National Marine Park, Bocas del Toro:** Cayos Zapatillas, or the "Slippers Islands" (so-called because they resemble footprints), not only fulfill the beach lover's fantasy with their soft sand backed by a tangle of jungle; they are also surrounded by a rich display of coral that attracts hordes of fish, providing good snorkeling. The park's main island, Isla Bastimentos, offers terrific beaches with clean sand and blue water, such as **Red Frog Beach, Wizard Beach,** and **Playa Larga,** which can be reached by a short walk or hike, or by boat during the calm-water season August through October. See p. 281.

- **Las Perlas Archipelago:** Despite this Pacific archipelago's proximity to Panama City, its top-notch snorkeling, white-sand beaches, and calm-water swimming conditions, the Pearl Islands are a relatively unsung beach destination perfect for families with young children. Outside of holidays and the hard-core summer, you won't find crowds here, even during weekends. It's also drier here during the rainy season. **Isla Contadora** offers lodging and day trips for fabulous snorkeling and visits to uninhabited beaches, and there is a luxury lodge, **Hacienda San José,** on Isla San José.

- **Isla Coiba National Park:** Beyond ranking as Panama's number-one diving site, Isla Coiba National Park boasts fine beaches backed by dense jungle. Tiny islands such as **Granito de Oro** are so idyllic that midsize cruise ships make a stop here (which could spoil your day if you're here independently). Even the beach fronting the park station seems too perfect to be true. See p. 252.

- **Las Lajas, Chiriquí Province:** It's not the most beautiful beach in Panama, but the water is the perfect temperature and produces just the right amount of waves for bodysurfing—though there's little current. All of which means that Las Lajas is ideal for swimming, and since the beach measures more than 13km (8 miles) in length, you can walk forever. Rustic shacks and cheap restaurants are clustered on the beach at the end of the road, but it's best to bring your own snacks. If you're looking for a beach closer to David (and Boquete), try **La Barqueta.** Strong currents at this black-sand beach mean the water is not ideal for swimming, but it is lengthy like Las Lajas and good for walking, and there is a nature reserve here, too. See p. 219.

○ **Playa Los Destiladores & Playa Venado, Azuero Peninsula:** Of the multitude of beaches lining the coast of the Azuero Peninsula, these two are the cleanest and the most attractive, and they are within a 20-minute drive from each other. However, given the deforestation in the area, they are less "tropical" than other Panamanian beaches. Currents will occasionally churn up the water along the golden sand at Playa Destiladores, but a protected cove at Playa Venado means it's calm enough for a toddler, and farther east crashing waves have converted the beach into a surfing hot spot. A major bonus here is the nearby picturesque town of Pedasí, and three gorgeous lodges. See p. 207.

○ **Boca Chica Beaches, Chiriquí:** In the Chiriquí lowlands, Boca Chica feels a world (and century) removed from the rest of Panama. This area is home to a number of attractive resorts and while the beaches themselves aren't the most beautiful, the area's utter seclusion and deeply isolated vibe make it a worthy off-the-beaten path destination, particularly for honeymooners looking to get away from it all.

○ **Santa Clara & Farallón, Pacific Coast:** These two are the most appealing beaches along the Pacific Coast, and the best for swimming. Best of all, they lie within a 2-hour drive of Panama City, so if you won't be going to one of Panama's better beaches, they're worth the drive. The beaches' water is bluer and the sand cleaner and whiter than its neighbors closer to the city. The Decameron Resort produces throngs of beachgoers at Farallón, but for the most part this long stretch of sand sees few crowds outside of weekends. Be warned, however, that swimming conditions can be treacherous due to large waves and strong riptides. Self-catering cabins, midrange bungalows, and seafood restaurants are abundant. See p. 179.

THE best ADVENTURES

○ **White-Water Rafting & Kayaking the Chiriquí and Chiriquí Viejo Rivers:** Depending on which section you raft, these two rivers produce serious white water ranging from technical Class III to Class V, some portions of which are so difficult they've been named "Fear" and "Get Out if You Can." There are plenty of tamer floats on Class II rivers, such as the Esti, for families and beginners. Virtual solitude, beautiful views, and lush surroundings are part of the tour, too. Contact **Chiriquí River Rafting** (© 720-1505; www.panama-rafting.com) in Boquete or, for kayaking, **Panama Rafters** (© 720-2712; www.panamarafters.com). See p. 235.

○ **Zipping Through the Treetops on a Canopy Adventure:** It's all the rage in Costa Rica, and now Panama has joined in to offer this adrenaline-fueled and exhilarating adventure. Participants climb high to a treetop platform, where they are strapped into a harness and then descend quickly using a pulley attached to a cable. Part of the experience is observing wildlife, mostly birds, from different vantage points in the forest. Both **Canopy Adventure** (© 264-5720;

www.canopylodge.com), in El Valle, and **Boquete Tree Trek** (© **720-1635;** www.canopypanama.com), in Boquete, offer canopy rides. See p. 236.

o **Surfing Bocas del Toro:** There are plenty of surfing hot spots along the Pacific Coast, especially at Santa Catalina, but Bocas is where surfers find everything from beginner-friendly waves to monster, Hawaii-style waves that reach more than 6m (20 ft.). What's special about Bocas, too, is that the water is clear blue, allowing you to see the reef as you race over it, and there are lots of lodging options, restaurants, and thumping nightlife, unlike in Santa Catalina. Another perk is that the Caribbean tides fluctuate only .9m (3 ft.), whereas the Pacific's fluctuate five times that amount. The waves here are powerful beach breaks, and long, barreling reef point breaks; for organized tours, contact **Panama Surf Tours** (© **6671-7777;** www.panamasurftours.com) or **La Buga Dive & Surf** (© **727-9594** or 6781-0755; www.bocasdeltorosurfschool.com). See p. 269.

o **Diving Around Isla Coiba:** This national park only recently opened to the traveling public—a notorious penal colony that closed here in 2004 kept tourists away, and now the park's virgin waters rate as *the* best diving site in Panama. Isla Coiba is often described as the Galápagos Islands of Panama, and although the snorkeling is outstanding, diving gets you close to pelagics such as white-tipped sharks, sailfish, turtles, manta rays, dolphins, and so much more. Coiba is home to one of the largest coral reefs in the Pacific Coast of the Americas. Day excursions involve a minimum of 3 hours round-trip to get here, which is why many multiday excursions include onboard lodging or a stay at the park ranger's cabins on the island. See p. 254.

o **Trekking the Camino Real:** Centuries before the Panama Canal, the Spanish built an 80km (50-mile) cobblestone path to transport looted gold from the Pacific to galleons waiting in the Caribbean Sea. You can trace their path, much of which still exists in stone, in about 3 days, beginning with a canoe ride up the Chagres River, an overnight in an Emberá Indian Village, and a tramp through earthy jungle full of birds and wildlife to Nombre de Dios, near Portobelo. Lodging is in tents, and the return trip is by railroad to give you an idea of how revolutionary the railroad's construction was to increasing coastal access. **Ancon Expeditions** (© **269-9415;** www.anconexpeditions.com) and **Advantage Tours Panama** (www.advantagepanama.com) both offer excursions. See chapter 7.

o **Reeling in a Billfish off the Pacific Coast:** Panama's Pacific Coast is legendary for sport fishing, and anglers can battle monster species such as marlin, sailfish, and tuna in the Gulf of Chiriquí and the Gulf of Panama. Near Piñas Bay, the **Tropic Star Lodge** has broken more International Game and Fish Association world records than anywhere else on the planet. There are a handful of fishing lodges at Boca Chica, near David, and as many live-aboard fishing operations that use charter yachts or barges as home base. See "Fishing" in chapter 5.

o **Kayaking in the Kuna Yala Comarca:** Considering that diving is prohibited in the Kuna Yala, kayaking fills the "sports void," and offers travelers a way to intimately explore the mangrove swamps and the undeveloped beauty of the tiny islands this region is famous for. Along the way, kayakers stop at traditional Kuna communities for cultural tours, land-based hiking, and snorkeling. **Xtrop** (© **317-1279** or 317-0530; www.xtrop.com), or "Expediciones Tropicales," is the company to call; they are a well-respected company and the only outfitters with special permission from the Kuna chief to kayak in the Kuna Yala. They employ local guides. See p. 292.

○ **Bird-Watching by Dugout Canoe on the Mogue River** (Darién Wilderness): The tour outfitter Ancon Expeditions offers a bird-watching and nature adventure near Punta Patiño that takes travelers up the Mogue River in a motorized dugout canoe, winding past dry forest and ancient mangrove swamps for an absolutely authentic jungle experience. From here, it's off to find the harpy eagle, Panama's national bird, and then spend the night with Emberá Indians in one of their rustic communities. For more information, contact Ancon (✆ **269-9415;** www.ancon expeditions.com). See p. 305.

○ **The Panama Rainforest Discovery Center** (near Panama City): A truly amazing experience, this 40m (120-ft.) tower overlooks the dense rainforest canopy on the edge of Soberanía National Park on Pipeline Road, a world-renowned bird-watching hot spot. But you don't have to be a bird-watcher to enjoy the Rainforest Discovery Center; you're bound to see plenty of monkeys, butterflies, sloths, plus dozens of tree and plant varieties—and there's really nothing like being 40m (120 ft.) above the rainforest. See p. 148.

THE best DAY HIKES & NATURE WALKS

○ **The Quetzal Trail** (Volcán Barú National Park): Panama's foremost day hike takes visitors around the northeastern flank of Volcán Barú and through primary and secondary tropical forest and cloud forest that provides a dazzling array of flora and fauna. The trail's namesake, the resplendent quetzal, lives here, too. The trail is mostly downhill from the Cerro Punta side to Boquete, and is the recommended direction unless you really crave a workout. What's unique about this trek is that travelers lodging around Cerro Punta can send their luggage to their next hotel in Boquete, and walk there. See p. 224.

○ **Walk to Pirre Mountain** (Darién National Park): This is a serious jungle trail, located in one of the most remote wildernesses in Central America. Pirre Mountain rises above the Cana Field Station in the Darién National Park, and is a moderate-to-difficult trail beloved by nature enthusiasts and bird-watchers for its dense concentration of fauna. Howler monkeys, spider monkeys, sloths, even snakes are easily and frequently spotted, but just as exciting is the wild sensation that comes from the magnificent jungle surrounding you. At the peak's summit, there is a lookout point with sweeping views. See p. 305.

○ **Pipeline Road** (Soberanía National Park): As mentioned elsewhere, Pipeline is a bird-watcher's haven, but this trail also provides outstanding opportunities to see wildlife and just to delve into steamy, wild jungle. The farther you walk or bike, the better your chances of seeing monkeys, coatimundis, sloths, and other mammals. The best time to go is early morning, before 9am if possible, when birds and animals are most active. See p. 142.

○ **Finca Suiza** (on the road btw. Almirante and David): The Swiss owners of this tiny ranch-style hostel offer some of the best hiking trails in Panama, both for beauty and because they are so well maintained and marked. There are three loop trails that connect with one another; all are moderate to difficult but worth the initial climb for the expansive views of the coast and lowlands of the Pacific, and into the peaks of Costa Rica. The trails pass through verdant rainforest, and there are waterfalls with bathing pools for taking a dip. You can visit for the day, or bunk in their simple but attractive rooms (© 6615-3774; www.panama.net.tc). See p. 247.

○ **La Amistad International Park** (Chiriquí Highlands): Visitors here can walk a quick 15-minute easy path near the ranger station, or an hour-long (but still easy) path through bamboo gardens and thick jungle, and past clear-water creeks. Another 2-hour hike takes visitors to a series of lookout points with mountain and valley views, and a crashing 49m (160-ft.) waterfall; a detour here to a lookout point offers a view that stretches to the Caribbean. Gung-ho hikers can hack through a narrow trail up to a peak for a coast-to-coast view. Finish off your hike with a delicious lunch at the local co-op cafe near the ranger station. See p. 225.

THE best BIRD-WATCHING

○ **Watching Macaws in Flight over the Forests of Darién National Park:** Few places in the world rival the Darién National Park for bird-watching. The .5 million hectares (1.3 million acres) of rainforest here provide a home for four species of macaws, including blue and gold, red and green, great green, and chestnut-fronted. These noisy and colorful birds sail over the **Cana Field Station,** a converted research facility and bird-watcher's sanctuary run by **Ancon Expeditions** (© 269-9415; www.anconexpeditions.com); they'll take you up Pirre Mountain, where, if you're lucky, you'll glimpse the golden-headed quetzal. Also expect to see a rainbow of tanagers, toucans, oropendolas, and black-tipped cotingas. See p. 304.

○ **Searching for the Elusive Harpy from a Traditional Emberá Village:** One of Panama's top bird-watching companies, **Advantage Tours Panama** (© 232-6944 or 6676-2466; www.advantagepanama.com), has a brand-new package tour in La Marea that allows travelers to stay in an Emberá village deep in the Darién, providing excellent bird-watching opportunities as well as the chance to sleep, eat, and even dance among the Emberás. Guides will happily accommodate jungle hikes to harpy eagle nesting sites as overnight camping expeditions deep in the jungle for smaller groups. See p. 302.

○ **Looking for More Than 500 Species of Birds Along Pipeline Road in Soberanía National Park:** This is the "celebrity" bird-watching trail for the immense number of species found here. In fact, for several years Pipeline Road has set the world record for 24-hour bird counts. Even non-birders can't help getting caught up in the action with so many colorful show birds fluttering about, such as mot mots, trogons, toucans, antbirds, colorful tanagers, and flycatchers. The farther you walk or bike along the rainforest trail, the better your chances of spotting rare birds. Contact **Advantage Tours Panama** (see above) to arrange a bird-watching tour. See p. 142.

○ **Catching Sight of the Resplendent Quetzal in the Cloud Forests of the Chiriquí Highlands:** The iridescent green resplendent quetzal is widely considered to be the most beautiful bird in the Americas, and it was revered by the Aztecs and the Mayans. From December to May, the best place to see a quetzal is in the cloud forests of **Volcán Barú National Park,** but if you want a near-guarantee that you'll see one, head to **Finca Lérida** (© 720-2285; www.fincalerida.com) in Boquete and have them book the bird-watching guide **Santiago "Chago" Caballero** (© 6626-2200; santiagochagotours@hotmail.com) or one of his protégés—they're the best in the quetzal-spotting business. If you're more of a general birder, be sure to contact Terry from **Coffee Adventures** (© **720-3852;** www.coffeeadventures.net). See chapter 9.

o **Being Taken Aback by the Size of the Harpy Eagle in Punta Patiño Nature Reserve:** The harpy eagle is Panama's national bird and one of the largest eagles in the world, with a wingspan that can reach more than 1.8m (6 ft.). You can't help being struck by this creature's size, though now that they're endangered, they're not the easiest bird to spot. Head to Punta Patiño, and your chances soar. **Ancon Expeditions** (© **269-9415;** www.anconexpeditions.com) has a lodge here and organizes bird-watching trips. Short on time? Call the Summit Zoo to find out if they have a harpy eagle on grounds; www.summitpanama.org), near Panama City. See p. 303.

o **Grabbing a Cab to View 200+ Species in the Metropolitan Park:** Panama City's Metropolitan Park is the only protected tropical forest found within the city limits of a major urban area in the Americas—a 10-minute cab ride and you're there, checking out orange-billed sparrows, green honeycreepers, rufous and white wrens, and thrush tanagers, among more than 200 other species. Head to the top of the Cerro Mono Titi hilltop to view canopy birds down the slope, not to mention a spectacular view of the city. See p. 121.

o **Discovering Trogons, Blue Cotingas, and Chestnut-Mandible Toucans on the Little-Known Achiote Road:** The Atlantic Coast village of Achiote, about a 1½-hour drive from Panama City, is quietly revered as a bird-watching mecca by those in the know—the Audubon Society holds its Atlantic Christmas Bird Count here and has counted up to 390 species in a single day. Also fluttering around Achiote are orange-chinned parakeets, barbets, and flocks of swallowtail kites. Check out their website at **www.panamaaudubon.org** to see if they've got any day trips planned to the area. See p. 152.

o **Delving into the World of Bird-Watching at the Canopy Lodge or Canopy Tower:** These two lodges live and breathe bird-watching, with day trips, viewing platforms, expert guides, and a fully stocked bird-watcher's library. The lodges are located in prime bird-watching spots in Soberanía National Park and the cloud-forest foothills of Valle de Antón (© **264-5720** or 6687-0291; www.canopytower. com). See p. 190 and 147.

THE best DESTINATIONS FOR FAMILIES

o **Panama City:** If you're using Panama City as a base for day excursions to the Canal Zone, the **Country Inn & Suites Causeway** (© **211-4500;** www.countryinns. com/panamacanalpan) is a good bet for families for its safe, quiet location, outdoor pools, bicycle rental, and long walking/jogging shoreline path that connects with the Amador Causeway. On the causeway, visit the Smithsonian's **Punta Culebra Marine Exhibit Center** (© **212-8793**) to view and touch sea creatures. The **Frank Gehry Biodiversity Museum** on the Amador Causeway will eventually be one of the best—if not the best—museum in all of Panama, but it's hard to tell if the museum will actually be open at publication time. Kids and adults get a kick out of seeing the colorful **Mercado de Mariscos (Fish Market),** full of both common and alien-looking sealife, and kids will like the **Kuna Cooperative,** where Kuna women affix their traditional beaded bands to the arms and legs of tourists. See p. 122. Kids and adults will also enjoy the architectural gems and decent museums in **Casco Viejo,** Panama City's historic quarter.

o **The Canal Zone:** The Panama Canal, Lake Gatún, and the surrounding rainforest overflow with kid-friendly activities, and parents can either base themselves in Panama City or at **Gamboa Rainforest Resort** (Gamboa; ✆ 877/800-1690; www.gamboaresort.com), a kid-pleaser for its swimming pools, games center, butterfly farm, reptile displays, and aerial tram. In fact, the Gamboa Rainforest Resort is probably the most family-friendly lodging option in Panama City. Families can also rent a bicycle for a ride up the Pipeline Road to view wildlife and birds. See p. 136.

o **Jungle Adventure Cruises:** Half-day jungle cruises are fun for families because of wildlife sightings, and also because cruises put participants shockingly close to massive tankers crossing the Panama Canal. Cruises visit Monkey Island, where it is almost guaranteed you'll see four different species; also keep an eye out for capybaras, crocodiles, and sloths. Gamboa Rainforest Resort (see above) has their own tour, or try **Ancon Expeditions** (✆ 269-9415) for their fun guides. See p. 144.

o **Summit Gardens Park & Zoo** (near Panama City; ✆ 232-4854): Wildlife is notorious for shying away from humans, but you can view jaguars, monkeys, tapirs, and other species endemic to Panama at this zoo. It's not a fancy attraction, but there are extensive lawns and gardens, and the zoo is undergoing a progressive renovation during the next few years. See p. 147.

o **Emberá Villages** (Chagres River, near Panama City): This adventurous trip is fun for kids because it involves traveling the jungle-choked Chagres River by motorized dugout canoe to an Emberá Indian village. Along the way, guides keep an eye out for wildlife. The Emberá's rustic villages, handicrafts, and temporary *jagua*-stain "tattoos" fascinate kids and adults alike. Give **Ecocircuitos** (✆ 314-1586 or 6450-1093; www.ecocircuitos.com), **Advantage Panama,** or **Ancon Expeditions** (see above) a call. See p. 145.

o **Isla Contadora** (Archipiélago de las Perlas): What's special about this island are the dozen beaches that offer calm-water swimming conditions, the best snorkeling in Panama, day excursions to uninhabited islands, fishing trips, and more. **Punta Galeón Resort** (✆ 250-4221 or 250-4234; www.puntagaleonhotel.com) is now the best family lodging option on the island now that Hotel Contadora Resort has shut its doors.

o **El Valle de Antón:** Just 2 hours from Panama City, this mountain village provides families with a host of activities, including horseback riding, hiking, canopy adventures, a serpentarium, and El Nispero Zoo, with its new amphibian center. The most family-friendly hotel here is the **Crater Valley Adventure Spa** (✆ 215-2328; www.crater-valley.com), with a climbing wall, bicycle rental, and kids' activities, as well as a nice pool and minispa for adults. See p. 184.

o **Bocas del Toro:** Three distinctively different lodges on Isla Bastimentos in Bocas offer family-friendly activities. Go to Bahía Honda to see bat caves, sloths, monkeys, and caimans; snorkel around Cayos Zapatilla; or kayak through mangroves or on a Class I inland river. Check out the **Jungle Lodge** (✆ 6592-5162 or 6619-5364; www.thejunglelodge.com), **Tranquilo** Bay (✆ 713/589-6952 in the

U.S. or 380-0721 in Panama; www.tranquilobay.com/home), and **Casa Cayuco** (℗ **509/996-4178** in the U.S. and 6113-6431 in Panama; www.casacayuco. com). Activities on Bocas del Toro tend to center around adventure sports and beaches are known for their strong riptides, so I don't recommend Bocas for children 10 and under. If you prefer more standard lodging, **Playa Tortuga** (℗ **302-5424;** www.hotelplayatortuga.com) is a good family hotel with plenty of amenities and services to keep the kids busy. See p. 260.

o **Chiriquí Highlands:** A short, kid-friendly trail is in La Amistad International Park. The **Quetzal Trail** offers fairyland rainforest and birds, and is downhill from west to east. If staying in Boquete or Bambito, book a Class II white-water rafting trip with **Chiriquí Rafting** (℗ **720-1505**) or **Boquete Outdoor Adventures** (℗ **720-2284;** www.boqueteoutdooradventures). See p. 225.

THE best LUXURY HOTELS & RESORTS

o **The Panama Marriott Hotel** (Panama City; ℗ **210-9100;** www.marriott.com/ PTYPA): Of all the upscale options in Panama City, the Marriott consistently outshines its competitors. The hotel is in excellent shape, chock-full of facilities and amenities; guest rooms are roomy and comfortable, and the staff provides outstanding service. A central location close to restaurants and shops is an added bonus. See p. 94.

o **The Bristol Panama** (Panama City; ℗ **265-7844;** www.thebristol.com): It's button-up luxury with conservative textures and hues, English furniture, and carpeted guest rooms, but still the ambience at the Bristol feels cozy rather than stuffy. The Bristol is known for its bend-over-backward service and fine dining at Las Barandas Restaurant, though it doesn't have a pool. See p. 93.

o **Bristol Buenaventura** (℗ **908-3333;** www.thebristol.com/buenaventura) Also on the Pacific Coast, the Bristol Buenaventura was built in a colonial Spanish hacienda, complete with courtyards and plazas, and offers tons of amenities and services considering there are just 114 rooms. The beaches on the Pacific might not be Panama's best, but the Bristol has an attractive, relatively secluded beach, a fantastic pool, and stylish, elegant rooms, all with a balcony overlooking the property. Best of all, the staff goes out of their way to make your stay pleasant and glitch-free. Despite its upscale elegance, the Bristol has a bit of "family hotel" vibe to it, perhaps because of its proximity to Panama City. See p. 181.

o **Islas Secas** (Isla Secas; ℗ **805/729-2737** in the U.S.; www.islassecas.com): Casual elegance and an eco-conscious design using deluxe, solar-powered yurts for lodging are the hallmarks of this exquisite boutique resort, located on a private island in the blue waters of the Gulf of Chiriquí. Expect outstanding cuisine, impeccable service, access to world-class sport fishing and diving, and the smug feeling of having escaped the crowds. Islas Secas offers a bevy of activities, or they can leave you "stranded" on an uninhabited island for the day or back at home base at their spa. See p. 251.

o **Coral Lodge** (Colón Province; ℗ **232-0200;** www.corallodge.com): Spread around a dreamy inlet ringed with white sand and backed by coconut palms and thick jungle, this is a diver's and snorkeler's paradise, and one of the more luxurious and handsome lodges in Panama (it's eco-conscious, too). Lodging is in cozy individual thatched-roof *casitas* with snorkeling just outside your door—and the property is close enough to the Comarca Kuna Yala to tie in a visit there. See p. 161.

o **Hacienda del Mar** (Isla San José; © 866/433-5627; www.haciendadelmar.net): If you're looking for a lodge in a pristine island setting that isn't too far from Panama City, but that offers plenty of outdoor activities—this place fills the bill. Accommodations are in individual bungalows spread across a promontory and offering dynamite views. The overall ambience is intimate and romantic, making it an ideal place for a honeymoon. See p. 170.

o **Villa Camilla** (Los Destiladores; © 232-6721; www.azueros.com): It's one of Panama's finest hotels and one of its most exclusive, tucked away on the wooded shore of the Azuero Peninsula. French architect Gilles Saint-Gilles employed traditional, local woodworking and iron casting techniques to build a gorgeous and sophisticated hybrid of a hacienda and Moroccan villa, with locally produced furniture, individually designed rooms, and a wide veranda with wonderful views out to the sea. Surprisingly, the hotel is little-known, and with so few guests you can expect a high level of intimacy and privacy. Villa Camilla prides itself on eco-friendly practices. See p. 209.

o **Tropic Star Lodge** (Piñas Bay, Darién Province; © 800/682-3424; www.tropic star.com): For more than 40 years, the Tropic Star Lodge has drawn VIPs, sports stars, and actors for its world-renowned sport fishing—which is the focus of this lodge. If you're not a VIP, that's okay; this lodge just wants fishing fans, and they openly welcome families to get the kids interested in this high-adrenaline sport. The luxurious Tropic Star is located in the Darién Province on the Pacific Coast, and must be reached by small plane. See p. 306.

THE best ECOLODGES & WILDERNESS RESORTS

Ecolodges, by definition, should employ environmentally sound practices such as proper waste management, and contribute back to the local economy through jobs and an incentive to protect the environment for tourism. Ecolodges should also offer guided nature tours and provide in-depth information. The Gamboa Resort is the least "eco" of the following lodges, but its location, guided tours, and wildlife displays still place it in this category.

o **Canopy Lodge & Canopy Tower** (El Valle de Antón & Soberanía National Park; © 264-5720; www.canopytower.com): Birders flock to these two ecolodges for their focus on bird-watching and their location in habitats friendly to a wide range of species. The **Canopy Tower,** a remodeled military radar station in thick jungle, is a cross between a stylish B&B and a scientific research center. It's just 25 minutes from Panama City but feels worlds away, and the 360-degree observation deck here provides stunning views and a platform with scopes. The **Canopy Lodge** is more luxurious, with minimalist design that blends into the forested surroundings. Outstanding birding guides, a well-stocked library, day trips, and chats are a part of the stay. See p. 190 and p. 147.

o **Gamboa Rainforest Resort** (Gamboa; © 877/800-1690; www.gamboaresort. com): They bill themselves as an eco-resort, but the Gamboa is better called a "destination megaresort" that appeals equally to travelers seeking contact with nature to those who just want to be surrounded by nature while kicking back at the pool. Guided nature tours include jungle boat cruises, an aerial tram ride through the rainforest, and a minizoo of reptile, butterfly, and marine species exhibits. There's also a full-service spa. See p. 148.

- **La Loma Jungle Lodge** (Bocas del Toro; ☎ **6592-5162;** www.thejunglelodge. com): No other lodge envelops you more in nature than this one—it's like playing Tarzan and Jane for a night. Sleeping in an open-air, thatched-roof bungalow, of course, is not for everyone, but the cabins are stylish, and two sit high in the forest canopy, with sweeping views and wildlife sightings. There are guided nature and cultural visits with Ngöbe-Buglé Indians, organic meals, and an on-site butterfly farm. See p. 284.

- **Cana Field Station** (Darién National Park; ☎ **269-9415;** www.anconexpeditions. com): Originally a research facility, this rustic lodge is nestled in the Darién, the wildest and most remote region of Panama and renowned as one of the best birding sites in the world. Ancon Expeditions owns and runs the lodge, but birding specialty tour operators book here, too. Rooms are basic, with shared bathrooms, and meals are shared communally. You can even book an overnight stay at the Pirre Tent Camp in the cloud forest. See p. 305.

- **Punta Patiño Lodge** (Darién Province, Gulf of San Miguel; ☎ **269-9415;** www. anconexpeditions.com): This hilltop lodge looks out over the Pacific, and though it's rustic, it is a step up in comfort compared to the Cana Field Station, with air-conditioning and private bathrooms. It's also owned by Ancon Expeditions, but international tour outfitters book here, too. The lodge puts travelers close to wetlands, Emberá indigenous communities, sightings of the harpy eagle, and adventurous jungle rides up rivers in dugout canoes. See p. 303.

- **Sierra Llorona Panama Lodge** (Colón Province; ☎ **442-8104;** www.sierra llorona.com): This intimate, family-run lodge is a good bet for birders seeking a less-expensive option than the Canopy Tower. The lodge is nestled in 202 hectares (500 acres) of lush rainforest that is home to more than 150 species of birds, and there are walking trails, a natural bathing pool, and day trips in the surrounding area. Rooms are simple but spotless. See p. 149.

- **Tranquilo Bay** (Bocas del Toro; ☎ **620-4179;** www.tranquilobay.com): Embraced by lush, vibrant jungle and fronted by a thicket of mangroves, this resort, a haven for adventurers, is the most upscale lodging option in Bocas del Toro. The idea here is to provide activities that go where no other tour operator goes, including river kayaking on the mainland, snorkeling in remote areas, jungle hikes, and visits to isolated beaches. The cabins, though simply designed, offer plush interiors with high-quality beds and spacious bathrooms. See p. 285.

- **Cerro La Vieja** (near Penonomé; ☎ **786/206-0219** in the U.S.; www.posadalavieja. com): The drop-dead views and the fact that this spa and lodge is known to few outside of Panama City make the Cerro La Vieja a real find. The lodge is nestled in thick, green jungle and dominated by a torlike hill called Cerro La Vieja. Spa services are reasonably priced, and there are walking trails, mule rides, and other outdoor excursions. They serve delicious, organic cuisine, too. See p. 195.

- **Los Quetzales Lodge & Spa** (Guadalupe; ☎ **771-2291;** www.losquetzales.com): Although the main lodge is in town, there are several rustic wooden cabins set deep in lush rainforest that swarm with colorful birds. The cabins are large enough for groups, and they provide travelers with the wildest independent lodging option in the country. The cabins can be self-catering, or they'll send a chef up to cook for you. Walking trails and horseback-riding trips are options for those who stay here. See p. 228.

○ **Cala Mia** (Isla Boca Brava; ✆ **6747-0111**; www.boutiquehotelcalamia.com): This new hotel is environmentally friendly in every sense of the term. Entirely solar-powered, the hotel grows many of its own fruit and vegetables, and there are even plans for a cheese farm. A honeymooners' dream come true, Calamia offers two private beaches and a host of activities. Everything from the charming bungalows to the attentive service to the delectable, top-notch cuisine is right on. Fussier travelers should note however, that environmentally friendly means no air-conditioning. But this shouldn't be too much of a problem as temperatures cool at night. See p. 249.

○ **Punta Caracol** (✆ **6612-1088**; www.puntacaracol.com): It may not be the most upscale lodging option on Bocas del Toro, but when it comes to eco-friendliness, Punta Caracol doesn't cut any corners. Solar panels provide power lights and fans, with no A/Cs or electricity to speak of. The property consists of nine well-designed, two-story bungalows. Guests can jump right in the water (literally at your feet) for a bit of snorkeling or rent a kayak for a couple hours. Punta Caracol is a great choice for honeymooners willing to rough it a bit because of its seclusion and romantic ambience. See p. 277.

○ **Rancho de Caldera** (Boquete; ✆ **772-8040**; www.rancholacaldera.com): This relatively new eco-resort is off most travelers' radar, but is an ideal spot for couples looking for a romantic getaway. Its nine luxury cabins are set on a beautiful property just outside Boquete. The owner grows her own fruit and vegetables and has done a wonderful job building a low-impact resort powered by wind, hydro, and solar panels. See p. 248.

THE best SMALL
HOTELS & B&BS

○ **The Coffee Estate Inn** (Boquete; ✆ **720-2211**; www.coffeeestateinn.com): Gorgeous views of Volcán Barú, cozy bungalows with full kitchens, and owner-managed, friendly service tailored to your needs are the hallmarks of the Coffee Estate Inn. The bungalows are enveloped in native forest, fruit trees, and flowers that attract myriad birds. The romantic ambience is ideal for honeymooners. See p. 241.

○ **Cielito Sur** (Nueva Suiza; ✆ **771-2038**; www.cielitosur.com): The first thing you'll notice at this lovely country inn is the dozens of hummingbirds whizzing around the property. The Cielito is an ideal place for travelers seeking a pastoral setting, snug guest rooms, and easy-to-plan excursions. The inn also has lots of common areas, including a living area with lounge chairs and a well-stocked library. See p. 227.

○ **Los Mandarinos Hotel and Spa** (El Valle de Antón; ✆ **983-6645**; www.losmandarinos.com): Perched on a gently sloping hill and offering picturesque views of the Antón crater, this deluxe boutique hotel is also home to one of Panama's best restaurants. The Tuscan-style hotel recently opened a spa, and they rent bikes and arrange tours. See p. 190.

- **Park Eden Bed & Breakfast** (El Valle de Antón; ☎ **983-6167**; www.parkeden. com): It's the true definition of a B&B: owner-run; lots of charming, country decor; hearty breakfasts; and warm, gracious service. The storybook setting is amid flowering gardens and forest. See p. 192.

- **Posada los Destiladores** (Playa los Destiladores; ☎ **995-2771**; www.panama bambu.net): These rustic yet ultrastylish, individual bungalows offer one of the most romantic places to stay on the Pacific Coast of Panama. Secluded among 8.1 hectares (20 acres) of tropical plants and teak trees, the bungalows feature bamboo, thatched roofs, and intricately carved, custom-made furniture using local materials. There is a pool and private access to a beautiful beach. See p. 209.

- **Villa Marina** (☎ **646/383-7486** in the U.S.): Best described as a family home that happens to rent out rooms, this beachfront B&B is a find, located on the shore of surfing beach Playa Venado. The colonial-style home, set on 89 hectares (220 acres) of private land and boasting beautiful sunsets, is elegantly appointed—but the ambience is easeful, not fussy. Villa Marina is best rented with a group, but individual reservations are accepted, too. See p. 211.

- **The Golden Frog Inn** (El Valle; ☎ **983-6117**; www.goldenfroginn.com): It has the best views in El Valle and the grounds truly make it feel like paradise on earth. The six rooms are all individually furnished and decorated to provide comfort and tranquillity, and owners Becky and Larry are usually around to make sure their guests are happy. There's no better place to watch the sunset while enjoying complimentary happy hour. See p. 191.

THE best RESTAURANTS

- **Manolo Caracol** (Panama City; ☎ **228-4640**): The city's most innovative restaurant features an adventurous and creative daily menu that embraces in-season products and the freshest and most exotic fish of any restaurant in town. Sit back in the colonial, artsy ambience and wait for a "surprise" of 12 courses to be slowly ushered to your table—you never know what you're going to get, but you know it will be good. See p. 105.

- **Market** (Panama City; ☎ 264-9401): This snazzy new restaurant is one of the most popular dining spots in Panama City, and it's easy to see why. Contemporary yet classy, Market serves up some of the best burgers and steaks in Panama City. See p. 103.

- **Las Barandas** (Panama City; ☎ **265-7844**): Panama City's best boutique hotel also has one of its best restaurants. At the helm is "Cuquita," nationally famous as the Martha Stewart of Panama, who adapts traditional Panamanian recipes to modern gourmet tastes, and serves her delicious creations in a cozy and sophisticated dining area. They serve Sunday brunch, too. See p. 107.

- **Madame Chang** (Panama City; ☎ **269-1313**): Few diners are aware that some of the best Chinese food outside of China is in Panama, and Madame Chang is where you come to savor it. The Peking duck is the restaurant's showcase dish. The owners have merged Old China with new, both in terms of cuisine and their smart-casual atmosphere. See p. 108.

- **La Casa de Lourdes** (El Valle de Antón; ℂ **983-6450**): The cuisine is so to-die-for good that some residents of Panama City endure the 4-hour round-trip to El Valle de Antón just to have Sunday lunch. Ultra-fresh ingredients and exotic fruit are used to create updated takes on Panamanian and Latin American fare. Dining is alfresco: under the archways of a Tuscan-style manor house, next to an outdoor swimming pool. See p. 193.
- **Restaurant Terrazas del Mar** (Vista Mar; ℂ **832-0577**): This restaurant is run by a renowned French chef, and sports a chic Moroccan decor, plus outdoor dining with ocean views. The Mediterranean-style seafood is well conceived and bursting with flavor. The restaurant is within the Vista Mar residential community, on the Pacific Coast. See p. 178.
- **Panamonte Inn Restaurant** (Boquete; ℂ **720-1324**): This sanctuary of gourmet cuisine is located within the clapboard walls of the oldest hotel in Boquete. The food is inventive and consistently good, and service is attentive and courteous. You can bypass their more formal dining area for a comfy seat in their fireside bar and still order off the main menu. See p. 245.
- **Guari Guari** (Isla Colon, Bocas del Toro; ℂ **6575-5513**): One my favorite dining experiences in Panama, this new Bocas restaurant is conceptually similar to Manolo Caracol in Panama City; each course is a surprise and the menu varies depending on what's in stock. The Spanish cook creates delicious, creative dishes that rarely disappoint, and the service is impeccable. Make sure to call ahead; dinner is by reservation only. See p. 275.
- **Cumana** (El Valle; ℂ **6667-5001**): It's not technically a restaurant, but this eatery run from the home of a German-Panamanian couple is quickly becoming El Valle de Anton's most in-demand place to dine, and you'll want to reserve on weekends and holidays. The menu changes every month and the Panamanian chef has a natural knack for diverse, mouthwatering dishes. If you're looking for an unforgettable dining experience (usually accompanied by musicians and a romantic atmosphere), there's no better place to dine in El Valle. See p. 192.
- **Restaurante Los Camisones** (ℂ **993-3622**; www.loscamisones.com): It's not exactly the crux of fine dining, but in my opinion, this is the best spot to stop for typical Panamanian fare on the Pan American Highway. There are plenty of seafood dishes to choose from and the Bohio-style restaurant—with its wooden tables, Spanish-style interior, and thatched roof—reminds you that you're in Central America, something you can easily forget when visiting Panama's many sleek American- or European-style restaurants. See p. 181.

PANAMA IN DEPTH

2

For many years, Panama remained off the radar of international travelers and investors, but those days have come to an end and Panama has come into its own. Panama now receives over one million visitors a year, quite impressive for a tiny country of just three and a half million people. Panama underwent a major boom in the mid-2000s, with new retirement communities, restaurants, and hotels seemingly breaking ground every week. Prices and speculation have finally come down, but Panama continues to thrive despite economic hardships in North America and Europe and is still very much a country on the rise. Escaping much of the tourism boom all too familiar to Costa Rica, likely because of the Noriega years, Panama is proudly making a name for itself as a must-see destination in Latin America. Rapidly emerging from Costa Rica's shadow, Panama has a geography similar to that of its neighbor to the north, including pristine rainforests, attractive beaches, mountain villages, and, as an added bonus, a vibrant, cosmopolitan city often compared to Miami. Traveling isn't as cheap as it was a decade ago, but Panama is still cheaper than Costa Rica.

Panama claims a history rich with Spanish conquistadores and colonists, pirates, gold miners and adventurers, canal engineering, international trade, and mass immigration from countries as close as Jamaica and as far away as China. The pastiche of European and African cultures blended with the country's seven indigenous groups has had a tangible effect on Panama's architecture, cuisine, language, and folklore. And now that the dust has long settled after the infamous Noriega era, political stability has taken hold and offered hope for the country's future.

Given Panama's compact size and diversity, visitors here can take part in wildly different experiences without having to travel very far. The growing expat and retirement community, as well as the large number of Chinese, Colombian, and Venezuelan immigrants, make Panama a fascinating country to visit. This chapter will help you understand a little more about Panama's history, people, and culture.

PANAMA TODAY

Panama has three million residents, and more than a third of them live in Panama City, Colón, and David, the country's three largest cities. The remaining population is concentrated mostly in small towns and villages in central Panama and the Azuero Peninsula. Officially roughly 70% of the population are *mestizo*, or a mix of Amerindians and Caucasians; 14% are African descent, 10% are white and other immigrant races, and 6% Amerindian. About 30% of the population is under the age of 14.

There are seven indigenous groups in Panama who, despite foreign influences and modern advancements, have, to differing degrees, held onto their culture and languages. Ethnic tribes such as the **Kuna,** who live along the central Caribbean coast, form a semiautonomous and insular society that has hardly changed over the last century. However, the eastern Kuna community, near the Darién, has adapted to modern society, wears Western clothing, and practices few native traditions. The **Ngöbe-Buglé** are two tribes that are culturally similar and collectively referred to as Guaymí. Ngöbe-Buglés live in the highlands of western Panama and eastern Costa Rica, and are the country's largest indigenous group; many travel nomadically and make their living in coffee production. Eastern Panama is home to two indigenous groups, the **Emberá** and the **Wounaan**—several Emberá communities are close enough to Panama City to be visited for the day. Tiny populations of **Teribe** (also called Naso) and **Bri Bri** live scattered around mainland Bocas del Toro.

People of African descent first came to Panama as slaves of the Spanish during the 16th century, and many escaped into Darién Province where they settled and became known as *cimarrones.* In and around Portobelo and the eastern Caribbean coast, they call themselves **Congos.** During the 19th century, jobs in canal building and banana plantations lured immigrants from Jamaica, Barbados, and Colombia, who settled along the western Caribbean coast and are commonly referred to as **Afro-Caribbeans** or *creoles.*

One thing you'll find about Panamanians is that they are warm and outgoing people who are eager to help strangers. Panamanians no longer indulge in afternoon siestas, but you will notice that things move at a languid pace. Given this and the country's nascent tourism infrastructure, even well-respected tour companies and other tourism establishments can't always be relied upon for punctuality. If you are an impatient person, or in a hurry, you will not fare well in Panama—so *relax.* You're on vacation, right?

Panama has a dollarized economy whose major natural resources are its rainforests, beaches, and oceans, making this country an irresistible draw for tourism. Panama's principal source of income is derived from the services sector, including the Panama Canal, the Colón Free Trade Zone, banking, and flagship registry among other "export" services, all of which account for about three-quarters of the country's GDP. The withdrawal of U.S. canal workers and military personnel in 2000 had a devastating effect on Panama City's local economy, but a growth explosion in the construction sector is currently underway thanks to juicy tax incentives, and glitzy skyscrapers seem to shoot up overnight along the city's shoreline. Panama has very effectively sold itself as a retirement haven, with its low cost of living, inexpensive land, and dollar-based economy, and many of those who were just passing through are now putting down stakes in gated communities or taking on new roles as hotel or restaurant owners. For many years, foreign investors lured by get-rich-quick schemes were snapping up property in a real-estate boom that had many locals grumbling about the soaring value of land; this has slowed down a bit in the last couple of years, but prices have remained high for a relatively poor population On the legislative side, the Panamanian government has reformed its tax structure, opened its borders to free trade with key nations like the U.S., and implemented a social security overhaul. Yet money laundering, political corruption, and cocaine transshipment continue to be problems, as is widespread unemployment, with indigenous groups and Colón residents faring the worst. As the nation grows economically, the split between the rich and the poor widens. Today, about 40% of the population is under the poverty level and lacks adequate housing, access to medical care, and proper nutrition.

The current president of Panama is Ricardo Martinelli, a member of the right-leaning Democratic Change Party and a former businessman who has vowed to cut corruption and reduce crime. Martinelli has a degree from the University of Arkansas, and many see his business background as a key to Panama's continued economic development. Because he is a popular president who won more than 60% of the vote in 2009, many Panamanians are counting on Martinelli to "clean up" Panama and move the country forward.

In 2007, a $5.5-billion expansion of the Panama Canal got underway, a move that caused much controversy, but that ultimately promises to keep the canal relevant. Worldwide tankers have grown too big to fit in the canal, and those ships that can fit must line up for hours to cross. The project is slated for completion in 2014.

LOOKING BACK AT PANAMA

Early History

Little is known about the ancient cultures that inhabited Panama before the arrival of the Spanish. The pre-Columbian cultures in this region did not build large cities or develop an advanced culture like the Mayans or the Incas did, and much of what was left behind has been stolen by looters or engulfed in jungle. We know that the most advanced cultures came from Central Panama, such as the Monagrillo (2500–1700 B.C.), who were one of the first pre-Columbian societies in the Americas to produce ceramics. Excavation of sites such as Conte, near Natá, have unearthed elaborate burial pits with *huacas* (ceremonial figurines) and jewelry, which demonstrates an early introduction to metallurgy during the first century, as well as trade with Colombia and even Mexico. What little remains of Panama's prized artifacts can be viewed at the Museo Antropológico Reina Torres de Araúz in Panama City.

Spain Conquers Panama

The first of many Spanish explorers to reach Panama was Rodrigo de Bastidas, who sailed from Venezuela along Panama's Caribbean coast in 1501 in search of gold. His first mate was Vasco Nuñez de Balboa, who would return later and seal his fate as one of Panama's most important historical figures. A year later, Christopher Columbus, on his fourth and final voyage to the New World, sailed into Bocas del Toro and stopped at various points along the isthmus, one of which he named Puerto Bello, now known as Portobelo. Estimates vary, but historians believe that between one and two million indigenous people were in Panama at that time. Groups such as the Kuna, the Chocó, and the Guaymí lived in small communities and were highly skilled in pottery making, stonecutting, and metallurgy. Because they frequently wore gold ornaments, Spanish explorers during the following years would be further convinced of the existence of fabled El Dorado, the city of gold. Columbus attempted to establish a colony, Santa María de Belen, near Río Belen, but was forced out after a raid by local Indians.

Meanwhile, Balboa had settled in the Dominican Republic but had racked up huge debts. In 1510, he escaped his creditors by hiding out as a stowaway on a boat bound for Panama. In the years since Columbus's failed attempt, many other Spaniards had tried to colonize the coast, but were thwarted by disease and indigenous raids. Balboa suggested settling at Antigua de Darién, where he became a tough but successful administrator who both subjugated Indians as well as befriended conquered tribes. Having listened to stories by Indians about another sea, Balboa set out in 1513 with Francisco Pizarro and a band of Indian slaves, and hacked his way through perilous jungle for 25 days until he arrived at the Pacific Coast, where he claimed the sea and all its shores for the king of Spain. Balboa was later beheaded by a jealous new governor, Pedro Arias de Avila (Pedrarias the Cruel), on a trumped-up charge of treason.

In 1519, Pedrarias settled a fishing village called Panama, which meant "plenty of fish" in the local language, and resettled Nombre de Dios on the Atlantic to create a passageway for transporting Peruvian gold and riches from the Pacific to Spanish galleons in the Caribbean Sea. The trail was called the Camino Real, or Royal Trail, but later a faster and easier route was established, called the Camino de las Cruces. The land portion of this trail was two-thirds shorter, and met with the Chagres River, which could be sailed out to the Caribbean Sea. This trail can be walked today, and portions of the stone-inlaid path still exist.

With Incan gold nearly exhausted, the Spanish turned their interests to the immense supply of silver found in Peruvian mines, and in 1537 they held their first trading fair, which would grow into one of the most important fairs in the world. With so much wealth changing hands on the isthmus, pirate attacks became increasingly common, and ports like Nombre de Dios declined in importance after having been raided by the English pirate Sir Francis Drake twice in 1572 and 1573. Portobelo was refortified and became the main port of trade. Panama City, on the other side of the isthmus, flourished with trade profits, and was considered one of the wealthiest cities in the Americas.

By the mid–17th century, dwindling supplies of silver and gold from the Peruvian mines and ongoing pirate attacks precipitated a severe decline in the amount of precious metals being transported to Spain. In 1671, the notorious Welsh buccaneer Henry Morgan sailed up the Chagres River, crossed the isthmus, and overpowered Panama City, sacking the city and leaving it in flames. Those who escaped the attack rebuilt Panama City 2 years later at what is now known as Casco Viejo.

Spain finally abandoned the isthmus crossing and Portobelo after the city was attacked by the British Admiral Edward Vernon, and returned to sailing around Cape Horn to reach Peru.

Independence from Spain & the Gold Rush

Spain granted independence to its Central America colonies in 1821, and Panama was absorbed into "Gran Colombia," a union led by liberator Simón Bolívar that included Colombia, Venezuela, and Ecuador. Panama attempted to split from Colombia three times during the 19th century, but wouldn't be successful until the U.S.-backed attempt in 1903.

Having been a colonial backwater since the pullout of the Spanish in the late 17th century, Panama was restored to prosperity from 1848 to 1869 during the height of the California Gold Rush. Given that crossing from the Atlantic to the Pacific of the U.S. was a long, arduous journey by wagon and prone to Indian attacks and other pitfalls, gold seekers chose to sail to Panama, cross the Las Cruces trail, and sail on to California. In 1855, an American group of financiers built the Panama Railroad, greatly reducing the travel time between coasts. In 20 years, a total of 600,000 people crossed the isthmus, and both Colón and Panama City benefited enormously from the business earned in hotels, restaurants, and other services.

The Panama Canal

The history of the canal dates back to 1539, when King Charles I of Spain dispatched a survey team to study the feasibility of a canal, but the team deemed such a pursuit impossible. The first real attempt at construction of a canal was begun in 1880 by the French, led by Ferdinand de Lesseps, the charismatic architect of the Suez Canal. De Lesseps had been convinced that a sea-level canal was the only option. Once workers broke ground, however, engineers soon saw the impracticality of a sea-level canal but were unable to convince the stubborn de Lesseps, and for years rumors flew, financial debts mounted, and nearly 20,000 workers perished before the endeavor collapsed. Few had anticipated the enormous challenge presented by the Panamanian jungle, with its mucky swamps, torrential downpours, landslides, floods, and, most debilitating of all, mosquito-borne diseases such as malaria and yellow fever.

Meanwhile, Panama was embroiled in political strife and a nonstop pursuit to separate itself from Colombia. Following the French failure with the canal, the U.S. expressed interest in taking over construction but was rebuffed by the Colombian government. In response, the U.S. backed a growing independence movement in Panama that declared its separation from Colombia on November 3, 1903. The U.S. officially recognized Panama, and sent its battleships to protect the new nation from Colombian troops, who turned back home after a few days.

A French canal engineer on the de Lesseps project, Philippe Bunau-Varilla, a major shareholder of the abandoned canal project, had been grudgingly given negotiating-envoy status by the Panamanian government for the new U.S.-built canal. His controversial Hay-Bunau-Varilla Treaty gave the U.S. overly generous rights that included the use, occupation, and sovereign control of a 16km-wide (10-mile) swath of land across the isthmus, and was entitled to annex more land if necessary to operate the canal. The U.S. would also be allowed to intervene in Panama's affairs.

The French had excavated ⅔ of the canal, built hospitals, and left behind machinery and the operating railway, as well as a sizeable workforce of Afro-Caribbeans. For the next 10 years, the U.S., having essentially eradicated tropical disease, pulled off what seemed impossible in terms of engineering: carving out a path through the Continental Divide, constructing an elevated canal system, and making the largest man-made lake in the world.

The 20th Century to the Present

A stormy political climate ensued in Panama for the following decades, with frequent changes of administration. Presidents and other political figures were typically *rabiblancos,* or wealthy, white elites loathed by the generally poor and dark-skinned public. One especially controversial character in the political scene was Arnulfo Arias, a racist yet populist, one-time sympathizer of the fascist movement who would be voted into and thrown out of the presidency three times. Increasingly, Panamanians were discontented with the U.S. presence and, in particular, its control of the canal. In 1964, several U.S. high-school students in the Canal Zone raised the American flag at their school, igniting protests by Panamanian college students. The protests culminated in the deaths of more than two dozen Panamanians, an event that is now called "Día de los Mártires," or Martyrs Day.

By 1974, the U.S. had begun to consider transferring the canal to Panama. Arias was once again voted into power and after strong-arming the National Guard, he was deposed in a military coup led by Omar Torrijos Herrera, a colonel of the National Guard. Torrijos was an authoritarian leader but a champion of the poor who espoused land redistribution and social programs—a "dictatorship with a heart," as he called it. His most popular achievement came in 1977, with the signing of a treaty with then-president Jimmy Carter that relinquished control of the canal to Panama on December 31, 1999. Also part of the treaty was the closing of U.S. military bases and the U.S. right to intervene only if it perceived a threat against the security of the canal. On July 31, 1981, Torrijos died in a plane accident.

By 1983, the National Guard, now renamed the Panamanian Defense Forces (PDF), was firmly controlled by Colonel Manuel Antonio Noriega, and continued to dominate political and everyday life in Panama. Noriega created the so-called Dignity Battalions that aimed to stifle citizen dissent through force and terrorize anyone who opposed the PDF. For the next 6 years, Noriega kept the Panamanian public in a state of virtual fear, running the country through presidents he had placed in power via rigged elections, killing and torturing his opponents, and involving himself in drug trafficking.

The U.S. imposed tough economic sanctions on Panama that included freezing government assets in U.S. banks, and withholding canal fees, spurring widespread protests against Noriega across Panama City. In 1989, a fresh set of presidential elections pitted the Noriega-picked candidate against Guillermo Endara. When Endara won, Noriega annulled the election amid widespread claims by foreign observers of fraud on the part of the Noriega regime.

With Panama veering out of control, the U.S. began sending troops to bases in the Canal Zone. On December 20, 1989, the U.S. launched Operation Just Cause, led by 25,000 soldiers who pounded the city for 6 days, leaving anywhere from 500 to 7,000 dead, depending on whom you asked. Noriega fled and hid in the offices of the Vatican *nuncio*, where he asked for asylum. He later surrendered and was flown to the U.S., where he was tried, charged, and sentenced to 40 years in prison. The sentence was later reduced, though his fate is up in the air as he fights extradition to France, where he faces charges for money-laundering. Though Noriega also faces jail time in Panama if he returns, Panamanians are justifiably nervous about his release.

In the wake of Noriega's extradition, Guillermo Endara was sworn in as president, where he presided over a country racked by instability. In 1994, a former Torrijos associate, Ernesto Pérez Balladares, was sworn in as president and instituted sweeping economic reforms and worked to rebuild Panama's relationship with the U.S., which still had control of the canal. The same year, the constitution was changed to ban the military in Panama. Balladares was followed by Mireya Moscoso in 1999, the ex-wife of Arias and Panama's first female president. During her 5 years in power, however, her approval ratings dropped to less than 30%; she was generally viewed as grossly incompetent and prone to cronyism and corruption. Moscoso oversaw the much-anticipated handover of the canal. Despite decades of protest against the U.S. presence, many Panamanians in the end expressed ambivalence about the pullout when faced with the economic impact on businesses and the loss of jobs. Still, the handover has defied everyone's expectations, and the canal is run today as well, if not better, than before. Panama's current president is Ricardo Martinelli, voted into office in 2009. Like many presidents before him, he has vowed to increase jobs and security, and to fight against corruption and poverty. So far, most Panamanians seem to think he's living up to his promise.

A FEAST OF LANGUAGES

Spanish is the official language, but other languages are spoken in pockets around Panama. The country's seven indigenous groups speak a variety of dialects of Wounaan, Teribe, Emberá, Kuna, and Ngöbe-Buglé (Guaymí), the latter two being the most common given that they are the largest indigenous communities in Panama. In the Bocas del Toro region, descendants of Jamaican immigrants who came to work on banana plantations speak what's known as "Guari Guari," alternatively spelled "Wari Wari." It is also sometimes referred to as creole English, but really the language is patois English blended with Spanish and Guaymí (Ngöbe-Buglé) words. Native English speakers have a difficult time understanding Guari Guari. A good place to hear Guari Guari is at Old Bank on Isla Bastimentos.

San Miguel creole French, spoken by immigrants from Santa Lucía during the 19th century, is a dying language in Panama that's rarely heard any longer. On the other hand, Chinese immigrants, many of whom work as merchants running corner stores and small markets called *chinos*, continue to speak their native tongue. Adding to this mélange is Arabic, spoken by immigrants from the Middle East. There is also a growing, English-speaking expat community in Panama City, Boquete, Bocas del Toro, and el Valle de Anton, and English is now a requirement in all public schools, meaning growing numbers of Panamanians are bilingual.

THE LAY OF THE LAND
Climatic Regions & Land Formations

Panama is tropical country, and as such, has distinct dry and wet seasons. Generally speaking, December to mid-April are the driest months, while October and November are the wettest. However, cooler mountainous regions such as the Chiriquí Highlands and the Valle de Anton see rain throughout the year, though it's usually limited to a light mist or *barenje* during the dry season. The Caribbean Coast also tends to be wetter than the Pacific, particularly Bocas del Toro, where it can rain anytime of the year. The Darién can be difficult at best in the rainy season, and you'll be hard-pressed to find a company willing to go in the rainiest months, though there are so many bugs during this time that it's unlikely you'd want to go anyway. The Azuero Peninsula is a bit drier than the rest of the country, and has been subject to much deforestation. The Kuna Yala Islands represent an interesting topography. Unlike most Panamanian islands, which are heavily forested, the more than 365 Kuna Islands are made up of sand and palm trees, and temperatures are often more comfortable here than other beach destination, with nights even getting a bit cool.

Flora & Fauna

Panama is the land bridge that connects Central and South America, and as such, it is home to an amazing array of flora and fauna native to both continents. In fact, the tiny country of Panama has more than 10,000 species of plants, more than 225 species of mammals, and over 940 identified species of birds. That's more bird species than that of the United States and Canada combined! Although Costa Rica, its neighbor to the north, is better known in terms of eco-tourism, nature lovers will feel quite at home in Panama. Bird-watchers have reportedly spotted up to 367 bird species on trails such as Pipeline road and the Achiote road, and there have even been sightings of the elusive harpy eagle.

It is Panama's incredible geographical diversity that makes this tiny sliver of a country a haven for thousands of species of flora and fauna. From tropical rainforests to rivers, lakes, beaches, mountainous cloud forests, and swampy mangroves, Panama is home to hundreds of ecosystems that make it a fascinating country to visit.

For more information and details on Panama flora and fauna, see chapter 15.

Panama's Ecosystems

Once covered almost entirely in dense rainforest, many of Panama's ecosystems have been irreversibly damaged by the onset of deforestation and development. However, recent government initiatives to protect natural habitats and ecosystems have slowed this irresponsible practice, and a new government focus on eco-minded tourism means Panama is taking measures to protect its natural resources.

Panama's **lowland rainforests** are true tropical jungles with sweltering, humid climates and up to 180 inches of rainfall per year. The most impressive lowland rainforests stretch from the vast Darién along the coastal Kuna Yala Comarca to the immediate Panama City surroundings to the Bocas del Toro archipelago.

The Darién, covering nearly 17,000 square miles, is Panama's largest province, and one of its least traveled. Bordering Colombia, it has an exaggerated reputation as a dangerous destination, and it is perhaps this reputation that has allowed the

Darién to thrive as one of the last bastions of pristine rainforest in the Americas, save for a few towns and a couple dozen Emberá settlements deep in the forest. Here you'll find pristine primary forests, chemically pure rivers, and intricate ecosystems that have been able to thrive due to little to no human contact. Thanks to the man-made Gatun Lake, the fourth-largest man-made lake in the world, the rainforest surrounding Gatun has also remained protected from the onset of development, and jungle river cruises are the perfect way to see monkeys, sloths, caymans, birds, and much more if you're sticking around Panama City. Panama's rainforests remain relatively dry between December and mid-April, with October and November being the rainiest months.

In the Chiriquí Highlands and the Valle de Anton, **cloud forests** are a major attraction, with frequent rain, cloudy days, and cooler temperatures. Because cloud forests are found in generally steep, mountainous terrain, the canopy here is lower and less uniform than in lowland rainforests, providing better chances for viewing elusive fauna. Panama's most impressive mountain parks and cloud forest is the **Amistad International Park** spread between the provinces of Chiriquí and Bocas del Toro, and actually sharing a border with Costa Rica. **Volcán Barú National Park** is another well-known destination for wildlife and bird-watching, home to **Volcán Barú,** Panama's only active volcano.

Along the coasts, primarily along the Pacific Coast where river mouths meet the ocean, you will find extensive **mangrove forests** and **swamps.** The mangroves of the **Cocle** province are well known as crustacean and salt factories, and there are also impressive mangroves along the islands of **Bocas del Toro.**

Isla de Coiba on the Pacific side has drawn comparisons to the Galápagos Islands because of its fascinating ecosystems, and in fact, the entire island has been declared a National Park.

Over the last decade or so, Panama has taken great strides toward protecting its rich biodiversity. About 22% of the country is protected within 14 national parks. However, natural habitats along the Pacific Coast are being rapidly replaced by high-rise condominiums and golf courses. The Azuero peninsula continues to be harvested and deforested at an alarming pace, meaning that this region is now much drier than the rest of the country, with its natural landscape permanently altered.

Wildlife of the Bocas del Toro

Around the seemingly monotonous tangles of roots of the mangroves lining the shores of the islands of the Bocas del Toro you'll find one of the most diverse and rich ecosystems in the country. All sorts of fish and crustaceans live in the brackish tidal waters. Caimans and crocodiles cruise the maze of rivers and unmarked canals, and hundreds of herons, ibises, egrets, and other marsh birds nest and feed along the silted banks. Mangrove swamps are often havens for water birds: cormorants, frigate birds, pelicans, and herons. The larger birds tend to nest up high in the canopy, while the smaller ones nestle in the underbrush. The mangroves in the province of Cocle are also believed to have medicinal and therapeutic properties.

TIPS FOR SEEING WILDLIFE

Seasoned bird-watchers and wildlife lovers know that the animal world is most active at sunrise and, to a lesser extent, at sunset. Birds are easier to spot in open areas and secondary forests than in primary forests. I recommend that you hire a guide if you're planning on trekking through the rainforest. A guide's local knowledge, and his or her ability not only to identify flora and fauna but to actually point it out, are invaluable.

Here are a few helpful hints on spotting wildlife:

- **Stay quiet.** Noise scares off animals and birds, so keep chatting to a minimum.
- **Listen.** Guides spot birds by listening to their call, and animals by listening to the sound of rustling leaves or anything else that indicates an animal is in the vicinity.
- **Bring binoculars.** Choose a quality pair with a long range, and learn how to use them before you get on the trail.

- **Be patient and don't try too hard.** Once you relax and soften your focus, you'll see animals and birds more readily.
- **Dress appropriately.** Wear comfortable clothing and good shoes or boots—neutral tones are recommended for blending in with your environment. The better camouflaged you are, the better your chances for spotting wildlife. Also, wear long pants and a long-sleeve shirt, and repellent.
- **Respect the wildlife.** Remember ecosystems are delicate and it is a privilege to visit wildlife in their native habitat. Do not poke, prod, scare or antagonize wildlife just so you can have a better look. It may sound obvious, but I've been on enough wildlife and birding excursions to know there are always a few people who don't seem to remember it's the animals' home, not ours.

In any one spot in Panama, temperatures remain relatively constant year-round. However, as seen above, they vary dramatically according to altitude, from hot and humid in the tropical lowlands to cool in the highlands.

PANAMA IN POPULAR CULTURE: BOOKS, MUSIC & FILMS

For a guide to English-language bookstores in Panama City, see "Fast Facts: Panama City," in chapter 6. For literature concerning the natural habitat of Panama, its forests, birds, insects, and wildlife, head straight to the **Corotu Bookstore** at the Smithsonian in Panama City on Roosevelt Avenue in Ancon (© **212-8000**); you won't find a better selection anywhere. Many of the books listed here can be ordered from a Web-based book dealer such as Amazon.

GENERAL INTEREST & HISTORY *Emperors in the Jungle,* by John Lindsay-Poland (Duke University Press, 2003), digs deep into the history of U.S. military involvement in Panama during the past century. *Panama,* by Kevin Buckley (Touchstone, 1992), is a gripping read by a former *Newsweek* correspondent who vividly describes the events leading to the overthrow of Manuel Noriega. Another probing insight into the failure of U.S. policy that led to the rise of Noriega and the invasion is *The Noriega Mess: The Drugs, the Canal, and Why America Invaded,* by Luis E. Murillo (Video Books, 1995), but prepare yourself for 900 pages.

CULTURE *A People Who Would Not Kneel: Panama, the United States and the San Blas Kuna,* by James Howe (Smithsonian Books, 1998), tells of the powerful resistance by the Kuna Indians to set their own terms against invading Europeans and a Panamanian government intent on flattening their culture and relegating them to inferior social status. *The Art of Being Kuna: Layers and Meaning Among the Kuna of Panama,* by Mari Lynn Salvador (University of Washington Press, 1997), is a beautifully illustrated guide to the arts and culture of the Kuna.

THE PANAMA CANAL *Path Between the Seas: The Creation of the Panama Canal, 1870–1914,* by David McCullough (Simon & Schuster, 1978), brings the epic history of the building of the canal to life with McCullough's meticulously researched book—but at 704 pages, it's a tremendously long read and a heavy book to carry. *How Wall Street Created a Nation: J.P. Morgan, Teddy Roosevelt, and the Panama Canal,* by Ovidio Díaz Espinoso (Four Walls Eight Windows, 2001), is a page-turning account of the intrigue and back-door dealings between a group of Wall Street bankers and lawyers who paved the way for the construction of the Panama Canal.

FIELD GUIDES Most lodges and hotels have a copy of *A Guide to the Birds of Panama,* by Robert S. Ridgley and John A. Gwynne (Princeton University Press, 1992), which is the layman's bible to identifying the many birds you'll see during your visit, and which includes tips on where you're most likely to see them. Most guides and nature lodges have a copy of this book on hand, although it's always best to have your own. A good all-around book to have is Carrol Henderson's *The Field Guide to the Wildlife of Costa Rica* (University of Texas Press, 2002). Although it's a Costa Rican guide, this book is useful in Panama since these two neighboring countries are home to much of the same fauna.

NATURAL HISTORY *Tropical Nature: Life and Death in the Rainforests of Central and South America,* by Adrian Forsyth and Ken Miyata (Touchstone Books, 1987), is a passionate, lucid exploration of the interrelationships of flora and fauna in the tropical rainforest. *The Neotropical Companion,* by John C. Kricher (Princeton University Press, 1999), is tremendously popular with field guides, giving a lively and readable overview of ecological processes at work in the neotropics. Juan Carlos Navarro, the mayor of Panama City, is the author of a glossy coffee-table book, *Parques Nacionales de Panamá* (Balboa Ediciones, 2001), featuring gorgeous photos of national parks in Panama and the flora and fauna found within. *The Tapir's Morning Bath,* by Elizabeth Royte (Mariner Books, 2002), is an engaging account of the joys and frustrations of scientific fieldwork by biologists at the canal's Barro Colorado Island.

MUSIC & FILMS **Ruben Blades** may be Panama's current Minister of Tourism, but he is better known as Panama's best-known salsa singer. He's made dozens of CDs, but you might want to check out *Maestro de la Fania* (2005), his latest creation, and *Lo Mejor vol. 1 and 2* (2004), featuring his greatest hits over his decades-long career.

The Panama Deception (1992) is an interesting documentary that aims to tell the truth about the 1989 invasion of Panama by the U.S.

The Tailor of Panama (2001) is an excellent spy-thriller starring Pierce Brosnan, Geoffrey Rush, and Jamie Lee Curtis and centers around the transfer of power of the canal from the Americans to the Panamanian people during the post-Noriega years.

The latest James Bond film, ***Quantum of Solace*** (2008), doesn't take place in Panama, but the Bolivia scenes were filmed in Casco Antiguo, and Colón doubles as Jamaica. Actor Daniel Craig stayed in the Canal House hotel (p. 99) in Casco Antiguo during much of the movie's filming.

EATING & DRINKING IN PANAMA

Panama is a melting pot of ethnicities, and its cuisine is accordingly influenced by its diverse population. Within Panama City, travelers will find something from every corner of the world, including French, Japanese, Italian, Thai, Middle Eastern, and Chinese food—all of it very good and true to its roots. In regional areas, traditional Panamanian cuisine is an overlapping mix of Afro-Caribbean, indigenous, and Spanish cooking influences incorporating a variety of tropical fruit, vegetables, and herbs. Most Panamanian restaurants are casual—diners, beachfront cafes, and roadside fondas (food stands). A large U.S. population has spawned North American cafes and bistros serving burgers and the like, and fast-food chains are plentiful in Panama City.

Meals & Dining Customs

Panamanian cuisine is tasty but can be repetitive given that every meal is based around coconut rice (rice made with coconut milk) and beans, and fried green plantains called patacones. A lot of Panamanian food is fried—just stop at a fonda and see for yourself. Even breakfast is a selection of fried meats and breads. Panamanian food is neither spicy nor heavily seasoned; in fact, salt is often the only seasoning used in many staple dishes.

Dining hours generally follow North American customs, with restaurants opening around 7 or 8am for breakfast, serving lunch from noon to 2pm, and dinner from 7 to 10pm. In smaller towns, you'll find that restaurants close as early as 9pm or sometimes even 8pm. Upscale restaurants in Panama City serve until 11pm.

Note: All Panamanian restaurants and bars recently became smoke-free, so smokers will have to take it outside.

BREAKFAST Start your day with a cup of fresh-brewed Panamanian joe. Breakfast menus around the country feature standbys like scrambled eggs, toast, and fruit, but Panamanians like their tortillas, too. These are not Mexican-style tortillas but deep-fried corn batter topped with eggs and cheese, something akin to huevos rancheros. *Hojaldras,* deep-fried bread sprinkled with powdered sugar like a Panamanian doughnut, are another common breakfast staple. Afro-Caribbeans eat greasy meats like pork with their breakfast; if your arteries can handle it, give it a try. A hearty breakfast of "Caribbean porridge," made of rice, beans, and pork, is called *gallo pinto,* or "spotted rooster," and can be found in local joints.

APPETIZERS & SNACKS Seviche, raw cubes of fish and onion marinated in lemon juice, is a popular dish throughout Latin America. It's usually made with sea bass or with shrimp or octopus. Crunchy cornmeal pastries stuffed with meat are called empanadas—greasy but good when they're fresh and hot. The yuca root, a Panama staple, when fried, substitutes for french fries. Yuca is also used for a *carimañola;* the yuca is mashed and formed into a roll stuffed with meat and boiled eggs, then deep-fried. Plantains are served in two varieties: *patacones,* or green plantains, cut in rounds, pounded and deep-fried, and salted; or *plátanos maduros,* ripe plantains, broiled or sautéed in oil. Ripe plantains are also called *plátanos en tentación* when they are slightly caramelized with sugar and cinnamon. Plantains and *patacones,* along with coconut rice *(arroz con coco)* and beans *(frijoles),* are the standard accompaniment to traditional Panamanian dishes. Another popular snack is a tamale; much like the Mexican version, tamales are cornmeal patties stuffed with meat and steamed in a banana leaf. Sandwiches in Panama are called *emparedados.*

MEAT & POULTRY　There is perhaps no dish more emblematic of Panama than the *sancocho,* a chicken stew made with a starchy root called *ñamé* and seasoned with a cilantro-like herb called culantro. Sancocho is said to put strength back into your body after a late night out. Meat is commonplace, served as a *bistec* (steak), or in a popular dish called *ropa vieja,* meaning "old clothes" and consisting of shredded beef with a spicy tomato sauce served over rice. Chicken is a staple, too, as is pork. In the Caribbean, some locals still eat turtle soup and turtle eggs, although it is usually kept under wraps due to vocal conservation efforts to protect turtles—these are endangered creatures, so refuse turtle if ever it is ever offered to you.

SEAFOOD　Panama, which means "abundance of fish," lives up to its name with lots of fresh delicacies from the sea, including *pargo* (red snapper), *corvina* (sea bass), *langostino* (jumbo shrimp), *langosta* (lobster), calamari, *cangrejo* (crab), and *pulpo* (octopus). Traditional Panamanian seafood dishes come four ways: fried, grilled, *al ajillo* (with a spicy garlic sauce), or *a la española* (sautéed with tomatoes and onions). Lobster and jumbo shrimp are expensive because of overfishing and dwindling supplies.

VEGETABLES　Panama's agricultural breadbasket is around the flank of Volcán Barú in the western Highlands; here the volcanic soil and high altitudes encourage year-round growing conditions, and vegetables are readily available. Elsewhere, the hot, humid weather is not conducive to growing vegetables, which is why you'll see so few served with meals. Salads are not hard to come by, but traditional Panamanian fare is typically only served with just a small cabbage salad topped with a slice of tomato. Sometimes you'll see corn, or the exotic root vegetables such as the aforementioned yuca and *ñamé.*

FRUIT　Panama has a wealth of tropical fruit, but the most common you'll see (especially at breakfast) are pineapple, papaya, banana, and melon. Other fruit are the *maracuyá,* or passion fruit, which is better as a juice than off the tree; *guanabana,* or soursop; and *guayaba,* or guava.

DESSERTS　*Pastel tres leches,* or "three-milk cake," is made with just that: evaporated, condensed, and regular milk, cooked into a rich, puddinglike cake. Flan is as popular here as it is all over Latin America. Street vendors in Panama City (especially on Av. Balboa or in Casco Viejo) sell *raspados,* or fruit-juice-flavored snow cones. Panamanians like to top the cone off with a dollop of condensed milk.

BEVERAGES   Major brands of soft drinks are available in Panama. You can't find a more fresh-off-the-tree beverage than a *pipa,* the sweet, clear liquid of an unripe coconut. Roadside vendors hack a hole in the crown of the coconut, pop in a straw, and for about 25¢ you have what some refer to as the "nectar of the gods." It is also said to aid digestion. *Chicha* is the common name for juice, and the variety of fresh fruit juices in Panama is a tasty and refreshing elixir on a hot day. *Chichas* come in a variety of common flavors such as watermelon and pineapple, but there are more exotic *chichas* such as *chicha con arroz y piña,* a beverage made from rice and boiled pineapple skins; *naranjilla,* a tropical fruit whose juice has the taste of apple cider; or *chicha de marañón,* a beverage made from the fruit of a cashew tree. A local favorite in the outskirts of Panama City (mostly sold at roadside stands) is *chicheme,* a corn-based beverage mixed with water, sugar, and cinnamon. Panamanians tout the drink for its nutritional properties.

Panama is known for its high-quality coffee, with Café Durán being the most common brand. Kotowa, the Jansen Family, and Café Ruiz are all excellent, too. *Café con leche* is coffee with milk (usually condensed) or cream.

BEER, WINE & LIQUOR   When in Panama, do as the locals do and down an icy cold local beer. Beer is Panama's most popular alcoholic drink, and there is a wide variety of national brands to sample, such as Balboa, Atlas, Panamá, Soberana, and Cristal—all light pale lagers, none of which are particularly outstanding, but all taste divine in a hot, sticky climate. International brands such as Heineken, Corona, and Guinness can be found even in small-town markets.

Panama's most famous drink is *seco,* a sugar-cane-distilled alcohol produced in Herrera and commonly served with milk and ice. You won't find *seco* in trendy bars or high-end restaurants; it's consumed mostly in rural communities and cantinas. Also popular in Panama are rum, vodka, and scotch. And you won't want to forget to purchase a couple of bottles of Abuelo, Panama's surprisingly tasty rum.

You'll find Chilean, U.S., and Spanish wines on most menus, but the selection is limited, and many restaurants serve red wines cold (must have something to do with the climate). But wine consumption is increasing in Panama, evidenced by the growing number of upscale restaurants that put time and thought into their wine lists, and there are a few wine-specialty stores popping up here and there.

PLANNING YOUR TRIP TO PANAMA

3

Panama is just starting to take off as a major tourist destination, and many areas remain deliciously free of crowds while offering the same pristine wilderness and action-packed adventure as its more popular neighbor, Costa Rica. Panama is but a thin squiggle of a country, but there is a wealth of diversity packed within its borders, from lush rainforests to sultry beaches to craggy mountain peaks—all of which can be reached by a short drive or flight. The Caribbean Sea and Pacific Ocean are so close to each other that you can swim in both in 1 day. If you're a nature lover, consider that Panama is a land bridge between North and South America, and hundreds of wildlife species—more than 900 species of birds alone—meet here at the isthmus, providing a rich environment for eco-travel.

Panama is a safe country, too, and Panamanians are some of the friendliest people in Latin America. So many residents speak English that it could almost be called Panama's second language. And in comparison to Costa Rica's, Panama's infrastructure and capital city are decidedly more modern, and travel budgeting is easier considering that the country's national monetary unit is the U.S. dollar.

So now the question isn't whether you should go, but when? What is the best time to visit, and which destinations should you visit? How can you preplan a trip and find cheap deals and other tantalizing offers? These are just a few of the questions that this chapter answers to help you plan an unforgettable vacation.

For additional help in planning your trip and for more on-the-ground resources in Panama, please see "Fast Facts: Panama" on p. 308.

WHEN TO GO

Panama lies between 7 degrees and 9 degrees above the Equator, which places it firmly within the Tropics. Accordingly, average year-round temperatures are a balmy 75°F to 85°F (24°C–29°C), varying only with altitude. The average temperature in the Chiriquí Highlands, for example, is 60°F (16°C), and it is the only area in Panama where you will likely feel cold.

Humidity is always high in Panama, and rainfall varies noticeably between the Pacific and Caribbean sides of the country, with some areas in the Caribbean receiving almost twice the yearly rainfall of Panama City. The best time to visit Panama is during the summer **dry season** from mid-December to mid-April. This is also **high season,** and some hotels and resorts charge higher rates during this period. Caribbean destinations such as Bocas del Toro have a shorter dry season, usually September/October and February/March, but really showers can occur on any day.

The Chiriquí Highlands experiences a variety of microclimates that can change drastically, sometimes even within a few miles. In Boquete, high winds and a peculiar misting rain called *bajareque* are common from mid-December to mid-February; January sees the occasional thunderstorm, and March to May are the sunniest months.

If you are unable to visit during the dry season, keep in mind that the early months (Apr–July) are characterized by sudden, heavy thunderstorms in the afternoon that are short in duration, and can happen every few days. Often, the skies are sunny in the morning or afternoon.

For up-to-date information on weather in Panama, go to **www.accuweather.com**.

Average Monthly Temperatures & Rainfall in Panama City

	JAN	FEB	MAR	APR	MAY	JUNE	JULY	AUG	SEPT	OCT	NOV	DEC
Temp. (°F)	82	82	82	82	80	80	81	81	81	80	81	82
Temp. (°C)	27	27	27	27	25	25	26	26	26	25	25	27
Days of Rain	4	2	1	6	15	16	15	15	16	18	18	12

Public Holidays

There is a saying in Panama that the only thing Panamanians take seriously are their holidays—and it's no joke. Nearly every business, including banks, offices, and many stores and restaurants, closes, making even Panama City feel like a ghost town. Official holidays that fall on a Saturday or Sunday are usually observed on Mondays, allowing for a long weekend. Transportation services are also greatly reduced. During holidays, most locals head for the beach or other getaway destinations, so if you plan to travel during this time, book lodging well in advance and make certain you have confirmed reservations.

Panama's most revered holiday is Carnaval, the 4 days that precede Ash Wednesday. (Though not officially a holiday, most call in sick to work to recover from Carnaval on Wed.) The largest celebrations take place in Panama City and the Azuero Peninsula, with parades, floats, drinking, costumes, and music. Note that celebrations in Panama City can be a bit raucous and aren't usually as classy as those on the Azuero Peninsula. The dates for upcoming Carnavales are March 5 through March 8 (2011), February 18 through February 21 (2012), and February 9 through February 12 (2013).

Official holidays in Panama include January 1 (New Year's Day), January 9 (Martyr's Day), Good Friday, Easter Sunday, May 1 (Labor Day), August 15 (Founding of Old Panama—observed in Panama City only), October 12 (Hispanic Day), November 2 (All Souls' Day), November 3 (Independence Day), November 4 (Flag Day), November 5 (Colón Day—observed in the city of Colón only), November 10 (First Call for Independence), November 28 (Independence from Spain), December 8 (Mother's Day), and December 25 (Christmas Day).

Panama Calendar of Events & Festivals

Many of the following listings are annual events whose exact dates vary from year to year, and the majority are local festivals. Call the **ATP tourism board** at $\textcircled{C}$ **800/962-1526,** or check their website at www.visitpanama.com, for more information.

For an exhaustive list of events beyond those listed here, check **http://events.frommers. com**, where you'll find a searchable, up-to-the-minute roster of what's happening in destinations all over the world.

JANUARY

Feria de las Flores y del Café (Flower and Coffee Festival), Boquete. This festival is one of the grandest celebrations of flowers in the world, drawing thousands of people to Boquete for 10 days. Expect lush flower displays, food stands, live music, amusement rides, handicrafts booths, and hotel rooms booked far in advance. Mid-January.

Jazz Festival, Panama City. For one 3-day weekend, Panama City throbs with live jazz performances by outstanding international musicians. Some events are held outdoors and are free; log on to www.panamajazz festival.com. Late January.

FEBRUARY

Carnaval (Carnival). Panama's largest yearly celebration (occasionally falling in early March) takes place during the 4 days that precede Ash Wednesday. The largest celebrations are in small towns on the Azuero Peninsula, such as Las Tablas, and Panama City, with parades, music, and dancing. Be prepared to get wet by *mojaderos,* or trucks that spray revelers with water.

MARCH

Semana Santa. During this week (Holy Week), parades, religious processions, and other special events take place across the country. Palm Sunday through Holy Saturday.

Feria de David. The Chiriquí capital's largest festival (www.feriadedavid.com) draws more than 500 exhibitors from around the world to display industrial products and new technology. During the 10-day event, the city hosts plentiful cultural and folkloric events. Mid-March.

APRIL

Feria de Orquídeas (Orchid Festival), Boquete. It's not as grand as the flower festival, but the Orchid Festival is enjoyable because it showcases thousands of varieties of these delicate flowers for public viewing. At the fairgrounds around mid-April.

Feria Internacional del Azuero, La Villa de Los Santos. This multiday festival is something akin to a county fair, with animal displays, food stalls, and lots of drinking. Mid-April.

JUNE

Festival Corpus Christi, La Villa de Los Santos. The town explodes with activity for a 2-week religious festival known for its elaborate dances led by men in devil masks. Forty days after Easter.

JULY

Festival Patronales de La Virgen de Santa Librada, Las Tablas. This festival is famous for its **Festival de la Pollera** on July 22, which showcases the region's most beautiful pollera dresses and elects the "Queen of the Pollera" for that year. July 20 to July 22.

Feria Internacional del Mar (International Festival of the Sea), Bocas del Toro. This 5-day event features food stands serving local cuisine, handicrafts booths, exhibits by the Smithsonian Institute and ANAM (the park service), folkloric presentations, and dances. Around the second week of September.

Festival de la Mejorana, Guararé. This nationally famous folkloric festival features hundreds of dancers, musicians, and singers coming together for a week of events and serious partying. Last week of September.

OCTOBER

Festival del Cristo Negro (Black Christ Festival), Portobelo. Thousands of pilgrims come to pay penance, perform other acts of devotion, and do some reveling at the Iglesia de San Felipe, home to a wooden black Christ effigy that is paraded around town on this day. October 21.

NOVEMBER

Independence Days. Panama celebrates three independence days. November 3 and 4 are Independence Day and Flag Day and the largest independence celebrations, featuring parades, fireworks, and other entertainment in Panama City and larger cities like David. November 10th is a holiday for the "First Call for Independence," as is November 28th honoring Independence Day from Spain, with some regional festivities—but nothing matching November 3 and 4.

Feria de las Tierras Altas, Volcán. This Highlands Festival is a 5-day celebration of agriculture, local arts, and culture. Around the last week of November.

ENTRY REQUIREMENTS

Passports

U.S. citizens traveling to Panama are required to present a valid passport. For information on obtaining a passport, see "Passports" in the "Fast Facts" section of chapter 13—the websites listed provide downloadable passport applications as well as the current fees for processing passport applications. For an up-to-date, country-by-country listing of passport requirements around the world, go to the "Foreign Entry Requirement" Web page of the U.S. State Department at **http://travel.state.gov**.

Important: When entering the country travelers must be able to demonstrate proof of sufficient funds if requested, and they must present an onward or return ticket. However, I've never been asked to present proof of either, and I've been to Panama eight times in the past 3 years. Keep in mind that Panama charges a departure tax of $20 at the airport, but the tax is probably already included in the price of your ticket.

In an effort to prevent international child abduction, many governments require a parent or legal guardian (or someone other than the parent) traveling alone with a child to provide documentary evidence of relationship and travel permission. Having such documentation on hand can facilitate entry/departure if immigration requests it, although it is not always required. Inquire when booking your airline ticket about updated entry/departure procedures for children.

Visas

Citizens of the United States, Canada, Great Britain, and most European nations may visit Panama for a maximum of 90 consecutive days. No visa is necessary. Carry your passport with you at all times. Police will sometimes ask for your documents, particularly on long bus rides on routine checks. The last thing you want to do is be detained by police for hours on your way somewhere, so be sure to have your passport with you. If you absolutely refuse to carry your passport, make a copy of your ID page and your Customs arrival stamp. Even in Panama City, police are known to take advantage of "gringos" without documents, threatening jail time or demanding a payment of whatever you have on you. (If you don't have enough on you, they'll be happy to drive you to the nearest ATM.) This little trick is most likely to happen to men walking around at night after a few too many drinks, but the bottom line is to *always* carry your passport or a copy of your ID and entry page.

Medical Requirements

There are no vaccination requirements when entering Panama. However, if you'll be traveling to the tropical lowlands or to the jungle, it's wise to get vaccinated for typhoid, yellow fever, and hepatitis A. All travelers should also be up to date on their tetanus immunizations. There has been a recent spike in dengue fever in recent years, so travelers will want to be especially careful during the rainy season. If you'll be going to the Darién, you may also want to take malaria pills, which should be prescribed by your doctor at least 10 days before your departure. However, if you're traveling during the dry season or won't be exploring the tropical lowlands or rainforests too much, your risk of tropical disease is relatively low.

Customs

WHAT YOU CAN BRING INTO PANAMA

Visitors to Panama may bring with them personal items such as jewelry, and professional equipment including cameras, computers, and electronics, as well as fishing and diving gear for personal use—all of which are permitted duty-free. Visitors may bring in up to 200 cigarettes and 3 bottles of liquor tax-free. Customs officials in Panama seldom check arriving tourists' luggage.

WHAT YOU CAN TAKE HOME FROM PANAMA

For information on what you're allowed to bring home, contact one of the following agencies:

U.S. Citizens: U.S. Customs & Border Protection (CBP), 1300 Pennsylvania Ave. NW, Washington, DC 20229 (© **877/287-8667;** www.cbp.gov).

Canadian Citizens: Canada Border Services Agency, Ottawa, Ontario, K1A 0L8 (© **800/461-9999** in Canada, or 204/983-3500; www.cbsa-asfc.gc.ca).

U.K. Citizens: HM Customs & Excise, Crownhill Court, Tailyour Road, Plymouth, PL6 5BZ (© **0845/010-9000;** from outside the U.K., 020/8929-0152; www.hmce.gov.uk).

Australian Citizens: Australian Customs Service, Customs House, 5 Constitution Ave., Canberra City, ACT 2601 (© **1300/363-263;** from outside Australia, 61/2-6275-6666; www.customs.gov.au).

New Zealand Citizens: New Zealand Customs, The Customhouse, 17–21 Whitmore St., Box 2218, Wellington, 6140 (© **04/473-6099** or 0800/ 428-786; www.customs.govt.nz).

GETTING THERE & GETTING AROUND

Getting to Panama

BY PLANE

All international flights land at **Tocumen International Airport** (PTY; ℂ **238-2700**). Air Panama flights from Costa Rica to Panama City land at the **Marcos A. Gelabert Airport** (PAC), which is more commonly referred to as **Albrook Airport**). There is also direct service from San José, Costa Rica, to the David and Bocas del Toro airports (see chapters 9 and 10, respectively). TACA Airlines (see below) has service from Costa Rica, arriving at Tocumen. An expansion of the David airport was recently approved, so flights from Florida and other international destinations will eventually be able to land in David, meaning travelers going directly to Bocas and Boquete won't have to fly into Panama City. However, this project is in the early stages and likely won't be finished for at least a couple years.

The following airlines serve Panama City from the United States, using the gateway cities listed. **American Airlines** (ℂ **800/433-7300** in the U.S., or 269-6022 in Panama; www.aa.com) has two daily flights from Miami; Copa Airlines (ℂ 800/359-2672 in the U.S., or 227-0116 in Panama; www.copaair.com) has two daily flights from Miami, and one daily flight from Orlando, New York, Los Angeles, and Washington, D.C. **Delta Airlines** (ℂ 800/241-4141 in the U.S., or 214-8118 in Panama; www.delta.com) offers one daily flight from Atlanta; TACA (ℂ 800/400-8222 in the U.S., or 360-2093 in Panama; www.taca.com) has one daily flight from all major U.S. hubs, but with a stopover in El Salvador or Costa Rica. Mexicana (ℂ 800/531-7921 in the U.S., or 264-9855 in Panama; www.mexicana.com) offers daily flights from Miami, Dallas, and Los Angeles; however, they connect with Copa Air in Mexico City, so you're better off with a direct flight with Copa. From Canada, flights to Panama City are available through American Airlines, with a connection in Miami. **Spirit Airlines** (ℂ **800/772-7117;** www.spiritair.com) offers nonstop service to Panama City from Fort Lauderdale.

From London, Iberia (ℂ **0870/609-0500** in the U.K., or 227-3966 in Panama; www.iberia.com) has daily flights to Panama City that connect in either Madrid or Costa Rica; American **Airlines** and **British Airways** have daily flights that connect in Miami; **Continental Airlines** has daily flights that connect in Orlando or Houston; **Delta** has a daily flight that connects in Atlanta or Newark.

From Australia, Qantas (ℂ **9691-3636;** www.qantasair.com) has daily flights in conjunction with Copa Air from Sydney, connecting in Honolulu or Los Angeles; Air New Zealand (ℂ **507-264-8756** in New Zealand; www.airnewzealand.com) also works in conjunction with Copa Air with one daily flight from Auckland, connecting in Los Angeles.

For information about getting into Panama City from the airport, see chapter 6.

Getting Around

Getting around Panama is relatively easy compared to other Latin American countries, and major roads are well-maintained and delightfully free of potholes, making it a good place to rent a car to get from destination to destination. In Panama City, taxis are the best way to get around: They're cheap, and you don't have to deal with the stress of chaotic city driving. I don't recommend buses, as their routes are confusing, they can be dangerous, and you'll get everywhere much faster by taxi. Panama City (except for the Casco Viejo neighborhood) isn't the best place to explore on foot, as most major tourist attractions aren't within walking distance from each other.

If you're traveling between cities or destinations, you can do so by bus, plane, or car. If you'll be driving, most destinations are off the paved and well-maintained Pan American Highway. Once you get off the highway, however, some secondary roads can be a bit rough. To enter or leave Panama City, you'll take the Puente de Las Americas or the newer Puente Centenario.

Bus travel between cities is relatively cheap, but slower than driving. Nearly all buses from Panama City to other destinations depart from the Terminal de buses by Albrook Airport.

BY PLANE

Aero Perlas (© 315-7500; www.aeroperlas.com) and **Air Panama** (© 316-9000; www.flyairpanama.com) are Panama's two carriers, servicing most destinations in the country. Air travel is safe, quick, and relatively inexpensive. If, like me, you're afraid of flying the 12-to-40 passenger planes used by Aero Perlas and Air Panama, they may not make you feel at ease as you shakily fly over the rainforest, but keep in mind there hasn't been a Panamanian airline crash in years. Check their websites for schedules and fares.

BY CAR

Driving in Panama allows you the most flexibility and if you can afford it, this is the best way to see Panama. Renting a car costs about as much as in the U.S., and gas is a little more expensive, so while this isn't the cheapest option, it allows you to enjoy the scenery, adhere to your own schedule, make pit stops, and visit destinations away from your hotel. Generally speaking, speed limits in Panama are about 60–80kmph on major roadways and slower on secondary roads. You'll want to stick to this limit, as police speed traps are common, and you don't want a speeding ticket to put a damper on your trip.

There are car-rental kiosks at both the Tocumen and Albrook airports (car-rental agencies at Tocumen are open 24 hr.; Albrook rental agencies are open 8am– 6:30pm), and each agency has a few locations in town. Tocumen Airport car-rental agency phone numbers are as follows: **Alamo** (© 238-4142; www.alamopanama. com), **Avis** (© 238-4056; www.avis.com), **Budget** (© 263-8777; www.budget panama.com), **Dollar** (© 270-0355; www.dollarpanama.com), **Hertz** (© 238-4081; www.hertz.com), **National** (© 238-4144; www.nationalpanama.com), and **Thrifty** (© 264-2613; www.thrifty.com).

When renting a car in Panama, you must purchase two basic insurances. The agency will also offer a variety of other full-coverage options, but generally, your credit card rental insurance should cover you, and you really only need the obligatory insurances.

Keep in mind that, depending on your destination, it's sometimes better to get a four-wheel-drive vehicle, as some of Panama's roads are unpaved and rocky. If you're staying close to Panama City or all your planned destinations are right off the Pan American Highway, you should be fine with a two-wheel-drive.

Getting There & Getting Around

PLANNING YOUR TRIP TO PANAMA

Although most Panamanians drive stick shift vehicles, automatics are readily available at all car-rental agencies, though you should expect to pay a bit more. Generally speaking, renting a car in Panama should cost you between $40 and $100 a day, depending on the kind of car and how you reserve. For the best deals, book through an online agency, such as Expedia, Hotels.com, or Kayak.com. You can also book directly through the car-rental agency's websites, as booking ahead of time generally gets you a better rate. The agency will give you a road map upon car rental.

Some distances are as follows:

Panama City to Colón: 1 hour
Panama City to Gamboa: 25 minutes
Panama City to Portobello: 1½ hours
Panama City to Cartí: 3 hours
Panama City to Boquete: 7 hours
Panama City to the Azuero Peninsula: 7 hours

There are also car-rental agencies in David, Colón, and other popular tourist destinations.

BY BUS

Bus routes between major and minor destinations in Panama are frequent and relatively inexpensive. Expect to pay about $2 to $4 per hour, depending on your destination. Panama City's bus terminal is located adjacent to Albrook Airport. It's not necessary to reserve your tickets ahead of time unless you are traveling on a holiday weekend or during December or Easter week. Be sure to arrive at the terminal at least 45 minutes ahead of time. You'll need a nickel to get on the bus, so make sure you have change. Long-distance buses are air-conditioned, comfortable, have an onboard bathroom, and usually show several movies. Shorter routes tend to use smaller, less comfortable buses, but are usually air-conditioned. If your route is 4 or more hours, the driver will make a pit stop about halfway through for lunch or dinner. Although buses are generally safe, I accidently left my purse on a bus recently and my passport, cash, and credit cards were stolen. It was my mistake—who leaves their purse on a Panamanian bus?—but try not to carry too many bags to reduce the risk of leaving anything behind. On the bright side, the kind thief did leave me $15 so I could get back to Panama City and start the 3am cancellation, application, and phone-call-to-mom process.

MONEY & COSTS

Currency

The unit of currency in Panama is the U.S. dollar, but the Panamanian balboa, which is pegged to the dollar at a 1:1 ratio, also circulates in denominations of 5¢, 10¢, 25¢, and 50¢ coins. (U.S. coins are in circulation as well.) Balboa coins are sized similarly to their U.S. counterparts, and travelers will have no trouble identifying their value.

Travelers with pounds or euros may exchange money at Banco Nacional, which has branches in the airport and across the nation. To save time, you may want to convert your money into dollars before arriving at Panama. At time of publication US$1 is equal to £.50 and .75€.

WHAT THINGS COST IN PANAMA	US$	EURO€	C$	UK£
Taxi from Tocumen Airport to downtown Panama City	25.00	20.00	29.00	14.00
Double room at moderately-priced hotel in Panama City	100.00	71.00	102.00	48.00
Taxi within Panama City	1.50–5.00	1.13–3.75	1.61–5.35	0.75–2.50
Three-course dinner for one, without alcohol, at a nice restaurant	15.00–35.00	10.00–26.00	16.00	7.50–18.00
Bottle of water	1.00	0.75	1.06	0.50
Cup of coffee	0.75	0.50	0.80	0.38
Can of soda	0.45	0.34	0.48	0.23

ATMs

The easiest and best way to get cash away from home is from an ATM (automated teller machine), available in banks and supermarkets, and identifiable by a red SISTEMA CLAVE sign with a white key. ATMs, called *cajeros automáticos,* can be found in larger towns only, so if you're visiting out-of-the-way destinations such as an off-shore island, plan to bring extra cash. Remember that you can usually only take up to $500 a day out of an ATM in Panama, so if you need a large sum of money, you'll need to start withdrawing a few days in advance. To find ATM locations in Panama, check out **www.sclave.com/english.html**.

Credit Cards

Businesses that accept credit cards always accept Visa and MasterCard, and to a lesser extent American Express. Diners Club is not widely accepted. Most businesses in Panama City and other major commerce centers accept credit cards. In small towns and more remote destinations, be sure to bring enough cash.

Traveler's Checks

They're practically extinct, but traveler's checks are still accepted at major hotels, and less so at budget hotels and restaurants. In fact, beyond major hotels and banks, businesses in Panama seem reluctant to accept traveler's checks and you're likely to draw blank stares. Use an ATM for cash if you can, and bring traveler's checks as a backup in the event of a lost or stolen card.

HEALTH

Staying Healthy

Travelers in Panama should have no problem staying healthy, as standards of hygiene are high, and tap water is safe to drink in most areas. Those with sensitive stomachs will want to drink bottled water when outside major hotels and cities. The most common health problems that affect travelers in Panama are sunburn and mosquito bites. Illnesses that once ravaged humans in the Tropics, such as yellow fever and malaria, are no longer epidemic in Panama. Viral infections and other illnesses are described in "Common Ailments," below. See "Medical Requirements," earlier in this chapter, for suggested vaccination information.

If you suffer from a chronic illness, consult your doctor before your departure. Pack **prescription medications** in your carry-on luggage, and carry them in their original containers, with pharmacy labels—otherwise they won't make it through airport security. Carry the generic name of prescription medicines in case a local pharmacist is unfamiliar with the brand name.

Contact the **International Association for Medical Assistance to Travelers (IAMAT; © 716/754-4883** or, in Canada, 416/652-0137; **www.iamat.org**) for tips on travel and current information about health concerns in Panama, and for lists of local, English-speaking doctors. The United States **Centers for Disease Control and Prevention (© 800/311-3435;** www.cdc.gov) provides up-to-date information on health hazards by region or country and offers tips on food safety. The website **www.tripprep.com**, sponsored by a consortium of travel medicine practitioners, may also offer helpful advice on traveling abroad. You can find listings of reliable clinics overseas at the **International Society of Travel Medicine** (www.istm.org).

Common Ailments

The most likely illness you'll face in Panama is traveler's diarrhea from unfamiliar foods or drinks. Even though the water in Panama is perfectly safe to drink almost everywhere, travelers with very delicate stomachs may want to stick to bottled water. Also, those with delicate stomachs may want to stick to moderate and high-end restaurants, and avoid raw vegetables and peeled fruit.

If you're traveling to the tropical lowlands or jungle areas, be sure to pack plenty of bug repellent with a high percentage of DEET, especially if you'll be hiking or spending most of your time outdoors. There's been a spike in dengue fever cases in the past few years, and the last thing you want is to have your trip ruined by a tropical disease. Also, if you'll be traveling in the Darién or another heavily forested area, bring light, long-sleeved clothing to avoid bug bites.

Most drugs can be bought over the counter at any pharmacy in Panama, and many prescription-only drugs in the U.S. are sold over the counter in pharmacies. Headache, anti-diarrheal, and other common OTC medications are readily available at all pharmacies.

TROPICAL ILLNESSES Travelers have a low risk of contracting a tropical disease while in Panama. **Yellow fever,** the mosquito-borne disease that decimated canal workers in the late 19th and early 20th century, is no longer epidemic and vaccinations are not required. However, if you're traveling to the Darién, Bocas del Toro, or other remote tropical destinations, you may want to consider getting vaccinated against yellow fever.

Governmental bulletins from the Centers for Disease Control (CDC) recommend that travelers planning to visit Bocas del Toro, Darién, or the San Blas Archipelago be vaccinated against **malaria**—yet cases of malaria are not common and mostly afflict rural citizens who live in remote areas, such as Ngöbe-Buglé Indian tribes. You might consider vaccination against malaria if you plan to spend extended periods in the jungle in the aforementioned areas. Malaria is a parasite that lives in red blood cells and is transmitted by the female anopheles mosquito. The symptoms are cycles of chills, fever, and sweating, sometimes accompanied by headache, backache, and vomiting. Check with your doctor for updated news about malaria outbreaks and what vaccine is best for the region you plan to visit (mosquitoes in the Darién, for example, are resistant to the common vaccine chloroquine).

More common is **dengue fever,** an infectious disease caused by an arbovirus transmitted by daytime mosquitoes. Symptoms of the disease appear suddenly and include a high fever, chills, swollen and painful eyes, a headache, and severe aches in the legs and joints—the reason dengue is commonly referred to as "breakbone fever." Symptoms last a week, and though most people recover fully, weakness and fatigue can continue for several weeks. Dengue fever outbreaks have been reported during the past few years in the Bocas del Toro and Colón provinces, mostly affecting locals who live near pools of stagnant water.

The most effective prevention against malaria and dengue fever is to protect yourself against mosquito bites (see "Bugs, Bites & Other Wildlife Concerns," below.)

DIETARY DISTRESS   **Hepatitis A** is a highly contagious viral disease and one of the most common travel-related infections in the developing world. It's transmitted by eating contaminated food, by fecal-oral contact, or by contact with unsanitary conditions. Outbreaks usually occur in poor regions such as the Colón Province, where more than 50 cases were reported in early 2006 due to a contaminated aqueduct and poor food-handling practices. Hepatitis A symptoms range from mild to severe, and can include fever, nausea, and jaundice; cases are normally resolved without complications. The vaccination is safe and effective, and is recommended for anyone traveling to Panama.

Leptospirosis is a disease caused by contact with animals infected with *leptospires,* or by ingesting, or swimming in, water contaminated with animal urine. It causes fever, chills, headache, muscle aches, vomiting, and diarrhea. Travelers become sick from between 2 days and 4 weeks after exposure to the bacteria, the catch being that it can often be misdiagnosed without a blood or urine sample. If you experience the aforementioned symptoms, contact your doctor, who can treat leptospirosis with antibiotics such as penicillin.

The most common illness that affects tourists is TD, or **traveler's diarrhea,** caused by microbes in food and water and typically affecting persons from a country with a high standard of sanitation traveling to an area with a less-advanced system of sanitation. In addition to diarrhea, affected persons may experience nausea and headaches. To prevent TD, avoid foods or beverages from street vendors that look iffy, avoid eating raw or undercooked meat and seafood, and drink bottled water when outside major hotels and restaurants.

BUGS, BITES & OTHER WILDLIFE CONCERNS   Panama is replete with bugs that bite, including chiggers, sand flies (also called no-see-ums, or *chitras*), mosquitoes, ticks, and ants. It is very important that you protect yourself against mosquitoes that may or may not carry a disease such as dengue fever. Mosquitoes are endemic, and in mountain ranges they can leave particularly large welts. Ticks are found mostly in the Darién jungle area during March and April. Chiggers leave a tiny bump that can itch for 2 weeks, but the gross-out factor is that these immature nymphs burrow their mouths into skin pores or hair follicles; you notice the bite after they've left. *Chitras* live in sand, and are more active during sunrise and sunset—but they can bite at any time of the day.

Panama City is the only area of the country where you won't have to worry too much about getting bitten. Otherwise, spray yourself with insect repellent every day, even if you are just stepping out for dinner at an outdoor café. In the jungle, wear long pants (tuck them into your socks) and give your ankle area and all exposed areas a coat of repellent that has at least 30% DEET. Some travelers soak their clothing with the insecticide Permethrin (some companies now sell adventure wear pre-soaked with Permethrin) to repel bugs. Above all, bring along a bite-soothing, anti-itch product like Sting-eeze. I didn't heed my own advice and wound up looking like I had the chickenpox for a couple of weeks; remember you're in the Tropics and the bugs here are relentless. Even though your chances of catching something are low, it's uncomfortable to walk around with hundreds of bug bites.

Panama is home to many poisonous snakes such as the pit viper, the fer-de-lance, and the patoca, but bites are rare. Nevertheless, protect yourself by wearing high boots if you're walking in remote jungle, and keep alert, scanning the trail in front of you. If you're bitten, cutting X-shaped gouges and sucking out the venom is old-fashioned nonsense that won't work; instead, remain calm (panic speeds the venom's diffusion), wash the wound with soap and water if you can, try to identify the species, and seek emergency medical help.

TROPICAL SUN The blistering, equatorial sun can burn your skin faster than you think—even on a cloudy day. Limit your exposure or apply, liberally, a high-factor sunscreen. The sun is especially strong from 11am to 2pm.

Sunstroke, or heatstroke, can afflict travelers in the Tropics when humidity interferes with the cooling of an overheated body. Sunstroke can be serious, so rest and cool off if you begin to feel dizzy or have a headache. Drink plenty of fluids to keep dehydration at bay.

If You Get Sick

Hospital quality in Panama City is on a par with that of the United States (most doctors are U.S.-trained), but medical service here is far more economical. Major cities such as David have at least one high-quality hospital, but in small towns, a medical clinic may be the extent of healthcare facilities in the area, and more serious cases must be treated in Panama City. For a list of the best hospitals in Panama City, see "Fast Facts: Panama City," in chapter 6.

English-speaking doctors are very common in Panama—your embassy can provide you with a list if you request one. **Hospitals** and **emergency numbers** are listed in "Fact Facts: Panama City," p. 88.

For travel abroad, you may have to pay all medical costs upfront and be reimbursed later. See "Insurance," in the "Fast Facts" in chapter 13.

SAFETY

Panama is one of the safest countries in Latin America, with a few exceptions. The ragged port town of **Colón** is dangerous day and night, except in the Colón 2000 cruise-ship and Zona Libre (Free Zone) areas. The northeastern region of the **Darién Province** near the Caribbean Sea is dangerous due to incidents of kidnapping, murder, and drug-running by Colombian guerrilla and paramilitary groups who have crossed the border into Panama. Other regions of the Darién are home to several lodges that are in a no-risk area.

Panama City is relatively safe, but crime rates are rising all over the city, particularly in neighborhoods such as El Chorrillo and Curundú; these neighborhoods should be avoided if possible. El Chorrillo surrounds Casco Viejo, to which visitors should take a taxi instead of walking. Panama City is a modern, clean city, yet a very visible poor underclass lives in run-down neighborhoods that feature prominently in the city's west side. As with any urban area, visitors should be alert, exercise caution when taking money out of an ATM, and not walk around with large sums of cash.

Visitors headed for the beach should be extremely cautious when swimming or surfing in both the Pacific and Caribbean oceans, where there are **strong riptides.** Often there are no warning signs; and tour guides rarely advise their clients of dangerous areas. Remember, no matter what happens, stay calm, and swim parallel to the shore and out of the current.

Illegal drugs are easy to buy in Panama, but stiff penalties apply to anyone caught with illegal substances.

For current security information about Panama, check the U.S. Department of State's Travel Advisory website at **http://travel.state.gov**.

SPECIALIZED TRAVEL RESOURCES

Travelers with Disabilities

Major hotels in Panama City offer wheelchair-accessible guest rooms, and many public bathrooms are accessible to those with limited mobility. However, sidewalks can be uneven and downright dangerous for those in wheelchairs and you'll have to rent a car to get around. Travel outside Panama City or major hotels and resorts can be difficult, and most small towns and out-of-the way destinations are not well equipped to handle travelers with disabilities. Also, travelers with disabilities will likely be subject to less-than-subtle staring, especially in smaller, more out-of-the-way destinations.

For information on organizations that offer resources to travelers with disabilities, go to www.frommers.com/planning.

Gay & Lesbian Travelers

Panama is more tolerant toward gays and lesbians than other more conservative Latin American societies, but discrimination exists, and displays of public affection are not common. The Catholic Church is the most vociferous anti-gay organization in Panama, rallying against events such as gay participation in Carnaval parades. Panama held its first gay-pride parade in 2005 without incident. A few hotels in Panama advertise **gay-friendly accommodations;** you can find them at www. purpleroofs.com. As long as you're discrete, no one should bother you.

For more gay and lesbian travel resources visit www.frommers.com/planning.

Senior Travel

Panama is one of the hottest retirement destinations in the world, and most Panama hotels and businesses offer discounts of up to 40% to seniors 60 and older (age varies from business to business). Yet some are reluctant to extend discounts to foreign travelers, and claim the discount is for Panamanian seniors and foreigners with a residential visa only. Nevertheless, it doesn't hurt to request senior rates or discounts when booking.

For more information and resources on travel for seniors, see www.frommers.com/planning.

Family Travel

Panama can be a fun destination for families, especially those with young children who are easily bored by stuffy museums. Jungle cruises, wildlife sightings, interactive marine museums, and outdoor activities such as snorkeling and kayaking are kid-pleasers. Hotel resorts are generally family-friendly, with children's swimming pools, playgrounds, and even kids' organized activities. A handful of resorts in Panama accept adults only, which is indicated in hotel reviews.

Unfortunately, though many hotels in Panama do not charge for kids 3 and under, they do charge extra for older kids, usually about $10 to $15 extra per child for a larger "triple" or "quadruple" with additional beds. Other hotels ask that you book a junior suite because a regular double does not have the space for an additional bed. Junior suites and suites have a sofa bed for one to two small children. Major hotels have rooms with connecting doors for two doubles; this can be a costlier option if a hotel doesn't offer a break in price. Ask anyway; you never know what they'll be willing to offer.

Take special care with the health of your kids. Sunburn, bug bites, and unfamiliar food can take its toll, so review the precautions under "Health," earlier in this chapter, before departing. Major hotels offer babysitting service, though it's less common at country-style inns—but ask anyway as they might have a reliable babysitter on hand.

To locate accommodations, restaurants, and attractions that are particularly kid-friendly, refer to the "Kids" icon throughout this guide.

Some tour operators can put together dynamic, activity-rich trips for families, either privately or as part of a larger travel group. See "Organized Adventure Trips" on p. 60.

For a list of more family-friendly travel resources, visit www.frommers.com/planning.

Women Travelers

Walking alone will probably earn you a couple of catcalls (in the form of hissing), but women traveling in Panama will not feel overwhelmed by a *macho* presence. The influx of foreigners in Panama has helped, too. The best defense toward an inappropriate comment is to just ignore it and keep walking. I've tried responding a couple times in the past, but men seem to take this as further invitation. In Panama

City, women dress up in spite of the heat (meaning no flip-flops and shorts), but skimpier wear is accepted in beach areas. However, the way I see it, unless you're wearing a full-body covering, you might as well dress comfortably for the heat, because you're going to get catcalled no matter what.

For general travel resources for women, go to www.frommers.com/planning.

RESPONSIBLE TOURISM

Responsible tourism is conscientious travel. It means being careful with the environments you explore, and respecting the communities you visit. Two overlapping components of sustainable travel are **eco-tourism** and **ethical tourism.** The **International Ecotourism Society** (TIES) defines eco-tourism as responsible travel to natural areas that conserves the environment and improves the well-being of local people. TIES suggests that eco-tourists follow these principles:

o Minimize environmental impact.
o Build environmental and cultural awareness and respect.
o Provide positive experiences for both visitors and hosts.
o Provide direct financial benefits for conservation and for local people.
o Raise sensitivity to host countries' political, environmental, and social climates.
o Support international human rights and labor agreements.

You can find some eco-friendly travel tips and statistics, as well as touring companies and associations—listed by destination under "Travel Choice"—at the **TIES** website, www.ecotourism.org. Also check out **Ecotravel.com**, which lets you search for sustainable touring companies in several categories (water-based, land-based, spiritually oriented, and so on).

While much of the focus of eco-tourism is about reducing impacts on the natural environment, ethical tourism concentrates on ways to preserve and enhance local economies and communities, regardless of location. You can embrace ethical tourism by staying at a locally owned hotel or shopping at a store that employs local workers and sells locally produced goods.

Responsible Travel (www.responsibletravel.com) is a great source of sustainable travel ideas; the site is run by a spokesperson for ethical tourism in the travel industry. **Sustainable Travel International** (www.sustainabletravelinternational.org) promotes ethical tourism practices, and manages an extensive directory of sustainable properties and tour operators around the world.

In the U.K., **Tourism Concern** (www.tourismconcern.org.uk) works to reduce social and environmental problems connected to tourism. The **Association of Independent Tour Operators** (AITO; www.aito.co.uk) is a group of specialist operators leading the field in making holidays sustainable.

Volunteer travel has become increasingly popular among those who want to venture beyond the standard group-tour experience to learn languages, interact with locals, and make a positive difference while on vacation. Volunteer travel usually doesn't require special skills—just a willingness to work hard—and programs vary in length from a few days to a number of weeks. Some programs provide free housing and food, but many require volunteers to pay for travel expenses, which can add up quickly.

It's Easy Being Green

In addition to the resources listed above, the following websites provide valuable wide-ranging information on sustainable travel.

- o Carbonfund (www.carbonfund.org), TerraPass (www.terrapass.org), and Cool Climate (http://coolclimate. berkeley.edu) provide info on "carbon offsetting," or offsetting the greenhouse gas emitted during flights.

- o Greenhotels (www.greenhotels.com) recommends green-rated member hotels around the world that fulfill the company's stringent environmental requirements. Environmentally Friendly Hotels (www.environmentally friendlyhotels.com) offers more green accommodations ratings.

For general info on volunteer travel, visit **www.volunteerabroad.org** and **www. idealist.org**. Ecologically oriented volunteer options in Panama are listed under "Ecologically Oriented Volunteer & Study Programs" in chapter 5.

Before you commit to a volunteer program, it's important to make sure any money you're giving is truly going back to the local community, and that the work you'll be doing will be a good fit for you. **Volunteer International** (www.volunteer international.org) has a helpful list of questions to ask to determine the intentions and the nature of a volunteer program.

STAYING CONNECTED

Telephones

Panama's country code is 507, but there are no local city or area codes in Panama. Whenever you're calling a land line Panama phone number while in Panama, simply dial the seven-digit number. Note that cellphones have eight digits, and all cellphone numbers begin with a 6.

Many moderate to budget hotels don't allow outgoing calls to cell numbers, so it is definitely a good idea to buy a cellphone in Panama. To dial an international number from a Panama phone, dial 00 + the country code + the area code + the seven-digit number. Most hotels charge steep fees for international calls, and some moderate and most budget hotels don't allow international calls. Some Internet cafes also provide phones for local and international calls, generally with better rates than you'd get at a hotel.

For more telephone dialing tips, see "Telephones" in the "Fast Facts" in chapter 13.

Cellphones

I strongly recommend buying a cellphone in Panama. It's expensive to call cellphones from land lines, meaning reaching taxi drivers, some restaurants, and even hotels can be difficult without a cellphone. Luckily, a cellphone in Panama can be obtained for as little as $10. You can buy calling cards starting at $5.

There are no phone-rental kiosks in the Panama City airport, and travelers who need to make a lot of local calls and receive international calls are better off **buying a phone** in Panama. Cellphones that accept prepaid phone cards are as cheap as $30 in electronics stores in Panama City (and come with a bonus of $20 in calls), and phone-card companies have nonstop promotions that double or triple the value of phone cards. Local calls are as low as 10¢ per minute, and incoming calls are free. While some higher-end hotels rent cellphones, it's probably cheaper just to buy a new one.

Prepaid phone cards can be purchased in just about any grocery store or pharmacy, and instructions for how to add credit are listed on the back of each card. The instructions are in Spanish, but whoever sells you the card can credit your account if you ask.

The major cellphone providers in Panama are **Movistar** and **Cable & Wireless.** Note that calling cards are service-provider specific, so you'll have to buy a different card depending on whether you have a Movistar or Cable & Wireless phone. If you are unsure what kind of phone you have, a salesperson can help you. Calling cards generally come in denominations of $5, $10, and $12.

Voice-Over Internet Protocol (VoIP)

If you have Web access while traveling, consider a broadband-based telephone service (in technical terms, **Voice-Over Internet Protocol,** or **VoIP**) such as Skype (www.skype.com) or Vonage (www.vonage.com), which allow you to make free international calls from your laptop or in a cybercafe. Neither service requires the people you're calling to also have that service (though there are fees if they do not). Check the websites for details. I've found Skype particularly helpful when my cellphone ran out of minutes or when I need to make an international call from Panama.

Internet & E-Mail

WITH YOUR OWN COMPUTER

More and more hotels, cafes, and retailers are signing on as Wi-Fi (wireless fidelity) "hot spots." To find public Wi-Fi hot spots at your destination, go to **www.jiwire.com**; its Hotspot Finder holds the world's largest directory of public wireless hot spots.

For dial-up access, most hotels offer dataports for laptop modems, and high-speed connection in their business centers. Most upscale hotels have stepped up to wireless connection in guest rooms, but it often costs $10 to $20 per day. Rates vary wildly from hotel to hotel (some even offer free service), so factor the price into your nightly stay if you're bringing your work with you and need ongoing access to the Internet. Moderate to budget hotels often offer free Wi-Fi, at least in their lobbies. Internet connections of any kind are more difficult to impossible to come by in more remote areas such as the Darién, some parts of Bocas del Toro, and the Kuna Yala Islands.

WITHOUT YOUR OWN COMPUTER

Many hotels have at least one computer hooked up to the Internet available for guests to use. For additional help locating cybercafes and other establishments where you can go for Internet access, see "Internet Access" in the "Fast Facts" in chapter 13. However, even the most remote destinations in Panama usually have at least one Internet cafe.

TIPS ON ACCOMMODATIONS

Panama offers a wide variety of lodging options, from five-star luxury ecolodges to well-known chains, to budget backpacker hostels. Outside of Panama City, there aren't many chain hotels, however. In Panama City, the Marriott, Radisson, and InterContinental are among the best chain hotels. Sprawling resorts are limited to the Pacific Coast, with the best bed-and-breakfasts in Boquete and the Valle de Anton.

The hotels listed in this book are categorized broadly by price: **Very Expensive,** $180 and up; **Expensive,** $110 to $180; **Moderate,** $60 to $110; and **Inexpensive,** under $60 for a double. *Rates in this book do not include a government-mandated 10% hotel tax, unless otherwise specified.* This tax could add considerably to the cost of your stay, especially at expensive hotels.

Hotels may include **breakfast** in the price, either continental or a full breakfast or breakfast buffet. If your hotel offers an all-inclusive package that includes meals, compare the package price against the room cost alone paired with ordering meals from their restaurant's menu—some hotels inexplicably gouge travelers when it comes to meals in all-inclusive packages. Also inquire as to whether a hotel includes round-trip transportation from the airport. If not, hotels can usually organize transportation for about $20 one-way.

Moderate and upscale accommodations in Panama are on par with hotels of similar caliber in the U.S., while budget options can range from scary hole-in-the-wall type places to charming *pensiones* and B&Bs. Though there are plenty of standard smaller hotels throughout Panama, I find that the abundance of delightful and reasonably priced ecolodges and B&Bs are your best bet for lodging, and one of the things that will make your vacation to Panama memorable.

Panama's strong suit is its **moderately priced hotels** in the $60 to $110 range. Hotels from $40 to $65 are lean on style, and mattresses are not orthopedic and fitted with high-thread-count sheets, but more budget-minded or bohemian travelers won't mind. These hotels usually have air-conditioning and TV, too. In the $65 to $100 per night range, you'll find outstanding hotels, ecolodges, and B&Bs that include all amenities and are usually located in beautiful surroundings. Few remote lodges have in-room amenities such as television, telephones, or hair dryers, and some solar-power-generated hotels may have electricity for a few hours only, or no electricity at all. Remote lodges usually have ceiling fans or cross ventilation instead of air-conditioning.

Panama is a world-class eco-tourism destination, and therefore there are many nature-oriented **ecolodges** throughout the country. These lodges are found in natural settings and frequently offer opportunities to see sloths, monkeys, and a host of birds, sometimes even from your bedroom window. Ecolodges are so called for their commitment to sustainable tourism, or because they are oriented around activities that involve learning about tropical forests or bird-watching. They range from spartan facilities in converted scientific research stations to luxury accommodations. Ecolodges can be quite expensive if you throw in the cost of a chartered plane, guided excursions, and meals. Also, consider the elements you'll be forced to put up with, including biting insects, heat and humidity, strenuous hikes, or rugged transportation to see wildlife.

In most of Panama, hotels with kitchenettes are referred to as **"aparthotels,"** an amalgam of apartment and hotel. Kitchenettes can be anything from a hot plate and microwave to a full-scale kitchen.

When booking a hotel room, be sure to ask if there is any construction going on nearby (this is especially true in Panama City); if so, ask for a room facing the interior of the hotel to reduce noise disturbances.

High season in Panama is the dry season, roughly **early December to late April.** Hotels in Panama City do not generally adhere to high- and low-season rates, but some hotels in popular tourist areas do. Price ranges listed in hotel reviews reflect a range encompassing low and high season; for example, $50 to $75 for a double means $50 from May to November and $75 from December to April. Precise start and end dates for high season may vary from hotel to hotel. A few of the more remote lodges may close entirely from April to October. Check with individual properties for details about rates.

For tips on surfing for hotel deals online, visit www.frommers.com/planning.

SUGGESTED PANAMA ITINERARIES

P anama is home to a staggering array of natural landscapes, each beautiful in its own way, and each
offering attractions and excursions that appeal to
different kinds of people. Scuba-diving fanatics or anglers
seeking to reel in boatloads of billfish, for example, might
plan their entire journey to Panama around their sport.
Multisport resorts have been popping up around the country, too, providing guests with a home base and roster of
activities as varied as kayaking, hiking, scuba diving, and
mountain biking. These range from pricey, boutique-style
lodges boasting "rustic elegance" to destination megaresorts, with 300 or more guest rooms.

4

Whatever your passion or desire, Panama has it all: a thriving metropolis;
endless stretches of pristine, hyper-diverse rainforest; legendary sport fishing; scuba diving in the Caribbean and Pacific (even diving both oceans in
1 day, if you wish); white-water rafting and trekking through rugged mountain highlands; cultural encounters with one of the country's seven indigenous groups; a round of golf on a world-class course; a river cruise on a
dugout canoe; or boating the Panama Canal. Of course, there are also
plenty of relaxing spots for travelers who just want to kick back on a chaise
longue or spend their afternoons taking walks along the beach.

The itineraries in this chapter are specific blueprints for memorable
vacations that can be adhered to explicitly, or modified according to your
desires and likes, or even expanded if you're lucky enough to have an
extended vacation. But before planning your itinerary, take some time to
better acquaint yourself with Panama's regions.

THE REGIONS IN BRIEF

Panama, an S-shaped **isthmus** that measures little more than 77,700 sq.
km (30,000 sq. miles), is just slightly smaller than South Carolina—yet

there is a huge diversity of landscapes and microclimates within this tiny nation. Costa Rica borders Panama to the west, Colombia to the east, and, in what can be vexing to the traveler with no sense of direction, the Pacific Ocean to the south and the Caribbean Sea to the north. Because Panama City faces southeast, travelers are presented with the uncommon view of the sun rising over the Pacific. At its narrowest point, Panama measures just 50km (31 miles) wide.

Besides the isthmus, Panama is made up of than 1,500 **islands,** many of them uninhabited and cloaked in thick vegetation. These islands are grouped into four regions. In the Caribbean Sea there are the Bocas del Toro and San Blas archipelagos; in the Pacific Ocean, Las Perlas Archipelago in the Gulf of Panama, and Coiba Island and its accompanying tiny islands in the Gulf of Chiriquí.

Panama is home to two **mountain ranges,** the Serranía del Darién in the east, and the Cordillera Central in the west, the latter of which is home to the highest peak in the country, the dormant Volcán Barú, at 3,475m (11,400 ft.). This is the only place in Panama where you are likely to experience brisk temperatures—the rest of the country averages 75°F to 85°F (24°C–29°C) year-round.

Panama is a centralized nation, with about a third of its population of three million living in Panama City; in comparison, the population of the second-largest city, Colón, is just under 200,000 residents. The country is divided into nine *provincias,* or provinces, three provincial-level indigenous territories called comarcas, and two sub-provincial comarcas. For the most part, chapters in this book are divided into general regions rather than provinces. See the map in this chapter for a visual guide to the regions outlined here.

PANAMA CITY, THE CANAL & SURROUNDINGS Beyond the urban streets of Panama City, the Canal Zone is characterized by a species-rich, dense tropical rainforest, hundreds of rivers, mangrove swamps, the Pacific Ocean coastline, and Las Perlas Archipelago in the Gulf of Panama. Thanks to the Panama Canal and its reliance on the local watershed, the rainforest in this area is protected as a series of national parks and reserves (Chagres, Soberanía, Sherman, and Camino de Cruces, for example). Visitors to Panama City are often surprised how quickly they can reach these parks and surround themselves in steamy jungle, and view a dazzling array of both North and South American birds and other wildlife. Near the city, the shore consists mostly of mud flats; visitors seeking beaches must head to the islands, or drive about 1 hour southwest (described in chapter 8).

CENTRAL PANAMA Considered the country's cultural heartland, Central Panama in this book covers Panama City beaches, the Coclé Province, and the Azuero Peninsula. In Coclé, city dwellers flock to popular El Valle de Antón, a verdant mountain hideaway located in the crater of an extinct volcano (1,173m/3,850 ft. at its highest peak). The area is blessed with a mild climate that is a welcome respite from the humid lowlands. The Pacific Coast southwest of the city is another popular weekend getaway for its beaches and a few all-inclusive resorts. Farther southwest, the Azuero Peninsula has been largely deforested, but it is still a popular destination for its traditional festivals, handicrafts, and Spanish villages whose architecture dates back to the medieval era. The beaches along the peninsula are blissfully uncrowded any time of year.

BOCAS DEL TORO ARCHIPELAGO Bocas del Toro is in the northwest corner of the country, near the border with Costa Rica, and it's one of the more popular

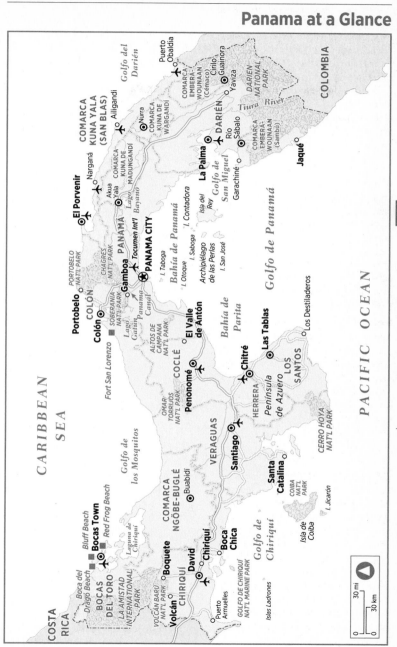

and easily accessed Caribbean destinations, with a wide variety of hotels and amenities. The region is characterized by an eclectic mix of indigenous groups, Spanish descendants, Afro-Caribbeans, and, more recently, American expats; it is also one of the wettest areas of Panama. Outside of brief dry seasons in September/October and February/March, the rain is constant, so bring an umbrella or waterproof gear. Although there are a few beautiful beaches here, there are also dangerous riptides, and visitors come more to scuba dive, snorkel, boat, see wildlife, or just soak in the bohemian vibe of Bocas Town, the capital city.

THE WESTERN HIGHLANDS & GULF OF CHIRIQUI   The Western Highlands—so-called for the region's location and its Cordillera Central range—is a veritable paradise of fertile peaks and valleys, crystal-clear rivers, mild temperatures, and fresh air. The region is undergoing a palpable growth spurt as hundreds of North Americans continue to buy second and retirement homes here, so expect to hear a lot of English. The region centers around the skirt of Volcán Barú, a dormant volcano capped by a moist cloud forest. Farther south are the humid lowlands, the capital city David, and the wondrous coast and islands of the Gulf of Chiriquí. This is Panama's up-and-coming beach/ocean destination, with its highlight being Coiba National Park, one of the most diverse and pristine islands for scuba diving and snorkeling in the world.

THE DARIEN   The easternmost region of Panama is known as the Darién Province, a swath of impenetrable rainforest and swampland that is undeveloped, save for a handful of tiny villages and indigenous settlements. It is Panama's wildest region and the most difficult to reach: This is the famous "missing link" of the Pan American Highway that runs from Alaska to Puerto Montt, Chile. The interior of the Darién can be reached only by foot, boat, or small plane—and herein lies the allure of adventure for travelers. Within the province lies the Darién National Park, most of it inaccessible except for the Cana Research Station, an area revered by birders worldwide for the abundance of endemic and "show-bird" species such as macaws and harpy eagles, the largest predator in the world. Along the Pacific shore is the famous Tropic Star Lodge, but otherwise, lodging in the Darién is in rustic shelters and tents.

THE COMARCA KUNA YALA (THE SAN BLAS ARCHIPELAGO)   Though commonly referred to as the San Blas Archipelago, this semiautonomous region, or comarca, is named for the Kuna Yala, perhaps Panama's most well-known indigenous group. The Kuna are recognized for their tightly knit culture, colorful clothing, and handicrafts such as *mola* tapestries. More than 300 lovely, palm-studded islands in turquoise Caribbean waters make up the archipelago in what is truly an unspoiled paradise. The San Blas is a very popular cruise stop. However, staying on the islands requires a sense of adventure because they can be reached only by a small plane or boat. Lodging is alfresco with rustic accommodations and little in the way of activities other than swimming and swaying in a hammock.

PANAMA IN 1 WEEK

Given Panama's compact size, and the short flights that quickly connect you to other destinations, travelers can pack a lot into a week here—but the timing is tight. This itinerary includes a 2-day visit to Bocas del Toro, but you might opt instead to spend

2 nights in Boca Chica, near David, and visit Isla Coiba the first day (a long day trip, but worth it), then head out to the Gulf of Chiriquí National Marine Park the next day for sport fishing or lounging on the beach of an uninhabited island.

Day 1: Getting to Know the City

Arrive and get settled in **Panama City.** If your flight arrives early, visit **Panama Viejo** (p. 114) to get your historical bearings, then head across town for a walking tour of **Casco Viejo** (p. 115). Travelers with little time will want to head straight to Casco Viejo. Dine on Panamanian food at **Las Tinajas** (p. 110) or **Las Barandas** (p. 107).

Day 2: Getting Deep in the Jungle

One of Panama's top parks for birding, hiking, and just immersing yourself in the earthy, steamy environs of thick rainforest is only 45 minutes from Panama City: **Soberanía National Park** (p. 142). Leave early and bring your binoculars to view hundreds of birds on a walk or mountain-bike ride along **Pipeline Road;** join a **jungle cruise** to see monkeys, crocodiles, and transiting ships on the Panama Canal (p. 144); ride a dugout canoe up the **Chagres River** to visit an Emberá village (p. 145). In the afternoon, pay a visit to the country's star attraction, the **Panama Canal,** at the **Miraflores Locks** (p. 137), where you can have lunch and tour their visitor center. Head back to Panama City and cool off with a stroll or bike ride along the **Amador Causeway.**

Days 3 & 4: To the Highlands

Fly to David and grab a taxi or rent a car for the 45-minute drive to **Boquete.** Settle into your hotel and spend the afternoon getting to know the town on foot or by bike, visiting the town's public gardens and other sights. Another option is to dive into an adventurous afternoon activity such as a canopy ride on the **Boquete Tree Trek** (p. 236) or a low-key booked visit to the **Kotowa coffee farm** (p. 237). The following day, hike the **Quetzal Trail** (p. 224), or spend the day **rafting** on a Class II to Class V river. You can also book a bird-watching tour that includes **Finca Lérida** (p. 238) and **Volcán Barú National Park** (p. 233).

Days 5 & 6: From the Highlands to the Lowlands

Catch an early-morning flight from David to **Bocas del Toro,** and settle in to a hotel in **Bocas Town,** on Isla Colón. Preplan an afternoon tour with your hotel or an outfitter to visit **Swan's Cay** and **Boca del Drago** beach (p. 265), or rent a bicycle and pedal out to **Bluff Beach,** or take a water taxi over to Isla Bastimentos, and then walk the 10 minutes to beautiful **Red Frog Beach** (p. 282). The next day, head out with **Starfleet Scuba** (p. 267), which can put together a snorkeling or diving trip to the region's top underwater playgrounds, and a cruise through mangrove swamps.

Day 7: Leaving Bocas del Toro

Spend the morning wandering around town and soaking up the Caribbean vibe, architecture, and culture. There are quite a few **souvenir shops** in Bocas where you can pick up gifts before your flight back to Panama City.

PANAMA IN 2 WEEKS

Travelers with 2 weeks will be able to see all of Panama's highlights without feeling as if they're on a tight schedule. This itinerary gives travelers an option of visiting the funky, laid-back region of **Bocas del Toro,** or of experiencing the rustic, indigenous culture of the **Comarca Kuna Yala** and its gorgeous islands. They are two very different island destinations that appeal to different kinds of people.

Days 1 & 2: Panama City & Environs

Follow **Days 1** and **2** in the above "Panama in 1 Week" itinerary, but skip the Emberá village trip because you'll visit one in the Darién.

Day 3: Pirates, Ruins & Gold

Ride the **train** (p. 139) along the historical trans-isthmus route to Colón, but skip the city and head out to visit the ruins of **Fuerte San Lorenzo** and **Portobelo** to learn about pirate raids and the historic gold trade (p. 149). Dine on fresh seafood while gazing out over the sea at **Los Cañones** (p. 158), near Portobelo. Drive across the canal and visit the **Gatún Locks** (p. 152) and **Gatún Dam** (p. 152). You can even plan a 1-day Caribbean **scuba-diving** adventure from Panama City, with a tour around Portobelo, by calling Panama Divers (p. 156).

Days 4 to 6: Wild Darién & Emberá Villages

Join **Ancon Expeditions** for their "Coastal Darién Explorer" that offers a taste of Central America's last great wilderness area (p. 303). You'll get there by small plane to La Palma, and fill the next 3 days with activities such as traveling the **Tuira River** by dugout canoe as you search for dolphins and a wealth of birds, visiting an **Emberá indigenous village,** and trekking through dense and diverse tropical forest. Nights are spent in their simple but comfortable lodge overlooking the Pacific Ocean.

Day 7: Off to the Islands

On this day you'll board an early flight from La Palma to **Panama City.** The next destination is the **Caribbean,** and here travelers have two options: Visit **Bocas del Toro** (p. 258) or the **Comarca Kuna Yala** (p. 287) and its gorgeous islands. Travelers to Bocas del Toro can grab a flight out on the same day (Day 7), and lodge anywhere of their choosing. Travelers to the Comarca will need a 6:30am flight out the next day (Day 8). In this case, do a little souvenir shopping and catch the Panama City sights you missed on your first days there.

Days 8 to 10: Caribbean Fun

Now for a little fun in the Caribbean sun. Stay in one of the Comarca's all-inclusive lodges such as **Sapibenega** (p. 298). Visit traditional **Kuna villages,** and spend the rest of your days swimming, snorkeling, or just swaying in a hammock. In Bocas, organize a scuba-diving and/or snorkeling trip to **Crawl Cay** (p. 282) or **Zapatillas Cay** (p. 267). Hike through jungle on **Isla Basti-mentos** and end at a long, empty beach. Visit the **Bahía Honda bat caves** (p. 282). You can also **sea kayak** or take a **surf lesson.** Or just take it easy; you deserve it.

Days 11 to 14: To the Highlands

Fly from Bocas to **David,** or from the Comarca to Panama City, and then to David. Grab a taxi or rent a car for the 45-minute drive to **Boquete.** Settle into your hotel and spend the afternoon getting to know town by foot or bike, visiting the town's public gardens and other sights. Aside from the region's trademark coffee tours at farms like **Kotowa** (p. 237), you'll be able to hike through cloud forest on the **Quetzal Trail** (p. 224), bird-watch at **Finca Lérida** (p. 238), zip through the trees on a canopy ride with **Boquete Tree Trek** (p. 236), or spend the day **rafting** on a Class II to Class V river. You can even see both oceans, clouds willing, from the summit of **Volcán Barú National Park** (p. 233), or plan a **sport-fishing** trip leaving from Boca Chica, on the Pacific Coast.

The final day you'll head back to Panama City from David.

PANAMA FOR FAMILIES IN 10 DAYS

Panama is a mixed bag as a kid-friendly destination. A share of B&Bs, luxury resorts, and boutique hotels do not accept children under 10 to 12 years of age, and discounts for children are rare. Also, few hotels outside of destination resorts offer activities specifically tailored to kids and teens—though it is easy to book day excursions like snorkeling, jungle treks, or rafting trips, all of which are kid pleasers. If you're not up to planning your own trip, see chapter 5 for the names of tour operators who can put together a family-oriented vacation for you. Conveniently, a wealth of kid-friendly activities can be found just outside of Panama City. If you have a few more days, add on a trip to the mountain highlands of **Boquete,** where you can white-water raft, ride a canopy zip line, and hike. The following itinerary is best completed in 8 days, with an extra day in Bocas del Toro.

Day 1: Arrival in Panama City

Head to the **Gamboa Rainforest Resort** (p. 148), near the Panama Canal, a 45-minute to 1-hour drive from the Tocumen International Airport. Gamboa has a games center, tours, a butterfly farm, and an aerial tram. If you want to stay in Panama City, book your family at the **Country Inn & Suites—Panama Canal** (p. 97), an oceanfront hotel with bike path and pool located near the Amador Causeway.

Day 2: Jungle Cruises & the Canal Zone

Join an early-morning **jungle cruise** on Lake Gatún to visit "Monkey Island" (p. 77), and view other wildlife like crocodiles, capybaras, and sloths, and motor past huge tankers transiting the canal. Alternatively, ride a dugout canoe up the jungle-shrouded **Chagres River** to visit an Emberá indigenous community and get painted with *jagua* juice. At the Gamboa, take a **bike ride** to Pipeline Road in the afternoon, or visit the resort's serpentarium and butterfly exhibits, and take a ride on their aerial tram. In Panama City, pedal a bike ride along the **Causeway** and stop at the **Punta Culebra Marine Exhibition Center** (p. 122).

Days 3 to 5: From Lowlands to Highlands

Visit the harpy eagle exhibition and see tapirs, ocelots, jaguars, and more at the **Summit Gardens Park & Zoo** (p. 147). Afterward, stop at the Panama Canal's **Miraflores Locks** (p. 137), tour the visitor center, and have an early lunch at their restaurant looking out over ships transiting the locks. After lunch, transfer to El Valle de Anton, 2 hours from the city, and stay at the **Crater Valley Adventure Spa** (p. 190). Relax, bike ride, or let the hotel-activities staff teach your kids to ascend their climbing wall or obstacles course while you have a massage. The following day, book a ride on the **Canopy Adventure** (p. 186) for a thrilling zip-line ride through the forest. Later, families can organize an easygoing horseback ride, bike ride on country lanes, walk to a waterfall, or explore the amphibian exhibit and minizoo at **El Nispero** (p. 187). Spend your last day wandering through the **handicrafts fair** for souvenirs and gifts to take home.

Day 6: Descent to the Beach

In the morning, transfer back to Panama City for an afternoon flight to the Pearl Islands from Albrook Airport. Settle into your hotel on **Isla Contadora,** or book an all-inclusive stay at the upscale **Hacienda del Mar** (p. 170) on Isla San José. On Contadora, kids get a kick out of renting an ATV or golf cart to zip around the island. Lodge at the **Punta Galeón** (p. 169) for its central location and swimming pool.

Days 7 & 8: Sun & Fun in the Pacific Ocean

Your first or second day, book an all-day tour to sail around the idyllic Pearl Islands for the outstanding **snorkeling** and **fishing.** Teens can join a day class to learn the basics of **scuba diving.** For young kids, book a ride in a **glass-bottom boat** to view the underwater world without getting wet. Spend the other day lounging on one of the island's dozen beaches, especially on the calm-water **Playa Larga Beach** (p. 166), where families can buy a day pass for kids to use the hotel's kayaks, snorkeling gear, swimming pool, and other watersports equipment.

Day 9: Flight to Panama City

Depending on your departing flight home, leave early or in the afternoon to make your connection. Remember that Albrook Airport is 45 minutes to 1 hour from Tocumen, so plan accordingly.

A HIGH-OCTANE WEEK OF ADVENTURES

Panama can hold its own against adventure-travel heavyweights like Costa Rica, giving you the opportunity to pack a lot of active and adrenaline-fueled excursions into a single week. This is simply an outline, which you should tailor to your interests: Sport fishermen will need to either plan a trip around fishing, or head out for the day from Boca Chica, near David, or from Isla Contadora. If mountain biking is your priority, substitute that for hiking.

Day 1: Arrive in Panama City

Arrive and get settled in Panama City. If your flight arrives early enough, head to the **Miraflores Locks** (p. 137) at the Panama Canal, tour the museum, and have lunch here while watching massive tankers pass through the locks. In the late afternoon, tour and photograph the picturesque streets of **Casco Viejo** (p. 115), planning your stroll late enough so that you end at **Manolo Caracol** (p. 105) for an adventurous, gourmet meal.

Day 2: Rumble in the Jungle

Join an adrenaline-charged trip deep into the rainforest of Chagres National Park with **Adventures in Panama** (p. 64). The trip kicks off with a ride in a dugout canoe followed by trekking along narrow trails through wild jungle, **rappelling** a rock face, and taking a cool dip in a creek. Finish with a hot lunch at an **Emberá Indian village** before heading home or a visit to the **Rainforest Discovery Center.** At night, check out live jazz music at **Bar Platea** (p. 131).

Day 3: Get Wet & Wild

Grab an early-morning flight from Panama City to David, where **Chiriquí River Rafting** (p. 235) can pick you up on their way to the put-in site at the **Chiriquí Viejo River;** here you'll raft wild Class III to Class V white-water rapids. Afterward, sit back and enjoy the scenery on the ride back to **Boquete,** where you'll settle into your hotel and later get out and stroll around town.

Day 4: Explore Volcán Barú

Go climb or 4WD to the top of **Volcán Barú,** the highest peak in Panama, for electrifying views spanning from the Caribbean to the Pacific (p. 233). It's a gung-ho, rocky, slippery trip that must be planned with a guide or a driver on tours that leave at sunrise or earlier. Or walk the **Quetzal Trail** (p. 224) through emerald rainforest, trekking uphill from Boquete or downhill from Cerro Punta. See if you can spot a **quetzal.** Book a massage at the **Haven Spa** (p. 233) in the late afternoon to recover from your day of adventure.

Day 5: Canopy Tour & Biking

Contact **Boquete Tree Trek** to plan a thrilling canopy zip-line ride through the rainforest (p. 236). Arrive early to witness the region's bounty of birds when they are most active. In the afternoon, join the company for a **mountain-bike tour** and downhill ride through the highlands of Boquete; or rent a bike and head out on your own, exploring backcountry roads.

Day 6: Explore the Underwater World

Wake up early and drive a little over an hour to the Pacific Coast and Boca Chica, where you can set off for a scuba-diving, snorkeling, or sport-fishing adventure around the idyllic waters and rocky outcrops of the **Chiriquí Gulf National Marine Park** (p. 248). Have lunch on a deserted island ringed with white sand and turquoise water.

Day 7: Take a Break & Head Home

Book a flight from David to **Panama City** for your flight home, but remember that you'll need extra time to travel from Albrook to Tocumen Airport. If you can, squeeze in a low-key visit to **Kotowa coffee farms** (p. 237) to see how coffee is produced and head home with a few bags of some of Panama's best beans.

PANAMA CITY IN 3 DAYS

Panama City is a vibrant metropolis whose proximity to two national parks and the famous canal and its environs makes it an ideal base for travelers who seek to pack in a lot of adventure and sightseeing, but who'd like to finish the day with gourmet dining, comfortable accommodations, and city nightlife.

Day 1: Getting to Know the City

Start your day at **Panama Viejo** (p. 114), to get your historical bearings and learn about Panama in the handsome visitor center. Browse the extensive handicrafts market here. Head to **Casco Viejo** for lunch at **Manolo Caracol** (p. 105), then walk it off with a tour around this picturesque neighborhood. Buy a *raspado* at the **Plaza Francia** and enjoy the sea breeze. Check with your hotel for live music and other nighttime events, or drop by a casino at the **Sheraton Panama Hotel and Convention Center** (p. 95) or **Veneto Hotel** (p. 95).

¡Buen Provecho! 🍴

Sample Panamanian food at Las Tinajas, Calle 51 in El Cangrejo (☎ 269-3840; p. 110) and be entertained by a folkloric dance show. Or go upscale with gourmet Panamanian fare at Las Barandas, Aquilino de la Guardia at Obarrio (☎ 265-7844; p. 107).

Day 2: Getting Deep in the Jungle

See Day 2 of "Panama in 1 Week," earlier in this chapter.

Day 3: Pirates, Ruins & Gold

See Day 3 of "Panama in 2 Weeks," above.

Dinner & All That Jazz 🍴

Dine on fabulous Peking duck at Madame Chang, Avenida 5A and Calle Uruguay (☎ 269-1313; p. 108), or soak up the tropical ambience at the restaurant La Posta, Calle 49 at Calle Uruguay (☎ 269-1076; p. 103). Finish with an evening of jazz at Bar Platea (p. 131) in Casco Viejo.

THE ACTIVE VACATION PLANNER

Panama is a tropical paradise for adventure-travel enthusiasts, offering the same outdoor activities and landscapes as Costa Rica—but with far fewer tourists. Yes, maybe Panama's western neighbor boasts a more developed infrastructure for active travel, but really any kind of sport or outdoor activity in Panama has at least one or two responsible and experienced tour operators that can put together an adventurous trip. A full 30% of Panama's natural habitat is protected, including the wildest jungle in all of Central America, the Darién. There are high peaks with misty cloud forests, primeval rainforest, the best bird-watching in North and Central America, white-water rivers, powdery beaches, and an underwater world packed with sea life. Plus, Panama is home to seven Indian groups, as well as Afro-Caribbeans and West African descendants, offering visitors a rich and memorable cultural experience.

Adventure- and active-travel journeys can be pieced together as day excursions, or your trip can be planned from start to finish by a tour operator. There are a handful of all-inclusive resorts and lodges around the country, too, which plan daily excursions that are either included in the daily rate or are an additional cost. Some of these resorts have bird-watching guides and scuba-diving pros as part of their staff; others subcontract a local outfit. When booking a vacation at an all-inclusive resort, confirm the professional certification of the resort's guides—if you're a fastidious bird-watcher who's come all the way to Panama to see a quetzal, you'll want the finest guide available, not just a guy who likes birds.

ORGANIZED ADVENTURE TRIPS

The advantages of traveling with an organized group are plentiful, especially for those who have limited time and resources. Tour operators take the headache out of planning a trip, and they iron out the wrinkles that invariably pop up along the way. The language barrier is less of an issue when you have a guide to translate for you, and a guide can interpret the culture and history of Panama and the natural surroundings of your destination. Most tours include guides, ground transportation, accommodations, meals, and gear. Independent travelers tend to view organized tours as antithetical to the joy of discovery, but leaving the details to someone else does free up substantial time to concentrate on something else. Besides, your traveling companions are likely to be kindred spirits with similar interests.

The best tours limit group size to 10 to 15 people, which allows for personal attention and a bit of breathing room—this is appreciated after a week on the road together. Ask about difficulty levels when you're choosing a tour. Most are focused on "soft" adventure, with light excursions that are suitable even for couch potatoes; be honest with yourself when considering more difficult journeys. A multiday adventure that includes trekking through virgin jungle might look great on paper, but are you physically up to it? Tour operators are responsible for their clients' well-being and safety, but that doesn't let you off the hook. Inquire about your guide's experience, safety record, and insurance policy. Remember, no adventure trip is 100% risk-free.

North American–Based Tour Operators

These agencies and operators specialize in well-organized, 7- to 15-day tours that allow travelers to pack in a lot of action and diversity in a short period of time. Do a little price comparison when shopping for a tour, as many U.S.-based operators subcontract Panamanian tour operators who can be reached directly. Also, some operators offer trips that are duplicitous in that they plan journeys around all-inclusive lodges that already provide guides and transportation. In other words, the operator is simply booking your reservations and providing a minder-guide to solve any glitches from one stop to the next. A few of the operators include luxury accommodations and gourmet dining as part of the travel itinerary, and are therefore *very* expensive. Note that the tour prices shown below do not include airfare! Solo travelers in most cases will be charged the dreaded single supplement that can run an additional $500 to $1,500.

A few tour operators offer custom-made journeys for travelers who wish to craft their itinerary according to their own tastes and interests. Depending on the destination, this option can be reasonably priced or very expensive (less so if you are traveling with a group of friends and meet minimum group size requirements). For more specific activity-oriented tour operators such as those focused on bird-watching, see "Activities A to Z," below. Destination-specific chapters list local guiding services or tour operators.

Abercrombie & Kent (© **800/554-7016** or 630/954-2944; www.abercrombie kent.com), an award-winning tour operator that caters to the luxury market, offers customized guided 10-day tours from $5,890 (per person, not including internal airfare). Upscale accommodations and gourmet dining are features of this low-key, culturally oriented trip.

Panama's National Parks & Protected Areas

CARIBBEAN SEA

Golfo del Darién

Puerto Obaldía

COLOMBIA

COMARCA KUNA YALA (SAN BLAS)

Puerto Obaldía

Cirilo Guainora

COMARCA EMBERÁ-WOUNAAN (Cémaco)

DARIÉN NATIONAL PARK

Niura

COMARCA KUNA DE WARGANDÍ

Meteti

DARIÉN

Yaviza

COMARCA EMBERÁ-WOUNAAN (Sambú)

El Porvenir

G. de San Blas

Narganá

Akua Yala

COMARCA KUNA DE MADUNGANDÍ

Chimán

Lago Bayano

La Palma

Río Sábalo

Jaqué

Golfo de San Miguel

Garachiné

BOCA DE SÁBALO FOREST RESERVE

PORTOBELO NAT'L PARK

CHAGRES NAT'L PARK

CAMINO DE CRUCES NAT'L PARK

METROPOLITANO NAT'L PARK

★ **PANAMA CITY**

ISLA TABOGA WILDLIFE PRESERVE

Bahía de Panamá

I. Otoque

I. Contadora

I. Saboga

Archipiélago de las Perlas

Isla del Rey

I. San José

Golfo de Panamá

Portobelo

Colón

COLÓN

SHERMAN FOREST RESERVE

SOBERANÍA NAT'L PARK

BARRO COLORADO NAT'L MONUMENT

Panamá Canal

PANAMÁ

El Valle de Antón

ALTOS DE CAMPANA NAT'L PARK

Antón

Bahía de Parita

PEÑÓN DE LA ONDA WILDLIFE PRESERVE

ISLA IGUANA WILDLIFE REFUGE

Pedasí

ISLA CAÑAS WILDLIFE PRESERVE

Aguadulce

Penonomé

COCLÉ

OMAR TORRIJOS NAT'L PARK

Divisá

SARIGUA NAT'L PARK

Chitré

HERRERA

Peninsula de Azuero

LOS SANTOS

Las Tablas

Golfo de los Mosquitos

Veraguas

Santa Fe

LA YEGUADA FOREST RESERVE

Santiago

VERAGUAS

Soná

MONTUOSO FOREST RESERVE

Mariato

LA TRONOSA FOREST RESERVE

CERRO HOYA NAT'L PARK

COIBA NAT'L PARK

I. Jicarón

Isla de Coiba

Golfo de Chiriquí

COSTA RICA

Changuinola

ISLA BASTIMENTOS NAT'L MARINE PARK

Archipiélago de Bocas del Toro

Bocas Town

BOCAS DEL TORO

LA AMISTAD INTERNATIONAL PARK

Laguna de Chiriquí

PALO SECO FOREST RESERVE

COMARCA NGÖBE-BUGLÉ

FORTUNA FOREST RESERVE

Buabidi

Tolé

VOLCÁN BARÚ NAT'L PARK

Volcán

Boquete

Chiriquí

CHIRIQUÍ

David

Puerto Armuelles

GOLFO DE CHIRIQUÍ NAT'L MARINE PARK

Islas Ladrones

PACIFIC OCEAN

Adventure Life Journeys (℘ 800/344-6118; www.adventure-life.com) is a Montana-based operator specializing in travel to Central and South America. Groups are limited to 8 to 12 people or less, and they only utilize locally run hotels and native guides (prices run $1,390–$2,425 per person). Their weeklong journeys include a trip that combines Panama with Costa Rica; they also offer a 15-day trip for $2,990 and 5- to 20-day cruises starting at $3,999.

Bike Hike Adventures (℘ 888/805-0061; www.bikehike.com) is a Toronto-based company specializing in multisport adventures for travelers who are in at least moderate shape. Their 10-day "Rumble in the Jungle" includes river rafting, mountain biking, hiking, snorkeling, and canopy rides, as well as visiting the Caribbean Sea, the Pacific Ocean, and the Chiriquí Highlands and costs $2,699.

Country Walkers (℘ 800/464-9255; www.countrywalkers.com) focuses on easy to moderate, 3.2 to 9.7km (2- to 6-mile) day hikes through Soberanía National Park, Boca Chica, and the Quetzal Trail in the Chiriquí Highlands, plus a few add-ons like a city tour and a boat cruise in the canal. Lodging is in upscale hotels. Their "Tropical Jewel" trip is 7 days and costs $3,298 per person.

International Expeditions (℘ 800/234-9620; www.ietravel.com) offers a 9-day journey that focuses on the Panama Canal region (including boat passage through the canal) and the Chiriquí Highlands with nature and culture excursions in Soberanía National Park, visits to Emberá indigenous villages, sights along the Caribbean area in the Colón Province, and coffee tours; the cost is $3,498 per person January through November and $3,698 in December. In-country airfare costs $252 in low season and $272 in high season. They can add on trips to the San Blas and Bocas del Toro islands.

Wildland Adventures (℘ 800/345-4453; www.wildland.com) is a well-respected tour operator, offering five journeys from 8 to 14 days that are focused on exploring nature as well as cultural interactions with indigenous groups. The exciting, well-organized trips cover a lot of ground. Wildland Adventures is one of the few U.S. companies to offer trips to the wild Darién jungle. Wildland also offers a 9-day "Family Adventure" with kid-friendly hikes and activities. Prices run $1,995 to $2,750.

U.K.-based Tour Operators

Journey Latin America ★ (℘ 020/8747-3108; www.journeylatinamerica.co.uk) is the U.K.'s largest tour operator that specializes in Latin American travel. They currently offer tailor-made itineraries as well as organized trips such as the Kuna Yala Kayaking Adventure, Highlights of Panama, Islands and Highlands, and Discover Coast to Coast Tours.

Reef and Rainforest Tours (℘ 018/0386-6965; www.reefandrainforest.co.uk) specializes in just that, providing small-scale, nature-oriented trips to the Caribbean Sea and the rainforest of the Darién Province (via small plane). The company has an excellent track record, and their trips, though not specifically oriented toward families, are kid-friendly. Their Panama at its Best tour lasts 11 days and costs approximately $3,650, and their Beautiful Birds and Wondrous Wildlife of Panama tour lasts 15 days and costs approximately $3,680.

Getting the Hotel You Want

Many boutique-style hotels and inns have complained recently that tour operators who receive a hefty commission from a particular hotel tend to steer clients toward that hotel—even if a client has requested different accommodations or is not a good match for the operator's choice of lodging. If a travel operator or agency tells you that a hotel is sold out, and you had your heart set on staying there, do your own investigation and see if this is indeed true.

Panamanian Tour Operators

Foreign tour operators usually subcontract a portion—and sometimes all—of their tours to established Panamanian companies. Some book their clients on prescheduled trips with other travelers who are not part of the client's tour, while others plan exclusive itineraries but rely on local guides and logistics planners to do the ground work for them. Contacting a local tour operator directly, and thereby cutting out the "middleman," may result in a small price savings.

There are few tour operators in Panama despite the burgeoning tourism industry and the potential that exists here. But the operations that do exist are tried-and-true companies with a staff of full-time, qualified guides, drivers, and customer service reps. Trips can be tailor-made, or operate on predetermined dates, and most offer **day excursions** and **short adventures** that last just a few days. Hotel tour desks can put together a day excursion, but the quality of service can vary dramatically, so it's best to book ahead with one of the companies listed below. Also, if you have a specific activity in mind, it pays to plan ahead because some tours leave only on preset dates or when they have a large enough group. All the companies below have a bilingual staff.

Ancon Expeditions (© **269-9415;** www.anconexpeditions.com) is the foremost tour operator in Panama, with a full-time staff of degreed naturalists and birdwatching experts, a handful of remote lodges, and offerings of day excursions and preset and custom-planned journeys to all corners of Panama. Ancon Expeditions began as the travel arm of the Asociación Nacional para la Conservación de la Naturaleza (ANCON), an NGO devoted to the preservation of natural resources and biodiversity; but the two are no longer related. Trips with preset dates can be guaranteed with just two to four people. A few of the more unique offerings are a trek across the isthmus following the old Spanish Camino Real, and Ancon's short adventures (1–5 nights) visiting the San Blas Archipelago, Bocas del Toro, or the Chiriquí Highlands. A few of their trips are based around their own lodges. Ancon specializes in trips that take adventurers deep into the heart of the Darién jungle; they have more trips to this region than any other operator. Day excursions such as a "Panama Canal Rainforest Boat Adventure" are highly recommended, especially for kids.

Ecocircuitos (© **314-0068-1586;** www.ecocircuitos.com) is run by a young, dynamic group of travel professionals who specialize in small groups (minimum four and maximum eight people), and who focus heavily on sustainable tourism with a low impact on the environment. They offer everything from a city tour through Casco Viejo to an 11-day bird-watching, trekking, and cultural journey through the San Blas Islands, the Chiriquí Highlands, and Bocas del Toro. Ecocircuitos also has a unique 4-day trip to the Darién that involves trekking through old-growth forest and tent lodging in a traditional Emberá Indian village. Their 9-day Family Fun and Adventures tour is a great option for families. Tours are either tailor-made or have a preset itinerary.

Adventures in Panama (© 315/849-5144 in the U.S., or 260-0044; www.adventuresinpanama.com), whose slogan is "No Tours, Just Adventures," is the operator to go to for active sports such as kayaking, rafting, mountain biking, and rock climbing around Panama, and day adventures around Panama City. Tamer adventures, like city tours and cultural encounters with Emberá Indians, are also available and can be combined with sports. One of the company's specialties is the San Blas region—they offer guided tours or can book difficult-to-contact hotels and hostels there. Adventures in Panama focuses on private trips with either a preset itinerary or a tailored adventure to suit your tastes; rates vary according to the size of your party.

Advantage Panama (© 6676-2466; www.advantagepanama.com) specializes in bird-watching trips but also does day trips to Emberá villages, the Canal Zone, and Lake Gatun. In addition, non-birding custom tours can be arranged to just about anywhere in Panama and prices are more affordable than better known Ancon Expeditions. Advantage guides are all bilingual and college educated, and owner Guido Berguido has a passion for birding and nature. Prices vary depending on the size of the group.

Futura Tours (© 360-2030 or 6674-6050; www.panamatraveltours.com) offers half-day, full-day, and overnight tours in the Panama City area. If you're short on time but want to visit the Kuna Yala Islands, Futura tours offers a 1-day/1-night trip to the islands.

Margo Tours (© 263-8888; www.margotours.com) is a relative newcomer to the tour scene and offers day and overnight tours as well as fishing excursions and a unique real-estate and lifestyle tour for travelers thinking about a move to Panama.

Pesantez Tours (© 366-9100; www.pesantez-tours.com) is an established company that can do all your booking for you if you're not looking to join a set tour. They focus more on traditional tours of Panama City, trips to El Valle de Antón, the canal, and Portobelo, and they even offer a half-day shopping tour.

ACTIVITIES A TO Z

This section is divided by activity, with listings of the prime destinations in Panama for doing each as well as the tour operators and outfitters who tailor trips to the specific activities. Tour operators have local knowledge and, more importantly, they provide guides and, in most cases, equipment. If you are planning to focus your trip to Panama around one sport or activity, these tour operators and outfitters are your best bet.

Adventure travel carries risks, and travelers should be well aware of dangers before participating in any tour. The operators mentioned in this chapter have been chosen for their safety records and reputations, but ask questions on your own. For example, if your adventure involves boating, what kind of vessel will they use? Dug-out canoe *pangas* are common and a colorful way to get around, but for long journeys they're uncomfortable, wet, and dangerous in choppy water; also, few local boat drivers carry radios or safety equipment.

Check individual chapters for smaller regional tour operators.

Biking

Mountain biking is relatively new in Panama. There are few places suitable for riding other than well-established paved and dirt roads, but many of these roads can be dangerous if there is a lot of vehicle traffic. Roads in Panama are curvy, often with hairpin turns, and do not have bike lanes or a proper road shoulder, so keep alert for speeding vehicles coming around a bend. If you just feel like getting out and pedaling around town, you'll find bicycle rentals in more touristy areas that rent for an average of $10 a day. Bicycle rental shops are listed in regional chapters within this book. There are no tour companies (yet) that offer multiday packages that focus entirely on biking entirely on Panama; however, the operators listed below can custom-build a trip for you.

In **Panama City,** the most popular and safest bike-riding area is the Amador Causeway, which is flat and has bike lanes—and a pretty spectacular view to boot. Outside the city, the Gamboa Resort rents bicycles for touring around; from here it's a couple of kilometers to the Pipeline Road Trail, a dirt-and-mud road that is flanked by tropical jungle. **El Valle de Anton** was made for bike riding: Vehicle traffic is light, roads are flat and paved, and a few steep, technical dirt roads offer a good workout. **Boquete,** too, has picturesque, winding roads that provide moderate terrain and pastoral views. Note that rental bicycles around Panama are *not* top-of-the-line models and usually lack shocks and other deluxe features.

Adventures in Panama (see above) offers two bike day trips around Panama City. Their day excursion to the Pipeline Road Trail gives cyclists a chance to get (a little) dirty and ride through jungle at one of the best bird-watching sites in Panama. Across the isthmus, they offer a day tour that begins with a bike ride across the Gatún Locks, connecting with a 6.4km (4-mile) dirt road to Fort San Lorenzo, a road known for birds and wildlife. The company **Bike Hike Adventures** (see above) combines biking on the Amador Causeway and near Fort San Lorenzo as part of their multisport package trips.

Bird-Watching

Panama ranks as one of the world's top bird-watching sites, with more than 950 registered species of resident and migrant birds—more than the U.S. and Canada combined. Because Panama is a land bridge connecting two continents, birders are privy to viewing species from both North and South America. Many of the birds found here are "showcase" birds such as toucans, macaws, and the resplendent quetzal, which delight even non-birders. Keen birders often return home having seen dozens of "life birds," or their first sighting of a bird species. If you head out with a qualified birding guide, expect to see upwards of 100 or more in a single day.

Lodges with the best bird-watching include **Canopy Tower** (p. 147) in Soberanía National Park, and its sister property **Canopy Lodge** (p. 190) in El Valle de Antón; **Sierra Llorona Panama Lodge** (p. 149) southeast of Colón and near Portobelo

National Park; **Cana Field Station** (p. 305) in Darién National Park; **Punta Patiño Lodge** (p. 303) in Darién Province near the Gulf of San Miguel; **Los Quetzales Lodge & Spa** (p. 228) on the edge of International Amistad and Volcán Barú national parks. Note that these lodges provide professional bird-watching guides either as part of an all-inclusive package or ordered a la carte. Tour operators listed below center their trips around these all-inclusive lodges, so really what you're getting is a 24-hour professional who is both problem-solver and educational guide.

Bird-watching hot spots include the **Darién Highlands** for macaws, large toucans, colorful tanagers, and endemics such as Pirre Warblers; the **Darién Lowlands,** especially known for harpy eagles; the **Nusagandi** region for speckled antshrikes and sapayoas; **Soberanía National Park** and Pipeline Road, home to more than 525 species including trogons, antbirds, blue cotingas, and other canopy dwellers; **Achiote Road,** near Fort San Lorenzo and Colón, for diurnal raptors and spot-crowned barbets, oropendolas, and pied puffbirds; **El Valle** for North American breeding warblers and black-crowned antpittas; and the neighboring national parks **International Amistad** and **Volcán Barú** (Chiriquí Highlands) for the resplendent quetzal, three-wattled bellbirds, trogons, long-tailed silky flycatchers, tapaculos, and Andean pygmy owls. Two popular birding areas here include **Finca Hartmann** and **Finca Lérida,** both coffee plantations with endemic and migratory species. Seabirds such as magnificent frigate birds nest on **Isla Iguana** in the Azuero; they also nest on **Swan's Cay** in Bocas, where you'll also find brown boobies and red-billed tropic birds.

U.S.-BASED TOUR OPERATORS

Caligo Ventures ★ (© 800/426-7781; www.caligoventures.com) specializes in bird-watching tours, with set itineraries for 9- to 11-day tours January through March to the Darién as well as the Canal Zone and the western highlands. Caligo uses local, expert birding guides. They also offer 9-day trips for independent travelers for $2,250 from May to November, and $2,295 from December to April.

Field Guides ★★ (© 800/728-4953 or 512/263-7295; www.fieldguides.com) is a specialty bird-watching travel operator, with highly esteemed and friendly guides. They offer four all-inclusive programs from December to March. Their "Wild Darién" visits the Cana and Cerro Punta Field Station and their "Panama's Fabulous Fortnight" tour focuses on the Chiriquí Highlands. There are also tours to the Canopy Lodge and the Canopy Tower. Tours cost an average of $3,175 to $5,550. Group size is limited to eight people.

Victor Emanuel Nature Tours ★★ (© 800/328-8368 or 512/328-5221; www.ventbird.com) is a well-respected tour operator and the largest company in the world specializing in bird tours. VENT offers not just December-to-March tours, but tours year-round either with one of their own guides or a local guide (or combination). Group limit is 10 people; tours average 7 nights and base around one destination (mostly the Canopy Tower) with optional add-on trips. Prices start at about $2,345.

PANAMANIAN BIRDING COMPANIES

For local independent guides, see the regional chapters in this book. These tour operators provide travelers with multiple-day journeys, but more importantly, they are the companies to contact for shorter day excursions, especially around Panama City. In addition to these operators, the **Panama Audubon Society** (© 232-5977; www.panamaaudubon.org) offers a bird-watching trip around Panama City once a month for nonmembers ($5 per person) and other trips and activities for members. Check their website for dates.

Ancon Expeditions (see "Panamanian Tour Operators," above) has the largest staff of professional birding guides, many of whom are contracted by international companies, and they own and run both the Cana Field Station and the Punta Patiño Lodge in the Darién.

Advantage Tours ★★ (© 6676-2466; www.advantagepanama.com), which runs the Soberanía Research Lodge in Gamboa, are the travel organizers and outfitters for the international Audubon Society. Their secret asset is Guido Berguido, a degreed bird-watching guide who is one of the friendliest and enthusiastic guides anywhere. Their year-round "Birdwatchers Paradise" tour combines Soberanía and Achiote Road with Volcán Barú.

Diving & Snorkeling

Isla Coiba, in the Chiriquí Gulf of the Pacific Ocean, is simply *the* best diving site in Panama, often described as a cross between the Cocos Islands in Costa Rica and the Galápagos Islands of Ecuador. Isla Coiba was the site of a notorious penitentiary until 2005, which kept visitors away, and therefore the surrounding waters are untouched. The snorkeling here is outstanding, too, but diving puts you close to pelagics such as white-tipped sharks, sailfish, manta rays, and dolphins. Coiba is also surrounded by one of the largest coral reefs on the Pacific Coast of the Americas. Other islands such as **Islas Secas,** and the islands within the **National Marine Park** in the Chiriquí Gulf, also provide outstanding diving.

On the Caribbean coast, **Bocas del Toro** is where you want to go to view some of the best and most colorful hard and soft coral in the world. In the Caribbean, visibility is best from March to May, and during September and October. The reef at **Baja Escribano,** between the San Blas and Colón, is the new talked-about dive site for its clear waters and colorful sponges.

Some of the best snorkeling in all of Panama is in the waters surrounding the **Pearl Islands,** for the abundance of marine life found here. Expect multitudinous schools of tropical fish and large pelagics such as white-tipped sharks. Bocas is billed as a top snorkeling site, but you'll need to get away from the standard tours to find the good stuff. **Isla Iguanas,** off the coast of Pedasí in the Pacific Ocean, is excellent for snorkeling, too.

The outfitters listed below offer diving trips around Panama, including multi-destination trips. For local dive operations, check the listings in regional chapters. The resort **Islas Secas** in the Chiriquí Gulf and the **Coral Lodge** in the Caribbean are two lodges with on-site dive shops and personalized tours for guests only. For diving in Bocas del Toro, see that chapter.

Panama Divers (© 448-2293, 314-0817, or 6613-4405; www.panamadivers.com) is the premier dive operation in Panama, based in Panama City and Portobelo. They also offer dives around Las Perlas and Kuna Yala. Panama Divers, which is fully insured, has decades of experience and a PADI instruction facility.

Panama Dive (✆ 910/452-1452; www.panamadive.net) also operates in Costa Rica and Nicaragua, but their Panama operation focuses on the Bocas del Toro area. PADI certification is offered.

Scuba Panama (✆ 261-3841; www.scubapanama.com) has a bicoastal dive that starts in the Caribbean Sea—visiting a sunken B-45 plane—and then goes to the Pacific Ocean for a dive there. They also have a unique (and spooky) dive in the Panama Canal, and dives around Portobelo and Isla Grande.

Pedasi Sports Club (✆ 995-2894 or 6741-7172; www.pedasisportsclub.com) is a relatively new operation that offers PADI certification and beginning through expert training on the Azuero Peninsula.

Fishing

Panama is a world-class fishing destination known for its fast and furious reeling-in of monster species such as blue, black, and striped marlin; yellowfin tuna; and wahoo and swordfish. Fishing takes place year-round; however, marlin and tuna are more abundant from January to April. The Pacific Ocean is where the best fishing is—there's also fishing in the Caribbean, but the infrastructure (marinas and such) isn't well developed. Anglers looking for a sure bet can't beat Lake Gatún for peacock bass—throw your line in and within minutes you'll snag one, guaranteed, making this a good excursion for kids (see chapter 7). In addition to the information provided below for Lake Gatún, **Gamboa Rainforest Resort** offers fishing trips for guests and even for visitors not lodging at the resort.

Fishing charters are available for day and multiday excursions, either as part of a trip organized by a competent operator, or by simply hiring a local boatman to take you out on the water. Custom sport-fishing tours head to the Pearl Islands, the Gulf of Chiriquí (around Coiba Island), and Piñas Bay—the latter is home to the Tropic Star Lodge (see below), and when they're sold out, a fishing charter is a good second option. Charters typically include transportation, meals, fishing gear, and bilingual or native-English-speaking guides.

FISHING CHARTERS

Pesca Panama (✆ 800/946-3474 in the U.S.; www.pescapanama.com) is a U.S.-based company that offers inshore and offshore sport fishing in the Gulf of Chiriquí, around Coiba and Hannibal Bank. Pesca guests stay aboard their "floating lodge," a 21 by 9.1m (70- by 30-ft.) barge with a maximum capacity of 12 guests (four beds per room). Rates range from $2,150 to $4,150 per person for 5 nights, and dates are set, not flexible.

Panama Fishing & Catching (✆ 6622-0212; www.panamafishingandcatching.com) has custom charters with prices that vary according to group size and desires, but on average they charge $450 to $490 for two for a day tour leaving from Panama City, and $1,200 to $3,000 for multiday offshore fishing charters (price runs from bare-bones to all-inclusive) depending on the size of the boat.

Cahill Fishing (✆ 877/800-1690 in the U.S., or 314-9000; www.gamboaresort.com) offers fishing excursions on Lake Gatún. **Pedasi Sports Club** (p. 208) offers fishing and spear-fishing charters in the Azuero Peninsula.

FISHING LODGES

Tropic Star Lodge ★★★ (Bahía Piña, Darién; ✆ **800/682-3424** in the U.S.; www.tropicstar.com). This prestigious fishing lodge is considered the best saltwater fishing resort in the world for its monster black and blue marlin, sailfish, and more. American-run, the lodge has been around since the early 1960s, and is located on the remote shore of Piñas Bay, in the Darién Province. The lodge draws famous VIPs, but is homey enough for families with kids. See p. 306 for a complete review.

Islas Secas ★★★ (Gulf of Chiriquí; ✆ **805/729-2737;** www.islassecas.com) is not a fishing lodge per se, but sport fishing and spear fishing for marlin, billfish, and tuna are among the most popular activities at this elegant ecolodge, situated on 16 private islands in the Pacific. See p. 251 for more information.

Gone Fishing ★★ (Boca Chica; ✆ **6573-0151;** www.gonefishing.com) is a fishing lodge with comfortable, ranch-style accommodations on the shore of Boca Chica, and friendly American owners. The focus is on fishing around the Gulf of Chiriquí, aboard one of their two 9.4m (31-ft.) open boats, and other activities for non-fishing guests. See p. 250 for a complete review.

Panama Big Game Sportfishing Club ★★ (Boca Chica; ✆ **866/281-1225** in the U.S.; www.panama-sportfishing.com), like the aforementioned lodges, is American-owned, in this case by two retired charter-boat skippers from Miami. The club is located near the Gone Fishing Lodge in Boca Chica, and they have four upscale teak cabins perched high on a hill, offering lovely views. The lodge has four fishing boats to accommodate all guests. See p. 250 for a complete review.

Golf

Panama isn't known for its spectacular golf courses, but that is quickly changing as more and more resorts build private courses. Panama provides golfers with a variety of championship courses, some of which are open for public day use, others as part of an all-inclusive resort. Close to Panama City, **Summit Golf & Resort** (✆ **232-4653;** www.summitgolfpanama.com) is the ideal venue for those staying in the capital; it's located on the east bank of the Panama Canal on the Gaillard Highway, and is accessible by taxi from the city for about $15 one-way. There is no hotel here, but there are swimming pools, a restaurant, and a pro shop. Designed by noted architect Jeffery Myers, the course is spread across rolling hills, with sweeping views of the Gaillard Cut of the Panama Canal. It's very classy, and there is a traditional 18-hole course as well as a 6-hole course for juniors and beginners. Rates Monday through Friday are $90 per person, Saturday and Sunday $100 per person, which includes a golf cart; and clubs are available for an additional $15. The course is open every day from 6am to 6pm; call ahead to book a tee time.

The **Coronado Golf & Beach Resort** (✆ **240-4444;** www.coronadoresort.com) is a long-standing, premier golf resort located on the Pacific Coast, about an hour from Panama City. Designed by Tom Fazio, this is the only seaside 18-hole course in the country; players can come for the day from Panama City, but the resort specializes in packages with lodging included. For more information, see the "Pacific Beaches" section of chapter 8.

Costa Blanca Golf & Villas (✆ **986-1915;** www.costablanca.com.pa) is located next to the Decameron Resort on the Pacific Coast, about 1½ hours from

Panama City. It has an 18-hole course that, because of its lights, you can play both day and night. The cost is closer to a bargain than other resorts: Monday through Friday it's $30 per person, with an additional $22 for a cart; weekends cost $72 per person (including cart). The course is within a residential development, and there are a clubhouse and restaurant.

An 18-hole golf course is scheduled to open at the Buenaventura Bristol (© **908-3333;** www.thebristol.com/buenaventura) on the Pacific Coast in 2011; it should be one of the nicest golf courses in Panama.

Horseback Riding

Horseback-riding outfits are sparsely distributed throughout the country, and the only lodge that focuses solely on riding is **Hacienda del Toro** (© **6612-9159;** www.haciendadeltoro.com), which offers short rides only, not full-day excursions. Still, it's a solid operation with high-quality horses (p. 286). One of the best places to ride is in **El Valle** with **Mitzila** (© **6646-5813**); she and her team charge $4 per hour and operate daily. Trails here wind through thick forest, offering some wide-open panoramas. They have guides, but speak limited English. In **Boquete,** horses can be rented from **Eduardo Cano** (© **720-1750** or 6628-0814) for $5 an hour for tours around the surrounding countryside. Horseback riding here takes place along mountain paths that provide riders with sweeping vistas of the Boquete valley. Eduardo speaks Spanish only, so depending on your own facility with *el español,* have your hotel make arrangements. Many higher-end hotels on the Pacific and the interior also rent horses.

Kayaking & White-Water Rafting

Panama has some of the most thrilling white-water rafting and kayaking in the Americas. The translucent rivers that pour down the Talamanca Mountain Range in the Chiriquí Highlands provide wild Class III and IV kayaking and rafting, principally on the **Chiriquí River** east of Volcán Barú, and the **Chiriquí Viejo River** west of the volcano, near the border with Costa Rica. Unfortunately, the Chiriquí Viejo is being threatened by a series of dams for a hydroelectric project, but for now it's a pristine river and a lot of fun to ride. There are tamer floats, too, such as the **Esti River,** a Class II, that is perfect for younger rafters, families, and beginners. What's special about the Chiriquí area is that relatively few paddlers have discovered it, so rafters and kayakers have the river, and lush mountain scenery full of birds and wildlife, all to themselves. There are two local rafting companies in Boquete with years of experience and expert knowledge of the region; an option is to book with a tour operator that can put together multiday, multi-destination, or instructional trips.

On the other side of the Talamanca, the Guarumo River has family-friendly Class I and II rapids that descend into the Caribbean Sea at Bocas del Toro; only two lodges offer this excursion, **Tranquilo Bay** (p. 285) and **Casa Cayuco** (p. 283).

Closer to Panama City, there is rafting on the Class II and Class III **Chagres River** with **Aventuras Panama** (see below), a 5-hour float through rainforest and past Emberá Indian villages (p. 146).

You'll find kayaks at many hotels and resorts that are located near the ocean, but multiday sea kayak trips have yet to take off in Panama except for in the San Blas

Archipelago (Kuna Yala), and even here it is a nascent industry considering that each company that operates here must be granted permission by Kuna Indian chiefs.

Chiriquí River Rafting (© 720-1505; www.panama-rafting.com) is owned and operated by Hector Sánchez, who has been rafting this region for more than 25 years. Hector and his professional crew offer year-round, half- and full-day rafting excursions around the Chiriquí, both for die-hards and families seeking an easy, fun float. Packages include lodging at their rustic bunkhouse or at the owner's private home and B&B.

Panama Rafters (© 720-2712; www.panamarafters.com) is a young company offering rafting and kayaking on the many rivers in the Chiriquí Highlands. They also teach beginning and intermediate kayaking. This company is especially good for rafters and kayakers seeking a wilder ride on the river.

Boquete Outdoor Adventures (© 720-2284; boqueteoutdooradventure.com) is a young, American-owned company offering rafting and kayaking on the many rivers in the Chiriquí Islands, as well as excursions to Isla Coiba and Boca Brava. The crew is professional and enthusiastic, and many day trips are family- and kid-friendly.

Xtrop (© 317-1279; www.xtrop.com), or "Expediciones Tropicales," is a well-respected company staffed by conservationists who use local, indigenous guides for their kayak adventures, focusing on multiday kayak trips to the San Blas Archipelago (camping or upscale lodging), as well as a sunset kayak trip around the mouth of the Panama Canal near the city.

Aventuras Panama (© 260-0044 or 315/849-5144 in the U.S.; www.aventuras panama.com), is one of Panama's top rafting and kayaking tour companies, offering rafting trips close to Panama City at the Chagres River and the Mamoni River (Class II–Class IV), as well as multiday trips to the Chiriquí Highlands, and 5-day sea kayaking trips in the San Blas.

Seakunga Adventures (© 800/781-2269 in the U.S. and Canada; www.seakunga.com) is a Canadian company with years of experience in Central America. They specialize in sea kayaking in the San Blas Archipelago, often working in conjunction with Aventuras (above) for their 8-day tour, including 3 nights in the San Blas and an overnight in an Emberá Indian village, with rafting on the Chagres.

Motorcycling

Motorcyclists with their own bikes should know that the lion's share of Panama roads are twisty-curvy, with the exception of the Pan American Highway. Also, most roads off this highway are peppered with potholes, and it is common to see farm animals blocking or sharing the road. The company **ACS Motorcycle Tours** (© 727/787-6278 in the U.S., or 236-7232 in Panama; www.acs-panama.com) offers 10-, 14-, and 21-day Panama–Costa Rica motorcycle tours with a support vehicle, and can include other Central American countries. Tours are offered September to January, and cost $2,850 to $3,500 (rider) and $1,550 to $1,950 (passenger) including everything except the flight to Panama.

Spas

There are no "destination" spas in Panama, but most resorts and a couple of upscale hotels have a top-of-the-line spa, or at the very least provide services such as massage, a gym, a sauna, and sometimes a steam room. I don't foresee a huge boom in this market, in spite of its rapid growth worldwide, but a few hotel owners are slowly catching on to this hot trend.

The **InterContinental Playa Bonita Resort & Spa ★★** (☎ 211-8600; www.ichotelsgroup.com) is located on the Pacific, just a 30-minute drive from Panama City. The plush beach resort has a sybaritic spa facility with all the trimmings; services are booked individually, or as part of a package that combines fruit- and chocolate-infused skin treatments, massage, aromatherapy, and body wraps.

Decapolis Radisson ★★ (☎ 215-5000; www.radisson.com), a sleek, trendy hotel, has the Aqua Spa, the top spa in Panama City in terms of service and hip decor, and you don't have to be a guest to book an appointment. They offer a full range of treatments and a stylish beauty parlor for one-stop makeovers.

Veneto Hotel & Casino ★★ (☎ 340-8888; www.venetocasino.com) has a building facade that screams Las Vegas, but inside it's as elegant as can be, and their Bamboo Sea Spa & Gym is a calm oasis that opens out onto a rooftop swimming pool. This is the spa with the widest range of treatments (Vichy style), including hot stone massage, mud baths, aromatherapy, hydrotherapy, and facials.

Gamboa Rainforest Resort ★ (☎ 314-9000; www.gamboaresort.com) is the best-known spa in Panama. The top-notch service, along with the recently renovated premises, make this one of the best spas in Panama. Expect traditional massages, body scrubs, and facials. If you're not staying at the resort, you can visit the spa anyway, and combine it with a bike ride and lunch.

Los Quetzales Lodge & Spa (☎ 771-2291; www.losquetzales.com) is a slight misnomer—there is a "spa" building here but it is small and services are not up to snuff. Massage rooms are shared, for example, unless you throw down extra cash for a private room. There is a sauna, and the spa center is backed by forest and a rushing river, but the center is more a lodge amenity than a spa destination.

Los Mandarinos Boutique Spa and Hotel (☎ 983-6645; www.losmandarinos.com) offers one of the nicer spas in Panama. Though the spa area is small, it offers a range of facials, massages, and body treatments, in addition to a thermal circuit including a sauna, Turkish bath, bio-thermal shower, and Jacuzzi. The spa is open to nonguests by appointment. **Yogini's Spa** (☎ 832-2430; www.yoguini.com/en/spa) also offers full spa services in a more casual, laid-back setting.

Haven Spa (☎ 730-9345; www.boquetespa.com) is a sprawling, recently opened Boquete spa offering every service you can imagine, from high-tech sauna and Turkish bath to relaxing massages. Plus there are exercise classes, a pool, and half a dozen guest rooms for those looking for a relaxing few days. Haven Spa is definitely one of the nicest spas in Panama.

The **Buenaventura Bristol** (see "Golf," above) has a high-end spa with massage rooms, Turkish bath, sauna, and more. This elegant spa is one of the better hotel spas in Panama, and the staff is particularly warm and inviting.

Surfing

The powerful swells and hollow reef breaks off the Pacific and Caribbean coasts make Panama *the* destination for a surfin' safari. The water's warm, the waves are uncrowded, and surfing here is consistent year-round, with the largest swells between April and October in the Pacific, and December to March in the

Caribbean. If you're a beginner or need tips on technique, a couple of camps specialize in surfing instruction.

Bocas del Toro is often compared to Tahiti or Hawaii for its huge swells—from December to March, and June and July—and monster waves such as **Dumpers** and **Silverbacks,** the latter a right-hand, reef-bottom point break comparable to Backdoor Pipeline in Oahu. Waves in Bocas range between 1.2 and 7.6m (4–25 ft.), and can be powerful beach breaks, big waves, reef point breaks, and spitting tubes. **Isla Grande** has powerful reef breaks and is a good bet if you want to surf the Caribbean but don't want to go as far as Bocas.

In the Chiriquí Gulf, the surf meccas are at **Morro Negrito** (see below), and **Santa Catalina,** internationally renowned among surfers and located straight across the bay from Isla Coiba, in the Pacific. Santa Catalina is a scruffy town, but the surfing is epic, with a consistent easy-to-line-up, rock-bottom point break that averages 1.5 to 6.1m (5–20 ft.). Farther east on the Azuero Peninsula are **Cambutal, Punta Negra, Dinosaurios,** and **Horcones,** other reliable spots for consistent breaks, including beach, point, and reef-bottom breaks that are sometimes even better than at Santa Catalina, and less crowded. The up-and-coming **Playa Venado,** near Pedasí, is a long beach break with lefts and rights and swells that can be as little as 1.5m (5 ft.) or as high as 4.6m (15 ft.). The Pacific beaches that lie between 1 and 2 hours from Panama City are beach breaks and point breaks.

If you just don't want to waste time planning your surf trip, or if you want a local's insider information on the best breaks, check **Panama Surf Tours** (✆ 6671-7777; www.panamasurftours.com), a respected company with flexible 1- and 5- to 8-day tours that run from economical to luxury. Be sure out smaller, regional surf schools and tours in the Central Panama and Bocas del Toro chapters. **Morro Negrito Surf Camp** (✆ 760/632-8014 in the U.S.; www.surferparadise.com) is located in an out-of-the-way region of the Chiriquí Gulf, about halfway between Santiago and David, on an island 3.2km (2 miles) off the coast. Guests are limited to 25, and with 10 different breaks (averaging 1.2–2.4m/4–8 ft.), you've pretty much got the whole wave to yourself here. Accommodations are one step above camping—the focus here is on waves, not luxury lodging. The camp has surf guides and lessons.

Río Mar Surf Camp (✆ 345-4010 or 6516-5031; www.riomarsurf.com) is just 1½ hours from Panama City, near San Carlos on the Pacific Coast. The camp has simple rooms (most with A/C) that can accommodate three guests, and surf lessons can be booked on an hourly basis. It's a good spot at which to brush up on your technique when you don't have much time in Panama.

Bocas Surf School (✆ 757-9057; www.bocassurfschool.com) offers a variety of beginner, intermediate, and advanced surfing courses, as well as more specialized courses such as "Women's Surf and Yoga." The school operates out of Lulu's Bed & Breakfast, where participants can stay for $55 a night for a double.

Yachting & Sailing

Panama Yacht Adventures (✆ 263-2673; www.panamayachtadventures.com) specializes in luxury yacht charters. The company has four boats of different sizes and also offers other activities such as parasailing, diving, sports fishing, and canal transits.

The **Panama Yacht Club** (© **6616-2408**; www.panamayachtclub.com), based out of Fort Amador Marina in Panama City, specializes in private excursions to the Pearl Islands, but can also be chartered for canal transits.

San Blas Sailing (© **314-1800** or 314-1288; www.sanblassailing.com), a French company, has a fleet of sailboats based in the San Blas Archipelago, offering 4- to 14-night all-inclusive adventures sailing around the islands, snorkeling, kayaking, and visiting Kuna villages.

Panama Sailing (© **866/324-4052**; www.panamasailingschool.com) offers guests a variety of multiple-day sailing classes. The company operates from the Amador Causeway in Panama City and also charters yachts for those who'd rather let someone else do the steering.

PANAMA'S TOP PARKS & RESERVES

Panama boasts one of the most complex ecosystems on the planet, its territory incorporating ancient rainforests, virgin beaches, islands, rugged peaks shrouded in cloud forests, and an underwater world replete with coral reefs and marine life. To protect all this wealth, the Panamanian government has designated 30% of the country as national parks, reserves, or wildlife refuges—about 2 million hectares (5 million acres) all told. The Autoridad Nacional de Ambiente (ANAM) administers Panama's parks and reserves, charging $3 to $10 for entrance fees (less for Panamanian residents). If camping is permitted, the fee is $5. ANAM is under-funded, however, and although park entrances have a token ranger station and maybe even a few bunks for rent, they do not provide visitors with a lot of information, nor do they give out trail maps.

What's interesting is how accessible some of Panama's parks and reserves are—there are five national parks located between 30 minutes and 2 hours of Panama City. And yet some parks are virtually inaccessible, such as the Darién, with its impenetrable jungle, or the north-facing rainforest of La Amistad International Park. Many wildlife refuges are off-limits to protect a breeding ground for birds or animals.

The following is a selective guide to Panama's national parks and reserves—the best in terms of accessibility or interest, or because of a particular sport (scuba diving in Coiba, for example). Detailed information about dining, lodging, activities, and more can be found in the regional chapters that follow.

The Canal Basin

SOBERANIA NATIONAL PARK   Spanning 19,425 hectares (48,000 acres) of undulating, pristine tropical rainforest, this is one of the most accessible, species-rich parks in the Americas—and it's just 40 minutes from Panama City. Wildlife from both continents converges here to create a hyper-diverse region that's home to an estimated 525 bird species and 105 mammal species. Expect to see coatimundi, three-toed sloths, howler monkeys, and Geoffrey's tamarins, which are tiny primates. Soberanía is home to Pipeline Road, the world-famous bird-watching trail, as well as to hiking trails such as the historic Camino de Cruces used by the Spanish to transport gold from the Pacific in the 16th century. **Location:** 25km (15 miles) north of Panama City, on the eastern shore of the canal. For more information, see "Soberanía National Park" in chapter 7.

ALTOS DE CAMPANA NATIONAL PARK In 1966, this became Panama's first national park, covering an area of 4,925 hectares (12,170 acres) of igneous landscape created by the extinct El Valle de Antón volcano. Altos de Campana is characterized by rugged peaks that are almost completely deforested on the Pacific side, and sloping rainforest on the Atlantic side, and there are high cliffs here that provide lookout points with dramatic views of the Canal Basin and Chame Bay. For bird-watching, the park is home to exotic species that can be difficult to view elsewhere, such as violet hummingbirds, white-tipped sicklebills, and orange-bellied trogons. **Location:** 90km (56 miles) west of Panama City. For more information, see "Altos de Campana National Park" in chapter 8.

Oceans & Islands

COIBA NATIONAL PARK Panama's largest national park is a gem that covers an astounding 270,128 hectares (667,500 acres) of mostly marine park, as well as Coiba Island. The park owes its pristine state to a notorious penal colony that was located here until 2005, which kept visitors away and the region virtually untouched by development. Coiba has been called the Galápagos of Central America, providing world-class diving and snorkeling around its coral reef and white-sand beaches. In addition to saltwater crocodiles, turtles, humpback whales, and howler monkeys, this is one of the few places where it is still possible to see a scarlet macaw in the wild. **Location:** Gulf of Chiriquí, 1½ hours by boat from Santa Catalina. For more information, see "Isla Coiba" in chapter 9.

GOLFO DE CHIRIQUI NATIONAL MARINE PARK This park incorporates two dozen hilly islands and outcrops, but mostly it protects the surrounding ocean area and its rich marine life and coral reefs. Few people visit here, which is surprising given its beauty and proximity to Boquete. A couple of upstart operations offer diving and snorkeling, as well as visits to uninhabited and perfect white-sand beaches; there are two fishing lodges based here, too. **Location:** Just off the southern shore of Boca Chica, in the Gulf of Chiriquí. For more information, see p. 248.

ISLA BASTIMENTOS NATIONAL MARINE PARK This national park is the reason to come to Bocas del Toro, for its virgin rainforest, turquoise sea replete with preserved hard and soft corals, and the idyllic Cayos Zapatillas, two castaway-type islands with white sand and outstanding snorkeling opportunities. The park also protects the largest area of Caribbean mangrove swamp in the country as well as important turtle-nesting sites. About 90% of the park is marine area and home to lots of colorful tropical fish, and there is decent bird-watching on the island, with 68 species. **Location:** Southeast of Isla Colón, 45 minutes by boat from Bocas Town or Bocas airport. For more information, see "Isla Bastimentos" in chapter 10.

ISLA IGUANA WILDLIFE REFUGE Only 55 hectares (136 acres), this refuge is surrounded with coral reef and clear blue sea ideal for snorkeling. As the name implies, it's also home to many green iguanas. From June to November, humpback whales breed in the area and are commonly seen by boat. The white-sand beach here is the best in the Azuero area, but unfortunately this region gets hit by currents that carry trash thrown overboard by boats all over the Pacific. **Location:** 3km (2 miles) from the shore near Pedasí, in the Pacific Ocean. For more information, see "Pedasí" in chapter 8.

BARRO COLORADO NATIONAL MONUMENT A former hilltop, this island was created by the flooding of Lake Gatún during the construction of the Panama Canal. It is now home to one of the most important—and oldest—biological research stations in the world, administered by the Smithsonian Tropical Research Institute (STRI). The monument actually comprises more than 55 hectares (136 acres) of land, including five surrounding mainland peninsulas, but the spotlight is on Barro Colorado Island for its "captive" biodiversity that provides an opportunity for scientists to conduct studies without being encroached upon by outside forces. The island can be visited as a day tour. **Location:** Lake Gatún, in the Canal Zone. For more information, see "Lago Gatún" in chapter 7.

The Highlands

LA AMISTAD INTERNATIONAL PARK Popularly known as PILA, this is one of the more unique parks in Panama because it is shared with neighboring Costa Rica. Unfortunately, the park is not as easily accessed on the Panamanian side, but there are a couple of trails at the administration area near Cerro Punta, in the Chiriquí Highlands, that put you deep in primeval rainforest. The UNESCO Heritage Site comprises 207,000 hectares (511,508 acres) of land spread across the Cordillera Central mountain range, with dramatic peaks, cliffs, and valleys. It's one of the wettest regions in the country, so bring your waterproof gear. **Location:** The park straddles the Costa Rica–Panama border, in the Chiriquí Highlands. For more information, see "What to See & Do in the Northwestern Highlands" in chapter 9.

VOLCAN BARU NATIONAL PARK This mountainous park is 87,451 hectares (35,390 acres) spread around the Barú Volcano, and it is home to the best short-haul day hike in Panama. The volcano's altitude and fertile soil provide for a bioclimatic "island" that is home to many endemic plants not seen anywhere else around Panama. From the top of the Barú Volcano, you can see the Pacific and Atlantic oceans, but a cloud forest usually blocks the view. More than 250 bird species have been recorded here, making this prime bird-watching territory, especially for the resplendent quetzal and the endemic black-cheeked warbler. **Location:** Barú Volcano in the Chiriquí Highlands, accessible from Boquete or Cerro Punta. For more information, see p. 233.

Eastern Panama

DARIEN NATIONAL PARK The Darién is mostly impenetrable wilderness that runs the length of the border with Colombia, in eastern Panama. It is the largest, and wildest, national park in Central America, and designated a UNESCO Biosphere Reserve, but it's the least-visited park because of travel logistics and lack of accessibility. The most popular (and really only) destination here is Cana, which draws nature lovers of all kinds, but the Darién is revered mostly by bird-watchers who come to view the outstanding array of 450-plus bird species, including showcase birds such as blue macaws, toucans, and harpy eagles. **Location:** Eastern end of the Darién Province, along the Panama–Colombia border. For more information, see chapter 12.

PUNTA PATIÑO NATURE RESERVE This reserve is managed by the conservation group ANCON, and because it is on the Gulf of San Miguel and surrounded by dense jungle, the only way to get here is by boat. Birders like Punta Patiño because it offers the best chance to spot harpy eagles, and visits here usually center

Monkey Business

No trip to Panama would be complete without at least one monkey sighting. Home to five distinct species of primates—the white-faced capuchin, Geoffrey's tamarin, and howler, spider, and night monkeys—Panama offers the opportunity for one of the world's most gratifying wildlife-viewing experiences. Just listen for the deep guttural call of a howler or the rustling of leaves overhead—telltale signs that monkeys are in your vicinity.

For a guaranteed monkey sighting, visit Monkey Island by boat on a jungle cruise, or the Summit Gardens Park & Zoo (see chapter 7). The Darién area is home to many primates that can be seen fairly easily, as are the Soberanía National Park and Isla Bastimentos. The alert traveler can usually see Geoffrey's tamarins in Panama City's Metropolitan Park as well (see chapter 6). *Remember:* Monkeys have specific diets and should never be fed human victuals, especially junk food, no matter how fun it may seem to do so. Boycott any tour that attracts monkeys with food, and let your fellow travelers and tour guide know that this is not acceptable practice if you see someone feeding a monkey.

around Emberá Indian villages and Punta Alegre, home to descendants of West African slaves. There are also hikes and canoe rides. **Location:** Darién Province, on the Gulf of San Miguel. For more information, see chapter 12.

Central Panama

SARIGUA NATIONAL PARK   It's the only "desert" in Panama, but it's not here as a result of natural forces. This park features a lunar landscape of eroded land, fissures, and fossil-like stumps, but more than anything the park provides a vivid example of the ecological ruin that occurs with heavy deforestation caused by man. Along the shore are mangrove swamps and pockets of the dry forest that once covered the nearly 8,094 hectares (20,000 acres) that make up the park. Also, archaeologists have recently been discovering artifacts here left by the oldest known indigenous group in Panama. **Location:** In the Herrera Province on Azuero Peninsula's Parita Bay. For more information, see p. 200.

TIPS ON ETIQUETTE & SAFETY IN THE WILDERNESS

Adventure travel is inherently riskier than travel by cruise ship or on a tour bus, and in addition to preparing yourself physically you should also double-check your medical coverage and insurance policies. For specific information about diseases and illnesses that can afflict you while trudging through the jungles of Panama, see "Health" in chapter 3.

It's hot in Panama day and night. However, higher up in the Chiriquí Highlands it gets chilly in the evening, especially if you're in the rainforest and have gotten wet. Even during the summer, the cloud forest here (as well as the Caribbean Coast in general) is damp throughout the year, so bring rain gear and a couple of extra layers of dry clothing if you plan to be outdoors all day.

On the other hand, the equatorial sun is very strong and you can burn fast, so liberally apply a high-factor sunscreen. Bug bites are so common that I recommend you buy a pleasant-smelling but powerful repellent and apply it every day if you are visiting any area outside of Panama City. The beaches in Panama are lovely, but lurking in the sand are *chitras,* or no-see-ums, that leave an irritating welt. Deep in the jungle, chiggers burrow into your skin and leave an itching welt that lasts for 2 weeks. Bring along cortisone or Benadryl cream to soothe itching, and try not to scratch your bites, which can lead to sores and infections; also, the welt goes away faster if you leave it alone.

Panama is home to some of the most frightening snakes on the planet, such as boa constrictors and fer-de-lances, though on the whole, snakebites are rare. Still, don't go poking under rocks or fallen branches, and always scan the trail in front of you for any slithering menace. If you encounter a snake, don't panic or make any sudden movements, and don't try to handle the snake. Also, avoid swimming in rivers unless you know it is safe or are with a guide who can vouch for the river's safety. Caimans and crocodiles hide along shorelines, especially in mangrove swamps and river mouths.

Responsible travel tips: Always tread lightly and pack everything out with you when in the wilderness—this means *everything,* including toilet paper. Do not uproot plants or take flowers, especially wild orchids. Do not buy anything that is made of animal skin or shells, and do not eat seafood such as lobster during mating season from March to July. Be wary of hotels or outfits that call themselves "eco-anything," as the term here has yet to be properly defined or regulated. I've seen hotels that call themselves "eco" for no other reason than that they are located in the forest. Some small-scale hotels in Panama are blazing the trail for sustainable tourism and have been quite successful at it, but unfortunately, others cling to damaging practices.

ECOLOGICALLY ORIENTED VOLUNTEER & STUDY PROGRAMS

Although the **Peace Corps** (www.peacecorps.gov) sends a handful of volunteers to Panama every year, there's really not much in the way of volunteer organizations here. The following are a few institutions and nonprofit groups that work on sustainable development or other environmental or social projects in Panama.

Global Works (© 800/784-6362; www.globalworksinc.com) is a U.S.-based teen volunteer organization that provides support and services to local communities all over the world. Their Panama–Costa Rica program lasts 5 weeks and costs just over $5,000. They work in Boquete with the Ngöbé-Buglés and in Kuna Yala with the Kunas before moving on to Costa Rica.

Summit Garden & Zoo (© 232-4854; www.summitpanama.org) has volunteer programs working in animal care or environmental education, as well as in their botanical garden, providing opportunities to learn about Panamanian flora and fauna and conservation issues, and to pick up new skills while helping the park.

Paradise Gardens (www.paradisegardenspanama.com) is a completely volunteer-run organization operating as an animal rescue and release program, taking in injured monkeys, macaws, and sloths, among others. A rotating crew of volunteers tends to the animals' needs. There is limited housing available on-site.

PANAMA CITY 6

L ong overshadowed by the Panama Canal and a reputation as a hub for drug-running, Panama City is not
only reinventing itself as the thriving commercial and
financial hub of Central America, it is asserting itself as a
burgeoning tourist destination. Panama City has a Miami-
meets-Vegas vibe and is one of those rare Latin American
capitals that appears to have it all: a relatively high standard of living, a seemingly endless supply of investment
from abroad, a surplus of natural beauty, and a rich cultural
brew of ethnicities and religions. There is a sizeable expat
presence in the city, as well as a growing Asian community,
which continues to change the face of Panama City.

Signs of Panama City's reinvention are everywhere. The Amador Causeway, formerly a U.S. military base, is ground zero for several multimillion-
dollar condominium and commercial-center developments, such as the
new Biodiversity Museum designed by famed architect Frank Gehry. The
run-down 19th-century buildings of Casco Viejo have been revitalized
with private and public funds and declared a World Heritage Site by
UNESCO. Along the coast, swiftly rising skyscrapers, spurred by an
irresistible 20-year tax exemption (and rumors of drug laundering), por-
tend a megalopolis in the making. Even the dirty Panama Bay is undergoing a $360-million cleanup.

But Panama City's visitors need not venture far from their air-conditioned hotels to immerse themselves in the wild tropical jungle that is
characteristic of this region. Even the city's Natural Metropolitan Park is
the protected home of more than 200 species of birds, mammals, and
reptiles. Dozens of remarkable destinations outside the city limits can be
reached in less than 2 hours, meaning travelers can spend the day exploring but head back to the city and be well fed and rested for the next day's
adventure. For more on the area's day-trip offerings, see chapter 7. Keep
in mind, however, that hard-core nature lovers may be put off my Panama
City's chaotic layout, traffic, pollution and noise and will probably just
want to use Panama City as a stopover before heading elsewhere.

Panama City is the oldest Spanish settlement on the mainland of the
Americas, founded in 1519 by Pedro Arias Dávila (Pedrarias the Cruel).
The settlement was used as a base for stealing Peruvian gold and silver

and transporting it back to Spain via a treacherous road that linked Panama City with the Caribbean Sea. The immense wealth that passed across the isthmus proved irresistible to treasure-thirsty pirates and buccaneers, who conducted raids throughout the region during the 16th and 17th centuries. In 1671, the Welsh buccaneer Henry Morgan sacked Panama City, and the settlement burned to the ground. The ruins of Panama Viejo, or Old Panama, can be toured today. (See "What to See & Do," later in this chapter.)

By 1673, Panama City had been rebuilt in what is now known as Casco Viejo; it was heavily fortified and the city was never taken again. However, raids on the Caribbean coast mounted, and the Spanish, defeated, returned to sailing around Cape Horn in 1746. Panama declared its independence from Spain in 1821, but declined in importance until the Gold Rush of the mid–19th century, when thousands of forty-niners used the isthmus as a shortcut from the East Coast of the U.S. to California. Later, when Panama seceded from Colombia in 1903, Panama City was designated the capital. With the opening of the canal in 1914, Panama City became the most important center of trade and commerce in the Americas.

Panama City's modern history was marred by the rise of strongman dictator Manuel Noriega and by the 1989 U.S.-led invasion to overthrow him, which left hundreds dead, most of whom lived in the poor Chorrillo neighborhood. But today, Panama City is one of Latin America's safer cities, although crime rates have risen in the last few years because of Panama City's increasing role as a money-laundering capital. However, the average tourist should feel perfectly secure walking the city's streets.

ORIENTATION
Getting There & Departing
BY PLANE

All international flights, except those from Costa Rica, land at **Tocumen International Airport** (PTY; ℂ **238-2700**), located 21km (13 miles) from Panama City. Flights from Costa Rica to Panama City land at Albrook Airport (see below), and there is direct service from San José to David and Bocas del Toro airports. (See chapters 9 and 10, respectively.) See chapter 3 for airlines that service Panama City.

There are **ATP visitors' kiosks** inside Tocumen's arrival terminal (one in baggage claim and another through the Customs gate), with information about Panama City and some brochures; it's recommended, though, that travelers research accommodations and make reservations before their arrival because hotels are often booked.

The unit of currency in Panama is the U.S. dollar, so for those coming from the United States there is no need to exchange money. If you are coming from elsewhere, there is nowhere to exchange currency at Tocumen Airport, so be sure to bring your debit card or exchange at least $30 before arriving to cover the cost of your taxi before exchanging in the city center.

A licensed taxi from Tocumen to Panama City costs $20 to $25, plus toll fees for a total of about $25 to $30. Many hotels offer free scheduled pickup and drop-off service, or you can arrange transportation for a cheaper price—inquire when booking at your hotel. Another option for taxis is with **Easy Travel Panama** (ℂ **6617-4122**; www.easytravelpanama.net). They offer high-quality vehicles and bilingual drivers, and cost about the same as regular taxis ($40) for one or two people and $50 for three or four people, tolls included, but you must reserve ahead of time. Easy Travel offers personalized ground transportation anywhere; contact them for prices for long-distance destinations (the beaches outside of Panama City, for example). My two favorite cabdrivers in Panama are Mondi (© **6625-4631**) and Hector (© **6686-8127**); both are always prompt and courteous. Neither speaks much English, but both have years of experience working with tourists. Make sure to call them a couple days ahead of time to schedule pickup.

All rental-car agencies have desks in the arrival terminal and are open 24 hours a day. See "Getting Around," below, for more information.

Domestic flights, flights to Costa Rica, and charter flights to the 150 or so air-strips located on Panama's islands and remote jungle areas leave from **Marcos A. Gelabert Airport** (PAC), which is more commonly referred to as **Albrook Airport** (© Albrook is located northwest of Cerro Ancón (Ancón hill) off Avenue Omar Tor-rijos Herrera, near the canal. A taxi costs $2.25 to $3 to downtown Panama City and takes about 20 minutes. There are usually taxis waiting at the airport, although you can also cross the street and hail a taxi for a shorter wait. Rental-car agencies here are generally open from 8am to 6:30pm. Each company offers a key drop-box for customers who need to return a vehicle when rental desks aren't open.

Tip: Travelers who arrive at Tocumen Airport and plan to head directly to another destination in Panama via a domestic flight must transfer to Albrook Airport, about a 45-minute drive (or longer during rush hour) from Tocumen. A taxi costs about $30.

BY BUS

If arriving by bus, you'll be dropped off at the Albrook bus terminal near the Albrook airport and shopping center. A taxi to town costs $2.25 to $3 and takes 10 to 15 minutes. A taxi to the Gamboa area costs $25 and takes 30 minutes.

BY CAR

Travelers arriving to Panama City by car will do so via the Pan American Highway from the west, first crossing the canal on the Puente de las Américas (Bridge of the Americas) and arriving in the Balboa district of the city. Follow signs to Avenida Balboa to reach downtown. Drivers headed to Panama City from the west may also use the new Puente Centenario (Centennial Bridge), which crosses the canal near Paraíso, and avoid traffic congestion on the Bridge of the Americas. The road that crosses this bridge is also known as Vía Benedicto XVI, named after Pope Benedict XVI. There are currently plans to build an underground tunnel to Puente de la Americas, which would make leaving Panama City much quicker, but there's no telling how long this project will take or when it will even get underway.

The Pan American Highway continues east toward Colombia and ends in Yaviza, in the Darién Region. It is not possible to reach Colombia by car, and at this book's publication there were no ferries for vehicles to Colombia, although there is talk that this service might be reinstated soon.

Visitor Information

The **Autoridad de Turismo de Panama (ATP)** main office is on Calle Samuel Lewis on the first floor of Edificio Central, across from the Camosa; although open

Panama City

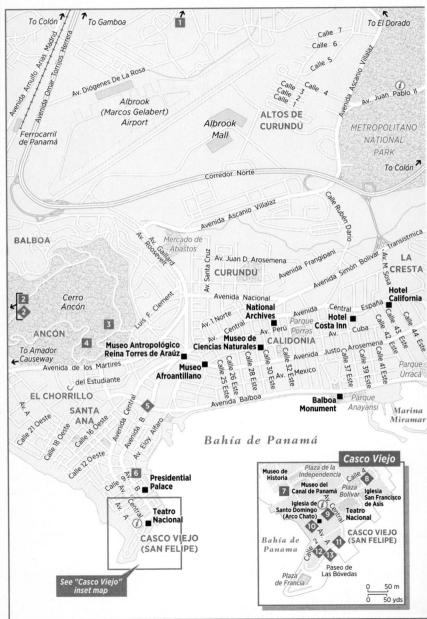

To Colón
To Gamboa
To El Dorado

Calle 7
Calle 6
Calle 5

Avenida Arnulfo Arias Madrid
Avenida Omar Torrijos Herrera

Av. Diógenes De La Rosa

Calle 4
Calle 3
Calle 2
Calle 1

Avenida Ascanio Villalaz

Av. Juan Pablo II

Albrook
(Marcos Gelabert)
Airport

Albrook
Mall

ALTOS DE
CURUNDÚ

METROPOLITANO
NATIONAL
PARK

Ferrocarril
de Panamá

To Colón

Corredor Norte

Avenida Ascanio Villalaz

Calle Rubén Darío

BALBOA

Cerro
Ancón

Mercado de
Abastos

Av. Santa Cruz

Av. Juan D. Arosemena

CURUNDÚ

Avenida Frangipani

Avenida Simón Bolívar

Transístmica

Av. M. Sosa

LA
CRESTA

Av. Gaillard
Av. Roosevelt

Avenida Nacional

Luis F. Clement

ANCÓN

Av. 1 Norte

National
Archives

Avenida

Central

Hotel
California

Hotel
Costa Inn

España

Calle 43 Este
Calle 42 Este
Calle 44 Este

To Amador
Causeway

Av. Perú
Parque
Porras

Av. Cuba

Central

Av.

Museo de
Ciencias Naturales

CALIDONIA

Calle 41 Este

Museo Antropológico
Reina Torres de Araúz

Avenida de los Mártires

C. del Estudiante

Museo
Afroantillano

Avenida

Justo

Arosemena

Calle 39 Este

Calle 37 Este

Parque
Urracá

Calle 25 Este
Calle 26 Este
Calle 28 Este
Calle 30 Este
Calle 32 Este

Av. México

EL CHORRILLO

SANTA
ANA

Avenida Balboa

Balboa
Monument

Parque
Anayansi

Marina
Miramar

Av. A

Calle 21 Oeste
Calle 18 Oeste
Calle 16 Oeste
Calle 12 Oeste

Calle 9

Avenida Central

Avenida B

Av. Eloy Alfaro

Bahía de Panamá

Calle 9
Av. B
Av. Central
Av. A

Presidential
Palace

Teatro
Nacional

CASCO VIEJO
(SAN FELIPE)

See "Casco Viejo"
inset map

Casco Viejo

Museo de
Historia

Plaza de la
Independencia

Calle 4

Museo del
Canal de Panamá

Plaza
Bolívar

Iglesia de
Santo Domingo
(Arco Chato)

Av. Central

Iglesia
San Francisco
de Asís

Teatro
Nacional

*Bahía de
Panamá*

Av. A

CASCO VIEJO
(SAN FELIPE)

Calle 2
Av. A

Plaza
de Francia

Paseo de
Las Bóvedas

0   50 m
0   50 yds

ACCOMMODATIONS ■
Albrook Inn **1**
Best Western Las Huacas **33**
Canal House **7**
Coral Suites Apartment **44**
Country Inn & Suites/
   Panama Canal **2**
Courtyard Panama
   Real Hotel **16**
Crown Plaza Panama **42**
Dos Palmitos **3**
Executive Hotel **28**
Hostal Familiar **2**
Hostal La Casa de Carmen **37**
Hotel DeVille **30**
Hotel El Parador **49**
Hotel Marbella **46**

Hotel Milan **48**
InterContinental Miramar **22**
La Estancia **4**
La Vegas Hotel Suites **53**
Le Meridien Hotel **20**
Luna's Castle **6**
Plaza Paitilla Inn **14**
Radisson Decapolis Hotel **15**
Riande Continental Hotel **41**
Sevilla Suites **52**
Sheraton Panama Hotel
   and Convention Center **40**
Suites Ambassador **45**
The Bristol **29**
The Panama
   Marriott Hotel **31**
Torres de Alba **50**
Veneto Hotel and Casino **43**

DINING ◆
Al Tambor de la Alegria **2**
Alberto's Pizza & Pasta **2**
Beirut **32**
Bucanero **2**
Café Belear **23**
Cafeteria Manolo's **35**
Caffe Pomodoro **51**
Crepes & Waffles **18**
Ego **8**
El Callejon del Gato **13**
El Trapiche **36**
Eurasia **24**
Greenhouse **21, 34**
La Posta **26**
Las Barandas **29**

Las Tinajas **25**
Lenos de Carbon **2**
Macarena **12**
Madame Chang **27**
Manolo Caracol **9**
Market **19**
Martin Fierro **47**
Mi Ranchito **2**
Mostaza **10**
Napoli **39**
Restaurante 1985/
   Rincon Suizo **42**
Restaurante Mercado
   Mariscos **5**
S'cena **11**
Sushi Itto **38**

El Cangrejo

Where the #@&!%$ Is It?

Ah, the aggravation of finding an address in Panama City. Just like in the U2 song, this is "Where the Streets Have No Name"—most of the residential streets, anyway. And of the streets that do have an appellation, they are either not signed or are referred to by two or three different names. Some say the reason is that Panama City has never had a postal delivery system (the postman only comes if you slip him some cash). Residents have post office boxes, called *apartados,* which is abbreviated as Apdo, or A.P.

Unbelievably, even taxi drivers are clueless when it comes to city street names beyond major avenues, even if they're labeled on a map. With taxi drivers, it is important that you give as much **detailed information** as possible such as the **cross street,** the **closest major intersection,** or better yet, a **recognizable landmark**—I've found that major hotels are helpful landmarks. When asking for directions, get as

much information as possible. Annoyingly, most buildings don't have numbers, so you'll have to rely on landmarks and main streets to get anywhere. If you're nuts enough to drive through Panama City, never do so without a map in your vehicle. Here you'll have double trouble because even major avenue and thoroughfare turn-offs are poorly marked. You'll most likely need to pull over periodically to see if you're still on track. Avenida Balboa runs from Casco Viejo to Panama Viejo and along the coast, and is the least-confusing route across town. Also, if you're new to driving in Panama City, it's probably best to practice during off-peak hours; you don't want your initiation to Panama's roads to be rush hour. I know this from personal experience. All that said, taxis are cheap and plentiful, so unless you love driving, there's really no need to rent a car in the city.

to the public, it does not have a proper information center (© **526-7000** or 526-7100; www.visitpanama.com). ATP has visitor centers at Vía España and Ricardo Arias (© **269-8011**), though they won't do much except give you a few brochures.

City Layout

Panama City lies on the eastern shore of the Panama Canal, and is bordered by the Pacific Ocean to the southeast, which can disorient first-time visitors unaccustomed to seeing the sun rise over the Pacific Ocean. Throw in a mesh of looping avenues and streets with two different names, or no name at all, and prepare to feel hopelessly lost during your first few days in Panama City. I've lived in Panama City, but I still can't make sense of the city layout—or lack of layout. Visitors rely on taxis, which are safe and cheap, about $1.50 to $3 for most locations in the city. Taxis from the city center to the Amador Causeway usually run about $5.

In very general terms, Panama can be divided into **four areas:** Old Panama (the ruins of the first settlement here); Casco Viejo, the city center during the late 19th and early 20th centuries; the former Canal Zone; and modern Panama, with its wide boulevards, glittering skyscrapers, and impoverished slums.

At the southwest end of the city lie the Amador Causeway, Casco Viejo, Cerro Ancón (Ancón hill), and the former Canal Zone. As a tourist, you'll probably spend most of your time here. From here, three principal avenues branch out across the city. Avenida Central, which begins in Casco Viejo as a thriving shopping center hawking cheap, imported goods, changes its name to Avenida Central España as it passes through Calidonia, and then becomes Vía España as it runs through the commercial area and financial district of El Cangrejo. Avenida Balboa extends the length of the coast, then forks into Vía Israel, later called Cincuentenario as it heads out to Old Panama. Corredor Sur, a fast-moving toll expressway, connects the city with Tocumen Airport. Avenida Simón Bolivar (also known as Av. 2da. Norte Transístmica) heads north to Colón; however, a new toll expressway, called the Corredor Norte, provides a faster route to Colón, eventually connecting with the Transístmica around Chilibre.

There are no beaches in the immediate area of the city—only mud flats—and visitors will need to travel northeast to the Caribbean or southwest to the Pacific beaches, about a 1- to 1½-hour drive from the city. The following Panama City neighborhoods run from west to east.

NEIGHBORHOODS IN BRIEF

Amador Causeway   This man-made peninsula on the south end of town is a popular recreation and dining area that provides sweeping views of the city skyline, and a reliable breeze that is a cool tonic on hot Panamanian days. It is also the site of several monstrous condominium and marina developments, as well as the new Frank Gehry museum dedicated to biodiversity. It may have a "manufactured" feel to it, but to me, Panama City's "boardwalk" is one of the most pleasant and peaceful areas of the city.

Balboa/Cerro Ancón/Albrook   These are three quiet residential neighborhoods located within the former Canal Zone. The domestic airport, Albrook, is here, occupying what once was the U.S. Air Force base, and many young professionals have moved into the "reverted area" for its trademark, sturdy wooden houses with wide verandas and lush foliage. Cerro Ancón hill is the most salient landmark here, offering a 360-degree view of the city and the canal from the lookout point up high. As a tourist, you're unlikely to spend much time in these three neighborhoods.

The neighborhoods El Chorrillo, Santa Ana, and Chinatown, on the eastern side of Cerro Ancón, are dangerous and not safe to visit, especially at night.

Calidonia/La Exposición   The shoreline that fronts these two neighborhoods is the future site of many of Panama City's most ambitious high-rise developments. There are many budget (and downright scary) lodging options here, but low-cost lodging can also be found in better neighborhoods like El Cangrejo. Avenida Balboa, which hugs the shore, is an excellent place for an afternoon stroll.

Casco Viejo/San Felipe   Panama's loveliest neighborhood was once a collection of homes built during the late 1800s and early 1900s, before it became fashionable to live elsewhere in the city. The historical barrio, now revitalized with public and private funds, boasts plenty of impressive historic homes and upscale bars and restaurants. Casco Viejo is undergoing a thorough renovation that prompted UNESCO to designate it a World Heritage Site. If you have time to visit just one neighborhood in Panama City, make it this one.

The Coastline: Marbella/Punta Paitilla/ Punta Pacífica   Residential towers and shopping malls are the identifying characteristics of this area, where there's a confluence of Panama's newly moneyed, illegally moneyed, and recently retired residents living in glitz-and-glass high-rises overlooking the sea. There are so many high-rises here, however, that I truly doubt there are enough investors or residents in all of Panama to buy all these shiny new apartments and office buildings, and many are almost empty. The new Cinta Costera, a boardwalk of sorts on the ocean side of Avenida Balboa, was finally completed last year and is a popular Friday and Saturday night hangout for Panamanians.

El Cangrejo/Area Bancaria/Bella Vista These three neighborhoods border each other, but they are so compact that they could be considered part of the financial/business district. Older El Cangrejo has a "lived-in" look and hilly streets that lend this neighborhood charm. Just to the south, the

Area Bancaria (Financial District), in addition to El Cangrejo, is where most travelers feel happiest lodging, as everything is within walking distance: top restaurants, shopping, and nightlife. Dozens of trendy eateries are concentrated in Bella Vista east of Avenida Frederico Boyd—the reason why Bella Vista is sometimes referred to as the Zona Rosa.

Panama Viejo On the eastern edge of the city are the ruins of Panama Viejo, the first settlement in Panama that later burned to the ground. Many visit as part of a guided tour, but the area also has a pleasant walking/jogging path along the shore and a self-guided interpretive trail that winds through the ruins.

GETTING AROUND

By Taxi

Taxis are inexpensive, safe, and plentiful—except when it is raining during rush hour and it seems that every worker heading to, or leaving, work is trying to flag one down. Quite often, a taxi will stop for another passenger if he or she is headed in your general direction, but the driver will usually deliver you to your destination first. Panama City taxis also have the infuriating habit of refusing to take you to pick you up if they don't feel like heading where you're headed, so you may have to hail a few cabs before one agrees to take you. Taxis charge $1.50 to $3 for most destinations within Panama City, but confirm the price beforehand as the "zones" that taxi drivers use for price reference are vague. Taxis from the city center to the Amador Causeway will run you about $5. Unscrupulous drivers may try to charge you more, especially to and from the Amador Causeway. What I do to prevent overcharging is simply pay the driver without asking how much I owe. I pretty much know that anywhere within El Cangrejo and the Area Bancaria should cost $1.50, Albrook $2.25 ($3 in traffic). I figure if the cabdriver thinks you know what you're doing, he's less likely to rip you off. *Tip:* Some taxis work directly for a hotel, and rip off guests by charging up to three times the going fare—and they're not going to budge when you contest the fare. These are the taxis that await guests directly at the front door. Simply walk out to the street and flag a taxi down for cheaper fare.

On Foot

Panama City is not easy to navigate on foot because of its interweaving streets, streets that are not signed, and lack of recognizable landmarks for visitors. Also, many neighborhoods aren't within walking distance of each other. To get around without a fuss, take a cab.

On the other hand, the best (really only) way to see **Casco Viejo** is on foot so that you can savor the neighborhood's colonial architecture, visit a museum, and

TIPS FOR drivers IN PANAMA CITY

If for some reason you must drive through town, consider the following advice:

- Prepare for abrupt stops when cars turn into or cross your lane, especially on wide avenues such as Balboa. You as a driver should be aggressive in this sense, too, and nose your way into oncoming traffic when making a left turn or merging into traffic—other cars will slow down for you, but this is a maneuver that is best learned from watching other drivers.

- Many streets are unsigned or not named, and often a one-way street is only advertised by the fact that all parked cars face one direction. First-time drivers in Panama City make a lot of U-turns and last-minute decisions, so don't lose patience.

- Keep cool under pressure and don't panic if an unexpected turn takes you into a spooky neighborhood. Have an open map at hand, keep your doors locked, and pull over if you need to find a route to get you headed in the right direction again.

- Cross walks in Panama City are poorly marked to nonexistent, so most pedestrians J-walk (or rather run) across the street when the coast is more or less clear. Keep this in mind if you'll be driving in Panama City because the last thing you want is to have your trip ruined by an unfortunate accident.

- Do not leave anything inside a parked vehicle.

- On some busy streets, a raggedy, self-styled "parking guard" might ask to watch your car. Pay him or her around 50¢. Some parking guards will demand payment of $1 or $2 before you leave your car in neighborhoods such as Casco Viejo or Bella Vista. Just do it. Do you really want to argue with a less than savory-looking character over $1?

stop for lunch. For a walking tour, see p. 116. Avenida Balboa has a long seafront walkway that starts near Punta Paitilla and ends at the Mercado de Marisco (the fish market). The Calzada de Amador (Amador Causeway) was designed for walking, jogging, and bicycling, with some 6.5km (4 miles) of landscaped pedestrian trails.

By Bus

The traveler in Panama City will feel more comfortable getting around by taxi than by bus. There are no printed bus routes, but the name of the bus's destination should appear on a sign in the front window. I lived in Panama City for over a year and never ventured on a bus because cabs are so cheap and they didn't seem worth the hassle. Panama City is supposedly overhauling its public transportation system, as the city's famous "Red Devils" are replaced by a modern fleet of coaches, but these plans have been in the works for years without any visible progress. Red Devils are retired U.S. school buses that drivers individualize with electric graffiti art, flashing lights, and other knickknacks, and they are driven until the wheels fall off. Though emblematic of the funky, vibrant culture that makes Panama what it is, Red Devils are often in the news for crashing and other unsafe practices, and "devil" drivers are notorious for their recklessness.

By Car

You do not need or want a rental car while visiting just Panama City, considering how economical taxis are. Admittedly, there are a lot of destinations and attractions outside the city, and independent travelers who desire a vehicle to see the sights on their own will have better luck renting at one of the airport terminals and heading straight out of the city on a well-signed thoroughfare. Pay attention to every sign on the road because some road signs are small and easy to miss; other times there is no "official" sign for a turnoff, but a couple of commercial signs with the town name, giving you only a vague idea of where you are. Travelers who have a basic command of Spanish and who can ask for directions will have the easiest time. Bring a good map and ask the rental agency exactly how to get to your destination. See "Tips for Drivers in Panama City," below.

There are car-rental kiosks at both the Tocumen and Albrook airports (car-rental agencies at Tocumen are open 24 hr.; Albrook rental agencies are open 8am–6:30pm), and each agency has a few locations in town. If you are renting a car to visit outlying areas such as the canal, Portobelo, or the Panamanian interior, have your rental agency show you, in detail, the quickest and most efficient route to your destination. For contact information for Tocumen Airport car-rental agencies, see "Getting There & Getting Around" in chapter 3.

[FastFACTS] PANAMA CITY

American Express American Express Travel Services has an emergency card pickup at Agencia de Viajes Fidanque in Centro Comercial Via Pacifica, local 9, in Punta Paitilla (© 265-2444).

Bookstores **Exedra Books,** on the corner of Vía Brasil and Vía España (© 264-4252; www.exedra books.com; Mon–Fri 9am–8:30pm and Sat 10am–7pm) is the top resource for English-language books, with dozens of titles, a cafe, a reading area, a children's corner, and Internet access. If you're spending extended time in Panama, you may order books on Exedra's

website and have them delivered for free for orders over $35. The Smithsonian's small but excellent **Corotu Bookstore,** at the Earl S. Tupper Research and Conference Center on Roosevelt Avenue in Ancón (© 212-8029; www.stri.org; Mon–Fri 10am–4:30pm) offers a comprehensive collection of books about Panama's flora, fauna, history, and culture, including large-format photo books, maps, and gifts. **El Hombre de la Mancha** (www. bookshombredelamancha. com) is a bookstore cafe with a small selection of English-language fiction and the best Panama City

map in town. They have locations in the Multiplaza, Multicentro, Albrook Mall, and the Centro Comercial Camino de Crucez Boulevar El Dorado, though the selection isn't exactly impressive. The **Gran Morrison** chain (Vía España at Calle 51 Este: © 269-2211; Punta Paitilla: © 264-5266), has a limited English-language book section and a variety of U.S. magazines such as *People* and *Time*.

Dentists & Doctors Panama City has no shortage of English-speaking dentists or doctors, most of whom trained in the U.S. For a list of dentists or doctors, contact your embassy, or see "Hospitals" below.

Drugstores Called *farmacias* in Spanish, drugstores are plentiful in Panama City. For 24-hour service, visit a branch of **El Rey** supermarket, the most central of which is on Vía España (℃ **223-1243**). Another reliable pharmacy is **Farmacias Arrocha** (℃ **360-4000**), with locations at Vía España in front of El Panama Hotel, Vía Argentina, and Punta Paitilla. You will probably be able to get most of your medication without a prescription, but bring an empty prescription container; medications often go by different names and an official prescription or prescription container can help the pharmacist figure out what medicine you're asking for.

Embassies & Consulates See "Fast Facts: Panama" on p. 308.

Emergencies For fire, dial ℃ **103;** for police dial **104;** for an ambulance, dial **Seguro Social** at ℃ **502-2532,** or **Cruz Roja** at ℃ **228-2187.**

Express Mail Services Many international courier and express-mail services have offices in Panama City, including **UPS** (℃ **269-9222**) in Obarrio (near El Cangrejo) at Calle 53 E in the Edificio Torre Swiss Bank; **Fed Ex** (℃ **800-1122**) on Calle 3 in Costa del Oeste; **Mail Boxes Etc.,** a one-stop service with

locations on Avenida Balboa in Paitilla in the Marisol Building, no. 1, next to McDonald's (℃ **264-7038**), on Vía España, next to Niko's Café in the Financial District (℃ **214-4620**), and in the Multiplaza Mall (℃ **302-4162**).

Eyeglasses Eyeglass shops are referred to as *ópticas.* **Optica López,** in Plaza Paitilla (℃ **269-0358**), and **Natural Vision,** in the Multicentro Mall (℃ **208-2648**), are dependable chains with other locations throughout the city. Both eyeglass shops offer repairs, exams, and name-brand eyewear.

Hospitals Many Panamanian doctors receive their medical degrees in the U.S.; therefore, many speak English. The best hospitals in Panama City are **Centro Médico Paitilla,** at Calle 53 and Avenida Balboa (℃ **265-8800**); **Clínica Hospital San Fernando,** at Avenida Central España (℃ **305-6300**); **Hospital Nacional,** at Avenida Cuba between Calle 38 and Calle 39 (℃ **207-8100** or 207-8102); and **Hospital Punta Pacífica,** at Calle 53 in Bella Vista (℃ **204-8000**). Punta Pacífica is the newest and most advanced hospital in the country and is affiliated with Johns Hopkins University. If you need to go to the hospital, do your best to wind up here.

Internet Access All hotels recommended in

this chapter have at least one computer with an Internet connection; some have wireless service in their lobby. Service in guest rooms is usually at an additional, and often expensive, price. Or try the best Internet cafe in town, **ClaroCOM,** at Avenida Eusebio A. Morales and Avenida Vía Veneto (℃ **200-0015;** Mon–Sat 8:45am–8:30pm), with wireless service if you have a laptop as well as plentiful computers. There are Internet cafes throughout El Cangrejo and the Area Bancaria as well as the el Dorado neighborhood northwest of downtown Panama and Via Argentina, all charging about $1 to $1.50 per hour.

Laundry & Dry Cleaning Most hotels offer dry cleaning and laundry services for an extra charge; if not, they can direct you to a nearby laundromat. **Lavandería Diamond Dry Cleaners Plus** (℃ **213-2216**) is at Calle J in El Cangrejo. **Lavandería Flash** (℃ **213-8092**) is at Vía Argentina. There's also **SUPERC-KLIN** in El Cangrejo in front of the Einstein statue at Calle F and Calle L-1 (℃ **223-5666**).

Post Office Postal service is scarce in Panama City; your best bet is to ask your hotel to mail something for you, or try Mail Boxes Etc. (see "Express Mail Services" above). The central post office (Correos y Telégrafos) is open Monday through Friday 8am to 4pm and Saturday 8am to 1pm, and is located on Avenida Central in front of the Mercado de Mariscos (✆ **212-7680**).

Restrooms There are few public restrooms in Panama City; your best bet is a hotel lobby or fast-food restaurant.

Safety Panama law requires that foreigners carry their passport with them at all times. I would say play it safe and carry a photocopy of only the opening pages and entrance stamp or tourist card, but police have been known to take in tourists not carrying their passport and the last thing you want is to end up in a Panamanian holding cell for a couple hours. During my time in Panama I was only asked to show ID once and of course, I had nothing on me, not even a

copy. I was taken to the officer's car and questioned extensively before he "kindly" decided to let me off with a warning. If you are carrying only a copy, *always* have a copy of your entrance stamp.

As Latin American cities go, Panama City is very safe for foreign travelers who stay out of bad neighborhoods such as Calidonia, Curundú, El Chorrillo, and Santa Ana. Chinatown is dangerous day and night as well. As in any major urban area, use common sense when it comes to safekeeping valuables—for example, don't put your wallet in your back pocket. Money and other valuables are best carried in hard-to-reach places, like deep pockets or a money belt, but purses are fine for women. Keep an eye out for suspicious characters who linger too close or follow too closely. Also, consider

taking money out of ATMs during the day to avoid stepping out from a brightly lit cashpoint into darkness. Scams are not common here; muggings and purse-snatchings happen, but not frequently. However, there have been cases of foreigners being shaken down by police or security guards late at night for not carrying their IDs. Basically, a police officer or security guard asks for your ID; if you don't have it on you, they threaten to take you to jail unless you pay up. There have also been a couple cases of foreigners reporting drugs being planted on them. Moral of the story? Don't go out late at night by yourself, especially if you've been drinking. If you park a car on the street, do not leave any valuables inside that could attract a thief, even if you park in a guarded parking lot.

WHERE TO STAY

Panama City is relatively small when compared to other major Latin American cities, but a chaotic city layout means you'll probably have to take a cab ride to get to most tourist destinations, unless you stay in Casco Viejo. Most hotels are concentrated in **El Cangrejo** and the **Area Bancaria (Financial District),** home to banking institutions, commercial services, shopping malls, and many of the city's best restaurants. For charm, you can't beat the cobblestone streets and renovated antique homes in **Casco Viejo,** which has apartment-style lodging units with kitchens. Cab-hailing, however, can be arduous in this neighborhood, especially at night, when raining, or during holidays, and walking to El Cangrejo or Bella Vista from here is out of the question. If you're staying in Casco Viejo, have your hotel provide you with the number of a radio taxi. This area also tends to get a bit seedy at night.

Elsewhere, there are excellent hotels scattered about the city in the **Marbella/Coastal** area, on the slope of leafy **Cerro Ancón** hill, and near the **Amador Causeway** (specific information about these neighborhoods can be found in each

Push-Buttons & the Pit Stop

Rent-by-the-hour hotels in Latin America are ubiquitous and largely patronized by young adults who still live with their parents, as well as by those carrying on the usual clandestine affairs. In Panama they're called "push-buttons." To admit to having patronized a push-button carries far less stigma here in Panama than it would in the U.S., but still, no one wants to be caught *in flagrante delicto,* and therein lies the origin of the name. Push-buttons are commonly found on the outskirts of towns and are clearly identifiable with cheesy names like "Lagoon of Love." Without getting out of the vehicle, a driver/client pushes an intercom button, and the gate opens. Each room has its own enclosed parking area and private entrance, and a small sliding partition that opens to the hallway means you can pay or order drinks without having to see or talk with anyone. Push-buttons come with all the romantic bells and whistles: heart-shaped tubs, mirrored ceilings, minibars—the works. To leave, the process is reversed, only the intercom button and exit area are called the "pit stop"—as the gate opens, the driver revs his engine, hits the gas, and quickly races to get out and avoid being seen.

lodging description). If cities aren't for you, you may want to consider staying in the comparatively quiet **Ancón** or **Amador** neighborhoods. **La Exposición** and **Calidonia** are home to mostly anonymous, divey hotels that seem better suited for a criminal hiding out from the feds than for a tourist seeing the sights. There are also quite a few "push-buttons" (see "Push-Buttons & the Pit Stop," below).

Although Panama City is best known for its high-end lodging options, there are a some budget gems for those turned off by the prospect of spending a couple hundred dollars a night on a hotel. **Hostal La Casa de Carmen,** Calle 1a between Vía Porras and Vía Brasil, El Carmen (© **263-4366;** www.lacasadecarmen.net), is a pleasant eight-room guesthouse on a quiet residential street just 1 block from the Via España. Rooms vary between hostel and B&B quality. Dorm rooms cost $15 a night and doubles with private bathroom run at $55 a night. All credit cards are accepted. Another good option, **Hostal Amador Familiar,** is housed in an older reverted canal home. There are dorm rooms and doubles available, ranging between $15 for a dorm room and $40 for a double with A/C. The Hostal Amador Familiar is a good option for families, the only drawback being that you'll have to take a taxi just about everywhere.

Tip: When booking a reservation at a local hotel (meaning not a chain hotel), always ask for the **corporate rate,** even if you're not on corporate business. A hotel may ask for the name of the company you work for, but most do not require any other identification or proof. Corporate rates are $20 to $30 cheaper than rack rates. Also, hotels listed below as "expensive" offer much cheaper rates for travelers booking through their websites. All hotels recommended in this chapter have **free parking** and at least one computer with an **Internet connection.** And if you're in town on a weekend, be sure to ask about weekend discount rates. Hotels in Panama City fill up during the week and empty out a bit on the weekends, and hotels are sometimes willing to negotiate weekend rates. Keep in mind that you'll probably get better rates when booking online than calling in person.

Aparthotels

Visitors on business, travelers on an extended stay in Panama City, or families with kids might consider renting an **aparthotel**, a self-catering unit with a kitchen that is rented nightly, weekly, or monthly (with rates based on length of stay). Aparthotels are high on function but low on style (they boast "luxury," but it's a stretch). A few have perks like gyms, swimming pools, and in-room laundry, but unfortunately, they charge up to $10 per day for an in-room Wi-Fi connection (it's sometimes cheaper to use their business center). The following aparthotels are located in El Cangrejo. Remember to ask for the corporate rate when booking, which could be cheaper than rack rates listed here.

Coral Suites Aparthotel ★   Tile floors, firm beds, and well-maintained rooms make this aparthotel a favorite. Rooms are cozy if not particularly luxurious, and the couches double as sofa beds. Their rooftop pool is well maintained and attractive, and their gym is small but complete. Their Coral Bay suites have terraces. Breakfast is included (but served in a cold, formal dining room).

Calle D at Vía Veneto. ✆ **269-2727.** www.coralsuites.net. 63 suites. $120–$140 executive suite; $130–$150 junior suite; $170 Coral Bay suite. AE, MC, V. **Amenities:** Gym; rooftop pool.. *In room:* A/C, TV, kitchen.

Las Vegas Hotel Suites   It's a shame the owners of the Las Vegas are blind to the retro-cool potential of this early-1970s building, having recently "renovated" with cheap furnishings and zero eye for style. Still, the suites have terraces, and the hotel rises high above the Caffè Pomodoro restaurant and the Wine Bar—convenient if you don't feel like walking far for a meal. This is the cheapest of the area's aparthotels, and service here is the friendliest. Some rooms have old, battered kitchens, others have just a hot plate and minifridge. Ask to see a few rooms—quality varies from one to the next, *especially* the quality of mattresses. All in all, the rooms are uninspired and mediocre.

Av. Eusebio A. Morales at Vía Veneto. ✆ **300-2020.** www.lasvegaspanama.com. 84 units. $85 studio; $110 suite. AE, MC, V. **Amenities:** Small gym. *In room:* A/C, TV, kitchenette, Wi-Fi.

Sevilla Suites   Slightly older but very clean with average beds, this aparthotel has modern kitchenettes and a pool with a view. Suites have two double beds or one queen-size and a separate living area; the junior suite is one open room. Rooms facing the street have the best views. The teensy gym has just a few machines. A continental breakfast is included and served in the ground-floor cafe.

Av. Eusebio A. Morales at Vía Veneto. ✆ **213-1312** or 213-0016. www.sevillasuites.com. 44 suites. $120 junior suite; $135 executive suite. AE, MC, V. **Amenities:** Small gym; Outdoor pool. *In room:* A/C, TV, kitchen, Wi-Fi.

Suites Ambassador   Located next door to Coral Suites, the Ambassador's rooms are darker owing to its location sandwiched between two buildings; ask for a room facing the back of the hotel. Rooms and bathrooms are clean but starting to show wear and tear. The principal difference between a studio and a suite is, in the latter, a dividing wall between the bedroom and living room (and a king-size versus a queen-size bed). The outdoor pool is uncomfortably close to the top flats of a nearby apartment, but breakfast is included, and the lobby-level breakfast nook is the coziest of all the aparthotels. The hotel is currently remodeling and updating all guest rooms.

Calle D at Vía Veneto. ✆ **263-7274.** 39 units. $120 studio; $120 suite. AE, MC, V. **Amenities:** Snack bar; babysitting; rooftop pool. *In room:* A/C, TV, Wi-Fi.

Torres del Alba   The old tower feels like a college dorm but the newer, more modern tower is more inviting and includes Wi-Fi and breakfast. Torres del Alba has a plant-filled rooftop patio and pool, and washers and dryers inside each apartment's spacious kitchen. Rooms come with a king-size or two double beds. Its location in El Cangrejo fronts several restaurants, the Veneto Casino, and Internet cafes. Ask for a quiet room—those overlooking the main street can be noisy both day and night. Better yet, request a room in the new tower.

49 B. Oeste at Av. Eusebio A. Morales. ✆ **269-7770** or 269-5180. www.torresdealba.com.pa. 204 suites. $129 suite in old tower; $159 suite in new tower. Breakfast included in new tower rates. AE, MC, V. **Amenities:** Fitness center; rooftop pool. *In room:* A/C, TV, hair dryer, kitchen, Wi-Fi in new tower.

El Cangrejo/Area Bancaria (Financial District)
VERY EXPENSIVE

In addition to the hotels listed below, the **Crowne Plaza,** Avenida Manuel Espinosa Batista at Eusebio A. Morales (✆ **206-5555;** www.ichotelsgroup.com), caters to business travelers and offers quiet rooms with double-paned windows and ergonomic beds in a central location. The **Courtyard Marriott** in Punta Pacifica (✆ **301-0101;** www.marriott.com) is adjacent to Multiplaza Mall—ultraconvenient if you plan to get in a lot of shopping on your trip—and quite stylish for a Courtyard.

The Bristol Panama ★★★   This boutique hotel is an excellent choice for business travelers and those seeking quiet, centrally located accommodations. The decor, uncharacteristic of tropical Panama City, is done in conservative, richly textured hues with mahogany furnishings—very English in style, and guest rooms have carpeted floors. The on-site restaurant is one of the best in town (see "Where to Dine," below). The eager-to-please staff can accommodate any need, including pressing a shirt or arranging a tour, and they issue all guests a set of business cards printed with their name and the hotel's info. The downsides: There's no pool, and the lobby is tiny (though the cozy bar serves 72 kinds of rum).

Aquilino de la Guardia at Obarrio. ✆ **265-7844.** www.thebristol.com. 56 units. $265 double; $395 junior suite. AE, DC, MC, V. **Amenities:** Restaurant; bar; piano bar; concierge; fitness center; room service. *In room:* A/C, TV/DVD/VHS, CD player, fax, hair dryer, minibar, Wi-Fi.

Four Points by Sheraton   The Four Points can be found in the heart of the Financial District, next to the World Trade Center, in a more antiseptic area of the city. The hotel is a bit nicer than the usual chain franchise, with spacious rooms, especially the suites, that come with two rooms, two bathrooms, and two televisions, making this a good bet for families. The decor consists of floral-chintz bedspreads, gauzy drapes, and purpose-built furniture—not very "wow," but nevertheless very comfortable. There is a range of amenities, too, including a nicely designed outdoor pool and icy-cold air-conditioning. I don't recommend the Sheraton's restaurant or bar, which are not particularly pleasant spots to hang out. Also, one drawback for business travelers is that Internet service is pricey. Check their website for deals.

Calle 53 at Av. 5A B Sur. ✆ **265-3636.** www.fourpoints.com/panamacity. 128 units. Doubles starting at $280; suites starting at $380. AE, DC, MC, V. **Amenities:** Restaurant; bar; concierge; fitness center w/ steam room; room service; tennis court. *In room:* A/C, TV, hair dryer, high-speed Internet, minibar.

Hotel DeVille ★   Centrally located on a leafy street close to the Financial District, the DeVille is a European-style, all-suites boutique hotel that boasts personalized service for a home-away-from-home feeling not provided by most chain hotels. The decor here is conservative, executive style, with historic canal-era photos and richly colored wallpaper and does not have the flashy, Miami vibe most Panama City hotels have. It could be said that the hotel lacks a bit of soul and vibrancy—you can literally hear a pin drop in their small, hushed lobby, but if you're looking for something a little more low-key, the DeVille is a good choice. Rooms are not carpeted, and their grand suites are two-story affairs that aren't suitable for families with small children. Luxurious bathrooms contain marble countertops and walk-in showers, and orthopedic beds have Egyptian-cotton sheets. Best of all, a full breakfast is included—and can be served to you in bed. The DeVille has an excellent on-site restaurant, the Ten Bistro. On the downside, there is no pool or gym at the hotel.

Calle 50 at Beatriz M. de Cabal. ✆ **206-3100** or 263-0303. www.devillehotel.com.pa. 33 units. $260 luxury suite; $275 junior suite; $400 grand suite. AE, DC, MC, V. **Amenities:** Restaurant; bar; concierge; room service. *In room:* A/C, TV, VD player, hair dryer high-speed Internet, minibar.

The Panama Marriott Hotel ★★   The Panama Marriott is the overall best grand hotel in the city. It's within walking distance of top restaurants and Internet cafes. Their high-tech fitness center is enormous, and the spa is extensive and reasonably priced. There are amenities galore, and the staff provides courteous, helpful service. The handsome, oversize lobby is generously appointed with huge bouquets of fresh flowers, and an ample, comfortable lounge is the perfect spot for reading the paper. The guest rooms are spacious and attractive; standard doubles have a couch and large bathroom. Executive rooms are higher up and nearly identical to standard rooms, but come with upgraded amenities such as a private lounge on the 19th floor with a dynamite view. The Marriott also has a casino for a little gaming action and disco nightlife, but one big word of caution: Rooms that end in even numbers suffer from the pounding of DJ music and partying on weekends.

Calle 52 at Ricardo Arias. ✆ **210-9100** or 800/228-9290 toll-free in the U.S. and Canada. www. marriott.com/PTYPA. 295 units. $275 double; $296 executive. AE, DC, MC, V. **Amenities:** Restaurant; deli; sports bar; casino; concierge; 24-hr. fitness center w/whirlpool, spa, steam room, and sauna; outdoor pool; Hertz and Copa Air desks; travel agency; room service; babysitting. *In room:* A/C, TV, high-speed Internet, minibar, hair dryer.

Radisson Decapolis Hotel ★★   Trendy 30-somethings will find their home at the deliciously fresh and fun Decapolis Radisson. Think glass and steel, a sleek martini-and-sushi bar, stark decoration, and hallways filled with a rainbow of ambient light. This is not a true luxury hotel, but it provides excellent value with its fashionable decor and wide range of amenities, including one of the city's best spas; full business services such as cellphone rental; chic restaurants; and a casino and shopping mall connected by a walkway. Bright, spacious guest rooms (with walk-in closets and big bathrooms) are mostly white with wood-grain paneling and touches of whimsical lime, orange, and leopard print. On weekends, there is a throbbing party atmosphere in the lobby-level lounge and fourth-floor pool, which draws the young glitterati of Panama City. If you're looking for quiet (and a view), book anything from the 10th floor up, or consider a different hotel. Check the website for deals.

Av. Balboa at the Multicentro Mall. ✆ **215-5000** or 888/201-1718 in the U.S. www.radisson.com. 240 units. $274 double standard; $295 executive double; $340 executive suite. AE, MC, V. **Amenities:**

Restaurant; martini/sushi bar and pub-style bar; babysitting; concierge; fitness center; room service; full-service spa. *In room:* A/C, TV, CD player, hair dryer, high-speed Internet, minibar.

Sheraton Panama Hotel and Convention Center ★

A perennial favorite with tourists and business travelers for its self-contained, resort-in-the-city feel and comfortable accommodations, the Sheraton Panama Hotel and Convention Center (previously the Caesar Park Hotel) is near the Atlapa Convention Center and a 5- to 10-minute cab ride from most sights and restaurants. Designed in a mock Spanish colonial style, with indoor fountains and arched doorways, the hotel has a lush, inviting outdoor pool fringed with palms; its upper-floor rooms have excellent city and ocean views, and there are plenty of restaurants and shops on the premises. The concierge desk, presumably accustomed to shuttling out passengers in cabs because of the hotel's distance from downtown, can accommodate any request for transportation or tours. The restaurants are excellent, making this a perfect hotel to head back to, after a long day of play or work, for a breather and a "night in." Ask for discounts during low season; they have a lot of rooms to fill and if no convention is in town the staff seems eager to make a deal.

Vía Israel at Calle 77. (℄ **305-5100** or 800/325-3535; www.sheratonpanama.com.pa. 362 units. $200 and up double; $425 junior suite. AE, MC, V. **Amenities:** 3 restaurants; 2 bars; babysitting; concierge; fitness center w/whirlpool, spa, steam room, and sauna outdoor pool; room service. *In room:* A/C, TV, hair dryer, minibar.

EXPENSIVE

Riande Continental Hotel

Located on busy Vía España, and convenient for shops and dining, the Riande has been well maintained since its opening in 1972, and the premises are spotless. The hotel rises high around a small, tropical-style outdoor pool fringed by lounge chairs. Rooms are spacious, but with run-of-the-mill decor on par with that of midrange American chain hotels. Rooms have small balconies, but access is blocked, management says, to avoid accidents. When booking, ask for a room in the back to escape late-night traffic noise from Vía España. One caveat about the hotel: The air-conditioning system is centrally controlled and therefore impossible to adjust; it's also a little loud. The Riande has a casino and a full list of amenities found at five-star hotels; however, this hotel is firmly within the four-star category. Book online for savings of as much as 50% off the rack rate.

Vía España at Ricardo Arías. (℄ **265-5114.** www.hotelesriande.com. 363 units. $180 double; $220 suite. AE, DC, MC, V. **Amenities:** 2 restaurants; bar; disco; concierge; gym; whirlpool; outdoor pool; room service. *In room:* A/C, TV, minibar, Wi-Fi.

Veneto Hotel & Casino ★

The Veneto likens itself to a Las Vegas–style hotel/casino, and from the garish exterior it's easy to see why—but step inside the wide, low-slung lobby and enter a hotel with a lot of style. During the day, their elegant casino on the mezzanine level is hardly noticeable unless you head up the escalator and pay a visit; but at night, the music pumps and the lobby takes on a very festive atmosphere. Strangely, the rooms here are all business, with conservative furniture and cool tones of blue; the beds are ultra-comfortable with crisp linens, duvets, and orthopedic mattresses, and there are luxurious marble-inlaid bathrooms. The pool here hints at resort glamour, and their spa is one of the most complete in Panama, but there are a few slight defects here and there that prevent it from feeling like a five-star hotel. Some doubles are an odd rectangular shape and feel a little claustrophobic; they vary in size so you might ask to see more than one.

Av. Eusebio A. Morales at Vía Veneto. 📞 **340-8888,** or 877/999-3223 in the U.S. www.vwgrand.com. 301 units. $200 double; $245 junior suite. AE, DC, MC, V. **Amenities:** 3 restaurants; pool bar and 24-hr. sports bar; babysitting; concierge; state-of-the-art spa and fitness center w/whirlpool, steam room, and sauna; outdoor pool; room service. *In room:* A/C, TV, minibar, Wi-Fi.

MODERATE

Best Western Las Huacas Hotel and Suites ☺ This small Best Western franchise hotel, a converted apartment building, is centrally located and features a playful, Panamanian-folklore decor and guest rooms with kitchenettes. It's not luxurious in any sense; indeed, you'll feel as if you're subletting someone's kooky apartment. Las Huacas probably most appeals to a young teen who thinks that the leopard-print-and-bamboo tropical style is cool, as well as to someone seeking a venue for a margarita-fueled bachelor party. On the other hand, this hotel doesn't have the mass-produced feel of chains, and the accommodations are spacious, the service friendly. When choosing a room, keep in mind that the lower floors facing the street can be noisy, and that those accommodations abutting the next-door apartment put you uncomfortably face-to-face with your neighbors. Buffet breakfast is included in rates.

49 A. Oeste, near Av. Eusebio Morales. 📞 **213-2222.** www.lashuacashotel.com. 33 units. $88 junior suite; $90–$130 suite. AE, DC, MC, V. **Amenities:** Restaurant; fitness center; room service. *In room:* A/C, TV, kitchenette, minibar.

Executive Hotel This place is like a time warp back to the 1970s—even the doorman is still dressed in a natty guayabera suit that looks like an original. The Executive was undoubtedly the hotel of choice for discerning travelers when it opened; but 35 years later, the rooms are a tad worn and the beds could stand to be replaced, even though on the whole the hotel has been well maintained. The best things about this spot are its location, in the heart of El Cangrejo; its 24-hour coffee shop, which is great for travelers arriving at odd hours; and some pretty stunning views from the tiny balconies attached to the rooms. (Incidentally, the fifth floor and above are definitely not for those who suffer from vertigo.) Guest rooms are spaced out motel-like in that they are joined by an outdoor walkway. There are a tiny gym with a big view, an outdoor pool at street level that is unfortunately shaded most of the day, and air-conditioning that could use a little more oomph. Service is very friendly here. Breakfast is included in rates.

Aquilino de la Guardia at Calle 52 E. 📞 **265-8011.** www.executivehotel-panama.com. 96 units. $125 double. AE, MC, V. **Amenities:** Restaurant; bar; concierge; fitness center; outdoor pool; room service. *In room:* A/C, TV, CD player, minifridge, hair dryer, Wi-Fi.

INEXPENSIVE

Hotel El Parador Hotel El Parador has two things going for it: Its central location in the El Cangrejo neighborhood and its price, far below what you'd pay almost anywhere else in downtown Panama. Other than that, El Parador boasts little character or soul and rooms are, for the most part, uninspired, bland, and not particularly memorable. However, larger rooms have a balcony, and in-room amenities are clean and comfortable enough. The hotel caters to a largely Panamanian crowd and is a relative newcomer on the El Cangrejo hotel scene. If you're just looking for a place to sleep and aren't particularly fussy, El Parador is a perfectly acceptable option. On the plus side, it does have an attractive rooftop pool with a view.

Calle Eusebio A. Morales, El Cangrejo. © **214-4588.** www.hotelparadorpanama.com. 85 units. $65 single; $85 double; $95 triple. AE, MC, V. **Amenities:** Restaurant, snack bar, rooftop pool. *In room:* TV, A/C.

Hotel Marbella ★ Because of its price and location, the Marbella is a popular hotel with budget travelers. It offers clean rooms that are in good shape if a bit on the small side—all are fitted with a double and twin bed that take up most of the space. Also, because there is no pool, this is an ideal hotel for travelers who plan to spend their days out and about, and simply need a comfortable place to sleep at night. The bathrooms are on the small side, too, but have large walk-in showers. The front desk staff is courteous and bilingual; there is a (slightly pricey) restaurant for breakfast. If you're staying for a few nights, ask for one of the small refrigerators in storage. Taxes are included in rates.

Calle D at Eusebio A. Morales. © **263-2220.** hmarbella@cableonda.net. 84 units. $55 double. MC, V. **Amenities:** Restaurant; room service. *In room:* A/C, TV.

Hotel Milan ⚑ This is a no-frills hotel, but it's relatively new and everything is fresh and works properly. For the price, you'd have a hard time finding a better deal when looking for a downtown hotel close to restaurants and shops. Rooms are plain, but the frilly bedspreads and aqua-blue guest-room walls add a touch of character. The "suite" is a large double with a minifridge and whirlpool bath (situated incongruously in a room behind a small bar), and not worth the extra cash. The lighting in guest rooms is awfully dim, so order a proper nightstand lamp from the front desk. Economy doubles are slightly smaller versions of doubles. The hotel is safe, clean, and a good lodging option if you're just looking for a place to sleep and ambience isn't high on your list of priorities. A 55-room addition is in the works, something to keep in mind if you're easily bothered by noise. Service is a bit lackluster and slow. You get a significant discount if you pay with cash.

Av. Eusebio A. Morales 31. © **263-6130.** hotelmilan@cwpanama.net. 53 units. $57–$77 economy double; $77–$90 suite. AE, MC, V. **Amenities:** Restaurant/bar; room service. *In room:* A/C, TV, high-speed Internet (in top 2 floors and all new rooms).

Cerro Ancón/Balboa
EXPENSIVE

Country Inn & Suites—Panama Canal ★ ☺ Located near the Amador Causeway and fronting Miraflores Locks of the Panama Canal, this hotel is worth considering if you have kids, seek quiet accommodations, and/or want plenty of space to walk, jog, or ride a bike. The hotel has a view that sweeps from the Bridge of the Americas to the Causeway, overlooking bobbing sailboats and ships awaiting the canal crossing. The decor is country-style and guest rooms look like any cookie-cutter hotel room, but with tile flooring. They all have terraces and kitchenettes, though, and there is an irresistible outdoor pool and a 3.2km (2-mile) walkway along the coast. You'll need a taxi to get anywhere ($3–$5; if you can, flag a regular taxi on the periphery of the hotel rather than take the hotel's taxi), or you can rent a bike and pedal out to the Amador Causeway for a meal. Insist on an oceanview room—it only costs $25 more, and the sparkling nighttime view of the bridge is the unique perk of this hotel.

Av. Amador at Av. Pelícano, Balboa. © **211-4500,** or 800/456-4000 in the U.S. www.panamacanalcountry.com/amador. 98 units. $135–$160 deluxe standard; $145–$180 junior suite; $215 master suite. AE, MC, V. **Amenities:** Restaurant; bar; bikes; kid's play area; gym; outdoor pool; spa; tennis courts; room service. *In room:* A/C, TV, Wi-Fi, fridge.

MODERATE

Albrook Inn ★ 📷 Housed in the old guesthouse for single officers, this converted canal home is one of the newest additions to Panama's City's lodging scene. Located in a leafy, upscale residential sector, you'll have to take a taxi to get almost everywhere, but if you're looking for privacy and quiet at a moderate price, the Albrook Inn is a good choice. Rooms are chain-like and not particularly memorable, but comfortable enough. The hotel is particularly attractive to bird-watchers and nature lovers because of the well-maintained gardens and prevalence of birds on the grounds. The reception staff doesn't speak much English and could stand to be a bit friendlier, but if you're just looking for a safe place to sleep at night, Albrook Inn is an excellent choice. Be sure to ask about any special deals as you can usually negotiate a price at least 25% lower than the prices listed below.

Calle Las Magnolias No. 14. ☎ **315-1789.** www.albrookinn.com. 30 units. $99 double; $145 junior suites. AE, MC, V. **Amenities:** Restaurant/bar; Jacuzzi; outdoor pool. *In room:* A/C, TV, kitchen (in suites).

INEXPENSIVE

Dos Palmitos Bed & Breakfast 📷 Also located on leafy Cerro Ancon, this delightful and new intimate B&B is ideal for those looking for a quiet reprieve far removed from the noise and chaos of downtown Panama City. Situated in a reverted canal house dating back from 1920, Dos Palmitos feels a bit like staying at a friend's house, and though rooms are not particularly fancy, they are clean, comfortable, and cozy and the owners do their best to make guests feel at home. Rooms vary in size and shape. The attractive and inviting living room is a good spot to mingle with other guests, and the on-site self-catering kitchen makes it a good choice for families with young children and extended stay guests. Dos Palmitos is one of the few hotels in Panama City that actually feels kid-friendly, and this European-owned and -operated B&B has a reputation for excellent, friendly service. Keep in mind you will have to take a taxi to most attractions.

Cerro Ancón, behind the Panama Canal Authority building. ☎ **6581-8132.** www.dospalmitos.com. 4 units. $96 double. No credit cards. **Amenities:** Kitchen, tours. *In room:* A/C, TV.

La Estancia ★ 🗡 Located on the forested slope of Cerro Ancón in a renovated 1960s Canal Zone home, La Estancia is a quiet refuge from the hustle and bustle of Panama City. You're likely to see plenty of birds, sloths, and even monkeys from one of the hotel's many balconies as you read the morning paper. The B&B has spotless, bright accommodations and personalized service that includes an on-site, reputable travel agency. There's nothing within walking distance, except the winding road up to the top of the hill, so you'll need a cab for sightseeing or dining out. Doubles are either en suite or have a bathroom just outside the door. (Choose the latter—the bathroom is for your use only, and these rooms have terraces.) The two suites are enormous, and have sleek kitchens and long outdoor terraces. The intimacy of La Estancia encourages socializing among guests—those seeking absolute privacy will be happiest in a suite or a second-floor room, which has its own common area. Rooms can be a bit musky.

Quarry Heights, Cerro Ancón. ☎ **314-1417.** www.bedandbreakfastpanama.com. 10 units. $83 double; $99 suite. MC, V. **Amenities:** Snack bar. *In room:* Hair dryer, Wi-Fi.

Casco Viejo

Despite its popularity as a major tourist draw in Panama City, there are few accommodations here, and even fewer recommendable lodging options. This will probably change as the Casco Viejo neighborhood continues to be renovated and revitalized, and in fact, a couple major hotel openings are planned in the near future and small guesthouses and B&Bs are slowly appearing through Casco. **Las Clementinas Hotelito** is scheduled to open by the time you read this and will be a six-suite hotel. **Central Hotel,** with a 2012 completion date, will be the first large hotel in Casco Viejo. Once Casco gets its act together, this will be *the* neighborhood in Panama City in which to stay. Although Casco Viejo isn't ultra dangerous, it does get a bit sketchy at night and you'll want to take a taxi around here if you're traveling alone or in a small group. It can be difficult to find a taxi in this neighborhood.

What Casco Viejo does offer travelers are lovingly restored apartments that can be rented nightly or weekly by **Arco Properties,** Calle 2A Oeste, Galería San Felipe (② 211-2548; www.arcoproperties.com). Rental properties are on a space-available basis (most owners live outside Panama City and visit for short periods during the year), and they feature daily maid service but limited parking. The cost for a one- to two-bedroom apartment ranges, per night, from $100 to $200 May to November, and $150 to $250 December to April. Check out the Arco Properties website for photos (some rentals are fancier than others), or e-mail for availability at clara@arcoproperties.com or patrizia@arcoproperties.com. **Los Cuatro Tulipanes ★★★** (② 211-0877; www.loscuatrotulipanes.com) offers 10 apartments housed in fully restored mansions and buildings scattered throughout Casco Viejo, and is a top-notch option in the old quarter for those seeking a memorable lodging experience.

Also, I usually wouldn't include hostels, but considering the lack of lodging options in Casco Viejo, I want to give readers as much choice as possible. **Luna Castle Hostel,** Calle 9na 3-28 (② 262-1540; www.lunascastlehostel.com), is popular with backpackers. It's a good place for those traveling alone to meet people, though those hoping to turn in early should know there's a popular nightclub below the hostel.

The Canal House ★★★ 🏠 This brand-new hotel in a 115-year-old renovated Spanish-style mansion offers the most unique accommodations in Panama City. Each room is different from the next, but all are elegant, with tasteful tropical decor, orthopedic beds, and stylish furniture. The best room is the expansive downstairs Mira Flores Suite, which feels more like an apartment than a hotel room, complete with separate sleeping, living, and work areas. The two upstairs bedrooms, the Gatun and San Miguel rooms, are comfortable and attractive but a bit dim. There is a large dining area with capacity for up to 14, perfect for business meetings or social gatherings. Perhaps the best thing about the Canal House is the service: Whether you want complete privacy or a more hands-on experience, the staff will accommodate your needs.

Calle 5ta. Ave. A. ② **228-1907.** www.canalhousepanama.com. 3 units. $155–$325, depending on room. MC, V. **Amenities:** Concierge; access to nearby gym; spa. *In room:* A/C, TV, MP3 docking station, Wi-Fi.

The Coast/Marbella

This quickly developing sector is home to some of Panama's glitziest skyscrapers and offers relative convenience to el Cangrejo, the Amador Causeway, and Casco

Antiguo. Aside from the options listed below, **Hotel Costa Inn,** Av. Peru y Calle 39 (© **227-1522;** www.hotelcostainn.com), on the seedier side of the Bella Vista neighborhood, offers decent if unremarkable guest rooms at low prices: Doubles start at $55 and four-person family suites run about $132 per night. **Hotel California,** Via Espana and Calle 43 (© **263-7736;** www.hotelcaliforniapanama.net), is not exactly located in the most reputable part of Via Espana, but for $44 a night for a double, you can't beat the price. The 60 guest rooms offer chain-like decor and standard amenities.

VERY EXPENSIVE

InterContinental Miramar ★   Towering 19 floors over the shore of Panama City, the InterContinental has a breathtaking view. But other components of the hotel could use some spit and polish: There are frequent complaints about lackluster service and inconsistency in maintenance of guest rooms. Standard guest rooms are spacious and have king-size beds and sofas, but the best accommodations here are on one of the five Club Floors because of their exclusive access to a glitzy rooftop pool and plush executive lounge. The shore-level deluxe outdoor pool receives high marks, especially from kids, and the state-of-the-art gym is one of the few in the area to offer yoga classes. The lobby, however, is simply too tiny for a hotel of this caliber.

Av. Balboa near Av. Frederico Boyd. © **206-8888.** www.miramarpanama.com.185 units. $290 double. AE, DC, MC, V. **Amenities:** 2 restaurants; bar; concierge; fitness center w/whirlpool, spa, steam room, and sauna; outdoor pool; tennis court;room service. *In room:* A/C, TV, hair dryer, high-speed Internet, minibar.

Le Meridien Hotel   I had great expectations for Le Meridien, but as with most supposedly world-class hotels in Panama City, I couldn't help being slightly disappointed. Yes, the lobby is over-the-top Las Vegas chic (if such a thing exists) and rooms are spacious, contemporary, and well designed with perfectly comfortable beds and phenomenal views, but I find the hotel a bit overpriced, the front desk can be a bit aloof and unhelpful, and subtle signs of sub-par craftsmanship are present. That said, overall, the Meridien is a sexy and sophisticated hotel and the architect should be commended for his stylish, provocative design, and its location on Avenida Balboa and Calle Uruguay means it's walking distance to dozens of shops and nightlife options.

Calle Uruguay and Av. Balboa. © **297-3200.** www.starwoodhotels.com/lemeridien. 111 units. $300 double; $450–$600 suites. AE, DC, MC, V. **Amenities:** Restaurant; bar; concierge; fitness center; outdoor pool; room service. *In room:* A/C, TV, hair dryer, high-speed Internet, minibar.

MODERATE

Plaza Paitilla Inn ✐   This hair-curler-shaped hotel is located in the high-rise residential community of Punta Paitilla—yet it is still only blocks from a few convenience shops and the Multicentro Mall. The best feature of the Plaza Paitilla is its striking view from floor-to-ceiling windows in each guest room. (Book a room with a city or ocean view; otherwise you'll look out onto a neighboring condo.) Many of the rooms have furniture that looks to have been scavenged or bought at a discount outlet sale. The staff is friendly enough but is not trained to provide top-notch service. The beds are firm and comfortable, and there is a nice swimming pool fronting the bay, though like the hotel as a whole, it is a little worn on the edges. Taxes are included in rates.

Vía Italia, Punta Paitilla. © **208-0600.** www.plazapaitillainn.com. 252 units. $116 double; $138 suites. AE, MC, V. **Amenities:** Restaurant; bar; concierge;small gym; outdoor pool; room service. *In room:* A/C, TV, minibar.

WHERE TO DINE

Like any port city worth its salt, Panama City has a gastronomic scene influenced by a melting pot of immigrants from around the world, and by its regional neighbors Colombia, Mexico, and Peru. Foodies will be overjoyed by what's on offer in this metropolitan city: Chinese food ranked by gourmets as the some of the best on this side of the Pacific, fine European cuisine, Middle Eastern eateries, Argentine steakhouses, English-style pubs, and, of course, Panamanian restaurants influenced by Afro-Caribbeans, indigenous groups, and Spanish descendants. Panamanian food is tasty, but a lot of it is fried—especially breakfast items like empanadas, *hojaldras* (fried bread), and tortillas. Most main courses are accompanied by a rice-beans-plantain combo that can become repetitive. In other words, if you're planning to visit other destinations in Panama, I say sample the rich variety of international and fusion-style restaurants here and savor Panamanian fare later.

Restaurant reviews here are divided by their individual neighborhood. The El Cangrejo district represents the area northwest of Vía España. The Financial District southeast of Vía España is included with the area "Bella Vista," which is south of Vía España and also referred to as Calle Uruguay (or Calle 48 Este, just to make it more confusing). Bella Vista is essentially a compact barrio of restaurants, shops, and bars.

Don't overlook hotel restaurants. The Hotel Deville's trendy **Ten Bistro** serves contemporary, French-influenced food where each main course costs—you guessed it—$10. **Monsoon,** the Sheraton Panama's Asian restaurant, has been honored with international culinary awards. Monsoon offers a sushi night on Tuesday, and shellfish specials on Friday. The Decapolis Radisson's **Fusion** restaurant and its hip sushi lounge is the trendiest see-and-be-seen venue in town for dining. Fusion has a reasonably priced menu and often features a fixed-price buffet lunch for under $20. The **Hotel Executive** serves breakfast 24 hours a day, as well as some of the best burgers in town. See later in this chapter for a review of the Bristol Panama's restaurant, **Las Barandas;** it offers some of the best Panamanian food in the city and is overseen by Panama's most famous chef. Limoncillo, one of Panama City's traditionally best restaurants, has moved and reopened in San Francisco under the name **Limoncillo Pony Club,** Calle 69 Este (© **270-0807;** www.limoncillo.com).

For cheap Panamanian food you can't beat the 24-hour chain **Niko's Café,** which, in addition to basic sandwiches, serves 100 snacks and items, such as a tamale or fried egg, for less than 90¢ each. Niko's can be found at Vía España and Calle Gerardo Ortega (Calle 51B Este, near the Continental Hotel), at the Albrook Bus Terminal, or on Calle 50 (Nicanor Obarrio). There are many hole in the walls and cafeterias that serve what's called *comida corriente,* or the cheap daily special that might include a beverage. One of the best spots for cheap food is **Casa Vegeteriana** with locations off of Via Veneto on Calle D and in El Dorado. Portions of anything cost 50¢, meaning you can eat to your heart's desire for $1.50 to $3. American fast-food chains, such as Dunkin' Donuts, Bennigan's, McDonald's, T.G.I. Friday's, and Subway, are everywhere. The Bennigan's on the Amador Causeway is particularly hopping on Friday and Saturday nights. Fast-food chains are clustered next to the Veneto Hotel and the Multicentro Mall. *Note:* All Panamanian restaurants and bars recently became smoke-free, so smokers will have to take it outside. Restaurants come and go in Panama with relative frequency, so you may want to call ahead to make sure newer restaurants are still open. Also, restaurants tend to come in and out of fashion quickly, so a place that was hopping a year ago may be empty most weeknights now.

Grocery & Specialty Stores The supermarket chain **El Rey** is Panama's largest, and most branches are open 24 hours a day. You can find national products plus a large selection of imported brands from the U.S. The most convenient location is on Vía España, near the Continental Riande; there is another in the Albrook area, on Avenida Omar Torrijos on the way to Gamboa. Another option is the Super 99 supermarket with many locations scattered all over the city, some open 24 hours a day. For more upscale shopping, head to the **Riva-Smith grocery store** in Bella Vista. Riva-Smith carries many organic and alternative products, though it's a bit more expensive than El Rey or Super 99. The premier wine store **Felipe Motta,** in Marbella on Calle 53 (© **302-5555**), is the most complete in Central America, and their prices are reasonable. For organic groceries and health products, try **Orgánica** in Marbella, at the Plaza Paitilla mall on Ramón H. Jurado (© **215-2400**) or **Super Gourmet** (© **212-3487**) behind the Canal Museum in the Casco Viejo neighborhood (Av. A and 6th St.), which offers many organic and healthy choices as a well as a deli serving up tasty sandwiches and lunch options. **Foodie** is the most upscale place in town to buy fruit and vegetables and is located in the Bal Harbour Plaza in Punta Paitilla, across from Multicentro.

Bella Vista/Area Bancaria (Financial District)
EXPENSIVE

Peruvian fusion restaurant **Lima Limon,** Calle 47 con Calle Uruguay (© 390-1609), serves some of the best pisco sours in town and you won't want to miss $3 Martini Night on Thursday. Lima Limon is also popular among expats for its trivia and beer pong nights. **Palms,** Calle 48 and Calle Uruguay (© **265-7256**), was once one of the hottest restaurants in town, but its star has faded in recent years. Even so, the grilled steaks and fish dishes are excellent, and **Urbanao,** the upstairs bar, makes some of the best cocktails in town. **Masala,** Calles 44 and 45, Bella Vista (© **225-0105**), serves delicious traditional Indian cuisine in a small, attractive converted house and is one of the few good options for vegetarian travelers.

Eurasia ★★★ FUSION One of Panama City's tonier restaurants, Eurasia is the only restaurant in Central America to receive a five-diamond rating from the American Academy of Hospitality, and continues to be a favorite among tourists and wealthier Panamanians looking for a unique dining experience. As the name implies, Eurasia's dishes are European with dashes of Asian flavors, stylishly presented. Daring and delicious, the food truly reflects the immigrant melting pot that is Panama City. The ambience is elegant, with papaya-colored walls, lavish art, heavy Spanish ironwork, and checkered marble floors; there is a slightly more casual dining area near the bar. Waiters in starched white shirts and shiny cummerbunds provide some of the best service in all of Panama. You can expect to find classics such as prawns in tamarind and coconut sauce with pilaf Eurasia, or grilled chateaubriand Indochine with petit potatoes and fine herbs. In addition, Eurasia offers a variety of mouthwatering desserts.

Edificio La Trona, Calle 48 btw. Parque Urraca and Federico Boyd Av., Bella Vista. © **264-7859.** eurasia_restaurant@hotmail.com. Reservations recommended for dinner. Main courses $7–$29. AE, MC, V. Mon–Fri noon–3pm and 7–10:30pm; Sat 7–11pm.

MODERATE

Can Oliver ★ SPANISH/STEAKHOUSE   Formerly Café Balear, the bulk of the menu at this Spanish-owned restaurant is, fittingly, Spanish—however, not everyone knows that Can Oliver is also one of the best steakhouses in the city. Chef Pedro Masoliver runs a tight ship here, and the service and quality of the food, especially his tender cuts of beef, are consistent—which is not true of most steakhouses in Panama City. The restaurant is in a converted chalet-style home and is neither formal nor casual, rather somewhere in between. Try the rib-eye with mushrooms, filet with anchovy sauce, a traditional paella (a Catalan-style seafood risotto), grilled octopus, or fresh tuna steak in peppercorn. Can Oliver has a well-chosen wine list, too, with mostly Spanish (along with a few Chilean and Californian) varieties.

Calle Colombia at Rogelio Alfaro. ✆ **269-2415.** Main courses $13–$30. AE, MC, V. Mon–Sat noon–3pm and 7–11pm.

Greenhouse ★ INTERNATIONAL   Like its name implies, this restaurant is full of lush vegetation and enclosed in glass—it tries to be a little hipper than it really is, but Greenhouse is contemporary and fresh, and cooled by a good air-conditioning system. It's better to stop here for lunch or an afternoon snack than for dinner; the place is very casual, and the sandwiches, wraps, and appetizers are better than the main courses. Greenhouse has more than a dozen hot and cold wraps—fresh tuna, smoked salmon, and falafel, among others; sandwiches are hearty and include a delicious portobello mushroom sandwich, and possibly the only veggie burger in Panama City. Fresh salads, shish kabobs, hummus, and antipasto platters, plus a couple of heavier fish and meat dishes round out the menu. I find this place to be a bit expensive for what you get, but it does offer a cool, calming ambience. Drinks are half off from 5 to 8pm. Greenhouse is best for lunch.

In Bella Vista, Calle Uruguay at Calle 47. ✆ **264-6846** (2nd location in El Cangrejo, on Vía Argentina at Calle Arturo Motta; ✆ **214-7475**). Main courses $9.25–$15; sandwiches $6.50–$8. AE, MC, V. Daily noon–midnight.

La Posta ★★ 🍴 INTERNATIONAL   The long-term popularity of this restaurant derives from the lively, 1950s Havana-style ambience as well as the tasty creations of its American-trained chef. La Posta has a gorgeous tropical decor, wicker ceiling fans, and plantation-style architecture. Although elegant, the restaurant does not feel pretentious. During the day, floor-to-ceiling windows separate the dining area from an outdoor patio (with outdoor seating), filled with vegetation, which provides for a bright and cheerful lunchtime setting. La Posta is inexpensive for such a lovely atmosphere but you'll definitely want to make reservations to avoid a long wait. Try the starters (there are more than a dozen, so you might consider ordering an assortment of these rather than an entree): yellowfin tuna seviche with capers; *mero* (a high-quality grouper) carpaccio; or fried polenta with Gorgonzola and portobello mushrooms. The thin-crust pizzas are delicious, as are the risottos. Seafood dishes are tasty but simple, such as jumbo prawns with passion fruit and rice pilaf.

Calle 49 at Calle Uruguay. ✆ **269-1076.** www.lapostapanama.com. Reservations recommended. Main courses $9.75–$16; pizzas $6.50–$9. AE, DC, MC, V. Daily noon–3pm and 7–10:30pm.

Market ★★★ STEAKHOUSE   Owner David Henessy's second Panama City restaurant (the first being La Posta), Market has made a place for itself as *the* place to dine in the city, filling up for breakfast, lunch, and dinner almost every day. Essentially,

Market is an upmarket burger joint with an ingredients-based menu. Try the tasty pork chops, grown locally by Chiriqui highlands farmers or the popular "sliders," miniature, delicious hamburgers. But whatever you decide to dine on, you probably won't be disappointed. The restaurant has a surprisingly good selection of delicious salads, a rarity in Panamanian restaurants, and unlike most restaurants of its caliber, Market opens for breakfast Monday through Friday and brunch on Sunday. The restaurant is divided into two distinct areas: the main room is reminiscent of an upscale market deli (hence the name) boasting a sleek bar, contemporary decor, and a cool cement floor. The second floor, known as the Zebra Room, is airy and fresh, and perfect for those looking for a bit more privacy.

Corner of Calle Urugay and Calle 47. ℂ **264-9401.** www.marketpanama.com. Reservations recommended. AE, MC, V. Main courses $5.75–$45. Mon–Fri 7:30am–midnight; Sat–Sun 11:30am–midnight.

Sushi Itto SUSHI   Despite Sushi Itto's being a chain franchise from Mexico, this is one of the most popular sushi spots in the city, and their ingredients are always fresh and high-quality. The restaurant is modern though not as flashy as the Decapolis's sushi bar; but Sushi Itto is cheaper, there's more variety, and they deliver. There are dozens of fanciful rolls, with sweet and spicy sauces, that go far beyond the classic California roll and fresh sashimi. They also serve teppanyaki, udon, and yakisoba noodles with meat and shellfish. For whatever reason, Sushi Itto feels a need to put cream cheese in all of their rolls, so make sure to say something if you don't want cream cheese.

Calle 55 este behind Plaza Obarrio, ℂ **265-1222;** Multiplaza Mall, Local A-240, ℂ **302-3704.** Sushi rolls $6–$8.50. AE, MC, V. Daily noon–1am.

INEXPENSIVE

Crepes & Waffles CONTINENTAL   Like the name says, this casual eatery specializes in crepes and waffles. It's best for lunch or a light meal in the early evening; they even offer a "menú light" during lunch that includes a beverage and crepe for $4.75. Order one of the pre-designed crepes or build your own from a long list of ingredients and sauces, including lots of vegetarian options. Crepes & Waffles also serves huge salads, soups, and sandwiches. They recently opened another restaurant in the Flamenco area of the Amador Causeway.

Calle 47 at Calle Aquilino de la Guardia, ℂ **269-1574;** other locations in Multiplaza Mall Food Court (3rd floor), ℂ **302-7630;** Albrook Mall (2nd floor, in front of movie theater), ℂ **305-6536.** Crepes $3–$9. MC, V. Tues–Sun noon–11pm.

Napoli ☺ ITALIAN   This bustling, casual Italian eatery in the Obarrio neighborhood is a longtime favorite with Panamanian families. The place lacks ambience and feels a bit like a cafeteria, but the smartly dressed staff is polite and helpful, and parents won't have to worry that their children are disturbing other diners as it can get pretty loud here. Dishes are tasty and hearty, particularly the spaghetti *al pescatore* (seafood spaghetti in tomato sauce) and the many pizza selections. The tiramisu is also good, and there's a decent selection of Italian and international wines.

Calle 57 Obarrio. ℂ **263-8800.** napoli@liberty-tech.net. Main courses $5–$11. AE, MC, V. Tues–Sun 11am–11pm.

Casco Viejo

Once shrugged off as a dying, forgotten quarter, Casco Viejo is quickly becoming one of Panama City's most important dining scenes, and in my opinion, boasts the city's

A Perfect Ice-Cream Stop

To combat the heat and humidity in Casco Viejo, head to **Granclement** (© 228-0737; www.granclement.com), a French-style gourmet ice-cream and sorbet shop. Though a bit pricey, it serves the best ice cream in Panama City and is the perfect place to take a break while sightseeing.

most colorful and characterful restaurants. In addition to the options listed below, **Café Rene,** Calle Pedro J. Sossa (© 262-3487), follows the same concept as Manolo Caracol—no ordering and a different menu every day—and in fact, Rene used to run Manolo Caracol. Café Rene is a bit cheaper than Manolo's but the dishes are just as good. **Puerta de la Tierra,** Avenida Central and Calle 9, serves Argentine-style steaks and offers excellent service. **Pony Rosso Café,** Avenida A between Calles 7 and 8, is another good lunchtime option serving mostly light fare. The cafe is located in the Diablo Rosso Art Gallery, and is a testament to Casco Viejo's growing art scene.

EXPENSIVE

Manolo Caracol ★★ INTERNATIONAL   This artistic eatery may not appeal to every diner, but I say give it a try. Manolo, the Spanish chef, professes "cooking with love," and his adventurous and creative daily menu embraces fresh, in-season products he finds every morning in the local market. There's no ordering here: Customers pay $15 for lunch and $20 for dinner (not including drinks), and sit back and wait for a vibrantly composed parade of up to 12 courses to be slowly ushered to their table. A day's offering might include sole carpaccio, green mango seviche, pork loin with pineapple, and gingery prawns. Meals range from delicious to mediocre depending on the menu and who's cooking, and service can be regular to shabby, accounting for the mixed reviews among customers. However, Manolo Caracol's modern, fixed-menu concept and the fact that it's been around for a while in Casco Viejo, where restaurants open and close with frequency, is a testament to its popularity among Panamanians and tourists alike. The dining area is within an antique colonial building, and is casual and warm, with wood tables, white stucco walls, and plenty of religious artifacts and local art.

Calle 3 at Av. Central Sur (in front of the National Theater). © **228-4640** or 228-9479. www.manolo caracol.net. Reservations recommended for dinner. Fixed-price lunch $15; fixed price dinner $20. AE, MC, V. Mon–Sat noon–3pm and 7–10:30pm.

Mostaza ★★ INTERNATIONAL   Featuring a cozy dining area with thick white tablecloths, candles, exposed brick walls, and tasty cuisine, this is another excellent eatery in Casco Viejo. Like any good Argentine, co-owner Jose Forestier knows his beef, and even imports cuts like rib-eye and filet mignon from the U.S. Mostaza serves pasta, fresh grilled fish, and a few chef's specialties such as *bacalao* (codfish), *osobuco Corleone* (Italian stew made with veal shank), and pork chops with passion fruit or guayaba sauce. The pasta dishes are also tasty.

Av. A at Calle 3. © **228-3341.** Reservations recommended for dinner. Main courses $9–$18. AE, MC, V. Tues–Fri noon–midnight; Sat–Sun 5pm–midnight.

S'cena ★★★ INTERNATIONAL   This sexy, sophisticated jazz club/upscale restaurant is the perfect spot for an all-in-one night out and is one of my favorite dining spots in Casco Viejo. The jazz club, Platea, is on the first floor, the restaurant on the second. The bar in Platea is a good place to start or end a meal, and they serve appetizers for less-hungry patrons. Upstairs, S'cena is casual elegance, with a New York vibe, with white table linens and exposed brick walls. The cuisine is very good and Mediterranean influenced, crafted by a talented young chef on loan from Spain. The meal begins with a complimentary *amuse-bouche,* a tiny appetizer to pique the taste buds. Order a bottle of wine from the well-chosen, and reasonably priced, wine list, and follow it with shellfish sautéed in Pernod or octopus caramelized in white wine. Main courses include fish and meat dishes, and a few pasta highlights such as "Grandmother's Catalan Cannellonis."

In front of old Club Union. ℂ **228-4011.** Reservations recommended. Main courses $9–$18. AE, MC, V. Tues–Sun noon–4pm and 7:30–11pm (bar until 1am on weekends).

MODERATE

Ego y Narcisco ★ TAPAS   Ego is a cosmopolitan bar/cafe, on a quiet corner of Plaza Bolívar, specializing in tapas. Make a meal out of hot chili seviche; a salad of arugula, fig, and Camembert cheese; and cilantro beef skewers. Nicely mixed cocktails, a long swooshing bar, and outdoor seating are a few of Ego's perks. (There's air-conditioned seating indoors.) Large, cold pitchers of sangria are also a treat.

Calle Antonio J. de Sucre, on the corner of Plaza Bolívar. ℂ **262-2045.** Tapas $4–$8.50. AE, DC, MC, V. Mon–Sat 5–11:30pm.

El Callejon del Gato ★★ SPANISH   This is one of the hottest new restaurants on the Casco scene and is owned and run by German chef Sajoscha Hamam, who lived and worked in Spain and Morocco, bringing these influences to his tapas and entrees. The restaurant could be described as Spanish Mediterranean with a touch of Moroccan, and it's been popular since its opening in early 2010. Tapas include *queso de oveja en aceite y finas hierbas* (sheep cheese in oil and fine herbs), Spanish tortilla, and *setas al ajillo* (mushrooms in garlic sauce). Popular main dishes include *Pulpo a la Gallega,* which features octopus in olive oil, paprika, and bay leaves; Pica Pica, a Mallorcan-style seafood paella; plus several chicken and beef dishes. The only downside to El Callejon del Gato is that there's no outdoor seating.

Calle 1, Edificio Universidad Club, San Felipe. ℂ **211-2886** or 6525-4246. Main courses $12–$28; tapas $5–$8. MC, V. Mon–Sat 6pm–midnight.

Macarena ★★ SPANISH   This cozy little restaurant is an ideal spot for a couple because most items on the menu are prepared for two. In the dining area of wood floors and brick walls, the Macarena's Spanish owner serves food typical of his homeland, including tapas that make an excellent light meal. The bulk of the menu consists of rice and seafood-based dishes including jumbo shrimp stew and more than five kinds of paella, as well as fresh tuna and gazpacho. The restaurant's chic bar features live music on Friday and Saturday.

Calle 1a near Plaza Francia. ℂ **228-0572.** Main courses $11–$14; paellas for 2 $20–$28; tapas $3–$4.50. AE, MC, V. Daily noon–3pm and 6:30–10:30pm (until 11:30pm Fri–Sat).

El Cangrejo
EXPENSIVE

In addition to the places listed below, **Costa Azul,** by the Marriott, specializes in seafood and Panamanian dishes, and is popular with business folks on their lunch

Restaurant Mercado del Marisco

To find the freshest seafood in Panama City, you have to visit the Mercado del Marisco (Fish Market) at Avenida Balboa and its unassuming little eatery on the second floor (② 212-3898). This market restaurant serves quite possibly the best seviche in town, perhaps because the owner is Peruvian and lends his special flavor to such an emblematic Latin American dish. The portions are hearty, the price reasonable and, best of all, you can see below in the market what your catch looked like before it got to your plate. It's open daily from 11am to 7pm, but come before 1pm or after 2pm because this place gets packed during the lunch hour. A word of caution: Fresh seafood means fresh seafood, so if you can't stand the smell of fish, this place is definitely not for you. *Tip:* If the restaurant is full or you are on the run, buy a $1-to-$2 generous portion of seviche from Shiela (you can identify her by her gold tooth.)

breaks. **New York Bagel,** off Via Argentina near La Cabeza de Einstein, is a popular expat hangout serving, as the name implies, bagel breakfasts, bagel sandwiches, bagel chips, and other breakfast and light lunch items. It feels a bit like a converted warehouse on the inside and is one of my favorite spots to go when I want to get work done. (For those traveling alone, New York Bagel is also a good spot to meet fellow travelers. You must purchase at least $4.25 to be able to connect to the Wi-Fi network.) **Machu Picchu,** Calle Eusebio A. Morales no. 16 (② **264-9308**), serves up some of the best Peruvian food in Panama City and has been a longtime favorite among Panamanians and expats alike. **Matsui** (② **264-9562;** Calle Eusebio A. Morales No. 12-A) is, in my opinion, the best sushi place in town, proved by its 30-year longevity on the Panama City dining scene.

Las Barandas ★★★ CONTEMPORARY PANAMANIAN   Cuquita, the chef at Las Barandas, is nationally famous as the Martha Stewart of Panama, producing her own line of culinary magazines in addition to a weekly cooking show. At Las Barandas, Cuquita is the creator of the restaurant's gourmet Panamanian food and oversees the kitchen staff. The restaurant, located inside the Bristol Panama, is a sleek and chic dining area with just a handful of tables—so book ahead. At Las Barandas, traditional recipes are updated to appeal to modern gourmet tastes, with dishes such as maize soup, plantain won tons, grouper in ginger, sea bass in tamarind, and chicken breast roasted with pumpkinseeds, all bursting with flavor yet not too over-the-top so as to appeal to more conservative tastes. In addition to an extensive menu, there is a special "South Beach" menu for dieters watching their waistlines. Of special note is Las Barandas's Sunday brunch from 10am to 3pm.

Aquilino de la Guardia at Obarrio, in the Bristol Panama Hotel. ② **265-7844.** Reservations recommended. Main courses $12–$25. AE, MC, V. Daily 6–10am breakfast, noon–3pm lunch, and 6:30–11pm dinner.

Restaurante 1985 & Rincón Suizo ★★★ FRENCH/SWISS   These are nationally famous chef Willy Diggelmann's two flagship restaurants, both of which are reviewed here since they are located in the same building, a rather incongruous Swiss-alpine-style chalet. Restaurante 1985, widely regarded as one of the best, and most expensive, in the city, is where Panamanians go for a special meal. The fare is predominantly French, with classic dishes such as pâté, escargot, and coquilles St.-Jacques, but there are also German touches such as Wiener schnitzel. The standout at 1985 is the tender veal cutlet in morel mushroom sauce, but the fresh catch of the day, lobster, calamari and scallop stew, and filet mignon in red-wine sauce are divine, too. There is also an extensive gourmet vegetarian menu. For a splurge, order the fixed-price dinner menu for $26. There is lighter fare, but you'll be tempted by many of the creamier, calorie-packed meals, which make up nearly half the menu. For dessert, don't miss the *guanábana* (a very sweet fruit with a rough green peel and a soft, chewy white inside) mousse. The ambience is country French.

Upstairs is **Rincón Suizo,** a slightly less-expensive place that pays homage to Switzerland; its waitresses wear dirndls and there's a cozy ambience with checkered tablecloths and soft light. Traditional dishes such as raclette, fondue, goulash, and bratwurst are the mainstays here, as well as rabbit in red wine and *cordon bleu.* Like 1985, Rincón Suizo is heavy on sauces, but there are also fresh salads and diet-friendly grilled fish. Both restaurants feature an outstanding selection of wine.

Eusebio A. Morales and Calle 49B Oeste, in front of Sevilla Suites. ✆ **263-8571** or 263-8310. www.1985. com. Reservations recommended for dinner. Main courses $12–$33. AE, MC, V. Mon–Fri 11am–midnight; Sat–Sun 5:30pm–midnight.

MODERATE

Beirut ★ LEBANESE   Beirut is always busy and enjoys popularity among Pana-manians, expats, and vacationers. This is an excellent spot for a couple or a larger group because it serves reasonably priced combo plates and appetizer platters. Combos come with dozens of little dishes and finger foods such as hummus, labre, baba ghanouj, fried kibbe, almond rice, and so on, offering a filling meal and varied sample of flavors. There are also salads, falafel and other sandwiches, and kabobs. Beirut's low ceilings, molded banquet seating, and exotic decor makes you feel as if you've actually stepped into Lebanon. Additionally, the food is light and fresh, and powerful air-conditioning provides a refreshing escape from the hot Panama City streets. The chef, a Lebanese immigrant, patrols the dining room for quality control, sometimes refilling the occasional guest's hookah pipe, which is de rigueur in this establishment. A Lebanese Table, with a selection of dishes, for four guests is $58; a special combo large enough to feed two is just $10.

Ricardo Arias at Calle 52, near the Marriott Hotel. ✆ **214-3815.** Main courses $6.50–$15. MC, V. Daily 11am–2pm.

Madame Chang ★★ CHINESE   Some of the best Chinese food found outside China is here in Panama, and Madame Chang is where you come to savor it. Few restaurants serve a more delectable Peking duck, but there are also the jumbo shrimp a la sal, the gingery San Blas crab, the prawn rolls, and clams in black-bean sauce—really, everything on the menu is worth recommending. The proprietor, Siu Mee Chang, and her daughter Yolanda have merged the old with the new: The elegant ambience is more smart-casual than button-up conservative, and the cuisine blends traditional recipes from all Chinese provinces, but with a contemporary touch. Madame Chang also shakes up killer martinis.

Av. 5A and Calle Uruguay. ✆ **269-1313.** Reservations recommended. Main courses $8–$22. AE, MC, V. Daily noon–3pm and 6–11pm.

Martín Fierro ★★ STEAKHOUSE   Named after Argentina's epic literary hero, a gaucho who wandered the pampa, this restaurant, accordingly, serves thick slabs of beef and other meats that would satisfy a gaucho or any weary traveler who's had a hard day and longs for a hearty, satisfying meal. Martín Fierro features meats cut Argentine style, but the price differs between domestic meat and that imported from the U.S. You'll find pastas and fish on the menu, but if you're not a carnivore there's really no reason to eat here. (They boast about their salad bar, but it's insubstantial and won't do much more than decorate your plate.) Martín Fierro strives to be an elegant eating establishment, but the bright lights and decor keep it decidedly casual.

Eusebio Morales, in front of Bonavel. ⓒ **264-1927.** Main courses $8–$25. AE, MC, V. Mon–Sat noon–3pm and 6–11pm; Sun noon–9:30pm.

INEXPENSIVE

Cafetería Manolo's PANAMANIAN   This neighborhood standby is a plain-as-Jane diner with uniformed waitresses and a long list of Panamanian dishes of varying quality. It's the kind of place you go for a quick, no-frills meal, or to kill time with a cold beer while sitting on the outdoor terrace. It therefore draws as many locals as tourists who can't be bothered with a serious sit-down restaurant. Manolo's sandwiches are your best bet here, but there are also quick-fry steaks, grilled fish, and local dishes such as *sancocho* (chicken stew). Try the sugary *churros* (a cornmeal pastry with gooey filling) for dessert. For breakfast try the Panamanian eggs and tortillas. There are two locations, but I like the Vía Veneto diner the best.

Calle 49B Oeste, in front of the Veneto Hotel. ⓒ **269-4514** (another location at Vía Argentina and Av. 2B Norte; ⓒ **264-3965**). Reservations not accepted. Main courses $6–$9; sandwiches $2.50–$4.50. AE, MC. Both locations daily 6am–1am.

Caffè Pomodoro ★ ITALIAN   Star chef Willy Diggelmann's third restaurant is a toned-down and moderately priced venue for a casual, tasty meal. The seating is outdoors, under umbrellas, but the dining area is completely enclosed by soaring buildings (and the Las Vegas Suites hotel), blocking the sun for the better part of the day and keeping temperatures down. The pasta here is fresh, homemade, and hearty, and you can build your own pasta dish by choosing from capellini, spaghetti, fettuccine, and so on, and pairing it with one of 15 sauces. I like the cannelloni with spinach, and the lasagna Bolognese, and there's also a fresh fish of the day and meats. Some of the vegetable dishes, like pasta primavera, are cooked so long that they resemble ragout; if you're looking for vegetables, stick with a fresh salad, of which there are many flavorful varieties such as fresh tomato with basil and mozzarella. At night, patrons can dine in the adjoining Wine Bar and order off Pomodoro's menu.

Calle Eusebio A. Morales and Calle 49B Oeste. ⓒ **269-5836.** Main courses $7–$15. AE, MC, V. Daily 7am–midnight.

El Trapiche PANAMANIAN   Ask anyone in Panama City where to savor great Panamanian food, and chances are the first place they say is El Trapiche. There's nothing palatial about it, but you can cool off in the air-conditioned dining room or people-watch from the outdoor sidewalk cafe. Newcomers to Panama should not miss the house specialty, the "Panamanian Fiesta" combination plate, which offers a taste of eight different local dishes. This is also where you'll want to try the hefty

Panamanian breakfast—order tasajo entomatado (beef jerky) with eggs and fried-bread hojaldras. The old-world sugar-mill decor comes from the name, El Trapiche, which refers to a press used to extract juice from sugar cane. Main courses, such as broiled sea bass or smoked pork chops with rice, beans, and fried plantains, are hearty and satisfy big appetites. Their fresh fruit juice blends are perfect on a hot day.

Vía Argentina at Av. 2a B Norte. ✆ **269-4353.** Main courses $3–$11. AE, MC, V. Sun–Thurs 7am–11pm; Fri–Sat 7am–midnight.

Las Tinajas ★ PANAMANIAN   Combining a taste of Panamanian flavors and folklore, Las Tinajas is certainly one of the more touristy restaurants in town, yet it shouldn't be pooh-poohed by those searching for authentic regional cuisine. Las Tinajas features costumed folkloric performances, which are enjoyable rather than hokey. They take place while diners go about tucking into some of the best Panamanian food in the city. It's no surprise, therefore, that Las Tinajas ranks high on many visitors' itineraries, so make reservations. Classic fare such as *ropa vieja* (spicy, shredded beef over rice), *carimañolas* (yuca rolls stuffed with meat), seviche, and creole-style sea bass highlight the extensive menu. Performances begin at 9pm on Tuesday, Thursday, Friday, and Saturday, and there is a $5 cover charge for the show as well as a minimum $10 consumption charge.

Calle 51 at Calle 22. ✆ **269-3840** or 263-7890. www.panamainfo.com/tinajas. Reservations recommended. Main courses $6–$14. AE, MC, V. Mon–Sat 11am–11pm.

Amador Causeway

In general, the food quality is not the highest on the Amador Causeway, but the places below serve pretty decent food.

EXPENSIVE

Bucanero ★ SEAFOOD   Bucanero, with its kitschy maritime decor, serves some of the area's best food. The restaurant is seriously overpriced, but the portions are hearty and the cuisine is a step above that of its neighbors. There are meats on the menu (including *parrilladas,* or barbecue meat platters), but the specialty is seafood. Start with a tangy seviche, and then have the stuffed sea bass, a rich Parmesan-cheese crab gratin, or jumbo shrimp in a vodka sauce. There are shared platters for groups. Dining is on a breezy veranda overlooking a parking lot and the Flamenco Shopping Plaza. Because the cruise-ship dock is nearby, some passengers stop at the Bucanero for meals. One caveat here has to do with the waiters, who are attentive but try to rip off guests by suggesting a higher quality seafood (jumbo shrimp, for example, as opposed to shrimp), thereby doubling the cost of the dish without warning the diner. Alas, the Flamenco area is a tourist trap anyway. Live jazz is featured on Wednesday, and salsa music on Thursday and Friday.

Flamenco Shopping area (end of the Amador Causeway). ✆ **314-1774.** Main courses $14–$26. AE, MC, V. Daily 11:30am–midnight.

Leños y Carbón ★ 📷 STEAKHOUSE   With its excellent bay views and warm, cozy ambience, Leños y Carbón is one of the most romantic spots for dinner in Panama City. Sit in the outside sitting area, admire the dozens of yachts in the marina, and let yourself pretend you're an international jet-setter. I recommend heading to Leños y Carbón for dinner and ordering the mixed meat platter, which includes beef, chicken, pork, sausage, potatoes, yucca, and plantains. Their grilled meat and fish dishes are also quite good, as is the service. No, it's not the best beef or fish you'll get in the city, but I found the restaurant to be quite reasonably priced: We ordered a large appetizer, mixed meat entree, wine, and dessert and paid just over $64 for four people.

Isla Flamenco, Amador. ⓒ **314-1650.** Main courses $12–$28. AE, MC, V. Daily noon–11pm.

MODERATE

Alberto's Pizza & Pasta ★ ☺ ITALIAN   This restaurant would have the best views on the Amador Causeway if only it didn't front a docking area for monster yachts. As it is, diners are treated only to a peek here and there of the city skyline in the distance. Nevertheless, Alberto's is always packed with tourists, and Panamanians head here for lunch alfresco—there is a lovely, cool breeze and ample outdoor seating. The menu is ridiculously long, with six pages of meats, pastas, pizzas, and seafood (the best bet is the pastas), but then again, Alberto's does offer something for everyone, and there's even a kids' menu. Peckish diners should try the Alberto's Bandeja, with an assortment of seafood and meat goodies. Despite the abundance of waiters in jaunty striped shirts, service can be erratic, even just plain bad. But most diners don't seem to care because no one here is in a rush to get in and out. There is an indoor dining room, but it's always empty.

Inside the Flamenco shopping area, facing the pier. ⓒ **314-1132.** Main courses $11–$20; pizzas $4–$8; pastas $5.50–$14. AE, MC, V. Daily noon–midnight.

Al Tambor de la Alegría PANAMANIAN   Giving Las Tinajas (see above) a run for its money, the new Al Tambor de la Alegría (Drum of Happiness) also offers a 1-hour folkloric dance presentation and good traditional cuisine. Indigenous Panamanians and women in traditional polleras provide a razzle-dazzle show that spans the history of the country, from the arrival of the Spanish to the construction of the canal. The menu features dishes named after the different regions of Panama, such as the Volcán Barú sampler platter (with *carimañolas,* tortillas, and other local delicacies), a Best of Boquete salad with fresh tomatoes and onions, and the Coiba Island octopus, among other themed seafood and meat dishes. The show is an additional $10, with no minimum consumption charge, and takes place at 9pm Monday through Saturday.

Brisas de Amador. ⓒ **314-3380.** Reservations recommended. Main courses $7–$15. AE, MC, V. Mon–Sat 6pm–midnight; Sun 9–11am, noon–3pm, and 6pm–midnight.

INEXPENSIVE

Mi Ranchito ★★ PANAMANIAN   This is certainly not the best Panamanian food in the city (El Trapiche, Las Barandas, Al Tambar de la Alegría, and Las Tinajas fill that bill), but nevertheless the great view of the Panama City skyline and the almost constant cool breeze that blows through accounts for its crazy popularity among tourists and Panamanians alike. And, to be quite honest, I love this place. The restaurant is open-air and under a massive thatched-roof *bohio* on Isla Naos, near the Smithsonian Museum. You'll find typical Panamanian dishes here such as grilled meat, prawns, sea bass, and snapper served in a garlic or tomato-and-onion sauce and paired with coconut rice and fried plantains. Mi Ranchito has an appetizer mix of Panamanian specialties such as empanadas, *patacones* (fried plantains), and *carimañolas,* but they are so deep-fried they almost all look and taste the same.

SPANISH-LANGUAGE programs

If you're moving to Panama, or if you plan to stay for an extended time, you'll need to pick up the local lingo. There are many language institutes in Panama, though these tend to vary in quality. Most offer group and private classes, though if you're low on time, I recommend working with a private tutor and calling around to decide which school is the best fit for you.

Spanish Panama, Calle 2a Norte, off Vía Argentina (© **213-3121** or 6590-2007; www.spanishpanama.com), is a Canadian-directed school with certified bilingual professors, offering crash courses, private classes either at the school or in your hotel, residence, or business; and a month-long program that includes excursions around town to place yourself in real-life situations where Spanish is necessary. They also have salsa dance classes, instruction in traditional Panamanian dance, and other cultural talks and activities. The Spanish Panama school has been modernized to include a space three times larger than their previous location, with spacious classrooms overlooking the tree-lined and fashionable Via Argentina. There is a lab and large city-view terrace and kitchen area. The staff is very friendly and professional. They offer three housing options that are suitable for all types. First, there are homestays with Panamanian families. Second, their Carmen's Realty finds efficiency suites and furnished apartments in the area (basic, at $500 a month, to luxury, at $1,300 a month) that can be rented weekly and monthly. They may also arrange better deals in any of the 16 major hotels within less than a 10-minute walk of the Spanish school. Finally, they have a number of rooms that can be had in the area that are often more economically priced. The ambience of Spanish Panama as well as its housing options is for fun but mature guests who are serious about learning. Group lessons plus homestay start at $500 per week to $1,650 for 4 weeks. Private lessons with homestay start at $595 per week to

Stick with the fresh fish and shellfish dishes, and an ice-cold beer. After lunch, you can rent a bike next door and go burn off all those calories.

Isla Naos. © **228-4909.** Reservations not accepted. Main courses $7–$10. MC, V. Mon–Sat 9:30am–12:30am; Sun 9:30am–11pm.

Around Town

Parus, Calle 67 y Calle 50 in the San Francisco neighborhood (© **270-3989**), is open between noon and midnight and occasionally hosts Martini and Latin jazz nights. The fact that there's a Russian restaurant in town shows just how far Panama City's restaurant scene has come. Try the borscht soup and the stroganoff.

WHAT TO SEE & DO

Few cities in the Americas can compete with Panama City when it comes to things to see and do. Some travelers spend their entire visit in and around Panama City, touring sights such as the historical ruins of Panama Viejo, walking the enchanting streets of Casco Viejo, visiting Natural Metropolitan Park, or strolling along the

$1,800 for 4 weeks. Spanish courses without accommodations start as low as $180 for a weeklong crash course.

Spanish Abroad, Inc. (© **888/722-7623;** www.spanishabroad.com) is located in the El Dorado neighborhood and offers group (max four) and private classes plus homestays with local Panamanian families. Classes focus on travel and professional Spanish and specialty courses, such as law, business, and medical Spanish, are also available. Group lessons run from $450 to $650 per week to $1,520 to $2,300 per month. Private lessons cost $580 to $780 per week and $2,320 to $3,120 per month. Classes are usually given between 8:30am and 12:30pm Monday through Friday. Cultural activities, homestays, books and learning materials, and two meals a day are included in all prices.

EPA! (© **391-4044;** www.studyspanishinpanama.com) offers semi-intensive, intensive, and super-intensive classes, as well as general Spanish and private classes. Located in the Plaza Paitilla shopping center in downtown Panama, classes start at $260 per month for general Spanish and $600 per month for semi-intensive Spanish. Check the website for class start dates. EPA! can also hook students up with accommodations options: Homestays range from $95 to $150 per student depending on whether you have a shared or private room, and shared apartments range from $63 to $100 per week. Internet access costs an additional $6.25 per week.

Languages in Action (www.languagesinaction.com) is one of your cheapest language school options and is located in the El Dorado neighborhood. Classes start at $350 per week without homestay to $525 with homestay. Monthly rates vary between $800 for just classes to $1,500 for classes with homestay. Rates include cultural activities and weekly lectures. There are also specialty Spanish courses for doctors, nurses, lawyers, and teachers.

Amador Causeway. Visitors can also head outside the city limits for day excursions such as boating in the canal, bird-watching and trekking in Soberanía National Park, and visiting Emberá Indian villages. Excursions outside the city limits are highlighted in chapter 7, "Around Panama City."

It is recommended that travelers book a city tour; transportation is included, and the experience is enriched by interpretative background provided by a bilingual guide. Half-day city tours include a morning visit to Old Panama and Casco Viejo; full-day tours head to the Miraflores Locks at the canal in the afternoon. **Ancon Expeditions** (© **269-9415;** www.anconexpeditions.com), **Gloria Mendez Tours** (© **263-6555;** www.viajesgloriamendez.com), **Panama Travel Experts** (© **6671-7923;** www.panamatravelexperts.com), **Pesantez Tours** (© **223-5374;** www.pesantez-tours.com), and **Margo Tours** (© **264-8888;** www.margotours.com) all offer full and half-day tours of Panama City and the surrounding area.

See "Panamanian Tour Operators" in chapter 5 for more details. If you want to see Panama City on your own, taxi drivers charge between $15 and $25 per hour. Every hotel has a personal recommendation for a private cab and can arrange the details.

Panama Viejo ★★

Panama Viejo, or Old Panama, comprises the ruins of the oldest capital in the Americas, and is a proud emblem—not to mention the most popular tourist attraction—in this historic city. The ruin site covers 23 hectares (57 acres) on the city's eastern edge, where visitors will find crumbling buildings sprinkled about and connected by paths with interpretive signs in both Spanish and English. The good view from this part of the city sweeps east to the Casco Viejo peninsula, and beyond Panama Viejo's significance as a culturally unique attraction it is also a pleasant park and recreation area that provides visitors with a chance to get out and stretch their legs. Some people come here for a sunrise jog along Panama Viejo's path, which hugs the seafront.

In 1519, Pedrarias Dávila arrived with his Spanish expedition; he found a village, which was called Panamá by the *cueva*-speaking indigenous group that lived here. Historians agree that Panama means "abundance," but whether it is abundance of fish, butterflies, or some other plentiful flora or fauna is still open to debate. Not much is known about the *cueva* except that their language was spoken among different indigenous groups all the way to the Darién (near the present-day border with Colombia). In 1521, the Spanish king, Ferdinand of Aragon, bestowed Panama with formal city status in an effort to secure the mainland of the Americas, then called Tierra Firme. Within 40 years, the *cueva* were wiped out. To this day, not much is known about them, but recent archaeological digs have unearthed artifacts shedding light on this ancient culture.

It is not clear why the Spaniards chose to build atop this swampy area with no clean drinking water—perhaps it was because the *cueva* represented an available labor force. The Spaniards first erected huts, followed by stone buildings around the end of the 16th century—these are the ruins you see today. In 1671, the famous buccaneer Henry Morgan sacked the city, and it burned to the ground. Panama City was then moved to what is now known as Casco Viejo, on the western side of the city.

This is the best-funded archaeological site in all of Panama and, accordingly, you'll find here a superb **Panama Viejo Visitors' Center & Museum ★★★** (🕻 **226-1757;** Tues–Sun 9am–5pm; combo museum and ruins tickets $6 adults, $5 seniors, and $3 students; entrance fee includes admission to both the museum and the Cathedral Tower ruin site). The two-story museum offers a thorough historical account, but is the right size so as not to overwhelm visitors with too much information (exhibits are in English and Spanish). There are handsomely displayed pre-Columbian artifacts dating from 700 to 500 years before the Spanish arrival, a model of the city in its 17th-century heyday, interactive video displays of what archaeologists imagine the buildings' interiors to have looked like, and colonial furnishings, clothing, pottery, and more. The best way to see the ruin site is to begin at the center, visit the museum, then walk to the Cathedral Tower. The visitor center and museum are located about 6.5km (4 miles) east of downtown Panama City, on Vía Israel. To get here, take a taxi from downtown for $2. Another transportation option is the blue minibuses that leave on the hour from the Albrook bus terminal and that cost 25¢.

After 5 years of labor, the renovation of the site's most important relic, **Torre de la Catedral (Cathedral Tower)** is now complete, with a steel interior staircase that visitors can climb for the first time in 335 years; at the top are expansive city views. The tower is too fragile to bear the weight of a replica of the old bell that rang out across the city during colonial times, so a speaker, which chimes at 6:30am, 12:30pm, and 6:30pm, has been installed. *Tip:* Visit the tower in the afternoon, when the morning tour buses have gone. Otherwise, you might find yourself waiting up to 20 minutes to enter. Spanish-speaking guides offer free tours of the tower. If you skip the museum, the cost to get in the area around the tower is $4 for adults, $3 for seniors, and $2 for students; it's open Tuesday to Sunday, 8:30am to 6pm. The cathedral is a good 15-minute walk from the museum.

One of the city's best **handicrafts markets** is at Panama Viejo, and has recently been relocated to the visitor center (no phone; call the visitor center for information; approx. 9am–5 or 6pm). *Note:* Even though the Cathedral Tower and museum are closed on Monday, you can still visit the ruins and walking paths.

Casco Viejo ★★★

Casco Viejo, the Old Quarter, is also referred to as Casco Antiguo or by its original and formal name, San Felipe. No trip to Panama City would be complete without a visit to this quintessentially charming neighborhood, with its narrow streets; its turn-of-the-19th-century Spanish-, Italian-, and French-influenced architecture; its bougainvillea-filled plazas; and its breezy promenade that juts out into the sea. Visitors often compare Casco Viejo to Havana or Cartagena. The neighborhood's historical importance and antique beauty spurred UNESCO, in 1997, to declare it a World Heritage Site. Because Casco Viejo provides such an ideal place to wander around and lose yourself in the antique splendor of the city streets, I've included a walking tour (see below). Within the walking tour are dozens of points of interest, and you can really begin and end wherever it suits you. Museums mentioned in the following itinerary are reviewed beginning on p. 123.

For the past century, Casco Viejo was nothing more than a run-down neighborhood whose antique mansions were left to rot after wealthy residents moved to other parts of Panama City. With the drop in land value, squatters and low-income families moved in, many of whom continue to live here but are being pushed out by a public and privately funded large-scale gentrification project. This is most evident along the southeastern tip of the neighborhood, where lovingly restored mansions line the streets; elsewhere renovation isn't happening as fast as was hoped when the project began more than 10 years ago. To combat the housing shortage, the government is offering funds to help resettle poor residents. Foundations such as the Oficina Casco Antiguo are working on a plan that will invest heavily in tourism, expanding services and even reinstalling the old streetcar that once ran along the city streets.

Safety note: In spite of Casco Viejo's renovation projects and the fact that both the mayor's *and* the president's offices are located here, tourists should stay alert and protect themselves from theft. Generally speaking, the peninsula of Casco Viejo, starting at Calle 11 Este and heading east and away from the Santa Ana neighborhood, is safe. There are two principal entryways into Casco Viejo but both pass through poor ghettos, so always take a **taxi** to get here. Taxis for a trip out of Casco Viejo can usually be found around the Plaza de la Independencia, or if you are dining here, have the restaurant call one for you. The Estación de Policía de Turismo (Tourism Police Station) is on Avenida Central at Calle 3a Este; the office is open 24 hours, and from Monday to Friday, 8am to 5pm, there is an English-speaking attendant.

Generally, they do a good job of patrolling Casco Viejo and are relatively helpful if you run into any problems.

Most important in this area is to tone down the "gringo look" if possible, meaning no shorts with 480 pockets or ostentatious clothing like Hawaiian shirts. And really, do you really need that fanny pack and khaki safari hat? Also, do not wear flashy jewelry or walk the streets brandishing your top-of-the-line camera.

WALKING TOUR: HISTORIC CASCO VIEJO

START:	**At Plaza Independencia.**
FINISH:	**At Iglesia de San José (a 2-block walk from Plaza Independencia).**
TIME:	**Approximately 1 to 2 hours.**
BEST TIMES:	**The streets are quieter on Sundays, and churches are most active. Some restaurants and museums are closed either Sunday or Monday.**

1 Plaza de la Independencia

Take a taxi to Plaza de la Independencia and begin your tour. This plaza is where Panama declared its independence from Colombia on November 3, 1903. There are several important landmarks here, notably the **Catedral Metropolitana (Metropolitan Cathedral),** easily recognizable by its contrasting gray, ashlar-stone facade flanked by two white neoclassical bell towers inlaid with mother-of-pearl. The cathedral took more than 100 years to build, and is one of the largest in Central America. On the south side of the plaza is the must-see **Museo del Canal Interoceánico** (p. 124). The neoclassical building was built in 1875 as the Gran Hotel, and converted into Canal Headquarters by the French in 1881; later it was used as offices for the U.S. canal commission. It is considered to be the finest example of French architecture in Casco Viejo. Next door, on the second floor of the Palacio Municipal, is the **Museo de la Historia de Panamá,** a ho-hum display of exhibits charting the history of the Panamanian republic. The **Hotel Central,** on the east side of the plaza, was once among the most luxurious hotels in the Americas, built in 1880. Today it sits abandoned while its two owners bicker about its fate.

Walk north on Calle 6a Este (from the middle of the plaza, toward the city skyline of Panama City) to Avenida Alfaro, and turn right.

2 Palacio Presidencial (Presidential Palace)

Calle 6a Este leads to the Presidential Palace, but you'll have to show your passport (or a copy) to the security guards on the street before they'll let you pass. This is the White House of Panama, the offices of Panama's President Torrijos, and it is a gorgeous Spanish mansion with a Moorish interior patio and fountain (you can't enter, but you can take a peek from the outside). Two African herons—whose Spanish name, *garza,* is the reason the palace is also called the Palacio de las Garzas—glide back and forth across the front patio. The city skyline views from this street are outstanding.

Turn right on Calle 5a Este, and head south 1 block, then turn left on Avenida B. Walk 1 block until you reach Parque Bolívar.

Walking Tour: Historic Casco Viejo

PANAMA CITY

Panama Canal

Area of detail

Bahía de Panamá

CASCO VIEJO (SAN FELIPE)

Avenida — Calle 10 Oeste

Av. Central

Calle 10 Este

Calle 9 Este

Iglesia de la Merced **8**

Plaza Herrera **9**

Calle 9 Oeste

Calle 8 Este

Av. Eloy Alfaro

Iglesia de San José (Altar de Oro)

10

Calle 8 Oeste

Calle P. J. Sosa

Catedral Metropolitana

Calle 7 Este

Palacio Presidencial **2**

1

Plaza de la Independencia

Avenida A

Calle 6 Oeste

Calle 4 Este

Avenida B

Plaza Bolívar **3**

Museo de Historia

Museo del Canal de Panamá

Calle 5 Oeste

Av. Central

Casa Góngora **7**

Calle 3 Este

Iglesia San Francisco de Asís & Salón Bolívar

Calle 4 Oeste

4 **Teatro Nacional**

Iglesia de Santo Domingo (Arco Chato) **6**

Calle 3 Oeste

Calle 2 Este

Museo de Arte Religioso

Calle 2 Oeste

Bahía de Panama

French Embassy

Calle 1 Oeste

5

Plaza de Francia

Paseo de Las Bóvedas

1 Plaza de la Independencia
2 Palacio Presidencial (Presidential Palace)
3 Plaza Bolívar
4 Teatro Nacional (National Theater)
5 Plaza de Francia
6 Iglesia de Santo Domingo & the Museo de Arte Religioso Colonial
7 Casa Góngora
8 Iglesia de la Merced
9 Plaza Herrera
10 Iglesia de San José

0 ___ 100 m
0 ___ 100 yds

3 Plaza Bolívar

One of Casco Viejo's prettiest spots, Plaza Bolívar and the buildings that surround it have undergone a face-lift over the past few years, and there are several cafes here for those who feel like stopping for a coffee or snack. The plaza originally was called Plaza de San Francisco, but was renamed in 1883 in honor of Simon Bolívar, widely considered in Latin America to be the hero of independence from Spain. There is a commemorative monument to Bolívar in the center of the plaza. The grand **Palacio Bolívar** (now the offices of the Ministry of Foreign Relations), on the northeast edge of the plaza, was built on the grounds of a former Franciscan monastery that succumbed to various fires. Of interest here is the totally restored **Salón Bolívar ★★** (© **228-9594;** Tues–Sat 9am–4pm, Sun 1–5pm; $1 adults, 25¢ students), site of the famous 1826 congress organized by Bolívar to discuss the unification of Colombia, Mexico, and Central America. The historical importance of this salon prompted UNESCO to declare Casco Viejo a World Heritage Site. During office hours (Mon–Fri 9am–3pm), it is possible to visit the courtyard inside the Palacio and admire the building's lovely architecture and tile work. Next to the Palacio is the **Iglesia y Convento de San Francisco de Asís (Church and Convent of St. Francis of Assisi)**, one of the original structures from Casco Viejo but nearly totally destroyed by fires in 1737 and 1756. It has most recently been restored in 1998.

Across the plaza, on Avenida B and Calle 4 Este (you'll pass it when arriving at the plaza), is the **Iglesia San Felipe de Neri,** one of the first churches built in Casco Viejo (1684–88). Though damaged by fires, the church has recently been restored and is worth checking out, at least from the outside. The church apparently opens to the public only twice a year.

Turn left on the south end of the plaza onto Avenida B to visit the:

4 Teatro Nacional (National Theater)

Built between 1905 and 1908, on the grounds of the old Concepción Monastery, the lovely Teatro Nacional hosts theater and classical-music and ballet performances; unfortunately, they do not have a website and their show calendar is available only by calling ℂ **262-3525,** or by visiting www.thepanama news.com and clicking on "Calendar." The theater opened in 1908 with a presentation of Verdi's *Aida*, and it is perhaps best known for the frescoes rendered by Panama's most famous painter, Roberto Lewis. Recent renovations have preserved both the frescoes and the baroque decor (scarlet and gilded tiered balconies, and a grand chandelier). The cost to enter and poke around is $1 per person. It's open Monday through Friday 8am to 4pm and sometimes on the weekends (but with no set schedule). Following Avenida B, behind the National Theater, is the **Ministerio de Gobierno y Justicia,** initially designed as a presidential building and built, in a neoclassical design, in 1908 in tandem with the National Theater by the Italian architect Genaro Ruggieri.

Continue along Avenida B (the street bends and changes names for 1 block to Calle 2da) until it ends at Avenida Central. Turn left on Avenida Central (Calle 1a) and follow until arriving at the stairs to the Esteban Huertas walkway. Walk up and circle the:

5 Plaza de Francia

The Plaza de Francia (French Plaza) is a Casco Viejo highlight, a historically important site and a delightful place to stroll around and crunch on a *raspado* (snow cone) from one of the several vendors. There is also a wonderful fresh breeze here. When you head down Calle 1a, the road turns into an inviting and lovely walkway called **Paseo Esteban Huertas,** which is partially covered by pretty bougainvillea. You're walking atop *las bóvedas,* or "the vaults," which originally functioned as a Spanish dungeon and later as a jail, storehouse, and offices. **Oficina Casco Antiguo** (ℂ **228-3664;** boveda1@cwpanama.net), offers free Saturday tours (in Spanish), leaving from its offices at 9:30am. This walkway also runs along the old defensive wall that once protected the city. From this vantage point you can see the Bridge of the Americas and ships lining up for their turn to enter the canal. Continue along the walkway and down to the French Plaza. Originally the main plaza (Plaza de Armas) of Panama City, it is now a commemorative monument to the failed French canal effort. Also here at the plaza is **INAC,** the National Institute of Culture, which has an art gallery (Mon–Fri 8am–5pm) and the French Embassy.

Head back to Avenida A and walk west until reaching Calle 3ra. Here you'll find the:

6 Iglesia de Santo Domingo & Museo de Arte Religioso Colonial

Only ruins remain of Iglesia de Santo Domingo, built in 1678 but victim of several fires including one in 1781, from which time it was never rebuilt. The church kept its fame, however, through the building's unusual supporting arch made of stone, which survived the fire. The arch, called Arco Chato, was unusual in that it was long and not very arching, seemingly defying gravity. When U.S. senators debated whether to build a canal in Panama or Nicaragua, they took the arch's longevity to mean that little earthquake activity made Panama a safer place to build. Next to the ruin site is the **Museo de Arte Religioso Colonial** (p. 124).

Continue 1 more block to Calle 4ta, turn right and walk 1 block to Avenida Central. Here on the east corner is:

7 Casa Góngora

This structure is the best preserved example of a Spanish colonial home in Casco Viejo. The house, built in 1760 by a wealthy merchant, was renovated with city funds, and much of its original woodwork, including ceiling beams, has been maintained. The Casa is also now home to the **Casa de la Cultura y del Artista Panameño** (✆ 506-5836), a cultural center for local artists, with occasional live jazz music, folkloric presentations, fashion shows, and changing art exhibitions. Drop by to see what's happening or check out the newspaper's calendar listings for shows.

Head up Avenida Central, crossing the Plaza de la Independencia (where you started). Continue on to Calle 9a to:

8 Iglesia de la Merced

Built in 1680, this church was transferred, stone by stone, from its Panama Viejo site. The facade is still an excellent example of one of Casco Viejo's oldest buildings.

Walk south down Calle 9a until you come to:

9 Plaza Herrera

The lively Plaza Herrera is dedicated to General Tomás Herrera, in honor of his battle for independence when Panama was still part of Colombia. Park benches here are good for people-watching or just for resting.

Walk 1 block east on Avenida A to Calle 8a. You'll come to:

10 Iglesia de San José

Your last stop is at the most famous of Casco Viejo's churches, the Iglesia de San José, and its baroque golden altar. The story goes that when pirate Henry Morgan raided Panama Viejo, a priest had the altar painted black to hide it from looters, later moving the altar to Casco Viejo. However, studies place the altar's stylistic details in the 18th century, casting doubt on this legend. It's a gorgeous work of art nevertheless, and worth a stop. From here you can head back to Plaza Independencia by walking 1 more block east on Avenida A, turning left on Calle 7, and walking 1 block.

Money Matters in Casco Viejo

There is only one cash machine here in Casco Viejo, and it's located within the National Theater (enter through the door on Calle 3A, not through the theater's main entrance). There is a restroom here as well. If the door to the ATM is locked or closed (Sun), enter through the Ministro de Gobierno y Justicia on the back side of the theater on Avenida Central, and ask the security guard to let you use the cash machine.

Cerro Ancón ★★

This conspicuous forested hill that rises 198m (650 ft.) above the city is another "reverted" property from the canal days that is now open to the public. The hill is bordered in the north by Heights and Culebra streets, and avenidas Arías and de los Mártires in the south. At the entrance to the office of the environmental organization ANCON, at Calle Quarry Heights, a winding, pedestrian-only road provides for a brisk uphill walk to a **lookout point ★★★**, with 360-degree views of the city center, Casco Viejo, and the canal. The hill is home to tiny Geoffrey's tamarins, *ñeques* (agoutis), and migratory birds. The **Museo de Arte Contemporáneo** is here (see "Museums," below).

Mi Pueblito ✋   Located at the southeastern foot of Cerro Ancón, Mi Pueblito is a mock village depicting three Panamanian cultures: Afro-Caribbean, the interior region, and indigenous groups. At the main entrance is a colonial Spanish hacienda-style building with displays of polleras, both antique and new, plus roped-off interiors with various and sundry antique household items placed to give visitors an idea of life during the 19th century. Here, at the entrance, one of several guides will approach you and offer to explain the historical and cultural significance of each display. Across the street are a few typical Caribbean-style homes, as well as the thatched-roof huts of Kuna and Emberá Indians. Altogether Mi Pueblito is a touristy, uninspiring attraction whose purpose seems less to educate travelers and more to hawk clothing and crafts at high prices. However, travelers who only plan to visit Panama City and are in the Cerro Ancón area might find it interesting to view the sharply contrasting cultural fabric of Panama displayed in the architectural design of the center's buildings.

Entrance at Cerro Ancón from Av. de los Mártires. ✆ **506-5725**. Free admission. Tues–Sun 9am–7pm. Reached by tour or taxi.

Panama Canal Murals ★   Located high on a grassy slope, the **Canal Administration Building** (✆ **272-7602**), built by the U.S. in 1914, houses the offices of the Autoridad del Canal de Panamá (Panama Canal Authority). At the bottom of the slope is the formidable Goethals Monument, dedicated to the chief canal engineer, George W. Goethals, who initiated construction of the Canal Building. Entering the building, visitors are taken aback by the beauty of the glass cupola, the focal point of the lobby. The cupola is encircled with handsome murals that narrate the heroism and relentless struggle to build the canal. The murals were done by William B. Van Ingen, a painter from New York who also did murals for the Library of Congress in Washington and the U.S. Mint in Philadelphia. There are four murals here. The first depicts the excavation of the Gaillard Cut; the second shows the construction of the Gatún Dam; the third the construction of the Gatún Locks; and, finally, the last is an impressive depiction of the building of the Miraflores Locks. Visitors may visit only this wing of the building, and entrance is free.

To put the Canal Zone in perspective, head out to the back of the building, facing the Goethals Monument. The flagpole here once displayed ensigns from both Panama and the United States, but today the only flag proudly flapping in the wind is Panamanian. There is a broad view of the Balboa neighborhood and the Bridge of the Americas beyond it. This area was a residential zone for American canal employees before the handover. Today, the buildings have been converted into residences for Panamanians, most of whom have no connection to the canal.

You may wish to visit the Canal Building before heading up to the top of Cerro Ancón because the road (via Quarry Heights) leads up from here.

Parque Natural Metropolitano ★

The Natural Metropolitan Park is the only protected tropical forest within the city limits of a major urban area in the Americas. In other words, one 5- to 10-minute taxi ride and you can delve into the earthy environs of thick jungle with a surprising array of fauna, more than 200 species of birds, and 40 species of mammals. Expect to see mostly birds and the occasional blue Morpho butterfly fluttering by. The park, roughly 265 hectares (655 acres), is located on the northern edge of Panama City, hemmed in by a few rather busy roads including the new and noisy Corredor Norte, which runs the eastern flank of the park. The park is overseen by the Smithsonian Tropical Research Institute, which carries out scientific studies here, and by the city, which maintains an administration center with maps, educational exhibits, and a bookstore. If you're planning to visit any regional national parks such as Soberanía, skip this attraction; if your visit to the country is limited to Panama City, this park is a must-see.

Three short trails give visitors a chance to get out and stretch their legs. **Los Momótides** trail is the shortest (30 min.) and therefore the most appropriate trail for young children and visitors in a hurry. It begins at the administration center, but you must cross busy Avenida Juan Pablo II, so be careful. **Mono Tití Road** heads up to Cedro Hill and a lookout point with sweeping views of the city; alert hikers occasionally catch sight of Geoffrey's tamarins, a pint-size primate, along this trail. The most difficult trail, and the longest at 2 hours round-trip, is **Cienequita Trail,** which begins just up the road from the center. It is possible to connect with Mono Tití Road after reaching the lookout point. If you'd prefer something more adventurous, **Ancon Expeditions** recently launched their **Metropolitan Nature Park and Smithsonian Rainforest Canopy Crane** tour, perfect for nature lovers and bird-watchers alike, especially if you won't be venturing far from the city. The tour consists of a 50-minute ride on the Smithsonian's 42m-high (138-ft.) research crane plus 2 hours of nature observation at Parque Metropolitano Natural's hiking trails. The guided tour is limited to groups of four, costs $99 per person, and includes transportation to and from any hotel in Panama City plus an English-speaking guide. For more information, e-mail canopycrane@anconexpeditions.com. **Advantage Panama** (www.advantagepanama.com) also does guided tours of the park.

The park is open daily from 6am to 6pm; the visitor center is open Monday to Friday 6:30am to 4:30pm and Saturday 8am to 1pm. Adult entrance is $2 per person, children 50¢. English tours are $10 per person with a reservation made at least 24 hours in advance (© **232-5516** or 232-5552; www.parquemetropolitano.org). There are also trail maps available for a small fee.

Calzada de Amador (Amador Causeway) ★★

The Amador Causeway is a series of three small islands—Naos, Perico, and Flamenco—connected by a road and pedestrian walkway that projects out into the Panama Bay, offering spectacular views of the glittering city skyline and a consistent breeze. The islands, once the haunt of pirates, were connected in the early 1900s with rock and dirt excavated from the Culebra Cut in the Panama Canal to form a breakwater for a protective harbor for ships waiting to enter the canal, and to prevent the buildup of sediment. Later, the United States militarized the promontory and fortified it with ordnance for protection during the two world wars. The causeway remained off-limits to Panamanians until 1999, when the canal handover opened this prime spot of real estate, much to the delight of walkers, joggers, bike riders, and diners. There is nothing like jogging or walking along the causeway early in the morning with the sun rising over the Pacific and casting its pastel hues on the glittering high-rises of downtown Panama City. The causeway is packed on Sundays.

Large-scale, multimillion dollar real-estate projects are on the horizon for the causeway, including a grand hotel, a casino, condo development, and new marinas.

By any measure, Panamanians are most excited about the opening of the new **Bridge of Life Biodiversity Museum,** designed by renowned architect Frank Gehry (who is married to a Panamanian), which features high-concept exhibitions about the relationship between nature and man. Check the website, **www.biomuseo panama.org**, for more information. The museum wasn't quite ready at press time and although I was told repeatedly it would open later in 2010, I wouldn't cross my fingers.

Punta Culebra Marine Exhibition Center ★★ ☺ Spread across a patch of dry forest on the tiny island of Naos, a former U.S. defense site during the two world wars, Punta Culebra is a kid-friendly attraction run by the Smithsonian Tropical Research Institute. It's a well-designed but small exhibition, with a short path that offers sweeping views and mounted telescopes that you can use to scan the horizon and get up-close views of ships waiting to transit the canal. The center will take a back seat to the Biodiversity Museum (once it opens). Really, if you're an adult without kids and you're having lunch at Mi Ranchito or riding a bike around, it makes sense to swing through here quickly—otherwise don't go out of your way to visit the center when there are so many other attractions in and around Panama City.

Within the center's grounds are a "touching pool" that allows kids to handle and closely examine aquatic life such as sea cucumbers, sea urchins, and starfish; an aquarium with tropical fish and a comparison between coral reefs of the Pacific and Atlantic; and an information center with videos. An interpretive trail winds through dry forest, which long ago was common up and down the Central American Pacific Coast; if you're lucky, you will catch sight of a sloth or an iguana. Call ahead for a guided tour. You'll see the Marine Exhibitions Center sign just before Mi Ranchito.

Isla Naos. © **212-8793.** www.stri.org. Admission $2 adults, 50¢ kids 11 and under, $1 seniors. Tues–Fri 1–6pm; Sat–Sun 10am–6pm. Around late Dec to Mar, the center opens for summer vacation daily 10am–6pm, but call ahead to confirm.

Biking Along the Causeway

While downtown Panama City's chaotic, potholed streets don't exactly lend
themselves to biking, the Amador
Causeway and the surrounding residential neighborhoods are a perfect spot
to spend a couple hours burning off
those *patacones* and *yucca fritas*. Most
shops also offer "family bikes" for up
to four people. **Bikes & More,** located
just past the Figali Convention Center
(✆ **314-0103;** daily 10am–9pm on
weekends and 8am–9pm on weekends)
rents bicycles for $2.50 to $3.50 for
children's bikes per hour and adult
bikes for $3.75 per hour, and motor
scooters for $30 an hour. **Bikes Moses,**
farther up the causeway (✆ **211-8579;**
Mon–Fri 8:30am–9pm and Sat–Sun
7am–9pm), rents bikes for about $3 to
$5 an hour, and kids' bikes at $1.50 to
$3. Bikes Moses also has "family bikes,"
pedal-operated carts for four, which
cost $14 an hour.

Museums

Museums across Panama are under-funded and poorly staffed, and the story here in
the capital isn't any different just because it's a metropolitan city. Things could
change when the Museo Antropológico Reina Torres fully reopens at its new location
on the edge of Parque Natural Metropolitano. The project is far behind schedule
and currently only one exhibition is open to the public, but the museum should be
up and running by the time you read this. The Canal Museum in Casco Viejo has
modernized its tours, with bilingual interpretive signs and guides.

Beyond this, most museums in Panama City are worth visiting only if you happen
to already be in the neighborhood. Perhaps local indifference to the city's museums
arises from the fact that many are closed on Saturday, Sunday, and holidays—the
very time when most locals are able to visit. Volunteers and nonprofit organizations
are the ones who keep the museums hanging in there, sometimes only by a thread.
Keep in mind that museums are closed on Monday and hours often change, so it's
wise to call ahead and verify.

Museo Afroantillano ★ A small museum housed in the 1910-era Iglesia de la
Misión Cristiana, the Museo Afroantillano (Afro-Antillian Museum) pays tribute to
the more than 30,000 West Indians who represented 85% of all foreign laborers
during the building of the canal. Afro-Antillians were relegated to the most menial
and treacherous of all work, and many lost their lives in the process. Within the
museum are reconstructed examples of their poor living quarters, and there are old
photos and other antiques from the early 1900s. It takes about 20 minutes to see
everything; which is good because the neighborhood here is awfully sketchy, and
doesn't induce you to linger or wander around. Take a cab directly to and from here.

Calle 24 Oeste and Av. Justo Arosemena (Av. 3 Sur). ✆ **501-4130.** Admission $1 adults, 25¢ children.
Tues–Sun 8:30am–4pm; closed holidays. Museum occasionally closes early; call ahead to verify hours.

Museo Antropológico Reina Torres de Araúz This was Panama's best
anthropology museum, with more than 15,000 pre-Columbian pieces, including
artifacts from the Barriles tribe, the earliest residents of Panama until 700 B.C. There
is also an interesting collection of gold *huacas,* the tiny ceremonial figures that were

buried with indigenous VIPs, as well as more modern pollera dresses and antique household items and farm tools.

However, the museum is undergoing perhaps the slowest reopening known to man at the Museo Tucán and there is currently only one exhibit actually open to the public and it really isn't worth a visit unless you're running out of things to do. Call ahead to find out if other exhibits have opened.

Av. Ascanio Villalaz, Natural Metropolitan Park. ℂ **501-4743.** $5 adults, $1 children, $2.50 seniors. Mon–Fri 9:15am–3:30pm; closed holidays.

Museo de Arte Contemporáneo The city's Contemporary Art Museum has improved over the years, but it is still erratic when it comes to the quality of temporary exhibitions. Their permanent collection features a selection of mostly water-color and oil paintings by well-known and up-and-coming Panamanians and other Latin Americans. It's a well-organized museum, operating a cultural center with painting classes for kids and adults and other art activities such as film nights. Check out their website for upcoming shows, or just pop in to see what's on when you're in the Cerro Ancón area.

Av. de los Mártires at Calle San Blas. ℂ **262-8012.** www.macpanama.org. Admission $5 adults, $3 seniors and students, $2 children. Tues–Sun 9am–5pm; closed holidays.

Museo de Arte Religioso Colonial ★ This small but vivid collection of 220 religious art pieces is housed in the old Santo Domingo convent, famous for the Arco Chato (see "Walking Tour: Historic Casco Viejo" on p. 116). The religious pieces are the last vestiges from the height of colonial baroque art in the Americas. Within this irregular but beautiful collection the visitor can find delicate wooden polychromatic sculptures, oil paintings on metal and leather, chalices, and church bells sent from as far away as Sevilla, Lima, and Mexico. Just like the ruins of the church, the pieces here date from the late 17th century to early 18th century. It is worth noting that the colonial baroque altar at the back of the museum was bathed in gold in the 1930s by an anonymous devotee. You'll need about 20 minutes or less to see everything here.

Av. A at Calle 3a, Casco Viejo. ℂ **501-4127.** Admission $1 adults, 75¢ seniors, 25¢ students and children. Tues–Sat 8am–4pm; Sun 1–5pm; closed holidays.

Museo de Ciencias Naturales ★ ☺ The permanent exhibition of the Museum of Natural Sciences is oriented toward kids and teens, and is reminiscent of the 1970s, with local stuffed animals in glass-enclosed displays of their "natural habitat," large plaster renditions of prehistoric sloths and mastodons, cardboard representations, and so forth. More unusual is the **International Specimen Salon,** an almost ironic, and sinister, display of donated hunting trophies—to enter you must pass beneath two gigantic elephant tusks. Mounted on the walls are dozens upon dozens of African, Asian, and American animal heads including leopards, elephants, grizzly bears, buffalos, and wolves. There is also a reptile and insect display of specimens found in Panama, and a library.

Av. Cuba btw. Calle 29 and Calle 30. ℂ **225-0645.** Admission $1 adults, 75¢ seniors, 25¢ children. Mon–Fri 8:15am–3:30pm; closed holidays.

Museo del Canal Interoceánico de Panamá ★ Housed in a fine antique building that was once the Gran Hotel and later the French canal headquarters, this was once the best museum in Panama City and an obligatory stop for every traveler;

however, the Miraflores Visitors' Center has dethroned the Museo del Canal. The museum is still well worth a visit if you're in the Casco Antiguo area. The museum gives you a good understanding of the isthmus as the center of world trade; it also provides (somewhat subjectively) an explanation of the effect of the isthmus and the canal on the Panamanian identity. Historical documents here include the 1977 Carter-Torrijos treaty that turned over control of the canal to Panama, multimedia and interactive exhibits, mock-household exhibits of everyday life during the history of the canal, a register of the U.S. Senate votes approving the canal, and a floor of old coins and stamps, including the famous Nicaragua stamp with an erupting volcano that was sent to senators to sway them from choosing that country to build a canal. This is an impeccable museum, with interpretive information in Spanish and English and on-site guides who give bilingual tours. The museum is wheelchair accessible. You could easily spend a full hour here.

Av. Central at Plaza Independencia. ⓒ **211-1649.** www.museodelcanal.com. Admission $2 adults. Tues-Sun 9am–5pm; closed holidays.

SPECTATOR SPORTS & RECREATION

Soccer never cast its spell over Panama as it has with the rest of Latin America—here baseball is king, yet stadium crowds and big-league games are not common. Games are mostly by national and local teams vying for regional championships. For spectator sports, check out the horse races (below) for a lively show and lots of colorful Panamanian characters. Walking and bicycling are best on the Amador Causeway, especially early in the morning with the sunrise.

BIRD-WATCHING   Serious birders will want to visit renowned sites such as Pipeline Road. This and other spots are highlighted in chapter 7. Within the city limits, **Natural Metropolitan Park** (p. 121) is a fine spot for glimpsing some of the more than 200 species found here. Check the Panama Audubon Society's website, **www.panamaaudobon.org**, for upcoming field trips to the park and other destinations around the city. **Ancon Expeditions** (ⓒ **269-9415**) and **Advantage Panama** (www.advantagepanama.com) both offer guided birding tours around Panama City.

HORSE RACING   The **Hipódromo Presidente Remón** (ⓒ **217-6060;** www.hipodromo.com) inaugurated more than a half-century ago, is a prestigious venue and a fun place to spend an afternoon. Races are held on Thursday, Saturday, Sunday, and holidays. To get here, take a taxi to Vía José Agustín Arango, on the way out to the airport. The Hipódromo can be reached via the Corredor Sur or by following Vía España until it turns into Vía Arango.

HOTEL SPAS & WORKOUT FACILITIES   Nearly every moderate to high-end hotel has a fitness center, and major hotels have full-service spas, which are the best in the city. Especially noteworthy are the spas at the **Veneto, Decapolis Radisson,** and **Marriott.** These hotels allow you to book a session even if you're not lodging there. **Vita Luxury Spa & Holistic Wellness Center** (ⓒ **390-9919** or 6677-6616; www.altavitaspa.com), located diagonally across from Multiplaza Shopping Center, offers chemical-free services and is one of the few high-quality stand-alone spas in Panama City.

SHOPPING

You'll hear a lot of talk about duty-free shopping in Panama, but it is exaggerated. Really, the only place you can duty-free shop is at the plethora of stores at the Tocumen Airport. Shopping complexes such as the **Flamingo Center** on the Amador Causeway limit duty-free purchases to cruisers landing at their port. Even the duty-free zone in Colón is overrated, as most wholesalers do not sell to independent travelers. The major shopping malls here offer excellent quality and national and international brands, though prices are comparable to those in the United States. A principal shopping avenue is **Vía España,** where both high- and low-end shops vie for business, as well as grocery stores and pharmacies. Designer stores are located around Calle 53 in Marbella and in the nearby World Trade Center's Centro de Comercio. Also try Plaza Paitilla in the Paitilla neighborhood. You'll find electronics shops around Vía Estronga, in the Financial District.

Modern Shopping Malls

Globalization and the rising demand for high-quality products have shifted the shopping scene to spacious megamalls that house international brands, cinemas, and a food court. **Multiplaza Pacific** (✆ 302-5380) offers the most in terms of selection and quality, yet it is the most expensive in town. Colombian-owned **Multicentro** (✆ 208-2500), conveniently located across from the Radisson on Avenida Balboa, has a number of Latin-diva-style boutiques; there's also a cinema and a casino. **Albrook Mall** (✆ 303-6333) is an air-conditioned shrine to low-cost outlet shopping, but you'll have to do a lot of digging around to find a gem. Because it is next to the bus terminal, it is busy with families who arrive from the interior of Panama, ready to shop. There is a cinema at Albrook Mall, too. **Metro Mall,** located on Avenida Domingo Diaz at Via Tocumen, is a brand-new mall located near the airport. You'll find designer and non-designer shops here, and because the mall always seems to be empty, most stores usually have 20%- to 75%-off sales.

Markets

The **Mercado de Mariscos ★★★**, located on Avenida Balboa and Calle 15 Este, is distribution headquarters for fresh seafood pulled from the Pacific and Caribbean. It's a vibrant market with lots of action as fishmongers shout while they deftly fillet corvina, tuna, octopus, and more. You can dine here at their upstairs restaurant. Several food stands sell seafood snacks like seviche. Next door is the brand-new **Mercado Público ★★**, the covered farmer's market of Panama City with exotic fruit and vegetables, meats, dried spices and nuts, and a food court of *fondas,* or cheap food stands serving Panamanian fare. Don't forget to bring your camera.

Artesanía, or indigenous handicrafts, are the number-one buy here in Panama (with the exception of real estate). *Molas,* the reversed appliqué panels made by Kuna Indian women, rank high on the list of popularity for souvenirs and gifts, either sewn onto a beach bag, as a shirt, or sold individually for you to frame or stitch onto anything you'd like (pillowcases are an ideally sized canvas). Other popular handicrafts, such as *tagua* nuts or vegetable ivory carved into tiny figurines, Ngöbe-Buglé dresses, and Emberá Indian baskets and masks, can be found at the following markets. These markets do not have phones, and all are open daily with the general hours 8 or 9am to 5 or 6pm (until about 2pm Sun). The **Mercado Nacional de**

WILDLIFE contraband: DON'T DESTROY WHAT YOU'VE COME SEEKING

International laws prohibit the trade of endangered plants or animals, or products made from endangered wildlife. Yet many travelers to Panama who purchase such goods rarely realize that what they are doing is illegal, nor do they understand the consequences of their purchase. Illegal trade destroys the very wildlife and habitat that travelers come here to enjoy. You could also set yourself up for being issued a heavy fine by law-enforcement officials upon your return. To help with wildlife conservation, ask yourself, Do I know what this product is made of? Do I know where this product came from? Do I need a special permit to bring this product home?

The World Wildlife Fund's trade monitoring network, TRAFFIC, and the U.S. Fish and Wildlife Service have a series of "Buyer Beware" brochures, including one aimed at travelers in the Caribbean, that you can download from their site at **www.worldwildlife.org/buyerbeware**. When in Panama, you should avoid purchasing:

- Products made from turtle shell (including jewelry)
- Leather products made from reptile skins
- Live birds including parrots, macaws, and toucans
- Live monkeys
- Certain coral products
- Orchids (except those grown commercially)

Artesanías ★★★, in Panama Viejo next to the visitor center, is expansive and sells handicrafts from around the country. In Balboa, on Avenida Arnulfo Arias Madrid and Amador, is a small **YMCA Handicrafts Market ★**, with mostly Kuna and Emberá indigenous arts and crafts, and clothing. A little farther east and up Avenida Arnulfo Arias Madrid is the **Kuna Cooperative ★★**, featuring Kuna handicrafts. This market is fun for kids because Kuna women offer to affix their traditional beaded bands onto the arms and legs of tourists, just as they themselves wear them.

For the more adventurous traveler seeking an "authentic" shopping experience, you can't beat **Avenida Central ★★**, a pedestrian street and market that stretches from where Justo Arosemena meets Vía España to the Santa Ana Plaza, and that is near Casco Viejo. It's a scrappy, run-down neighborhood, with cheap stores, outdoor fruit and vegetable markets, and a bustling fusion of ethnic groups shopping for a bargain. Visually, it's the most colorful neighborhood in town. Apart from $1-and-under kind of shops, vendors lining the streets hawk clothing, accessories, plastic gizmos, and knickknacks. Shopkeepers like to blare music or announce their deals through megaphones to pull buyers in. It's a slice of everyday Panama, but it's also street theater and people-watching as fascinating as catching sight of Kuna Indian women lining up at McDonald's. Don't wander too far off Avenida Central, and keep an eye on your personal belongings. This area is patrolled by police and is generally safe during the day. Kuna women have handicraft stands throughout Casco Viejo with many vendors concentrated on Paseo Esteban Huertas. Though it's not an official market, you can find plenty of high-quality molas and handicrafts in Casco Viejo.

The brand-new **Flamenco Shopping Plaza** is on the Amador Causeway (☎ **314-0908;** www.fuerteamador.com; hours vary, but generally noon–11pm). It caters predominantly to cruisers docking here, but shops are open to the general public (except the duty-free shop). The Plaza is a high-end, one-stop shopping area for souvenirs, jewelry, and upscale handicrafts. Come prepared: Visit their website and print out their discount coupons worth a savings of 10% to 15%, depending on the store.

Shopping A to Z
ART GALLERIES

Panama City is by no means an art city, but things are starting to change, with new galleries popping up every once in a while, particularly in the Casco Viejo neighborhood. The following art galleries showcase Panamanian contemporary artists and other well-known Latin American artists. Check www.thepanamanews.com and its Calendar listing for upcoming shows and special events. **Imagen Galería de Arte,** located at Calle 50 and Calle 77 (☎ **226-2649**), displays mostly paintings and sculpture by local artists, and offers professional framing. **Galería y Enmarcado Habitante,** at Calle 47 and Uruguay, has a small collection and is worth stopping at only if you're in the Bella Vista neighborhood; they also offer framing. As the name states, **Arts & Antiques** (☎ **264-8121**) sells antiques and art antiques representing Spanish colonial, Art Deco, Victorian, and other epochs. The store is located in the Balboa Plaza on Avenida Balboa at Calle Anastacio Ruiz. **Diablo Ross Gallery,** Av. A y Calle 7 (☎ **257-7674**), is a cutting-edge gallery in Casco Viejo showcasing the works of emerging artists. New shows open every month, and the gallery is home to the Pony Rosso Café and Restaurant, which also doubles as an indie movie house.

HANDICRAFTS

The widest selection of handicrafts in Panama City can be found at one of several markets (see above). Otherwise, an outstanding selection of *molas* can be found at **Flory Saltzman Molas,** located at Via Espana and Via Veneto (☎ **223-6963;** www.florymolas.com). Flory also sells bedspreads made of sewn-together molas, but

---

 Panama Hats: Not Very Panamanian, After All

Despite the name, Panama hats did not originate in Panama but in Ecuador, and were traditionally made by the Ecuadorian indigenous group from the Manabí Province using fibers from the *toquilla* palm. The hat was first popularized by Ferdinand de Lesseps during the French canal effort, and later during the canal building by the U.S., when thousands were imported from Ecuador and given to workers for protection from the blistering tropical sun. Hence, the name "Panama hat" stuck. The hat became fashionable not only in the U.S. but also among the English haberdashery and European royalty. Really, you'd have the best luck ordering a high-quality hat over the Internet from a reputable importer, though Panama does its own version called the *sombrero pintado,* in the Penonomé region. You'll find a range of hats at the stands at Plaza Cinco de Mayo, as well as a limited selection at the YMCA Handicrafts Market in Balboa.

the laborious work required for such an extensive, intricate piece of work means you'll pay top dollar. Another "designer" handicraft boutique is **Breebaart,** at Calle 50 and Calle 39 (℗ **264-5937**), owned by one Hélène Breebaart, who came to Panama as a representative of Christian Dior 30 years ago and stayed on. Breebaart creates designer fashion and accessories that incorporate contemporary looks with Kuna art (she has a crew of Kuna seamstresses on-site), mostly for Panama's rich and prominent women. There are some things for sale here, but Breebaart's specialty is custom-made pieces that take about a week to make.

The **Gran Morrison** variety/department store chain is located at Vía España and Calle 51 Este (℗ **202-0029** or 202-0030; www.granmorrison.com), El Dorado (℗ 202-0038), and the Marriott Hotel (℗ 210-9215); it has a selection of handicrafts. In Casco Viejo, about a dozen stores sell indigenous crafts and other Panamathemed souvenirs. **Galería de Arte Indígena,** 844 Calle 1a (℗ **6634-7064,** 6677-8045, or 228-9557; daily 9am–8pm), sells high-quality indigenous arts and crafts, and features folkloric dancing on Friday and Saturday nights from 6 to 8pm. Down the road from the Galería, on Calle 1era in Casco Viejo, is the shop **La Ronda** (℗ **211-1001;** daily 9am–7pm), with an outstanding selection of high-quality arts and crafts, hats, and paintings. There are shops at the **Mi Pueblito** cultural center (see "Cerro Ancón," under "What to See & Do," earlier in this chapter), but the selection is better elsewhere. Those looking for more upscale souvenirs and pre-Columbian reproductions should head to **La Reprosa** (www.reprosa.com) with locations on Avenida Samuel Lewis and Calle 54 (℗ **269-0457**); Casco Antiguo, Edificio Art Deco, Avenida A (℗ **228-4913**); and Costa del Este in Parque Industrial (℗ **271-0033**). Reprosa is pricey, but the quality is high.

JEWELRY

During the centuries before the arrival of the Spanish, indigenous groups produced decorative gold pieces called *huacas,* which they laid to rest with the dead to protect their souls in the afterlife. The word comes from the Incas, meaning something that is revered, such as an ancestor or a god. Spurred by the theft of *huacas* from the national anthropology museum, an American living in Panama during the 1970s set up **Reprosa** (see above), which makes elaborate and stunning jewelry casts using the "lost wax" process of the ancient indigenous groups. If you're searching for a one-of-a-kind, luxury gift for someone special, come here. Reprosa has several more demure collections that include orchids, treasures from the sea, and so forth.

Reprosa also offers a popular factory tour to demonstrate the casting and assembly process. The factory can be found just off the Costa del Este exit near Panama Vieja, and just after turning left on the first street next to the Felipe Motta shop. Englishlanguage tours cost $10 per person and must be booked at least 1 day in advance; call Monica at ℗ **271-0033.**

OUTDOOR GEAR & CLOTHING

It's best to buy your outdoor gear and equipment before your trip—there isn't a wide selection of outdoor products in Panama and you won't pay any less than you would at home. The chain store **Outdoors** (℗ **302-4828** or 208-2647) represents the brands Columbia and Caterpillar, and their stores carry clothing and footwear, sleeping bags, and accessories for biking, fishing, bird-watching, and other adventure sports. Outdoors has stores in the Multicentro, Multiplaza, and a low-cost outlet store in the Albrook Mall. **Sportline** at Albrook Mall also sells outdoor gear and equipment.

PANAMA AFTER DARK

You don't have to experience 5 days of Carnaval to know that Panamanians are party-loving people. When the sun goes down, Panama City lights up with a vibrant scene that caters to all ages, interests, and levels of stamina. Nightspots are concentrated in four neighborhoods: Bella Vista (also called Calle Uruguay), the Amador Causeway, Marbella (Calle 53 Este), Casco Viejo and the new "Zona Viva," located a couple miles before the Amador Causeway, but underground dance clubs pop up across town like mushrooms, and can be best found by asking your concierge or checking out the Weekend supplement in Thursday's *La Prensa* newspaper. *La Prensa* has a daily section called Vivir + which lists nightly events, but in Spanish only. Also try the calendar at **www.thepanamanews.com**.

Visitors should be aware that Panamanians are more open-minded about sex than Americans. Prostitution is legal in Panama, and therefore it is common to see prostitutes not just on seedier streets and in brothels but in the nicer parts of town such as El Cangrejo. They're also often at hotel lobby bars, or employed by one of the many "anything goes" massage parlors around town. If you're a foreign-looking guy or group of guys, women may approach you, but for the most part, prostitutes tend to sit by themselves or groups and wait for men to approach. Government authorities demand a weekly health check for all prostitutes, among other regulations, but cases of AIDS and other sexually transmitted diseases are swiftly multiplying in Panama so be sure to be safe 100% of the time.

The Performing Arts

THEATER, BALLET & CLASSICAL MUSIC

Theater tickets can be purchased by calling the theater directly, or you can buy tickets at **Blockbuster** locations and at the bookstore **El Hombre de la Mancha** or **Exedra Books** (see "Bookstores" in "Fast Facts: Panama City" on p. 88). All theater productions are in Spanish, with the exception of the **Ancón Theater Guild** (© 212-0060; www.tga-panama.com; admission donation around $10). The well-respected guild has been around for more than a half-century, first opening its doors in Colón to provide entertainment to U.S. troops during World War II. The guild normally produces contemporary dramas and comedy with a mix of native English speakers and Panamanian actors trained in English-language schools.

Classical music productions, plays, and ballet take place at Panama City's turn-of-the-20th-century **National Theater,** on Avenida B in Casco Viejo (see "Walking Tour: Historic Casco Viejo" on p. 116), but shows are infrequent. The best Spanish-language theater productions can be found at **Teatro la Quadra,** on Calle D in El Cangrejo (© 214-3695; www.teatroquadra.com; tickets average $10). This cultural center was founded to promote and develop the art of theater in Panama, and they receive acclaim for their nightly performances of well-known plays and children's theater. **Teatro ABA** at Avenida Simon Bolívar (Transístmica), near Avenida de los Periodistas in front of the Riba Smith supermarket (© 260-6316; tickets cost an average of $5), produces half its own shows and rents out its 200-person theater to independent groups; productions are mostly comedy, drama, and well-established plays. Check www.prensa.com for theater listings here. **Teatro en Círculo,** on Avenida 6C Norte at Vía Brasil (© 261-5375; www.teatroencirculo.com), is an esteemed playhouse with original Panamanian productions and classic international productions. The historic **Teatro Anita Villalaz** (*© 501-5020;* tickets average $10), on Plaza Francia in Casco Viejo, is administered by the National Cultural Institute (INAC); the intimate theater is home to folkloric productions, concerts, and plays, some of which are produced by the University of Panama students.

The Club & Music Scene

The nightclubs listed below open at 10pm but don't really get going until midnight or later; during the first hours of operation, however, nightclubs typically offer drink specials. Ladies' night specials are a bargain for women, giving them free drinks and entry. Otherwise, expect to pay between $7 and $10 for a cover charge, more if there is live music. Nightclub partyers tend to dress smartly for the occasion, so don your slinkiest or sharpest outfit or risk being refused entry (or just feeling out of place).

For folkloric presentations in a less-trendy environment, try **Las Tinajas** or **Al Tambor a la Alegría.** Large stadium bands play at the **Figali Convention Center,** on the Amador Causeway (*© 314-1414;* www.figaliconventioncenter.com), or at the **Atlapa Convention Center,** on the east side of town (*© 226-7000;* www. atlapa.gob.pa). For schedules, call or check *La Prensa*'s weekend supplement. Most clubs in Panama City are located in Casco Viejo, Calle Uruguay, or the new Zona Viva. Because of local residents tired of loud, all-night partyers on Calle Uruguay, many clubs have moved to the Zona Viva, located just before the Amador Causeway.

Bar Platea ★ A Casco Viejo Spot with plenty of soul, jazz is alive and well at this sophisticated bar/club, located on the ground floor of a colonial town house in Casco Viejo. The club shares the building with its partner S'cena restaurant (p. 105). Platea is cozy and classy, and appeals to a diverse crowd of Panamanians and foreigners young and old. Doors open at 7pm, except on Mondays, and live music begins at 10pm on Thursdays, Fridays, and Saturdays. Often, Platea hosts hot salsa bands. Platea is known for its Jazz Thursdays and Salsa Saturdays. In front of Old Club Union, Casco Viejo. *© 228-4011.* www.scenaplatea.com.

Habana Panama ★★ 👬 This salsa hot spot in the San Felipe neighborhood right outside Casco Viejo hosts live bands every Thursday, Friday, and Saturday and is, in my opinion, the best and most authentic place to listen to and dance salsa in Panama City. The great thing about Habana Panama is that most of the patrons are actually Panamanian and it has more character and soul than most Panama nightclubs put together. The club considers itself a homage to the early 20th-century "golden age of Salsa" era and brings out a talented, salsa-loving crowd with impressive, sultry moves. This area can be a bit dodgy at night, so be sure to have the club call a cab if you're leaving unaccompanied. Calle Eloy Alfaro y Calle 12 Este, Barrio San Felipe, Casco Antiguo. *© 6780-2183.* www.habanapanama.com.

Liquid Lots of steel and neon tube lighting accent a dark ambience at this popular dance club. It's chic and cool but laid-back, catering to a well-heeled crowd but without the velvet-rope attitude of big-city clubs. Liquid is the place to go for dancing, featuring one of the largest dance floors in the city. The music here ranges from thumping beats to rock. Calle 50 at Calle Jose de la Cruz, in front of the World Trade Center, Marbella. *© 265-3210.*

Moods This very happening club has weekday no-cover nights with free entry and an older crowd (late 20s–40s), mostly the collared-shirt and tight-jeans-with-heels partyers who sweat to primarily reggae and Latin music—on Saturdays, the reggae is often live. If you arrive late, expect to wait and be given the once-over by bouncers. Calle 48 and Calle Uruguay, Bella Vista. ✆ **263-4923.**

Next It's the biggest dance club in Panama—some say in all of Central America—and it's everything you'd expect in a full-scale, throbbing *discoteca:* spacious dance floor, electronic house music, and a full bar and lounge. Thursday is "crossover" night with more musical variety. The *discoteca* offers drink specials until midnight. Av. Balboa, Marbella. ✆ **265-8746.**

Oz Bar and Lounge Oz draws Panama City's elite 20-somethings for its chic decor, live DJ music (mostly house and chill-out), and popular Tuesday karaoke nights. On Friday from 9 to 11pm, it's ladies' night with free shots, and Saturday "Cocktail" night means free sangria for women until midnight. Calle 53 Este, Marbella. ✆ **265-2805.**

Wasabi Sushi Lounge Located behind Liquid (see above) in Bella Vista, Wasabi is '60s pop-retro, with low-to-the-ground white tulip chairs, mosaic walls, and orange transparent acrylic furniture. It's trendy and lively, especially on Wednesdays, when women drink free sangria until midnight and snack on sushi. There are several different salons, each with individual music. DJs spin house music and reggae. Look for a green *w* outside the door. Calle 54 at Calle 50, Marbella. ✆ **264-1863.**

BARS

Differentiating between a bar and a nightclub can be difficult these days in Panama City because so many bars have live DJ music, occasional live music, and maybe even a small dance floor and chill-out lounge. Popular hotel bars include the Decapolis (see below), the Peach Monkeys Lounge at the Sheraton Panama, and the Veneto Hotel's lobby bar. See "Casinos," below, for more information about hotel bars. Happy hours are the norm here. Office workers spill into bars after work for their 5-to-7pm happy hours; the best deals, however, are at bars that cater to late-night revelers: To reel people in before the late crowd, these bars offer happy hours from 10pm to midnight, and even free drinks (usually for women).

The Amador Causeway is an up-and-coming nightlife spot, with new bars and restaurants opening monthly. Many bars on Calle Uruguay and in other locations are moving to the new "Zona Viva" as it's called. As a nightspot, the area tends to draw groups of friends, and an upscale, older crowd. The **Wine Bar** (see below) has the same offerings as their El Cangrejo location, but with a better view (located at the Brisas del Amador area). At the end of the Causeway, within the Flamenco Shopping Plaza, are a handful of bars, dance spots, and live-music venues such as **Traffic Island,** with Latin music and cocktails, and a wind-swept veranda with city views; or try **Bar Baviera,** the **Ancla Sport Bar,** or **Karnak.** These nightspots are all next to each other in an American-style minimall—you could head here and stroll around until you find something to your liking. Closer to the city and the Figali Convention Center is **Las Pencas,** with live music on weekends and folkloric presentations every Wednesday at 8pm. **Bennigan's Irish Grill** at the end of the Amador Causeway is also a well-known nighttime hot spot with Panamanians and foreigners alike.

Most sit-down, full-service restaurants in Casco Viejo—and most of Panama City for that matter—turn into bars in the evening. Some of the best Casco Viejo spots to grab a drink are **Casa Blanca,** Plaza Bolivar (✆ **212-0040**); **Buzios,** Calle 1era (✆ **228-9045**); and **Ego & Narciso,** Plaza de Bolivar (✆ **262-2045**). The outdoor patio at Buzios has a fantastic Panama City skyline and is a great spot for couples; think bossa nova, caipirinhas, and glittering ocean and skyline sunset views.

Anemos Late in the evening, Anemos picks up the tempo with live DJ music and a jabbering crowd (a mix of office workers and university students), but before the clock strikes midnight, this modern, stylish bar can seem relatively empty—and so they offer unbelievable free-drink specials and cheap happy hours early on. It's a wonder they make any money at all, especially considering there never is a cover charge. Thursday night has "orgasmic" cocktails, recommended only for the brave. Calle Uruguay, Limoncillo. ☏ **214-6038.**

Blu Room Martini Lounge Panama City is undergoing a love affair with cool lounges, cocktails, and ambient DJ music, and the Blu Room was one of the first to kick-start this trend. It's actually a rather small bar, dark and intimate, with monster martinis and other vodka-mixed drinks. If you're looking to get soused in a more elegant environment, this is your place. You'll hear Latin house music and hip-hop during the week, and house during the weekends. Calle 1, Casco Viejo. ☏ **228-9059.**

Café Havana ★★ 🍴 This small Casco Viejo Bar is a tribute to Cuban music, and everything from the dark-wood interior and classic bar to the hundreds of photographs and artworks that decorate the walls is right on. Cuban music videos play on a TV in this little hole-in-the-wall bar where Cuba comes to life. Light fare such as seviche and calamari are available, but it's the mojitos and other tropical cocktails that are particularly good, if a bit overpriced. Café Habana attracts a mostly foreign crowd and for whatever reason, is empty more often than not. However, it's still my favorite bar in Casco Viejo. Calle 5 (corner) and Calle San Jeronimo, Casco Viejo. ☏ **212-3873.**

Decapolis Radisson Sushi Bar & Martini Lounge This popular upscale bar is located on the lobby level of the Decapolis Hotel. The ultra-chic ambience draws an upscale crowd that spans a range of ages, making this a good bet for travelers seeking a refined, hip bar without the post-teen crowd. Live DJ music, and a second, poolside bar keep the party going well into the night. The scene gets started a little earlier here than in other city bars and nightclubs. Av. Balboa at the Multicentro Mall. ☏ **215-5000.**

El Pavo Real The "Peacock" is a traditional British pub with pints of lager and Guinness, pub grub, dartboards and pool, and lots of dark wood. It's a local hangout for the English-speaking expat crowd in Panama, so expect to hear a lot of it here. The atmosphere is laid-back, but things pick up on weekends when live music starts at 11pm. Calle 51 and Calle 50, around the corner from the Marriott. ☏ **262-2448.**

La Casona de las Brujas An arty cultural center–cum–bar located on Plaza Herrera, La Casona is one of the new hip venues popping up around Casco Viejo. Out back, a patio and stage provide space for the bar's live music on weekends; you'll also find art exhibitions and other cultural goings-on. The scene here is mellow, and they're open during the day. The crowd depends on what kind of entertainment is scheduled that night. Saturdays often feature jazz. Plaza Herrera, Casco Viejo. ☏ **211-0740.**

The Londoner ★ The crowd here is almost exclusively foreign. This English-style pub is one of the top hangouts for the expat crowd, and on some nights, it seems like everyone knows everyone else. There's a pool table inside and popular outdoor bench deck seating. The beer and drinks here are reasonably priced. The Londoner attracts a mostly 25+ crowd, so it's a good place to try out if your idea of a good time doesn't include drinking cosmopolitans alongside 18-year-olds. Calle Uruguay. © **214-4883.**

RELIC RELIC is the new place to see and be seen in Casco Viejo. Located underneath the popular Luna Castle Hostel, Luna has a bustling, outdoor beer garden–style patio and a crowded, air-conditioned interior. The crowd here is about 75% expat and tourists, mostly of the backpacker variety—expect dreadlocks, plenty of beer, and under-30s. If you're a solo traveler, it is a good spot to mingle and meet fellow travelers. Calle 9na, Casco Viejo. © **262-1540.** www.relicbar.com.

Wine Bar Catering to wine lovers, this spot serves more than 200 varieties from Europe, Chile, and California. It's mostly midrange wine, but there are a few gems on the menu. The Wine Bar is like an Italian tavern, with vine-and-trellis ceilings and trattoria tables. The mood picks up with their live music, usually a one-man act. There is an appetizer menu with cheese platters, but you can order off the menu from the Wine Bar's partner restaurant, Caffè Pomodoro, next door. I personally prefer the Wine Bar at the Amador Causeway because of its ultra laid-back ambience and great skyline views (© **314-3340**). Av. Eusebio A. Morales, next to the Las Vegas Suites. © **265-4701.**

THE GAY & LESBIAN SCENE

Panama is a mostly Catholic country and although the gay and lesbian scene here is not underground, it is discreet. There are a couple of clubs in the city that operate without much fanfare, and attacks, raids, harassment, and so on are thankfully not very common. For a calendar of gay and lesbian events, check out **www.farraurbana. com.** There are few, if any, venues or events directed at the lesbian-only scene, yet lesbians are welcome at gay venues. Clubs are open at 10pm Wednesday through Sunday; weeknight cover charges are around $3 to $5, $8 to $10 on weekends. Early arrivals can take advantage of happy-hour drink specials.

The most established gay clubs are **BLG,** at Calle 49 and Calle Uruguay (© **265-1624**), with dancing to top DJ music Thursday to Saturday, and other special events like Gay Pride Nights on weekdays; **Lips** (no phone) at Avenida Manuel Espinoza Batista, next to Café Duran, has nightly drag shows on weeknights and dancing on Fridays and Saturdays. The largest gay dance club is called **Glam: The Club** (© **265-1624**), which features nightly drag shows, fashion shows, and more, followed by late-night dancing until dawn (the best nights are Fri and Sat). To get here, you need a taxi; the club is at Tumba Muerto (in the Urb. Industrial La Esperanza neighborhood) on Vía Ricardo J. Alfaro. **Punta G,** at Calle D in El Cangrejo (next to Ginza Teppanyaki; © **265-1624**), has barmen in spandex, DJ music, and a dance floor.

CASINOS

Gambling is legal in Panama, and virtually every major hotel in the city has an adjoining casino. You'll find slot machines, video poker, gaming tables, sports betting, and special shows and parties. The hottest casino at the moment is at the **Veneto Hotel & Casino.** The Veneto has a sophisticated gaming area and often hosts over-the-top parties such as E! Entertainment's *Wild On.* There is a sushi bar here, too. The **Marriott's Fiesta Casino** is popular with foreigners and expats thanks to its convenient central location, and **El Panama Hotel** has one of the newer centrally located casinos, which offers cheap drink specials for women. The **Sheraton Hotel and Convention Center** hotel has a large, elegant casino, but its out-of-the-way location means it's really only visited by guests. The bar here, though, is popular with young Panamanians.

AROUND PANAMA CITY

This chapter incorporates a sizeable region around Panama City, including the **Panama Canal, Canal Zone, Central Caribbean Coast** (including Colón and its surroundings), and **Gulf of Panama.** At first glance, it seems like a lot of ground to cover, but these destinations can be reached by a short drive, a puddle-jump flight, or a boat ride from the city, and some attractions are even close enough to visit by taxi. With its high level of services and amenities, Panama City is an ideal base from which to explore this region, and many travelers, especially those with limited time, plan their entire trips around this area, owing to its surprisingly diverse range of attractions.

The Canal Zone dry season is December to April, while the Caribbean coast sees substantially more rain; showers can occur during the so-called dry season at any time.

Temperatures in the islands off the Pacific Coast are consistently a few degrees cooler than those in Panama City, and less rain falls there.

EXPLORING THE REGION   A trip to Panama wouldn't be the same without visiting one of the engineering marvels of the world, the **Panama Canal.** There are several ways to do this: at the viewing platform in Miraflores, on a jungle cruise or partial canal transit, or at the Gatún Locks near Colón. Along the Canal Zone corridor, the national park **Soberanía** puts you in a thick rainforest teeming with birds and wildlife, and you can visit an Emberá Indian village nearby or raft the Chagres River. Near Colón, **Portobelo** pays homage to the Spanish colonial era with its forts and ruins, as well as **Fort San Lorenzo,** on the canal's western side. Around the area, there are a couple of cool ecolodges and resorts that offer accommodations in natural surroundings yet are still close to Panama City—a tantalizing option for travelers deciding where to stay. This chapter also covers the **Archipelago de las Perlas (Pearl Islands)** and **Isla Taboga,** which are located in the Pacific, off the coast of Panama City. Even if your travels won't take you too far from the city, you can visit everything from popular beaches to mountain villages, to idyllic islands, all within a 2-hour drive, thanks to Panama's incredible geographical diversity.

Keeping the Kids Happy

The area surrounding Panama City is packed with a lot of fun and exciting attractions that are ideal for families with kids. From the Summit Garden & Zoo, to canoe trips on the Chagres River, jungle cruises on Lake Gatún, rainforest expeditions, and beach sports, you can keep your kids busy learning or having fun for at least a week. The most kid-friendly hotel in the area is **Gamboa Rainforest Resort,** which has a huge pool and game center—but even better, the resort has an **aerial tram** that sails passengers through the rainforest to a high lookout platform. Also featured are a butterfly farm, reptile and aquatic life display, bike rental, and more—and these facilities can be used even by nonguests for the day. If you're lodging here, it's easy to plan trips with the company's on-site tour desk. If you're not staying here but would like someone to put together a couple of days' or a week's worth of family activities, even using Panama City as a base, check out one of the Panama City tour operators listed in chapter 5.

THE PANAMA CANAL

77km (48 miles) long from Panama City to Colón

The construction of the Panama Canal was one of the grandest engineering feats in the history of the world, an epic tale of ingenuity and courage but marked by episodes of tragedy. When it was finally completed in 1914, the canal cut travel distances by more than half for ships that previously had had to round South America's Cape Horn. Today, the canal is one of the world's most traveled waterways, annually handling around 13,000 ships that represent 5% of global trade.

The history of the canal dates back to the 16th century, when Vasco Núñez de Balboa discovered that Panama was just a narrow strip of land separating the Caribbean from the Pacific. In 1539, King Charles I of Spain dispatched a survey team to study the feasibility of building a waterway connecting the two oceans, but the team deemed such a pursuit impossible.

The first real attempt to construct a canal was begun by the French in 1880, led by Ferdinand de Lesseps, the charismatic architect of the Suez Canal. The Gallic endeavor failed miserably, however, as few had anticipated the enormous challenge presented by the Panamanian jungle, with its mucky swamps, torrential downpours, landslides, floods, and, most debilitating of all, mosquito-borne diseases such as malaria and yellow fever. In the end, more than 20,000 perished.

In 1903, the United States bought out the French and backed Panama in its secession from Colombia in exchange for control of the Canal Zone. For the next 10 years, the U.S., having essentially eradicated tropical disease, pulled off what seemed impossible in terms of engineering: It carved out a 14km (9-mile) path through the Continental Divide and constructed an elevated canal system and a series of locks to lift ships from sea level up to 26m (85 ft.) at Lake Gatún. The lake, created after construction crews dammed the Chagres River near the Gatún Locks, was at the time the largest man-made lake in the world.

In 1977, U.S. President Jimmy Carter and President Omar Torrijos of Panama signed a treaty that would relinquish control of the canal to the Panamanians on December 31, 1999. It was a controversial move because most Americans did not believe that Panama was up to the task—but those concerns have proved to be unfounded. As an autonomous corporation, the Panama Canal Authority has reduced safety problems and improved maintenance and productivity to the point where the canal basically runs itself.

It takes between 8 and 10 hours to transit the entire canal. There are three locks, the **Miraflores, Pedro Miguel,** and **Gatún,** whose maximum size is 320m (1,050 ft.) in length and 34m (110 ft.) in width. Ships built to fit through these locks are referred to as **Panamax** ships, which set the size standard until the 1990s, with the building of post-Panamax ships (mostly oil tankers) that are up to 49m (160 ft.) wide. The Panama Canal Authority, seeking to avoid becoming obsolete, is constructing two multibillion-dollar three-chamber locks to increase traffic and allow for wider ships.

Seeing the Panama Canal in Action

For information about visiting the canal at the Gatún Locks, see "Colón," later in this chapter. There is no viewing area at the Pedro Miguel Locks.

MIRAFLORES LOCKS ★★★

The best land-based platform from which to see the Panama Canal at work is at **Miraflores Visitors Center** (© **276-8325;** www.pancanal.com), located about a 15-minute drive from the heart of the city. The center is an absorbing attraction for both kids and adults, with four floors of exhibitions and interactive displays—and a theater—providing information about the canal's history and its impact on world trade, plus explanations of how the region's natural environment is crucial to the function of the canal. Ships can also be viewed from an observation deck. In fact, it's probably Panama's best museum. ***Tip:*** You'll have better luck catching sight of enormous Panamax ships in the afternoon around 11am or around 3pm. I recommend calling the Visitors Center ahead of time to find out what time large ships are expected to cross.

As you view ships in the locks, a monologue (in Spanish and English) piped through a loudspeaker, indicates what a ship is carrying, where it is registered, where it is going, and how much it paid; the speaker is cheerleader-like and tends to qualify the experience by saying such things as, "Can you *believe* they spent $200,000 to transit the canal, man?" There are also a snack bar and gift shop. The center is open daily from 9am to 5pm (ticket office closes at 4pm). Admission to the center's exhibitions and observation terrace is $8 adults, $5 children and students with ID, and free for children 4 and under; or $5 adults, $3 children to visit only the restaurant and gift shop.

Best of all, there is the **Miraflores Visitors Center Restaurant ★★★** (daily 11am–11pm; main courses $7–$20), which gets three stars because of its extremely unique location; the food is not particularly memorable, but you can dine while watching colossal ships transit the locks just 30m (100 ft.) away. Lunch is the most popular time to eat here, so arrive early or make a reservation, and try to get a table as close to the railing as possible. At night, the locks are well lit and provide clear views of the ships.

GETTING THERE & DEPARTING   City tours of Panama usually include a 2-hour stop at Miraflores, or you can take a taxi for $25 to $30 round-trip for a 45-minute to 1-hour visit. However, keep in mind that the increasing price of gas is making transportation more and more expensive in Panama, so prices are subject to change. Agree on a price with the driver beforehand. For buses, see "Getting There & Departing," below, under "Gamboa & the Canal Zone."

TRANSITING THE PANAMA CANAL ★★★

Visitors to Panama who are not part of a long-haul cruise can still transit the canal by boat on a journey from Panama City to Colón, or they can do a partial transit from Gamboa to the Pacific or vice versa. Beyond the thrill of transiting locks is the opportunity to get close to colossal Panamax-size ships en route from one ocean to the other. Partial tours are by far the most popular because they pass through the Pedro Miguel and Miraflores locks, and sail under the grand span of the Bridge of the Americas, which is enough for most visitors. Transiting a lock can take up to 2 hours, which can grow tiresome on full-transit journeys. In fact, unless you're an engineer or transiting the canal has been a lifelong dream, you'll probably get bored on a full-transit tour, so bring a good book; at least you'll be able to say you crossed the Panama Canal. The companies below are all reputable and offer excellent partial and full transit tours of the canal. Remember that if you book a canal transit through the Gamboa Resort (www.gamboatours.com), you will pay more than reserving directly with a company.

Panama Marine Adventures (✆ **226-8917;** www.pmatours.net) offers partial canal transit with a shuttle leaving from the Flamenco Resort and Marina on the Amador Causeway at 10am and going to their *Pacific Queen,* docked at Gamboa. Trips leave every Saturday year-round, and every Thursday and Friday from January to April. The company offers full transit of the canal one Saturday every month (check the website for dates) leaving at 7:30am, first passing through the Miraflores locks and finishing at the Gatún Locks; the company provides transportation by vehicle back to Panama City. Partial transit, which lasts 4 to 6 hours depending on traffic, costs $115 for adults and $65 for kids 11 and under; full transit costs $165 for adults and $75 kids 11 and under; it lasts 10 to 12 hours. The price includes all transportation, a bilingual guide, and lunch and soft drinks. The *Pacific Queen* has a capacity of 300 passengers.

Canal & Bay Tours ★★★ (✆ **209-2009** or 209-2010; www.canalandbaytours. com) is a pioneer in canal tourism, offering transit aboard one of two boats, the refurbished *Isla Morada,* a wooden boat with a capacity of 100 guests, or the *Fantasía del Mar,* a steel boat with a capacity of 500 passengers. The company offers full-day transit of the canal the first Saturday of every month for $165 adults, $75 children 11 and under; and partial transit every Saturday for $115 adults, $60 children 11 and under. Canal & Bay has full transit and partial transit (you pick) the third Tuesday of every month from January to April. Tours leave at 7:30am from the Flamenco Marina, docking in Gamboa or Gatún, depending on the tour. They also offer Saturday-evening **"Rumba in the Bay"** tours of the Bay of Panama, leaving at 9:30pm from their pier, with live music and an open bar.

Ancon Expeditions (✆ **269-9415;** www.anconexpeditions.com) also offers full and partial transits of the canal. Ancon offers early morning hotel pickup to the Port of Balboa, where you'll board a passenger ferry. Partial transits cost $95 for adults

7

The Panama Canal

AROUND PANAMA CITY

and full transits cost $150. Full transits are offered the first and third Saturday of every month with one additional Thursday departure in January, and partial transits depart every Thursday and Friday January through March and every Saturday year-round. After transiting, a bus will take you back to your hotel. **Margo Tours** (© 264-8888; www.margotours.com) also offers partial and complete canal transits. Partial transits cost $115 and leave every Saturday from La Playita de Amador on the Causeway. Complete transit costs $165, but they only happen once a month, so call ahead and find out when the next scheduled transit is. Complimentary hotel pickup is available.

THE PANAMA CANAL RAILWAY ★★

The **Panama Canal Railway** (© 317-6070; www.panarail.com) is the most picturesque mode of travel between Panama City and Colón. It gives passengers a chance to relive the experience of the California Gold Rush. The railway was first built in 1855 to meet the demands of forty-niners seeking quick passage from the east coast of the U.S. to the west. It later was rebuilt along more or less the same lines to transport workers and equipment during the building and maintenance of the canal. The train was relaunched in 2001, and features executive and tourist service and renovated coaches modeled after their 19th-century counterparts, with carpeted floors, wood paneling, and blinds. The trains have air-conditioning, and there are open-air viewing platforms. The journey lasts about an hour and borders the canal, racing through lush rainforest, past canal locks, and along slender causeways across Gatún Lake. Round-trip fare is $38 adults, $19 children; one-way fare is $22 adults, $11 children, and $15 seniors. The Corozal Train Station in Panama City is located in Albrook, and is a $3 taxi ride from downtown Panama. The trip takes 1 hour.

See "Tour Operators," below, for organized trips that include a ride on the train. The major issue for do-it-yourself travelers is departure times. From Panama City, the train leaves at 7:15am, with the return trip leaving Colón at 5:15pm—meaning round-trip travelers need to hire a taxi at the Colón station to get to attractions like Portobelo, which can be expensive. Killing an afternoon in the city of **Colón** (p. 149) is out of the question: First, there's really nothing to see, and second, it's dangerous. Consider riding the train one-way at the beginning or end of a journey to or from the Caribbean (in other words, after staying at the Meliá Panamá Canal or at a Portobelo hotel). Cruisers docking in Colón are offered this journey, but the ships charter an entire train for their passengers. Groups of 10 or more should call ahead of time to make reservations.

GAMBOA & THE CANAL ZONE

Gamboa is 20km (13 miles) from the Miraflores Locks

This is one of the most exciting natural areas to explore in Panama, if not in the Americas, and most of it is less than an hour's drive from the city. North America meets South America here in a confluence of hyper-diversity and, accordingly, the bird-watching is epic and easy to access in places like Soberanía National Park. There are also a birder's ecolodge, a recreational park and zoo, spots for white-water rafting, and opportunities to visit with Emberá Indian tribes. Gamboa, formerly an American Canal Zone residential area for workers in the canal's dredging division, is also the name for a full-scale resort here. It sits on the shore of Gatún Lake, home to the Smithsonian's Barro Colorado Nature Monument, where visitors can learn about the rich biodiversity of this area. Travelers either lodge here or simply visit the region's highlights by tour, taxi, or rental vehicle.

Essentials

GETTING THERE & DEPARTING   By Taxi or Tour   The Gamboa Resort and Canopy Tower offers transportation to and from its property. Nearly every visitor to the Canal Zone is part of a planned tour with a guide, or visitors can hire a taxi for a full- or half-day tour for around $15 to $25 an hour, depending on the number of passengers and the deal you're able to strike with your driver. The road to Gamboa ends at that town, and is about a 40-minute drive from the Cerro Ancón/Balboa area of Panama City.

If you're not taking part in an organized tour of the Canal Zone and Gamboa, and would like to visit the area on your own, taxi drivers Mondi (✆ **6625-4631**) and Hector (✆ **6686-8127**) are both honest and dependable. Though neither speaks much English, I have only great things to say about them: Both drivers are always on time, drive safely, are used to working with foreigners, and will charge you a fair price. From Panama City expect to pay $60 one-way to Colón, $120 round-trip (including waiting time); $25 one-way to Gamboa, $45 round-trip; $70 one-way to Portobelo, $100 round-trip; and one-way to Isla Grande $70, round-trip $120. From Colón to Portobelo expect to pay $50 one-way and $80 round-trip.

BY BUS   Buses headed to Gamboa leave from the SACA station at the Palacio Legislativo at Plaza Cinco de Mayo, near Avenida Central, not from the main terminal in Albrook. The cost is 65¢ adults, 35¢ children. This bus drops passengers off at stops along the Gaillard Highway and Gamboa Road, including at the Miraflores Locks. However, the stop for Miraflores is an 8- to 10-minute walk from the visitor center. Buses leave weekdays at 5, 5:45, 6:30, 8, and 10am, noon, 1, 2, 3, 4:30, 6:30, 8, and 10:30pm; on Saturday and Sunday buses leave at 6, 7, 8, and 10am, noon, 2, 4:30, 6:30, 8, and 10:30pm. I really don't recommend this option; I tried it once and waited for a bus outside the Miraflores Visitor Center for nearly an hour and a half, not a particularly enjoyable wait in 90-degree weather.

BY CAR   To get to Gamboa and the Canal Zone, head out of Panama City toward Albrook to the Gaillard Highway, which runs along the canal and passes the Miraflores Locks. The road continues on past the Pedro Miguel locks and the Summit Golf Course until it forks at the ANAM ranger station just after you pass under a railway bridge. To get to Gamboa, the Gamboa Resort, Barro Colorado Island, the Canopy Tower, El Charco Trail, or Pipeline Road, take a left here on Gamboa Road. To get to the Camino de Cruces trail, continue straight on a lovely, jungle-fringed road that cuts through Soberanía National Park and eventually connects with the road to Colón. The sign for the Cruces trail is clearly marked at an off-road picnic site.

What to See & Do

Travelers to the Canal Zone have two options: Visit on **day excursions** and lodge in Panama City, where you'll be closer to shops and services; or base yourself at one of the **resorts** or **hostels** (highlighted below) and take part in their in-house tours. (If they don't offer the tour themselves, they can book an outside tour for you.)

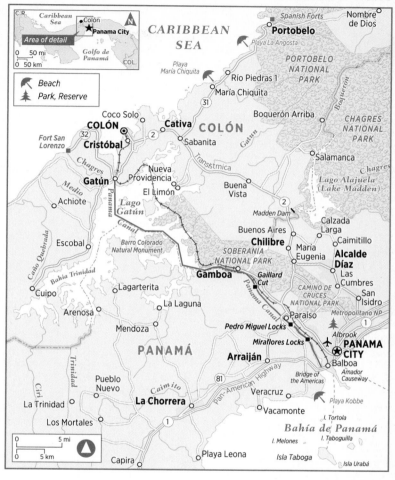

TOUR OPERATORS It makes sense to hire a guide or join a day tour, especially if you don't have your own car; things are far apart in the Canal Zone, making getting around without a car nearly impossible. Transportation, a bilingual nature guide, equipment (if necessary), and often lunch are included in the price, and it may be cheaper and more efficient than trying to see all the area's attractions on your own.

For contact information about **tour companies** mentioned here, see "Panamanian Tour Operators," on p. 63. Be sure to check tour companies' websites for detailed excursion information, recently added tours, and updated prices.

SOBERANIA NATIONAL PARK ★★★

Soberanía National Park comprises 19,425 hectares (48,000 acres) of undulating, pristine tropical rainforest on the eastern shore of the Panama Canal. It is undoubtedly Panama's most important national park in terms of tourism and economics: Not only is Soberanía one of the most accessible, species-rich parks in the Americas, it is also part of the watershed that provides hundreds of millions of gallons of water to keep the Panama Canal in operation and the cogs of international commerce greased and moving. The park is just 40 minutes from Panama City, but it feels worlds away.

Wildlife from North and South America, including migratory birds, meets here in Soberanía, creating a diverse natural wonderland. The park has 105 species of mammals and a staggering number of bird species—525 at last count. There are jaguars, yes, and collared peccaries and night monkeys, too, but you're more likely to catch sight of a coatimundi, three-toed sloth, or diminutive tamarin monkey. Bring binoculars even if you're not an avid birder.

There are several ways to see the park. ANAM, the park ranger service, has several excellent hiking trails for day excursions that range from easy to difficult; there are a full-scale resort, a birder's ecolodge, a recreational park and zoo, and the Pipeline Road, a site revered for its abundant diversity of birds. Soberanía National Park is open daily from 6am to 5pm, and costs $3 per person to enter (free for kids 11 and under). Paying is tricky; they ask that you stop at the ranger station to pay because there isn't anyone to collect money at the trail head—but it's unlikely that every visitor does this. Play it safe, though, and stop to pay; the pass permits you to use any trails within the space of a day.

The park can be accessed by rental vehicle or taxi, or by joining a tour. If you take a taxi, plan a time for the driver to pick you up or have the driver wait. For more information, call the park's office at ℂ **232-4192;** the website, www.anam.gob.pa, has limited park info in Spanish. The park office is open from 7am to 7pm daily, but if no one is inside, check around out back.

HIKING & BIRD-WATCHING TRAILS **Sendero El Plantación (Plantation Trail),** located at the turnoff for the Canopy Tower lodge on the road to Gamboa, is a moderate, 6.4m (4-mile) trail that ends at the intersection for the Camino de Cruces trail. This is not a loop trail, so hikers will either need to return via the same trail or, with a little preplanning, arrange to be dropped off at the Camino de Cruces trail on the road to Colón, hike northwest and connect with the Plantation Trail, and finish near the Canopy Tower, or vice versa (see Camino de Cruces, below). The Plantation Trail follows a road built in the 1910s by La Cascadas Plantation, the largest in the old Canal Zone during that period, producing cacao, coffee, and rubber. Alert hikers will spot remnants of these crops, especially the cacao plant. This trail is popular with birdwatchers, but mammals such as tamarins are frequently seen, too.

Continuing on the road to Gamboa, and to the right, is the trail head for **Sendero Charco (Pond Trail),** an ultra-easy, 20-minute loop that follows the Sardinilla River. The trail gives even the most reluctant walkers a brilliant opportunity to immerse themselves in thick tropical rainforest.

A little more than a mile past the bridge and turnoff to Gamboa Resort is **Camino de Oleoducto,** better known as **Pipeline Road,** the celebrity trail for bird-watching in Panama, renowned worldwide as a record-setting site for 24-hour bird counts. Even non-birders can't help getting caught up in the action with so many colorful show birds fluttering about, such as mot mots, trogons, toucans, antbirds, a rainbow of tanagers, and flycatchers. Bird-watching starts at the crack of dawn, when the avian world is at its busiest, so try to make it here at least before 9am, if not earlier. In spite of the name, the Pipeline Road is not drivable. More than half the bird-watchers who visit here walk only a mile or so, but if you like to hike or mountain bike (see below), push on because the chances of spotting rare birds and wildlife increase the farther you go. To get here by vehicle, pass the Gamboa Resort turnoff, and continue until you reach a fork. Turn left here onto a gravel road and continue until you see the Pipeline Road sign.

Soberanía's other prime attraction is historic **Camino de Cruces (Las Cruces Trail).** Before the railway and the canal existed, the only path from the Caribbean to the Pacific was the Chagres River to what's now called Venta de Cruces, followed by a treacherous walk along Las Cruces Trail. The Spanish used this route during the 16th century to transport looted treasure to the Caribbean and onward to Spain. In some areas, the cobblestone remains of the trail still exist or have been restored, and can be seen even if you walk just 10 or 20 minutes from the picnic area and trail head off Madden Road. The trail is moderate to difficult, and is about 9.7km (6 miles) to its terminus at Venta de Cruces. From here, a local boat can pick you up and drop you off at the Gamboa Resort, but you'll need a guide (a tour or your hotel can arrange this for you). Also, hikers may lose their way because the trail becomes somewhat indecipherable the closer you get to Venta las Cruces, another reason to have a guide. Backpackers can camp along the trail, but must pay a $5 fee at the park-ranger station beforehand. If this trail really piques your interest, check out Ancon Expeditions' 8-day "Camino Real Tour," which gives travelers a taste of what it was like to cross the isthmus by foot during the Gold Rush era, and includes tent lodging in the rainforest and at an Emberá Indian village. Ancon Expeditions (see above), Advantage Panama (p. 64), and **Panama Pete Adventures** (✆ 888/726-6222; www.panamapete adventures.com) all offer bird-watching, hiking, and Emberá village day tours, as does **Adventures Panama Canal** (✆ 6636-4647).

The second alternative is to hike the trail and turn into the Plantation Trail, which finishes near Canopy Tower and the road to Gamboa. This hike takes around 5 hours to complete and is a moderately difficult trek. To get to the trail head, continue straight at the fork in the road to Gamboa on what's known as Madden Road (but not signed as such). The road presents a lovely drive through the park along a road flanked with towering rainforest canopy. About 6km (3¾ miles) past the fork there are covered picnic tables and the trail head.

MOUNTAIN BIKING   The tour company **Adventures in Panama** offers a unique half-day mountain-bike trip on the Pipeline Road, leaving Panama City at 8am and returning at 1:30pm (cost averages $95 per person, and includes transportation, equipment, and a box lunch). The bike terrain is sand, pavement, packed dirt, and mud, and is classified as moderate to difficult. Your group can bike up to 29km (18 miles) round-trip or less depending on your appetite for riding. The minimum age for this bike trip is 8 years old. See p. 64.

Panama Pete Adventures (see above) also offers a similar mountain-bike trip for $76 per person, including transportation, equipment, box lunch, and bilingual guide. This day trip is for experienced bikers only and children must be at least 12 years old to participate.

LAGO GATUN

Engineers understood that the only feasible way to build the Panama Canal was to employ a system of locks to lift ships up and over higher altitudes on the isthmus, and central to this was the creation of Gatún Lake. The lake was formed in 1913 with the completion of the Gatún Dam, which staunched the powerful Chagres River—a tremendous feat considering that Gatún Dam and Gatún Lake were the largest earth dam and largest man-made lake of their time. The lake flooded roughly 425 sq. km (164 sq. miles), an area slightly larger than Detroit, creating islands out of hilltops and submerging entire forests and villages.

The thick rainforest that cloaks the shoreline provides water for Gatún Lake, which in turn provides water for the canal locks, and therefore the Canal Authority is keen to keep deforestation at bay. This is good news for eco-travelers—wildlife sightings are common. Ships traverse 38km (24 miles) across the lake from the Gatún Locks to the Gaillard Cut, and travelers can take part in this experience with a partial canal transit (see "Transiting the Panama Canal," earlier), or take part in a jungle cruise on the lake. There is also fishing, or you can visit Barro Colorado Island (see "Learn About the Rainforest with the Smithsonian Institute," below). Getting on the lake provides a more intimate view of the canal than a visit to the Miraflores Locks does.

JUNGLE CRUISES ★★★ ☺ Half-day jungle cruises in Lake Gatún are mini-adventures that are as fun for kids as for adults, and they are dependable ways to catch sight of monkeys such as white-faced capuchins, howler monkeys, and Geoffrey's tamarins up-close and in their natural habitat. Expect also to see sloths, crocodiles, caimans, turtles, and even *capybaras,* the world's largest rodents. The boat ride also allows passengers to get unusually close to monster tankers and ships transiting the canal. The **Gamboa Resort** offers a jungle cruise as part of their in-house excursions; others leave from the Gamboa pier and provide land transportation to and from Panama City. Guides provide passengers with an entertaining account of the history of the canal, the mechanisms that operate the canal, and fun anecdotes, while ducking in and out of island passageways searching for birds and wildlife. **Ancon Expeditions** (see "Panamanian Tour Operators," in chapter 5) has the best guides and service, not to mention the most experience in the area. Their Panama Canal Rainforest Boat Adventure leaves early from Panama City and returns in the mid-afternoon; the cost is $110 adults, $65 kids 12 and under, which includes lunch, naturalist guides, and all transportation. **Advantage Panama** (see "Panamanian Tour Operators," in chapter 5) also offers a rainforest land and water tour including a stroll through Soberanía National Park before boarding their aquatic vessel. The tour lasts about 6 hours, includes drinks and snacks, and costs $87.

Jungle Land Explorers, part of Panama City Tours (✆ **209-5657;** www.gatun explorer.com), offers an interesting motorboat tour of Gatún Lake and a stop at their anchored, double-decker *Gatún Explorer* houseboat, where guests have lunch and kick back in the middle of the jungle; kayaking and fishing are also options. They have a library with educational videos and books, too. The tour leaves from La Represa dock on the west side of the canal; however, round-trip transportation from Panama City is included, leaving at 8am and returning at 4:30pm. Tours cost $95 per person. Call ahead for tour days and availability.

FISHING ★★★ I give this three stars because in Gatún Lake you're guaranteed a fish—or your money back. The lake is packed with peacock bass, and all you need to do is just casually throw a line in and you'll easily snag one, sometimes within minutes. Fishermen tell stories of catching not dozens but hundreds of peacock bass and tarpon, which also reside here. Also, like a jungle cruise, you can get relatively close to ships on the canal and enjoy wild surroundings. **Panama Canal Fishing** (© 315-1905 or 6678-2653; www.panamacanalfishing.com; the easiest way to reach Panama Canal Fishing is to e-mail them at info@panamacanalfishing.com) has a 5.5m (18-ft.) Fun Deck with a 115-horsepower motor, live bait box, and fishing rods. The cost is $395 a day for two people plus $20 each additional angler, with lures, rods, snacks, and beer included. They recently began offering ocean boats for inshore fishing. The operation is run by Richard Cahill, a Panamanian-American who knows the lake inside and out. Rich recently added fishing tours to the Bayana River for snook and tarpon fishing ($550 all-inclusive), which is located about 1½ hours from Panama City. If you're looking for something cheaper, he can put you in touch with a local boat operator who will charge $80 a day for a 4.9m (16-ft.) boat, but rods and food are extra (and local guides speak limited English). Local boat operators charge about $120 a day. **Adventures Panama Canal** (© 6636-4614) can also organize fishing excursions. **Gamboa Tours** (www.gamboatours.com) at the Gamboa Resort can charter private fishing excursions, though you should expect to pay a bit more.

RIO CHAGRES & EMBERA VILLAGES

The Chagres River flows from the San Blas Cordillera down into Gatún Lake near Gamboa—on the other side of the lake, the river is blocked by the Gatún Dam, which created its namesake lake. Travelers visit this river for two reasons: cultural tours of Emberá Indian villages, or intermediate-level white-water rafting. Along the way, the jungle-draped riverbanks teem with birds, animals, and fluttering butterflies, providing an exciting sense of adventure without an investment of a lot of time or money.

EMBERA INDIANS VILLAGE TOUR ★★ ☺ Emberá Indians are native to the Darién Province, but many groups have resettled here on the banks of the Chagres River. For the most part, they continue to live life much as they have for centuries, traveling by dugout canoe, wearing nothing more than a skirt or sheath, and sleeping under thatched-roof huts. To earn income, the Emberá villages Parara Puru, Emberá Puru, and Emberá Drua, which are close to the mouth of the Chagres River, have opened to tourism, allowing visitors to share in their culture and see how they live. In the true sense, the villages are not pristine examples of Emberá life, and I can't help but feel that they exist as a sort of "Disneyworld" of indigenous culture; but the chance to travel by dugout canoe, interact with this fascinating culture and, yes, buy a few of their intricately woven baskets and other handicrafts is an informative and delightful experience. For a few bucks, you can have an Emberá hand paint a traditional "tattoo" with *jagua* vegetable dye on a part of your body (kids love this), but keep in mind that it takes 10 to 14 days for the stain to go away! Part of the tour includes a typical Emberá lunch and watching a folkloric dance show; like most folkloric shows, these are demonstrations of rituals long gone, but the music and dancing are still entertaining. Bring your swimsuit because tours include a walk to a cascade for a dip in cool water. All Panamanian tour operators offer this Emberá trip, though prices vary. **Ancon Expeditions** charges $130 for this half-day trip, while **Advantage Panama** charges $81. (See "Panamanian Tour Operators," in chapter 5 for details). **Panama Pete Adventures** (p. 143) charges $95, and **Margo Tours** (p. 64) charges $85.

LEARN ABOUT THE rainforest WITH THE SMITHSONIAN INSTITUTE

The **Barro Colorado Nature Monument** is home to one of the most important—and oldest—biological research stations in the world, administered by the Smithsonian Tropical Research Institute (STRI). It contains more than 5,261 hectares (13,000 acres) of land, including five surrounding mainland peninsulas, but the spotlight is on Barro Colorado Island in Gatún Lake, a short boat ride away from Gamboa. The forested island is the largest in the lake, and it was once a hill called West Hill that became a 16-sq.-km (6-sq.-mile) island after the surrounding area was flooded during the creation of Gatún Lake. The island is essentially a capsule of biodiversity that provides an opportunity for scientists to monitor population changes and test diversity theories about the rainforest without having their studies encroached upon by loggers, developers, poachers, or farmers. Each year, between 200 and 400 international scientists visit Barro Colorado, making this one of the most well-studied forests in the world. Scientists have so far discovered 1,200 plants, 120 mammals, and innumerable insects on the island, but really the chances of your spotting wildlife here are the same as at any rainforest in Panama (but count on seeing howler monkeys at Barro Colorado).

What's unique here is that the average layman can visit the island and see what's going on in the world of tropical science. It's an outstanding tour—part boat ride, part hike, part learning experience—and the price includes a delicious buffet lunch and access to the visitor center and Espavé bookstore. The only downside to the tour is that it is expensive ($70 adults, $40 students) and nonrefundable—don't even think about showing up late for the boat ride or you'll be left behind. Reservations should be made more than 2 weeks in advance, but you can always call and see if there is a last-minute cancellation. If you're short on time or not up to giving tropical rainforests more than a cursory glance, this is probably not the best tour for you.

The tour leaves at 7:15am on weekdays and 8am on weekends from STRI's dock located just past the turnoff to the Gamboa Resort (heading left at the fork and onto a gravel road). The boat ride to the island takes 45 minutes. Once there, a guided tour takes visitors on a 2- to 3-hour hike along a sometimes steep trail through forest, ending at the visitor center for lunch, followed by a Q and A session. At 3:40pm on weekdays and 2:30pm on weekends (you can see that a weekday tour is longer), the boat takes visitors back to the pier. They do not provide transportation to/from the pier, so you'll need a taxi ($15–$20 each way from Panama City), or a bus to Gamboa (see "Getting There & Departing," earlier in this chapter). Bring proper walking shoes, bug repellent, your passport, and your confirmation letter from STRI, and wear long pants, not shorts. Complete information is available from STRI (✆ **202/633-4014** in the U.S., or 212-8000 in Panama; www.stri.org). You can reserve and pay by credit card on their site.

RAFTING AND KAYAKING ★★ The tour company **Aventuras Panama** (✆ 260-0044; www.aventuraspanama.com) specializes in what it calls the "Chagres Challenge," with a hiking and rafting trip down the Class II and III river. It's a long float but technically not difficult, and it starts early, leaving Panama City at 5am by

4WD and going to the village San Cristóbal. From here you hike for more than an hour to the put-in site on the Chagres. The rafting portion lasts about 5 hours, but included in that along the way is a picnic lunch on the river. Travelers pass by Emberá villages but do not spend much time there. Expect to arrive back in Panama City around 7pm. The cost is $165 per person, and includes transportation, breakfast, and lunch, and all equipment. You must be between the ages of 12 and 70 to participate.

Aventuras Panama and **Panama Pete Adventures** both offer kayaking adventures. Aventuras Panama offers guided excursions of the Chagres River and Lake Gatún for $150 per person, and Panama Pete offers Lake Gatún excursions at $76 per person. Both tours leave Panama around 8am and return around 3:30pm.

SUMMIT GARDENS PARK & ZOO ★★

There's a lot of wildlife in the jungles of Panama, but almost all species shy from the public and are close to impossible to spot in their natural environment. If you're in Panama for the first time, or if you don't have much time here, **Summit Gardens Park & Zoo** is a good introduction to the flora and fauna native to the country. For kids, there are a lot of wide, grassy areas on which to run around, and enough animals on view to delight all ages. It isn't a fancy, state-of-the-art zoo by U.S. standards, however Summit recently hired a new director to refocus and revamp the zoo and gardens and to create a cohesive exhibition that illustrates biodiversity using animals, birds, and reptile displays.

The zoo has a wonderful display of "showcase" wildlife, including tapirs, white-faced capuchins and spider monkeys, ocelots, a jaguar, puma, collared peccaries, and more, some of which have been rescued from unscrupulous wildlife poachers (the young tapir "Lucia" was saved during a sting operation that nabbed two Panamanians trying to sell her on the Internet). But without a doubt the **harpy eagle** takes center stage here with its own interpretive center. The harpy is Panama's national bird and the largest eagle in the world, about half the size of an average human—it really is worth a visit just to see the size of this regal bird.

Summit began as a botanical garden in 1923, created by the U.S. in an effort to reproduce and distribute tropical plants from around the world. It is now home to the world's leading collection of palms, among other exotic species. Because Panama City has few green spaces for a picnic or a chance to let the kids run free, Summit is popular with families on weekends. The grassy picnic area and park are free, or you can pay $8 for a covered eating area and barbecue pit. The zoo costs $1 for adults and teens, kids 12 and under get in free, and it's open daily from 9am to 5pm. Call ✆ **232-4854** for more information, or check out their site at www.summitpanama.org.

Where to Stay & Dine

Lodging and dining options are limited and relatively expensive in the Gamboa area, which is why many people choose to visit as part of a day tour.

Canopy Tower ★★ 📷 Canopy Tower is an ex-U.S.-military radar station that has been converted into a fantasy lodge for bird-watchers—something like a cross between a stylish B&B and a scientific research center. There is a 360-degree observation deck that provides stunning views and serves as a platform for observing the 400-plus species of birds; there's also a comfy social lounge with wraparound windows that are flush with the trees. In the morning, the spooky roar of howler monkeys serves as a wake-up call. The best room here is the Blue Cotinga Suite, one of

Rainforest Discovery Center ★ ★ ★

The **Rainforest Discovery Center** (*☎ 264-6266; www.pipelineroad.org) is run by the Fundacion Avifauna and opened in 2008. The center is home to 3km of hiking trails, a visitor center, cafeteria, and tower; the tower overlooks lush rainforest and is a must-do for serious birders, who can expect to see the most species between 6am and 10am. Keep in mind it's 172 steps to the top, so less fit visitors may not enjoy this activity. Only 25 people are allowed up the tower at the time and you are pretty much guaranteed to see birds and other wildlife. The center is open daily (except Christmas and New Year's) between 6am and 4pm. Entrance is $20. For an extra-special experience, book a "special night hours" guided tour; night tours require a five-person minimum, and all reservations should be made 48 hours in advance. If you don't have a car, the easiest way to get here is by contracting a cab for a few hours to take you and drop you back off in Panama City.

two "suites," which are really large doubles with a hammock and private bathroom. Doubles on the second floor are comfortably spaced; however, the pie-slice single rooms are tiny and noisy in the morning (starting at 5:30am). No rooms have curtains; single rooms have shared bathrooms. The prices include meals, but tours—with the exception of bird-watching around the lodge—are an additional cost.

Road to Gamboa. *☎ **264-5720,** 263-2784, or 6613-7220. www.canopytower.com. 12 units. $100–$130 single; $125–$175 per person double; $145–$200 per person suite. AE, MC, V. **Amenities:** Restaurant; bar. *In room:* No phone, Wi-Fi.

Gamboa Rainforest Resort ★ ★ ☺

Sprawled along the shore of the Chagres River in Soberanía National Park, the Gamboa Rainforest Resort is an ideal destination for families with kids, given the resort's jungle boat cruises, aerial tram ride through the rainforest, and minizoo of reptile, butterfly, and marine species exhibits. Every amenity under the tropical sun is offered here, such as a full-service spa, guided tours, and several restaurants. Very spacious double rooms have garden or river views (with private balconies) and a pleasant yet anonymous chainlike decor; attractive suites have Indonesian furniture and large living areas. The bathrooms are elegant and spacious.

The 1930s-era clapboard homes at the resort's entrance have one- and two-bedroom apartments with kitchenettes. The apartments are quite appealing in a historical sense, with their hardwood floors and wicker furniture, but they are the cheapest lodging options because they do not have a view and are a short walk or minivan transfer from the main hotel. Book one of the newly renovated units in no. 253, 255, 256, or 258.

Gamboa. *☎ **314-5000** or 877/800-1690 in the U.S. www.gamboaresort.com. 107 units. $175–$250 double with garden view; $195–$285 double with river view; $290–$350 junior suite; $150–$215 1-bedroom apt. AE, MC, V. **Amenities:** 3 restaurants; 2 bars; bike and kayak rental; concierge; fitness center w/whirlpool, spa, steam, and massage; outdoor pool; room service; tennis courts. *In room:* A/C, TV, hair dryer, minibar.

Soberanía Lodge ★ ✎

This hostel is owned and operated by Advantage Tours and is divided into two parts: two studio rooms for scientists on long-term study projects with the Smithsonian Institute, the other for regular guests. If they're not too busy, two can book a room intended for three to six guests for the price of a double. The interior is pretty rustic, though all rooms have private bathrooms, hot water, and A/C. The public areas include a library, computer, Wi-Fi, and a public telephone. Advantage recently remodeled the hostel so all rooms have A/C and hot water. A taxi here costs $20 to $30 from Panama City; or you can take a bus to Gamboa and the end of the line, and walk a couple blocks. Contact Advantage Tours for information about packages that include tours.

Gamboa. © **6676-2466.** www.advantagepanama.com/soberania.html. 10 units. $30 small double; $55 larger double; $85 studio. Rates include breakfast. No credit cards. **Amenities:** Cafeteria. *In room:* No phone , Wi-Fi.

A NATURE LODGE ON THE WAY TO COLON

Sierra Llorona Panama Lodge ★★ Sierra Llorona, which means "crying mountain," is a converted home nestled in a gorgeous setting of 202 hectares (499 acres) of private rainforest, home to 150 bird species, and ideal for traveling bird-watchers. But Sierra Llorona really appeals to any traveler looking for a peaceful place to commune with nature. The lodge is family run and family style, with very friendly, personalized service and group meals. Guest rooms, like the lodge as a whole, are simply furnished but attractive and neat as a pin.

Off the main area, along Nance's Trail, is a camping space with a covered dining table and fire pit, but you'll need to bring your own gear. Room rates include lodging, meals, and a walk around the area with a local guide; but they have lodging-only rates also that include just breakfast. The staff can arrange transportation to the lodge for $80 for two from Panama City ($25 for each extra person).

Road to Santa Rita Arriba, near Sabanitas. © **442-8104** or 6614-8191. www.sierrallorona.com. 8 units. $75 single; $130 double; $130–$150 suites; all-inclusive packages available upon request. AE, MC, V. **Amenities:** Restaurant; bar.

COLÓN

76km (47 miles) NW of Panama City

Spread across a square peninsula at the mouth of the northern canal gateway is **Colón,** capital of the larger Colón Province that runs along Panama's Central Caribbean Coast. Most residents here are Afro-Caribbean descendants of canal workers who arrived around the turn of the 20th century. In spite of its status as the largest **duty-free zone** in the Americas with billions in annual sales, its profits do not trickle down to locals, and the city is rife with poverty and crime. A splashy $45-million cruise-ship port, called **Colón 2000,** has also failed to alleviate mass unemployment or improve living conditions. There is not much of interest in the actual city of Colón, and although stories of muggings and purse snatchings have been greatly exaggerated, Colón is definitely not one of Panama's safer cities. A drive through the city streets provokes shock, sadness, or just a very uncomfortable feeling at how impoverished Colón's residents are.

But don't let Colón scare you from visiting some of Panama's most important historical attractions that lie within a 30-minute to 1-hour drive from the city, such as **Portobelo** and **Fort San Lorenzo,** as well as the impressive **Gatún Locks** and **Gatún Dam** (see "The Panama Canal," earlier in this chapter). The translucent Caribbean Sea also beguiles visitors with outstanding **diving** and **snorkeling** opportunities, and the province is home to several oceanfront hotels and resorts that are popular weekend getaways for Panama City residents.

Colón was founded in 1850 during the California Gold Rush. At the time, crossing the United States from coast to coast was dangerous and time-consuming; a far better option was to take a ship to Panama, cross the isthmus via the Panama Railroad, and board a ship for California. Economically, the city flourished with businesses and hotels catering to travelers until 1869, with the completion of the transcontinental railway in the U.S. The arrival of the French, and later the U.S., around the turn of the 20th century, brought new prosperity to the city, and much of the architecture here dates from that era. Most of these buildings today are dilapidated shells of their former glory, the city having fallen on hard times when the focus turned to Panama City.

Essentials

GETTING THERE & DEPARTING **By Plane** **Aeroperlas** (www.aeroperlas. com) no longer offers regular flights from Panama City to Colón. For information regarding charter flights with Aeroperlas, call ✆ **315-2770.**

BY BUS The Colón bus terminal is located at Calle Terminal and Avenida Bolívar. There is daily service to and from the Albrook Terminal in Panama City leaving every 20 minutes from 6am to 10pm; the trip is just under 2 hours and costs $2 one-way. Buses headed to Portobelo leave every 15 minutes from 6:30am to 8:45pm; the ride is 1 hour and costs $1.50. I really don't recommend you take a bus to Colón unless you have a taxi driver waiting to take you to your hotel at the bus terminal. To reach Portobelo from Panama City, it is not necessary to transfer in Colón; instead, take a bus to Sabanitas and transfer to a bus headed to Portobelo (catch the transfer on the corner at the El Rey supermarket in Sabanitas). The fare is $3.

BY TRAIN By far the most picturesque journey to Colón is aboard the **Panama Canal Railway** (see "The Panama Canal Railway" in "The Panama Canal," earlier in this chapter).

BY CAR Driving here can be a little tricky because most streets are not signed. There are two ways to Colón from Panama City: The easiest is via the Corredor Norte, which connects to the Boyd-Roosevelt Highway, also known as the Transístmica Highway, at Chilibre. The other, more scenic route is to go through Soberanía National Park and then connect to the Boyd-Roosevelt highway—follow the Omar-Torrijos Avenue to the Gaillard Highway toward Gamboa, but continue straight rather than turning left at the park ranger's office and the sign for Gamboa and Summit Gardens.

GETTING AROUND If you are not part of a tour and do not have a vehicle, a taxi (which fits up to four people) is your best bet. Taxis are not metered—expect a driver to set a flat fee for visits to multiple destinations in the area. The Colón 2000 port has set rates for taxis, and even though you may be hiring one from the bus or train terminal, drivers like to adhere to these general rates for all tourists. I recommend having your hotel call a cab for you rather than taking one off the street. Average rates are $60 to $80 for Portobelo (3 hr.) and $120 for the Gatún Locks and Portobelo. Negotiate and you might get a better price. Most taxi drivers speak little English and are not tour guides. Considering this, you might want to stick with a bilingual tour.

GENERAL TOUR OPERATORS The tour operators listed in chapter 5 can put together custom day and multiple-day tours in the central Caribbean region. Typical day tours begin with a ride on the Panama Railroad to Colón, and are followed by minivan transportation to the Gatún Locks and Fort San Lorenzo, a historical tour of Portobelo, and finally return ground transportation to Panama City. **Ancon Expeditions** offers a unique, 7-night "Camino Real Tour" following the old Spanish-built cobblestone trail across the isthmus. The tour involves several days of moderate trekking and overnights in tents and hotels. **Ecocircuitos** has a 7-night "Caribbean Escapade" with hiking in Portobelo National Park, snorkeling and kayaking, and overnights in Bananas Resort. **Adventures in Panama** has tours in the area with add-on extension trips to the San Blas Islands.

What to See & Do

There are two principal attractions here in Colón. The **Colón Free Zone** (www. colónfreezone.com; no central phone) is a walled-in, city-within-a-city located on the southeastern edge of town. Its 1,600 showrooms are for wholesalers and retailers in Central and South America who travel here to buy consumer products at cost. The Free Zone is open to the public, but most showrooms sell to wholesalers only, and others only reluctantly sell to individual tourists. Really, you can't buy anything here that isn't available in an airport duty-free store, and legally, any purchase here must be sent by the retailer to the airport for pickup, which is another hassle. To visit, you'll need to sign in and show your passport at the Free Zone office, located at the right of the Free Zone entrance at Calle 13 near Avenida Roosevelt.

Running the length of the city's eastern shore is the modern cruise-ship port, **Colón 2000,** with two restaurants, a grocery store, and a dozen shops selling duty-free electronics, jewelry, and other handicrafts. There's really nothing interesting enough to keep you here, and the port is more of a jumping-off point to explore the area outside Colón. Excursions for cruise ships are provided by the port-owned **Aventuras 2000** tour agency.

Tip: ATMs in the central Caribbean region are scarce. Major hotels and most restaurants accept credit cards, but your best (and safest) bet is to use the ATM inside the grocery store in the Colón 2000 cruise-ship port; there is also an HSBC cash machine at the Gatún Locks, next to the entrance at the visitor center; or bring enough cash to cover your visit.

Where to Stay

There is a scarcity of decent, safe hotels in Colón and I recommend you lodge outside the city. Aside from the options listed below, **Davis Suites,** Edif. 27 Davis Cristobal (© **473-0639**), is a pleasant, all-suite hotel in a quiet setting in former Fort Davis. Rooms start at $55 per night and the hotel is a 10-minute drive from the Colón Free Trade Zone. The **Harbor Inn B&B,** in the Espinar neighborhood (© **470-0640;** www.harborinnpanama.com), is a pleasant, inexpensive alternative for those looking for more intimate lodging right in Colón.

New Washington Hotel   I only recommend you stay at this hotel if you absolutely, positively need to spend a night in Colón—otherwise head out to the Meliá Panama Canal hotel (see below) or elsewhere. The New Washington is a hotel grande dame, built in 1913 and considered luxury lodging during its time. Over the years, the hotel has been renovated and well maintained; rooms are clean but bland. The hotel is tucked back near the sea on a large, fenced-in lot in the least dangerous part of the city. A casino and a disco are located here, too, as is an outdoor pool, but the hotel almost always seems empty. For the price, it's a bargain, but unless you plan to spend a lot of time in Colón's Free Zone, there really isn't much of a reason to stay here.

Calle 2. ☎ **441-7133.** www.newwashingtonhotel.net. 124 units. $55 double; $65 suite. AE, MC, V. **Amenities:** Restaurant; bar; casino; disco; outdoor pool; room service. *In room:* A/C, TV.

Radisson Colón 2000 ★   I give this a star because it's the nicest place to stay right in Colón city. This relative newcomer on the Colón lodging scene caters to a mostly business crowd and is a standard, full-service hotel with comfortable and spacious—if not particularly memorable—rooms. It's really not worth staying here unless you plan to spend a lot of time in the Free Trade Zone, but the Radisson is by far the best hotel within Colón. On the plus side, the Radisson has a two-green leaf eco rating from iStayGreen.org.

Paseo Gorgas, Calle 13. ☎ **446-2000** or 800/395-7046 in the U.S. www.radisson.com/colonpan. 102 rooms. $120 double; $170 suite. AE, MC, V. **Amenities:** Restaurant; fitness center; outdoor pool; room service. *In room:* A/C, TV, hair dryer, minibar, minifridge, Wi-Fi.

West of Colón

GATUN LOCKS & DAM ★★★

The Gatún Locks, located at the Caribbean entrance of the canal about 10km (6 miles), or a 20-minute drive, from Colón, are the canal's busiest because there is just one set of locks here instead of the two at Miraflores—meaning you have a better chance of seeing Panamax ships backed up here and waiting their turn to enter the canal. These locks are also the most impressive because they lift ships and tankers up 26m (85 ft.) to the level of Lake Gatún in three steps (taking about 1½ hr. to complete), where they continue for 37km (23 miles) before reaching the Pedro Miguel Locks. The neat thing here is that you can **drive over the canal** at near-water level on your way out to Fort San Lorenzo (see "Colón," above). The **Gatún Locks Visitors Pavilion** (daily 9am–4pm; free admission) has a viewing platform, reached by a long flight of stairs, that offers a high perch for excellent photo opportunities. Apart from a model of the canal and a bilingual brochure, there are no other tourist facilities here. The visitor center is not well signed; to get here, head left just at the canal vehicle bridge until you see a parking lot to your right (pass around traffic if there is a line waiting to cross the canal bridge).

About 2km (1¼ miles) from the Gatún Locks is **Gatún Dam,** a tremendous earthen dam across Chagres River that was, at its completion, the largest in the world and one of the finest engineering achievements in history. The dam was built to create the artificial Lake Gatún, crossed by ships to reach Pedro Miguel Locks. During the rainy season from April to December, you'll want to visit when the spillway is open, but there are no regular hours so ask at the visitor center at the Gatún Locks.

The majority of visitors here are on shore excursions from the cruise-ship port at Colón or are staying at the Meliá Panama Canal hotel. If you're coming from Colón or the train station (in Panama City), a round-trip taxi ride will cost between $20 and $30 for an hour, or $40 to $50 for 2 hours (to see both the dam and the locks).

FORT SAN LORENZO & ACHIOTE ROAD ★★

Continuing past the Gatún Locks, the road hugs the edge of the Sherman Forest Reserve until reaching the old U.S. military base Fort Sherman, a part of which was torn down to make way for a new Decameron Resort that never happened. If you're driving your own vehicle, the police guard at the gate may ask to see your passport.

Continue for 8.9km (5½ miles) on a paved/unpaved road shrouded in tropical greenery, until the road ends and the view opens onto the Caribbean Sea and the mouth of the Chagres River. The Chagres has been called the "world's most valuable river," for it was here that the Spanish transported staggering quantities of Incan gold, later followed by forty-niners passing through with millions of dollars of mined treasure, and now the river's immense value is derived by the fact that the Chagres provides the necessary water to keep the Panama Canal in operation. Most intriguing here is **Fort San Lorenzo** (© **226-6602;** www.sanlorenzo.org.pa), a Spanish defensive fort first built in 1595 but subsequently sacked and burned three times and finally rebuilt in 1761—the version you see today. It was later used as a prison and, for a brief period, a campground for forty-niners during the Gold Rush. Fort San Lorenzo is a UNESCO World Heritage Site, and with its well-preserved state—rusty cannons pointed at enemies long gone, walls made of thick coral and rock, and a grassy moat—it's a worthwhile detour. However, if you're short on time and already planning to visit the forts at Portobelo, you might skip San Lorenzo because of the 1½-hour drive from Colón (unless you're a bird-watcher—see below). The fort is open daily 9am to 4pm, and you must be back out of the police guard station by 6pm. The cost is $3 per person.

The village of **Achiote** lies midway between Piña and Escobal on the Achiote Road, quietly revered as a bird-watching mecca by those in the know—the Audubon Society holds their Atlantic Christmas Bird Count here and has counted up to 390 species in 1 day, including the black-throated trogon, bare-crowned antbirds, white hawks, blue cotingas, and chestnut-mandible toucans. The area is just now developing as an eco-tourism site as a way to support the small local community, and there is a new **Centro El Tucán** (no phone; Mon–Fri 8am–4pm) in Achiote with interpretive exhibits. The best way to visit is with a birding guide who can arrange transportation; try **Advantage Panama** or **Ancon Expeditions** (see "Panamanian Tour Operators," in chapter 5), both offer Achiote Road/Parque Nacional San Lorenzo excursions, or check the Audubon Society's site, **www.panamaaudubon.org**, to see if they've got any day trips planned to the area.

WHERE TO STAY & DINE

Meliá Panama Canal ★★ ☺   The Meliá is housed in the old quarters of the Escuela de las Americas, the notorious military school that spawned Manuel Noriega. For the most part, people spend their time poolside, but there are kayaks for paddling around, a canopy-style zip line, day excursions offered to Portobelo and Fort San Lorenzo, and a fairly empty casino—but not much more. The soaring lobby is staffed by attentive, friendly personnel, and decorated with Spanish colonial art reproductions. The rooms have king-size beds and marble bathrooms, and suites are very spacious, with a marginally frumpy, classic decor. The hotel is centered on two fabulous, resort-style pools, with a swim-up bar, lounge chairs, and an activity center.

The resort sells packages that include meals, but do a price comparison because their nightly rate (which includes breakfast) coupled with ordering meals a la carte can be substantially cheaper. Also, skip the Duty Free Trade Zone shopping tour, which is overrated.

Gatún Lake, Colón. © **470-1100** or 470-1916, or 888/956-3542 in the U.S. www.solmelia.com or www.meliapanamacanal.com. 285 units. $120 double; $150 suite. AE, MC, V. **Amenities:** Restaurant; piano bar and pool bar; babysitting; kids' activities; concierge; fitness center; massage; 2 outdoor pools; room service; tennis court; sports equipment; kayaks. *In room:* A/C, TV, hair dryer, minibar, Wi-Fi.

PORTOBELO ★★

99km (62 miles) from Panama City; 43km (27 miles) from Colón

Portobelo is a modest seaside village made of clapboard homes built around and among the ruins of what was one of Spain's richest and liveliest ports from the mid–16th to early 18th century. The village, squeezed tightly between thick jungle and the blue Caribbean Sea, is less than an hour from Colón, and it's a very popular destination on the Central Caribbean Coast for day excursions. You wouldn't know it today, but this historic site was once the scene of the famous Portobelo fairs that took place for 2 centuries, when Spain's plundered gold and silver from South America passed through here. Around Portobelo are well-preserved forts that are splendid examples of 17th- and 18th-century military architecture, as well as a recently restored Customs House. The ruins, along with Fort San Lorenzo (see above), were named World Heritage Sites by UNESCO in 1980.

Portobelo's residents call themselves *congos*, and are descendants of African slaves brought here during the Spanish colonial era; they are culturally different from the Afro-Caribbeans in Colón. The *congos* possess a rich folkloric expression that arose from slavery and African traditions and religion fused with Catholicism, and which is now best expressed by their colorful costumes and devil masks that they don during festivals such as Carnaval and the famous **Black Christ Festival** on October 21 (see "Iglesia de San Felipe & the Black Christ," below).

Sailors and yachties like to anchor in the calm Portobelo bay, and you'll see lots of boats bobbing in the turquoise sea. There is decent scuba diving and snorkeling around here, too. Portobelo is not exceedingly dangerous, but it is an economically depressed town with run-down homes and a worn-out central plaza, and there are always a lot of people hanging around without much to do. If you use common sense and don't flash expensive equipment or money, you shouldn't have any problems.

Essentials

GETTING THERE & DEPARTING **By Car** Drivers from Panama City should take the Corredor Norte, a modern toll road that ends at Chilibre; from here head

The London–Panama Connection

Portobelo was named "Puerto Bello" (Beautiful Port) by Christopher Columbus on his first visit here in 1502, a name that gradually became known as Portobelo. Known for its 3-month-long, grand and lively trade fairs and the hordes of gold and silver that flowed through here, Portobelo was irresistible to pirates. But it's a battle led by British Adm. Edward Vernon in 1739 for which the town is most remembered. Vernon attacked Portobelo during the War of Jenkins' Ear, a 9-year British war against the Spanish, and his victory resulted in the use of "Portobello" as a commemorative name for a well-known farm in what is now the Notting Hill neighborhood of London. The road leading to the farm was called Portobello Road—today this road is itself internationally famous for its own lively market. Vernon is also associated with the term "grog," which was his moniker and therefore the name his sailors gave to the watered-down rum he served them to avoid drunkenness.

right then turn left on the Transístmica Highway and drive about 40km (25 miles) to the town of Sabanitas. Keep your eyes open for El Rey supermarket and turn right on the road just past it. Follow the signs for Portobelo, located about 33km (20 miles) from Sabanitas.

BY BUS   Buses from Panama City leave from the Albrook Terminal. You'll want a bus to Sabanitas, or a bus to Colón that stops in Sabanitas (verify this with the driver; the cost is $2), and to transfer at the El Rey supermarket on the highway for a bus to Portobelo ($1.25). To get back to Panama City, you'll need to get a bus to Sabanitas, cross the highway, and flag down a bus headed to Panama City. Buses to and from Colón leave every half-hour. I recommend getting here by car or taxi.

BY TAXI   Taxis from Colón to Portobelo average $40 to $45 for the one-way trip, and $20 per hour thereafter (in the event that you'd like the driver to wait while you tour the ruins).

VISITOR INFORMATION   See "Colón," earlier in this chapter, for tour operators.

What to See & Do

FORT RUINS & THE CUSTOMS HOUSE ★★

If you're a history buff, plan on spending about 2 hours touring the ruins and the Custom House—more if you take a water taxi to the ruins at Fuerte San Fernando across the bay. You'll only need an hour if you plan to just walk around a bit and snap a few photos. Portobelo is tiny enough to see all sites on foot.

Entering town, the first site you'll encounter on your left-hand side is the **Batería Santiago,** a defensive fort built after the famous raid on Portobelo by the British Admiral Edward Vernon in 1739. The fort is remarkably well preserved, with rusty cannons, ramps, and a sentry box. Across the road is a short uphill path to **Casa Fuerte Santiago,** which overlooked the bay and was a depository for ammunition.

Farther into town is **Castillo San** [...] **la Gloria,** built in 1600 but destroyed after an attack by Henry Morgan, [...] sacked Panama City. The fort was rebuilt, but attacked again by Vernon; a [...] is the fort was left in ruins and abandoned. From here you can take a water [...] the pier ($2.50) to **Fuerte San Fernando,** which really i[...] longer because much of the fort's stone was taken and [...] canal by the U.S. Leading up from the Castillo is another sho[...] ike [...] **Mirador el Perú,** a lookout offering a lofty view of the Portobelo bay.

The **Real Aduana de Portobelo** (Customs House), located in front of the *parque* (plaza) in the center of town [...] highlight of Portobelo. There is also a small museum here (no phone; daily 8am[...]pm). This fine old building is the restored version of what was known as the "counting house" during the Spanish colonial days, so-named for the gold and silver that was counted, registered, and distributed here. For a century, a third of all the gold in the world passed through this spot. The Spanish built the Customs House in 1630, but it was damaged in both 1744 (by a cannon) and 1882 (by an earthquake). The museum will hold your attention for about 15 minutes—there's really nothing much to see in the main section except a jumbled collection of clipped articles about Portobelo, cannonballs, coin collections, and other items that are not very representative of the Spanish colonial days. A free map of Portobelo is available here, however. The museum has a short informational video, in Spanish and English, for $1 per person. On the second floor is a Spanish-only folkloric display.

The best-preserved fort in town is **Fuerte San Jerónimo,** next to the Customs House. Like the other forts of Portobelo, this one, originally built in 1664, was attacked by Vernon and rebuilt using a more streamlined design.

IGLESIA DE SAN FELIPE ★ & THE BLACK CHRIST

One of the most curious churches in Panama is **Iglesia de San Felipe,** home to the famous "Black Christ" statue and the source of Portobelo's largest yearly festival, on October 21. Legend has it that a ship headed to Cartagena, Colombia, left the statue behind in Portobelo either to lighten its load or because the crew believed that the statue was causing them bad luck. Later, Portobelo residents prayed to the statue to spare them from a cholera epidemic—and indeed they were spared. Praying to the statue has become so widespread that every year pilgrims don ornate purple robes and walk to San Felipe Church, sometimes from as far away as Sabanitas and beyond, either to give thanks or pray for something they need in their lives. It's a spectacle, and not always as religious as you might suspect, with music and drinking thrown into the mix. The best way to see this festival is with a guided tour, because parking is impossible and you might need someone to get you out after a long day.

Behind San Felipe Church is **Iglesia de San Juan,** the original hospital of Portobelo that eventually became a church. Now it holds a small **museum** that displays dozens of the purple robes used by pilgrims during the Black Christ Festival. It's open daily from 8:30am to about 3:30pm.

Adventure Activities

SCUBA DIVING & SNORKELING

The waters off Portobelo do not provide divers with the rich diversity of marine life found in places such as Coiba in the Chiriquí Gulf, but diving is one of the main draws to this area beyond touring the ruins in town. One of the most well-respected dive operators, **Panama Divers** (© **448-2293** or 6613-4405; www.panamadivers.com), has a base at the Octopus Garden Hotel. They offer day trips, multiday trips, and PADI instruction courses. The good news about diving off the Central Caribbean Coast is that it is surprisingly accessible, even if you're lodging in Panama City; the bad news is that visibility is poor when the sea gets churned up (Dec–Feb), or when it rains. On a good day, expect visibility depths of about 40m (131 ft.). Popular dive spots include Drake's Island, with sponges in a rainbow of colors, Buffet Reef, and Iron Castle. Divers can also visit a submerged plane. Panama Divers is a competent, fully licensed, and insured operation with professional guides and travel assistance.

Farther away from Portobelo, heading east toward the San Blas Archipelago, is the relatively undiscovered island **Escribano,** with superb diving opportunities— "Discovery Channel" stuff, as they like to say. Dives in this region require lodging at the Coral Lodge (see "Isla Grande," below). Contact them for more information, or for custom packages. Panama Divers includes a tour of the ruins at Portobelo as part of their scuba excursions. For snorkeling, the best place in the area is Playa Blanca, reached by a 20-minute boat ride from the pier.

If you're just looking to rent snorkeling or diving equipment, try **Scubaportobelo** (© **261-3841** or 261-4064; www.scubapanama.com), located before Coco Plum. It's an a la carte operation whereby equipment and boat rides are charged individually. Prices are cheaper than nearby Panama Divers, with snorkel rental for $10 a day and diving-gear rental for about $30 per day. Tank refills are $4. They have a cafe here and a couple of basic cabins, too, for $35 to $50 a night.

BEACHES & BOAT TOURS

Local boatmen operate at the pier near the Castillo Santiago de la Gloria, ferrying passengers to the empty **Playa Blanca,** located on the coast north of Portobelo. It's one of the best beaches in the area—if you're looking for a little beach time, this is your place. The cost to get there is about $15 to $20, though this is changing quickly due to increasing gas prices. There is a two-person minimum.

LAND-BASED ACTIVITIES

An upstart tour company run by a couple of friendly locals, called **Selvaventuras** (*©* **442-1042** or 6680-7309) takes visitors on hiking trips through the rainforest in neighboring Portobelo National Park, visiting the waterfall at Río Piedra, among others. They can even put together a horseback-riding trip, or any custom itinerary, but they speak limited English. A half-day trip averages $20 per person.

Where to Stay

Coco Plum Cabañas   The Coco Plum Cabañas are a congenial slice of Caribbean tranquillity tucked away on the seashore, about a 5-minute drive from Portobelo. All said, it's a cute little place painted in bold, primary colors, with a hammock-strung common building and an on-site restaurant, Las Anclas (see below). The *"cabañas"* are simple, connecting rooms decorated with marine-themed knickknacks and stenciled art; though clean and cozy, most rooms are dark. Also, there is no hot water in the showers, and the shower head is just a spigot jutting out of a wall. It's not luxury, but it's not a backpackers' haven, either. There are rooms for two, three, and five guests.

About 5km (3 miles) before Portobelo. *©* **448-2102** or 448-2309. www.cocoplum-panama.com. 12 units. $35 single, $69 single with meals included; $50 double, $90 double with meals included. No credit cards. **Amenities:** Restaurant; on-site dive shop. *In room:* A/C, TV.

Finca Don Flor de Café ★★   Finca Don Flor is by far my favorite lodging option in Portobelo. The "Finca" is made up of two simple but attractively appointed bungalows in the middle of Portobelo National Park. Owners Gerard and Michele obviously put a lot of thought and love into both bungalows, and guests can expect to see plenty of birds and other wildlife just outside their window. Unlike other hotels that cater mostly to divers, Finca Don Flor is a good choice for families and couples alike and horseback riding, hiking, snorkeling and surfing excursions are available. Finca Don Flor de Café is also home to Caballo Loco, Portobelo's best restaurant (see review below).

Parque Nacional Portobelo. *©* **448-2291** or 6512-8664. www.flordecafe.com. 2 bungalows. $50 for 4-person bungalow; $60 for 6-person bungalow. No credit cards. **Amenities:** Restaurant; spa. *In room:* Mosquito net, hot water.

Octopus Garden Hotel   Panama Divers moved out of Coco Plum Cabanas and built their own hotel, which also bills itself as a dive resort. The hotel caters almost exclusively to divers, but also offers snorkeling, kayaking, beach and historic excursions, and tours. Rooms here are colorful, bright, and airy, but don't expect luxury by any means. There's a decent on-site restaurant.

10 min. before Portobelo. ✆ **448-2293.** www.panamadivers.com. 8 rooms. $60 double. MC, V. **Amenities:** Restaurant. *In room:* A/C, complimentary Wi-Fi.

Sunset Cabins   Sunset Cabins bills itself as a dive resort and is owned and operated by the same people who run Scuba Portobello. While calling itself a resort is a bit of stretch, Sunset Cabins is the only lodging option in Portobelo with an on-site beach and its own private island reserve, and it has one of the best and most attractive settings in Portobelo. There are five comfortable, clean, and attractive rooms on-site but the one- and two-bedroom cabins are a better bargain. Sunset Cabins is occupied mostly by divers taking part in multiday Scuba Portobello excursions.

Portobelo. ✆ **261-3841** or 261-4064. www.scubapanama.com. 5 rooms, 6 cabins. $45 rooms; $55 1-bedroom cabin; $65 2-bedroom cabin. AE, MC, V. **Amenities:** Restaurant; dive center. *In room:* No phone.

Where to Dine

During the high season (Dec–Apr), restaurants in Portobelo are open according to the times listed in each review. Outside of high season, and sometimes even during high season when tourism is sluggish, restaurants will shut their doors around 5pm. In addition to the places listed below, around the Iglesia de San Felipe, there are several modest restaurants serving up delicious Caribbean seafood dishes, another good option if you want to get a taste of the local culture.

Restaurante Caballo Loco ★★ FRENCH   Located in the middle of Parque Nacional Portobelo at Finca Don Flor de Café, Restaurante Caballo Loco is far and away the best (and most expensive) restaurant in Portobelo. The restaurant is surrounded by lush jungle vegetation and seating is on an attractive outdoor patio. Chef Lionel has years of experience with French cuisine and you'll find dishes such as duck with vanilla, octopus with coconut sauce, and pork in sweet-and-sour sauce. The Caballo Loco is an excellent choice if you're looking for something besides typical Panamanian fare and makes for a romantic meal.

Parque Nacional Portobelo. ✆ **448-2291** or 6512-8664. Reservations recommended. Main courses $12–$32. No credit cards. Fri–Sun noon–9pm.

Restaurante Los Cañones ★ SEAFOOD   This is the best restaurant in the area for seafood. It's located a little under 6km (3½ miles) from Portobelo on the left side of the road. The restaurant sits over the water, facing a pretty cove, so guests dine while gazing out onto the sea. The highlights here are *cambombia* (conch) in coconut milk, and octopus—a very common dish in the area. Their fried snapper, or whatever's fresh on the menu and fried, is good, but not, of course, for dieters.

About 6km (3¾ miles) from Portobelo. ✆ **448-2980.** Main courses $5–$10. No credit cards. Daily 8am–7 or 8pm.

Restaurant Las Anclas PANAMANIAN   Las Anclas is located on the left side of the road just before Portobelo, next to the Coco Plum Cabañas. The fun ambience comes with a cluttered, marine-kitsch decor; Just plan for enough time because busy or slow, it takes 20 minutes or more to be served once you order. Expect seafood stew in coconut milk, squid in pineapple and ginger, tangy seviche, meats, and the usual dishes prepared with garlic, breaded and fried, or done creole style. Their bargain lunch is a fixed-price "tourist menu" with fried snapper, coconut rice, fried plantain *patacones,* and a salad and soft drink for $7. Las Anclas serves full breakfasts, too.

Next to the Coco Plum, about 5km (3 miles) before town. © **448-2102.** Main courses $5–$10. No credit cards. Daily 7:30am–7:30pm, sometimes until 8:30pm on Fri–Sat.

Restaurant La Torre PANAMANIAN/COLOMBIAN   Known for their "cheeseburgers in paradise," this friendly, Colombian-owned roadside restaurant serves sandwiches and fresh seafood, and is open principally for breakfast and lunch. Jumbo shrimp, sea bass, and a mixed seafood platter (octopus and clams) can be prepared with lemon and basil, creole style, or battered and fried. There is also fried chicken as well as snack platters with empanadas and fried *patacones*. Wash it all down with a fresh natural juice or a *pipa,* which is a hacked-open coconut with a straw.

Just before Portobelo, on right-hand side. © **448-2039.** Reservations not accepted. Main courses $6.25–$10; burgers $3. MC, V. Daily 9:30am–5:30pm.

ISLA GRANDE

20km (13 miles) from Portobelo; 105km (65 miles) from Panama City

Isla Grande is a Caribbean island getaway frequented by residents of Panama City because it's close enough to get to without flying. A tiny village stretches along the western shore, and there are no roads—residents get around by foot or water taxi. During high season and some weekends Isla Grande can get very festive, with drinking and loud reggae music; weekdays are often dead. The largest beach is in front of the Hotel Isla Grande, which has a day-use fee of $3 per person; otherwise you'll need to walk along the shoreline trail or hire a water taxi for a couple of bucks to take you to the beach on the north shore of the island. A short boat ride to Isla Mamey will put you on an uninhabited beach, and there are other boat tours, too, but mostly people come here just to unplug for a day or two. The last time I visited Isla Grande it felt like things had gone downhill, so I think it's best for travelers who'd like a taste of the Caribbean but are not planning to visit other island destinations in Panama.

Essentials

GETTING THERE & DEPARTING   By Car or Taxi   To get to Isla Grande, you'll want to continue past Portobelo along a pockmarked road for about 20km (13 miles) to **La Guaira,** an impoverished fishing village with two piers: one with boats to the Bananas Resort and, 2km (1¼ miles) beyond it, the pier for boats to Isla Grande. You can park at either dock, but the Isla Grande dock charges a $2-per-day fee. And upon your return, you can count on some slacker or young kid hanging around and asking for a $1 or $2 for additional "security" when you leave—and they're not nice if you decide not to pay. If you really want to get out of paying this "fee," simply ask how your car looks. Likely, they have no idea.

There are few taxis in Portobelo to get you here, but if you find one, expect to pay around $10. Taxis from Panama City run about $120 round-trip and $70 one-way.

BY BUS   For buses from Colón or Panama City to La Guaira, you'll need to follow the same procedure you would for Portobelo (see "Getting There & Departing" in "Portobelo," above), but catch a bus to La Guaira instead of Portobelo when transferring in Sabanitas. You'll be dropped off at a small port from where you'll have to take a $1.50 water taxi to Isla Grande.

BY WATER TAXI The Bananas Resort includes water-taxi service to their resort for guests staying there, or for those visiting on a day pass. Boat taxis at the public pier charge $1.50 one-way to Isla Grande, or $3 per person to Bananas. (They'll sometimes charge a $10 minimum if there aren't enough people.) When the sea is rough, you might get a little wet.

Fun in the Water

SCUBA DIVING & SNORKELING

Panama Divers (p. 156), based out of Portobelo, can put together a day excursion from Isla Grande (reservations required).

BEACHES & BOATING

There is no "day tour" center with a roster of excursions and set prices; instead, you'll need to hire a local boatman and negotiate a price. If you're staying on the island, your hotel can organize a boat tour for you with a local, or in a pinch you can find a boat and driver at the main dock near Cabañas Jackson, or at the pier in La Guaira. It's best to plan ahead and reserve a time with a local boat, but on slow days you shouldn't have a problem finding a willing captain. Also, check the pier at the Hotel Isla Grande, or check with the staff there to see if they have boat trips planned.

Day boat tours usually include a zip through a mangrove swamp and a visit to one of the offshore islands such as **Mamey Island,** a private island up for sale but still open to day visitors. There is a fine white-sand beach here with good snorkeling opportunities, but you'll need to bring your own gear. This trip can range between $35 and $50, depending on the amount of time you'd like to stay on the beach (in the event that they drop you off and pick you up later).

Where to Stay & Dine

Hotels and cabins on Isla Grande fill during weekends and the high season, from late November to early April. Outside of these dates, it's difficult to find a restaurant that is open, so stick with the hotels mentioned below, or try the restaurant at **Villa En Sueño** (© 448-2964), or the reggae bar **Club Punta Proa** (no phone) in the village, both of which serve midrange Panamanian fare (seafood or chicken) with coconut rice, beans, and plantains. The **Candy Rose** (© 448-2947) has simple meals and dining on a seafront deck. By far the most unique dining experience on Isla Grande is **El Nido del Postre** ★★ (© 448-2061 or 6684-4088; www.elnidodel postre.com), a cafe and reservations-only restaurant popular for weddings, graduations, and other special events. The lovingly maintained gardens and gourmet meals also make it the perfect place for a romantic dinner on Isla Grande. Be sure to call a few days in advance for dinner reservations, as there are no walk-ins allowed. The cafe, which sells mostly coffee, pastries, and desserts, is generally open between 9am and 6pm, though this too can change depending how many people are on the island.

Aside from the lodging options listed below, **Cabanas La Cholita** (© 232-4561 or 6653-9056; www.hotellacholita.com) offers comfortable, air-conditioned cabins and enjoys an attractive beachfront location. Another lodging option not listed below is **Hotel Isla Grande** (© 448-2019). It gets a mention because it offers the best beachfront location on Isla Grande, but it would be an understatement to say Hotel Isla Grande is in bad shape. The rooms smell like mold and are seriously overpriced considering their condition, and the restaurant does not seem to adhere to any kind of hygienic standards. That said, if you absolutely have to be on the beach, it's doable for a night or two.

If you're not staying at the **Bananas Resort,** but would like to take advantage of their many activities, they offer a **day pass** to visit the resort and use their pool and facilities; the cost is $35 per person, $25 for kids ages 3 to 12, and includes round-trip boat transportation, lunch, and a cocktail. This also means that weekends are busier here, so think about visiting on a weekday. In general, service is friendly but lackadaisical, and the food is hit-or-miss (usually depending on what's in season), but it's still the best on the island. Their collection of small bird cages holding ratty macaws and toucans is a little unsettling to eco-conscious travelers.

Bananas Resort ★ ☺   Located on a secluded shore of Isla Grande, this "boutique" resort is not luxurious, but it is the nicest place on the island. There are two cabin-like stand-alone units near the water, each housing two attractive suites that have a kitchenette. The rest of the guest rooms at the resort are within cheery, lemon-yellow A-frame units set slightly above the pool and activities area, each with three spacious rooms with two double beds. If you're a couple, choose the top floor, which provides the most privacy. Swimming conditions at the narrow beach are less than ideal owing to lots of rock and coral, and sometimes the sea here can be too choppy. But there's a pool, volleyball court, and plenty of games to keep kids occupied. All rates include boat transportation, lodging, and breakfast, with meals and excursions ordered a la carte. Transportation from Panama City is once a day in the morning, for $20 per person, with a minimum of four passengers. A single steep trail leads to the village on the other side of the island; otherwise, you'll need a $3 water taxi.

Isla Grande. © **263-9510.** www.bananasresort.com. 28 units. $139 double Sun–Thurs, $169 Fri–Sat; $169 suite Sun–Thurs, $199 Fri–Sat. AE, MC, V. **Amenities:** Restaurant; bar; outdoor pool; volleyball court; kayaks; free snorkeling gear. *In room:* A/C, TV, hair dryer, no phone.

Sister Moon Hotel ★   Perched on a hilly slope and surrounded by arching palms, the Sister Moon is on a more secluded area of the island, about a 20-minute walk from the village. It's a funky, eco-centric, castaway-style place ideal for easygoing travelers who don't need much more than a bed, a hammock, and the sound of the crashing sea. Guest rooms are divided into cabin units. The quality of guest rooms here varies, but all are stripped-down, with stone floors, a basic bed, and a private bathroom. There are also bunk-bed units for backpackers who don't mind sharing. The property has places to just lounge around: on a terrace over the sea or beside their compact pool. There are never a lot of people here so you have a sense of freedom. The boat ride here is $2.50 per person, doubled in the evening. Snorkeling gear is not for rent, so you'll need to bring your own. The hotel is a 2- to 3-minute walk from the pier. Ask about low-season discounts.

Isla Grande. © **6948-1990** or 6674-1403. www.hotelsistermoon.com. 17 units. $72 double. MC, V. **Amenities:** Restaurant; bar; outdoor pool. *In room:* No phone.

A Luxury Ecolodge East of Isla Grande

Coral Lodge ★★★ 📷   This boutique eco-resort gets it right. The lodge sits midway between Isla Grande and the San Blas Archipelago, spread around a tiny, dreamy inlet ringed with white sand and backed by coconut palms and thick jungle. It's a model of resort development, protecting the environment and working with local people while providing guests with all the creature comforts and an unforgettable experience. The units are handsome, individual thatched-hut *casitas* (little houses) strung over turquoise water and a coral bed, meaning you can snorkel just outside your door. Like the rest of the buildings here, they are painted in neutral tones of chocolate and ecru, and decorated with Indonesian furnishings and art. The rooms feature fine bedding, walk-in showers, a large, in-bedroom whirlpool tub, and air-conditioning. Glass sliding doors open onto a small deck with a hammock and chaise longue. On the other side of the inlet, there is an indoor fine-dining restaurant fronted by an outdoor infinity pool; there is also an over-the-water, open-air dining area for lunch or afternoon cocktails. The cuisine here is to die for, and the staff truly makes you feel at home.

Of course, it's not cheap, and getting here is part of the adventure. You must fly by small plane into Porvenir, in the San Blas Islands, then take a powerboat for 45 minutes to the lodge. Alternatively, there is a 40-minute boat ride east from the lodge to the village Miramar, where you can return to (or arrive from) Panama City, 2½ hours away. Rates include all meals and use of their kayaks and snorkeling equipment; however, transportation to the lodge (an additional $360 for two, round-trip) and diving excursions are an additional cost.

Note: Coral Lodge does not accept children 11 and under.

Colón Province, 45 min. by boat from Miramar. © 232-0200 or 6681-2360. www.corallodge.com. 6 units. $215 per person, based on double occupancy. AE, MC, V. **Amenities:** 2 restaurants; bar; outdoor pool; cultural excursions in San Blas; diving excursions; kayaks; free snorkeling gear. *In room:* A/C, no phone.

ISLA TABOGA ★★

19km (12 miles) from Panama City, in the Bay of Panama

Isla Taboga, known as the "Island of Flowers" for its lush bougainvillea, hibiscus, and jasmine, isn't a destination with adventurous offerings; instead, it's a place to escape the streets of Panama City, enjoy the fresh sea breeze, get a little beach time in, and enjoy a lazy lunch. The island is only 19km (12 miles) off the coast, and the ferry ride here provides passengers with a dazzling view of Panama City and ships waiting to transit the canal. The drowsy, charming village here is a nice place to stroll; you'll find a couple of restaurants and hotels, but really this is a very low-key excursion and best as a day trip. If your Panama travel plans include a beach destination such as Bocas or the San Blas Peninsula, skip Isla Taboga. But if you've got a lot of time in Panama City and are looking for a quick excursion, this is a do-it-yourself trip that doesn't require a tour operator or a lot of advance planning—just show up at the ferry dock and head over.

Isla Taboga is one of the most important historical sites in Panama. The village was founded in 1524, and later conquistador Francisco Pizarro pushed off from here on his way to conquer Peru. During the 17th century, the island became the haunt of pirates in search of treasure, and in the 19th century it was a port for the Pacific Steamship Navigation Company, which brought over hundreds of Irish, whose Anglo-Saxon names can be seen on gravestones here. The United States even used Isla Taboga as a training ground for military practice during World War II. Today the village is home to about 1,000 residents.

Essentials

GETTING THERE & AROUND   Ferry service to Isla Taboga is provided by **Barcos Calypso Queen** (© 314-1730), which leaves from the Isla Naos pier on the Amador Causeway, next to the Smithsonian's Centro de Exhibiciones. From Panama City to Isla Taboga, the ferry goes Monday, Wednesday, and Friday at 8:30am and 3pm; Tuesday and Thursday at 8:30am only; and Saturday, Sunday, and holidays at 8am, 10:30am, and 4pm. Service from Isla Taboga to Panama City is Monday, Wednesday, and Friday at 9:30am and 4:30pm; Tuesday and Thursday at 4:30pm; and Saturday, Sunday, and holidays at 9am, 3pm, and 5pm. The cost is $11 adults, $7 children 12 and under, and $7 seniors. Arrive at the pier 1 hour before departure. There is a cafe at the dock.

You'll get around Isla Taboga primarily on walking paths. There are also a few roads for the three service vehicles on the island. (They occasionally double as taxis.) Nearly everyone here walks, but a few residents get around by golf cart.

Note: There are no ATMs on Isla Taboga, and except for Hotel Vereda, no establishments accept credit cards. Be sure to bring enough cash to get you through your stay.

What to See & Do

There's not much to do here other than amble around the little village and snap photos. When you arrive, head left from the pier into the village—the streets are hilly so you'll do a lot of walking up and down. At the town center is **Iglesia San Pedro,** the second-oldest Spanish colonial church in the Western Hemisphere; it's rarely open, however, so you'll probably have to make do admiring the facade. In the plaza, locals meet to chat and play games. If you're okay with walking, continue southeast toward Cerro de las Cruces, and continue up a moderate path to a lookout point that offers a sweeping view of the sea and other islands in the area. The west side of the island is the **Taboga Wildlife Refuge** that protects nesting brown pelicans, but it's mostly off-limits.

Beaches here aren't secluded and can get a little busy on weekends, but they offer soft sand and blue water. The best beach here is **Playa Restinga,** in front of the old Hotel Taboga (closed), going past the pier after the end of town. Like all beaches on the island, this beach is free; the hotels mentioned below will either rent snorkel gear or put you in touch with someone who does. Playa Honda is the beach that fronts the village.

Where to Stay & Dine

Despite its proximity to Panama City and its popularity as a weekend-getaway destination, there aren't too many good dining and lodging options on Isla Taboga, which is another reason to make this destination a day trip; I actually recommend you bring a picnic lunch. In fact, Isla Taboga is almost eerily underdeveloped despite being a short ferry ride away from Panama City. By far, the best food in town is at **Vereda Tropical Hotel**'s restaurant (see below). For inexpensive but good Panamanian-style fare in an open-air setting, try **Donde Pope Si Hay** (no phone), open Thursday through Sunday. **El Aquario,** to the left of the pier, is open 8am to 8pm daily, and though the food isn't bad, expect zero ambience. Both restaurants offer seafood and meats served with rice and *patacones* (fried plantains) for about $3.50 to $8. **El Mirador** and **Fonda Mundi** to the right of the pier serve up inexpensive, okay food for $3 to $7.

Cerrito Tropical   The Cerrito Tropical has delightful apartments with kitchenettes for independent travelers or for long-term stays. The property sits up on a hillside, offering sea views from two of the four apartments, the Palma and the

Mango (two-bedroom and three-bedroom units, respectively). The other apartments have views of the forest and mango trees, and all rooms open onto a balcony with a hammock. Accommodations are very clean, and the owners of the Cerrito Tropical, a couple from Canada and the Dutch Caribbean, are warm and friendly. The garden features an open-air patio. Although there is no on-site restaurant, caretaker and chef Artistedes offers his services to guests who want to enjoy a tasty meal—a real plus considering the lackluster dining options on the island. Apartments are usually rented weekly, but you can ask about shorter stays. A one-bedroom unit can be rented by the day. With advance notice, the hotel can also arrange snorkeling, fishing, and walking tours of the island.

Isla Taboga. © **6489-0074.** www.cerritotropicalpanama.com. 5 units. $100–$270 depending on apt. Rates include breakfast. MC, V (only for online deposits); on-site, cash only. *In room:* A/C, no phone, Wi-Fi.

Vereda Tropical Hotel   This hotel is the best lodging on Taboga. Perched high on a hill and overlooking Playa Honda near the pier, the Vereda Tropical has stunning views of the sea. (You can even make out Panama City from here.) The decor is eclectic but leans toward Mexican style, with bold colors, ceramic tile floors, arched doorways, and swirling iron balustrades; an atrium lights the interior patio and its fountain. Rooms are decorated in a variety of styles; some open onto balconies. They all are comfy and have good beds and high ceilings. The **Pelicanos Bar** is on-site, but the big bonus is the **restaurant**—definitely the best and most atmospheric on Taboga. The view from their open-air veranda is dynamite. They serve tasty, fusion-style cuisine and wonderfully refreshing fruit drinks. Try their Vereda Tropical cocktail with passion fruit juice and *seco*. The menu has pastas, pizzas, and fresh seafood dishes and salads.

Isla Taboga. © **250-2154.** www.veredatropicalhotel.com. 12 units. $90 double with sea view and A/C; $75 double with town view. MC, V. **Amenities:** Restaurant; bar; Internet desk. *In room:* A/C (in some), TV, no phone.

ARCHIPIÉLAGO DE LAS PERLAS

64km (40 miles) S of Panama City, in the Pacific Ocean

Historically famous for its pearls and more recently as the island Shangri-La for television's *Survivor* series in 2003 and 2006, the Archipiélago de las Perlas (Pearl Islands) is nevertheless an unsung beach destination that has taken a back seat to places such as Bocas del Toro. Perhaps residents have done a bad job promoting the Pearl Islands as a getaway destination—or perhaps keeping the masses at bay has always been the goal. Whatever the reason, the archipelago deserves a look. It's surprisingly close to Panama City, just 20 minutes by small plane. The rich aquatic life here offers great snorkeling on sunny days—sometimes manta rays and schools of tropical fish can be seen by just popping on a mask and walking out from the beach. The cerulean sea laps at picture-postcard white- and golden-sand beaches backed by a forest canopy. And the big-game sport fishing around the islands is revered by fishers around the world—you're pretty much guaranteed to catch something. Need I say more?

The archipelago is composed of more than 200 islands and islets, the majority of which are unnamed and uninhabited. The most developed of the islands is Isla Contadora, with a full range of amenities including hotels and B&Bs, restaurants, tour companies, and daily flights. Isla San José is privately owned and home to one luxury resort, the Hacienda del Mar, but that's it. There are plans for a hotel on Isla del Rey, the largest island in the archipelago and the site of a forthcoming residential development. Beyond these islands there is nowhere else to stay in the archipelago, though small islands and islets can be visited as part of a day trip.

Tip: Here in the Pearl Islands, the weather is drier than in the rest of Panama, meaning that low season (May–Dec) can be quite enjoyable and cooler, with showers lasting an hour or so rather than the all-day downpours other parts of the country experience. Lodging rates drop during this time, and there are so few people on Isla Contadora it almost feels deserted.

Isla Contadora

Isla Contadora is one of Panama's most underrated vacation destinations; it's a relatively tiny island with a dozen white-sand beaches including Panama's only nude beach, Playa Suecas. The island harbors a reputation as the exclusive playground for the Panamanian elite and international figures such as Christian Dior, Julio Iglesias, and the deposed Shah of Iran, all of whom constructed palatial mansions here during the past 50 years. Isla Contadora once offered only a couple of funky hotels, but now several attractive and affordable B&Bs have opened their doors, providing comfortable lodging and services to more demanding travelers. Still, those seeking world-class luxury will want to head straight to **Hacienda del Mar** (see "Isla San José," below).

Isla Contadora is so-named because of its historical role as the "counting house," a colonial-era distribution center that recorded and classified pearls before they were shipped to Spain. African slaves were brought to Isla Contadora to harvest pearls, and their descendants still work here, although most cannot afford to live on Isla Contadora and instead live on neighboring Isla Saboga, a 10-minute ferry ride away.

The island's center of activity is at the end of the airport runway on the northeastern side of the island; here you'll find public telephones, a few restaurants and bars, grocery stores, and a basic medical clinic (© **250-4209**). Walk around to the back of the clinic if no one answers the door. There is an Internet cafe next to the dive center across from the airstrip; there's also Internet service inside Restaurant Sagitario. The island doesn't have a post office, and although credit cards are accepted at hotels, there are no ATMs—so you'll want to bring enough cash to cover expenses. No need to pack your snazziest outfits, as the look here is beach casual.

ESSENTIALS
Getting There & Departing
BY PLANE Aeroperlas (© **378-6000;** www.aeroperlas.com) has daily flights to Isla Contadora leaving Panama City at 8:45am and 5pm; return flights leave at 9:39am and 5:50pm. **Air Panama** (© **316-9000;** www.flyairpanama.com) offers flights daily departing at approximately 10am, with an extra 5pm flight on Fridays. Their return flights are daily at 10:30am with an extra return flight at 5pm on Friday. Both Aeroperlas and Air Panama charge $112; both fares are round-trip and include taxes. When boarding your flight back to Panama City, you'll need to stop by the Aeroperlas or Air Panama offices by the airstrip to confirm your flight and check in. Flight availability and times can change depending on demand, also bear in mind flights rarely leave or arrive on time.

Some of the boating and yacht companies mentioned in chapter 5 can also offer shared catamaran or sailing excursions to and from the Islas de Perlas. While some of these are all-inclusive, you can request only pickup and drop-off as well. Keep in mind that this option will be much more expensive than flying.

GETTING AROUND   Isla Contadora is a compact island, and though most roads are paved there are few vehicles—and no taxis—on the island. People get around by walking, by bicycle, or, more popularly, by ATV or golf cart. A cheaper transportation option is to rent a mountain bike from **Casa del Sol** (© **250-4212**) for $15 a day. Ask your hotel about a multiple-day discount for a golf cart, or if they provide drop-off and pickup service around town. Most visitors get a kick out of coasting the island on a cart, searching out the perfect beach or ogling the stately vacation homes that line the streets. If your hotel doesn't have a vehicle for rent, **Bill Carney** (© **6513-9064;** bill@perlareal.com) at the Perla Real Inn has a fleet of golf carts he rents out for $50 for 24 hours or $20 per hour. Casa del Sol rents out Kawasaki Mule carts (which can go down dirt roads golf carts can't) for $100 per day as well as Suzuki ATVs for $50 a day. Nearby Contadora Island Inn has six golf carts; they rent for $70 a day.

WHAT TO SEE & DO

BEACHES   The principal activity on Isla Contadora is spending sun-drenched days lounging on the beach, reading a book, and cooling off with a dip in the turquoise sea. There are no strong riptides and powerful waves here so swimming is safe, even for kids. Surfers, however, should look elsewhere. There are 13 beaches on the island, all perfectly lovely and virtually empty every day except for weekends and holidays. Panama's sole nude beach, **Playa Suecas (Swedish Beach),** is located on Isla Contadora and can be reached by taking the dirt road at the end of **Playa Larga (Long Beach),** the strip of beach that fronts the Hotel Contadora Resort. This beach, like its neighbor, **Playa Galeón,** is convenient for its proximity to restaurants and shops. Both beaches are also recommended for snorkeling, and outfitters rent snorkel equipment, jet skis, and other marine toys. There are also a couple of beachfront bars. **Playa Ejecutiva** is a pretty beach on a tiny cove on the north side of the island, and **Playa Cacique** (often referred to as "Playa Hawaii") is another good option for solitude and beautiful tropical surroundings. During the high season, you'll find the fewest people on Playa Suecas.

Beyond the beaches at Isla Contadora, the region is replete with uninhabited islands with isolated and heavenly beaches—those seeking to really get away from other people will find this a tantalizing option. There's a substantial economic gap between native islanders and wealthier expats on Contadora, so socially conscience tourists looking for less formal snorkeling or fishing options can support the local economy by hiring one of the local boatmen who hang around Playa Larga, Playa Cacique, or Playa Galeón. Most charge between $25 and $30 an hour and offer island, fishing, and snorkeling tours.

You can visit other islands either by hiring a local boatman or taking part in a half-day or full-day excursion. **Isla Chapera** has a couple of empty beaches that are surrounded with a rich variety and abundance of marine life that provides some of the best snorkeling in the area, and it's located straight across from Playa Cacique, about a 10-minute boat ride away. A local boatman can take you here in a wooden *cayuco* for about $25 to $30 per hour (if he waits for you), or about $50 if you want drop-off and pickup; the cost depends on the fluctuating price of gas. Bring a picnic lunch and beverages because there are no stores or restaurants here. Local boatmen can be found at the beach at Punta Galeón. For organized excursions and charter-boat rentals, see "Snorkeling," below.

DIVING   **Coral Dreams** (© 6536-1776; www.coral-dreams.com), at the airport runway, is Isla Contadora's only full-fledged scuba operation, run by a friendly young Argentine couple. Dives take place around the island and never exceed 18m (60 ft.), with visibilities of 4.5 to 9.1m (15–30 ft.) of mostly sponges, some brain and fan coral, and an abundance of marine life. Two-tank dives cost $95 for certified divers. Coral Dreams also offers course instruction, including their intensive Discover Scuba course ($75), which lasts 1½ days and is for beginners who are short on time or who just want a taste of the diving experience; there's also a 4- to 5-day course for full scuba certification ($425). They also offer 3-hour snorkeling excursions and whale-watching between July and October around the area for $40 per person; snorkel equipment rental is $20 per day.

FISHING   The Pearl Islands are legendary for deep-sea fishing. If you want to get out and cast a line for an hour or so, negotiate with local boatmen at Punta Galeón beach; they often have a few beat-up poles lying around and charge lower rates. *Tip:* If you've caught fish but don't have a kitchen, most restaurants will prepare your fish for you and your friends at a negotiated price.

SHOPPING FOR PEARLS   **Casaya Island** is home to a very humble village with no electricity, and residents collect and sell pearls to visitors from their homes. There are no "stores" here; typically, when residents see a tourist walking by, they'll pop out with their glass jars and matchboxes that they use to store loose pearls, which are teeny-tiny, irregularly shaped, and varying in luster, costing from $5 to $25. Don't expect to find any gems—residents contact expert buyers as soon as they find anything valuable, so what's left over for tourists isn't particularly impressive. However, pearl buying can be fun, and it's a good way to support the floundering local economy. On Sunday, residents pour into the streets, drink a lot of warm beer (there's no electricity, remember), and hold cockfights that usually either repel or fascinate visitors. Otherwise, this is a low-key excursion, recommended more as a pleasant 1-hour boat ride to get to the Casaya and make contact with the locals. The average cost is $60 round-trip for a maximum of four people; ask your hotel to hook you up with a boatman, or find one at the Punta Galeón dock.

SNORKELING   Isla Contadora offers excellent snorkeling opportunities, with five coral fields encircling the island, which attract a wealth of marine life, including schools of tropical fish, white-tipped reef sharks, manta rays, and turtles. At Playa Larga, the Hotel Contadora rents snorkel gear for about $5; from here you can reach one of the best snorkeling spots on the island at Punta Verde, located at the southeastern end of Playa Larga. Other prime spots include Playa Ejecutiva and Punta Galeón.

    Coral Dreams (see "Diving," above) rents quality snorkel gear for $10 a day, and they offer snorkeling and bird-watching trips around the area for $35 per person.

WHERE TO STAY

A slow-moving (some would say stagnant) tourism economy means many hotel owners are willing to drop their prices on weekdays and during the low season. The price for a weeklong stay or longer can also be negotiated.

Casa del Sol ★ This attractive B&B is located in the home of a young German-British couple who opened their doors in 2004 with just one guest room, but there is now a small double, a studio, and a rental house, all thoughtfully decorated and bright and cheery. The B&B is located in a quiet residential neighborhood on the western side of the island, next to the Perla Inn and the Contadora Island Inn, and about a 20-minute walk from the airfield. The couple is on-site to cater to all guests' needs, including arranging tours and providing information about the area. ATVs are available for guest use for a discounted rate. They offer free Wi-Fi and will let you use their laptop if you don't have one. Price includes a full breakfast.

Located on the western side of the island. ✆ **250-4164.** www.panama-isla-contadora.com. 2 units; 1 rental house. $80 double; $100 studio; $200 house (rates based on double occupancy). AE, MC, V. **Amenities:** ATV and mountain-bike rentals. *In room:* No phone, Wi-Fi.

Contadora Island Inn ★ This delightful inn is more aptly called a B&B since it is located within two converted, low-slung homes without a full-time "front desk" staff—but the charming American owners live down the road and are on call 24 hours a day, and they pop in frequently. The setting is blissfully tranquil, especially if you're staying in one of the rooms that open onto the back patio, and there are plenty of common areas that give guests enough breathing room to relax and do their own thing. Nights are so quiet that the only sound is the soft chirping of crickets. If you need absolute privacy, a hotel is a better bet for you, but most travelers enjoy the light camaraderie that can develop between guests over a delicious breakfast, which includes freshly baked bread. Because the B&B has been totally renovated, rooms are modern, with contemporary decor, ample closet space, and spotlessly clean bathrooms. Many visitors choose to spend days, sometimes weeks, here, especially if booking the Frigata Magnífico room, which is spacious and has a kitchenette and French doors that open onto a back patio. Their Guayacama room has private access. They'll rent out either of the houses for $350 for the smaller one and $450 for the larger one per night.

Located on the western side of the island. ✆ **250-4164.** www.contadoraislandinn.com. 10 units. $55 double; $125 deluxe room with kitchenette. AE, MC, V. **Amenities:** Full kitchen (in common area). *In room:* A/C, Wi-Fi.

Perla Real Inn ★ 🐾 The young owners of the Perla Real hail from California, and the style of their new inn is heavily influenced by the Spanish missions of that state. The rose-colored building has two stories that center around a small patio courtyard with a bubbling fountain. Rooms have cool white stucco walls accented with stencil art, Mexican ceramic floors and countertops, and handmade furniture. There are just four doubles, and their two suites have a full kitchen for independent travelers or extended stays (room rates are discounted for stays of 7 nights or more). Each room has a comfy queen-size bed with crisp sheets, French doors, and a private entrance. The Perla Real is located next to the Casa del Sol and Contadora Island Inn in a whisper-quiet residential area, about a 20-minute walk to the airstrip. Continental breakfast is included. Guests can rent golf carts for $35; use of snorkeling equipment and beach towels is complimentary.

Larger families may enjoy the new Spanish-style two-bedroom villa with kitchen, living area, complimentary Wi-Fi, and satellite TV for $165 a night.

Located on the western side of the island. ✆ **250-4095** or 6513-9064. For reservations, call their U.S.-based number at 949/228-8851. www.perlareal.com. 6 units. $81–$99 double; $108–$133 suite. MC, V. **Amenities:** Complimentary Wi-Fi. *In room:* A/C, minibar.

Punta Galeón Resort & Restaurant ★★   This is the best full-service hotel on the island, and one of the better options for dining on Isla Contadora. What I like best about the Punta Galeón is that all rooms are in a one-story building spread across a bluff, and all have direct ocean views, sliding glass doors that open onto individual patios, and an elevated wooden boardwalk with benches that hug the cliff and wrap the property. There's also a cool breeze on this side of the island. Guest rooms are a little kooky, look slightly 1970s, and have the feel of a submarine with cantilevered bed platforms, whitewashed walls, and okay mattresses. Rooms are also on the small side, but the connecting patio adds space. Breakfast is included.

    The hotel has two mediocre restaurants, the year-round outdoor **La Popa,** open from 7am to 11:30pm, which offers simple meals, salads, and pastas for $6 to $14. Their weekend and high-season restaurant, **Pelicano's,** is open for dinner only from 3 to 11:30pm, and serves fish and meat with creative sauces for $10 to $16. It's the only restaurant on the island with air-conditioning. The hotel rents jet skis for $85 per hour.

Isla Contadora. © **250-4234** or 250-4221. www.puntagaleon.com. 48 units. $195 all meals included; $135 no meals. AE, MC, V. **Amenities:** 2 restaurants; concierge; outdoor pool; room service; sauna; Turkish bath; sports equipment. *In room:* A/C, TV, minibar.

Villa Romántica   Seaside kitsch, 1970s love-motel renaissance, or a tribute to cheesy *telenovelas?* It's difficult to fathom what the Austrian owner of Villa Romántica envisioned when he converted his holiday home into a full-service hotel. Certainly there is no other hotel in Panama like it. Perched above Playa Cacique, a secluded beach with soft golden sand, the hotel also has a popular, breezy restaurant with sea views—it could be said that the hotel and restaurant's location is the best on the island. But it all runs downhill from there. Rooms are spacious enough, but the decor is busy and tragically mismatched—think pink tile frescoes, blue lamps, and a silhouette of a naked woman on your shower door. The owner, a gregarious expat who is colorful enough to be known all over the islands, recently landscaped the front of the hotel with a funky little miniature golf course that undoubtedly will appeal to kids, and he offers boat rides in the area and day excursions. Service is erratic and could use some polishing.

    Restaurante Romántico ★ serves mostly seafood with a choice of sauces such as curry pineapple or garlic, as well as meat dishes and salads. The food quality depends on who's cooking and what's brought in that day, but the view here is lovely. The restaurant is open daily from 7am to 3pm and 6 to 10pm; main courses run $10 to $20.

Playa Cacique. © **250-4067.** www.villa-romantica.com. High season doubles $84–$96, $156 suite; low season doubles $96–$114, $250 suite. MC, V. **Amenities:** Restaurant; sports equipment. *In room:* A/C, TV, no phone.

WHERE TO DINE

Restaurants on the island are expensive, and most do not serve memorable meals. If you want something cheap, try Restaurante Sagitario (see below); or try the little joint that adjoins the **minimarket Duty Free**—their simple *comida corriente* costs about $2 to $3. The place is always full of construction workers so you know it must be good.

Restaurante Geralds ★ GERMAN/PANAMANIAN   It's the best restaurant on Isla Contadora, but you'll pay to enjoy it. Geralds serves mostly European dishes with dashes of Panamanian flavor. The restaurant is open-air and tastefully designed, with wood tables and a bar, and is located on a sloping hill near the airport. There isn't a view, but the ambience is pleasant and refined. You can have the fresh catch of the day with a choice of sauces such as hollandaise or white wine; jumbo prawns fried in beer batter or served with pineapple juice and cucumber ragout; filet mignon with green pepper sauce; or beef stroganoff. Their fish stew is a delicious starter or light meal. During busy weekends, it's best to make dinner reservations.

Near the airport. ℂ **6588-1046.** Main courses $14–$23. MC, V. Mon–Fri 11am–3pm and 6pm–midnight; Sat–Sun 11am–midnight.

Restaurante Sagitario ★ PANAMANIAN   Where the locals go for home cooking and cheap prices, Sagitario, sometimes called "Matilde's" after the owner, often serves fresh jumbo prawns for as low as $6. There's also sea bass, seviche, chicken, and stewed pork. All dishes come with rice and beans. The special of the day costs $2.50.

Paseo Urraca, near the health clinic. ℂ **250-4091.** Reservations not accepted. Main courses $2–$7. No credit cards. Daily 7am–9pm (Fri–Sat until 10pm).

Isla San José

This private island is quite large at 44 sq. km (17 sq. miles). It is almost totally covered with forest, save for a luxury lodge, an airstrip, and more than 97km (60 miles) of roads built by the U.S. military when it held training operations and weapons testing from World War II and onward here. Today the owner of the island is the Panamanian George Novey, who is also the owner of Air Panama. The Hacienda del Mar (see below) arranges flights on Air Panama for visitors.

WHERE TO STAY & DINE

Hacienda del Mar ★★★   Despite Hacienda del Mar's remoteness it's surprisingly easy to get here via a short plane ride from Panama City—making it an upscale beach resort for discriminating travelers who aren't looking to journey far from the capital. The bungalows are best described as rustically elegant, built predominantly out of the handsome bamboolike *caña blanca*. Each bungalow has ocean views, and a balcony/deck with chaise longue chairs to kick back on and enjoy the unsurpassed beauty of the island's surroundings. The front door opens onto flowering hibiscus and jasmine. For the price, it's best said that the rooms are not so much luxurious as they are ultra-comfortable, and like most eco-oriented lodges, there is no TV or Internet in the rooms, encouraging guests to unplug from the modern world. Junior-suite bungalows have an additional couch and a little more room, and their VIP suites have a separate living room. Each bungalow is sold as a unit, not per person. Breakfast is included, with other meals a la carte.

If you're into sport fishing, this is your place. The Hacienda has five boats that can take you shore or deep-sea fishing (they'll cook up whatever you catch back at the lodge) for wahoo, amberjack, sailfish, and tuna. This, as with most excursions here that involve a boat or guide, costs extra. There are also wildlife and bird-watching tours, ATV tours across the island, canoeing and kayaking, scuba diving and snorkeling, jet-ski tours, and mountain bike riding. Because this is a private island, wildlife has been allowed to flourish, so don't be surprised to see a collared peccary or brocket deer during your stay. The meals here are absolutely delicious—made using fresh seafood and organic fruit and vegetables—and are served on an open-air deck infused with sunset colors and candlelight. Prices below do not include airfare (an extra $125 round-trip), and reflect low to high season rates. Check their website, as they often lower prices by $50 or more if booking between Sunday and Wednesday.

Isla San José. © **269-6634,** 832-0214 on weekends, or 866/433-5627 in the U.S. www.haciendadelmar. net. 14 units. $330–$650 low season; $375–$700 high season, depending on type of suite. AE, MC, V. **Amenities:** Restaurant; 2 bars; fitness center; outdoor pool; sauna; sports equipment rental. *In room:* A/C, minibar (some units), no phone.

EAST OF PANAMA CITY

East of Panama City, the Pan American Highway travels toward the renowned Darién region, but not before passing the turnoff to the only road that connects the Comarca Kuna Yala and the eastern Caribbean coast with central Panama. The 37km (23-mile) road begins just past the town of El Llano, and ends at Cartí Suitupo, passing through hilly country cloaked in thick rainforest, much of it unexplored and replete with wildlife. This is one of Panama's best bird-watching spots, and sightings of monkeys are common, too. Additionally, at intervening points sweeping views provide a chance to see both the Pacific Ocean and the Caribbean Sea. There is no bus service along this route, and though the road is in good shape, it still requires a 4WD vehicle. The lodge below can provide transportation to the Kuna coast, where it is possible to hire a *cayuco* boat to go to one of the islands in the comarca.

A Nature Lodge in the Wilderness

Burbayar Lodge ★★   Rated as one of Panama's top bird-watching lodges for both its location and its quality of guides, the Burbayar is a pared-down lodge that envelops travelers in wild, natural surroundings. The Burbayar is best described as rustic adventure, but the accommodations and the property are so well designed that rusticity feels 100% appropriate in such lush jungle surroundings. The Burbayar is a good bet for travelers seeking to delve into the rainforest without having to travel far from Panama City, and the price here is cheaper than that of its counterparts near the canal. The lodge comprises five thatched-roof, stylish cabins built of recycled local woods and palms (each cabin has a private bathroom) and a main dining/lounge area, strung along the ridge of a hill. The lodge offers treks to the Caribbean coast, and to Lake Bayano for a boat ride to an Emberá Indian community. Meals are hearty and served family style. The service at the Burbayar is a highlight; the Spanish owner, Iñaki, is exceptionally attentive to his guests.

El Llano. © **393-7340** or 6674-2964. www.burbayar.com. 5 units. $135 per person, all-inclusive. No credit cards. **Amenities:** Restaurant; no electricity. *In room:* No phone.

CENTRAL PANAMA

8

Central Panama in this guide is defined by the Panamá and Coclé provinces west of Panama City, and the Herrera and Los Santos provinces that make up what's known as the Azuero Peninsula. The Central region includes **El Valle de Antón,** a lovely mountain village located in the center of a volcanic crater; **Pacific Beaches,** with an array of lodging accommodations from rustic cabins to all-inclusive destination resorts; and the charm of Panama's cultural "heartland," the **Azuero Peninsula,** dotted with colonial villages and home to the liveliest festivals in Panama. What these destinations all have in common is that they are reached by vehicle (or bus) from Panama City, not by plane—unless, of course, you charter a plane to fly to Pedasí, at the tip of the peninsula. This region begs to be explored by car, so consider renting a vehicle, which will give you the freedom to plan your own itinerary and wander at your own pace, stopping off at villages and attractions that interest you and buying gastronomic treats from vendors that line the highway.

The Interamerican Highway (Pan American Highway) and the Carretera Nacional are modern roads that are easy to drive and do not require any kind of special considerations or a 4WD. Distance is measured by markers that show the kilometers from Panama City—this is how locals give directions, for instance: "Turn at kilometer 54." The markers are white and look like oversize dominoes.

El Valle de Antón is characterized by year-round spring weather conditions, and a cooler cloud forest in higher areas; the Pacific Beaches are driest from January to March; and, because of mass deforestation, the Azuero Peninsula is very dry in comparison to the rest of Panama.

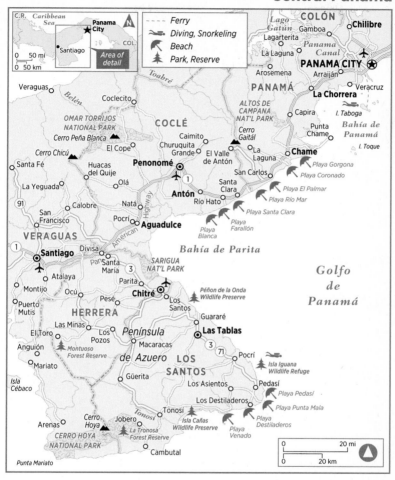

PACIFIC BEACHES

Every weekend, hordes of residents from Panama City and the interior head out to the Pacific Coast to frolic on the beaches of the Panamá and Coclé provinces. Until a decade ago, this long stretch of beach backed by dusty cliffs was the home of fishermen and humble people who moved here after their villages were flooded with the building of the Panama Canal. But the beaches' proximity to Panama City (just 30 min.–2 hr. from downtown) has proved tempting to well-heeled Panamanians and foreign retirees, and now the coast is the haunt of extravagant homes, manicured residential communities, and a few splashy megaresorts. There are three exclusive seaside golf courses—Playa Coronado, Tucan Country Club, and the Mantaray course near the Decameron—and a couple of surf schools with packages or day lessons if you're short on time. And Panama's only RV park is located here, close to Santa Clara. Most coastal destinations in this section see few people outside of weekends, and at some beaches during low season, weekends can be relatively free of crowds. Despite their popularity with weekend city dwellers, the Central Pacific beaches are certainly not Panama's most attractive beaches, and are really only worth visiting if you don't have time to visit some of Panama's better beaches or if you're taking part in an all-inclusive vacation at one of the resorts along the coast. Personally, I find the rapid overdevelopment and "planned community" feel of the Central Pacific Coast a bit disconcerting, but if you're looking for an all-inclusive package or want to spend your holiday playing golf, you'll feel right at home here.

The modern, four-lane Interamericana (also called Panamericana) Highway connects the city with the coast's beaches, which are listed in this section in descending southwest order: Playa Bonita, Gorgona, Coronado, Santa Clara, and Farallón (Playa Blanca). The farther you drive from Panama City, the whiter the sand turns and the bluer the sea. The sands of some of the beaches have a lot of iron and are blackish.

Important note: The Pacific beaches have strong riptides and choppy swimming conditions, so they aren't the best choice for families with small children.

Getting There & Departing

There are two exit routes from the city: the Puente de las Américas (Bridge of the Americas) that spans the mouth of the canal; and the newer cable-stayed span bridge Puente Centenario, built in 2004, that crosses the canal at the Gaillard (Culebra) Cut,

---

ROADSIDE gastronomy

If you're like me and relish sampling local delicacies, especially those found at cheap road stops and hole in the walls that usually go unnoticed by tourists, try these culinary gems. **Bollos Chorreranos** (no phone; Fri–Sat 8am–8pm, Sun–Thurs 8am–6pm) is an open-air dive recognizable by the dozens of parked cars of Panamanians out front. It's on the highway outside Chorrera, 35km (22 miles) west of Panama City. Every Panama City resident, it seems, stops here for local specialties that include *tasajo,* an out-of-this-world gooey smoked beef; *bollos,* tamale-like corn patties filled with chicken or coconut; *chichas,* fresh juices such as passion fruit and the exotic guanabana; and the regionally famous *chicheme,* a thick, sweet beverage made with corn

and cinnamon, and said to "put hair on your chest" and "pump you up." Farther down the road, at kilometer 57, next to the defunct Texaco station, is **Queso Chela** (no phone; daily 7am–8pm) with heavenly light fresh cheeses, fresh yogurt (even *chicheme* yogurt), soft egg bread, warm beef and chicken empanadas, and *chichas* to wash it all down. Don't miss the fresh roasted cashews sold at the front door—this is what cashews were meant to taste like. The town of Chorrera is known for its juicy pineapple. If pineapple is in season, road vendors often sell three for $1; a little farther past Chorrera, vendors sell mango and papaya. At Antón, vendors sell sweet treats such as candies and coconut cakes.

the section of the canal whose excavation cost the most lives during its construction. Both routes are nearly the same in terms of distance, and each has a toll of 50¢. Do not leave Panama City from 3:30 to 6:30pm, or return between 7 and 9am, when heavy traffic jams could add an extra 30 minutes to an hour to your travel time.

BY CAR   I suggest renting a car to get around the Pacific Coast, especially if you don't want to be stuck at your resort or hotel because tours and excursions can be pricey. For the Bridge of the Americas, take Avenida de los Mártires along Cerro Ancón, which connects with the Panamericana and the bridge. For the Puente Centenario, head out past the Miraflores Locks until you see the bridge entrance. The four-lane Interamericana Highway is in good shape, and turnoffs are marked by either a municipal sign or promotional billboard.

BY BUS OR TAXI   Buses leave from the Albrook Terminal. Buses will drop you off at the turnoff for each beach, where cheap taxis (about $3) wait for the quick ride to the beach. Taxis from the city charge an average of $50 for transportation to all beaches listed in this section, less if heading to the Intercontinental Resort in nearby Playa Bonita. Some resorts here provide transportation for guests from the airports or from any hotel in Panama City. **Pesantez Tours** (© **263-7577;** www. pesantez-tours.com) has round-trip transportation, dropping off and picking up on different dates, for $56 per person to beaches like Santa Clara.

Playa Kobbe (Bonita)

The formal name for this area is Playa Kobbe, but with the opening of the Intercontinental the area is also commonly referred to as Playa Bonita. This is the closest beach to Panama City. Take the first exit after the Bridge of the Americas and follow the road 6.5km (4 miles) to get here. A taxi from downtown will cost you about $45 one-way, or $65 from the international airport. Apart from the resort and an upscale residential community with an 18-hole golf course, there is Playa Kobbe—the public beach (with a lifeguard), which charges $7 (price includes a snack), and at which you can rent boats.

A LUXURY RESORT

InterContinental Playa Bonita Resort & Spa ★★★   The InterContinental is one of the most luxurious and relaxing resorts in Panama, and a tad more exclusive than the Playa Blanca and Decameron resorts in Farallón. The InterContinental's whitewashed exteriors feel Mediterranean, and the interior decor is tropical Indonesian, with lots of neutral tones like dark chocolate and ecru. A vast lobby with floor-to-ceiling windows looks out onto the heart of the resort, a palm-fringed maze of pools with a swim-up bar, restaurants, a beach volleyball court, Jet Skis, and an activity center that rents snorkeling equipment and kayaks. My only caveat with this resort is that when the tide is low, there is no beach—just a lot of goopy mud.

All guest rooms are exquisite, with plush beds and stocked, marble-inlaid bathrooms. Balconies overlook the pool, the beach, and, farther beyond, Isla Taboga and ships waiting to enter the canal. The bright and enthusiastic staff provides some of the best customer service of anywhere in Panama. The elegant spa is also one of the country's best, with a full range of exotic treatments. And the food is delicious, too. There are excursions to the Gamboa Rainforest Resort, or you can play a round of golf at the world-class Tucán Golf Course nearby.

Playa Kobbe, Punta Bruja. ©️ **211-8600,** or 800/424-6835 in the U.S. www.ichotelsgroup.com. 303 units. $250 double; $300 Club Room, $650 suite. AE, MC, V. **Amenities:** 3 restaurants; 2 bars; babysitting; kids' activities; access to Tucán Golf Course; fitness center w/whirlpool, spa, steam, and sauna; 5 outdoor pools; room service; sports equipment rental. *In room:* A/C, TV/DVD, CD player, hair dryer, minibar,.

Playa Gorgona

This is the next stretch of sand on the coast, but it's quite a drive from Playa Bonita—about 79km (49 miles) from the Bridge of the Americas or Puente Centenario. Gorgona is a small town with three salt-and-pepper sand beaches, including Playa Malibu, a popular surf spot (you'll need a 4WD to get to this beach); Arena Negra, a charcoal-sand beach commonly used by fishermen; and the Gorgona Beach itself. During the winter, strong currents create poor swimming conditions here. These are not the nicest beaches on the coast, and accommodations consist mostly of inexpensive, weathered *cabañas*.

WHERE TO STAY

Aside from the options listed below, **Cabañas de Playa Gorgona** (©️ **240-5314;** www.propanama.com/gorgona) consists of 40 uninspiring, low-cost self-catering cabins popular with Panamanian families on the weekends. The cabins are clean enough, but it's not really worth staying here unless you can't afford one of the area's all-inclusives. **Cabañas Villanita** (©️ **240-5314**) is a slightly better option consisting of four cinder-block cabins for up to six people located right on the beach. Again, it's nothing fancy, but a better option than Cabañas de Playa Gorgona.

Hotel Canadian ★ 🔧   This hotel is not located on the beach—in fact, it's a couple of blocks off the highway in Chame, just before Gorgona. The hotel acts as a base for travelers taking part in a host of outdoor activities in both El Valle and the surrounding coastal area. The Canadian-owned guesthouse is very tranquil and sits atop a knoll, offering views of lush coastal forest. Of the seven units, five are doubles and two are family-size units. Guest rooms are simple but tidy and well-maintained, with decent beds and lots of closet space. The friendly owners Katie and Ralph can put together one of 21 different tours for guests, or get you to the beach in Gorgona if you'd just like to kick back on the sand. They have an open-air bar and restaurant, and breakfast is included in the price of a room.

Chame. ©️ **240-6066** or 867/536-2272. www.hotelcanadianpanama.com. 7 units. $45–$55 double. No credit cards. **Amenities:** Restaurant; bar; outdoor pool. *In room:* TV, no phone.

WHERE TO DINE

Rincón Catracho ★★ 🍴 INTERNATIONAL   Catracho serves delicious food, and is a real find in such a modest town. The menu features dishes such as filet mignon, veal cutlets, seafood dishes, pastas, and even tacos, which are all very tasty and reasonably priced. The owner, a German, is a retired international chef who sought to open his own place—and good thing he did because this area needed a solid dining option. During the low season, call ahead to let them know you're coming.

Follow paved road, right at grocery store. ©️ **240-5807.** Reservations recommended for dinner. Main courses $5–$10. No credit cards. Fri–Sun 7am–9pm.

Playa Coronado

Playa Coronado is the oldest community on the coast, and the most developed, with a sprawling residential area and full range of services such as a 24-hour El Rey supermarket, shops, and restaurants. It's located 83km (51 miles) from Panama City, and 3km (1¾ miles) from the highway. There are quite a lot of residential homes here that have been around long enough to give off that lived-in feel, unlike other beach areas that are mostly modern condo developments. Both Panamanians and expats like Coronado for its services and for its lengthy beach, though this is certainly not the best beach on the coast—the sand here contains a lot of iron and is dark. There is a controlled security gate to keep the crowds at bay—even if you're not registered at a hotel, tell the gate attendant that you are headed to the Coronado Beach Resort so that he'll let you pass.

WHERE TO STAY

Club Gaviota ✦ For pleasant budget accommodations, this is your best bet in Coronado. There are nine guest rooms in a motel-like building close to the beach, but not close enough to offer ocean views. Rooms are modest but clean, with either one or two double beds; ask for a newer room because their two older units are depressing. Prices are nightly, or as a package with meals for $45 per person, but considering that a double costs $61 to $77 per night, you might be better off opting for the meal package if you're a couple. Their on-site restaurant serves decent, simple meals, with a la carte options priced at $5 to $12. There are adult and kids' pools with a good view of the sea.

Paseo George Smith. © **240-4526** or 224-9056 in Panama City. www.hotelgaviotapanama.com. 10 units. $49–$61 double; $45 per person with 3 meals a day. MC, V. **Amenities:** Restaurant; 2 outdoor pools. *In room:* A/C, TV, no phone.

Coronado Golf & Beach Resort ★★ ☺ With the feel of a stuffy country club, the Coronado would more aptly be called a golf resort than a beach resort. People who stay here are principally families and older guests. One highlight at the Coronado is the guest rooms, all of which are very spacious and nicely appointed "suites." Garden suites, their standard option, are 53 sq. m (570 sq. ft.) in size, with a master bedroom, sitting area with two sofa beds, and a dining table; their Royal Suites are the same as Garden Suites but have a second story with an extra bedroom, two queen-size beds (for a total of six guests), and a balcony. Residential Suites are for a maximum of six, with the addition of a kitchenette. At the beach, the Coronado has a covered activities area with a restaurant and sports equipment for guests only. The Equestrian Club offers horseback riding for $20 an hour, but is open on Saturdays only. There is an excellent steakhouse next to the club, but again it's open to guests only. The staff here is friendly for the most part, but the quality of service is lackluster. The resort claims it has all-inclusive packages, though the prices are really for rooms only, and everything is an additional price—so keep tabs on your tab or you'll be left with an expensive surprise when you check out.

Av. Punta Prieta, Coronado. © **264-3164** or 866/465-3207 from the U.S. www.coronadoresort.com. 75 units. $305 Garden Suite for 2; $405 Royal Suite for 2; $605 Residential Suite for 4 (additional guests are $15 per person; children 12 and under stay free). Ask about discounts during off season. AE, DC, MC, V. **Amenities:** 5 restaurants; 2 bars; disco; bike rental; kids' playground; kids' miniclub w/activities; fitness center w/sauna, spa whirlpools, and Jacuzzis; Olympic-size pool; kids' pool; tennis courts; ATV rental. *In room:* A/C, TV, hair dryer, kitchenette (Residential Suites only), minibar, Wi-Fi (some units).

Corowalk Inn ★ I really only recommend this hotel if you're in a pinch because it's located next to the highway behind El Rey supermarket and shopping area and is a 5-minute drive to the beach (much too far to walk, though). Still, the contemporary hotel with country decor is a very clean establishment, with attractive rooms and amicable service. Make sure you book a room with windows, as a few do not have them. A continental breakfast is included in the price.

Av. Roberto Eisenmann, 1 block from highway. ℂ **240-1516** or 240-1517. www.hostalesdelpacifico.com. 14 units. $77 double; $130 suite or apt up to 4 people. MC, V. *In room:* A/C, TV.

WHERE TO DINE

Rincon del Chef ★ CONTEMPORARY PANAMANIAN   Located almost next door to Don Chacho, in a country-style wooden building that's part of a handicrafts market, this restaurant serves excellent meals prepared by a chef who once ran the kitchen at the Coronado Resort. You'll find traditional dishes, but mostly the food here consists of creative takes on locally available ingredients, such as shrimp and green plantains, and curried seafood; grilled meats and lighter fare are available. The prices are very reasonable, and the waitstaff is attentive. The only problem with Rincon is that they often do not adhere to their posted hours during the low season. Once you turn off the highway, you'll see the restaurant on your right-hand side.

Av. Roberto Eisenmann. ℂ **240-1941.** Main courses $5–$10. MC, V. Tues 8am–4pm; Wed–Thurs 8am–8pm; Fri–Sun 7am–10pm.

AN ELEGANT RESTAURANT IN VISTA MAR

Restaurant Terrazas del Mar ★★★ MEDITERRANEAN   The Vista Mar Resort is a new, private residential community whose Restaurant Terrazas del Mar I highly recommend. If you're in the coastal area and seeking an upscale dining experience with delicious, gourmet cuisine, this is your place. The dining area is fresh and chic, with a Moroccan decor and whitewashed walls. The outstanding French chef, Pascual Finet, has created a Mediterranean-influenced menu that incorporates French, Spanish, and Italian dishes. Highlights include duck confit, Galician octopus, and calamari stuffed with crabmeat. Everything is fresh, and flavors are well combined. They have a solid wine list, too. You can dine indoors or outdoors on their terraced patio that overlooks the sea. Vista Mar is located 90km (56 miles) from Panama City, and 2km (1¼ miles) from the highway turnoff.

Road to Vista Mar. ℂ **832-0577.** Main courses $7–$15. AE, MC, V. Thurs–Tues 11am–10pm (to 11pm Fri–Sat).

Playa El Palmar

The turnoff for Playa El Palmar is 95km (59 miles) from Panama City, just past the town of San Carlos, which has services such as a supermarket. El Palmar is a gray-sand beach popular with surfers and weekenders from the interior. Along the coastal area are oceanfront properties, and there are two midrange places to stay: the Palmar and the Bay View Resort (see below). The water, depending on the tide, can be blue or dark; also, be aware of riptides when the surf is pounding. Day visitors should look into the Bay View's day pass (see below).

WHERE TO STAY & DINE

Hard-core surfers may want to head to the **Palmar Surfcamp** (ℂ **240-8004**), which fills up with a mostly younger crowd on the weekends.

Bay View Resort ★ ☺   The Bay View is not the most elegant "resort" on the coast, but it is a good place to bring the kids and let them splash around in the pool while you take surf lessons or lounge on the pleasant beachfront terrace, and its prices are reasonable. The Bay View is simple and somewhat funky, with leafy green vegetation centered around a fish-shaped swimming pool. A wooden bridge connects this area with a promenade-like terrace where you can gaze out at the sea view, dine, or enjoy the sunset with a cocktail. Guest rooms are pretty basic, with thin curtains and bedspreads, two double beds of so-so quality, and tiled floors. The grounds are nicely landscaped for the most part, and there are campsites for $10 per night. Note that at high tide there is virtually no beach in front of the resort.

Day visitors may use the pool for $10 adults and $5 kids. The Bay View Restaurant sits atop a hill and has a sweeping view of the ocean. They serve mostly seafood, including seviche, lobster, and fresh sea bass and snapper; they also serve barbecued meats, fresh fruit juices, and a kids' menu. Prices below are for accommodations only, but the resort offers packages that include meals.

Playa El Palmar. ✆ **240-9621.** 30 units. May–Nov $70–$90 double. MC, V. **Amenities:** Restaurant (w/free Wi-Fi); bar; outdoor pool; soft surfboards for rent; volleyball. *In room:* A/C, TV, no phone.

Santa Clara

Santa Clara and its neighbor down the road, Farallón, are home to the nicest beaches in this Pacific coastal area, though even here you won't find any particularly breathtaking beaches; however, the sand is clean and white and the swimming conditions are relatively good. There are relatively few people in Santa Clara—the area has a ban on weekend "Coaster" buses that transport rowdy beachgoers to the coastal region. Santa Clara doesn't have much of a town to speak of, and consists mostly of tourist lodgings and residential and weekend homes for urbanites. It's a little farther from Panama City than other beaches mentioned earlier in this chapter, but it's worth the extra effort to get here, especially if you plan on spending the night. The turnoff for Santa Clara is 113km (70 miles) from Panama City; keep your eyes open as it's easy to miss the turnoff. After turning, the road forks—head left for Las Sirenas, right for Las Veraneras and the public beach.

OUTDOOR ACTIVITIES

Most visitors come to Santa Clara just to kick back on the beach and relax. Locals rent **horses** on the beach, but there isn't a corral or specific place to head to—rather, horse owners wander the beach looking for potential riders. The lodging options mentioned below or the day area at the Balneario Santa Clara can put you in touch with a horse-renting local; the cost is $3 per hour. If you want to rent a bike, your hotel should be able to put you in touch with a local bike-rental outfit.

WHERE TO STAY

Las Sirenas ★★ Las Sirenas is a top choice for travelers seeking private cottages with a full kitchen rather than an all-inclusive package. Half the cottages are perched on a bluff and offer cool breeze and sea views, and the other half are smack-dab on the beach itself; all are light and fresh and painted white with a splash of yellow and blue in a somewhat nautical decor. The grounds at Las Sirenas are abloom with pretty bougainvillea, and the sea is decidedly bluer here than at other beaches closer to Panama City. The cottages have a patio with hammocks and a barbecue that they'll fire up for you when you're ready to cook. The charming, English-speaking family that runs Las Sirenas is very accommodating, and can help with any dinner plans and even provide meals to heat up if you give them enough notice. There are one- and two-bedroom cottages on the bluff, and those on the beach have one bedroom with a double bed as well as a loftlike floor with a single. Maid service happens only once every 3 days.

Santa Clara. ✆ **223-0132** in Santa Clara, or 993-3235 in Panama City. www.lasirenas.com. 11 units. $130 1-bedroom (up to 4 guests); $180 2-bedroom (up to 6 guests). MC, V. **Amenities:** Kids' playground; volleyball court; Ping-Pong table. *In room:* A/C (bedrooms only), TV, kitchen, no phone, Wi-Fi (some units).

Las Veraneras This place is overpriced for what you get. Las Veraneras is a restaurant/bar/hotel complex with cabins with kitchens, individual rooms, and a few rather dreary houses nestled in tropical jungle. The best units here are the two-story, five-person cabins with kitchenettes set back and above the beach; three are made of wood with thatched roofs and small balconies that have partial views of the sea, and the other four have no views and are made of cement. Altogether, it's a very tight squeeze for five people, and there's no hot water. The spacious, open-air restaurant has five rooms on stilts above the restaurant/dance floor, and although the new management claims that party nights (something the place has been known for) have been toned down, you can still expect to hear a lot of noise on weekend nights and during the summer. Elsewhere on the property, farther back from the beach and nestled in tropical jungle, are houses for up to 10 guests—but I wouldn't recommend them. On the plus side, there is a huge, circular pool. Las Veraneras is for younger, more bohemian travelers. The restaurant here is open daily from 7am to 9pm, and serves seafood and Panamanian dishes.

Santa Clara. ✆ **993-3313.** http://lasveraneras.aventuraspanama.com/lasveraneras. 15 units. $76 cabin for 5 with fan; $87 cabin for 5 with A/C; $200 house for 10 with fan; $220 house for 10 with A/C. MC, V. **Amenities:** Restaurant; bar; outdoor pool. *In room:* A/C (some cabins), TV, no phone.

XS Memories ★ It's an RV park and they serve the best burgers on the Pacific Coast. Sounds a little incongruous in Panama, and as you might have guessed it's American-owned. They tend to get a lot of day visitors to their restaurant, and a fair number of hardy American RV travelers who drive all the way from the U.S. to the end of the road in the Darién. They have 22 motor-home hookups, with water, electricity, and septic-tank service, for $10 per day. There's also a campground, and three simple, terra-cotta-tiled cabins; one has a kitchenette and is sized for two guests, another has two double beds, and the third has three double beds. Within the walled complex are a pool; a small zoo; and a restaurant and sports bar with a large-screen TV, kitschy decor, and good, American-style cuisine but no beach access. The restaurant is open Sunday through Monday and Wednesday to Thursday 8am to 8pm, and Friday and Saturday 8am to 10pm

North side of the Interamericana, near Santa Clara. ✆ **993-3069.** www.xsmemories.com. $50 cabin for 2. MC, V. **Amenities:** Restaurant; sports bar; outdoor pool. *In room:* A/C, TV, fan, no phone.

WHERE TO DINE

Restaurante Balneario Santa Clara ★ PANAMANIAN If you'd like to visit Santa Clara for the day, this is where you go. This complex has a decent restaurant, a long row of beachfront picnic tables with thatched roofs (called *ranchos*), a campground, public bathrooms, showers and, on busy weekends, a lifeguard. *Ranchos* cost $5 to rent, hammocks $2. The restaurant specializes in fresh seafood, with crayfish, garlicky clams, and octopus as their specialty, but they also have burgers and a kids' menu. The Balneario is next to Las Veraneras.

Santa Clara. No phone. Reservations not accepted. Main courses $6–$14. No credit cards. Mon–Thurs 10am–7pm; Fri 10am–8pm; Sat–Sun 8am–8pm.

Restaurante Los Camisones ★★ PANAMANIAN   This is the best restaurant in the area, though it's not directly on the coast. It's situated just off the Interamericana Highway at kilometer 104, about a 10-minute drive back toward Panama City from Santa Clara. It's a casual, open-air restaurant housed under a tremendous thatched roof, and the seafood here is straight-from-the-boat fresh. Los Camisones is Spanish-owned, evidenced by dishes such as Galician octopus sautéed with olive oil and red peppers, and Iberian sausage. There's also Angus beef filet, lamb stew, steamed mussels, breaded oysters, and yummy crepes for dessert. The freshest, most delicious jumbo prawns I have ever sampled in Panama were here at Los Camisones. In fact, the food is so good, the U.S. ambassador to Panama often stops in for a meal. Service can be slow.

Km 104. ✆ **993-3622.** www.loscamisones.com. Main courses $7–$18. AE, MC, V. Mon–Thurs 9:30am–9pm; Fri–Sun 9:30am–11pm.

Farallón

Farallón is often referred to as Playa Blanca, for the lovely white-sand beach that stretches along the coastal area here. It's mostly known for the gigantic Decameron Resort and the Playa Blanca Resort (see below); there is also a poor village whose residents, to be honest, are resentful of their new resort neighbors. It's not common, but those with a rental vehicle might encounter a bit of rankling from locals on the roads here (usually kids throwing trash at passing vehicles). It's anyone's guess how this area will look in a decade, given the fact that it is a hot property for retirement and weekend homes.

OUTDOOR ADVENTURES

The all-inclusives on Playa Farallón and Playa Blanca have activities desks that can help arrange outdoor adventure tours and excursions.

WHERE TO STAY & DINE

Breezes Resort & Spa   This resort is a relative newcomer on the Playa Fallaron all-inclusive scene. Breezes calls itself the first "super-inclusive all-inclusive" in Central America and is housed in three attractive if rather generic buildings. Rooms are decked out in bright pastel colors giving them a family vibe. Most have a terrace or balcony with ocean and mountain views, but only suites have minibars. Although there are four restaurants on-site, the food is not particularly memorable and there are often long lines at mealtimes. The staff is friendly and tries to be attentive but can be a bit slow, though this might be attributed to the hotel's newness. Overall, I feel that Breezes has potential to be a great all-inclusive but for now, I find it a bit overpriced for what you get.

Playa Blanca. ✆ **877/273-3937.** www.breezes.com/resorts/breezes-panama. 294 units. $310–$350 double; suites start at $420. AE, MC, V. **Amenities:** 4 restaurants; 4 bars; Internet cafe; kids' activities; 3 pools; room service; spa; tennis courts. *In room:* A/C, TV, hair dryer, minibar in suites, balcony or terrace in most rooms,.

Bristol Buenaventura ★★★   The Bristol is technically situated on Buenaventura Beach and it's the only high-end non-all-inclusive on Playa Farallón. This beautifully designed hotel has a spacious, tropical chic lobby and is laid out like a Spanish hacienda with courtyards and mini-plazas, making it feel much larger than 114 guest rooms. Rooms are delightful with ultra-comfortable and lovingly carved colonial-style mahogany wood beds, spacious bathrooms, a sitting area, and a balcony or terrace overlooking the pool and the ocean farther away. There are also suites and detached rental villas available. The staff here is attentive and helpful, perhaps because of the hotel's more manageable size, and the food at the main restaurant is quite good with strong Peruvian influences. The great thing about the Bristol is that it's intimate and unique enough to appeal to couples, but there are enough activities to keep families busy as well; there's even a petting zoo and horse stables! But if you're looking for romance, I recommend booking during the week, as the hotel fills up with Panamanian families on high-season weekends. The only problem I have with the Bristol is that the property on the whole seems a bit unfinished; a golf course is in the works and much of the land is as yet undeveloped and unlandscaped. Luckily, the grounds are so large than any future construction noise won't be a problem in the guest rooms.

Playa Buenaventura. (C) **908-3333.** www.thebristol.com/buenaventura. 114 units. $395–$515 doubles; $900 suite; $1,000 Bristol Suite; $2,000 villas. AE, MC, V. **Amenities:** 3 restaurants; bar; kids' activities; fitness room; 3 pools; room service; spa; Wi-Fi (at additional cost). *In room:* TV, hair dryer, minibar/minifridge, balcony or terrace.

Playa Blanca Resort ★★   The Playa Blanca is more manageable than the Decameron, yet still offers a bounty of things to see and do (including doing nothing at all). The entire property is painted white, with cerulean-blue awnings and trim, and is centered around trim gardens and the resort's two pool areas, one more of a party scene, the other peaceful and relatively empty. The 220 rooms look out onto the beach, the pools, or gardens; they are not as extravagant as you would expect from a self-billed five-star resort, but they are roomy and well attended. Standards come with two queen-sizes or a king-size, and suites have a living area and luxury bathroom. The evening entertainment and food—even buffet food—are above par, and there are day activities galore, including excursions to areas like El Valle. All-inclusive prices include three daily meals and use of all facilities; the price does not include sport-gear rental, day excursions, tips, or services like massages.

Note that day visitors not lodging at the resort can pay $45 per person on weekends or $35 on weekdays to use their swimming pools and facilities (does not include gear rental), and the price includes lunch and beverages. For transportation for day trips to the resort from Panama City, call **Pesantez Tours** ((C) **223-5374** or 336-9100; www.pesantez-tours.com), which charges $30 per person round-trip.

Centro Comercial Paitilla, Av. Balboa. (C) **264-6444.** www.playablancaresort.com. 220 units. $190 double. AE, MC, V. **Amenities:** 4 restaurants; bar; disco; babysitting; kids' activities; 9-hole putting range; 2 outdoor whirlpools; 2 outdoor pools; room service; tennis courts; watersports equipment rental. *In room:* A/C, TV, hair dryer, minibar.

Royal Decameron Beach Resort, Golf, Spa & Casino ★★★ ☺   With seven swimming pools, an 18-hole golf course, casino, spa, marina, and a host of other facilities, the resort is almost like an amusement park you must navigate with a map. The Colombian-owned Decameron has handsomely designed interiors and immaculately landscaped, lush tropical grounds. All guest rooms are essentially the same, and come with two queen-size beds or a king-size. They are comfortable and bright, but note that a lot of stairs connect the units to facilities, so if you're not able to climb stairs, ask for a room that has shuttle transportation or is in a convenient location. Do not book a room by the pools unless you want to hear thumping Latin music day and

Pipa's ★★

If you're not staying at the aforementioned resorts, or if you are but would like to get out and find a more "local" experience than lining up at a buffet, walk down to Pipa's (© 6575-7386)—it's located between both resorts. (You can also reach the restaurant by driving to the Decameron, turning right, and continuing on for about 2km/1¼ miles.)

Pipa's is owned by a laid-back California couple who serve some of the most delicious seafood found along the coast, like fresh jumbo shrimp and lobster. At night they'll sometimes fire up a beach bonfire. Pipa's is normally pretty mellow, but get enough patrons filled with booze and the mood can turn festive. It's open daily from 11am to 8 or 9pm.

night. Also, sometimes there are a lot of kids running around and screaming, another reason to book far away from the hullabaloo. As an all-inclusive resort, meals, all drinks (alcohol included), nonmotorized watersports equipment, entertainment, kids' activities, and tips are included. The most common complaint heard here is that during busy weeks it is a never-ending lineup to book a reservation in a specialty restaurant (as opposed to the buffets), or to book a day excursion, and so on.

For an additional cost, guests have access to the beautiful **Mantaray Golf Course ★★★**, designed by Randall Thompsen and featuring 18 holes spread across rolling hills, with some sea views. There are driving ranges, a practice putting green, and six flood-lit par-3 holes for nighttime playing.

Playa Blanca. © **993-2255** (resort) or 206-5324 (reservations). www.decameron.com. 820 units. Rates per person based on double occupancy: $89 adults, $49 children. AE, MC, V. **Amenities:** 2 buffet restaurants; 6 specialty restaurants; 2 snack bars; 7 bars (1 swim-up); casino; disco; babysitting; kids' activities; 18-hole golf course; fitness center and spa; 7 outdoor pools; room service; tennis courts; watersports equipment; volleyball. *In room:* A/C, TV, hair dryer, minibar.

ALTOS DE CAMPANA NATIONAL PARK

90km (56 miles) W of Panama City

This is Panama's first national park, established in 1966 and covering about 4,925 hectares (12,170 acres) of mostly igneous terrain created by the extinct El Valle de Antón Volcano. The park is characterized by rugged peaks—almost completely deforested on the Pacific side—and sloping rainforest on the Atlantic side. There are dramatic cliffs, lava fields, and one of the most extraordinary lookout points in Panama at Chame Peak, from which visitors can marvel at sweeping views of the Canal Basin, the Chame River, and the Chame Bay. Unless you're an avid bird-watcher, this is the major reason to visit the park, since hiking and other adventure activities are in short supply here. Past the turnoff for Altos de Campana, drive about 4km (2½ miles) to an ANAM **ranger station** (© **254-2848;** or try the local office in Coclé © 997-7538), pay the $3 per person entrance fee, and walk up to the lookout. ANAM has developed a mostly uphill hiking trail here called **Sendero La Cruz,** but you'll need a 4WD to reach the trail head. The park station sometimes has copies of a good illustrated guide to the trail. Bird-watchers should know that the park is home to exotic species that can be difficult to view elsewhere, such as **violet hummingbirds, white-tipped sicklebills,** and **orange-bellied trogons.** Taking a public bus here is next to impossible; you'll need a rental vehicle or arrangements with your tour company to make a detour here on your way out to other destinations in the area. A campground here charges $5 per night.

EL VALLE DE ANTÓN

124km (77 miles) W of Panama City

Nestled in the crater of the world's second-largest extinct volcano, El Valle de Antón—popularly known as El Valle—is a delightful and relaxing destination popular with urbanites escaping the heat and hectic pace of Panama City. It's about 2 hours from the city, and can be easily reached by rental vehicle or by bus. El Valle is ringed by steep, verdant peaks, and its streets are abloom with flowers and lined with stately weekend homes that open onto well-manicured gardens and lawns. Best of all, El Valle enjoys springtime conditions year-round due to its altitude at 762m (2,500 ft.), with temperatures that vary between 68° and 80°F (20°–27°C).

On Sundays, the main street comes alive when vendors come to town to sell handicrafts, vegetables, and ornamental flowers at the town's famous market, but otherwise El Valle moves at a languid pace, offering low-key activities like bird-watching and bike riding through town. Visitors seeking a little more action can hike through rainforest, race through the forest on a zip line at the Canopy Adventure, or horseback-ride high up to a lookout point. American and Canadian retirees are beginning to discover El Valle, but for now it still has a distinctly Panamanian feel.

Essentials

GETTING THERE & DEPARTING

If you are lodging in El Valle, ask your hotel about transportation to and from Panama City, which they can arrange for you for a price (about the same price as a taxi, or less).

BY CAR It's easy to drive to El Valle because the road is well maintained and suitable for any kind of vehicle (unlike many destinations in Panama, you won't need a 4WD). To get here, take the Interamericana Highway west for 98km (60 miles) until you see the turnoff for El Valle. From the Interamericana, it's 28km (17 miles) to El Valle, along a very curvy road. Drive slowly and keep an eye out for people and animals walking on the road, especially at night. The road is quite scenic, and you'll want to stop occasionally to snap a photo or two.

BY BUS Buses leave from the Albrook Terminal near the national airport every 40 minutes to an hour, depending on demand. The trip takes a little less than 2 hours and costs $3.50 one-way. Buses are surprisingly convenient because drivers will drop you off at your hotel if you let them know ahead of time; otherwise, buses stop at the market on Avenida Principal. There aren't many taxis in El Valle, though, so getting dropped off at your hotel really is the better option, especially at night. Direct buses run from 6am to 6pm, or you can catch a later bus until 9pm and be dropped off at the highway, where you can flag down any bus headed for Panama City.

BY TAXI A taxi from Panama City costs around $70 to $90 one-way or about $150 round-trip. A taxi to any one of the beaches from El Valle costs around $30 to $40 one-way. Again, this is subject to change due to the ever-increasing cost of gas.

GETTING AROUND

BY TAXI There are only a handful of taxis in El Valle, and on weekends the wait can be up to an hour if your hotel calls one for you. If you're lucky, you might be able to flag one down on the main street. The cost to travel around El Valle is $1 to $2. **Domingo** (© 6832-3639) is a quiet, respectful official driver. **Mito** (© 6744-0098) drives an unofficial taxi, but his enthusiasm and friendliness are contagious and he's my cabdriver of choice. Both men speak limited English, so you'll have to brush up on your Spanish.

ORIENTATION

There is an **ATP visitors' kiosk** (© 983-6474; daily 9am–4pm) at the handicrafts market on Avenida Principal across La Victoria Grocery store, but they speak limited English and usually have few materials to hand out other than brochures about Panama destinations in general. They can however, call a cab to get you to your hotel when you when you get into town. **Don Pepe** (see "Shopping," below) has maps of El Valle for sale.

FAST FACTS

There is a 24-hour **ATM** inside Banco Nacional on Avenida Principal. There is also an ATM inside the red supermarket on the main street, but this closes around 7 or 8pm when the grocery store closes. The **medical clinic** is located directly behind the Iglesia San José, and is open from 7am to 3pm (© 983-6112 for 24-hr. emergencies). There is a large natural medicine health complex in the works as well. The **post office** is located adjacent to the police station and fire brigade on Carlos Arosemna Guardia. There is **Internet service** at FSR Technology Services next to the Supercentro NG on Avenida Principal (Mon–Fri 8am–noon and 1:30–6pm; Sat 8am–5pm; Sun 11am–3pm). Right next door is a **laundry** service, open daily from 10am to 6pm. Maria Candelaria's hostel (see below) also has an Internet cafe, but it's a bit outside of town. There is a public library across the street from the Anton Valley Hotel; the book selection's minimal, but if you have your own laptop, you can connect to the Internet here for $1 an hour. When I last visited El Valle, a recreation center, **Donde Daniel** (© 6615-5511), had just opened. It hosts movie nights, children's games, and barbecues, and it has a restaurant, cafe, and bar with live music. This ambitious project is set in an attractive house off the main street.

What to See & Do
OUTDOOR ACTIVITIES

BIKING There's no better way to get around El Valle than by bicycle. The terrain is perfectly flat and mostly paved, with some bumpy side roads that have potholes and rocks. Around the edge of town, a couple of dirt roads head high into the hills, if you're looking for more of a workout. Many hotels rent bicycles to their guests, or you can rent from **Don Pepe** (© 983-6425), for $3 per hour, $6 half a day, or $12 full day; or from **Residencial El Valle** (© 983-6536) for $3 per hour, or $10 for a full day. Both locations are next to each other on Avenida Principal.

CANOPY ADVENTURE   This exhilarating, adrenaline-fueled activity involves zipping from tree to tree while strapped in a harness connected to a pulley on a steel cable. The adventure begins with a 30-minute walk to a high platform that is flush with the canopy (the uppermost branches of the forest). A guide gives instructions and demonstrates how the equipment works and how to put on the brakes using a thick leather glove; from here you let gravity do the work. The full tour includes four "zips," which are connected by platforms that gradually descend from the canopy, allowing you to appreciate tropical vegetation from different vantage points. You also get to ride over the 150-foot Macho Falls. If you don't have much time, you can do a quick zip (15 min.) closer to the Canopy Adventure entrance, for $11 per person. The full tour takes about 1½ hours, although the actual cumulative time you ride is less than 15 minutes. Part of the experience is spending time on the platform to observe wildlife, the reason the canopy opens daily at 8am, when the animal world is most active (they close at 4pm). The full tour costs $52 per person, and children must be at least 6 years old to participate. Canopy Adventure also offers an easy-to-moderate guided hike through the rainforest for $25 per person, or you can pay $3.50 for a 15- minute walk near the waterfall, where you will be able to swim, close to the water wall. There is a trail with signs offering education about the cloud forest. Wear sneakers or hiking boots, not flip-flops, and long pants or shorts that are long enough not to ride up while you're seated in the harness. It should go without saying that skirts are not the ideal garb. The Canopy Adventure (© **264-5720;** www.canopylodge.com) is owned by Canopy Lodge (see "Where to Stay," below), and it is located at the Chorro El Macho on the west side of town, about 3km (1¾ miles) from the market. It is recommended that you make a reservation on weekends or during the high season for groups of four or more.

HIKING & BIRD-WATCHING   More than 350 species of birds have been recorded in El Valle, placing the lush valley on the list as one of the top five spots in Panama for bird-watching. Canopy Tower, a bird-watching lodge, recently built their second property here to offer a place to view birds commonly found in foothills, rainforest, and cloud forest. A prime spot for bird-watching here is at **Cerro Gaital National Monument ★★★**, which covers the northern slope of El Valle. This national monument also offers one of the **best hikes** in the area, a 2½-hour, easy-to-moderate loop trail that reaches a lookout point where, weather permitting, you can see the Pacific and Atlantic oceans, and even as far as the Panama Canal. The trail is pretty straightforward, but it's always better with a guide who can point out wildlife and make sure you don't get lost (see below). Cerro Gaital is administered by the ANAM park service, which charges a $3.50 entrance fee per person.

The second hiking area is a 3-hour, moderate trail at **La India Dormida ★★**, which means "Sleeping Indian Woman" and refers to the outline of the western peaks that locals claim resembles a reclining woman. (Have someone point it out to you—it's hard to make out at first.) It is advisable that you walk this trail with a guide as it is not clearly marked. There is a swimming hole along the way, so bring your swimsuit.

If you're interested in bird-watching, I recommend staying at the Canopy Lodge, a bird-watching lodge located just outside town, owned and run by fellow bird-watcher Raul Arias, but if you're staying elsewhere, the lodge should be able to recommend a good guide.

HORSEBACK RIDING   Riding horseback is one of the best ways to appreciate El Valle's gorgeous mountain views. Rent horses from a woman named **Mitzila** (© **6646-5813**); she and her team offer horseback riding for $8 per hour (minimum 1 hr.), plus $8 an hour if you want a guide. **Rosa Carvajal** (© **6622-4374**) also rents horses for the same rates. Horseback rides lope along for beginners, while advanced riders note that rocky trails for the most part prohibit full-tilt gallops.

HOT SPRINGS   Pozos Termales ★ (no phone) are springs without the hot—that is, there are a couple of muddy, tepid pools with minerals that ostensibly alleviate ailments like arthritis and rheumatism. What Pozos promotes is fangotherapy, or caking yourself in mineral-rich mud, waiting on a metal bench for it to plaster, and washing it off in a shower. The end result is much softer skin, but although the complex is neat as a pin, this is no glamour spa, rather a public concession with picnic tables, a meandering stream, and a couple of tiny pools that can get too close for comfort on weekends when dozens of visitors come to soak their aches away. As far as hot springs go, there's nothing particularly memorable about the Pozos Termales, but they're a fun option if you're short on activities. The complex is open daily from 8am to 5pm, and costs $2 adults, 50¢ children under 12, 75¢ seniors.

ADVENTURE TOUR OPERATORS

Mario Urriola, a biologist who runs the Serpentario (see "Zoos & Museums," below), is an excellent nature guide, and he heads a group of bilingual bird-watching guides and conservationists who can put together hikes and other outdoor activities. Birding tours cost $25 per person for a half-day; hiking tours cost $30 for a half-day for up to five guests (© **6559-2676**; chombond1@latinmail.com).

The **Panama Explorer Club** operates out of the Crater Valley Adventure Spa (see below), where they have an "Adventure Center" with a rock-climbing wall and obstacle course, plus bike rental and organized tours available to the general public (© **983-6942** in El Valle, or 215-2330 in Panama City to talk to someone who speaks English; www.pexclub.com). Their half-day excursions include rappelling down a waterfall ($20), mountain-bike tours ($10–$33), and kayaking and rafting nearby rivers ($88–$116), one of which is Class I and suitable for kids.

ZOOS & MUSEUMS

Aprovaca Orquídeas   The Asociación de Productores de Orquídeas El Valle y Cabuya (APROVACA) is a nonprofit agency that strives to cultivate and conserve endangered local and regional orchids. At their site there are 147 species on display. The place has been spruced up recently, but is really only worth a visit if you're an orchid aficionado.

Off Av. Principal near the entrance to town, next to the ANAM office. © **983-6472.** Free admission. Daily 10am–3pm.

El Nispero Zoo ★★ ☺   The Nispero Zoo never planned to be a zoo; it just happened. The owner, an agronomist who runs a small for-profit nursery here, had a large collection of animals and birds, and over time so many people donated abandoned or sick animals that it just made sense to open a zoo. The 2.8-hectare (7-acre) El Nispero sits at the foot of Cerro Gaital National Monument. There are 55 species of birds, both exotic imports from Asia and Africa such as golden pheasants and white peacocks, as well as a few tropical species not seen in any zoo outside Panama.

A good representation of endemic animals includes a white-faced capuchin and spider monkey, an ocelot and trigillo margay, and a couple of tapirs rescued from Manuel Noriega's home after the invasion. Note that there are no protective railings between you and the cages, and children (and adults!) should be careful not to stick their hands through the chain-link fence that guards the animals. El Nispero's bucolic property has shade trees and a botanical garden that offer quiet spots for reading a book or just reflecting on nature.

El Nispero is also home to the brand-new **Centro de Conservación de Anfibios de El Valle (EVACC),** an amphibian study center sponsored by the Houston, San Antonio, and San Diego zoos. The center will study the bacteria that are wiping out the golden frog, among other amphibians, and work to ensure the amphibians' survival (see "End of the Golden Era for the Golden Frog?" below). The center has aquariums, exhibits, and a video and reading center.

Turn up Carlos Arosemna Guardia St. and follow signs to El Nispero. © **983-6142.** Admission $2 adults, $1 children 3–12, free for children 2 and under. Daily 7am–5pm.

El Rincon de la Biodiversidad ★   This small organic farm run by the very knowledgeable Tomas Garcia is an example of sustainable farming. You can pick your own vegetables here, as well as learn a bit about the organic farming process. There are also some handicrafts for sale. Long and short-term volunteer opportunities are available for those who wish to contribute their time, and discounted (and even free) lodging can be negotiated with Tomas.

Located in front of the Casa de Lourdes Restaurant of Los Mandarinos Hotel. © **6706-1271.** Free admission. Daily during daylight hours.

Museo del Valle   It's usually closed, and this museum is worth a look only if you've run out of things to do in El Valle or if you're at the market on Sunday. Located behind the church, the museum has a small collection of pre-Columbian ceramics, colonial religious art, petroglyphs, and domestic utensils.

Av. Principal, behind the church. No phone. Admission 25¢. Sun 10am–2pm.

Serpentario ★ ☺   This modest serpentarium makes for a quick and fun place to learn about snakes. There are 14 different snakes on display, including a boa constrictor that they'll let you hold while you have your picture taken. A local biologist gives interpretive information.

Av. Principal. © **983-6680.** Admission $1 adults, 50¢ kids 12 and under. Mon–Thurs 8:30am–5pm; Fri–Sat 8:30am–7pm; Sun 8:30am–4pm (hours sometimes reduced during low season).

SPAS

Crater Valley Adventure Spa (see below) has a limited-service spa that offers massages, a tiny sauna, and an outdoor whirlpool, and they have an attractive outdoor pool, ringed with hammocks and lounge chairs, that they'll let you use even if you are not lodging at the hotel. (Crater Valley prefers low-key day visitors and no groups.) Surely the best spa in the area is the **Casa de Lourdes,** which opened recently. This elegant hotel has a full spa including massage, whirlpool, Turkish bath, fangotherapy, and a solarium. If you come in the morning, you can lunch at their fabulous restaurant afterward (the pool here is at their restaurant and not private enough to encourage swimming). **Yogini Spa** (© **832-2436** or 6676-8111) is a relatively new spa located on Main Street at the intersection of "Millionaires Avenue." It's run by friendly

End of the Golden Era for the Golden Frog?

Animal extinction is normally a result of habitat loss, but El Valle's amphibians are facing a more insidious enemy: *Batrachochytrium dendrobatidis.* It's a fungus that infects an amphibian and blocks the creature's ability to breathe, and it is spreading so quickly across Panama that conservationists from the U.S. have recently collected and relocated hundreds of amphibians in a Noah's Ark–style evacuation to prevent a mass extinction. Central to this tragedy is the **Golden Frog** *(Atelopus zeteki),* a beloved cultural symbol in Panama not unlike the bald eagle in the U.S. This little frog can be found on T-shirts, posters, and even lottery tickets, and historically it was considered good luck by pre-Columbian cultures. You can see the frog, among other amphibians, at El Nispero Zoo's new amphibian center. (See "What to See & Do," above.)

Canadian Michael Duchamp and offers massages, facials, and yoga classes. The place might not look like El Valle's best spa from the outside, but it's my favorite; I had an amazing 2-hour massage here, and Michael is sure to put you at ease. I recommend Yogini's after a day of hiking, biking, or rafting. There's also a holistic wellness center in the works, but it wasn't yet open at press time.

Shopping

SUNDAY MARKET ★★

El Valle is regionally famous for its Sunday Market that takes place along the town's main Avenida Principal. It's not a grand bazaar but a colorful and lively event that draws vendors, many of whom are Ngöbe-Buglé and Emberá Indians from around the area who come to hawk traditional clothing, handicrafts, baskets, ceramics, vegetables, orchids, food items, and more. There is a scaled-down version of the market open every day—Saturdays are often quite happening. Hours for the market are 8am to 5pm.

Next to the market is the **Tienda Artesanía Don Pepe** (② 983-6425; daily 8am–6pm), which has an extensive selection of well-made indigenous art and handicrafts from around Panama, plus other trinkets, souvenirs, and maps. Next door to Don Pepe is the Residencial El Valle and its ground-level shop **David's** (② 983-6536; daily 7am–7pm), with a similar, high-quality selection of handicrafts, many of which are made on the premises.

Where to Stay

There is something for every wallet in El Valle, with good budget accommodations, B&Bs, and two upscale hotels. Park Eden, Casa de Lourdes, and Los Capitanes hotels have rooms for those with disabilities, which is not common in Panama. Note that some hotels jack up their prices on weekends, even during low season. In addition to the lodging options listed below, the **Residencial el Valle** (② 983-6536 or 6615-9616; www.hotelresidencialelvalle.com) on the main street in town offers 17 basic but comfortable rooms starting at $49 a night. There is also a handicraft store downstairs. **Hotel Don Pepe** (② 983-6425) next door offers slightly cheaper prices and similar accommodations. **Hostal Cariguana** (② 983-6269 or 6761-6294; http://hostalcariguana.galeon.com) is owned and run by 101-year-old Maria

Candelaria, who also happens to be a natural medicine expert and can help you out with a cold, aches, and pains and even food poisoning. It's a humble hostel, but it has the town's best Internet cafe and some of the cheapest rates: $28 for a double, $44 for a quad. There are about 2 acres of medicinal plants behind the property.

EXPENSIVE

Canopy Lodge ★★★ ▣ Like its sister property, the Canopy Tower, this lodge caters predominately to serious bird-watchers—though its stylish sensibilities and its prime location in the lush foothills will appeal to any traveler. Unlike the Canopy Tower, there is no early-morning noise to wake up guests who are less than enthusiastic about bird-watching. Set on the shore of a meandering stream, Canopy Lodge is fresh and airy, almost minimalist, with most of the property built with river rock, wood, and glass. Guest rooms have whitewashed walls accented with just a dollop of color from Kuna Indian *mola* art. Six rooms have two queen-size beds with fluffy down comforters, two have king-size beds and bathrooms with walk-in showers, and four single rooms have a private bathroom. Glass-paneled doors open onto a long balcony, promoting a sense of oneness with the natural surroundings. Canopy Lodge sells bird-watching packages that include airport transfers, guided tours, and meals. Contact them for nightly pricing if you'd like lodging only. Keep in mind that rooms are rustic, with no TV or phone.

Road to Chorro El Macho. ✆ **264-5720** or 263-2784. www.canopylodge.com. 12 units. Packages are per person, based on 3 nights/4 days: $567–$876. AE, MC, V. **Amenities:** Restaurant; library; bird-watching and other tours. *In room:* No phone, Wi-Fi.

Los Mandarinos Hotel and Spa ★★★ The motif here is Tuscany with a touch of Panama, and all rooms are decorated with heavy wood sleigh beds and thick curtains; spare, pastel-washed walls; and white-tile floors. The bathrooms have beautiful showers tiled with river rock. There are three "villas" with a total of 18 guest rooms; the three-story villa has suites and Superior rooms with French doors that open onto terraces, and these are the best rooms for their accompanying views. Executives are standard doubles with two twins or one king-size bed. Guest rooms feature all the creature comforts of an upscale hotel, but Los Mandarinos Hotel and Spa is run somewhat like a B&B, with one 24-hour dedicated manager and a light staff, but no front desk. A 14-room tower was recently built; there are a pool, snack bar, and game area here. O'Pedros is the on-site Irish pub, serving up typical Irish fare, but it has more of a bar feel.

Calle El Ciclo. ✆ **983-6645.** 31 units. $125 executive; $155 superior; $205 junior suite. MC, V. **Amenities:** Restaurant; sports bar; babysitting; fitness center w/whirlpool, steam room, and spa; outdoor pool; room service; library. *In room:* A/C, TV, minibar.

MODERATE

Crater Valley Adventure Spa ☺ The Crater Valley Adventure Spa has lost its luster in recent years and isn't the great hotel it was before, but it's still the best lodging option for families with children, who will enjoy the climbing wall, obstacle course, and other activities. There are eight contemporary guest rooms, but each is different from the next, and some are darker than others. For the asking price, management could stand to tighten the screws on service and maintenance, repairing niggling details such as chipped tiles and ripped curtains that hang around the massage salon. Also, the hotel charges extra for every activity and amenity—so know what you're being charged for ahead of time. The hotel's sister operation, Panama Explorer Club, organizes outdoor activities. (See "Adventure Tour Operators," above.) All in all, the Crater Valley Adventure Spa has gone downhill in quality in the last few years, but is still the best option for families with young children.

Vía Ranita de Oro. © **983-6942** or 215-2325. www.crater-valley.com. 8 units. $84–$125 (up to 4 guests); $102–$128 (up to 6 guests). 2 breakfasts included in rates. AE, MC, V. **Amenities:** Cafe; bar; bike rental; kids' activities; outdoor whirlpool; outdoor pool; sauna; spa. *In room:* TV, Internet.

The Golden Frog Inn ★★ 🎁

This peaceful hotel offers six comfortable rooms with excellent beds and is one of my top lodging options in El Valle. Rooms vary in size and style, so you may want to poke your head into a couple before deciding; a few rooms have shared bathrooms. Suite no. 3 is the best for families, with its spacious interior and private veranda offering great views. What really makes this place special are the breathtaking views and meticulously maintained grounds. The small lobby, which has Wi-Fi access and a book exchange, makes a great place to enjoy the complimentary happy hour and watch the sunset. A well-stocked kitchen is available for guest use. The helpful owners, Larry and Becky Thormahlen live on-site, and are happy to help you arrange tours and excursions in the Valle de Anton region.

Calle Los Veraneras, El Hato neighborhood. Follow signs from Texaco Station at beginning of El Valle. © **983-6117** or 6565-8307. www.goldenfroginn.com. 6 units. $60–$150 double. Rates include 5-course breakfast. No credit cards. **Amenities:** Outdoor pool; Wi-Fi. *In room:* No phone.

Hotel & Restaurante Los Capitanes ☺

Set on an open space with good views of the peaks surrounding El Valle, this hotel has both budget accommodations and spacious "family" suites, as well as manicured gardens and a friendly atmosphere. The German who runs Los Capitanes was once a sea captain himself, hence the name. There are three stucco buildings. One building is divided into polygon rooms that are differently sized and decorated; some buildings are kid-friendly with bunks and cubbyhole type rooms; one building has a loftlike, second-floor sleeping area perfect for kids. Rooms on the second floor have balconies. All rooms here are clean but modest and some have a slight mildew smell, so you may want to see a couple of rooms first. Around the property are seating areas with outdoor tables, and they have one of the best (and most popular) restaurants in town. (See "Where to Dine," below.) Note that the owner has begun organizing fun, full-day mule rides for guests, which no other hotel offers. Like the Crater Valley Hotel, Los Capitanes has a bit of an abandoned feel to it and could use a bit of a rejuvenation.

Calle de la Coopertiva. © **983-6080.** www.los-capitanes.com. 14 units. $66 double; $88 junior suite. Rates include breakfast. MC, V. **Amenities:** Restaurant; bar; bicycle rental; kids' pool; Internet room; room service. *In room:* TV, fridge.

Hotel Rincón Vallero

The Rincón Vallero has some of the best suites and junior suites in El Valle, but it also has kennel-like double rooms that are not much value, probably because the hotel complex has been adding units like patchwork without maintaining quality. It's altogether a funky but friendly place, with a kids' play area, ponds, and tiny streams that meander through the property, and ceramic toadstools and other decor that make the complex feel a little like a fairyland. The low-slung building has ground-floor rooms only, with separate cabinlike units in the back, behind their popular restaurant. The suites are large enough to feel like a spacious one-bedroom apartment, especially room no. 1, which like the other suites has sloping, bamboo-inlaid ceilings and interesting sunken showers tiled entirely in chipped rock and fitted with a skylight. Doubles are cramped, with small bathrooms, and they don't feature the quality craftsmanship found in the suites.

Calle Espavé. © **983-6167** or 6695-6190. www.hotelrinconvallero.com. 17 units. $83 standard; $105 junior suite; $138 suite. AE, MC, V. **Amenities:** Restaurant; bar; kids' playground; outdoor pool and kids' pool; room service; billiard table; Ping-Pong table. *In room:* A/C, TV, minibar.

Park Eden Bed & Breakfast ★★ 📔   I absolutely love the Park Eden. It exemplifies the true definition of a B&B: lots of charming, country decor; hearty breakfasts; and warm, gracious service provided by Lionel and Monica, the couple who have owned the property for more than 20 years. Every room is different from the next and will appeal to different kinds of people. There is a two-story, snug house with room for four guests and a full kitchen; other rooms come with refrigerators, microwaves, and coffeemakers. The Limoneros room is more masculine and has a small private patio, while two others are done in pastels and decorated with figurines and lacy curtains. All units have private entrances. Although they do not have a restaurant, if you arrange it in advance, they will happily serve lunch or a romantic candlelit dinner. Park Eden is popular with bird-watchers and receives lots of return visitors.

Calle Espavé #7. © **983-6167** or 6695-6190. www.parkeden.com. 8 units. $100 double; $135 room with full kitchen; $225 house for 4. AE, MC, V. **Amenities:** Bike rentals; tours. *In room:* A/C, TV, fridge, hair dryer, microwave, no phone.

INEXPENSIVE

Anton Valley Hotel 🖋   Previously the Golden Valley Hotel, this is an excellent choice for those who don't have a car or would rather be in town. The hotel is on the main road, and rooms are small but fresh, with a choice of queen-size or twin orthopedic beds. There is also a decently sized family suite. Though not luxurious, this hotel's bright rooms, common barbecue area, and cheerful decor make it a good value for the money. The peaceful breakfast cafe serves delicious and cheap Panamanian and American breakfast fare. Bruschetta's Restaurant has relocated here.

Av. Principal. © **983-6097.** www.antonvalleyhotel.com. 10 units. $50–$65 double; $75–$85 suite. MC, V. **Amenities:** Restaurant (breakfast only); bike rental; room service. *In room:* TV, fridge, Wi-Fi.

Where to Dine

If you're just looking for a snack, a cup of coffee, or even a to-go sandwich or picnic lunch, stop off at **El Valle Gourmet & Coffee Shop** on the main street (© **6715-5785;** Fri noon–9pm, Sat 9am–10:30pm, and Sun and holidays 9am–6pm). The shop has juices, coffee, imported cheeses and cold cuts, sandwiches, frozen meals, jams, tinned delicacies, and more. **Santa Librada** on the main street also serves up generous portions of tasty local Panamanian fare. For breakfast, you can't beat the **Anton Valley Hotel** breakfast, where $2 or $3 will get you a very tasty traditional American or Panamanian breakfast. **Bambusillo** (© **983-5004**) doubles as an art gallery and cafeteria and is a good option for light and healthy vegetarian fare. **Juice Bar,** Calle la Pintada (© **6414-5223;** open daily 10am–8pm), sells all kinds of fruit juices for $1.25 to $2.50.

EXPENSIVE

Cumana ★★★ INTERNATIONAL   The hottest restaurant in town is actually located in a humble home owned by a German/Panamanian couple. The menu changes monthly, and there is almost always live music. The restaurant only opens Thursday, Fridays, and Saturdays, so it's best to make a reservation if you're in town during high season, as the place tends to fill up pretty quickly. For a flat rate of $25, you get an appetizer, main course, and dessert. Expect tasty specialities such as pork shoulder in brandy and strawberry sauce, peanut-crusted fish filet with spinach purée, or veal steak in fig and blue cheese sauce. This unique dining experience is considered one of the best places to eat by locals and is quickly toppling La Casa de Lourdes' claim as the best place to eat in El Valle. There is often live music and a lively crowd of mostly expats and tourists.

Calle LaReforma, just before the Cabañas Potosí. ℂ **6667-5001.** Reservations recommended. Multi-course meal $28. No credit cards. Fri–Sat 7pm until last guest leaves; Sun noon until the last guest leaves.

La Casa de Lourdes ★★★ CONTEMPORARY PANAMANIAN Some diners drive from Panama City to El Valle (2 hr. each way) just to dine at this regionally famous place. Lourdes Fábrega de Ward studied with Martha Stewart and Paul Prudhomme, and her well-honed flair and technique are evident in every dish she prepares. What I like best is how she uses so many exotic Panamanian fruit and vegetables in her meals, such as roast pork with guayabera sauce, or Sunday morning mimosas with marayón (a little like passion fruit). Do not miss the yuca croquettes, clam chowder, or any of the seafood dishes, which change weekly but could include sole with trout mousse, or a blackened sea bass in tamarind sauce. The mostly outdoor dining area is under giant arches of a Tuscan-style manor house, next to an outdoor pool. Saturdays and Sundays are absolutely packed, so come with a reservation if you can. Keep in mind that gourmet means smaller portions, so if you're very hungry you may want to look elsewhere.

Calle El Ciclo. ℂ **983-6450.** www.lacasadelourdes.com. Reservations required on weekends and recommended for all other days. Main courses $8–$18. AE, MC, V. Wed–Mon 7:30am–9pm (to 10pm Fri–Sat).

MODERATE

El Rincón Vallero PERUVIAN/PANAMANIAN The best thing about Rincón Vallero is that it's usually open when other restaurants are closed. At dinner, low-hanging lamps provide for a cozy, warm ambience, but the dining area is a little oddball with flagstone floors that wrap around three interior fishponds—be careful where you walk or you might fall in. The menu features a lot of dishes that can be prepared multiple ways, including grilled sea bass with nine different preparations, and pastas including ravioli, cannelloni, and spaghetti with a variety of sauces. Their Panamanian classics, such as jumbo shrimp with garlic and spices, are quite good, as are their Peruvian dishes—a carry-over from the days when a Peruvian owned the hotel/restaurant.

Calle Espavé. ℂ **983-6167.** Main courses $5–$12. AE, MC, V. Daily 7:30–10:30am, noon–3:30pm, and 6–9pm.

Los Capitanes ★ GERMAN Part of the Los Capitanes hotel, the restaurant and bar here are quite popular with locals and tourists alike. It's a 10-minute walk from the main street. The restaurant is housed in a stone-and-metal *bohio;* an outdoor dining area is the site of weekend barbecues during the summer. The food is hearty and good, consisting mostly of German dishes such as smoked pork chops with sauerkraut, *leberkäse* (a German meatloaf), and meat or seafood platters for a group (priced per person: $6.75 paella, $12 meat, $13 seafood). The breakfast menu offers tasty fare such as German pancakes with apples.

Calle de la Coopertiva. ℂ **983-6080.** Main courses $7.75–$10. MC, V. Daily 8am–9pm.

INEXPENSIVE

Don Pepe ★ PANAMANIAN   If you're looking for a cheap, quick, and simple meal, this is your place. It's a bit like a diner, but the staff is very friendly and the prices are low. Everything from Chinese food to Panamanian dishes to hamburgers is on offer; try their *ropa vieja,* a stewed beef dish, or carrot mousse flan. Also on the menu are sandwiches, vegetarian items, and fresh fruit juices and shakes.

Av. Principal. © **983-6425.** Reservations not accepted. Main courses $3–$8. MC, V. Mon–Thurs 7am–9pm; Fri–Sun 7am–11pm.

Pizzería Pinocchio's PIZZA   Pizzeria Pinocchio's recently changed locations, but thin-crust pizzas baked in a wood oven are still the specialty here, and they are the best pizzas in town, with a dozen varieties to choose from. Rounding out the menu are traditional pastas, such as lasagna and spaghetti. The ambience is cafeteria-like—if it doesn't suit you, order your pizza to go.

Calle del Hato, on road to Hotel Campestre. © **983-6715.** Reservations not accepted. Pizzas $4–$5.50. No credit cards. Fri 4–9pm; Sat–Sun and holidays noon–9pm.

WESTERN COCLÉ PROVINCE & PENONOMÉ

145km (90 miles) W of Panama City

The Coclé Province from Penonomé to Aguadulce is scarcely visited by foreign tourists, and although local municipalities have initiated the first stages of organized tourism, the region is not yet poised to become a hot spot. Historical, cultural, and natural attractions are scattered around in such a fashion that renting a vehicle or booking a custom tour is key to exploring the area, unless you're headed straight for the Cerro La Vieja outside of Penonomé. Travelers normally visit this area on their way to the Azuero Peninsula, or as a side trip from the Pacific Coast. In this section, villages are highlighted only if they have at least one worthwhile attraction.

The capital of the Coclé Province is **Penonomé,** a town that for a few years during the 17th century was the nation's capital after Panama City had been sacked by the pirate Henry Morgan. Little of the town's colonial history is evident today, and really there isn't much to do and see in Penonomé apart from visiting the **Mercado de Artesanías** and **Museo de Penonomé.**

The **Mercado de Artesanías** (Mon–Fri 9am–5pm) is located on the Interamericana Highway just before the exit for Penonomé. You'll find a limited selection of mostly Ngöbe-Buglé indigenous handicrafts and clothing. If you're driving to the Azuero Peninsula, you might consider a quick stop to see what they have here and continue on your way. Near the plaza is the small yet interesting **Museo de Penonomé** ★ (© **997-8490;** Mon–Sat 9am–12:30pm and 1:30–4pm, Sun 9:30am–1pm; $1 adults, 25¢ kids) on Calle San Antonio at Parque Rubén Darío Carles in what's left of the San Antonio colonial neighborhood. The museum occupies four adjoining homes and displays colonial religious art, pre-Columbian artifacts, and artifacts from the town's initial stages.

I don't recommend that you lodge in Penonomé—there are far better options on the Pacific Coast or at the Cerro La Vieja or La Iguana (see below). You'll only find utilitarian lodging in Penonomé, and most of it is located along the not-so-glamorous

Interamericana Highway. If you are in a pinch, and really need an inexpensive place to lay your head down, try the **Hotel La Pradera,** which has clean, modern rooms, a restaurant, and a pool (© **991-0106;** $35 Mon–Thurs, $43 Fri–Sun; MasterCard and Visa are accepted). You'll see it near the western entrance to Penonomé.

Heading north out of Penonomé, **La Pintada** village (see below) is regionally known for its own handicrafts fair and especially for its locally renowned straw hats and its cigar factory.

Getting There & Departing

BY BUS   Buses leave every 20 minutes from Panama City's Albrook Terminal to Penonomé; it takes a little over 2 hours and costs $4. You'll be dropped off on the Interamericana Highway on the opposite side of the Hotel Dos Continentes. From here, there are local buses to La Pintada that leave every 20 minutes and cost $1. You can also grab a taxi to take you to La Pintada for $3.

BY CAR   The drive to Penonomé takes 2 hours. The exit is clearly signed and is at the Hotel Dos Continentes.

La Pintada

About 20 minutes from Penonomé is the charming, sleepy village of La Pintada, known for its *sombreros pintados,* or "painted hats," made from intricately hand-woven black and white fibers of the *bellota* plant. It's a long, arduous task to create this traditional hat, and prices average $75 to $80, twice that amount if bought in Panama City. You'll find a good selection of *sombreros pintados* at the **Mercado de Artesanías La Pintada ★** (Tues–Sun 9am–5pm), as well as *montuño* embroidered shirts, woven rugs, dolls dressed in folkloric dresses such as the pollera, and other regional knickknacks. The market is on the left side of the main road from Penonomé, once you enter La Pintada.

Another unique attraction is a factory tour of **Cigarros de Panamá ★** (© **6896-7120**). These are the only premium cigars in Panama made with Cuban-seed tobacco. Miriam Padilla launched her cigar operation in the early 1980s with Cuban partners who eventually moved on. After a hiatus for many years, Miriam rebuilt the business and now each month produces more than 300,000 fine cigars, handcrafted in the Cuban tradition, for export. A box of 25 of her cigars sells for about $85 in the U.S., but you can buy them wholesale here. You'll see the factory, which is well signed, just before you enter La Pintada.

TWO ECOLODGES OUTSIDE OF PENONOME

Both lodges mentioned here are located on the road to Churuquita Grande and Caimito. To get here, turn into Penonomé at Hotel Dos Continentes on the Interamericana Highway, then turn right (northeast) onto the road to Churuquita and Caimito. La Iguana is 14km (8½ miles) from the turnoff; the Cerro La Vieja is about the same distance from La Iguana (28km/17 miles from the turnoff to Caimito). Cerro La Vieja will pick you up in Penonomé; for the La Iguana, take a taxi from Penonomé.

Cerro La Vieja ★★ 🛏️   The undulating landscape that surrounds the lodge is cloaked in thick, green jungle and dominated by a tor-like hill called Cerro La Vieja, among other peaks in the distance. The property comprises 19 spacious rooms divided into thatched-roof cabins, with four rooms to each cabin. Guest rooms are not ultra-deluxe and the decor is spare—yet they're perfectly comfortable and have quality beds. By far the best rooms are the Turega and Chichibalí units because of the views and balconies; these units are considered "Premier" rooms and are more expensive even though they're the same size as a standard, but they have a view. There are several trails around the property for hiking, and unique mule rides can be organized, among other excursions. Rates are nightly and include breakfast; sample 2-night packages include three daily meals consisting of delicious organic cuisine, two spa treatments, and two eco-tours for $183 per person.

Caimito, Coclé Province. ⓒ **983-8905** in Panama, or 786/206-0219 in the U.S. www.posadalavieja.com. 18 units. $79 double standard; $109 double premier. MC, V. **Amenities:** Restaurant; bar; full-service spa w/massage, facials, and thermal baths. *In room:* A/C (some units), no phone.

La Iguana Eco-Resort ☺ This ecolodge does not offer luxury or a spa, but it does offer pleasant nature trails, a river, a pool for swimming, a minizoo, a playground, and other outdoor activities like horseback riding—all in all, it's an ideal place for kids, but with so few people here, couples will feel perfectly comfortable, too. La Iguana is very inexpensive and nothing fancy, but the new administration recently spruced up the property and repainted guest rooms; each has two double beds and three singles in a loftlike second floor, for a total of five people. Bathrooms are private but without hot water. The owners of La Iguana love nature, and even the minizoo is part of their effort to repopulate the area with endemic species that have been in decline. The lodge's restaurant specializes in barbecued meats and seafood, and though simple, the meals are quite good. For an additional price, they'll organize tours around the Coclé area.

Churuquita Grande. ⓒ **991-0879** or 6785-7550. www.laiguanaresort.com. 8 units. $25–$35 for 2 people; each additional person is $5. No credit cards. **Amenities:** Restaurant; kids' playground; outdoor pool. *In room:* A/C (in some rooms, and for an additional price), no phone.

Parque Arqueológico El Caño

El Caño Archaeological Park displays the excavated burial grounds and artifacts of indigenous groups that inhabited this region from A.D. 500 to 1500. Considering that it is one of the most important archaeological sites in Panama, it's surprising that you don't even need a full hour to take it all in—much of what was found was shipped to the U.S. when an American amateur archaeologist excavated the site in the 1920s. More importantly, it is estimated that many unearthed burial sites still exist here, yet there is little interpretive information about these or other items. Nevertheless, if you're in the area, this 8.1-hectare (20-acre) park makes for an interesting stop. There are burial mounds and a burial pit with skeletons still intact; a small museum with pottery, tools, and other artifacts taken from burial sites; and a reproduction of what the site is imagined to have originally looked like. (Hours are Tues–Sat 9am–noon and 12:30–4pm, Sun 9am–1pm; admission $1 adults, 25¢ kids.) To get here, take the exit for El Caño, about 27km (19 miles) west of Penonomé, and continue for 3km (1¾ miles), always keeping to the left until you reach the site. If you don't have a vehicle, you'll need to take a taxi from Natá.

Natá

Natá is the oldest village in Panama, founded by the Spanish in 1522 and named after the powerful *cacique* Natá who once ruled this region. Natá is known for its venerable church **Basilica Menor Santiago Apostal de Natá,** which was erected during the same year and is therefore considered to be the oldest surviving church in the Americas. Extensive renovations took place during the 1990s, yet visitors can still appreciate the church's original wooden columns, altars, and artwork. The church is located on the plaza, about a half-mile from the Interamericana Highway. Natá is 180km (112 miles) from Panama City, and 31km (20 miles) from Penonomé.

LA PENÍNSULA DE AZUERO

From Panama City: Chitré is 250km (155 miles), Las Tablas is 282km (175 miles), and Pedasí is 324km (201 miles)

Entering the Azuero Peninsula past Divisa, you'll feel as if you've gone back in time a hundred years. The Azuero Peninsula is considered the cradle of Panamanian folklore and rural culture, passed down from Spanish colonists who settled here during the 17th and 18th centuries. The region is dotted with terra-cotta-tile-and-gingerbread representations of early Spanish villas, and everything is very, very slowly paced—except when residents join together for the raucous festivities for which this region is famous. Nowhere in Panama is **Carnaval** celebrated with as much gusto as it is here in the Azuero, especially in towns such as Las Tablas and Chitré; and religious festivals honoring saints are livened with fireworks, music, and costumed folkloric dances that are as pagan as they are Catholic. Really, the best time to visit the peninsula is during Carnaval, though you'll want to be sure to book your hotel in advance. The Azuero Peninsula is the birthplace of the pollera, widely considered to be one of the most beautiful traditional dresses in the world. *Seco,* the sugar-cane alcohol and national drink, hails from this region, too. But what makes the Azuero Peninsula special are its people. Panamanians are remarkably friendly, but Azuero residents are beguiling in their fondness for greeting strangers, so practice your *"buenos días"* and get ready to smile.

The Azuero Peninsula protrudes south from the Panamanian isthmus into the Pacific Ocean, separating the Gulf of Panama to the east and the Gulf of Chiriquí to the west; most of the peninsula is within the Herrera and Los Santos provinces. It is about 100km (60 miles) wide and 90km (55 miles) long and, sadly, most of the terrain has been completely denuded because of the region's large-scale cattle production. Indeed, a visitor who has just come from the green and lush panorama farther north is in for a surprise here in the Azuero. Some areas, such as Sarigua National Park, have been so thoroughly stripped of vegetation that they are now considered a desert. Oddly, most towns sit inland despite the beautiful coastline here—but investors and foreigners are starting to move in, especially near Pedasí and Playa Venado. This pristine coast could see changes during the next few decades.

So where to go and how to best see this region? You'll notice that destinations or towns in this section seem to include only the highlights, but in most cases there is just one museum or one church to see in each village. Also, decent lodging is scarce here, the reason you won't see much listed outside of Chitré and Pedasí. My advice

FESTIVALS & events IN THE AZUERO PENINSULA

Residents of the Azuero Peninsula seemingly live for festivals, and here they are livelier than anywhere else in the country. The following are the major festivals, but the list is by no means comprehensive. Check the ATP tourism board's website at **www.visit panama.com** for information about all events taking place during your visit.

February: Carnaval kicks off the Friday before Ash Wednesday and continues until the following Tuesday in this nationwide event—and it's at its rowdiest and most colorful here in the Azuero. See "Party On! Carnaval in the Azuero Peninsula" on p. 204.

March/April: Semana Santa's most colorful celebration is in La Villa de Los Santos and Guararé.

Late April: Feria Internacional del Azuero in La Villa de Los Santos. As at a county fair, this features animal displays, food stalls, and drinking.

June: Festival Corpus Christi in La Villa de Los Santos. This village explodes with activity for the 2-week festival known for its elaborate dances led by men in devil masks.

July 20 to July 22: Festival Patronales de La Virgen de Santa Librada in Las Tablas. This festival is famous for its **Festival de la Pollera** on July 22, which showcases the region's most beautiful polleras and elects the year's "Queen of the Pollera."

September 24: Festival de la Mejorana in Guararé. This nationally famous folkloric festival sees hundreds of dancers, musicians, and singers converging for a week of events and serious partying.

October 19: Fundación del Distrito de Chitré in Chitré. A large festival with parades celebrates the founding of the city.

November 10: Grito de la Villa, or "Cry of Independence," in Villa de Los Santos. Commemorates this national independence holiday with parades and music.

is to rent a car in Panama City or Chitré and take in the sights at your own pace, stopping from town to town and lodging near Pedasí. This picturesque village has the widest range of lodging and dining options, is close to beaches, and has snorkeling, surfing, and diving, too. If you have a car, you'll also be able to stop at roadside stands that dot the Carretera Nacional and sell everything from fresh watermelon to sausages; there are *fondas,* or cheap food stands, too, with fried Panamanian snacks, as well as open-air cantinas that sell three beers for $1. There are no commercial flights to Chitré and Pedasí (though there are charter flights). Bus service is inexpensive, but you'll need a taxi to get around from the station. It takes more than 4 hours to reach Pedasí by vehicle from Panama City; those with enough time might consider breaking up the trip with a stay in El Valle or on the Pacific Coast.

Parita

About 25km (16 miles) after Divisa is Parita, one of the most charming villages in Panama. It's a very humble place, but the streets are lined with well-preserved examples of Spanish colonial architecture. At the plaza is the **Iglesia de Santo**

Domingo de Guzmán, but apart from this there really aren't any attractions here other than city streets to be wandered and photographed. If you're driving along the Azuero Peninsula, make this a quick stop on your itinerary.

Chitré

Chitré is the capital of Herrera Province, and it is the largest town on the Azuero Peninsula, founded in 1848. Many of the streets here ooze charm, yet on the whole Chitré isn't as picturesque as Pedasí. Many of its colonial buildings have been replaced by more utilitarian structures, and the downtown bustles with shops hawking cheap plastic goods and clothing. Chitré does offer plentiful services, including lodging and car rental, and it can be a convenient base for exploring the region, but don't expect 17th century colonial charm. Visitors during Carnaval will find higher-quality lodging here than in Las Tablas, but this option is better for those with a rental vehicle (don't forget that Chitré is pretty lively, too, during Carnaval). Before arriving at Chitré, you'll pass through the tiny village of La Arena, which is described below in "What to See & Do."

You'll see an **ATP tourism office** just before you enter La Arena, but the location is not very convenient, on Calle 19 de Octubre—when the road forks in La Arena, head right toward La Villa los Santos (✆ **974-4532;** daily 8:30am–4:30pm). The tourism office has a helpful staff and a limited amount of printed information about the history of the area and attractions.

FAST FACTS   Banks: There are 24-hour ATMs at HSBC bank on Avenida Herrera, ½ block north from the plaza; and Banco Nacional on Paseo Enrique Greenzier, near the Hotel Versailles. **Internet:** Sanchi (✆ **996-2134**), at Calle Aminta Burgos de Amado, 1 block west from the plaza, is open daily from 8am to 11pm. **Laundry:** Lavandería Express is on Avenida Herrera, ½ block from the plaza. **Police:** ✆ **996-4333.**

GETTING THERE & DEPARTING   By Plane   At press time, there were no regularly scheduled commercial flights between Panama City and Chitré. To charter a private flight, contact **Air Panama** (✆ **316-9043**); **Aeroperlas** also does charters (✆ **315-7570**).

BY BUS & TAXI   The **Transportes de Herrera bus terminal,** a $1.15 taxi ride from the center of town, is located on Calle 19 de Octubre (also called Av. Roberto Ramírez de Diego). The turnoff for this street is next to the Hotel Hong Kong. Buses to and from Panama City cost $7 and run every hour between 6am and 6pm; the trip is 3½ hours. Buses to Las Tablas leave every 15 minutes from 6am to 6:30pm and cost $1.25. For buses to Pedasí, you'll need a bus to Las Tablas, and then you must transfer to a Pedasí-bound bus. Or you can take a taxi for $25.

BY CAR   When you arrive at La Arena, just before Chitré, the road forks; take the left road and continue along the Carretera Nacional, which will take you directly into the center of town. If you turn right at the plaza, the road will funnel back into the Carretera Nacional south to La Villa de los Santos. Chitré is 37km (23 miles) from the start of the Carretera Nacional at Divisa, and 252km (157 miles) from Panama City.

For **rental cars** in Chitré, **Thrifty** (✆ **996-9565;** www.thrifty.com), is on Paseo Enrique Geenzier, just west of the Hotel Versalles.

WHAT TO SEE & DO

There really isn't much to do in the town itself, other than pay a quick visit to the **Museo de Herrera** (© 996-0077; Tues–Sat 9am–4pm; admission $1 at press time) at Calle Manuel María Correa and Avenida Julio Arjona; you'll recognize the whitewashed colonial building—it sticks out from its more modern neighbors. The museum staff has put a lot of effort into providing visitors with a better understanding of the anthropology and ecology of the Herrera Province, but however well-meaning the staff is, the museum is clearly under-funded. Still, there are a few gems here, including pottery dating back to 2500 B.C., and folkloric costumes and polleras. There is a small library with research books about the region; signs are in Spanish only, but the staff is working on an English-language informational brochure.

Take a step into the lovely **Catedral de San Juan Bautista** on the plaza, built at the turn of the 20th century with a bold stone exterior and exposed-wood interior with stained glass and chandeliers.

La Arena

This tiny artisans' village is almost entirely dedicated to pottery making, which began during pre-Columbian times. Most of the vendors who hawk their ceramics along the two principal streets here sell gaily painted pots called *tinajas,* which traditionally were used as all-purpose storage vases but are now primarily decorative. There are also wall hangings, flowerpots, and animal figurines, but the best buy here: reproductions of terra-cotta-colored pre-Columbian vases and other such storage vessels. You'll have to look around to find these since it seems that the artisans are opting to create more modern styles, most of which are a little gaudy and not particularly attractive. For a good selection, head to the **Mercado de Artesanías** in the large, white building found where the road divides near the center of town (no phone; daily 9am–4:30pm). For traditional, pre-Columbian-influenced pottery, visit **Cerámica Calderón** (© 974-4946; daily 7am–5pm), whose owner, Angel Calderón, has been handcrafting beautiful, museum-quality pieces for half a century. Angel and his artisans offer to show visitors how the pieces are made, from pottery wheel to the voluminous ovens out back. The workshop is on the right just as you enter town. La Arena is only 2km (1¼ miles) west of Chitré.

Parque Nacional Sarigua (Sarigua National Park)

Ranking as one of the more bizarre national parks in Panama, Sarigua National Park protects nearly 809 hectares (2,000 acres) of lunarlike wasteland caused by the total destruction of native forest by settlers clearing land for cattle. The park protects large mangrove swamps along the coast, but mostly the protected area is something akin to a desert—or so they'd like you to believe, but really, a visit here provides you with a vivid example of the devastation that occurs when indiscriminate deforestation takes place. After settlers cleared the region of its coastal forests, the forces of wind, ebbing tides, and rain eroded the acidic soil here, leaving deep fissures and oddly shaped land formations. The fascinating sight is, more than anything, a good lesson about protection of forests.

The park lies along the coast and is reached by a well-signed road off the Carretera Nacional, about 10km (6 miles) from Chitré; after the turnoff continue following the signs. There is an ANAM park-ranger station with a lookout point over the expanse of Sarigua (admission $3), and that's about it. But if you've got the time, stop for a quick look.

WHERE TO STAY & DINE

Hotel Guayacanes ★ ☺   It isn't luxurious, but it is the most upscale hotel in Chitré. The Guayacanes is close to the bus terminal and about a 5-minute drive or taxi ride from the main drag, which is ideal if you're looking for a tucked-away location to repair to after a day on the streets—but not ideal if you want close contact with the local scene. It is set on a spacious property and has a casino, an outdoor pool (which can get busy on weekends), gardens, and a kids' play area, among other amenities. Guests are allowed access to the Chitré Golf Club, too. The guest rooms are within a couple of cookie-cutter buildings fanned around a pleasant, artificial lagoon. The rooms are average size, with a country decor and ceramic floors. Farther south are certainly more interesting places to stay, but considering the amenities offered here and the price, this hotel is an excellent value. There are two good, open-air/indoor restaurants that serve international dishes (daily 7am–11pm), and they allow **day visits** to their pool for $6.30 adults, $4.75 kids, which includes a snack between 10am and 6pm.

Vía Circunvalación. ℂ **996-9758.** www.losguayacanes.com. 64 units. $99 double; $116 triple. Breakfast included in rates. AE, MC, V. **Amenities:** 2 restaurants; 2 bars; disco; casino; kids' play area; gym; outdoor pool; tennis courts. *In room:* A/C, TV, hair dryer.

Hotel Hong Kong ☺   Situated on the busy Carretera Nacional, this hotel does not claim the most glamorous of locations, but kids love their on-site aquatic park. Notwithstanding its Chinese-style roof, the hotel exterior looks like any run-of-the-mill U.S. chain; inside, the Hong Kong motif continues with Chinese art and furnishings. Guest rooms are clean and comfortable, with decent, but slightly garish, furniture, and the price is nice. You can't really walk anywhere except to a McDonald's and other strip-mall-style stores. The aquatic park has three swimming pools and a large, tubular water slide. On weekends, this is a popular place for kids celebrating their birthdays, so expect crowds. The restaurant serves Chinese and international dishes, but is not particularly memorable.

Carretera Nacional at Vía Circunvalación. ℂ **996-4483** or 996-9180. www.hotelhongkongpanama. com. 30 units. $55 double; $100 during festivals. AE, MC, V. **Amenities:** Restaurant; bar; aquatic park. *In room:* A/C, TV.

Hotel Rex ★   I like this hotel because it is right on the plaza, it has a decent on-site restaurant and mini–business center with Internet access. There's nothing fancy about the place; the rooms are spartan and the beds are average, but there is hot water and even cable TV. Try to get a brighter room on one of the top floors, but if you can't, you can use the common terrace to look out onto the plaza. Finicky travelers should go elsewhere, but if you're trying to curb your costs, this is your place.

I also recommend their ground-floor restaurant **El Mesón,** which overlooks the plaza and features a lengthy menu with something for everyone, including seafood, traditional Panamanian and Spanish dishes, tacos, pasta, sandwiches, and a kids' menu. If you're really hungry, order one of their *parrilladas*, a selection of meats served on a mini-barbecue. The restaurant is open daily from 7am to 1pm; prices are about $4.50 to $9.

Central plaza *(parque)*. ℂ **996-4310.** hotelrexchitre@hotmail.com. 32 units. $44 double; $55 double with king-size bed; $90–$110 during Carnaval and other festivals. AE, MC, V. **Amenities:** Restaurant. *In room:* A/C, TV.

Hotel Versalles   Despite its boxy, bland exterior, the Hotel Versalles has a sooth-ing lobby full of plants and a central patio with a small outdoor pool, giving you the sensation of being in the Tropics and not in the dry city of Chitré. Guest rooms are modern and clean, but a little musty and with run-of-the-mill decor commonly found in midrange chain hotels. Indeed, there's not a lot of charm here, but it's a good value nonetheless. Amenities such as assistance with rental vehicles and admission to the local Chitré Golf Club are available. To get to the town center, you'll need to walk about 10 minutes along a busy road. Doubles have either one or two queen-size beds. The **restaurant** is one of the better dining options in town, serving national dishes such as tasty grilled and fried seafood with rice and beans, and international dishes with a little more flair, plus sandwiches and snacks. The restaurant is open daily from 6:30am to 10:30pm.

Paseo Enrique Geenzier. ✆ **996-4422** or 996-3133. www.hotelversalles.com. 60 units. $50–$66 dou-ble. AE, MC, V. **Amenities:** Restaurant; bar; access to the Chitré Golf Club; outdoor pool; room service. *In room:* A/C, TV, Wi-Fi.

La Villa de los Santos

Just 4km (2½ miles) south of Chitré, you'll cross over Río la Villa and into Los Santos Province. A few minutes later, you'll arrive at the colonial town La Villa de Los Santos, often referred to simply as "Los Santos." This is the site of the famous "Cry of Inde-pendence," when Panamanians issued the first official request to liberate themselves from Spanish rule. The letter of request was signed on November 10, 1821, inside what is now the **Museo de la Nacionalidad** (✆ **966-8192;** Tues–Sat 8am–4pm; admission $1 adults, 75¢ students, 25¢ kids 11 and under). The most interesting aspect of the museum, located on the northwest side of Parque Simon Bolívar, is the lovely building it is housed in, with lofty ceilings and handmade ceramic floors. The curators have set up the room to show how it would have looked during the signing of the declaration. There is also a display of pre-Columbian ceramics and other odds and ends, but not enough to keep you here more than 15 minutes.

More worthwhile is a visit to the most beautiful church in the Azuero Peninsula, **Iglesia de San Atanacio,** also located on the Bolívar plaza. This baroque, statu-esque church was declared a national monument because most of the interior deco-rative work is intact from the year it opened, 1782. Some features of the church are even older—the church was built in stages beginning with the retablo (the structure forming the back of the altar) in 1721, and the ornamented archway in 1733. The altar and archway are simply gorgeous, intricately carved with cherubs and flowers that are almost completely covered with gold leaf and decorative paint. There is also a wooden, full-scale sculpture of Christ, as well as plaques designating the names of priests who are buried here.

WHERE TO STAY & DINE

Hotel la Villa ★   This midsize hotel is laid out in a motel-like fashion, and offers modest yet pleasant accommodations at a good price. The highlight here is the swimming pool, surrounded by palm trees and leafy vegetation, but the rooms are okay, too—if you book in their newer wing (avoid the dingy, older wing). They're nothing fancy, but the beds are decent, and the clean rooms feature a bit of folkloric art and a good air-conditioning system. There's a restaurant on-site. Just before entering Las Villas, you'll see signs for the hotel and the Restaurant Las Palmeras.

The national dress, the pollera, is from the Azuero Peninsula and is considered to be one of the most beautiful traditional dresses in the world. It consists of a full, gathered skirt over several petticoats, and a flounced top, intricately embroidered with floral designs and trimmed with lace. The pollera is worn during special occasions, and would not be complete without *mosquetas* and *tembelques,* or gold and pearl jewelry, as well as hair combs encrusted with pearls. A pollera takes several months to a year to make, and can cost thousands of dollars.

La Villa de los Santos. ☏ **966-8201.** Fax 966-8201. 38 units. $40–$99 double in new wing; $26 double in older units. V. **Amenities:** Restaurant; outdoor pool. *In room:* A/C, TV.

Kiosco El Ciruelo PANAMANIAN   This roadside, cantina-style restaurant is the locals' favorite. Food is cooked over a wood fire, so it's definitely rustic. Expect Panamanian specialties: El Ciruelo is known for its spicy, pork-filled tamales, and there are soups and barbecued meats, too.

La Villa de los Santos. 3km (1¾ miles) southeast of town. No phone. Main courses $1.50–$6. No credit cards. Days and hours vary, although typically daily 11am–8pm.

Guarare

This blink-and-you-miss-it village is nationally famous for its yearly **La Mejorana** festival (see "Festivals & Events in the Azuero Peninsula" on p. 198); you'll notice the permanent stage set up in the plaza. Guararé has its charms, but the village is so tranquil it feels almost abandoned. If you're driving past, take a quick spin through town and visit the **Museo Manuel F. Zarate** (☏ 994-5644; Tues–Sat 8am–4pm; admission 75¢ adults, 25¢ kids 12 and under), on Calle 21, 2 blocks behind the church. Located within the graceful old home of the founder of La Mejorana festival, this quaint folkloric museum, like all the region's museums, strives to do more but is under-funded. Expect to find dusty displays of polleras from the early 1900s, devil masks, and photos of past reigning queens of La Mejorana festival. Guararé is located 26km (16 miles) south of Chitré; turn on the road at the grocery store.

Las Tablas

Las Tablas is the provincial capital of Los Santos, known as the "cradle of national folklore" chiefly for its famous **Carnaval** festivities (see "Party on! Carnaval in the Azuero Peninsula," below). The spruce town is made of adobe colonial homes with iron balustrades and terra-cotta roofs, interspersed with more modern, utilitarian architecture and service-oriented businesses. It has more of a city feel to it than even Chitré, but really, it's a quiet place without much to see or do except wander the streets and relax in the plaza with an ice-cream cone. Most tourists visit Las Tablas only for Carnaval, or on their way south to Pedasí.

The town's sole museum, **Museo de Belisario Porras** (☏ 994-6326; Tues–Sat 8am–4pm; admission 50¢ adults, 25¢ kids), located on the south side of the plaza, pays homage to Panama's national hero and three-term president Dr. Belisario Porras, who died in 1942. The museum is inside Porras's old home, and features military decorations, stamps with his likeness, and documents pertaining to his time spent as a national leader, but this museum is easily skipped.

GETTING THERE & DEPARTING

BY BUS OR TAXI The bus terminal is located about 5 blocks north of the plaza, on the Carretera Nacional and Avenida Dr. Emilio Castro. Buses to Las Tablas from Panama City leave every hour from 6am to 7pm. Buses to Panama City generally leave every hour from 6am until about 5:30pm. Hours change frequently, so it's a good idea to pop in and buy your ticket and check schedules; the fare is $8 for buses with air-conditioning. To Pedasí, buses run every 45 minutes from 6am to 7pm, and cost $2. Taxis are plentiful in Las Tablas; there are taxis at the bus terminal and also at the taxi stand at Calle 2 and the Carretera Nacional, next to the Banco Nacional. A taxi to Pedasí costs about $20.

BY CAR Las Tablas is 282km (175 miles) from Panama City, and 32km (20 miles) from Chitré. The Carretera Nacional funnels into town and passes the main plaza; if continuing on, you'll need to hang a left at the end of the plaza (Calle Belisario Porras) to keep following the Carretera Nacional out of town.

WHERE TO STAY

Hotel Piamonte y Restaurante This is as good as it gets in Las Tablas, but really this hotel is just a step above backpacker lodging. The Piamonte is clean, with cheery lemon-yellow halls and friendly service, but guest rooms are very spare, with

PARTY ON! carnaval IN THE AZUERO PENINSULA

Some say the only thing that Panamanians take seriously is Carnaval, and here in the Azuero, especially in **Las Tablas,** it's celebrated with a fervor unseen elsewhere in Panama. For old-timers who lament that Carnaval has marched toward vulgarity in Panama City, the festival in the Azuero has maintained its folkloric traditions. It begins the Saturday before Ash Wednesday and continues for 4 days with dancing, drinking, music, and parades. The atmosphere is enlivened by the famous rivalry between Calle Arriba and Calle Abajo (High St. and Low St., respectively), whereby the town is divided into two groups that try to outdo each other with the fanciest costumes and floats, and even their own queens, who are specially chosen for the event. Other highlights include the parade of the polleras. Be forewarned that *mojaderos,* guys who spray passersby with water from pistols, garden hoses, buckets, and even fire hoses, are out before noon, so be prepared to get drenched.

Carnaval is a tremendously enjoyable cultural and party event, but keep in mind that in Las Tablas it is also a raucous and sometimes disorderly event that might be too much for some people. For this reason, many tourists opt to lodge elsewhere and visit Las Tablas for the day. Or, for a low-key version of Carnaval, head to a quieter town such as Pedasí or La Villa de los Santos. *Note:* Hotels in Las Tablas and Chitré, and many others around the Azuero, sell 4- and 5-night Carnaval packages at prices that are about double the standard rate. You will need reservations at least a month in advance, and most hotels will expect you to pay 100% upfront.

low-quality mattresses, well-worn bedding, and a lack of windows. The best two rooms are called "junior suites"—a misnomer since they are just more spacious doubles with bureaus and better lighting, but they face the road and are noisier. During Carnaval, the Piamonte sells only 5-night packages for $400 to $500, lodging only, which is pretty steep given the basic accommodations. Still, the hotel has a ground-floor restaurant that is one of the better eateries in town, serving everything from tacos to Panamanian-style meats and seafood to Chinese food. The restaurant is open daily from 7am to 11pm. They'll provide room service, but it's hard to imagine wanting to eat in your room.

Av. Belisario Porras. © **923-1603.** 16 units. $33 double; $40 junior suite. AE, MC, V. **Amenities:** Restaurant. *In room:* A/C, TV, no phone.

Residencial Piamonte Formerly the Residencial Mariela, the neighboring Piamonte recently bought out this property. It's the kind of hotel that builds character in those who brave its spartan guest rooms—but if you're a budget-minded traveler perhaps you won't mind. Fronting the original Piamonte, and located on the second floor above an appliance and kitchen store, this hotel is dirt-cheap, about the same in quality as the original Piamonte, but with brighter rooms. Beds are cots with low-quality mattresses. The owner is very amicable and helpful, and there's satellite TV, a big bonus. The front rooms are the best for their large windows, and they are next to a terrace overlooking the street. Five-night Carnaval packages go for $350 to $450, lodging only.

Av. Belisario Porras. © **923-1603.** 13 units. $25–$39 double. No credit cards.

WHERE TO DINE

Pizzeria Portofino PIZZERIA This takeout-style pizzeria does brisk business because of its cheap thin-crust pizzas, burgers, and sandwiches. It's a good spot for a meal on the run (there are a few tables), or you can order to go. There are also good fresh fruit juices and shakes.

Av. Belisario Porras. No phone. Pizzas $3–$5. No credit cards. Mon–Sat 9am–10pm; Sun 11am–10pm.

Restaurant & Pizzería El Caserón ★ PANAMANIAN/PIZZERIA Just off the main street, on a tranquil corner surrounded by colonial homes, this restaurant is housed in a hacienda-style building and offers a pleasant ambience that provokes you to linger a little longer than usual after your meal. Another plus is its extensive menu, with typical Panamanian dishes like barbecued meats in homemade sauce. (Most meats are prepared with local ingredients such as chicken with pineapple, prunes, and cherries, or with mushrooms and almonds.) Pastas, such as their tasty lasagna, are served in large portions, and there are simple pizzas, sandwiches, and farm-style breakfasts. The service is attentive and friendly. Note that the restaurant does not serve alcohol.

Calle Agustín Batista at Calle Moisés Espino. © **994-6066.** Main courses $3–$9. No credit cards. Daily 7am–11pm.

Restaurante Los Faroles ★ ☺ PANAMANIAN The newest restaurant in the area is located outside of town on the road to Chitré—just before entering Las Tablas, you'll see an orangey, hacienda-style building on your left side. There is a breezy wraparound terrace, like the one at El Caserón, which offers an enjoyable ambience, but its location is more isolated and it overlooks the National Highway.

Still, the food is a notch above El Caserón's. Hearty platters of barbecued meats and seafood are the specialty here, and there are salads and kids' items. There is also a playground.

Carretera Nacional. © **994-0777.** Main courses $4–$12. MC, V. Tues–Sun 10am–11pm.

Pedasí

Arguably the region's prettiest town, this is without a doubt the choice destination in the region, and I hesitate to say that because it is one of those special places you want to remain a secret. Pedasí is the kind of small town where no passing visitor goes ungreeted—usually locals camped out on their front porch give a pleasant wave to any stranger passing by. The autochthonous architecture is well preserved, and residents have recently painted and spiffed up most of the facades of residential buildings. The town is one long main street called Avenida Central, with a tidy plaza 2 blocks from the main road. The paved and signed streets and other well-tended civic structures exist because the former president Mireya Moscoso is from here—you'll see her bust in the plaza. Note that this is a languid town without many services other than a bank (Banco Nacional, at the town's entrance) and two restaurants.

A little farther south in the village of **Los Destiladores,** you'll find luxury lodging; and to the southwest in **Playa Venado,** there's high-end beachfront lodging. The region is known for its beaches, surfing, fishing, and Isla Laguna Wildlife refuge. There is even a scuba-diving operation.

VISITOR INFORMATION & ORIENTATION

There is a helpful **ATP visitor center** (© **995-2339;** Mon–Fri 8:30am–4:30pm, Sat–Sun and holidays 8:30am–1:30pm) with brochures about regions throughout Panama, and they occasionally have maps. The staff isn't overly occupied and will eagerly help you with any transportation or logistics problems. The office is at the entrance to town, on the road to Playa Arenal.

GETTING THERE & DEPARTING

BY PLANE At press time, there are no scheduled commercial flights between Panama City and Pedasí. **Air Panama** (© 316-9043) or **Aeroperlas** (© 315-7570) can organize a charter flight for you; however, this option is expensive and not really worth it unless you're traveling with a large group or money is no object.

BY CAR To continue through Las Tablas to Pedasí, follow the Carretera Nacional until it dead-ends at Avenida Belisario Porras, turn left, and drive until the road turns back into the Carretera Nacional. The road from Las Tablas to Pedasí is straightforward. *Warning:* Mind your speed along this road. It is common knowledge that the police set up speed traps and then demand a bribe, usually about $5. If you are a tourist, they will probably let you go with a warning.

BY BUS & TAXI Buses from Panama City or Chitré change in Las Tablas. Buses from Panama City to Las Tablas are $8; from Las Tablas to Pedasí it is $2. A taxi from Chitré to Pedasí costs around $20.

GETTING AROUND

BY TAXI Taxis do not cruise the streets frequently, but if you wait long enough on a corner one will eventually pass by. If not, call © **995-2275,** or have the ATP office call for you.

FUN IN THE OCEAN
Beaches
There are a lot of fine beaches in this region, but unfortunately, they are receptacles for trash that currents deposit throughout the year. Sometimes it's just a few pieces here and there; other times it's a poor man's beachcomber's paradise. When the tide is low, you won't notice this as much. **Playa Arenal,** about a mile from the main street in Pedasí, is a prime example, and visitors might only want to stop here briefly before carrying on to the Isla Laguna Wildlife Refuge, which is reached by boat from here—take the road past the scuba shop near the ATP office. **Playa del Toro** has good swimming conditions but its murky waters are not very inviting. The best beach here is in **Los Destiladores,** another 10km (6 miles) south of Pedasí. The waves pound, but the beach is cleaner and altogether more beautiful. Also, see "Playa Venado," below. Like most beaches on the Pacific, the beaches of the Azuero Peninsula aren't the most attractive in Panama, but the availability of comfortable lodging makes them a good choice for those who don't want to go as far as Bocas del Toro or don't want to rough it in Kuna Yala.

Isla Iguana Wildlife Refuge
This island refuge is reached by boat from Playa Arenal, and is about 3km (1¾ miles) from shore. Isla Iguana is only about 55 hectares (136 acres), and it is surrounded by an extensive coral reef that attracts thousands of colorful fish—the blue sea here is ideal for snorkeling. Unfortunately, a lot of trash washes up onshore, carried by currents and left by negligent tourists. The island was also used as target practice by the U.S. military, and it's said that unexploded bombs are still occasionally found here, so be careful and stick to main beaches and trails.

The island is home to green iguanas; and if you're lucky enough to be here from June to November, humpback whales breed in the area and are commonly seen by boat. The refuge can be reached by hiring a local boatman at Playa Arenal, or you can book a trip with Buzos de Azuero (see below)—you'll need to rent snorkel gear from them anyway, so you might as well plan your trip here. The cost is $50 for a half-day, and boats run from 8am to 6pm. The boat ride out is smoothest from April to December; if you've come between January and March, you may not be able to reach the island because of strong winds. There aren't any services on the island, so pack a picnic lunch.

Snorkeling, Diving & Fishing
Canadian-run **Buzos de Azuero** is now located in the Pedasí Sports Club, which is a B&B (see below). Buzos de Azuero offers activities that include PADI diver training, scuba-diving adventures, spear fishing, sport fishing, kayak tours, and snorkel tours to Isla Iguana. Two-tank dives cost $95 to Isla Iguana and $115 to Isla Frailes. All-inclusive snorkeling tours to Isla Iguana cost $55 per person. All tours include all equipment, transportation, and lunch.

WHERE TO STAY
Casa Margarita ★★   Casa Margarita is Pedasí's best and most upscale hotel. Rooms are casually elegant with comfortable orthopedic beds, handmade teak closets, attractive artwork, and soothing, warm colors. This boutique hotel is the place to stay if you're looking for memorable lodging, and best of all, a delicious buffet breakfast is included in room rates. There are two guest rooms on the

ground level and three on the third level; all are comfortable, quiet, and tactfully decorated. Also, the on-site restaurant is open to the public Friday and Saturday night, but guests can request private meals. Casita Margarita offers tours to Isla Iguana, "No B.S." real-estate tours, and can help guests arrange fishing and diving excursions.

End of Av. Central. ✆ **995-2898.** www.pedasihotel.com. $89–$129 double. Buffet breakfast included in rates. MC, V. **Amenities:** Restaurant; honor bar. *In room:* A/C, TV, Wi-Fi.

Dim's Hostal ★   Located in a converted old home at the entrance to town, this is a very popular hostel in Pedasí. Rooms are en suite but simple, and are a big step above the rooms at Residencial Moscoso (see below). The owners are exceptionally friendly and hospitable. They include breakfast with the already low price, which is served in a pleasant back patio. It's often difficult to get a room if you just show up (especially during high season), so try to book in advance. There's a computer with Internet hookup available for guest use and Wi-Fi in rooms.

Av. Central. ✆ **995-2303.** mirely@iname.com. 9 units. $30 single; $45 double. Breakfast included in rates. No credit cards. **Amenities:** Kitchen. *In room:* A/C, TV, no phone, Wi-Fi.

Pedasí Sports Club ★   It's not luxurious, but it's one of the nicest lodging options in Pedasí. The hotel was built in 2008 and is housed in a colonial-style building and run by the same people who run Buzos de Azuero. Rooms are bright, spacious and comfortable, and there is a large family suite available with a fully equipped kitchen, satellite TV, and a separate living area. The Pedasí Sports Club is a 20-minute walk from Playa Arenal and a 5-minute walk from downtown Pedasí. There's a dive shop and PADI pro dive shop on-site, as well as a pleasant lounge area. Pedasí Sports Club also offers 6-day/5-night packaged vacation tours for all of the above activities at very reasonable prices and is more than willing to tailor a package specifically to meet your needs. Package prices start as low as $995 per person.

Pedasí. ✆ **995-2894.** www.pedasisportsclub.com. 10 units. $55 single; $66 double; $77 triple; $88 quad; $125 suite. Breakfast included in rates. No credit cards. **Amenities:** Restaurant; bar; lounge area; outdoor pool; dive shop; complimentary Wi-Fi. *In room:* A/C, TV.

Residencial Moscoso   Frequented by surfers on the cheap, Moscoso's rooms are about as spartan as an insane asylum's. To stay here, you have to find your bohemian side or at the very least be an easygoing traveler who doesn't fuss much with accommodations. Really, for the price it's hard to expect much more. Showers are spigots that shoot out cold water from the wall. But there is a computer so guests can check their e-mail.

Av. Central at Calle Ofelia Reliz. ✆ **995-2203.** 19 units. $25 double; $35–$40 quadruple. No credit cards. *In room:* A/C, TV (2 local channels).

Residencial Pedasí   Despite the name "residencial," accommodations here are hotel rooms laid out in a motel-like building that looks more attractive from the outside than from the inside. The guest rooms have small windows that let in little light, with basic decor and firm beds. The hotel attracts mostly foreign visitors who come here to fish. Service is friendly, and there's a computer with Internet access available for public use.

Av. Central. ✆ **995-2490.** 15 units. $30 double. No credit cards. **Amenities:** Restaurant. *In room:* A/C, TV, no phone.

WHERE TO DINE

Aside from the dining options listed below, **Pasta e Vino** (road to Playa el Toro) offers tasty and affordable Italian dishes and **Maudy's Café** (btw. Calle Principal and Calle la Policai) serves light fare and coffee and has free Wi-Fi.

Dulcerías Yely ★ 🎂 PASTRIES/SANDWICHES This delightful little bakery is owned by the amiable Mrs. Dalila Vera de Quintero, who is as sweet as her confections. Dalila puts a lot of love and care into her homemade cakes and sandwiches, and every visitor to Pedasí makes at least one stop here to sample her delicacies. The *queques,* or pound cakes, come in a variety of flavors such as almond, coconut, chocolate, or anise, and are not too sugary. She also has a creamy flan made with condensed milk. But Dalila's specialty is *chicheme,* a drink made of mashed corn and milk and infused with vanilla—it's delicious and filling. There are also fresh *chichas,* or juices, made from local fruit such as *uva,* a cross between a grape and cherry; much of these fruit is taken from her backyard. For lunch, don't miss her $1.25 sandwiches of either ginger chicken, roast pork, or roast beef and cheese.

Calle Ofelia Reluz at Av. Central. ℂ **995-2205.** Reservations not accepted. Sandwiches $1.25; cakes 30¢ a slice. No credit cards. Daily 7am–8:30pm.

LUXURY LODGING IN LOS DESTILADORES

Los Destiladores is a tiny hamlet about a 5-minute drive from Pedasí. Its two fine resorts offer travelers the most upscale accommodations on the Azuero Peninsula. The beach here is also the best in the area—with the exception of Playa Venado, which has its own deluxe B&B (see below). A taxi to town from here costs $5.

Posada los Destiladores ★★★ 📷 The property is owned and run by French expats; Philippe is the former owner of Las Bóvedas restaurant in Panama City, and Jean Francois is a talented furniture maker who has bestowed unique artistic craftsmanship to the bungalows and main building that form the property. Secluded among 8.1 hectares (20 acres) of tropical plants and teak trees, the bungalows feature bamboo, thatched roofs, and intricately carved custom-made furniture using local materials. Other details include cobblestone floors, palm-thatched walls, and bathrooms with large, walk-in showers and carved wooden sinks (note that water is tepid, not hot). The largest and best bungalows are Itzania and Ariel, each with two stories under an A-frame roof, and a terrace strung with hammocks. Beds feature comfortable mattresses; some are on a raised Zen-like platform. Two sun decks jut over the beach, perfect for relaxing to the sounds of the sea. Meals are served in the artistically decorated main lodge.

Los Destiladores. ℂ **995-2771** or 6673-9262. www.panamabambu.net. 9 units. $75–$200 double bungalow. MC, V. **Amenities:** Restaurant; outdoor pool; horse rental; tours. *In room:* A/C (some units), no phone.

Villa Camilla ★★★ 📷 There is perhaps no finer or more exclusive hotel in Panama than the Villa Camilla. Villa Camilla is owned by the celebrated French architect Gilles Saint-Gilles and his wife Camille, both of whom fell in love with this slice of paradise on the Azuero Peninsula. Their goal is to create a local economy producing furniture and providing living means for local residents. All seven rooms are sophisticated and fresh, with handsome hardwood floors, molded half-walls, hand-carved furniture, and wrought-iron door frames. The guest rooms were built with an emphasis on privacy. There is a cottage for families with children (children are not accepted in the other guest rooms). The elegant lounge, with Wi-Fi access, is mostly open-air and faces the sea and an inviting pool, although it is a 15-minute walk to get to the mostly private beach. The grounds are lushly landscaped: Giles has been reforesting the area to restore its natural luster. Delicious meals made with organic ingredients from their garden are included in the price; breakfast and lunch are served at individual tables, and dinner is served family style at a formal dining table.

Los Destiladores. (✆ **232-6721.** www.azueros.com. 7 units. $180–$450 double (steep discounts on weekdays). AE, MC, V. **Amenities:** Restaurant; bikes; outdoor pool; tennis courts; tours. *In room:* A/C, hair dryer.

Playa Venado

Playa Venado (often called "Venao") is an up-and-coming destination notable for its surfing and half-moon sandy beach. The surf here breaks left and right, great for both pros and beginners. (For information about surf tours here, see chapter 5.) There's no sign to Playa Venado, so keep your eyes open for the turnoff, about 1.5km (1 mile) from the Playita Resort. If you don't have a vehicle, you'll need a taxi, which will charge around $15. Like most of the beaches in this area, currents bring in trash—also, during high tide the sand fills with crabs, making swimming unpleasant. Low tide brings better swimming conditions. The beach at La Playita (see below) is more suitable for swimming, but they charge $3 to use it. During surf competitions this area can take on a party atmosphere.

The coastline of the Azuero Peninsula is rich with marine life and pelagic fish like tuna—so much so that it is often called the "tuna coast." Here at Playa Venado, the Inter-American Tropical Tuna Commission (IATTC), which monitors tuna fishing to prevent its depletion, has a research facility, **Achotines Laboratory** (✆ **995-8166;** www.iattc.org), that offers educational tours. It sounds dry, but it's actually fascinating to see the various stages of tuna reproduction (among other fish like sea bass and snapper), and especially to witness the frenzy that occurs when the staff feed huge broodstock yellowfin tuna. Kids love it. Visiting hours are Monday through Friday from 8:30am to noon and from 1 to 4:30pm. You must make advance arrangements.

About 11km (6½ miles) from Playa Venado is the **Refugio de Vida Silvestre Isla de Cañas,** an island village that receives more nesting turtles than any other location on the Pacific Coast. From April to October, hundreds of thousands of Pacific green, olive ridley, leatherback, loggerhead, and hawksbill turtles arrive here to lay eggs, but there is no surefire date that guarantees you'll see any. The view of Isla de Cañas, a barrier island reached by boat, is worth seeing even if you do not visit the island itself. Getting here is difficult because there is only one local boat that can take you from the mainland (it leaves from the end of the road); if you show up, it may or may not be there; the aforementioned Buzos de Azuero offers tours to the island.

WHERE TO STAY & DINE

Beside the hotels listed below, **Eco Venao** (✆ **832-0530;** www.ecovenao.com) is a 346-acre reforestation project that offers three simple but attractive low-impact guesthouses and an ecolodge with doubles and dorm rooms. Guesthouses run $50 to $300 during high season, doubles $25, and dorms $12. **Hotel Sereia do Mar** (✆ **6523-8758;** www.sereiadomar.net) is an pleasant B&B located in the tiny village of Ciruelo with four simple but comfortable rooms, all with A/C, TV, and fridge. Breakfast is included in rates.

La Playita ☺   This is one of the funkiest places on the coast, run by a Panamanian/American horse jockey with a serious penchant for kitsch. La Playita is located on a gorgeous blue-water inlet with tan sand and tranquil swimming conditions. The beach is open to the public, and on weekends this area is packed with Panamanian families. That, along with their multitude of birds (including a free-roaming ostrich and two very vocal scarlet macaws), give the property a zoolike ambience. The landscaped grounds, however, are well-tended. There are five rooms whose interiors, oddly, have the feel of an alpine lodge, with chipped-stone-and- fossilized-wood walls and knobby-wood headboards; three of the rooms can fit up to five people. They have an on-site restaurant, but meals are not included in the price; you can also use their kitchen to cook for yourself.

Playa Venado. ✆ **996-6551** or 6615-3898. www.playitaresort.com. 5 units. $80 double. No credit cards. **Amenities:** Restaurant; bar; surfboard and snorkel rental; tours. *In room:* A/C, no phone.

Villa Marina ★★★ 🛅   It's difficult to imagine a more idyllic location, set on 89 hectares (220 acres) of private coastal land that allows guests to step directly onto the beach. The stunning evening sunsets can be enjoyed from a breezy veranda or from a thatched-roof *bohio* strung with hammocks. There are 10 elegantly appointed rooms with antiques, French windows, and fine bedding, but the ambience is easeful, not fussy, and the amicable staff strives to make guests at home. The hacienda-style B&B has a terra-cotta-tiled roof, and is painted white and cerulean blue, which gives it a fresh, airy feel. Because the common area is shared by guests, this place would be ideal if rented by a group of friends or a family, but individuals and couples are welcomed, too. (It's best to book in advance.) What I especially like about Villa Marina is that you can swim, surf, or horseback ride right outside the door, meaning that you don't have to book a tour. The Villa Marina has three putting greens and a driving range for golf, and can put together fishing trips. If camaraderie grows between guests, meals are served family style; otherwise they are served individually on the veranda. The food is delicious, hearty, and fresh, and they have a full Argentine barbecue.

Playa Venado. ✆ **211-2277** or 646/383-7486 in the U.S. 9 units. $150 double; $25 per person additional for meals. MC, V. **Amenities:** Outdoor pool; putting green; free surfboards and snorkel gear; horseback riding; fishing trips. *In room:* A/C, TV.

THE WESTERN HIGHLANDS & THE GULF OF CHIRIQUÍ

9

Western Panama is home to the cool highlands of the Chiriquí Province, a tropical mountain paradise brimming with lush rainforest and trout-filled streams, and dotted with storybook villages nestled on the verdant slopes of the region's dominant peak, the 3,478m (11,410-ft.) Barú Volcano. Given the region's fertile soil and ideal year-round temperatures, the Chiriquí area is Panama's agricultural breadbasket, and many of the mountain's valleys and hillsides are blanketed with a colorful patchwork of fruit trees, vegetable fields, and coffee plantations—one of the country's signature products. The air is fresh and sweet here, and the roads that wind through the peaks and valleys overflow with pretty pink and white impatiens and exotic flowers.

The Chiriquí Highlands region is a mecca for adventure, and travelers can participate in activities such as white-water rafting and kayaking Class II to Class V rivers, canopy rides, or hiking through primeval forest dripping with vines and bromeliads and interlaced with creeks. Laid-back activities include scenic drives and tours of coffee plantations or orchid farms. The Chiriquí region is well known as a hot spot for **bird-watching,** and hundreds of species have been recorded in the area, including showcase birds such as the resplendent quetzal, blue cotinga, trogons, and toucans. The area is a corridor for migratory species that pass through from November to April.

The eastern side of the Barú Volcano is home to **Boquete,** an enchanting valley town that has received a lot of press lately as a top retirement area. Indeed, it's not uncommon to see a number of foreigners

The Western Highlands & the Gulf of Chiriquí

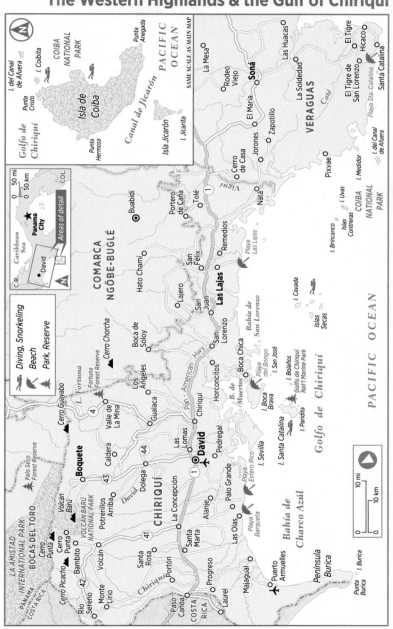

here. On the volcano's western side are picturesque agricultural communities such as **Cerro Punta.** Both towns are linked by the Los Quetzales Trail that winds through the gorgeous forests of **Parque Nacional Volcán Barú.** Additionally, the western side offers access to one of the most important parks in Central America, **Parque Internacional La Amistad,** which Panama shares with Costa Rica.

The Highlands are accessed from the province's capital **David,** a service-oriented city located on the hot and humid lowlands. A little farther south is the Gulf of Chiriquí, Panama's up-and-coming travel destination that offers outstanding scuba diving, snorkeling, and sport fishing in the crystalline waters around such revered sites as **Isla Coiba,** and the islands in and around **Parque Nacional Golfo Marino.** This chapter covers the extensive region that includes the Highlands, the Gulf, and even the remote village Santa Catalina, for its epic surfing and direct access to Isla Coiba.

The Chiriquí Highlands have microclimates that produce cloud forests and phenomena such as the misting rain *bajareque,* so it is important that you bring clothing that is waterproof if you plan to spend time outdoors. Also, temperatures here are decidedly cooler than in the rest of Panama.

DAVID

440km (274 miles) W of Panama City; 40km (25 miles) south of Boquete

David, Panama's third-largest city, with a population of 125,000, has an economy based around commercial services and Chiriquí Province's thriving farming industry. At just 45 minutes from the Costa Rica border, the city has the ambience of a frontier town, and there is little here to offer travelers other than a transportation hub and services. Travelers on their way to Costa Rica often stop in David for the night, but with so little to see and do in town they are up and packing early the following day. Also, owing to David's location on a coastal plain, the heat and humidity here can be suffocating—another reason so many residents escape to the beach or the highlands during weekends, and so few tourists base themselves out of the city. It's a pleasant enough city, but I recommend using David as a jumping-off point to other destinations.

Essentials

GETTING THERE & DEPARTING

BY PLANE   The Aeropuerto Enrique Malek (DAV) is about 4.8km (3 miles) from the city center and is serviced by **Air Panama** (© 316-9000; www.flyairpanama. com), with flights to and from Panama City, Bocas del Toro, and even San José, Costa Rica. There are three daily round-trip flights from Panama City daily at 6:30am, 9:15am, and 6:30pm. The cost is about $206 round-trip including taxes. There are flights from Bocas del Toro to David on Monday, Wednesday, and Friday at 8:35am, with return flights at 1pm. Flights from San José are on Monday, Wednesday, and Friday, at 10am, with the return trip from David leaving at 9:30am.

Aeroperlas (© 378-6000; www.aeroperlas.com) has three daily flights from **Panama City** to David from Monday to Saturday at 6:30am 10:30am and 5:30pm and two flights on Sunday at 10:30am and 5:30pm. The cost is $206 round-trip including taxes. From **Bocas del Toro,** there is one flight per day from Monday to Friday, leaving Bocas del Toro at 8:25am and returning from David at 9am.

There are currently plans to expand the David airport to allow incoming flights from the U.S., meaning travelers headed for Boquete and the Chiriquí Highlands can fly directly into David rather than Panama City; however, there is no concrete completion date on this project.

There is an **ATP visitor center** booth at the airport (no phone; daily 7am–3pm), manned by a helpful and friendly representative who has a limited number of brochures and maps. A taxi into town costs $2 per person.

BY BUS The **Terminal de Transportes** is located on Avenida Estudiante. Daily service to and from Panama City is offered by the bus line **Terminal David–Panama** (© 775-7074), with regular service leaving every hour daily from 6am to 8pm, and express service leaving daily at 10:45pm, midnight, and 3am. I recommend buying your tickets a day in advance for overnight trips. **Panafront** has regular bus service at 7:30, 8:45, 9:45, and 11am, 12:45, 2, 3:15, 6, and 7:45pm; express buses leave at 10:45pm and midnight. Both companies charge $13 for regular service (7 hr.), and $15 for express service (5½ hr.). The Panafront office is not located in the David terminal; if you are leaving with Panafront, ask your cabdriver to drop you off at the Panafront offices, not the terminal. Note that bus drivers on this route like to turn the A/C on full blast, so be sure to bring a sweater. Call ahead to confirm departure times.

Volcán–Cerro Punta–Guadalupe buses from David leave every 35 minutes from 5am to 7pm ($2–$3); and buses to **Boquete** leave every 15 minutes from 4:15am to 9pm ($1.45). Buses to Costa Rica via the Paso Canoa border are available from **Panaline** (© 314-6383) and **Tica Bus** (© 314-6385); both companies charge the same price from David as from Panama City ($25 one-way); they leave David for Costa Rica around 5:30pm daily. *Note:* Travelers to and from Costa Rica will need to show proof of onward travel. If you do not posses such proof, you will be required to buy a round-trip ticket.

BY CAR David is reached from Panama City via the Interamericana Highway (Pan American Highway), which skirts the edge of town and continues on to the Paso Canoa border with Costa Rica. If you are heading on to Boquete or Volcán, see "Getting There & Departing," later in this chapter. Personally, I find renting a car to be the best option, because it allows you to explore the Boquete/Cerro Punta region.

GETTING AROUND

BY TAXI Taxis are plentiful in David. The fare for a taxi from the airport to the city center is $2 per person; to Boquete it is $25; to Volcán it is $40; and to Guadalupe it is $50. Around town, fares cost $1 to $2.

BY CAR Rental vehicles are available at the David airport, including **Alamo** (© 236-5777; www.alamopanama.com), **Budget** (© 263-8777; www.budgetpanama. com), **Hertz** (© 721-3345; www.hertz.com), **National** (© 721-0974; www.national panama.com), and **Thrifty** (© 721-2477; www.thrifty.com). If you'll be exploring the surrounding Chiriquí Highlands, I recommend you get a 4WD for difficult, unpaved road if you'll be exploring off the beaten track.

FAST FACTS You'll find banks with ATMs on the streets around the plaza; **Banco Nacional** is at Calle B Norte and Avenida 3 Este/Bolívar on the plaza; **Global Bank** is at Calle A Norte and Avenida 1 Este; and **HSBC** is at Avenida 1era Oeste and Calle D Norte. Cybercafes are plentiful in David, and all hotels offer Internet service to their

The Feria Internacional de San José de David is the largest commercial, industrial, agricultural, ranching, and folkloric festival in Panama, taking place every year around the middle of March. The weeklong event draws 300,000 people, most of whom come to visit the booths of international companies and catch up on the newest technology, but folklore, culture, and handicrafts play a large role, delighting tourists, too. Check the website **www. feriadedavid.com** for exact dates.

customers. Also try **American Copy** at Calle Este Norte and Avenida 1 Este; or **Naveg@net** at Avenida 2 Este and Calle A Norte. There are two excellent hospitals here, the **Mae Lewis Hospital** (© 775-4620; www.maelewis.net) and the **Hospital Chiriquí** (© 774-0128; www.hospitalchiriqui.net). For the **police,** dial © 771-4231. The **post office** can be found 1 block northeast of the plaza on Avenida 4 Este and Calle C Norte, and is open Monday through Saturday from 7am to 5:30pm.

There is an **ATP visitor center** at Avenida Central and Calle B Norte (© 775-9021; Mon–Fri 8:30am–5:30pm), but it is largely useless except for maps, which are in short supply. The staff here oddly does not provide the public with much tourist information, nor does it seem to know David well enough to give recommendations.

What to See & Do in & Around David

Despite the fact that David is one of Panama's largest cities, it has surprisingly few attractions to keep a tourist occupied for more than an afternoon—which is why most use the city as a jumping-off point. Also, the "border town" feel combined with the heat and humidity (David is Panama's hottest city) doesn't exactly encourage you to spend afternoons strolling city blocks. In 2006, the local government began a half-million-dollar renovation of the historic **Parque Miguel de Cervantes** plaza, and this is one of the rare areas in David that offers shade trees and a respite from the oppressive heat, and vendors sell ice cream, fresh coconut juice, and cold beverages.

Take a stroll down to **Barrio Bolívar** by following Calle A Norte west of the plaza to Avenida 8 Este. This is "old town," with a couple of blocks that boast the last vestiges of colonial architecture from David's early days. On Avenida 8 Este you'll find the **Museo de Historia y de Arte José de Obaldía** (© 775-1217; Tues–Sat 9am–5pm; admission $1 adults, 25¢ children), housed within an 1834 building that once belonged to the founder of the Chiriquí Province, José Domingo de Obaldía. It's a humble museum that requires just 15 minutes to see the odds and ends on display, including archaeological artifacts from the Chiriquí area and pieces from the colonial period.

The **Nuevo Centro Artesanal de David** has a good selection of Panamanian handicrafts for sale, and is located on Vía Boquete, in front of the Autoservicios de Chiriquí (no phone; daily 10am–8pm).

Residents of David escape the heat by heading to **Playa Barqueta,** about 30 minutes' drive from town. This long, black-sand beach is often breezy, and the ocean can be too choppy for swimming (beware of riptides here). Also here is the **Refugio de Vida Silvestre,** a nature preserve that is an excellent spot to view wildlife and birds. It is a turtle-nesting site from about August to October. **Las Olas Resort** is here (see "Where to Stay & Dine," below), and although they have a restaurant, another option is to bring a picnic lunch.

NIGHTLIFE & ENTERTAINMENT

The newly expanded, 24-hour **Fiesta Casino** (© 775-6534), opposite the Gran Nacional Hotel, has slots and gaming tables, a restaurant, and a bar. There are two cinemas, the **Alhambra** at the Gran Hotel Nacional (see below), and the **Chiriquí Mall** on the Interamericana Highway (© 774-5648); both cinemas have six screens and show mostly American movies, mostly of the action and horror variety. There are also quite a few clubs and bars, but most of these also have a border town feel, and aren't highly recommendable. If you really want to go out, I recommend heading to the bar at the Gran Hotel Nacional (see below).

Where to Stay & Dine

Hotels and B&Bs in the Chiriquí Highlands and the Boca Chica region offer much more ambience and character, but if you absolutely need to spend a night in David, the hotels below are your best bet. If you're just looking for a cheap place to stay, head to the **Purple House Hostel** (© 774-4059; www.purplehousehostel.com). It's a mostly backpacker crowd, but rooms are clean and comfortable enough and you can get a double with A/C for $30 a night. Plus, Andrea, the American owner, has lived in David for 11 years and can offer plenty of advice on what to do in and around the city. Another good option is the midrange **Hotel Castilla** (© 774-5236; www.hotelcastilla.com) with clean, comfortable rooms costing $55 to $88, and **Hotel Puerta del Sol** (© 774-8422; www.hotelpuertadelsol.com.pa) caters to Panamanian families and business folks and charges $70 to $170 a room, but steep discounts of nearly 50% are usually available.

In terms of food, David isn't exactly known as a gastronomic capital, but things are getting better. Aside from the places listed below, **Casa Vegeteriana** offers dirt-cheap Chinese vegetarian options and there is a popular **McDonald's** in town if you're craving a Big Mac and full-blast A/C. **T.G.I.F.** is the new hot spot to dine in David and is considered fine dining by the locals.

Best Western ★ 🍴 A newcomer on the David hotel scene, the Best Western has some of the nicest rooms in David and says a lot about how fast David is growing and changing. All guest rooms have orthopedic beds, standard chain decor and furnishings, and modern amenities such as flatscreen TVs. The suites in particular are a good deal for families with children. It's the best value in David, the only drawback being that there's no pool. The hotel caters to Panamanian and Latin American business folks and foreign tourists. The staff is polite and friendly, and does a better job than most David hotels in being attentive. There's also a pretty good Italian restaurant on-site.

3era entre Calle A y B. © **777-0000.** www.bestwestern.com. 108 units. $50 double; $88 suite. AE, MC, V. **Amenities:** Restaurant/bar; fitness center; room service. *In room:* A/C, TV, Wi-Fi.

Gran Hotel Nacional ★ This 60-year-old hotel, with its attractive, mock-colonial facade, has some of the fanciest accommodations in David. The Hotel Gran Nacional also offers the most amenities, including a casino, a cinema, an outdoor swimming pool, and three restaurants. Guest rooms are fresh and clean, with tiled floors, orthopedic mattress beds, and run-of-the-mill, chain-hotel decor.

The Gran Nacional hosts mostly businessmen and travelers taking a break during the drive to either Costa Rica or Bocas del Toro. David's humid weather makes the swimming pool key, and their on-site restaurants are decent, serving mostly Panamanian dishes, pizzas, and pastas. Given the dearth of decent restaurants in David, consider **dining** at the hotel even if you're not lodging here. Every day from 5:30 to 10:30pm, the hotel's outdoor restaurant has a barbecue special with beef, chicken, and seafood.

Av. Central. ✆ **775-2221** or 775-2222. www.hotelnacionalpanama.com. 75 units. $78 standard double; $84 junior suite; $145 master suite. AE, MC, V. **Amenities:** 3 restaurants; bar; cinema; casino; outdoor pool; room service. *In room:* A/C, TV, Wi-Fi.

Restaurante El Palacio Oriental ★ 🍴 CHINESE   The menu at this Chinese restaurant is as thick as a book, and with so many options it is difficult to decide what you'd like. The menu features traditional dishes such as chop suey and chow mein, but given the amount of fresh fish available on the Pacific Coast you might want to opt for a seafood meal. The fare is delicious, and the portions are hearty—two could easily order an appetizer and split a main course if they weren't absolutely starving. The restaurant is often busy and the ambience is lively.

Calle E Norte and Av. Central. ✆ **777-2410.** Reservations not accepted. Main courses $3–$7. MC, V. Daily 10am–11pm.

Taverna Libanesa MEDITERRANEAN   Taverna Libanesa is a good choice as far as David restaurants go, especially if you're tired of typical Panamanian fare. The Taverna Libanesa offers and extensive menu of mostly typical Mediterranean specialties such as baba ghanouj, hummus and pita, kibbee and sambusek, as well as pasta, steaks, and seafood. The restaurant itself is air-conditioned and attractive enough with indoor and outdoor seating, though it can be a bit empty on weekdays.

Calle F-Sur. ✆ **774-2700.** Main courses $8–$16. MC, V. Daily noon–9pm.

A BEACH RESORT OUTSIDE OF DAVID

Las Olas Resort   This the only moderately upscale lodging option along this stretch of the Pacific Coast. The best thing about Las Olas is Playa Barqueta, the lengthy, undeveloped black-sand beach that it fronts If you do not need luxury—and if you just want to spend a night or two on the coast and take long strolls along the beach, join a yoga class, or maybe take a boat ride to an uninhabited island—this is your place. (All excursions and classes are an additional price.) The resort sells all-inclusive packages that include lodging, meals, drinks, and use of the facilities, or you can book for the night and order meals a la carte, but the latter is more expensive. The guest rooms and common areas are tidy and well-kept, though starting to show slight signs of wear and tear. Standard rooms feature oceanview terraces, but the rooms are on the small side. A small spa offers massages and facials. Wi-Fi is available in public areas.

Las Olas recently opened **Las Brisas del Mar** condos, a good choice for families or those who plan to stay for at least a couple of weeks. These 42 condos are fully equipped with standard modern amenities.

Playa Barqueta. ✆ **800/535-2513** in the U.S., or 772-3000. www.lasolasresort.com. 90 units. $55–$140 double; $75–$180 suite; $1,000–$1,700 per week condos. AE, MC, V. **Amenities:** Restaurant; bar; bikes; gym; outdoor pool; room service; sauna; spa; horseback riding. *In room:* A/C, TV, fridge, hair dryer.

A Side Trip to Las Lajas

Las Lajas is popular for its long, 10km (6-mile) stretch of tan-sand beach. The current here is not strong, so swimming conditions are better than at many other Pacific Coast beaches. The beach is 70km (44 miles) east of David, along a potholed but paved road from the Interamericana Highway. Along the beach you'll find cabins, thatched *bohío* picnic sites, and a couple of cheap restaurants—but it's all a bit weather-beaten and half-open unless it is a summer weekend. Las Lajas is best done as a day trip from Panama City or the Valle de Anton. Most hotels in El Valle de Anton can arrange tours or provide guidance for day trips to Las Lajas.

To get to Las Lajas beach, head east from David on the Interamericana Highway and turn at the signed road at Las Cruces. Continue for 13km (8 miles), passing through the village Las Lajas, until you reach the beach. The cabins are to the right, but the road peters out and you need to drive across a stretch of sand.

A Remote Surf Camp

Morro Negrito Surf Camp ★★   Located on Isla Ensenada 3.2km (2 miles) off the coast of the Chiriquí Gulf, about halfway between Santiago and David, this surf camp limits its guests to 25 to keep waves uncrowded. The accommodations are just a step above camping, with rustic cabins that overlook the Pacific Ocean and neighbor a small community—the focus here is on surfing, not luxury lodging. Transportation from Panama City (5 hr. by bus; 30 min. by jeep or boat), meals, lessons, and other activities are included in the price. The camp sells weeklong packages only, but they are reasonably priced at $550 per person. For surfing, 10 different breaks average between 1.2 and 2.4m (4–8 ft.). Sand breaks with small waves are good for beginners learning how to ride. You can also fish, ride horses, or just chill out in a hammock.

Isla Ensenada. (℮ **760/632-8014** in the U.S. www.surferparadise.com. 10 units. $650 all-inclusive weeklong package. No credit cards accepted at camp. **Amenities:** Restaurant; bar; surf lessons and surfboard rental; boat rides; horseback riding; TV rooms for video playback. *In room:* No phone.

VOLCÁN

33km (21 miles) N of David

The road from La Concepción to Volcán slowly winds 34km (21 miles) up from the humid lowlands and into a cooler climate and a landscape characterized by a patchwork of *fincas,* or dairy and cattle ranching farms. Eventually, the road opens up to a wide plateau and the village of Volcán, the highlands center for services such as banks, pharmacies, grocery stores, and just about everything else. While Volcán isn't as picturesque as Cerro Punta or Guadalupe, the fresh mountain air and open views of rugged landscape give Volcán a decidedly alpine atmosphere, part of the reason so many European immigrants chose to settle around here in the early 1900s. The town sits at the skirt of the Barú Volcano and offers grand views of that peak, although it is commonly shrouded with a layer of clouds and hidden from view. Considering Volcán's location at the axis of the roads to Guadalupe and Río Sereno, near the Costa Rica–Panama border, the town is a convenient base from which to explore the western highlands area. Volcán is centered around a blink-and-you-miss-it main street, Avenida Central, which forks in the center. Head right to continue on to Guadalupe and Cerro Punta, and straight ahead for the road to Río Sereno and the Costa Rica.

Like Boquete, its neighbor to the west, foreigners are beginning to discover Volcán and the surrounding mountain communities, which is evident in the new, foreign-owned restaurants that seem to be popping up all over the place. For now, Volcán still retains a distinctly Panamanian feel, but how long this will last is anyone's guess.

I strongly recommend you rent a car if visiting this area, because attractions are not within walking distance and using a taxi will cost you just as much or more than renting a car. A 4WD vehicle will give you more freedom to visit some of the region's more remote and difficult-to-reach attractions.

Essentials

GETTING THERE & DEPARTING

BY BUS & TAXI Buses to **Volcán, Cerro Punta,** and **Guadalupe** leave from the Terminal de Transportes in David every 35 minutes from 5am to 7pm ($2–$3). If traveling from Costa Rica, Panama City, or elsewhere, you'll need to transfer in David. A taxi from David to Volcán is $40, and to Guadalupe it is $50.

BY CAR From the David airport, turn left and drive 3.4km (2 miles), then turn left again, onto Calle Miguel Brenes (also called Calle F Sur). Continue for 1.8km (1 mile) until you reach the Interamericana Highway. Turn left and continue to Concepción, 21km (13 miles) after passing the Chiriquí Mall, and turn onto the road to Volcán and Cerro Punta. The turnoff is easy to miss; keep your eyes open for a Shell gas station and turn right after it. The drive from Concepción to Volcán is 34km (21 miles).

FAST FACTS There is an ATM at **Banco Nacional** (© 771-4282), located on the main street in front of the police station, after the road forks and at HSBC Bank diagonal to **Farmacia Volcán** (© 771-4651), open Sunday through Thursday 7:30am to 10pm; Friday 7:30am to 6pm; and Saturday 6 to 10pm. Fast Internet service is available at **Hotel Don Tavo** (© 771-4055) on main street near the church, open from 8am to 11pm daily. The **post office** can be found on the right-hand side of the road to Guadalupe, just after turning on the fork. It's open every day, except Sunday, from 7am to noon and 2 to 6pm.

TOUR OUTFITTERS **Western Wind Nature** (© 771-5049 or 6775-0118; westernwindnature@yahoo.com), operated by the friendly and knowledgeable birding and naturalist guide Nariño Aizpurua, offers a variety of outdoor excursions including hiking in La Amistad and Volcán Barú parks, canoeing in Lagunas de

Volcán, and horseback riding and bird-watching. Nariño's brother, Gonzalo Aizpurua (© **6685-1682**) is also a competent nature guide who can customize any outdoor excursion around Volcán. Both speak enough English to be understood. Prices average $60 for a half-day excursion for two, including transportation. A full-day tour with transportation, lunch, park entrance, and bilingual guide starts at about $110 a day. He runs **Highlands—Adventures/Turismo Ecologico** (© **771-4413** or 6685-1682; ecoaizpurua@hotmail.com), which also offers tours of Volcán and the surrounding area. Also, your hotel should be able to put you in contact with individual tour guides if you're looking for a custom tour.

Considering that the renowned Chiriquí Viejo River is on this side of the volcano, travelers can take part in absolutely thrilling white-water rafting offered by the Boquete-based companies **Chiriquí River Rafting** and **Panama Rafters** (see "What to See & Do" under "West of Volcán Barú: Boquete," later in this chapter). Contact these companies directly if possible—hotels in the area have been known to tack on a booking fee.

What to Do & See Around Volcán

For information about Volcán Barú and La Amistad parks, see "Bambito, Cerro Punta & Guadalupe," p. 224.

Sitio Barriles ★ Located 5.5km (3½ miles) southwest of Volcán, Sitio Barriles (© **6607-5438**; $6 donation) is an archaeological site on the private land of the Landau family, whose grandfather discovered hundreds of artifacts when excavating to build a coffee plantation. The artifacts are from the Barriles culture, an indigenous population that lived in the area from 600 B.C. to 300 B.C. before being forced to evacuate after the eruption of Volcán Barú. It's a curious attraction because hardly anything is known about the culture, and, accordingly, there's little interpretive information available to visitors. Artifacts include a burial tomb with funeral urns, pottery, and tools made of basalt. One basalt slab, when doused with water, shows ancient etchings. The site is open daily from 7am to 5pm, and can be reached by following the Río Sereno road west out of Volcán; the turnoff is on the left. The Landau family sells fresh cheese and homemade jams, too.

Lagunas de Volcán ★★ About a 15-minute drive from Volcán, along a rough, poorly maintained road, sit the highest wetlands in Panama: Lagunas de Volcán. The wetlands comprise two lakes surrounded by exuberant forest, with dramatic views of Volcán Barú rising in the distance. It's a lovely spot to visit, but it especially draws bird-watchers who come to see northern jacanas, tanagers, collared trogons, emerald toucanets, masked ducks, and the rose-throated becard, among others. Western Wind Nature offers canoe trips here, too (see above). To get here you'll need a 4WD vehicle. Turn left off the main road at the sign for Vía Aeropuerto at the Agroquímicas Volcán building, and follow the signs for Lagunas de Volcán. There is no entrance fee. Considering that the Lagunas are close to La Torcaza Estate coffee farm (see below), you might want to tie in a visit to both.

La Torcaza Estate ★★ The Janson Family produces extraordinary coffee, and a visit to their estate gives connoisseurs a chance to learn how coffee is processed (and, of course, to sample and buy coffee at the on-site shop). The splendid views of Volcán Barú and the Janson's lovely farm are worth the visit alone. The Jansons pride themselves on environmental protection, producing shade-grown, organic beans that are handpicked and roasted in small batches, then packed up and shipped overseas to the U.S. and Europe. Their tour is in Spanish and English, and lasts about an hour; tours include a visit to their production facility, followed by coffee tasting. To get here, head west on the main road and turn left at the sign for the Vía Aeropuerto, at the Agroquímicas Volcán building; continue until you see the sign for Janson Family Coffee, turn right, and continue to the airport strip, where you'll turn right and follow the signs. The tour is $5 per person (children 9 and under free), or you can visit the coffee shop for free (© **771-4306;** www.estatecoffee.com; Mon–Fri 8am–5pm, Sat 8:30am–1:30pm).

Los Pozos Termales ★   It's not Baden Baden, but these natural hot springs do offer a place to soak your sore muscles after a day of adventure. The hot springs are located west from Volcán on the road to Río Sereno, 8.5km (5 miles) from the Berard Supermarket. You'll need a 4WD to get through a couple of sticky ruts as you get closer to the hot springs, and because a river crosses the road, it can be impossible to cross after heavy rain.

Shopping for Handicrafts   Just before entering Volcán, on your left-hand side is **Artesanías Cruz Volcán ★★★** (© **6622-1502**), a shop that showcases exquisite woodworking and glasswork crafted by the talented José de la Cruz, who studied his craft in Italy. He's usually there between 8am and noon and 1 and 5pm, but call ahead to make sure he'll be there. You can watch him work for as long as you like. José has many ready-made items for sale, but given a few days he'll also custom-carve everything from signs to furniture to doors, which can be shipped or picked up later—so stop here on your way into the area rather than on your way out. You can also pick up handicrafts at the gift shop at **San Benito Crafts School** in town, which donates proceeds to the school. The Crafts School holds a market every weekend.

A NATURE SANCTUARY & COFFEE FARM WEST OF VOLCAN

Part of the allure of a visit to **Finca Hartmann ★★★** (© **6450-1853;** www. fincahartmann.com) is the drive there, which surely ranks among the top-five scenic drives in Panama. The twisting road requires that you take it slowly to avoid oncoming traffic, which whips around hairpin turns; you'll pass through beautiful dense forest that opens periodically for sweeping views. If you have a rental vehicle, this is a highly recommended day trip—or a tour operator can provide transportation.

Finca Hartmann is a boutique coffee farm producing shade-grown, high-quality beans typically sold to small specialty distributors. What's fascinating about their tours is the care that goes into producing such flavorful beans, and the Hartmann family's devotion and passion for the natural environment that surrounds them. More than anything else, the *finca* (farm) is known for is its position in the north-south corridor of migrating birds, thus ranking it as one of Panama's **bird-watching hot spots,** and many specialty bird-watching tours include this as part of their itinerary. Finca Hartman sits on the edge of La Amistad Parque Internacional; though they are not "official," hiking trails do exist and can be walked if reservations are made in advance so that a guide can accompany you. The only people you will see around the *finca* and along the trails—if you see anyone at all—are traditional Ngöbe-Buglé Indians.

There is a wooden *rancho* with an attractive coffee-tasting area and a small museum containing extensive bug collections and indigenous artifacts collected in the century that the Hartmanns have lived here. Coffee tours cost $10 per person, but a better bet is to plan a walking-and-coffee tour that includes lunch—contact Finca Hartmann for prices as each full-day tour is organized and priced individually. The Hartmanns have two picturesque but rustic cabins (with hot water but no electricity) tucked away in a small cloud forest at the end of a very rough road. Finca Hartmann is located in the tiny community of Santa Clara, on the road to Río Sereno. The turnoff is 27km (17 miles) from Volcán. Turn at the signed road and drive 1km (½ mile) until you reach the *finca*.

Where to Stay & Dine

Note: Restaurants close very early in Volcán, usually at 9pm (or earlier when tourism's low). The Hotel Dos Ríos has a restaurant and pizzeria, and the Hotel Don Tavo has inexpensive meals. Aside from the lodging options listed below, the **Mountain River Lake Inn** (✆ **771-5998** or 6585-6953; www.mountainriverlakeinn.com), located 20m (66 ft.) from the Hotel Dos Ríos on the road to the Rio Sereno, offers cabins, aparthotels, and long-term rental homes for $70 to $160 per night depending on the season and the type of accommodations, as well as a popular American bar/restaurant. For typical Panamanian food, head to **Restaurante Mary** (✆ **6704-1237**; Edificio Don Julio). Popular with locals, this no-frills restaurant is open 6:30 to 9pm every day. Don't expect top-notch service, but portions are big and the food is good. **Polineth** (✆ **6594-8113**) specializes in Thai food and is open daily from 11am to 9pm. Aside from offering some of the tastiest dishes in the Volcán area, there is also an interesting display of carnivorous plants here. Paul Votova, the owner and chef, asks for a $1 donation if visiting the carnivorous plant garden.

Hotel Dos Ríos ☺   The Hotel Dos Ríos offers the most upscale lodging in Volcán. That's not saying much, but considering the amenities offered and the friendly, helpful service, it's a good base for seeing the sights around the area. Guest rooms are average size and boast polished wooden floors and artistic, stenciled wall paintings; double rooms have two double beds, and there are triples with a double bed and a bunk bed. The quietest, and largest, rooms are the two suites at the end of the building, which come with a bed and a sofa bed. (Karaoke can be a problem on weekends, so if you want quiet, book one of these rooms.) Kids love the enclosed butterfly garden, and there is a kids' play area and a lot of grassy areas to run around in. The hotel's moderately priced, on-site restaurant, **Estrella Volcanera Restaurant,** serves decent international fare, mostly meats, pasta, and fish, and they have a pizzeria with takeout service (daily 7am–10pm). The staff can put together tours for guests.

Vía Río Sereno, west end of town. ✆ **771-5555** or 771-4271. www.dosrios.com.pa. 18 units. $77 double; $99 junior suite; $169 suite. AE, MC, V. **Amenities:** Restaurant; bar; kids' play area; Internet access; room service. *In room:* TV, hair dryer.

Hotel y Restaurante Don Tavo ✦   For budget accommodations, you can't beat Hotel Don Tavo. It's located on the main drag and is more attractive than the facade would lead you to believe because it is centered around a pleasant backyard patio garden adorned with a landscape mural and bougainvillea. Rooms are nothing fancy, but simple and clean, with hot-water showers (not typical for budget lodging in Panama). They have an Internet center with fast connections on the premises. The restaurant here, which serves basic Panamanian dishes, is open daily from 7am to 11pm.

Av. Central, near the church. ✆ **771-5144.** www.hoteldontavo.com. $29–$38 double; $66 quadruple. No credit cards. **Amenities:** Restaurant; Internet center. *In room:* TV, no phone.

Il Forno Restaurant ★★ ITALIAN   This Italian restaurant, with its cozy wooden interior, warm colors, and quiet Spanish music, is among my favorites in Volcán. Il Forno serves flavorful lasagnas, pastas, and pizzas. All pastas and raviolis are made on-site from scratch, as is the ricotta cheese. There is an excellent wine list, and be sure to save room for a tasty dessert.

Off the main avenue via Hotel California, 2nd house on the street. ☎ **771-5731.** $5.50–$8. No credit cards. Mon and Wed–Sat noon–3pm and 5–9pm; Sun noon–8:30pm.

Restaurante Cerro Brujo ★★ 🎁CONTEMPORARY PANAMANIAN   Tucked away in a residential area about 1km (½ mile) from the main road, this tiny restaurant, with an arty ambience, serves gourmet food, and is one of the better dining options west of Volcán Barú. The restaurant serves from a fixed-price menu that changes daily according to what is fresh and available on any given day. When I dined here, the offerings were homemade pea soup, tossed green salad with dill vinaigrette, and a choice of chicken in coconut and curry, or grilled beef filet. They have a limited wine list with mostly Chilean varieties. Service is a bit absent-minded, but the owner, Patty, is a delight and likes to personally greet her customers.

Heading west, turn right at restaurant sign before the road forks. ☎ **6669-9196.** Reservations recommended for lunch and dinner. Fixed-price menu $11–$13 per person. No credit cards. Daily noon–3pm and 6–9pm. (Call to verify open days during low season.)

BAMBITO, CERRO PUNTA & GUADALUPE ★★★

Bambito is 18km (11 miles) N of Volcán; Cerro Punta is 7km (4½ miles) from Bambito; Guadalupe is 2.5km (1½ miles) from Cerro Punta

Bambito, Cerro Punta, and Guadalupe are three of a dozen or so tiny farming communities nestled in a bucolic, alpine paradise. The area is characterized by rugged hills and peaks cloaked in thick emerald forest that is speckled with flowers and interspersed with a patchwork of colorful fields. Bambito is just a sprinkling of homes and services along the road. Cerro Punta is located in the crater of an extinct volcano, and is the epicenter of agricultural production. Cerro Punta sits at 1,800m (5,900 ft.), looking out over a fertile valley and craggy peaks beyond, and provides for a quick scenic drive past strawberry and flower farms. Guadalupe, too, has flower-filled streets and is flanked by quilt-like farms that slope up the surrounding hills. From here, the roads branch out to La Amistad International Park and Volcán Barú National Park. This is truly the loveliest alpine region in Panama.

What to See & Do in the Northwestern Highlands

For information about hiking in **Volcán Barú National Park,** see "What to See & Do," in the Boquete section, later in this chapter. Hikers on this side of the park are usually headed to Boquete along the stunning **Quetzal Trail.** The trail from this side of the volcano to Boquete is mostly downhill, and it's recommended that hikers walk the trail in this direction unless they're looking for a strenuous workout. If you don't plan on hiking this trail in its entirety, it's worth walking a portion of it and then heading back when you've had enough. The Respingo ranger station can be reached by walking 45 minutes up a rutted road from the main road near Bajo Grande, or by driving a 4WD to the station, where you'll find a high-altitude picnic site with views. For bird-watching and hiking tours here, see "Tour Outfitters," under "Volcán," earlier in this chapter.

Several farms in Cerro Punta are open to the public for visits; there are no regular hours, so just pop by if you're in the area. Turn at the first left just before Cerro Punta at the sign for the International Park and continue until you see **Finca Fresas Pariente,** a strawberry farm that will sell their fruit to passersby. Take a left at the road just past Pariente to **Panaflores,** an extensive flower farm with rows upon rows of flowers in a rainbow of colors, and an excellent spot for taking photos.

HIKING IN PARQUE INTERNACIONAL LA AMISTAD ★★★

La Amistad Park, popularly known by the Spanish acronym PILA, is "international" in that half the park is located in Costa Rica. La Amistad was formed in 1988 by the Panamanian and Costa Rican governments to protect the virgin forests and fragile ecosystems of the rugged Talamanca Range and its surrounding lowland buffer zones, and to protect one of the most biodiverse areas in the Americas. UNESCO designated the park a World Heritage Site in 1990, but, sadly, this hasn't been 100% effective in staunching encroachment by ranchers and hunters. Still, for the most part the park is totally untouched, creating a home for an extraordinary array of more than 100 mammal species, including endangered tapirs, jaguars, ocelots, pumas, and howler monkeys. There are also more than 400 species of birds like resplendent quetzals, crested eagles, harpy eagles, three-wattled bell birds, and a rare umbrella bird. The Panama side of the park encompasses 207,000 hectares (511,500 acres), the majority of which are part of the Bocas del Toro Province—but it is here at the administration area near Cerro Punta where hikers can access the primeval rainforest that is this park's characteristic feature. This is one of the wettest regions in Panama, so prepare yourself for damp conditions with waterproof clothing and shoes.

What I enjoy about La Amistad is that there are several trails for all levels of ability (and all weather conditions), and there are usually few people here. Also, after a morning of hiking through rainforest, you can have an inexpensive, delicious lunch at a cooperative cafe near the park ranger station, located just past the hamlet of Las Nubes. Three trails leave from the ranger station, and one trail currently under repair (Sendero los Antepasados), which might be open by the time you read this. **Sendero Puma Verde** is the easiest walk here and can be completed in 15 minutes. **Sendero El Retoño** is 2.1km (1.3 miles) and an easy 1-hour loop trail that is mostly flat. The trail is simply gorgeous, taking hikers through a dense jungle and a bamboo tunnel, and across babbling brooks. There are signs along the way identifying trees and other plants. **Sendero La Cascada** is 3.5km (2 miles) and about a 2-hour round-trip hike to a series of lookout points with mountain and valley views, and a crashing 49m (160-ft.) waterfall. Along the way is a detour to a lookout point that, on a very clear day, offers a view that stretches to the Caribbean. Taking this detour will add an extra 1½ hours to your trip; take a left at the fork at the Mirador Barranco. About half of this hike is uphill, and therefore moderately strenuous.

Lastly, **Sendero Cerro Picacho** takes gung-ho hikers along a narrow and poorly marked trail through primary forest up to a peak at 2,937m (9,635 ft.), where you can see from the Pacific to the Caribbean—and you can even spend the night here in a rustic hut. This trail is uphill, about 4km (2.5 miles), and a strenuous slog that should not be attempted without a guide. If you're not already booked with a guide,

THE WESTERN HIGHLANDS & THE GULF OF CHIRIQUÍ | Bambito & Gaudalupe call the co-op near the ranger station (see below for number) and they can arrange one for you. It takes about 3½ hours each way for this trail.

ANAM charges $5 per person to enter the park. Hours are daily from 7:45am to 4pm. There is very rustic lodging in bunks at the station for $15 per person, but you'll need a sleeping bag. They have a grungy kitchen for cooking meals, or you can visit the **Asociación Agroecoturística La Amistad (ASAELA)** co-op near the station. The small cafe serves daily specials such as stewed chicken, beans, and rice for $4.50; hot soup for 75¢; and breakfast. They also sell locally produced preserves and other goodies (✆ **771-2620**; daily 8am–4pm). There is also camping available for $6 per person.

FINCA DRACULA ★★

Despite the spooky name, this *finca* is revered as one of the most important orchid farms in Central America, with more than 2,000 species on display that are cloned to produce 250,000 plants yearly. The farm claims to have the most complete collection of rare American orchid species, some of which no longer exist in their natural habitat. The farm is owned by master orchid horticulturist Andres Maduro, who bought the property in 1969 and has allowed the former cattle ranch to reforest and return to its natural, exuberantly tropical state. The name of the *finca* refers to the Dracula orchid, an elegant purple flower that droops and hides itself during daylight. Tours of the orchid farm are best in April, when there's a higher incidence of blooming orchids, but on any day you're bound to see dozens of orchids in full bloom. Tours cost $10 per person, but they include a thorough guided tour of the facilities and laboratory to illustrate the delicate process involved in cloning. Tours for groups of eight or more are $7 per person. If you wish to visit the facilities without a guide, the cost is $5. Finca Dracula (✆ **771-2070**; www.fincadracula.com) is open Monday through Friday from 8 to 11:30am and 1 to 5pm.

TRUCHAS BAMBITO

This is less of an attraction and more of a place to reel in a fresh trout for dinner, if you have kitchen facilities or if your hotel's restaurant is willing to cook one up for you. Truchas Bambito is part of the Hotel Bambito (see below), but located on the other side of the road. Three pools here are packed with swimming trout; throw a line in and within minutes, or even seconds, you'll be reeling in a fish. Young kids, of course, really get a kick out of this attraction. The cost to rent a pole is $2.50; the cost per pound for a trout is $1.65. It's $3 per pound to have the fish gutted and filleted. Truchas Bambito is open daily from 8am to 3pm; they accept Visa or cash only.

Where to Stay & Dine

In contrast to Volcán, the lodging options below are nestled in forested areas that put travelers closer to natural surroundings (with the exception of Hotel Cerro Punta) and the two parks. Aside from the options included below, the **Cabanas Fistonich** (✆ **771-2115** or 6636-2244) offer simple cabins with TV and hot water, picturesquely situated on the edge of a river in the Nueva Suiza community. The cabins go from $65 for three to $100 for 10. **Cabañas Kucikas** (✆ **771-4245;** www.kucikas.com) offers 18 stand-alone units for $66 to $133, but you'll need to bring your own soap, toilet paper, and any other dispensable items.

There's not much in the way of restaurants in this area, meaning hotel restaurants are your best bets.

Casa Grande ★ ☺ Casa Grande is spread along a 121-hectare (300-acre) forested property and surrounded by a large lawn, neatly manicured gardens, and a river backed by forest. It's a beautiful location, and there are walking trails and dirt roads for bicycling. Guest rooms boast handsome teak and pine paneling and polished wood floors; some have wicker furniture (most are quite dark). Outside, there is a resort-style pool, an artificial lagoon with novelty trout fishing, a kids' play area, and a zip-line canopy ride for a fast thrill. The **spa** here is very complete, reasonably priced, and open to the public with advance notice. The resort has staff guides and can put you in touch with a specialty guide if they're booked.

The very pleasant **Blue Garden Restaurant** serves tasty fare with main courses ranging from $5 to $15, and has a slight Asian feel to it, though it serves international fare. Restaurant hours are 7am to 10pm.

Bambito. ⓒ **201-5555** or 771-5126. www.casagrandebambito.com. 20 units. $160–$184 garden suite; $154–$221 junior suite; $196–$265 royal suite. AE, MC, V. **Amenities:** Restaurant; bar; bikes; kids' play area; outdoor adult and kids' pools; room service; full-service spa. *In room:* TV, hair dryer.

Cielito Sur ★★ 👜 There are just four spacious but cozy rooms here, each decorated in a country style paired with indigenous artwork. Two rooms are slightly larger and feature kitchenettes, and two have king-size beds that can be divided into two twins. The rooms face the back garden and a long patio terrace where 12 species of hummingbirds whiz about. What I like is the plenitude of common areas so that you don't feel trapped in your room. There's a short trail that winds through the property, a thatched *bohio* hut with hammocks, a little house with an indoor whirlpool, and a comfy living room with reclining chairs and a well-stocked library. A hearty breakfast is included. Janet and Glenn can help plan daily excursions, and they seemingly know more about the highlands area than anyone I've met. The Cielito Sur is in Nueva Suiza, 10km (6¼ miles) from Volcán and just before Cerro Punta.

Nueva Suiza. ⓒ **771-2038.** www.cielitosur.com. 4 units. $80–$90 double. MC, V. Closed Oct. Children age 11 and under not accepted. **Amenities:** Bikes; whirlpool; Wi-Fi. *In room:* Hair dryer, kitchenette (some rooms).

Hotel Bambito ★ The guest rooms here are comfortable and spaciously appointed with a small sitting area and two double beds. There are also apartment suites with two stories and a living area. The hotel has fresh white exteriors accented with river rock and A-frame eaves in a vaguely Swiss style, and it is surrounded by handsomely landscaped and tidy grounds that include an artificial lagoon and creek. The restaurant serves decent international food, but they really could stand to spruce up their bar a bit and charge less for drinks. If you catch a fish at their neighboring trout farm (see "What to See & Do," below), they'll prepare it for your evening meal. The hotel is popular with Europeans and Panamanians, and sees its fair share of conventions and weddings. The hotel offers its own tours for an additional price. Breakfast is included in rates. Steep discounts are available in low season.

Bambito. ⓒ **771-4265.** www.hotelbambito.com. 45 units. $110 double; $125 junior suites; $160 master suites; $150 cabin. AE, MC, V. **Amenities:** Restaurant; bar; small gym; Internet access; heated pool; room service; tennis courts; whirlpool; sauna. *In room:* TV.

Hotel Cerro Punta It's a little low on style, but Hotel Cerro Punta is clean and inexpensive. The hotel, built in 1983, is on the Cerro Punta's main drag, and has a couple of rooms with mountain views (others are darker and do not have views). Guest rooms have a double bed and a twin that are reasonably comfortable. The Cerro Punta locals who run this hotel are nice people, and the restaurant here serves local dishes that cost between $4 and $9. My only caveat is that the owner is a hunter, and he's decorated his restaurant with the mounted animal heads and skins of native fauna—which might rub nature lovers the wrong way.

Cerro Punta. (C) **771-2020.** 10 units. $25 single; $30 double. MC, V. **Amenities:** Restaurant. *In room:* No phone.

Las Plumas ★ 🗝   The Dutch owners of Las Plumas offer five homes with full kitchens and living rooms that are truly a bargain. The spacious, stand-alone homes are spread across 2.4 hectares (6 acres) on landscaped gardens surrounded by forest. The homes can be rented nightly (3-night minimum) or long-term. The largest home, Quetzal, is a whopping 223 sq. m (2,400 sq. ft.), and contains three bedrooms, a fireplace, and terrace; the Woodpecker and Tanager houses have less than half the square footage, with two bedrooms each and a gazebo; Motmot and Hawk have three bedrooms each. Sparkling clean and fitted with contemporary furniture and fixtures, the houses have high-speed Internet and contain orthopedic beds and tiled floors.

Paso Ancho btw. Volcán and Cerro Punta. (C) **771-5541** or 6527-3848. www.las-plumas.com. 5 units. $60–$130 per night, house for 4–6 guests. Weekly and monthly rates also available. MC, V. *In room:* TV, high-speed Internet, kitchen, no phone.

Los Quetzales Lodge & Spa ★   Los Quetzales Lodge & Spa is a destination mountain lodge with guest rooms and backcountry cabins that appeal to hikers, nature lovers, and especially bird-watchers. Los Quetzales leads you to believe that their lodge is tucked away in a national forest, but it is really their handful of rustic wooden cabins that are nestled within the cloud forest of Volcán Barú National Park, about a 25-minute drive away from the lodge and up a brutal road. (They provide transportation to and from the lodge.) The lodge itself sits on the main road of the village of Guadalupe, next to a river and on a grassy property whose landscaping could use a lot of TLC.

The standard double guest rooms are cramped and dark. The spacious junior and master suites, as well as the stand-alone "duplex," are the best rooms, with wood-paneled walls, kitchenettes, and fireplaces (suites only). The suites can fit four to six people, but be aware that the suites have only one bathroom. There are two cheaper dormitories for up to eight, but they share just one bathroom. Of the six cabins available, I highly recommend only two: units 2 and 3. These rustic cabins are in stunning rainforest swirling with birds, and are attractively designed with patio terraces. They also are near trail heads for hiking. The other cabins are located too far up the road, and are dirty and not well maintained.

The service at Los Quetzales is at best absent-minded (or just absent). Rarely will you find anyone in reception, and when you do, prices are given arbitrarily, reservations are lost, and the staff is grossly unknowledgeable.

Guadalupe. (C) **771-2291.** www.losquetzales.com. 22 units, 6 cabins. All-inclusive packages cost, per person, based on double occupancy, $170 per person. Nightly rates are $75–$85 double; $95–$110 suite; $100–$175 cabin; $39 economy room. AE, MC, V. **Amenities:** Restaurant; bar; bikes; cybercafe; spa; horseback riding; volleyball. *In room:* No phone.

WEST OF VOLCÁN BARÚ: BOQUETE ★★★

40km (25 miles) from David; 473km (293 miles) from Panama City

This is the destination of choice for most tourists visiting the Chiriquí Highlands, and with nearly 25% of the population hailing from the United States, Canada, or Europe, it feels somewhat like a tropical colony—you'll find plenty of foreign-owned, international restaurants here, and you'll get along just fine even if you don't speak a word of Spanish. Boquete is one of the fastest changing destinations in Panama, with new restaurants, hotels, and real estate agencies opening left and right. Boquete is located in a steep-walled, green, and flower-filled valley on the flank of the Barú Volcano and at the shore of the Caldera River. Despite Boquete's somewhat utilitarian downtown made of cheap, concrete-poured buildings, the town on the whole oozes charm and offers a bounty of activities for travelers. Recently Boquete has climbed the charts to become one of the top-five retirement destinations in the world, and large-scale gated communities have begun their spread on the city's outskirts, much to the chagrin of longtime residents. With so many foreigners living in the area, Boquete has indeed taken on a more international feel than its counterpart Cerro Punta on the other side of the volcano. But, given the bounty of services, tours, attractions, gourmet restaurants, and a wide scale of lodging options, Boquete makes an ideal base for exploring the Chiriquí Highlands. Travelers who are keen to hike the Quetzal Trail would do well to visit Cerro Punta on the western side of the volcano first, and then walk to Boquete, sending their luggage around by vehicle.

Essentials

GETTING THERE & DEPARTING   Most hotels either provide transportation from the David airport or can arrange for you to be picked up by an independent taxi driver for the 45-minute drive to Boquete.

BY BUS & TAXI   Buses for Boquete leave from the David bus terminal every 25 minutes, take approximately 1 hour, and cost $1.45 one-way. You can catch a bus from Boquete to David from the north side of the main plaza. If you're coming from Bocas del Toro or from Panama City, you'll need to transfer in David. It takes 7 hours by bus from Panama City, and costs $13. A taxi from David to Boquete costs approximately $15 to $20 one-way, or you can contact **Boquete Shuttle Services** (© **720-0570**), which charges $15 each way.

BY CAR   If you're driving from Panama City, you'll turn right on the signed turnoff for Boquete before entering David, at the intersection next to the Shell gas station.

From the airport in David, turn right onto the main road and drive until you arrive at the intersection with the Shell station, then turn left. Drive until you reach a stop sign at the four-lane highway, turn right, and continue until you reach the intersection at the Super Barú supermarket. Turn left and continue onward to Boquete.

The road to Boquete is well paved; there are two side roads that provide shortcuts if you're driving from the Bocas del Toro area.

GETTING AROUND   If you're a do-it-yourself traveler who likes to explore at your own pace, you'll want to rent a vehicle to get around—but you'll have to do it from the David airport (p. 214); alternatively, some hotels can arrange for a rental car to be

Bajareque

The *bajareque* is a unique weather phenomenon that occurs from December to March, when a fine misting rain is pushed over from the Atlantic and into the highlands. The mist is so soft it "caresses the face," as locals like to say. The combination of sun, wind, and *bajareque* provides endless rainbows.

delivered to you in Boquete for an additional $30. I strongly recommend renting a car in Boquete, as it's the best way to explore the countryside.

Taxis around town cost $1 to $3; unless your hotel is located in the town center, you'll need one to get back and forth. If you're looking for a fluent English-speaking taxi driver for a half- or full-day tour around Boquete, try **Daniel Higgins** (© 6617-0570); he charges $15 per hour.

Local buses cruise Avenida Central and the hilly roads around Boquete, but taxis are so cheap that you'll invariably end up hailing a cab before a bus.

ORIENTATION   Boquete's **CEFATI visitor center** (© 720-4060; daily 9am–4:30pm) is the large building on your right just before you enter town. Call ahead about weekend hours. With its location high above the Río Caldera, the visitor center provides sweeping views of town. You'll find **Café Kotowa** here, too, with a small shop. On the center's second floor is an interpretive display (in Spanish) of the history and anthropology of the region. Ask for a representative here to give you a quick tour and translate the displays. The center isn't within walking distance from downtown, so you'll need to take a cab ($1) or a local bus (25¢).

Boquete sits in a fertile valley below the Barú Volcano, and is bisected by the Caldera River. A recent flood redirected the river, and when I was in town, there was currently construction going on to avoid future flooding. The main street, Avenida Central, runs the length of town from north to south, and businesses and transportation services are clustered around the main plaza on streets that run east-west. From downtown, a series of paved and gravel roads climb the hilly terrain surrounding Boquete.

FAST FACTS   For the **police,** dial © 104; for the **fire department,** dial © 720-1224. The **Centro Médico San Juan Bautista,** located on Avenida Central, 2 blocks up the road past the Hotel Panamonte, has English-speaking doctors; for serious health problems, you'll need to head to the hospital in David. The **post office** is located on the plaza, and is open Monday to Friday 8am to 5:45pm, and Saturday 8am to 4:45pm; for fast service go to **Mailboxes Etc** (© 720-2684) on Avenida Central, in front of the Almacén Reina.

Twenty-four-hour ATMs can be found at **Banco Nacional** and **Global Bank,** which lie across from each other on Avenida Central and Calle 5 Sur (Mon–Fri 8am–3pm, Sat 9am–noon). There is also an ATM in **Los Establos Plaza** in downtown. Most hotels have a computer with Internet access or Wi-Fi for their guests, or try **Java Juice** on Avenida Central.

What to See & Do

There's no shortage of things to see and do in Boquete: adrenaline-pumping outdoor adventures, quiet forays in the rainforest seeking the elusive quetzal, and walks among perfume-scented flowers at public gardens; you can learn how to make a good cup of joe and about the local Ngöbe-Buglé tribe . . . and the list goes on. As

Boquete

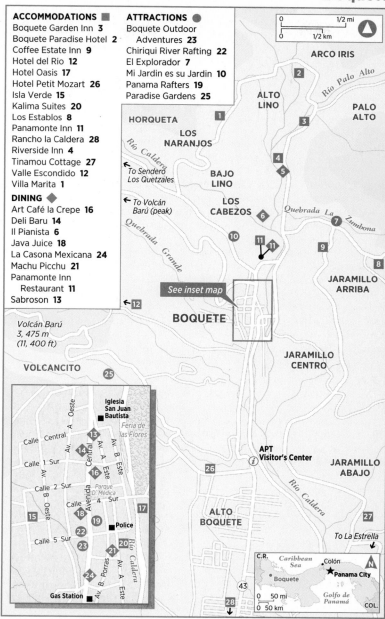

ACCOMMODATIONS ■
Boquete Garden Inn **3**
Boquete Paradise Hotel **2**
Coffee Estate Inn **9**
Hotel del Rio **12**
Hotel Oasis **17**
Hotel Petit Mozart **26**
Isla Verde **15**
Kalima Suites **20**
Los Establos **8**
Panamonte Inn **11**
Rancho la Caldera **28**
Riverside Inn **4**
Tinamou Cottage **27**
Valle Escondido **12**
Villa Marita **1**

DINING ◆
Art Café la Crepe **16**
Deli Baru **14**
Il Pianista **6**
Java Juice **18**
La Casona Mexicana **24**
Machu Picchu **21**
Panamonte Inn
  Restaurant **11**
Sabroson **13**

ATTRACTIONS ●
Boquete Outdoor
  Adventures **23**
Chiriqui River Rafting **22**
El Explorador **7**
Mi Jardin es su Jardin **10**
Panama Rafters **19**
Paradise Gardens **25**

0 ——— 1/2 mi
0 ——— 1/2 km

ARCO IRIS

Río Palo Alto

ALTO LINO

PALO ALTO

HORQUETA

LOS NARANJOS

Río Caldera

To Sendero
Los Quetzales →

← To Volcán
Barú (peak)

Quebrada Grande

BAJO LINO

LOS CABEZOS

Quebrada La Zumbona

JARAMILLO ARRIBA

See inset map

BOQUETE

Volcán Barú
3, 475 m
(11, 400 ft)

JARAMILLO CENTRO

VOLCANCITO

Iglesia
San Juan
Bautista

Feria de
las Flores

Calle Central

Av. A Oeste

Av. A Este

Av. B Este

Av. Central

APT
Visitor's Center

JARAMILLO ABAJO

Río Caldera

Calle 1 Sur

Parque
D. Médica

Calle 2 Sur

Avenida B Oeste

Calle 4 Sur

Calle Central

ALTO BOQUETE

Calle 5 Sur

Police

Av. B Porras

Av. A Este

Río Caldera

To La Estrella ↓

Gas Station

C.R.   Caribbean
            Sea   Colón
                          ★ Panama City
      Boquete
                    Golfo de
                    Panamá
0 ——— 50 mi   COL.
0 ——— 50 km

9

THE WESTERN HIGHLANDS & THE GULF OF CHIRIQUÍ | West of Volcán Barú mentioned throughout this chapter, a lot of visitors opt to rent a car—the area offers so many beautiful scenic drives. Here are a few:

The **Bajo Mono Loop** takes you high above the town along a newly asphalted road for panoramic vistas and beautiful forest scenery. This is a good drive from which to get your bearings and see why everyone's gone wild about living in Boquete. To get here, follow the main road past the church and head left at the fork, passing Café Ruiz and staying left until you see the sign for BAJO MONO. Just as pretty is the **Volcancito Loop**—to get here, follow the main road out of town and when you see the CEFATI visitor center, turn right and follow the loop until you arrive back at town. You can bike these loops as well. (See "Biking," below.)

One of the most beautiful drives in Panama heads to **Finca Suiza** (p. 247) on the main road to the Atlantic Coast, in the Bocas del Toro Province. The scenic drive winds through mountain forests and open fields with sweeping views, and farther down to the lush lowlands and rainforest of Bocas Province. Take the left turn to Caldera 16km (10 miles) south of Boquete and continue along paved/gravel road, until you hit the major road to Bocas. You can also take a completely paved, easier-to-follow road by heading toward David and turning left toward Gualaca.

Boquete Mountain Safari Tours (© **6627-8829** or 6742-6614; www.boquetemountainsafaritours.com) is a relatively new company well known for their bilingual, open-air yellow jeep tours. They offer wildlife tours ($80 full day), as well as half-day tours to the Caldera Hot Springs ($35) and the Boquete Mountains ($35) among others. Their latest offering is called the Grand Coffee Adventure, in which you travel through the lush cloud forest and mountainsides to visit various boutique coffee estates for tastings, as well as a new horseback riding tour and horseback riding and coffee-tasting tour for $60. Boquete Mountain Safari Tours is a professional operation, and all tour guides speak English. Check their website for a full listing of full- and half-day excursions.

HIKING & BIRD-WATCHING OUTFITTERS/GUIDES

The following tour outfitters and local guides offer hiking, bird-watching, and other general excursions to destinations and attractions listed below in this section. With their new office in Boquete, the reputable Panama City–based adventure company **Ecocircuitos** recently closed their Boquete office, but their Boquete representative can be reached at **6617-6566.** Ecocircuitos is a one-stop shop for short adventures in the Chiriquí area; they offer kayaking, hiking, family-adventures, and bird-watching day trips and focus on green tourism that promotes local communities. Another company, **Coffee Adventures** (see "Coffee Tours," below), offers guided excursions around Boquete and their bird-watching tours are particularly good. Coffee Adventures offers cultural excursions to a Ngöbe-Buglé community near the Caribbean coast, guided hikes on Los Quetzales Trail from Boquete to Cerro Punta (or vice versa), and low-key excursions like bird-watching and trips to the Caldera Hot Springs. **Aventurist** (p. 236) also offers hiking tours of Boquete, the surrounding area, and the Chiriquí lowlands. **Feliciano González** is a local guide with more than 20 years' experience in the Boquete area (© **6632-8645** or 6624-9940; www.geocities.com/boquete_tours). He has a 4WD vehicle, speaks basic English, and can customize tours of Boquete as well as day hikes on the Quetzales Trail, the Pianista Trail, and the full-day hike to the summit of Volcano Barú ($100 for up to four people). Based in Volcán,

Nariño Aizpurua (© 771-5049 or 6775-0118; westernwindnature@yahoo.com or nature_tour@yahoo.com) is a fun and friendly guide who specializes in bird-watching; he is a recommended guide for Los Quetzales Trail if you plan to start on that side. Half-day tours start at $60. Transportation isn't included in prices. (See "Volcán," earlier in this chapter, for more information about his other trips.)

For birding, you can't beat local guide **Santiago "Chago" Caballero** (© 6626-2200; santiagochagotours@hotmail.com) or one of his protégés. Want to see a quetzal? If you're here from December to May, Santiago can guarantee you will—the reason he is such a valued guide in the region. Santiago typically takes birders to Finca Lérida but can customize tours, including searches for wild orchids in the rainforest. Terry from Coffee Adventures offers private bird-watching tours and her knowledge is unbeat in Boquete.

SPAS

The best spa in town is the new **Haven Spa** (© 730-9345; www.boquetespa.com), located just left of the Accel gas station. Boquete's best gym is also here, and you can take part in exercise and aquatic classes, use their whirlpool and infrared sauna, or enjoy a hot stone or traditional massage. Most of the staff speaks English. There are also five smallish but elegant rooms on-site with more in the plans if you want to focus your visit to Boquete on Haven Spa. They offer day passes for $25 and week passes for $50, which allows guests to use the pool, gym, sauna, and whirlpool. There is also a spa at Valle Escondido (p. 242).

EXPLORING EL PARQUE NACIONAL VOLCAN BARU

As the name states, this national park is centered around the 3,475m (11,500-ft.) extinct **Barú Volcano,** the highest point in the country and the beloved center of adventurous outdoor pursuits for bird-watchers, hikers, rafters, and nature lovers. The park is situated on the Pacific-facing side of the Talamanca Mountain Range, and encompasses 14,000 hectares (34,600 acres) of rugged topography cloaked in primary and secondary rainforest. This rainforest provides a home to nearly 250 species of birds, the most notable of which is the **resplendent quetzal,** whose extraordinary beauty puts the bird in the number-one spot on many a bird-watching list. Other rare birds here include the silky flycatcher, the three-wattled bellbird, and the hairy woodpecker. Owing to the volcano's height and isolation, this area is considered a "bioclimatic island." Its forest is home to unique species of orchids and uncommon flora such as magnolia and giant oak trees, some of which are between 600 and 900 years old. You'll also see wild bamboo gardens and gigantic, gnarled trees dripping with vines and sprouting prehistoric-looking bromeliads from their trunks. In higher reaches, an intermittent cloud forest provokes an eerie ambience. All said, it's a wonderful place to hike and immerse yourself in wild beauty, but come prepared with waterproof outerwear and shoes and a dry change of clothes just in case. In this national park, temperatures average 50° to 60°F (10°–16°C).

Natural beauty aside, the park is economically important because it protects the headwaters that provide irrigation to the country's prime agricultural region, concentrated in the fertile areas of the volcano's skirt. These rivers are also revered by rafters and kayakers for their Class III to Class V rapids, which provide thrills and a sense of remote solitude—a sure recipe for adventure. For more information about rafting, see below.

Volcán Barú National Park is administered by ANAM, which has ranger stations at the Los Quetzales trail heads in both Boquete (Alto Chiquero) and Cerro Punta (El Respingo), and charges a $3-per-person entrance fee. Both ranger stations have a handful of truly rustic bunks with shared bathrooms, which cost $5 per bed. There's not much ambience at the Boquete station to encourage even the hardiest of nature lovers to lodge there, however. A taxi to the ranger station, about 8km (5 miles) from Boquete, costs $3. Volcán Barú is a tough hike, and unfortunately, the views are not as fantastic as one would hope; however, fit hikers who want to challenge themselves will enjoy the hike.

HIKING   By any measure, the most popular trail is **Sendero Los Quetzales ★★★**, a superb, short-haul day hike—regarded as the best in Panama by most visitors to the country. The rainforest here is thick and lush and dazzling with its array of colorful birds, panoramic lookout points, and crystalline streams rushing across velvety moss-covered rocks. Most important, and most unique, is the fact that the trail connects Cerro Punta (and Guadalupe) with Boquete, allowing hikers to have their baggage sent from one town to the other, and to arrive by foot at their next destination. If you're physically up to it, I recommend the entire trek as one of the region's highlights—but there are *a few things to consider* before setting out. First, Cerro Punta's altitude is 1,981m (6,500 ft.), while Boquete's is 975m (3,200 ft.)—so the trail is mostly downhill from Cerro Punta. Now, a lot of Boquete residents and tour guides will pooh-pooh the level of difficulty and stamina needed to complete the uphill trail from Boquete to Cerro Punta, but every hiker I saw doing the trail uphill looked just frazzled. In other words, if you're fit and looking for a workout, walk Boquete to Cerro Punta; if not, either plan your trip so that you visit the western region of the volcano first and then Boquete or, if you only plan to walk the trail for the day, leave early and drive to Cerro Punta. For those who want to just get out and hike around a little, you'll be okay because the first couple of kilometers from the Boquete ranger station are relatively flat, offer outstanding opportunities to see birds (especially the quetzal), and put you in the middle of a stream-lined forest. You can walk as little or as much as you like and then turn around and head back.

The Quetzales Trail from Boquete begins with a 45-minute walk from the ranger station on a semi-paved road. After the sign for the trail head, the trail continues for about 2 hours before heading up into a steep ascent. Midway up the ascent is a picnic area with tables. Farther up, about halfway along the trail, is a sweeping lookout point, with a roofed eating area and a couple of campsites.

From the Cerro Punta ranger station, a rutted road requiring a 4WD heads downhill for almost 3km (2 miles) until it reaches the paved road to Cerro Punta. Tour operators and taxis with 4WD traction can make it up and down this road, but few seem willing—so prepare yourself to walk this portion. The total number of trail miles is anyone's guess, as park signs, rangers, and tour guides all disagree on the distance; it's estimated that the trail is about 9.7km (6 miles). From station to station, plan on 6 to 7 hours if walking uphill, and 4½ hours if walking downhill, plus another 45 minutes to 1 hour for the last leg of the Cerro Punta ranger station to the road.

Keen adventurers might be interested in the trail to the **volcano's summit,** a very arduous climb that puts visitors at the highest point in Panama and offers electrifying views from the Caribbean Sea to the Pacific Ocean. Although this trail can be reached from the Cerro Punta side, the trail from the Boquete side is far easier and better marked. You don't want to get lost on the volcano and spend the night freezing in the wet rainforest. This is but one of the serious considerations you must make when attempting to summit the volcano. The trail, an old service road, is ragged and rough, and even the most agile hikers often slip and fall on the slick downhill trip. Second, the trail is confusing in some areas, so it's highly recommended that you hire a guide. Lastly, the peak is shrouded in thick clouds with such frequency that the chances of seeing the view are not particularly good; but even on good-weather days you'll want to begin the hike at the crack of dawn to increase your chances of clear skies. The trail takes between 5 and 6 hours to climb, and about 4 to 5 hours to descend.

Keep in mind that the Qutezal trail hasn't been all that well maintained, meaning hiking can be difficult in some areas where the vegetation is thicker and the trail less visible.

RIVER RAFTING & KAYAKING

The translucent rivers that pour down the Talamanca Mountain Range in the Chiriquí Highlands provide for thrilling Class III to V white-water kayaking and rafting, and gentler floats for the whole family. What's special about the Chiriquí area is that relatively few paddlers have discovered it, so rafters and kayakers have the crystalline river and pristine, tropical mountain scenery—replete with birds and wild animals—all to themselves. Also, the variety and number of rivers in this area provide fanatics with enough white-water options to fill a week with rafting or kayaking.

Technical rides that are 2 to 5 hours in duration with Class III to Class V conditions are principally on the **Chiriquí River** east of Volcán Barú and close to Boquete, and the **Chiriquí Viejo River** west of the volcano, near the Costa Rica border. The Chiriquí Viejo River is revered by rafters for its challenging rapids and exuberant scenery, but it is a full-day trip that requires a scenic drive to the other side of the volcano. (Visitors to Volcán or Cerro Punta are closer to the put-in site for this river.) Unfortunately, the Chiriquí Viejo is being threatened by a series of dams for a hydroelectric project—but for now it's pristine and a lot of fun to ride. There are tamer floats, too, such as the **Esti River,** a Class II that is perfect for young rafters, families, and beginners; and there's the **Gariche River,** with Class II and III rapids that are suitable for beginners but a bit more technical and adrenaline-charged than an easy float. Many rivers can be rafted year-round, but others, like the Chiriquí and the Gariche, are rafted from July to November when the rivers are full.

Two reputable rafting companies in Boquete have years of experience and expert knowledge of the region. **Chiriquí River Rafting,** on Avenida Central (© **720-1505** or 6618-0846; www.panama-rafting.com), is run by Héctor Sanchez, a rafting pioneer in the Chiriquí Highlands, with more than 2 decades of experience and an excellent safety record. Héctor and his guides are fluent in English. Depending on the river and logistics, rafting trips cost between $85 and $105, and require a minimum of four guests (a few trips require only three guests); trips include all gear, transportation, and lunch. Héctor can also plan multiple-day packages that include rafting, hiking, fishing, and more. Note that Chiriquí River Rafting offers accommodations at **El Bajareque Lodge,** a hostel-like spot with dynamite views, simple bunks, and communal meals; Héctor also offers more upscale rooms in his private home.

Panama Rafters (© **720-2712;** www.panamarafters.com), with offices next to Java Juice on Avenida Central offers kayaking on the many rivers of the Chiriquí Highlands, and they offer beginning and intermediate kayaking instruction. Panama

Rafters employs highly qualified guides that adhere to strict Canadian standards. Rafting trips cost an average of $75 for a half-day trip, $90 for a full-day trip—which includes transportation, gear, and lunch. Check out their website or contact them for multiple-day rafting packages with outdoors camping.

Boquete Outdoor Adventures (© **720-2284** or 6630-1453; www.boquete outdooradventures.com) is run by the friendly and enthusiastic Jim Omer and specializes in white-water kayaking trips, and offers a number of different excursions in the Chiriquí Highlands as well as the Boca Chica Region. Some of their sea kayak excursions include Boca Brava and the 1-day white-water kayak sampler, which serves as an introduction to white-water kayaking. There are motorboat excursions to the Laguna de Chiriquí and the Golfo de Chiriquí, as well excellent excursions to Isla Coiba. Trips range from $60 to $80 per person.

OTHER OUTDOOR ACTIVITIES IN THE AREA

BIKING   Boquete provides visitors with kilometer upon kilometer of picturesque, winding roads; moderate terrain; and pastoral views. Bicyclists on main paved roads will need to keep an eye open for speeding motorists, as there are virtually no shoulders and lots of blind curves. For bike rental, check out Panama Rafters on Avenida Central (see above) or Boquete Tree Trek (see "Canopy Tours," below). The cost to rent is $3 per hour. A half-day bike tour around Boquete is offered by **Aventurist** (© **720-1635** or 6615-3300; www.aventurist.com). Tours begin by traveling by vehicle to the scenic heights at Alto Quiel, where bicyclists and their guide descend for 2 hours for a total of 26km (16 miles) until they reach town. Tours leave at 7am and 1pm, and cost $25 per person.

CANOPY TOURS   Canopy tours, the adventure fad of zipping through the tree-tops suspended by a harness attached to a cable, are available through **Boquete Tree Trek** at Avenida Central (© **720-1635;** www.aventurist.com). This exhilarating ride is appropriate for kids as young as 3, and the weight limit for each rider is 113 kilograms (250 lb.) for men, and 77 kilograms (170 lb.) for women. The zip line is 3km (1¾ miles) long, with a drop of 351m (1,150 ft.), and is located in the upper reaches of the Palo Alto valley, about 45 minutes from town. A 2½- to 3-hour canopy adventure costs $60. Women should avoid wearing skirts because of the harness seat. The best attire is long pants or shorts that do not ride up too high and closed-toe shoes like sneakers or hiking boots.

HORSEBACK RIDING   **Eduardo Caño** (© **720-1750** or 6629-0814), a local guide from Boquete, is the man to go for horseback riding tours of 2 to 5 hours, loping along trails on the outskirts of Boquete in areas such as Volcancito and Jaramillo. The views of Boquete and the surrounding area are simply splendid, but Eduardo speaks limited English, so unless you know Spanish, you'll need your hotel to call and make arrangements. Sample prices for two are $5 per person per hour. Also, contact **Ecocircuitos** (see "Hiking & Bird-Watching Outfitters/Guides," above) for horseback riding or to hire an English-speaking nature guide to accompany you and Eduardo on your ride. Boquete Mountain Safari tours offer $40 horseback rides around town, $60 for horseback riding and coffee tasting.

HOT SPRINGS   The **Caldera Hot Springs** comprises four undeveloped pools in natural surroundings, with mineral water in varying temperature grades. It's worth a stop if you're a huge fan of hot springs, are already in the area, or are looking for a pretty low-key activity—otherwise, I can't figure out what the big to-do about Caldera is, especially considering that it's a good half-hour drive from Boquete. The hot springs are next to the Caldera River, which you can bathe in as well. To get here, you'll need to be part of a tour, or have a 4WD (you might make it in a regular car, but just barely). Head south from Boquete, and 11km (7 miles) later, turn left at the sign for Caldera; once you arrive in Caldera keep driving until you see a sign for the hot springs. Follow a rather brutal dirt road to the end and then walk about 10 minutes to the hot springs.

COFFEE TOURS

Did you know that Panama produces some of the most flavorful coffee in the world? A relatively new player on the gourmet-coffee market, the country produces traditional shade-grown-coffee varieties that are generally considered to be more complex and distinctive than those produced by its more famous neighbor, Costa Rica. Most coffee plantations in Panama are centered around Boquete because of the high altitude required for prime coffee growing, and because of the region's fertile volcanic soil. Coffee tours are available and highly recommended—really, you'll never look at your morning cup of joe the same once you've taken a tour with one of the companies below. Even coffee snobs will glean insight not only into the meticulous growing process but into the economics of the local Ngöbe-Buglé indigenous labor and culture, the "shade-grown" theory to protect the environment and to grow a better bean, the effect coffee has on the world, and what coffee producers really think about Starbucks. Tours are capped off with a "cupping," which, much like a wine-tasting (and *almost* as fun), gives you a chance to sample different flavors, strengths, and roasts. In addition to the following companies, see Finca Lérida's tours below.

Casa Ruiz, S.A. Café Ruiz ★★ (② 720-1000 or 6672-3786; www.caferuiz-boquete.com) is one of the oldest and most respected coffee producers in the country and the national top-quality coffee-roasting organization. A guided visit entails a three-stop visit to the plantation, the processing plant, and the roasting-and-packaging facility. This is an ideal visit for those interested in seeing large-scale production that includes boutique operation and quality traceability. Visits, led by a jovial and bilingual local Ngöbe-Buglé descendant Indian guide, are offered Monday through Saturday from 9am to noon, or from 1 to 4pm; the cost is $30 per person. Alternatively, you can visit the roasting facility for a 45-minute informational general session on high-end quality coffee; the cost is $9 per person. Casa Ruiz, S.A. is the largest specialty green coffee exporter of Panama.

Café Kotowa ★★ (② 720-1430; www.kotowacoffee.com) is a boutique coffee farm founded nearly a century ago by a Scottish immigrant, and it's still run by the same family. Kotowa, the indigenous word for "mountain," has earned a reputation for producing award-winning coffee beans, and though they've since moved on to modern production means, the farm's antique, water-powered mill still exists and is part of their fascinating tour. Visits to Kotowa are one-stop—first you amble through the coffee plantation behind the mill, then you tour the production-and-roasting facility, and finally you have a cupping in the old mill. The tour is led by Hans and Terry of **Coffee Adventures** (② 720-3852; www.coffeeadventures.net), who pioneered coffee tours in Boquete and who are animated and amusing. Tours are Monday through Saturday at 2pm and cost $20 per person, which includes transportation from Boquete to their farm in Palo Alto. Children must be 10 or older, unless they're part of a private tour. Private tours cost $45 per person but can be scheduled at any time, including Sundays. This is the best coffee tour in Boquete.

Finca Lérida ★★★ (see below) also offers coffee tours.

SPANISH-LANGUAGE PROGRAMS

Habla Ya Spanish School, located on Avenida Central above the Global Bank (*©* **730-8344;** www.hablayapanama.com), offers intensive "survival" Spanish courses, as well as more advanced conversational and fluency courses. Beginner survival courses are ideal for the traveling monolinguals with little time in Boquete but who'd love to speak enough to get around; weekly group classes cost $50 for 4 hours, $225 for 20 hours; weekly private courses cost $60 for 4 hours and $295 for 20 hours.

ATTRACTIONS IN & AROUND TOWN

Finca Lérida ★★★ (*©* **720-2285;** www.fincalerida.com; open daily sunrise–sunset) is a lovely 324-hectare (800-acre) coffee plantation and nature reserve located 10 minutes from Boquete in the lofty alpine setting of Alto Quiel. The *finca* is widely regarded as one of the most important bird-watching sites in Panama, not only because of the sheer numbers of species on view here but because it is a hot spot for seeing the resplendent quetzal, among other rare birds. The Finca Lérida has stepped up operations lately, building an 11-room ecolodge on their property and a new exhibit showcasing their highly rated coffee growing process, and giving information about the biodiversity of their property and the surrounding region.

They've also standardized their tours. Finca Lérida has three nature trails (one easy, two moderate) that offer a chance to put yourself in the middle of pristine primary and secondary forest. Independent visitors are charged $10 per person for access to the trails, and though they're marked, there are no maps or interpretive information available. The *finca* works with the best local birding and naturalist guides, if you need one (it's highly recommended if you come to bird-watch); the cost is an additional $25. Or you can book a 2-hour coffee tour for $16 per person, and take to the trails following the tour. For the complete (and somewhat pricey) package, a full-day tour includes a guide, bird-watching, coffee tour, gourmet lunch, transportation to and from Boquete, and access to trails for $310 for two guests.

Mi Jardín es Su Jardín ★★, or "My Garden is Your Garden," refers to the lavish private gardens of the González family, who live on the property but have opened their grounds to the public. These gardens are some of the most exquisite in Panama, with hundreds of varieties of flowers expertly tended and cared for. But, weirdly, the whole spread is chockablock with nutty figurines and statues of windmills, dinosaurs, a blue cow, wee little castles, cutouts of frolicking children, and other oddball decorative items. The garden was built by a family with a Down syndrome child; legend has it the family hid the child for years until they saw her playing with some of the workers' children and realized their mistake. They then decided to build a children's garden for their daughter and other children. There is a children's playground on the property, too. Admission is free, and the garden is open daily during daylight hours. To get here, head up the main street past the church, and stay left at the fork and continue until you see the gardens on your right-hand side.

One of the more curious attractions in Boquete is **El Explorador** gardens (*©* **720-1989**), which provide visitors with splendid panoramic views enhanced by classical background music. But what's really the attraction here are the eccentric gardens sprinkled with vernacular, artlike recycled items: old television sets, a sewing

Stop & Smell the Flowers: Festivals in Boquete

Boquete's largest annual festival is the **Feria de las Flores y del Café (Flowers and Coffee Festival),** which coincides with the coffee-harvesting season and takes place at the local fairgrounds in mid-January. The festival is one of the grandest celebrations of flowers in the world, drawing thousands of people to Boquete, clogging roads, and filling up hotels (book well ahead of time). During the 10-day festival, the fairgrounds fill with lushly landscaped and intricately designed flower displays that stretch the length of the facilities. Local residents follow suit and spruce up their gardens, too, giving Boquete the feel of a horticultural Xanadu. Coffee plays a big role, with tastings of local java and sales of coffee by the bag and by the cup. There are other festival-oriented attractions like food stands, live music, amusement rides, handicrafts booths, and more—these activities take place only during the festival, but from January to April the flower exhibits are on display daily; entrance fee is $1.

Later, in mid-April, Boquete holds the same kind of festival but on a reduced scale, the 4-day **Feria de Orquídeas (Orchid Festival),** when local orchid growers showcase thousands of varieties of these delicate flowers for public viewing (many orchids bloom in Apr). Other large-scale festivals in Boquete are celebrated nationally; however, considering Boquete's charm and desirable ambience, many Panamanians head here for a few days of respite. Book your hotel well ahead of time during these dates: Carnaval (Feb), Semana Santa (Holy Week before Easter), and Independence celebrations (weekends of Nov 3, 10, and 28).

machine, boots used as planters, shopping carts, old bottles, and more. For example, there is a bush clipped to resemble a cartoonish animal, and in its mouth is a plastic doll—but what this means is anyone's guess. The main purpose of the gardens is to offer a place for quiet reflection and "spiritual renewal." To this end, the gardens feature signs (in Spanish only) with uplifting quotes to boost a visitor's self-esteem. As hokey as it seems, you do leave El Explorador feeling a little better. The garden park is owned by the Miranda family, who bought this property and began decorating it according to whim until it grew into a public venue. There is a cafe here with snacks, fresh fruit juices, and coffee. El Explorador costs $1 per person, and is open daily from 9am to 6pm. To get here, stay right at the fork on the main road and follow the signs.

Paradise Gardens ★ (© **6657-5555;** paradisegardensboquete@gmail.com) is a wild animal rescue and rehabilitation center where you'll find animals such as monkeys, tamarins, macaws, parrots, jaguars, and more that have been injured in the wild or abandoned by their owners. Most of the animals stay here for a little while until they're well enough to be released into the wild, but others that have lived in captivity all their lives or that have been seriously injured are permanent residents here. Begun by a British couple, Paradise Gardens is now a completely volunteer-run organization. Aside from the animal life found here, there are also lovely gardens, a butterfly house, and a lavastone fountain. There is a minimum $5 entrance fee when visiting Paradise Gardens. The center is located past Fresas Mary on the road to Volcancito. Inquire about volunteer opportunities.

SHOPPING

Coffee is the local product you won't want to leave Boquete without, and bagged beans are sold all around town in cafes and grocery stores. **Café Kotowam,** at the visitor center just before town, sells top-rated blends and souvenir and gift packs. No stores in the Tocuman International Airport sell coffee, so don't put off until the last minute buying a few bags of Panama's best. The **Harmony Gift Shop** on Avenida Central has arts and crafts, jewelry, and other gift items for sale. **Souvenir El Cacique,** on Avenida Central at the plaza, has indigenous handicrafts made by the Ngöbe-Buglé, Kuna, and Emberá indigenous groups, plus handicrafts from indigenous groups around Central America. **Ingana Art Shop** (✆ 720-1699) sells ethnic handicrafts and art from all over the world, and the **Galeria de Arte** (✆ 6769-6090), adjacent to Art Café La Crepe, 150m north of the church, sells jewelry, molas, ceramics, and paintings by international artists. **Boquete Mountain Safari Tours** (p. 232) recently opened a store in Los Establos Plaza (✆ 720-1147) that sells Panama-made handicrafts, Boquete maps, souvenirs, and coffee.

Where to Stay

Travelers can opt to stay in town and be close to services and restaurants, or outside of the town center in a more forested setting. No hotel mentioned here is farther than a 10-minute drive from town. Air-conditioning is available at some hotels but is really not necessary given the elevation of Boquete. Breakfast is included in the price unless otherwise specified. Note that some hotels sell out for the Flower and Coffee Festival in January, so you'll need to plan ahead. In addition, **Valle del Rio Inn,** located just down the road from the Valle Escondido Resort (✆ 720-2525; www.elvalledelrio boquete.com) offers 25 standard chain-like doubles and one three-bedroom suite. There's nothing special about this hotel, but there are two excellent restaurants on grounds, the **Pomodoro** and **the Wine Bar,** which are both open to the public. **Finca Lérida** (p. 238) has an attractive ecolodge with 11 comfortable and bright rooms for $80 to $90 a night; this is the best spot in Boquete for bird-watchers. If you're just looking for a cheap place to put your head down right in town, **Kalima Suites** (✆ 720-2884) offers six uninspired but clean suites starting at $40 a night.

EXPENSIVE

Boquete Garden Inn ★★   This irresistible inn is one of my favorites in Boquete, although it's actually five cabin bungalows, a central reception building, and a gazebo lounge scattered around a lovely, well-tended garden on the shore of the Palo Alto River. The octagon-shaped, ocher-colored cabins, most of which are framed with a riot of bougainvillea, are connected by narrow paths that wind through lushly landscaped grounds. Each cabin has two stories, with a separate guest room on each floor for up to four guests. The renovated cabins are very cozy, offer plenty of space, and come with kitchenettes, a dining table, complimentary Wi-Fi, cable TV, and dehumidifier. The beds are feather soft and fitted with fine linens and duvets. It's quite a deal for the price, which includes a hearty, delicious breakfast and drink at their popular social hour. The inn is located in the forested Palo Alto section of Boquete, just under 3km (2 miles) from downtown, so you'll need a taxi or a rental vehicle to get back and forth.

Palo Alto. ✆ **720-2376.** www.boquetegardeninn.com. 10 units. $89 queen; $99 king; $20 additional person. MC, V. **Amenities:** Cafe; bar; Internet service. *In room:* Kitchenette, no phone.

Boquete Paradise Suites ★ Formerly the Rio Alto Suites Hotel, the Boquete Paradise offers 12 tastefully decorated bungalow-like units that are similar to those at the Boquete Garden Inn. The beds here are comfortable and, although there's nothing particularly memorable about the rooms themselves, the lovely gardens and great mountain and river views more than make up for this. The hotel is beautifully situated in front of the Rio Alto River and, like the name implies, feels a bit like a piece of paradise broke off and found its way to the Boquete Mountains. All rooms have their own terrace, but no. 11 offers attractive views of the Rio Palo Alto and the Boquete Mountains. The downside here is that the bathrooms are a bit small and oddly shaped, the small lobby is a bit dim, and the rooms are in need of a bit of light maintenance. All suites have kitchens and fridges.

Boquete. ⓒ **720-2278.** www.panamatropicalvacations.com/boquete_paradise.php. 12 units. $79–$189. AE, MC, V. **Amenities:** Wi-Fi. *In room:* A/C, TV, kitchen.

The Coffee Estate Inn ★★★ 📷 Cozy yet spacious accommodations with all the trimmings, gorgeous views of Volcán Barú, and truly personalized service are the hallmarks of the Coffee Estate Inn, which is my favorite place to stay in Boquete and is located 2.5km (1½ miles) from downtown Boquete, on a very steep slope overlooking the lush valley below. Owners Jane and Barry go out of their way to help guests feel welcome and relaxed; if you're looking for a real treat, request Barry's "no-frills" and "date night" dinners, beautifully presented on a flower-strewn table on your balcony with gorgeous views of the Boquete mountains. Three contemporary and cheery cabins contain a bedroom for two guests, a living area, a fully stocked kitchen, and an outdoor terrace. One bungalow has a twin hideaway. The cabins are enveloped in native forest, fruit trees, and flowers that attract myriad birds. The owners recommend that guests rent a vehicle (they'll set this up for you), and they'll provide maps, directions, contacts for the best guides in the area, and anything else you need for a day of adventure. There are 1.5km (1 mile) of hiking trails on the property. There's a daily breakfast of homemade breads, estate fresh-roasted coffee and fruit, and an on-site coffee tour with Barry.

Jaramillo Arriba. ⓒ **720-2211.** www.coffeeestateinn.com. 3 units. $145 double, $50 for an additional guest. MC, V. Children age 14 and under not accepted. **Amenities:** Library; Wi-Fi; optional daily dinner service. *In room:* TV/DVD, CD player, hair dryer, kitchenette.

Los Establos ★★ Another of my favorites, this ranch-style hotel is situated high above Boquete on a spacious, grassy property with splendid views of the valley and Volcán Barú—possibly the best in town. The accommodations are deluxe, but only the suites come with a view, though a wide patio and plenty of common areas give all guests a place from which to take in the vista. The decor is elegant and reminiscent of rural Spain, with a terra-cotta-tiled roof, heavy iron chandeliers, and cowhide rugs; guest rooms have a country decor and fine bedding. The two suites each contain a glass-enclosed seating area with expansive views and four-poster beds. The standard rooms are comfortable, but are on the ground floor and open onto the main foyer. Service is personable and accommodating. The price range below reflects the range from low season to high season (low season is Apr 16–Oct 31). My only problem with Los Establos is that the rooms sometimes smell a bit musty, but I suppose this is to be accepted in such a rainy, humid climate. An additional wing with three coffee cottages opened in 2010.

Jaramillo Arriba. ☏ **720-2685.** www.losestablos.net. 9 units. $110–$130 double and coffee cottages; $175–$230 suite. AE, MC, V. Children age 13 and under not accepted. **Amenities:** Bar; Internet access. *In room:* TV/DVD, no phone.

Panamonte Inn & Spa ★   Boquete's landmark hotel, built in 1914 and the first lodging here in town, offers storybook charm and beautifully tended gardens. It's a country-style inn, painted sky blue and surrounded by a white picket fence, and decorated with chintz and country-manor furnishings. The larger *cabañas* have been replaced by an additional wing with more guest rooms, which, although lovingly decorated, don't offer as much privacy as those in the old wing. Still, there are several reasons to consider staying here: The location is in town and convenient for travelers without a car; the finest restaurant in Boquete is part of the hotel and it has a terrific open-air bar with a roaring fireplace (see "Where to Dine," below); and there is a full-service spa on the premises.

Av. Central (take a right at the fork). ☏ **720-1324** or 720-1327. www.panamonteinnandspa.com. 31 units. $65 standard double; $132 cabin. AE, MC, V. **Amenities:** Restaurant; bar; full-service spa w/sauna and steam room; Wi-Fi. *In room:* A/C, TV.

Riverside Inn ★★   This boutique hotel, formerly called the Palo Alto, is sophisticated and gives discriminating travelers the highest level of accommodations available in Boquete—but you wouldn't know it from the hotel's exterior, which looks a little like a country-style inn. Located on the shore of the Palo Alto River, the hotel is next to the Rock, its gourmet restaurant. There are only six guest rooms, the best of which are in back, overlooking the river. A bit of color has recently been added to the once neutral rooms, giving the inn a well-done mini-face-lift. Standard decor consists of exposed wooden beams, stark walls, Indonesian teak furniture, and luxurious bathrooms. All rooms have king-size beds with Egyptian cotton sheets. Guest rooms feature lots of amenities, including a whirlpool tub in the master suite. My favorite thing about the Palo Alto is the common areas where guests can sit and read or converse.

Palo Alto. ☏ **720-1076.** www.riversideinnboquete.com. 6 units. Low season $80 suite, $105 master suite; high season $165 suite, $195 master suite. MC, V. **Amenities:** Restaurant; bar; tours; spa; Wi-Fi. *In room:* TV/DVD, minibar.

Tinamou Cottage Jungle Lodge ★   Hans and Terry of Coffee Adventure Tours own and operate this delightful eco-friendly lodge a short drive up from Boquete and recently expanded the property to include a total of three cabins, all surrounded by dense cloud forest. Two cabins have a balcony; Little Tinamou, the original and smallest of the cabins, has a small patio. There are several kilometers of hiking trails on the property, as well as a 4-acre organic coffee farm. Cabins are simple but comfortable and spacious, all decorated in a country style and all are well equipped for longer-term stays. Serious birders in particular will enjoy staying here and participating in guided bird-watching tours with Terry, one of Boquete's best bird-watching guides, for an extra fee. Rates vary depending on how many nights you stay.

Jaramillo Abajo, near Boquete. ☏ **720-3852** or 6634-4698. www.coffeeadventures.net. 3 units. $85 Little Tinamou; $105 larger cabins. MC, V. *In room:* Kitchen, Wi-Fi.

Valle Escondido ★   This resort community/hotel isn't for everyone, but it does have a 9-hole golf course, pool, the most complete spa in Boquete, and several restaurants. Valle Escondido is primarily an upscale residential community that's home to many Americans and Canadians, but the hotel guests can use the community amenities for an additional price. Valle Escondido offers 39 chain-like units, or you can book one of the 12 stand-alone bungalows, good for two to four people. Rooms are comfortable and high-end and most come with views, but they lack character and soul. Valle Escondido can arrange tours as well, and the staff is bilingual and helpful, if a bit snooty. They offer $40 transfers from David per couple, which may be the best option if people are flying into David to get to Boquete.

From the main avenue, take a right at the National bank, make a right after the Al Baraya Restaurant, and then follow the Valle Escondido signs to the left. © **720-2454** or 720-1327. www.valleescondido. biz. 37 units. $160–$250 double; $224–$376 bungalow. AE, MC, V. **Amenities:** 2 restaurants; bar; golf course and driving range; 3 pools; full-service spa w/sauna and steam room; horse stables. *In room:* A/C, TV/DVD, high-speed Internet.

MODERATE

Cabanas Momentum B&B ★ Located 6km (3.7 miles) before the Boquete town center, and reached by following a left-hand turnoff before arriving in Boquete, this hotel is for independent travelers who desire a lot of open outdoor areas and trails on which to walk or jog. This is also the only hotel in Boquete that has a heated swimming pool and a gym. There are five free-standing cabins spread across a neatly trimmed grassy area with views of the distant Volcán Barú, and two guest rooms within a main building. Though very clean and roomy, the cabins are starkly decorated. Travelers with a rental vehicle will be happiest here, although the Momentum will organize transfers and tours. This is a gay- and lesbian-friendly establishment.

Bajo Boquete. © **720-4385.** www.momentum-panama.com. 7 units. $75 cabin for 2; $60 double B&B room; $450 weekly cabin rates. No credit cards. **Amenities:** Gym; outdoor pool; volleyball. *In room:*Kitchen (in cabins), no phone, Wi-Fi.

Isla Verde Hotel ★ ☺ This is the best hotel walking distance from town. Located in a residential area about a 3-minute walk from Boquete, the German-owned Isla Verde features six cheery cabins, called "roundhouses." Half the cabins are for four guests, and half are quite spacious with a capacity for up to six guests (though they're ideal for a group of just four). There is a queen-size bed on the ground floor (but not separate from the living area), and a loft with a double bed; the additional "beds" for the six-person units are comfortable sleeper sofas. Isla Verde recently added four fetching suites for couples, each with a terrific outdoor patio that offers forest views, especially from the second-floor units, which are more expensive. The suites have a bedroom and independent living area, and kitchenettes; the cabins as well as all the roundhouses have full kitchens.

Calle 2 Sur Bajo Boquete. © **720-2533** or 6677-4009. www.islaverdepanama.com. 10 units. Prices based on double occupancy: $100 big roundhouse; $80 small roundhouse; $80–$100 suite. Children 4 and under stay for free; children 5–18 $10; extra adult $20. MC, V. **Amenities:** Internet service. *In room:* Cable TV, kitchen or kitchenette, no phone, Wi-Fi.

Villa Marita ★ Perched high on a plateau above a twisting road 3.5km (2 miles) from town, this hotel is strong in panoramic views of Volcán Barú and the river valley below. It's too far to walk to town, so if you don't mind taking a taxi or driving, the reasonably priced cabins here are an attractive lodging option. There are six mustard-colored cabins, for up to four guests (one bedroom and a sofa bed), which are outfitted with a fridge. French doors open onto a roofed terrace with the dynamite view. There are also three newer and comfortable hotel rooms in a new wing adjacent to the main building, which is a converted home with a lived-in and homey ambience. Families might be interested in their "Big House" unit that sleeps six to eight guests and has a kitchen, but no view. The friendly, knowledgeable host and his wife will gladly serve you a home-cooked meal with ingredients from their on-site organic greenhouse. The owners have lived in this area for 40 years and can help with tours and information about the area.

Alto Lino. ℂ 720-2165. www.villamarita.com. 10 units. $50 double hotel room; $80 cabin; $130 family house. AE, MC, V. **Amenities:** Restaurant; Wi-Fi. *In room:* TV, fridge (in cabins), no phone.

INEXPENSIVE

Hotel Oasis ★ This simple, low-cost hotel run by a local family has a riverfront location close to the Boquete fairgrounds, offering more scenic accommodations than most budget hotels. You want to book either room no. 1, 2, 4, 5, 11, or 12—they all offer views of the volcano and the river; room no. 4 is the only one with a king-size bed (the others have doubles and twins). Breakfast, which is included, is served on an outdoor patio, and there's a common area with a coffeemaker and microwave. Service is very friendly and helpful, and Hotel Oasis is close to the Flower Festival (when it's going on, in mid-Jan). I especially recommend the spacious and bright suites, part of a second-floor addition; all have great views. Prices below reflect low season-high season rates.

Av. Buenos Aires, across the bridge. ℂ 720-1586. www.oasisboquete.com. 17 units. $70–$95 double; $110–$200 suites. MC, V. **Amenities:** Restaurant; Internet. *In room:* TV, no phone.

Hotel Petit Mozart ★ Located on the outskirts of town in a tranquil and forested residential neighborhood, the Petit Mozart offers rooms with a view that stretches out to the Pacific Ocean. There are freshly painted, folksy cabins and guest rooms, a couple of which have a kitchenette for longer-term visitors and can be rented by the week or month. There are a total of three units, one with full kitchen. The Petit Mozart is German-owned and operated by an artist who uses much of the main building as a painting and jewelry-making studio and offers painting classes. The 2.5-hectare (5-acre) property has a small coffee plantation and fruit trees, and a lawn that slopes out from a pleasant patio terrace. This is a good lodging option for travelers seeking private and tranquil accommodations away from town, but it's a good idea to have your own vehicle; otherwise you'll need to depend on taxis. Breakfast is $6.50.

Volcancito. ℂ 720-3764 or 6487-7042. 3 units. $35 Colibri; $45–$50 Girasol; $390–$450 La Casita. No credit cards. *In room:* TV, fridge (some rooms), kitchenette, microwave, Wi-Fi, no phone.

Where to Dine

Given that many of Boquete's residents are retired folks who tend to dine in or not stay out too late, the restaurants mentioned below can unexpectedly close early or for the night during the low season, from May to November. Also, in addition to the places reviewed below, several kiosks and cafes offer quick meals and are worth considering.

Worth a stop is the locally famous **Fresas Mary** (ℂ 720-3394; daily 9:30am–7pm), which you'll find on the left side of the road to Volcancito, reached by turning onto the road opposite the CEFATI visitor center. The specialties here are *batidos*, or fresh fruit drinks, made with strawberries and local fruit such as *guanábana* (soursop); they also make fresh yogurt and *duros*, or frozen fruit sherbet. Sandwiches and hamburgers go for $1.50.

The **Deli Barú** (© 720-2619; Tues–Sun 9am–8pm) is a gourmet deli with sandwiches, soups, and salads, and a market with an excellent selection of cheeses, cold cuts, wine, fresh bread, and specialty goodies. For fresh fruit juices and cheap sandwiches in town, try **Java Juice** on Avenida Central, next to Panama Rafters (© 720-2116; daily 10am–10pm). A mango smoothie and hamburger here cost less than $2. **Café Punto de Encuentro** (© 720-2123; daily 7am–noon), located on Calle 6A S, near Avenida Belisario Porras, and often referred to as "Olga's Place," is *the* spot for breakfast. Have your omelets, fruit pancakes, and fresh coffee on their pleasant outdoor patio. **Restaurante Lourdes** on the main avenue serves typical Panamanian fare at low prices. **Sugar & Spice** is a new bakery in town with cookies, fresh baked breads, and other tasty baked books. **Tammy's**, located across from Sugar & Spice when entering town (© 6524-1013; Tues–Sun 11:30am–10pm), serves the best Mediterranean vegetarian platter in Panama; it's definitely not fancy but it's popular with locals.

MODERATE

Il Pianista ★ SICILIAN   This restaurant is owned and operated by chef Giovanno Sontorno and his Panamanian wife, both very friendly and attentive, and it's one of the most atmospheric places in town to dine. The cozy stone interior lends itself for a nice romantic meal out, or you can sit outside by the river. Specialties here include the vegetable lasagna, Sicilian-style seafood, fettuccini del chef, and the pasta fresco. Giovanni recently added an authentic wooden oven for extra-tasty pizzas and calzones. There is also a large selection of reasonably priced Italian wines.

On Alto Lino Loop by Palo Alto River. © **720-2728.** Main courses $7–$16. No credit cards. Tues–Sun noon–11pm.

Machu Picchu ★★ PERUVIAN   Peruvian chef Aristóteles first achieved fame for his tantalizing cuisine at his restaurant in Panama City, also called Machu Picchu, and decided to test his luck on the Boquete dining scene. The restaurant specializes in fare that combines fresh local products with traditional recipes. There are more than 25 appetizers (and double that in entrees); you might want to start with the stuffed potatoes or a "Piqueo Especial Inti Raymi" platter with a diverse sample of seafood delicacies. For a main course, the sea bass with black butter and capers is top-notch, as are the creamy jumbo prawns gratin. There are meat and chicken dishes, too. During weekdays, a fixed-price lunch costs $5.50. The ambience is warm—the restaurant is painted yellow and blue and accented with Peruvian art. Don't miss the sugary-sweet Suspiro Limeño, a classic caramel-like Peruvian dessert.

Av. Belisario Porras. © **264-9308.** Reservations recommended for groups. Main courses $6.50–$14. MC, V. Daily 11am–3pm and 6–11pm.

Panamonte Inn Restaurant ★★★ INTERNATIONAL   This sanctuary of gourmet cuisine is hands-down the best restaurant in Boquete. The food is inventive and consistently good, and service is attentive and courteous. Diners are given the option of dining in the 1940s-style, formal dining area, with its floral motif, but I like to order from their main menu and sit at a table in the ultra-cozy bar/lounge next to a roaring fire. The chef, Charlie Collins, is one of Panama's best. His dishes adapt local products with Scandinavian and New American cooking styles, and he utilizes the freshest and highest-quality ingredients available, such as local Black Angus beef and trout caught from the Caldera River. Trout, it could be said, is the restaurant's trademark dish, served in a variety of ways such as with a garlic and herb sauce. Order a trio of appetizers (such as a raw tuna cocktail) if you're feeling peckish, or dive into a wild-mushroom polenta, pork chops with onion ragout and veal stock and wine sauce, or seafood stew. Polish it off with pie made with a lemon-orange hybrid from the Panamonte's gardens. The bar menu has lighter fare and casual meals like burgers, empanadas, and chicken brochettes, as well as an excellent wine list.

Av. Central. ✆ **720-1324** or 720-1327. Reservations recommended for main dining area. Main courses $9–$12. AE, MC, V. Daily 7–9:30am, 12:30–3pm, and 6–10pm. Bar daily 8am–11:30pm.

The Rock ★★ INTERNATIONAL   If you're looking for a refined yet tranquil atmosphere where you can dine on fresh trout, a juicy rib-eye or New York steak, barbecue baby back ribs, or a light pasta primavera, this is your place. Located in a stand-alone building on the shore of a scenic river, about a 3-minute drive from town, the Palo Alto is a handsome, upscale eatery serving some of the best cuisine in Boquete. The dining area is Mediterranean style, and fresh and airy, with brick floors, glass walls, a zinc roof strung with iron chandeliers, and local art. The menu features mostly North American cuisine and pasta, though there are also delicious appetizers such as Thai spring rolls with a fish sauce, kabobs, and Greek *ladopsomo* (pita bread with feta). For lunch there are salads and sandwiches. Service is attentive but not overwhelming. Their wine list is mostly Spanish, with a few Chilean varieties.

Road to Palo Alto. ✆ **720-1076.** paloalto@cwpanama.net. Reservations recommended. Main courses $6.50–$14. AE, MC, V. Daily noon–9:30pm.

INEXPENSIVE

Art Café La Crepe ★ ⛏ CREPES/FRENCH   This creperie doubles as an art gallery (see "Shopping," earlier in this chapter) and is a fun, funky place for a light meal or afternoon snack. The place is lively and colorful with poster artwork decorating the yellow and red walls. As an added bonus, there are vegetarian options here—particularly good is *L'Argenteuil,* a fresh asparagus crepe served with Béchamel sauce and cheese. For those craving something a little bit sweeter, *La Symphonie* with fruit, almonds, strawberries, and vanilla ice cream is delicious, as is the Profiterole with chocolate sauce.

Calle Principal, next to Zanzibar. ✆ **6769-6090** or 6789-9430. Main courses $5–$7. No credit cards. Tues–Sun 10am–9pm.

La Casona Mexicana ★ MEXICAN   This restaurant has a good selection of authentic Mexican dishes in addition to Tex-Mex fare. Hearty and well prepared, the food consists of tasty roasted pork *carnitas,* and a sour cream and chili-based Michoacán chicken, as well as burritos, fajitas, and chimichangas paired with rice and black beans. What they don't have is guacamole, but then you rarely see avocado anywhere in Panama. The dining area is very casual, with the usual Mexican motif: fiery red and orange walls festooned with sombreros.

Av. Central. ✆ **720-1274.** Main courses $3.75–$7. MC, V. Daily noon–10:30pm.

Sabrosón PANAMANIAN   For cheap, local fare, you can't beat this cafeteria-style restaurant. The ambience is no-frills, and the food is simply prepared but filling and tasty. Just pop in, stand in line, and when you get to the buffet point at what you'd like behind the glass—they'll heap it on your plate. I like the stewed chicken with rice and a bean salad, but their fresh trout, served fried or sautéed, is okay, too.

Av. Central, near the church. © **720-2147.** Main courses $2–$4. No credit cards. Mon–Thurs 6:30am–10pm; Fri–Sun 6:30am–11pm.

Boquete After Dark

Most Boquete residents are tucked into bed by 11pm, but there are a couple of places for a nightcap or a night out. **Zanzíbar,** located on Avenida Central on the right side past the church, is an attractively decorated bar with African odds and ends. It's a cozy place for a cocktail (open Tues–Sun until midnight), and my favorite nightspot in Boquete. **Las Cabanas Lounge,** located 3.2km (2 miles) outside of town on the road to the Coffee Estate Inn, is a newer bar/dance club popular with Boquete's younger crowd. It gets crowded Friday and Saturday nights after Zanzibar closes.

A Nature Lodge with Hiking Trails

The simple, Swiss-owned **Finca Suiza ★★** is one of the best lodges in Panama to spend the night or visit for the day if you're an avid hiker, because the trails are so well maintained and marked (probably better than any others in the country), and because the scenery and views along the trails are dazzling. Also, you don't need a guide. Finca Suiza is truly a find, located on 81 hectares (200 acres) of land about 56km (35 miles) north of David, on the road to Chiriquí Grande. From the lodge there are three loop trails through dense, emerald tropical forest to lookout points, waterfalls, and through cloud forest. If you're in Boquete for a lengthy period and looking for a day-hiking trip, or if you're traveling from Bocas del Toro and want to stop for the day before heading to David, you'll have to arrive and start hiking between 7 and 10am, and be out of the finca by 4pm during the dry season (mid-Apr to Nov), by 2pm during the rainy season. Admission is $8 per person, paid to the Ngöbe-Buglé woman at the entrance to the finca; you'll need to park your vehicle here and walk up the road until you reach the trail head. If you're staying in the lodge and have a 4WD that can make it up their dirt road, advise them of when you're coming because they let their guard dogs out at night.

All trails are moderate, with easy portions, but there's a lot of uphill walking during the first stretch. The **Small Circuit** takes 3½ hours; or you can continue on and complete the **Large Circuit** for a total of 6½ hours, with the option of walking an extra hour to the Mirador Alta Vista lookout point. This lookout point is breathtaking, stretching as far as the mountains of Costa Rica and the Pacific Ocean. Those with a full day can tack on the 3-hour hike through the cloud forest. It is common to hear howler monkeys here, and hikers report having seen white-faced capuchin monkeys and coatimundis. The forest provides nesting sites for many species of birds, but the finca is not specifically known as a hot bird-watching spot—the focus here is on hiking. Hikers walking the Large Circuit and the cloud-forest circuit must be in good physical shape, and children 11 and under are not allowed on the trails. July and August, when everything is green, are the best months to come; March and April are drier months with less foliage.

The **Finca Suiza Lodge** (© **6615-3774;** www.panama.net.tc), with its clapboard walls and wooden shutters, looks out toward the Pacific with sweeping, sunset-facing views framed by blooming bougainvillea. There are two spotless guest rooms, each with two twin beds and a private bathroom. The rooms lean more toward comfort than rusticity, but this lodge will appeal more to easygoing nature lovers. There is a cozy living/dining area with a fireplace where meals are served (breakfast $4; dinner $11). Meals are tasty and healthy, made with organic ingredients from the *finca*'s garden. Bring snacks and picnic lunch items with you, and alcohol, as none of these items are available. Rates for a minimum of 2 nights are $44 for the first night, $35 for the second, and credit cards are not accepted. The Swiss owners, Monika and Herbert, answer their phone only from 7 to 9pm, and check e-mails once a week only. Note that the lodge and the trails are closed during June, September, and October.

Another excellent lodging option if you have your own car and don't mind being 25 minutes outside downtown Boquete is **Rancho de Caldera ★★** (© **772-8040;** www.ranchodecaldera.com). This small, relatively new eco-resort is offers nine luxury cabins and two discount rooms. Cabins are spacious and tastefully decorated with fantastic views of the Boquete countryside. The on-site pool also offers breathtaking mountain views. Cabins cost $160 to $220 in high season and $150 to $200 in low season. Cabins have modern amenities such as flatscreen TV, A/C, microwave, refrigerator, toaster, and complimentary Wi-Fi. Note that cabin no. 6 does not have a TV. The two discount rooms share a bathroom and do not have TV, A/C, or private deck, but are nevertheless nicely appointed and run for $55 during low season and $60 during high season. The resort is run completely on solar, hydro and wind power, and much of the food served at the excellent Madre restaurant is produced on-site. To get to Rancho de Caldera, drive down Via Boquete and turn at the Caldera turn. After 9.5km (6 miles), turn left on the church, then turn left onto Rancho de Caldera's driveway and drive 1.3km (less than a mile) more before arriving.

PARQUE NACIONAL MARINO GOLFO DE CHIRIQUÍ & ISLAS SECAS ★★★

The Chiriquí Gulf National Marine Park is one of Panama's best-kept secrets—but it won't be for long, given its proximity to Boquete and the wave of retirees and expats moving to that area every year. At Boca Chica, the closest town to the park, there are no high-rises, golf courses, or gated communities, just a couple of lodges and a tiny fishing community—and a lot of thick vegetation and crystalline water. The Boca Chica area is actually one of my favorite regions in Panama and has a bit of a "back in the day" feel to it. The dirt road down to the pier was recently paved, meaning you no longer need a four-wheel-drive to get here. The Marine Park was founded in 1994 to protect 14,730 hectares (36,400 acres) of extensive coral reef, mangrove swamps, and marine meadows—the park's most salient characteristics. Another significant feature of this park is its dozens of picturesque rocky outcrops sprinkled across the gulf, as well as its idyllic islands carpeted in forest and lined with slender coconut palms. Several of these islands boast tropical-paradise white-sand beaches lapped by turquoise waters (unlike the Pacific Coast beaches on the mainland), especially **Isla Gámez** and **Isla Bolaños.** While out in the gulf, you can see the purple silhouette of Volcán Barú rising high in the background. The air is fresh and balmy, unlike the interior humid lowlands.

The sea is rich in marine life, providing **scuba divers** and **snorkelers** with the opportunity to see huge schools of colorful tropical fish, as well as large pelagic fish like white-tipped sharks. Scuba divers and snorkelers will need to book a boat tour to get to the offshore islands, where visibility is better than it is near shore (expect up to 15m/50 ft. offshore). The shore near Boca Chica and the pier is shrouded in mangrove and the water is cloudy, not suitable for underwater sports.

As with Coiba, the **sport fishing** in the Chiriquí Gulf beyond the national park is legendary, especially around Islas Ladrones, Islas Secas, and Islas Contreras. Islas Secas is a cluster of 16 private islands that are part of a luxury ecolodge (p. 251), one of the most gorgeous in all of Panama.

Boca Chica fronts a large island called Boca Brava; here two lodges and a restaurant share space with howler monkeys, agoutis, raccoons, and other wildlife, and there are walking trails through the forest. You can reach the island via a $1 water-taxi ride from shore.

Essentials

GETTING THERE & DEPARTING

BY PLANE   The closest airport to Boca Chica is in David (see "Getting There & Departing" under "David," earlier in this chapter).

BY BUS   There is frequent bus service from David to the town of Horconcitos, but bus service from there to Boca Chica is spotty. Considering that Boca Chica is the jumping-off point for the gulf, nearly every traveler here has arranged accommodations in the area or a day or multiple-day excursion that includes transportation to Boca Chica.

BY CAR   Heading east from David, drive 38km (24 miles) and turn right on the turnoff for Horconcitos. Drive about 4.8km (3 miles) to Horconcitos, when the road forks; stay right and turn at the sign for Boca Chica. The road continues from here for 16km (10 miles) to Boca Chica. This portion of the road is unpaved and quite dusty, though does not require a 4WD unless it's raining.

Fun in & on the Water

FISHING, SNORKELING & SCUBA DIVING

Private overnight fishing and scuba-diving charters that operate around Isla Coiba are described below (under "Isla Coiba"); these charters normally leave from the Pedregal pier near David, or from Puerto Mutis southwest of Santiago. Your lodge or hotel will be able to arrange kayaking, snorkeling, and fishing excursions for you. For lodges in Boca Chica that specialize in fishing, see below.

Boca Brava Divers (© 775-3185 or 6600-6191; www.scubadiving-panama.com) is a locally based scuba-diving operation run by a friendly English-speaking Colombian named Carlos, who is a PADI dive master and has lived and dived in the Marine Park region for years. Boca Brava offers a full-day diving trip that can go as far as Islas Secas or Isla Ladrones, leaving at 7am and returning at 4pm; the cost is $150 per person, with a four-person minimum. Boca Brava's boat, a 14m (46-ft.) converted commercial-fishing vessel, has live-aboard accommodations for five guests for multi-day scuba-diving trips around the Gulf of Chiriquí, including to Isla Coiba.

Where to Stay & Dine

Cala Mia ★★★ 📷   Located on a small island fronting two small but attractive beaches, this eco-resort offers 11 solar-powered bungalows best for honeymooners or couples looking for a secluded, romantic getaway. The bungalows themselves are spacious and comfortable, with furnishings designed by local artisans and decorated in a tropical chic style. An environmentally conscientious operation, Cala Mia plans to produce its own fruit, vegetables, and cheese in the future and—here's the catch—there's no air-conditioning, so lounging in your room during the daytime may be uncomfortable. Luckily, there is a cool breeze at night that makes the heat bearable. The large, tiled showers are open and unique, and each bungalow has a small terrace complete with a couch and hammock, the perfect place to spend the afternoon lounging around and listening to the sounds of the sea. Meals, which are absolutely delicious, are served in an elegant dining area with views of the ocean.

The hotel offers free pickup and drop-off before 8pm. There are also local boatmen that can get you to the hotel for about $25. Note that if you arrive late at night, it's unlikely that there will be any boatmen at the port to take you. Call the hotel and let them know of your approximate arrival time so they can arrange to pick you up. Prices below reflect low-season rates.

Isla Brava. ℂ **851-0059** or 6747-0111. www.boutiquehotelcalamia.com. $180–$200 bungalow suite; $300–$370 double bungalow suites; $320–$400 deluxe suite. Rates include breakfast. AE, MC, V. **Amenities:** Restaurant; bar; pool; spa; kayaks; surfing and snorkeling equipment. *In room:* No phone.

Gone Fishing ★ The lodge's focus is on fishing around the Gulf of Chiriquí, both inshore and offshore, aboard one of their two 9.4m (31-ft.) custom open fishing vessels. However, the lodge is for non-fishers, too, who want to come and hang out in natural surroundings and snorkel or dive the region. Considering this, and the fact that they have a large swimming pool and a small strip of beach, this is an ideal lodge for fishers traveling with non-fishing spouses. There are two stand-alone cabins and two hotel rooms that are not luxurious—but they aren't basic either, sporting artfully painted walls with colorful marine and jungle murals. The lodge's **restaurant and bar,** which serves American and Panamanian food, is open to the public; they have a breezy terrace with sunset views. Guests pay a nightly fee and order meals and excursions a la carte; daily fishing trips are $1,200 for up to four anglers. You'll see the entrance to Gone Fishing on your left side, just before entering Boca Chica.

Boca Chica. ℂ **851-0104** or 786/393-5882 in the U.S. www.gonefishingpanama.com. 6 units. $175–$130 double. MC, V. **Amenities:** Restaurant; bar; outdoor pool; fishing excursions; boat trips. *In room:* A/C, no phone, Wi-Fi.

Pacific Bay Resort ★★ This rustic resort offers some of the best vistas and beaches of any lodging option on Boca Chica, and its five cottages each have two rooms and room for up to eight people. The resort is set on 140 picturesque acres, though only 17 of these are developed, meaning wildlife is free to roam in the remaining 123. The resort can set up excursions to nearby islands or take guests on whale and dolphin-watching tours; most activities, such as kayaking and snorkeling, are free. There are three beaches on the property, all open to guests; the best of these is the white-sand North Beach.

Punta Bejuco, Boca Chica. ℂ **6678-1000** or 6095-1651. www.pacificbayresort.org. 5 units. $99 per cottage, based on double occupancy. No credit cards. *In room:* No phone.

Panama Big Game Sportfishing Club ★★ Perched high on a hilltop on Boca Brava Island, a couple of minutes from Boca Chica by boat, and accessed by a long flight of stairs or a funicular-style people-mover, Big Game boasts sweeping views of the area and is backed by wooded surroundings teeming with wildlife. The resort is owned by two retired charter-boat skippers and restaurateurs from Miami. The Sportfishing Club consists of a main building with a bar/dining area centered around a large, curved teak bar, and four attractive cabins. The cabins are surprisingly roomy (56 sq. m/600 sq. ft.) and thoroughly contemporary, accented with colorful cushions and tiled with locally produced ceramics; these units can sleep up to six. The lodge has four fishing boats to accommodate all guests. Prices include transportation from the David airport, lodging, fishing, meals, and beverages. Three-day packages start on Monday and Thursday, and 5-day packages start on Monday. From June 1 to November 30, guests pay for 3 days of fishing and get 4.

Boca Brava Island. © **866/281-1225** in the U.S. www.panama-sportfishing.com. 4 units. 3-day packages $3,481 per person, based on 2 anglers; $2,461 per person, based on 4 anglers; 5-day packages $5,040 per person, based on 2 anglers, and $3,364 per person, based on 4 anglers. MC, V. **Amenities:** Restaurant; bar; fishing excursions. *In room:* A/C, no phone.

Seagull Cove Lodge ★★   This hotel isn't quite as romantic as Cala Mia (see above), but it does offer creature comforts such as air-conditioning, Wi-Fi, and TV for travelers not quite willing to get away from it all. Best of all, the hotel boasts a small, attractive beach good for swimming and tanning. The stand-alone units here each have a small terrace; one has mountain views, while the others have ocean views. Rooms are comfortable if a bit small, and furnished with expensive furniture and imported towels. There is a full-service restaurant, and if you are tanning by the ocean and don't feel like climbing all the way up to the restaurant for drinks (it's a steep climb) the staff will be happy to bring your drinks down to you. If you're here on Saturday or Sunday, the restaurant cooks up delicious gourmet Italian meals. The prices below reflect low- to high-season rates.

Boca Chica. © **851-0036** or 786/735-1475 in the U.S. www.seagullcovelodge.com. $145–$175 standard doubles. AE, MC, V. Children age 10 and under not accepted. **Amenities:** Restaurant; bar; pool. *In room:* A/C, TV, Wi-Fi.

A LUXURY ECOLODGE ON A REMOTE PRIVATE ISLAND

Islas Secas ★★★ 📷   It is difficult to describe Islas Secas without lapsing into superlatives, so here it goes. The service and the cuisine are the best of any resort in Panama. The staff provides impeccable service and anticipates your needs to the point where you wonder if they are reading your mind. The gourmet cuisine is out-of-this-world delicious, even down to the picnic lunches served on day excursions. Whatever your whim on any given day, the staff can fulfill your desire: sport fishing, surfing, scuba diving, snorkeling, walking through pristine forest, kayaking, or just having the boat captain drop you off on an uninhabited island to play castaway for a day. With tropical views this idyllic and a scattering of wooden *rancho* outdoor lounges, stretching out with a good book can be an enticing activity, too. Upon return to home base, you can pamper yourself with a massage, or have cocktails and watch the sunset. The *casitas* are 6.1 by 6.1m (20- by 20-ft.) yurts that have a low impact on the environment and boast an aesthetic that is both spare and very stylish, appealing equally to the eco-conscious jet set and to honeymooners (who receive 2 nights free if they book for 8 nights). There is no air-conditioning, though yurts have an insulation layer that keeps the heat out, and there is also a ceiling fan. The American owner of Islas Secas is a tech wizard with a healthy appetite for the outdoors; when he's not around, his deluxe *casita* with a full kitchen, satellite Internet hookup, and a full deck can be rented. The *casitas* are elegantly appointed and feature ultra-comfortable beds draped in mosquito netting, deluxe bathrooms, and a small sitting area.

To get here, you'll need to fly by small plane from Panama City, which costs an additional $400 round-trip. Everything else is included, except spa services and fishing charters. Islas Secas is open from mid-December to April only.

Islas Secas. © **805/729-2737** in the U.S. www.islassecas.com. 6 units. All-inclusive packages based on double occupancy are $495 per person, per night; the large *casita* is $695 per person, per night. AE, MC, V. Children age 9 and under not accepted. **Amenities:** Restaurant; bar; Internet service; spa; kayaks. *In room:* Ceiling fan, minibar, no phone.

ISLA COIBA ★★★

SE Gulf of Chiriquí

Once the haunt of pirates, and in recent times an island feared by convicted criminals who were sent there, Isla Coiba (© **998-4271** or 998-0615; www.coibanationalpark. com) is now a treasured national park, UNESCO World Heritage Site, and nature lover's, fisherman's, and scuba-diver's dream destination. Given Isla Coiba's astounding natural diversity, rich sea life, and rare species, it is frequently referred to as the Galápagos of Central America. Isla Coiba is the largest island in Panama, but the national park spreads beyond the main island, encompassing 38 islands and islets and marine waters for a total of 270,128 hectares (667,500 acres). The area is home to the second-largest coral reef in the eastern Pacific, at **Bahía Damas,** and its waters teem with huge schools of colorful fish, hammerhead and nurse sharks, dolphins, manta rays, tuna, turtles, whales, and other gigantic marine species. Onshore, there are 36 species of mammals and 39 species of reptiles, including saltwater crocodiles. Beyond these impressive numbers, Coiba is one of the last places on earth where it is possible to see a scarlet macaw in the wild. Indeed, few places in the Americas are as wild, remote, and full of life as Isla Coiba National Park.

The island and its surrounding waters owe their pristine state to a notorious penal colony that existed on the island from 1919 to 2004, which kept tourists and developers at bay. Panama sent its most hardened criminals to the island, who considered the isolated penal colony the most punishing sentence the government could hand down. There's talk that the government might reopen the prison for Alcatraz-style tours. Having only recently opened itself to tourism, the island takes a little work to get to for the day, or an expensive all-inclusive package to spend a few nights in the area. The majority of visitors to the island are "temporary" travelers who descend en masse from small to midsize cruise ships to spend a couple of hours snorkeling around **Granito de Oro,** or for a quick walk through the island's jungle trails. Granito de Oro is a tiny island whose waters offer outstanding snorkeling and a picture-postcard white-sand beach, but the waters surrounding Coiba are still virgin territory, and snorkeling and diving outfits have yet to discover all of Coiba's treasures. Expect new "hot spots" to come to the public's attention soon.

The park is administered by ANAM, which has a ranger station (© **998-0615**) and the only lodging on the island, consisting of several basic air-conditioned cabins on a glorious white-sand and turquoise-water beach. The cost to visit Coiba National Park is $10 per person. The cabins are used by fishing, diving, and snorkeling tour outfitters (or by those with a private boat). Day visits to Coiba go through operators in Santa Catalina (see below). There is a landing strip on Coiba, but for charter flights only.

Outdoor Adventures in Coiba

HIKING

There are two short trails at the ANAM station that lead to lookout points, but each is less than .4km (.25-mile) long. **Sendero de los Monos (Trail of the Monkeys)** is located on the shore in front of Granito de Oro Island. You must walk this trail very early to see monkeys; otherwise it's just an easy, 45-minute walk through dense forest that starts and ends at different points—you need a boat to get there and be picked up. If you've only got a day here, you might want to skip it.

FISHING

The fishing around Coiba and the Gulf of Chiriquí is legendary, but keep in mind that ANAM only allows catch-and-release fishing within 1.6km (1 mile) of the boundary of the national park–protected area. ANAM only recently began enforcing fishing laws, and after a few misunderstandings, charter boat captains are now aware of restrictions and adhere by them. Fishermen consider this area special due to the size and variety of fish, and the sheer number of fishing sites that could not be covered even in a week. By far the most renowned sport-fishing areas near Coiba are Hannibal Bank, which is something like an underwater mountain, and Isla Montuosa, but there are plenty of other sites with underwater mountains and deep ledges that attract black marlin, roosterfish, cubera snapper, bluefin trevally, and other very big fish.

Coiba Adventure (© 998-5073 or 800/800-0907 in the U.S.; www.coib adventure.com) is operated by American Tom Yust, who is considered Panama's most renowned sport-fishing captain and has been sport fishing the Coiba area since 1991. Coiba Adventure has two boats, the Joker, a 9.4m (31-ft.) Bertram, and a 6.4m (22-ft.) Mako. Guests are flown to the Coiba landing strip on a chartered plane from Panama City, and lodging is on the island in the ANAM air-conditioned cabins (a generator is used for backup). Five-night all-inclusive packages cost $3,000 per person. Lower rates and shorter stays are offered June through November.

The **M/V *Coral Star*** (© 866/924-2837 in the U.S.; www.coralstar.com) is a deluxe, air-conditioned, 35m (115-ft.) mother ship with mahogany and teak interiors and so many amenities that it feels like a floating fishing lodge. The *Coral Star* can accommodate 16 guests, and they also have seven sport-fishing boats for daily excursions. Beyond fishing, the *Coral Star* offers scuba diving, snorkeling, kayaking, and eco-tours, and they can put together a custom canal transit for groups. Itineraries run from Saturday to Thursday and leave from the Pedregal marina in David. All-inclusive packages, based on four anglers, are $4,000 per person from January to April, and $3,200 per person the rest of the year; rates include hotel stay in Panama City and round-trip flights to David. Occasionally, *Coral Star* has "specialty weeks," during which they invite a fishing "celebrity" along to teach the tricks of the trade.

Pesca Panama (© 800/946-3474 in the U.S.; www.pescapanama.com) is a U.S.-based company that offers inshore and offshore sport fishing in the Gulf of Chiriquí, around Coiba and Hannibal Bank. Pesca guests stay aboard their floating lodge, a 21-by-9.1m (70-by-30-ft.) barge with a maximum of 16 guests (four beds per room), with five boats and five cabins, and take day fishing trips aboard 8.2m (27-ft.) Ocean Master boats. Rates range from $2,150 to $4,295 per person for 5 nights' fishing and 7 nights' lodging; itineraries are set, but they do offer charter trips. They also offer day fishing trips from Pedregal, near David.

Boquete Outdoor Adventures (p. 236) also offers multiday excursions to Isla Coiba.

SCUBA DIVING & SNORKELING

The *Coral Star* ship (above) offers scuba diving on its fishing expeditions. Alternatively, you can organize day scuba and snorkeling excursions to Isla Coiba with an outfitter in Santa Catalina (see "Scuba Diving," below, under "Santa Catalina").

Panama Divers (© **314-0817** or 6613-4405; www.panamadivers.com) is the country's foremost scuba-diving company based out of Panama City and Portobelo. Panama Divers is fully insured and has decades of experience; their 5-night/6-day diving trips include 2 nights in Panama City, and 3 nights of lodging in the cabins at the ANAM ranger station, with ground transportation to their 7.9m (26-ft.) boat at Puerto Mutis. As part of the trip, they also offer fishing, whale-watching, snorkeling, and kayaking. The cost is $1,275 per person, with a maximum of eight divers.

SANTA CATALINA ★

300km (186 miles) SE of David; 360km (223 miles) from Panama City; 110km (68 miles) from Santiago

Santa Catalina is a surfing mecca and humble fishing village in the Veraguas Province, located at the end of a pressed-dirt road south of Santiago and southeast of David. The waves here are epic, with a couple of perfect and easy-to-line-up point breaks that average 1.5 to 6.1m (5–20 ft.). Most of the waves are for advanced surfers only, but a sandy break has waves suitable for beginners and intermediates surfing with a local guide. Offshore islands such as Isla Cebaco also have excellent surfing conditions. Beyond surfing, Santa Catalina has accommodations and services and is close enough to Isla Coiba to reach on a day excursion for scuba diving, snorkeling, or eco-adventures. Local boatmen in *pangas*, or fiberglass boats with 70-horsepower outboard engines, hang around the shore waiting for customers, but it's better to go with one of the two scuba-diving outfits here (see "Scuba Diving," below), which put together day trips and packages with an overnight on Isla Coiba.

Santa Catalina is a scruffy and remote community whose residents generally earn less than $10 a day and live in cinder-block homes. The recent introduction of plastic bottles and packaged products and no garbage service means that the streets are sprinkled with trash. A lot of locals pass the day hanging around the shoreline and waiting for work, or playing soccer. Given that the village sits across from Isla Coiba, and has some of the best waves in Central America, Santa Catalina has that up-and-coming feeling, with the first young adventurers from the U.S. and Europe anchoring themselves here with a hostel or cafe, and grudgingly watching the region slowly develop for tourism. At the moment, Santa Catalina's accommodations are budget-oriented, and some are downright rustic, but you'll find a couple of surprisingly good restaurants here.

The main road from Soná funnels into what is considered "downtown"; heading left will take you along a dirt road to an open coastal area, and to restaurants, hotels, and hostels in a more natural setting. There is a decent, palm-lined beach near the Oasis Hotel, but it is certainly not the prettiest in Panama. Note that there is no public phone in Santa Catalina, and no local public transportation, so you'll need to walk if you don't have a rental vehicle.

Essentials

GETTING THERE & AWAY

BY BUS   Santa Catalina can be reached by public bus from David or Santiago (if coming from Panama City). From Panama City, take the San Isidro bus line to Soná (5 hr.; $6 one-way); from David, take a bus to Soná ($6; about 5 hr.). Buses from Soná to Santa Catalina leave at 5:15am, noon, and 4pm, and cost $3.75 one-way; or you can take a taxi for $25.

BY CAR   The best way to arrive is by rental car so that you can stop and take photos with some truly beautiful surroundings. But getting here by car from David and following the logical shortcut through Las Palmas to Soná is not easy—there is an absolute lack of road signs. From Panama City, it is a little more straightforward. Drive the Interamericana Highway west to Santiago, about 3 hours. Drive through town and past the cathedral, and 2 blocks later turn left. Drive 45km (28 miles), almost to Soná, turning left at a well-signed exit for Santa Catalina. Drive another 45km (28 miles) and turn left at the sign for Santa Catalina at El Tigre Amarillo, continuing for 20km (12 miles) more until you reach Santa Catalina.

>
> ### Guayamí Indian Handicrafts
>
> **Ngöbe-Buglé (Guayamí) Indians sell copies of their traditional, flouncy dresses, beaded jewelry, and other handicrafts at stalls along the roadside in Tolé.** If you're driving from David, stop 97km (60 miles) east of David.

From David, the right-hand turnoff to Soná is just past El Piro. (If you pass the left-hand turnoff for El Prado, you've gone too far.) The road is tiresomely potholed, and though it is supposedly a straight line to Soná, there are many paved and semipaved roads that branch off and can be confusing before you reach Soná—but then again, the countryside is lovely, with tiny villages dotting the road. If you don't want to hassle with getting lost or dealing with unpaved roads, drive the extra 56km (35 miles) toward Santiago, turning right at the sign for Soná and La Peña, and continue following the directions from Panama City.

Fun in the Ocean

SCUBA DIVING

Isla Coiba is not only the best place to scuba dive and snorkel in the area; it's the best place to dive and snorkel in all of Panama. Day excursions to this island and its surrounding waters are available only from local operations based out of Santa Catalina. It's not cheap, and it takes nearly 1½ hours to get there—which is why you might want to check into spending the night on the island at the park-ranger station. (Both outfitters mentioned below can organize this.) Local boat operators will do the round-trip to Isla Coiba for about $250 to $300, but that's without rental equipment, and drivers are not schooled in even rudimentary first aid, nor do they carry radios or much safety equipment. It's a long, bumpy ride over open water, so it pays to play it safe. Closer to Santa Catalina is **Isla Cebaco,** which offers excellent diving and snorkeling around an extensive coral reef; it only takes about a half-hour to get here, and the fare is less.

   Scuba Charters (© **6565-7200;** www.scuba-charters.com) is owned and operated by two Americans who are fully certified and boast years of diving experience (they hail from Florida). The company offers day trips to Coiba aboard their rigid inflatable tunnel hull, including two-tank dives for $95 per person, and snorkeling for $75 per person. Local diving trips near Santa Catalina cost $60 per person, and $40 per person for snorkeling. They'll put together an eco-tour combined with scuba diving at Coiba, too. They're also dive instructors and offer PADI-certified instruction courses for travelers spending 4 or 5 days in the area. You can buy snorkel gear, underwater camera cases, and other marine-related goodies from Scuba Charters.

Scuba Coiba (✆ **6575-0122** or 6429-3560; www.scubacoiba.com) is a local operation run by an Austrian expat named Herbie Sunk (yes, it's true), with scuba diving, snorkeling, and eco-tours to Isla Coiba. Using local *panga* boats to get to the island gives Scuba Coiba a by-the-seat-of-your-pants feel to the operation, and though Herbie is *way* laid-back to the point of being unenthusiastic, he is fully certified and he offers 2- and 3-night-stay packages on Isla Coiba that include eco-tours to the interior of the island. Two-dive trips to Coiba cost $95 per person; 2-day all-inclusive packages with stays on Coiba (six dives total) are $390 per person.

SURFING

Panama Surf Tours (✆ **6671-7777**; www.panamasurftours.com), a respected company, can plan multiple-day tours to a variety of surf spots, including Santa Catalina, with transportation. They offer flexible 5- to 8-day tours that range from economical to luxury.

Otherwise, if you're interested in surfing with a guide or need lessons, you'll want to book with a surf camp such as **Punta Brava** or **Oasis** (see below).

Where to Stay

Aside from the lodging options listed below, German-owned **Hotel Hibiscus Garden** (✆ **6615-6097**; www.hibiscusgarden.com) offers simple but clean dirt-cheap lodging (just $15 per person!) on Playa Lagartero about 10 minutes from Santa Catalina. The lodge attracts bird-watchers and those interested in horse riding, as well as the usual surfer crowd.

La Buena Vida ★   This attractive hotel offers three simple but comfortable stand-alone villas, all a good value and all with A/C and fridge and most with hammocks. Butterfly, Bird, and Gecko Villa are ideal for visitors who plan to stick around the Santa Catalina area for at least a week and there are hostel-type accommodations available as well for budget-minded travelers. Like most hotels to this area, La Buena Vida attracts a mostly surfer crowd, but non-surfers are welcome as well. Their restaurant is open for breakfast and lunch and offers a good selection of healthy dishes and even vegetarian fare, a rare option in these parts. This is one of the better lodging options in the area.

Santa Catalina. ✆ **6635-1895** or 6572-0664. www.labuenavida.biz. 3 units (plus dorm lodging). $55 Butterfly Villa; $66 Bird Villa; $75 Gecko Villa. No credit cards. **Amenities:** Restaurant; surfboard rental; fishing tours. *In room amenities:* A/C, ceiling fan (in Gecko), fridge, hot water, no phone.

Oasis Surf Camp ★   I like this surf camp/hostel because it is the only lodging option that actually sits on the Playa Estero beach. It's nice to be able to walk outside to the ocean's edge and feel the sea breeze in the afternoons. The rooms are nothing special, with double and triple units that are basically a cement cabin with beds, but for the price it's hard to ask for more. The surf camp rents boards and gives lessons for $20 an hour, and they offer day surfing trips around the area for experienced surfers. The owners are a young Italian couple, and they serve excellent meals—Panamanian lunches and Italian dinners—under a thatched *bohio*; it's $5 per meal. You can camp on grounds for $5 per person. To get here, take the only turnoff road east of the village, follow it to the end, then drive across a creek, on the other side of which is Oasis.

Playa Estero, Santa Catalina. No phone. www.oasissurfcamp.com. 6 units. $35 double; $50 triple; $60–$70 4–6 person bungalow (no A/C). No credit cards. **Amenities:** Restaurant; surfboard rental. *In room:* No phone.

Where to Dine

There are a couple of solid dining options in Santa Catalina, and all are located east of town along the road that dead-ends at the Oasis. Otherwise, hotels and hostels here include meals with their packages, or have kitchens for independent cooking. None of the restaurants has a telephone or accepts credit cards; hours are only guidelines, never firmly adhered to during slower weeks; and though restaurants are open daily, they sometimes close on Mondays.

Blanca's is a local joint and the first that you'll pass on the road. They serve delicious breakfasts, but are not open frequently. Italian-owned **Penquino's** is a good spot for seafood and is located at the end of the road to Santa Catalina. Lunch and dinner dishes are the usual Panamanian-style meat or fish with rice and beans. **Jamming** is an Italian-owned pizzeria, with a dozen or so combinations of mouthwatering thin-crust pizzas baked in a clay oven. The vibe here is reggae-and-rum, and there are a bar and a couple of tables in an open-air thatched-hut *rancho*—this restaurant is a meeting point and what passes for nightlife in town. Jamming is open from around 6:30 to 10 or 10:30pm. There is a **Parrilla Argentina,** owned by two Argentine surfers, with delicious grilled meats and fish paired with salad and potatoes. When I was last there, they did not yet have an alcohol license, so it could still be BYOB. It's open from 7 to 10pm.

BOCAS DEL TORO ARCHIPELAGO

10

The Bocas del Toro Archipelago is a scattering of seven islands and more than 200 islets off the northwestern coast of Panama, near the border with Costa Rica. The region has all the trappings of a Caribbean fantasy: dreamy beaches, thatched-roofed huts, aquamarine sea, thick rainforest, and soft ocean breeze. Add to that a funky, carefree ambience and a large English-speaking population, and it's easy to see why Bocas del Toro is quickly emerging as an eco-tourism hot spot faster than any other part of Panama.

But scratch the surface and you will find an island destination that is as much a paradox as it is paradise. Backpackers and surfers first discovered Bocas, lured by big waves, an underwater playground, and cheap accommodations. Midrange hotels and restaurants moved in, and retirees and expats with disposable income followed, snapping up beachfront properties and building their own tropical Xanadu. Considering that Bocas consists mostly of Ngöbe-Buglé and Teribe Indians plying the waters in dugout canoes, as well as Afro-Caribbeans who go about living much as they have for nearly a century, the contrast between the mix of ethnicities and nationalities here is striking.

The principal island in the region is Isla Colón, 62 sq. km (24 sq. miles) and home to **Bocas Town,** the regional capital and the center of activity in the archipelago. A smaller island called Isla Carenero neighbors Isla Colón, and is a quieter location with a few hotels and restaurants just a minute or two away from Bocas Town by water taxi. Isla Bastimentos and Isla Cristóbal offer accommodations and amenities, and are better choices than Bocas Town for travelers seeking a more intimate, castaway-like experience in wild, natural surroundings. Visitors to island lodges also benefit from in-house tours planned by proprietors with local knowledge, but there are plenty of tour operators in Bocas Town to fill your days if you choose to stay closer to shopping, restaurants, and nightlife.

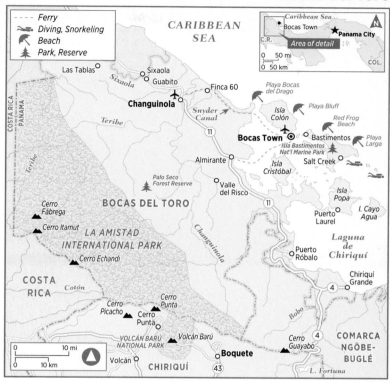

Bocas can hold its own against nearby Costa Rica when it comes to adventure travel in the Caribbean. The diving and snorkeling are outstanding in this region—Bocas is home to some of the best-preserved hard and soft coral on the planet—but make sure your tour operator is willing to take you to the finest examples instead of bleached-out coral in "typical" tourist spots. There are sailing tours, boat tours to deserted islands and visits to Indian communities, hiking through luxuriant rainforest in Isla Bastimentos Park, and riding waves in what is largely considered the surfing epicenter of the southwest Caribbean.

Historically there has always been a rough, end-of-the-line feel to Bocas del Toro, which is perceptible even today. Weathered, plantation-style homes—many of which look as if a good sneeze would level them—line dirt streets; Jimmy Buffett types hold court at waterfront dive bars; and residents and foreign visitors languidly stroll from one point to another, or kill entire afternoons on a park bench in the town's central plaza, which is choked with overgrown tropical foliage. But underneath this are the rumblings of an upcoming boom in tourism, with multimillion-dollar hotels, gated residential communities, and waterfront condominiums either

🔖 A WORD ABOUT water

The major drawback to Bocas del Toro as a destination is its climate. While the rest of Panama enjoys a generally predictable dry season from December to April, Bocas can experience cloudy skies and **downpours** any time of the year. The most trustworthy months for sunshine are late August to mid-October, and February and March.

Tourists with sensitive digestive tracts should stick to **bottled water** when in Bocas Town. Tap water is treated but not to the same standards as it is in the rest of Panama. Hotels on outlying islands use filtered rainwater that is okay to drink—but you still might want to play it safe and drink bottled water only.

Visitors should be extremely careful when swimming in the ocean because of strong **riptides.** The day before I went to Red Frog beach, a 26-year-old tourist was caught in a riptide and died. Even my experienced, native Bocas guide got caught in a riptide and had to struggle to keep his head above water. It can be the scariest moment of your life, and can affect anyone regardless of his or her abilities as a swimmer. At a beach, find a section of the water that isn't being churned up by looking for clear, not sandy, waves. If you're caught in a riptide, don't panic, no matter how much the waves are tossing you around. Swim parallel to the shore until you feel yourself released from the current, then head back to shore. To play it safe, stick close to the shore at beaches with strong waves and riptides.

in the works or already breaking ground. Still, the laid-back friendliness that characterizes Bocas del Toro endures.

ISLA COLÓN: BOCAS TOWN ★

30 min. by boat from Almirante; 1 hr. by boat from Changuinola; 1 hr. by plane from Panama City

Christopher Columbus arrived at what is now known as Bocas del Toro in October 1502, on his fourth and final voyage to the New World. It is said that he repaired his ships at Isla Carenero (thus the moniker "Careening Cay") before continuing on to present-day Portobelo and back to the Veraguas coast in the never-ending quest for gold and riches for the Spanish crown. Columbus never found the fabled gold mines of the highlands backing Bocas del Toro, and the area therefore piqued little interest in the region for the Spanish. By the 17th century the archipelago became the haunt of renegade pirates and buccaneers.

The United Fruit Company first settled Isla Colón in the early 1900s for large-scale banana production, designating **Bocas Town** as headquarters and regional capital. A wave of immigrants from Jamaica, as well as from San Andrés and Providencia, Colombia, followed, so that by the 1920s, Bocas Town had more than 20,000 residents. It ranked as one of the most prosperous regions in Panama, but when a banana blight forced the company to shut down in the 1930s and move operations to the mainland, Bocas Town retreated into a state of relative anonymity.

Fast-forward to the 21st century, and really there hasn't been much change in Bocas Town. But not for long: Tourism, though nascent, is alive on Main Street, and developers have their eye on the waterfront. Yet, there is still little in the way of

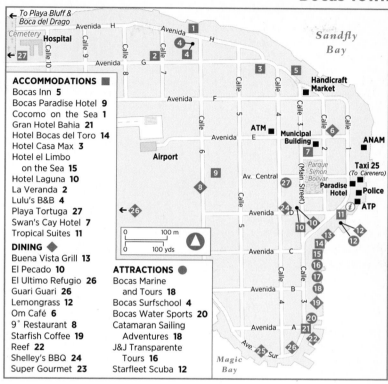

ACCOMMODATIONS ■
Bocas Inn **5**
Bocas Paradise Hotel **9**
Cocomo on the Sea **1**
Gran Hotel Bahia **21**
Hotel Bocas del Toro **14**
Hotel Casa Max **3**
Hotel el Limbo
  on the Sea **15**
Hotel Laguna **10**
La Veranda **2**
Lulu's B&B **4**
Playa Tortuga **27**
Swan's Cay Hotel **7**
Tropical Suites **11**

DINING ◆
Buena Vista Grill **13**
El Pecado **10**
El Ultimo Refugio **26**
Guari Guari **26**
Lemongrass **12**
Om Café **6**
9° Restaurant **8**
Starfish Coffee **19**
Reef **22**
Shelley's BBQ **24**
Super Gourmet **23**

ATTRACTIONS ●
Bocas Marine
  and Tours **18**
Bocas Surfschool **4**
Bocas Water Sports **20**
Catamaran Sailing
  Adventures **18**
J&J Transparente
  Tours **16**
Starfleet Scuba **12**

Map labels: To Playa Bluff & Boca del Drago; Cemetery; Hospital; Sandfly Bay; Handicraft Market; Avenida H; Avenida; Calle 9; Calle 10; Avenida G; Avenida F; ATM; Municipal Building; ANAM; Airport; Parque Simon Bolivar; Taxi 25 (To Carenero); Av. Central; Paradise Hotel; Police; ATP; Avenida D; Avenida C; Avenida B; Avenida A; Ave. Sur; Magic Bay; (Main Street); 0 100 m; 0 100 yds

10

BOCAS DEL TORO ARCHIPELAGO | Isla Colón: Bocas Town

upscale accommodations and services here. Finicky travelers will be happiest visiting Bocas Town only as a jumping-off point to a lodge away from the hustle and bustle.

Essentials

GETTING THERE & DEPARTING   There are two ways to get to Bocas del Toro: via a land/sea combination, or by air. Considering the short flight (1 hr. from Panama City), most travelers opt to fly. If crossing into Bocas del Toro from Costa Rica by land, travelers head to Changuinola, where they can grab a boat shuttle to Bocas (1 hr.) or hop over on a small plane from Changuinola (10 min.). **Tip:** If traveling from Costa Rica, remember that Costa Rica is **1 hour ahead** of Panama.

BY PLANE   The basic but spruce **Bocas International Airport** (*©* **757-9208**) is serviced by daily flights from Panama City, David, Changuinola, and Costa Rica. Both Airlines charge about $180 (including taxes) for a round-trip ticket from Panama City to Bocas Town, but again, gas prices mean this is likely to go up.

   Air Panama (*©* **316-9000;** www.flyairpanama.com) has service to Bocas del Toro from Panama City, David, and San José, Costa Rica (for Costa Rica flights, see

Being Grounded

Air Panama and Aeroperlas occasionally **cancel flights** when there are not enough passengers to make the flight profitable, or for any other unforeseen problem. It is a frustrating aspect of local air travel in Panama, especially when flights are canceled with short notice. If traveling to Boquete or David from Bocas, your second option is to take a boat to Almirante, and negotiate a fee with a local taxi driver at the dock (around $80 one-way). It is about the same price as a one-way flight for two, and takes around 3 hours. Don't hesitate to negotiate the price and be certain to settle on a fee beforehand.

From Costa Rica by Plane, below). From Panama City, there are two daily flights leaving at 6:30am and 6:30pm from Panama City, though flights are added when demand is high. Return flights from Bocas to Panama City leave 8am (Mon–Sat); 9:15am (Sun); 1:45pm (Mon, Wed, Fri); and 4:30pm (daily), but call ahead to confirm times.

Aeroperlas (✆ **378-6000;** www.aeroperlas.com) offers two daily flights from **Panama City** to Bocas, weekdays at 3:45pm and 4pm; the return trip to Panama City leaves at 9am and 5:20pm. From **David,** flights leave once daily, on Mondays, Wednesdays, and Fridays only at 11:20am; the flight from Bocas is at noon.

BY BOAT **Bocas Marine & Tours** (✆ **757-9033** in Bocas, 758-4085 in Almirante; www.bocasmarinetours.com) has daily boat service between Almirante and Bocas every 30 to 40 minutes, from 6am to 6:30pm (6:30am–6:30pm from Bocas to Almirante). *Note:* Owing to the increase in fuel costs, Bocas Marine & Tours operates with a minimum of six passengers; this means that when business is slow they might not leave on schedule.

Taxi 25 (✆ **757-9028**) also operates between Almirante and Bocas, leaving every half-hour from 6am to 6:30pm. Both companies charge $4 per person, one-way, and leave from the Almirante dock; Bocas Marine & Tours is on Main Street in Bocas, and Taxi 25 can be found next to the ATP office. If you have a vehicle, there is parking for $3 a day at the lot at the Almirante boat dock. To get to the Almirante bus station for the 4-hour bus ride to David, take a $1 taxi that waits at the port.

FROM COSTA RICA BY PLANE **Nature Air,** a Costa Rican airline (✆ **506/2299-6000** in Costa Rica, or 800/235-9272 in the U.S. and Canada; www.natureair.com), has one flight to Bocas from San José (with connections from Quepos, Liberia, and Puerto Jiménez) on Sunday, Wednesday, and Friday leaving at 11am and returning from Bocas at 1:30pm; the flight costs $111 to $139 one-way, $222 to $278 round-trip. Note that Nature Air is known to increase prices during the high season (Dec 1–Apr 20).

FROM COSTA RICA BY ROAD Travelers entering Panama from Costa Rica by road at the Sixaola-Guabito border can take a taxi (about $15) to **Changuinola,** then a boat to Bocas del Toro with **Taxi 25** (see above). Have your taxi driver take you to the dock at Finca 60, just outside of Changuinola. The boat journey passes through the San San Pond Sak wetlands and an old banana plantation canal, and is so scenic it could be considered a low-price tour. From Changuinola, boats leave daily at 8am, 9:30am, 11am, 12:30pm, 2pm, 3:30pm, and 5pm. From Bocas Town to Changuinola, boats leave at 7am, 8am, 9:30am, 11am, 12:30pm, 2pm, 3:30pm, and 4:30pm. The cost is $5 per person one-way. Remember, if you're crossing into Panama from Costa Rica, you'll have to go through immigration. This can take a long time on a 50-passenger bus, so be prepared for a 1- to 2-hour process. If you're arriving by car, immigration should only take 15 to 20 minutes.

VISITOR INFORMATION   There is an **ATP visitor center** (© **757-9642;** Mon–Fri 9am–12:45pm and 1:45–4pm) in a barn-size yellow building on the waterfront at Calle 1, near the police station. It appears that ATP blew its budget on this sparkling new office, because English-speaking, trained information officers, maps, and brochures are all in short supply. Around lunchtime, you'll be lucky to find anyone staffing the desk, though on the second floor you'll find a display on the natural history of Bocas, and there are public bathrooms here, too. For additional information about Bocas, try the Web portal **www.bocas.com**, which has links to hotels, tourism services, transportation information, and more.

Note: Though not dangerous by any means, there has been a slight increase in theft in Bocas Town, mostly due to the lack of economic opportunity for the native Afro-Caribbean population paired with the comparative affluence of expats and tourists. Just keep an eye on your personal belongings like you would anywhere else; you are highly unlikely to be violently assaulted, but if you're careless with your wallet or camera you may not find it where you left it.

GETTING AROUND   Everything in Bocas Town is within walking distance, but collective taxis are plentiful if you need one. Most hotels arrange pickup and dropoff for guests arriving by air, but there are also taxis waiting for every arrival at the airport. If arriving by boat, find out where your hotel is in relation to the dock—you may already be close enough to walk. Taxis cost between $1 and $2. There are two principal roads on the island: One runs along the coast and ends at Playa Bluff; the other crosses the island to Boca del Drago.

There are **bicycle** rentals on Main Street across from the plaza; all charge $1 an hour, or $5 to $8 a day. Informal **water taxis** are available at the dock next to the ATP office, with service to neighboring Isla Carenero ($1.50 one-way) and Isla Bastimentos ($11 one-way to Red Frog Beach). Hours are irregular, with service generally running from 7am to 9pm. Most people visit Isla Bastimentos as part of a day tour; resorts on that island include round-trip transportation in the price and an extra charge for additional trips.

For beaches outside of Bocas Town, see "What to See & Do," below.

 Money

Many hotels and restaurants in Bocas del Toro do not accept credit cards, and of those that do, it's mostly **Visa** and **MasterCard only.** Some hotels will request that you pay your deposit via PayPal or a bank deposit in your home country, then pay cash or traveler's checks for the remaining balance. There is a 24-hour ATM at Banco Nacional de Panamá, located at the corner of Calle 4 and Avenida E, and an ATM in the Expreso Taxi 25 building—but bring extra cash in case both are down, which can happen here, especially during high season.

ORIENTATION Bocas is the only town on Isla Colón, centered around a bustling (though far from picturesque) Main Street (Calle 3) and Simon Bolívar Plaza. There are fewer than two dozen streets in Bocas, and most are unpaved. The airport is just a couple of blocks away from the main plaza, meaning you could walk to your hotel if you felt like it. Calles 1 through 10 run west-east and Avenidas A to H run north-south. There is no "downtown," but most hotels and restaurants are concentrated on the south end where Calle 1 meets Main Street. Internet cafes and shops are along Main Street between Avenidas E and D.

[FastFACTS] BOCAS TOWN

Banks See "Money," above.

Bookstore There's a small new bookstore in town (© **6452-5905**) selling used and new books with a decent selection of English-language titles; it's located right next to Om Café. Movie rentals are also available.

Emergency For an ambulance, call © **757-9814;** for fire, dial © **103;** police, dial © **104** or 757-9217.

Hospital There is a basic hospital clinic in

Bocas, located at Calle 10 and Avenida G (© **757-9201**), with a 24-hour emergency room. However, service is limited and those with more serious health problems will need to seek medical care in Panama City or David.

Internet Access There are multiple Internet cafes on Bocas's main street, and many hotels also offer free Wi-Fi.

Laundry There are coin-operated machines and drop-off laundry

services including pickup and delivery at **Bubbles** on Avenida C at Main Street (© **6591-3814;** Mon–Sat 8am–6pm).

Post Office The post office is located at Calle A and Avenida 2; no phone. It's run by a no-nonsense woman who maintains hours Monday through Friday from 8am to noon and 2 to 4pm (some days 3–4pm "when I feel like taking a long lunch"), and Saturday 8am to noon.

What to See & Do

The Bocas del Toro Archipelago, despite its location in the warm, cerulean Caribbean Sea, is not a quintessential beach destination. That's not to say that there are no beaches here; in fact, there are a handful of idyllic beaches straight from the pages of a travel magazine—it just takes a little effort to reach them. Also, most beaches in Bocas offer poor swimming conditions because of strong riptides. (See "A Word About Water," above.) For this reason, those traveling with small children may want to consider another beach destination, or stick to **Boca del Drago** and **Starfish Beach,** which both have calm waters and excellent swimming conditions.

The closest decent beach to Bocas Town (Bluff Beach) is an 8km (5-mile) bike or taxi ride away, and the beaches on Isla Bastimentos can only be reached by boat, followed by a short to medium-long walk. During the calm-water months (early Sept to early Nov), it's possible to arrive directly by boat at the beaches of Isla Bastimentos.

If you don't have an all-inclusive package with your hotel, or if your hotel simply does not offer trips, there are plenty of tour agencies to fulfill your excursion needs. Bocas is a good base for exploring the archipelago—nearly every kind of excursion and destination can be reached from here, including spots for watersports and cultural visits. Trips to Isla Bastimentos and the Zapatilla Cays are better with fast boats that offer flexible itineraries. If you have a group or can afford a private-boat rental, do so because it offers you the freedom to plan your own itinerary.

Tip: The old cliché "You get what you pay for" rings true in Bocas. There are plenty of agencies pitching the same day tour to the masses, usually for dirt-cheap prices. These companies cut corners by hiring semi-qualified guides with little concern for the environment; others try to save on gas by not taking clients far enough to the best snorkeling and diving sites—providing less-than-memorable experiences and the dreaded cattle-herd sensation. To avoid disappointments, when booking, ask detailed questions about destinations, snorkeling and diving sites, safety precautions, and schedules.

BEACHES & OTHER NATURAL ATTRACTIONS
Boca del Drago Beach, Starfish Beach & Swan's Cay ★★
Boca del Drago is the best beach on Isla Colón for swimming, and when the sea is calm visitors can snorkel from the shore. However, often there isn't much beach to speak of—just a couple of feet or so for throwing down a towel or beach chair, but it's a lovely spot. The beach is on the north shore of Isla Colón. Tour companies include Boca del Drago as part of their standard day tour, including a visit to nearby **Swan's Cay,** a picturesque rocky outcrop and bird sanctuary that attracts nesting boobies, frigates, and the magnificent red-billed tropic bird. There is no coral reef at Swan's Cay, but the sea-battered rocks are still an interesting place to snorkel. Do not disturb nesting birds by going ashore. You can also get to Boca del Drago from Bocas Town by road in a taxi, which costs $25 round-trip and takes 30 minutes, or you can take a $2 bus that stops in front of the park. **Starfish Beach,** located right next to Boca del Drago Beach, is one of my favorite beaches for its calm, crystal-clear waters, and the hundreds of starfish that dot the bottom of the ocean floor. To get here, simply keep walking after you pass Boca del Drago beach. There's not much of a beach at **Starfish Beach** either, but swimming conditions are perfect. Both beaches are home to schools of colorful fish and make for good informal snorkeling time. You'll have to bring your own snorkeling gear however, because **Yasinori,** the seafood restaurant on Boca del Drago Beach, no longer rents snorkel equipment.

Bluff Beach ★
This golden-sand beach would be perfect if it weren't for a light sprinkling of trash. It's still the prettiest beach close to town for catching some rays—but don't plan on getting more than your feet wet here because the ocean is fraught with riptides. The beach is about 8km (5 miles) from the city center and can be reached by taxi for $10 one-way. Some drivers are willing to hang around if you plan on staying an hour or two; if not, you'll need to arrange for pickup later. In this case, negotiate to pay when the driver returns (to make sure that he comes back). You can also rent a bicycle and pedal there, which is quite a pleasant ride if you're up to it. Rain can wreak havoc on the road, so be prepared for lots of puddles. (Incidentally, taxi drivers often inflate their price when the road calls for a 4WD.) On the way out of town you'll pass by the less-scenic **Punch Beach,** which is popular with surfers. Punch is known for its right and left breaks, reef bottom, and swells that average 1.5 to 1.6m (5–6 ft.).

Emergency Treatment

Healthcare in Bocas del Toro is less than adequate, particularly if you suffer an emergency or a catastrophic accident. For any serious conditions, you'll likely have to be transported to David or even Panama City. **Evac Americas** (© 261-0024 or 6633-1156; www.evacamericas.com) offers 90-day tourist packages for $10 and will airlift you to Panama City or the nearest major airport appropriate for treatment at no cost after the $10 initial payment. In fact, Evac Americas works anywhere there is an airstrip in Panama, making it a good investment for travelers who will be visiting remote areas of Panama if your insurance does not fully cover ambulance or air medical transfer. No medical exam or insurance is required to purchase 90-day coverage. There are also $26/month plans available to year-round residents.

San San Pond Sak Wetlands ★★★

The San San Pond Sak Wetlands, covering nearly 16,187 hectares (40,000 acres), are located on the coast about 4.8km (3 miles) north of Changuinola. The wetlands are home to sloths, white-faced capuchin monkeys, and caimans, but more importantly, San San is the natural habitat of the manatee, an aquatic, elephant-like mammal that weighs between 363 and 544 kilograms (800 and 1,200 lb.). Previously it was difficult to visit San San, but **Starfleet Scuba** (see "Scuba Diving & Snorkeling," below) now offers a full-day excursion (7am–5pm) that provides for an out-of-the-ordinary experience. Because there is so little human traffic in this region, your chances of spotting a manatee are very good, but please note that manatees are protected animals. Do not chase, pet, or harass these magnificent creatures—and report anyone who does. The Starfleet tour takes visitors to the coast, where they are transported by minibus to the put-in site for the *cayuco* (dug-out canoe) to paddle quietly through the wetlands. There is also an easy nature trail for getting out and stretching your legs. The cost includes a full lunch, park entrance fees, guides, and transportation; contact Starfleet for prices.

The Soposo Rainforest ★★

The Soposo Rainforest is home to the Naso culture, the only culture in the Americas still governed by a king. Though the Naso number only about 4,000, they are a proud people hoping to hold on to their traditions by promoting sustainable tourism in their native lands and sharing their culture and traditions with visitors. The rainforest on the Bocas del Toro mainland sees few visitors, so like the San San Pond Sak Wetlands above, the likelihood of spotting wildlife is high here. **Soposo Rainforest Adventures** (© 6631-2222; www.soposo.com) offers day trips as well as weeklong adventures. Day trips cost $90 per person for three or more people, 2-night/3-day trips cost $500 per person for up to six people, and 5-night/6-day adventures cost $900 for three to six people. Prices are higher for smaller groups. Expect to see sloths, frogs, monkeys, and other wildlife. The highlight of the trip, however, is the opportunity to interact with and experience the Naso culture.

OTHER ATTRACTIONS
Scuba Diving & Snorkeling

Scuba diving and snorkeling are among the most popular activities in Bocas del Toro, owing to well-preserved displays of hard and soft coral, mangrove swamps, volcanic-rock walls, underwater caves—and balmy water temperatures that average around 86°F (30°C). Beyond tropical reef fish, divers are privy to larger species such as nurse sharks, spotted eagle rays and southern rays, turtles, and more unusual species such as batfish and toadfish. You might also see colorful sponges, and there is even an underwater landing craft that was sunk to create an artificial reef. Snorkeling and diving sites that are recommended are **Crawl Cay** (or Coral Cay), with shallow waters and some of the best coral formations in the area; **Hospital Point,** just a 10-minute boat ride from Bocas and easy to reach by water taxi; **Polo Beach,** a shallow system of caves suitable for snorkelers but reachable only 6 months of the year; **Swan's Cay,** with interesting rock formations created by battering waves and also a migratory-bird site; and **Cayos Zapatillas,** two delicate islands with white-sand beaches surrounded by an extensive reef system that attracts lots of tropical fish. Cayos Zapatillas, it should be noted, has currents and is for strong swimmers only. Divers also head to **Buoy Line** near Isla Solarte, which is a deepwater channel where pelagic and larger marine species can be seen; the same is true of **Tiger Rock,** an offshore site and rocky outcrop whose long distance from Bocas Town keeps the crowds away. Adventurous divers and snorkelers really looking to get away from other travelers might consider visiting **Isla Escudo de Veraguas,** which is a full-day trip and a fairly large undertaking (available usually only Sept–Oct). The beaches here are generally considered to be the loveliest in the entire region.

The principal shortcoming of Bocas del Toro as a diving and snorkeling destination is the **unpredictability of the weather,** with spontaneous downpours and wind gusts that can churn up the sea and cloud visibility. If the focus of your trip is diving and snorkeling, come from September to early November, when the sea is tranquil and flat. Other months with better visibility are March and April, but rain and wind can occur at any time during these months. Dive sites with deeper water and larger species (mostly offshore sites such as Tiger Rock) can be visited only during these more tranquil months.

Bocas Water Sports, Main Street (✆ **757-9541;** www.bocaswatersports.com), is the oldest operation in town, and has recently been taken over by new American owners. Dive trips include all gear; a two-dive trip is $60 per person, a one-dive trip $35 per person. Trips last 3 hours and depart at 9am and 2:30pm. Dives to Tiger Rock and Cayos Zapatillas are $75 per person and only available during calm months. Night dives from 6:30 to 8:30pm are $50 per person. Snorkeling tours are $17 to $20 for a full day, not including lunch.

Starfleet Scuba, at Calle 1A (✆ **757-9630;** www.starfleetscuba.com), has a spotless record and a British owner who last ran diving operations in Indonesia. Starfleet has three boats plus a new, 80kmph (50-mph) inflatable Zodiac boat that gives the company the edge in terms of more quickly getting to remote destinations like Tiger Rock ($90 for minimum of four people; lunch included). Two-tank dives cost $50, a one-tank dive $35; snorkeling tours are $20 per person. Starfleet works in conjunction with the U.K.-based **Ocean Pulse,** a marine-research group that offers 2-week "eco-ventures" to travelers with advanced diving experience. Participants accompany marine biologists exploring new dive sites to monitor for conservation, and are treated to lectures and presentations about species and habitats throughout the day. Packages vary depending on accommodations requirements, so it's best to contact them for prices ((*C* **0175/220-2101** in the U.K.; www.oceanpulse.co.uk).

La Buga Dive and Surf, next to Farmacia Rosa Blanco ((*C* **757-9534;** www.labugapanama.com), offers PADI certification as well as dive excursions. A two-tank half-day dive costs $60 and night dives cost $50. A 3-day PADI-certification course will cost you $235; however, Bocas Water Sports and Starfleet are a bit more reputable. In addition to diving, La Buga also offers surfing, snorkeling, and kayaking excursions.

Several companies offer snorkeling and diving trips in addition to the two companies mentioned above. Day trips include equipment; lunch is extra so bring cash for a local restaurant, or bring your own food. There are plenty of operators along the waterfront; **J & J Transparente Boat Tours** offers trips to all the islands, but they're garden-variety. Tours cost $17 to $22 per person, and suffer from a get-em-in and get-em-out mentality. However, J & J is the company to call for charter-boat rentals, which cost $200 for a full day, not including lunch.

Catamaran Sailing Adventures at Main Street ((*C* **757-9710** or 6637-9064; www.bocassailing.com) has a 12m (40-ft.) catamaran for laid-back and enjoyable full-day snorkeling trips to Bocas del Drago or around Isla Bastimentos for $30 per person (four-person minimum, 18 maximum), including a sack lunch. Charter rentals cost $250 a day. The catamaran has little protection from the sun, so bring sunscreen and a hat.

Tip: Ask a lot of questions before embarking on the standard, full-day snorkeling tour that starts in Dolphin Bay and ends at Hospital Point. Boat drivers and guides on these tours practice poor environmental management by racing around a dolphin breeding site, and then they dump guests at an expensive restaurant where they are left to "snorkel" around dead coral and bits of trash. See "What to See & Do" in "Isla Bastimentos," later in this chapter.

Watersports

Bocas Water Sports (see above) offers water-skiing for $45 for 1 hour, gear included, using their 7.6m (25-ft.) tour boat (maximum four people). There are many mangrove-fringed canals in the area that provide for glassy water year-round. Full-day water-skiing trips can be arranged; contact the company for price information. Bocas Water Sports also rents one-person kayaks that cost $3 per hour, or $10 half-day. During bad-weather days, you'll only be able to navigate around mangrove swamps and the coast, but on calm days experienced kayakers can make it all the way to Hospital Point. Other providers along the waterfront also offer watersports, some for a lower price, but be sure to ask a lot of questions.

Boating & Sailing

For catamaran tours, see **Catamaran Sailing Adventures,** under "Scuba Diving & Snorkeling," above. **Boteros Bocatoreños** ((*C* **757-9760;** boterosbocas@yahoo.com) is a group of local boatmen who have banded together in the face of encroaching competition—they can provide custom tours at slightly lower prices than outfitters. Most speak at least some English and have local knowledge, and they can be found on the Via Principal by the ATP office. **Boteros Nuestra Senora del Carmen**

NEXT VACATION: PICK UP A skill

Take advantage of your trip to Bocas del Toro to learn a new skill. Scuba courses taught in swimming pools may earn you the basic dive certification you need, but they don't give you much practical experience in open water. Starfleet Scuba and Bocas Water Sports (see "Scuba Diving & Snorkeling," above) offer well-respected **scuba training academies** for everyone from absolute beginners to divers seeking to brush up—and even for those who want to be certified as instructors. The **Discover Scuba** course is a half-day introduction to scuba diving for $65 to $85 per person; the **Scuba Diver** course is 1½ to 2 days for a partial certification program that allows you to dive up to 12m (39 ft.) with a certified dive master, and costs $185 per person; the **Open Water Course** that is the standard certification program for worldwide independent diving takes 3 to 4 days and costs $210 to $235 per person. Contact the companies for more information about Rescue Diver and Instructor programs. Bocas Water Sports also offers an advanced open water class and a divemaster class.

Stop blaming your rusty Spanish for misunderstandings with locals, and start doing something about it. **Spanish-by-the-Sea language classes,** Calle 4, behind Hotel Bahía (© 757-9518; www.spanish atlocations.com), has inexpensive classes that are as long or intensive as you want them to be. Weekly programs (5 days only) include group lessons at $150 to $185 per week (20 hr.), and private customized courses are also available. Spanish-by-the-Sea also has packages that include lodging in their comfortable hostel that caters to younger adults, as well as $230 open-water dive excursions and 3-day $135 surfing classes. Home-stays can also be arranged.

(© 757-9039) is another group of local operators. They require a minimum of five people and tours usually cost $3 to $20 per person, though Cayos Zapatilla costs $25 per person. You can find them at Calle 3 next to Catamaran Tours. They have snorkeling equipment. Another good source for local boatmen is **Ancon Expeditions** (see Bocas Inn under "Where to Stay in Bocas Town," below).

Surfing

Bocas experiences the largest and most consistent swells from December to March, and during June and July, with reef point breaks, beach breaks, and huge, challenging waves recommended only for experienced surfers. The waves in Bocas are more suitable for shortboarding and bodyboarding; if you're bringing your own board, check with your airline about requirements because some smaller planes may not accept a long board. **Del Toro Surf** (© 6570-8277; deltorosurf@yahoo.com.ar) offers surf lessons and board rentals to clients participating in lessons. To rent a surfboard, try **Tropix,** located on Main Street across from the plaza, or **Flow** surf shop (no phone) on Avenida H below the Om Restaurant. All offer tips and maps to the best surf spots in the area, as well as information on how to get there. **La Buga** (see "Scuba Diving & Snorkeling," above) offers surf trips from $10 to $20 for those who already know how to surf, half-day surf trips for $49, and full-day surf trips for $99 for those interested in learning. The **Best of Both Adventures for Women** (see "Spas," below) offers women-only surf tours. **Bocas Surf School** (© 6852-5291 or 757-9057;

www.bocassurfschool.com) is owned and operated by Bryan and Jana Hudson at Lula's B&B (see later in this chapter), who set-up beginner through advanced surfing courses and surfing excursions from.

OTHER ACTIVITIES IN BOCAS TOWN
Scientific Visits
The **Smithsonian Tropical Research Institute** has a base in Bocas del Toro, and is open to the public every Friday from 3 to 5pm. If you're lucky, you'll be around for one of their monthly chats led by a scientist who highlights the center's work and discoveries in the region. Contact the institute at ✆ **212-8000,** or visit their site, www.stri.org, for information about upcoming lectures.

Local Events
The **Fería Internacional del Mar (International Festival of the Sea),** which takes place around the second week of September, is a 5-day event featuring handicrafts booths, food stands serving local cuisine, and exhibits by the Smithsonian Institute and ANAM (the park service), with displays of animals and natural history information. Nightly events include folkloric presentations and dances, all culminating with the crowning of the Sea Fair Queen. Contact the ATP office for exact dates. The **Fundación de la Provincia de Bocas del Toro (Founding Day of Bocas del Toro)** takes place on November 16, and is celebrated with parades and other events; on November 23, residents of Isla Bastimentos celebrate **Bastimentos Day,** with parades and live music. There is a maypole dance in Bocas and on Isla Bastimentos for **Palo de Mayo,** which takes place on May 1. Lastly, on July 16 is the **Día de la Virgen del Carmen,** which honors the patron saint of Bocas with a parade; the following Sunday hundreds make the pilgrimage across the island to visit the shrine of the virgin at La Gruta.

Spas
If you're winding down from a day of activity (and a hammock isn't doing the trick), try Donna at **Spa Flora Bella** (✆ **6591-3814;** islagirly@yahoo.com), which offers deep tissue massages, reflexology, and hot-stone treatments, as well as an assortment of beauty services such as hair cuts and facials. Donna has two locations, but give her a call or send her an e-mail to set up an appointment. Several massage therapists provide in-hotel services; try **Holistic Alternative Therapy** (✆ 6686-0235), which has Zen Shiatsu massage and Thai foot massages. **Starfleet Scuba** (✆ **757-9630;** see "Scuba Diving & Snorkeling," above) now has a low-key day spa above their in-town office. Thirty-minute massages cost $40, and 1-hour massages $60. Pedicures, manicures, and waxing are also available, or you can head to **Danuta's Holistic Therapy** (✆ **757-9308** or 6676-0235). The **Best of Both Adventures for Women** (www.bestofbothadventures.com) offers women-only adventures throughout Panama (and Latin America), which feature yoga, spa, and massage treatment. For more information, call Dez Bartelt at ✆ **787/823-0610** or check out the website.

If you want to get a bit of exercise in during your vacation, contact Laura Kay of **Bocas Yoga,** Casa Morada, 4th Street (✆ **658-1355;** www.bocasyoga.com). Drop-ins are available for $5 plus a 50¢ mat fee, or you can purchase a 10-class pass for $45.

Where to Stay in Bocas Town
The brand-new **Playa Tortuga Resort,** part of the Country-Inn and Suites Chain, is really the only remotely upscale lodging option on Isla Colon. Travelers seeking

true luxury accommodations will be happier at a lodge such as Tranquilo Bay on Isla Bastimentos (see later in this chapter). Easygoing travelers enjoy the laid-back Caribbean vibe in Bocas Town, and its proximity to restaurants, bars, and shopping, not to mention people-watching and cultural encounters. But loud music and other street noise is a factor, and travelers seeking peaceful isolation will do better lodging elsewhere. Neighboring Isla Carenero is close enough that you can occasionally hear music on particularly loud party nights in Bocas, but it still gives travelers an option for being near Bocas without actually staying in it.

Nearly every hotel sits over the water, so try to get a view if you can. The north shore of town is usually breezier, which is a definite plus in the Bocas heat. If a price range is shown, it indicates that a hotel applies high- and low-season rates. Low season is generally mid-April to December. Lodging in Bocas tends to be more expensive for what you get compared to other destinations in Panama, and hotels are unlikely to drop their prices during high season. Be sure to make reservations at least a few weeks in advance outside of April through December, as hotels here fill up quickly.

Aside from the options listed below, **Bocas Inn** (© **757-9600;** www.ancon expeditions.com) offers basic but comfortable rooms and a prime location. The hotel is owned and operated by Ancon Expeditions and the staff can help guests with tours and excursions. Doubles start at $66.

VERY EXPENSIVE

Playa Tortuga Resort ★ ☺   The Playa Tortuga resort is really more a medium-size hotel with lots of amenities and services. Located about 3.2km (2 miles) from Bocas town, the resort fronts a small, relatively calm beach and is perfect for families and those looking for comfort and convenience. The lobby is a bit dim and unwelcoming, but the cheerful, friendly (and bilingual) staff makes up for this. Rooms have a familiar, chain-like decor, but all have their own balcony, complete with a hammock and sitting area, many with great ocean views. The best things about the Playa Tortuga Resort is its impressive, cascading pool, complete with a pool bar and restaurant. The hotel's service desk offers snorkeling, fishing, and wildlife excursions for those looking for a little bit of adventure and is especially great for kids. Though it may not provide a world-class resort experience, there's really nothing else like it on the island, and it will suffice for those used to more upscale accommodations.

Playa Big Creek. © **302-5424** or 757-9050. www.hotelplayatortuga.com. 118 units. $135 double; $150 1-bedroom suite; $300 grand master suite; $600 Almirante suite. Rates include breakfast. AE, MC, V. **Amenities:** Restaurant; 2 bars; room service. *In room:* A/C, TV, minibar, Wi-Fi.

EXPENSIVE

Tropical Suites ★ ☺   The best thing about this condo-style hotel is how sparkling clean its rooms are. Considering that Tropical Suites rents by the night, week, and month, this is an ideal place for long-term visitors searching the area for property to buy. Half the guest rooms have lovely waterfront views and terraces, and are absolutely worth the $35 extra per night, especially considering that other rooms face the street. Guest rooms are like studio apartments in that the kitchenette and bed are in the same room. The kitchenettes are spotless and stocked with all the utensils you'll need for cooking. A fully stocked dock with a water slide, kayaks, and jet skis is available for guest use, and there's a small bar. The setup is perfect for families, although the fold-out couch is large enough for one child only. The hotel allows guests to tie their boats at their dock. Steep discounts are available in low season.

Calle 1. ☎ **757-9081.** www.tropical-suites.com. 16 units. $175 island-view double; $225 sea-view double. Rates include breakfast. AE, MC, V. **Amenities:** Watersports equipment. *In room:* A/C, TV, hair dryer, kitchenette, Wi-Fi.

MODERATE

Bocas Paradise Hotel This relative newcomer on the Isla Colon hotel scene offers 30 rooms of varying quality and sizes. All rooms are perfectly comfortable and clean, but nos. 306, 307, 205 and 206 are the largest and nicest, with attractive sea views and a bit more style and pizazz than the other rooms. It's definitely worth paying the extra $30 for one of these. The staff here is a bit friendlier and more attentive than at other Bocas hotels, and the room quality is slightly higher than similarly priced hotels. The front desk can help guests arrange snorkeling, diving, and fishing tours.

☎ **757-9708** or 6780-0063. www.bocasparadisehotel.com. 30 units. $66 double; $99 suite. No credit cards. **Amenities:** Restaurant. *In room:* A/C, TV, kitchenette (some rooms), Wi-Fi (all rooms).

Cocomo-on-the-Sea ★ The Cocomo is a pleasant little hotel tucked away behind a white picket fence and a lush garden, about a 5-minute walk to the central part of town. The hotel sits on the waterfront, and feels cool and fresh even on a muggy day. There are only four rooms, all pretty close to each other but bright and airy; each comes with a double bed and a twin. The bathrooms are clean but small. There is a spacious deck, with hammocks and lounge chairs, which is partially covered in case of rain. The hotel staff is friendly, and the American owner can help you plan any tour in the area—although he's not around very much, so try to grab him when you can. Rate includes a good, hearty breakfast, and they have kayaks for guest use.

Av. Norte at 6A St. ☎/fax **757-9259.** www.panamainfo.com/cocomo. 4 units. $70 double. MC, V. **Amenities:** Bar; kayaks. *In room:* A/C, no phone.

Gran Hotel Bahía ★ This is the town's most historic hotel, located in the old United Fruit Company headquarters. Although it is not located on the waterfront, nor does it have ocean views, it's a lovely example of Caribbean architecture, with breeze-swept verandas, built in 1905. Vestiges of the building's original purpose remain, such as the front desk's barred windows and an enormous steel safe; and the long hall with polished pine floors is antique splendor. Superior doubles are better than standards because they have been recently renovated, but even the standards were recently painted colors and country-style teak furniture was added. Nevertheless, the superiors are comfortable and have a lot of amenities. The Hotel Bahía has very friendly service. Note that the hotel closes in June. Steep discounts are available in low season.

South end of Main St. ☎ **757-9626.** www.ghbahia.com. 18 units. $80 double; $90 superior double. MC, V. **Amenities:** Restaurant. *In room:* A/C, TV, Wi-Fi at an additional cost.

Hotel Bocas del Toro ★ With its full-service restaurant and dock furnished with lounge chairs, this place is one of the best places to stay on Isla Colon, and the staff here is a bit more attentive than in other similarly priced hotels. Hotel Bocas del Toro features beautiful wood craftsmanship and a fresh, nautical decor, but some of the standard doubles that do not face the water or the street are dark and small; "premium" rooms have balconies. The third-floor "Luxury Room" is one of the best rooms in town for its ample size, long balcony, and water view; and it has a queen-size and a double bed for up to three guests. If you have a laptop, you'll enjoy the free Wi-Fi service in their restaurant. Like the Limbo, this is not a particularly loud hotel, but a lot of action in the area means it's not whisper-quiet, either.

Calle 1 at Main St. ✆ **757-9018** or 757-9771. www.hotelbocasdeltoro.com. 11 units. $126–$145 double with street view; $140–$195 double with ocean view; $270 luxury room. AE, MC, V. **Amenities:** Restaurant; bar; massage. *In room:* A/C, TV.

Hotel El Limbo on the Sea ★   This oceanfront hotel, centrally located and near restaurants, tour operators, and water taxis, is virtually identical to the neighboring Hotel Bocas del Toro (see above). Hotel Limbo has the edge, however, with brighter rooms, but the service here can run from inattentive to downright unfriendly. Guest rooms are not luxurious, but they are neat as a pin and attractively decorated in nautical style, with cooling blues and whites, polished wood floors, and wood paneling. This is one of the only hotels in town with bathtubs in guest rooms. The best rooms are the two with balconies that overlook the water; they provide particularly relaxing places to have drinks or order meals in, but if you can't get one, take advantage of the Limbo's good restaurant and bar on the first floor.

Calle 1 at Main St. ✆ **757-9062**. www.ellimbo.com. 15 units. $90 double standard; $125 double with balcony and street view; $180 double with balcony and sea view. Rates include breakfast. AE, MC, V. **Amenities:** Restaurant; bar; room service. *In room:* A/C, TV/DVD, minibar.

Hotel Laguna   None of the rooms come with views, but this hotel does have comfortable rooms in a pretty white building with gingerbread-carved details and wide awnings. The hotel is centrally located just steps from the plaza, and is the only hotel in Bocas Town with purified tap water, if that matters to you. Guest rooms, paneled entirely in wood and decorated with simple furniture, have orthopedic beds. There is one deluxe suite and one slightly larger apartment with a kitchenette and private balcony for those seeking independence; these units can sleep up to six. The hotel has a popular first-floor restaurant, El Pecado (see "Where to Dine in Bocas Town," below).

Main St. at Av. D. ✆ **757-9091**. www.bocas.com/hotellaguna.htm. 22 units. $50–$85 double; $85–$135 junior suite; $100–$185 suite with kitchenette. Breakfast included in rates. AE, MC, V. **Amenities:** Restaurant; bar. *In room:* A/C, TV, kitchenette (2 units only), Wi-Fi.

Swan's Cay Hotel   The Swan's Cay Hotel has a convenient location next to the plaza, a waterfront swimming pool, and a lovingly restored antique lobby decorated with lots of dark mahogany wood, Persian rugs, and intricate Italian furnishings. The elegance of the common areas, which include a handsome, manicured outdoor patio and carved-wood balconies, certainly gives a promising first impression. But the hotel seems to have run out of steam when it got to the guest rooms. Standard doubles are terribly small and dark, with fluorescent bulbs for lighting. Deluxe suites have a balcony facing the street. The hotel staff have an offhand way of making you feel more like a nuisance than a welcome guest, lending a certain Fawlty Towers feel to the establishment. Perhaps that is why the hotel never seems full. The above-ground, kid-friendly swimming pool is 2 blocks away from the shore. They have a full-service restaurant with good local and international dishes.

Calle 3 at Av. E. ✆ **757-9090**. www.swanscayhotel.com. 46 units. $85 standard double; $99 deluxe double; $220 suite. AE, MC, V. **Amenities:** Restaurant; pool. *In room:* A/C, TV, minibar (in deluxe rooms).

INEXPENSIVE

Hotel Casa Max   This Dutch-owned hostel is housed in a Caribbean-style, two-story turquoise wooden building, with a barlike common area spread across the ground floor. On the whole, Casa Max offers good value for low-budget travelers, with tasteful but small rooms that are kept very clean. Five more rooms with A/C,

TV, and minibar have been added above the relatively new Indonesian/international restaurant. The service is accommodating and friendly. My only caveat is that Casa Max is in front of the surf bar Mondo Taitu, and light sleepers may be disturbed by late-night music.

Av. G. ☏ **757-9120.** casamax1@hotmail.com. 16 units. $30–$40 double with fan; $45–$60 double with A/C. No credit cards. *In room:* No phone.

La Veranda ★   Housed in a lovely, converted home built in 1910, this is one of the best economy hotels in Bocas. It's about a 5-minute walk on a paved road to the main strip, but there's an open-air, communal kitchen if you'd like to cook and dine in. The rooms are mostly simple, with mosquito nets, pastel-colored walls, and polished floors. Rooms with a private bathroom cost more, but they are well worth the investment because they are larger and brighter than room nos. 4 and 5. The perk at this hotel is its spacious, pleasant veranda, for which the hotel is named. It's a very relaxing place, giving travelers on a shoestring a place to just sleep, while they do their unwinding elsewhere.

Calle G. ☏ **757-9211.** http://laverandapanama.tripod.com. 7 units. $30–$49 double with shared bathroom; $30–$59 double with private bathroom; $10 per extra person. No credit cards. **Amenities:** Communal kitchen. *In room:* A/C (some units), no phone, Wi-Fi.

Lula's Bed & Breakfast ★   This American-run B&B fronts the Cocomo-on-the-Sea and is across a now-paved street from the waterfront, about a 5-minute walk to town. The B&B offers simple, squeaky-clean guest rooms notable for their polished wood floors and wall paneling. The most appealing aspect of Lula's is its "Turtle Deck" balcony, which receives cool breezes. In general, guest rooms are on the small side, but not so small as to seem cramped, and the friendly service here makes guests feel at home. The owner grew up in Bocas and can provide in-depth information and excursion-planning information about the area. A tasty cooked breakfast is included in the price with veggie/cheese omelets alternating with pancakes and homemade jams and syrups. Bocas Surf School (see above) operates out of Lula's B&B.

Av. H at Calle 6. ☏ **757-9057.** www.lulabb.com. 6 units. $50 double; $60 triple. AE, MC, V. *In room:* A/C, no phone, Wi-Fi.

Where to Dine in Bocas Town

Believe it or not, tiny Bocas is home to one of the few gourmet supermarkets in the country, **Super Gourmet** (☏ **757-9357**; Mon–Sat 9am–7pm), with imported foods, vegetarian and organic products, and very expensive produce. Super Gourmet, which has a full-service delicatessen, is located next to the Hotel Bahía on the south end of Main Street by the ATP office. You'll find good coffee drinks and lots of reading material at **Starfish Coffee** on Main Street next to El Encanto bar, and good breakfasts on a waterfront dock at the **Coffee Bar** inside Hotel El Limbo on the Sea (see "Where to Stay in Bocas Town," above). For cheap, gringo-style fast food, try **McDouglas' Golden Grill** (daily 7:30am–11pm) on Main Street across from the plaza.

You should keep in mind that like lodging, dining in Bocas tends to be more expensive than other regions in Panama, and many restaurants do not accept credit cards, so make sure you have plenty of cash.

EXPENSIVE

Guari Guari ★★★ 🎁 INTERNATIONAL   This romantic restaurant is a short taxi ride away from Bocas Town and offers some of the best food on the island. The restaurant is run by a German/Spanish couple and open for dinner only. You must make reservations. There is a set menu that changes daily depending on what the Spanish chef decides to make. Conceptually similar to Manolo Caracol in Panama City (p. 105), you'll be brought six courses, which may include specialties such as Thai chicken, tuna sashimi, and leek and potato soup. The restaurant isn't particularly fancy, but the cozy ambience and attentive service (some of the best in Bocas) makes you feel right at home. Be sure to call ahead to let the chef know if you have any food allergies. The best way to get here is by taxi (have your hotel call for you). While there aren't any ocean views, you'll dine to the sound of waves gently crashing on the shore.

2km (1.2 miles) outside Bocas town on the main road. ✆ **6575-5513.** Reservations required. $19. No credit cards. Thurs–Tues 6:30-10:30pm.

9° Restaurant and Market ★ INTERNATIONAL   This relatively new establishment is the most upscale dining option in Bocas Town and also features a high-end fruit, vegetable, and meat market, as well as attractive outdoor restaurant serving international food. It has the "classiest" bar in Bocas Town and great ocean views. The restaurant's chic exterior seems out of place among Bocas's clapboard Caribbean-style buildings, but it is a testament to the quickly changing face of the island. You can dine on sushi, steaks, and seafood dishes here. Personally, I prefer to do my high-end dining in Panama City and enjoy Bocas's beach-style seafood restaurants, but if you're looking for something a little fancier, 9° is a good choice.

Calle Primera at the back of Tropical Markets. ✆ **757-9400.** www.9degreespanama.com. Main courses $14–$35. MC, V. Mon–Sat 3-10pm.

MODERATE

El Pecado ★ INTERNATIONAL   El Pecado is now located at the Hotel Laguna, a good thing because diners no longer have to worry about the balcony collapsing beneath them. This is one of my favorite restaurants in town and serves Thai, Mexican, Lebanese, and Panamanian food. It is a favorite with locals and travelers alike. It may sound like fusion-confusion, but the food comes together well despite its wide-ranging influences. Main courses are mostly seafood such as grilled tuna, snapper, sea bass, and jumbo shrimp served in sauces such as coconut-curry or spicy garlic, and their Thai soup is highly recommended. Light reggae music sets a funky mood, and the staff couldn't be friendlier.

Hotel Laguna. ✆ **6852-3600.** Main courses $9–$17. No credit cards. Tues–Sat 7am-10:30pm.

El Ultimo Refugio ★★ 🎁 CARIBBEAN/INTERNATIONAL   One of the most atmospheric restaurants in Bocas, El Ultimo Refugio feels a bit like a tiki bar with a fun, tropical bar area and laid-back island decor. The Christmas lights and ocean views add a particularly festive touch. The menu changes frequently depending on the daily catch and whatever the chef feels like preparing, but can include tasty dishes such as seared tuna, Cajun-style chicken, and chicken in peanut sauce. El Ultimo Refugio is popular with tourists and expats alike, and the American owner is friendly and helpful. It may not be the fanciest dining option in Bocas, but the energy here is right and you won't leave disappointed.

100m (109 yds.) past the ferry dock on the water. ✆ **6726-9851.** Main courses $7–$15. No credit cards. Mon–Fri 6-10pm.

Lemongrass ★ ASIAN   Lemongrass fills the bill both in terms of innovative, delicious cuisine and waterfront view. Located above the Starfleet Scuba shop, Lemongrass is the brainchild of expat Mike Thompson, who earned his stripes working in restaurants in Thailand and Indonesia. The menu focuses on Asian cuisine using local ingredients as inspiration. Spicy crab cakes, Thai tacos with red-curry chicken, and fresh trout glazed in chili and ginger are a few mouthwatering items on the menu. Lemongrass is the only restaurant with an elevated waterfront view—really the best view of any restaurant in town—and there is a comfy lounge area, occasional live music, and very friendly service.

Calle 1 at Calle 2. ⓒ **6721-6445** or 757-9630. Main courses $5–$12 lunch, $10–$17 dinner. MC, V. Fri–Wed noon–midnight for drinks, noon–3pm for lunch, and 6–10pm for dinner.

Om Café ★★ INDIAN   The welcoming feeling of this eatery, coupled with the mellow vibe that runs throughout, is pure Bocas. The restaurant is located on the second floor, with an open-air dining area and street-facing balcony for watching the world go by. Om Café serves delicious and healthy Indian cuisine such as tandoori chicken, and a host of vegetarian dishes. The restaurant is closed for lunch, but not for breakfast—and this is where the restaurant really shines, serving strong coffee, waffles, fruit pancakes, and Indian-style dishes like eggs vindaloo. They also serve refreshing fruit juices and yogurt shakes. If you're looking for something a little stronger, Om Café has a nightly martini bar and a "ladies' night" every Tuesday with reduced drink prices for women. The restaurant is closed in May and June.

Av. E at Calle 2. ⓒ **6624-0898** or 6516-3817. Main courses $5–$9. No credit cards. Thurs–Tues 8am–noon and 5:30–10pm.

INEXPENSIVE

Buena Vista Grill ★ AMERICAN   For more than 10 years Buena Vista has been serving casual, North American fare to homesick expats and travelers seeking food with which they are familiar. On the lengthy menu you'll find Philly cheese steaks, hot Reuben and BLT sandwiches, and arguably the best hamburger in town. Heartier appetites can dig into a surf-and-turf platter of filet mignon and garlic shrimp, or snack on a variety of appetizers such as nachos or fried calamari. With a happy hour from 5 to 7pm, some come to "waste away in Margaritaville." Food is served throughout the day, but dinner only after 5pm.

Calle 1 at Calle 2. ⓒ **757-9336.** Main courses $8–$14; sandwiches $5–$6. MC, V. Wed–Mon noon–9:30pm.

Reef PANAMANIAN   The Reef is a local dive serving ultra-fresh Panamanian seafood in a rough-and-tumble, saltwater ambience. You can't get any closer to the waterfront than at a table at the Reef—one false move and you'll tumble into the sea. This is pure home-style cooking, mostly seafood with the usual choice of garlic, creole style, or fried, with rice, beans, and *patacones*. These dishes are simple yet pleasing, but stay away from their bland sandwiches. I like the Reef for its seafaring Panamanian flavor; here in Bocas, it just feels right.

Main St. on the south end of town. No phone. Main courses $4–$10. No credit cards. Daily 7am–11pm.

Shelley's BBQ ★ MEXICAN ROTISSERIE   This is definitely a hole in the wall, but a delicious one. Shelley's serves slow-cooked barbecue beef, chicken, and baby back ribs by the pound ($8), or as a meal with rice, beans, and salad. More popular are Shelley's outstanding tacos and quesadillas; at dinner they offer Mexican specialties such as chicken mole and *enchiladas verdes*. There isn't much to this place, just a walk-up ordering counter and a few bar-stool tables, making this the best spot for a quick but filling meal. Shelley's also sells food to go.

Corner of Calle 4 and Av. D. ✆ **6710-1200** or 6705-3586. Main courses $8–$10; taco meals $4–$7. No credit cards. Mon–Sat 10am–10pm.

Where to Stay & Dine Around Isla Colon

Playa Mango Resort ☺ This relatively new "resort" is really just a small hotel perfect for families with kids because of its attractive pool, comfortable, standard rooms, and watersport opportunities. The hotel is decorated in a tropical, beachy style and rooms are all painted bright yellow, with casual light-wood furniture; rooms are not particularly memorable, but they should more than satisfy families and those looking for a comfortable place to sleep. Prices below reflect low to high season rates. The best thing about the Mango Resort is that it's out of town, but it's close enough that in-town restaurants and bars are just a 25-minute walk or 5-minute cab ride away. Note that every extra guest is $20 in doubles and $25 in apartments and office suite.

Big Creek Ranch 2 miles north of town. ✆ **6788-9191** or 6679-3956. www.playamango.com. 15 units (12 doubles, 2 apartments, 1 office suite). $79–$99 double; $250 1-bedrooms apt; $280 3-bedroom apt. MC, V. **Amenities:** Restaurant, bar; outdoor pool; room service; watersports; excursions. *In room:* A/C, Wi-Fi.

Punta Caracol ★★ 📷 Playa Caracol is a string of stylish, thatched-roofed bungalows that gently curve across a sky-blue Caribbean Sea. The owner should be applauded for his eco-friendly concept of architecture that treads lightly on the environment (using solar panels for light, for example). The nine tropical-chic bungalows are painted in cheery lime and yellow, and fitted with elegant furnishings and French doors that open onto a veranda overlooking the blue sea. The big perk, then, is that you can swim and snorkel just outside your door. During sunny, calm days, there's no better hangout spot than the chaise longue or hammock on the veranda, where the water laps at your feet. Considering that there is no beach here and nowhere else to walk to, a sense of claustrophobia can set in, so good day excursions are a must. A 15-minute water taxi to Bocas is $20. It can get stuffy in the cabins on steamy hot nights, and in inclement weather, rain and heavy winds can batter the bungalows and make the walk to the restaurant a slippery adventure for older, less-agile guests. The Punta Caracol is best for honeymooners or those seeking a bit of secluded romance, though I do find it to be a bit overpriced.

15 min. by boat from town. ✆ **6612-1088** or 6676-7186. www.puntacaracol.com.pa. 9 units. $172–$289 per person, double occupancy. AE, MC, V. Children age 13 and under not accepted. **Amenities:** Restaurant; bar; snorkeling equipment. *In room:* Ceiling fan, no phone.

Restaurant Yasinori PANAMANIAN This thatched-roof restaurant serves tasty Panamanian and creole cuisine on the island, as well as fresh-from-the-boat seafood. Choose from red snapper, dorado, jumbo shrimp, octopus, and crab, and have it your way either grilled or with a garlicky sauce, slightly sweet oyster sauce, or onions and tomatoes, but note dishes are sometimes not available. They also serve grilled chicken, vegetarian plates, and sandwiches. All meals come with coconut rice, coleslaw, and fried plantains. Don't miss the passion fruit (*maracuyá*) juice, or any of their fresh fruit juices. The open-air ambience goes well with the Caribbean Sea setting.

Bocas del Drago. No phone. Main courses $5–$16. No credit cards. Daily 8am–7pm.

Shopping

High-quality handicrafts and fashionable beachwear can be found at **Pachamana,** located on Main Street on the waterfront next to Starfish Coffee at Avenida B (Tues–Sat 9am–12:30pm and 3–6pm). **Artesanía Bri-Bri Emanuel,** at Main Street and Avenida B (Mon–Sat 10am–8pm), specializes in indigenous handicrafts from around Panama. A varied and ultra-cool selection of beachwear, flip-flops, and surf gear can be found at **Flow** (daily 10am–5pm) at Avenue H, below the Om restaurant. You'll find a good selection of handicrafts, including Kuna Indian-made *molas,* at the compact **open-air market** at the end of Main Street and Avenida H.

Nightlife

Bocas Town is Party Central for the archipelago, but there are plenty of low-key venues for a quiet drink, and the town's laid-back, friendly atmosphere creates an environment that encourages meeting fellow travelers and locals. Nearly every bar and restaurant offers happy hour for about 4 hours, generally sometime between 4 and 8pm, with beer priced as low as 50¢. **Iguana Bar and Surf Club,** on Calle 1, is a good all-around bar, with a cool surfer theme and a wood-hewn, comfy ambience that's good for conversation and suitable for all ages, though late in the evening the party can pick up. **Buena Vista** is the old-school expat hangout, with a long wooden bar, lapping seafront, and decent cocktails (see "Where to Dine in Bocas Town," earlier in this chapter.) The open-air waterfront bar **Barco Hundido (Shipwreck Bar),** on Calle 1, is the all-out party zone with late nights and dancing that culminate with one or two drunk guys jumping into the water on a dare. The bar often has live DJs or bands with a cover charge. **Mondo Taitu,** on Avenida G, caters to 20-something surfers and backpackers, and has cheap drinks and good music late into the night. The awful-sounding **Blue Nasty Mermaid,** on Main Street at Avenida A, has a happy hour from 4 to 6pm and, to keep you going, another from 10 to 11pm; they also have open-mic nights and a sand-floor seating area over the water.

> **Note:** During high season, the **Sunset Cruise ★★★**, a yellow-and-purple banana boat, leaves from the Barco Hundido Bar. This is one of the most fun ways to see the sunset over the Caribbean Ocean. For $2, you get to party with and interact with other tourists of all ages, while drinking rum and coke, piña coladas, beer, or just about any drink of your choice from the onboard bar. If you're a solo traveler, this is a great way to meet fellow travelers and have a great time.

ISLA CARENERO (CAREENING CAY)

Isla Carenero practically adjoins Isla Colón, and is about a 2-minute water-taxi ride away. It is a more tranquil location to spend the night than Bocas, meaning you can be close to the action, but get away from it when you choose. Water-taxi service only runs until about 9pm, unless you arrange transportation ahead of time (and even then, taxis aren't enthusiastic about providing service past 10:30pm or so). There are no roads on the island, and it is technically possible to walk around Isla Carenero, though the narrow beach disappears at points and a meandering stroll can become more of a hike across rocks and up and down a few muddy slopes. There are a few hotels and restaurants here, but most of the structures are the very modest homes of local Bocatorinos. Everything on the island is located on the waterfront, but only the hotels on the island's east side face a strip of beach (which, little by little, is disappearing). *Chitras,* those no-see-ums that bite like mad, are common on the island, so come armed with repellent.

Where to Stay & Dine

Aside from the lodging options listed below, **Hotel Doña Mara** (℃ **757-9551;** www.donamar.com) offers six motel-like rooms on a small beach fringed with palms; the **Doña Mara Restaurant** specializes in Panamanian dishes and a few vegetarian options. Rates, including breakfast, run between $55 and $85 per night.

Careening Cay ★★   The friendly, welcoming American owners who purchased this small complex in 2005 have put an extraordinary amount of thought into building their vision of a "magical botanical paradise," offering bountiful amenities, personalized service, and cabins surrounded by 6½ acres of lush, orchid-studded landscaping and whizzing hummingbirds. Butterflies are the theme here: There are butterflies inlaid in the walkways, the shop sells original jewelry and crafts, and there's even a butterfly farm in the works. For children there is a playground and fort. Careening Cay has eight fully equipped wood cabins, four with two bedrooms with queen-size bed and bunks. There's also Careening Cay's Cosmic Crab Café, which you'll want to try even if you don't stay here; set on the waterfront, the Cosmic Crab serves tasty, gringo-style food—including banana-leaf-wrapped snapper with papaya salsa, ribs, and burgers—as well as original cocktails like a frozen "Sex in the Mud" and huge selection of exotic martinis.

Isla Carenero. ℃ **757-9157.** www.careeningcay.com. $29–$59 small cabin (1-room cabin for 2 guests); $79–$99 large cabin for up to 6. MC, V. **Amenities:** Restaurant; bar; sports equipment; Wi-Fi. *In room:* A/C, TV/DVD, no phone.

Casa Acuario ★ 🔥   This four-room, baby-blue-colored hotel features "suites over the sea," and in fact the entire property is propped on stilts over water. This is not a secluded hideaway—the oceanfront location feels more exposed than it does at most hotels—but, on the flip side, the guest rooms are huge, like small apartments without a kitchen. (They'll let you use their kitchen.) One step outside your door and you're on a wooden veranda where you can sway in a hammock, admire the spectacular views, or take a swim in the crystal-clear water. The owners are American, but the architectural style of the building is pure Caribbean—clapboard walls and carved wooden details. There's a new Chino on Carnero, so no need to stock up on supplies or take a water taxi in to Bocas for meals.

Isla Carenero. ℃ **757-9565.** www.bocas.com/casa-acuario.htm. $77–$88 suites Apr, $87–$99 suites rest of year. No credit cards. **Amenities:** Wi-Fi, kitchen. *In room:* A/C, TV, no phone.

Tierra Verde ★   Tucked away behind a stand of tall palms on the eastern side of the island, Tierra Verde is owned by two Panamanian surfers, Cookie and Ivan, who can organize surf expeditions for guests. It's a tremendously pleasant location, and there is a small beach fronting the property, but Tierra Verde is more guesthouse than hotel, and nothing is close enough that it doesn't require a water taxi—so bring supplies. The hotel interior is attractively paneled in tropical woods, but guest rooms are tiny and dark, and offer no views, except for the suite, which has a wraparound terrace. The room size, coupled with the isolation of the hotel, means that the quality of your stay could be influenced by other guests lodging at the same time. There is a cheery lobby with an Internet desk, a communal television, and a beverage bar. Service is very informal but friendly, and they can put together any kind of tour.

Isla Carenero. ⒸⒸ **757-9903.** www.hoteltierraverde.com. 7 units. $50–$65 double; $150 suite. Rates include breakfast. No credit cards. **Amenities:** Beverage bar; Internet station. *In room:* A/C, no phone.

ISLA BASTIMENTOS

Isla Bastimentos is the second-largest island in the archipelago, and it is one of the region's most popular destinations for its outstanding snorkeling and diving. It is also home to **Isla Bastimentos National Marine Park,** a boomerang-shaped park that protects a species-rich tropical jungle, pristine coral formations, and two tiny Robinson Crusoe–style islands ringed with powdery white sand. There are also a few highly recommended lodges here that put travelers far away from the hustle and bustle of Bocas Town, and closer to the aforementioned attractions.

Taking the island as a whole, Isla Bastimentos is a curious microcosm of ethnicities and income levels, of pristine landscapes and overdeveloped hamlets. There is one town here, the second largest in the Bocas Archipelago, called **Bastimentos Town.** Locals often refer to the town as Old Bank, and it can be found on the western tip of the island, about a 15-minute boat ride from Bocas Town. The community of 200 is principally Afro-Caribbean (many prefer to be called *creole*) descendants from the banana plantation days. It's a little like Jamaica in the 1950s, and the poverty here can be equally heartbreaking and frightening: a collapsed pier, piles of garbage, women playing cards, men drinking beer or lurking about. The official industry here is tourism, but you'd have to be an adventurous soul to brave spending a night here, or even visiting the town's restaurant **Roots** (ⒸⒸ **6662-1442**) for its popular "Blue Mondays" night with cold beer and reggae music. Still, Bocas residents consider Roots *the* local restaurant in the area, for its Caribbean vibe and inexpensive creole food, arguably the best creole food in the Bocas area. **Wizard Beach,** also called First Beach, is a popular surf spot for beginners for its smaller waves and absence of rocks; it can be reached by landing in Bastimentos Town and following a short path, but beware of youths who skulk at the path's entrance, demanding bribes to pass. The beach can also be reached by walking west from **Playa Segunda,** or Second Beach, home of the controversial new **Red Frog Beach Club** (ⒸⒸ **757-4559;** www.redfrogbeach. com), a luxury resort development whose two-bedroom homes and condos start at $400,000. Both Playa Segunda and Wizard Beach can be reached by walking from Red Frog Beach.

Beyond Afro-Caribbeans and wealthy foreigners, the island is also home to the Ngöbe-Buglé indigenous group, who live in two tiny communities in **Bahía Honda** and **Salt Creek Village,** the latter located on the southeastern shore and consisting of a cluster of thatched-roof huts, a small school, and a store.

What to See & Do

PARQUE NACIONAL MARINO ISLA BASTIMENTOS

A do-not-miss highlight in Bocas del Toro, this national park is an irregularly shaped swath of virgin tropical forest, pristine coral reef, and two white-sand islands called **Cayos Zapatillas,** or "Little Shoes Cays" (so-named for their resemblance to two footprints). There is no development here save a small park-service hut and a ranger who may or may not charge the $10 per-person entry fee to walk on the islands. The more westerly island has an easy nature path called the "forest behind the reef."

The national park covers 12,950 hectares (32,000 acres), more than ¾ of which is marine park with a complex and diverse array of underwater life that makes an outstanding site for snorkeling and diving. Expect to see healthy brain, lettuce, and Elkhorn coral; tropical reef fish such as parrotfish and angelfish; and, in deeper water, spotted eagle rays. The wealth of coral species, fish, and marine invertebrates makes this one of the most extraordinary national parks in Panama. The park is also home to the largest concentration of mangrove swamp on the Caribbean coast. *Note:* When the sea is choppy, swimming and snorkeling here require extra work, and visibility is poor.

On land, the national park protects a portion of the island's dense tropical rainforest and endangered and threatened reptile species such as the Jurassic-era leatherback turtles and hawksbill turtles, which nest along with three other turtle species on **Playa Larga ★★**, a 5.6km-long (3½-mile) beach on the northern shore. The trail to this beach is one of the unsung excursions in Bocas del Toro, starting in the indigenous village **Salt Creek,** at Old Point, continuing through thick steamy jungle, and ending on a beach with (usually) no one else around. Along the way you might see sloths or white-faced capuchin monkeys, and view many of the island's 68 species of birds. The trail is moderate, with undulations that can be difficult in some areas, requiring hands and shoes sturdier than sandals. Most tour operators offer this trek in conjunction with a visit to Salt Creek; or the village can be visited in conjunction with Zapatilla Cays; also contact Ancon Expeditions (p. 63).

Quebrada de Sal, or Salt Creek, is a village community of Ngöbe-Buglé Indians who no longer practice many of their traditions—even the women here no longer wear the billowy, colorful dresses they are known for. Apart from a few cement buildings, a collection of thatched-roof huts, and a tiny souvenir shop, there isn't much to see here—but combined with the enjoyable boat ride and hike to Playa Larga, this is a pleasant full-day trip if coming from Bocas Town. Visitors are charged $1 to enter. A round-trip boat ride from Bocas town to Cayos Zapatillos will cost you at least $90, and this is likely to increase if the price of gas continues to go up.

BEACHES

The loveliest beaches in Bocas del Toro can be found here at Isla Bastimentos and at the Cayos Zapatillas on the eastern tip (part of the national park; see above). Island beaches here play a critical role as the nesting sites for four of Panama's five kinds of marine turtles. From late August to October, when calmer weather prevails, visitors can get to Isla Bastimentos's beaches by taking a boat directly at the shore; the rest of the year you'll have to walk. The easiest beach to reach is **Red Frog Beach,** a heavenly stretch of white sand, arching palms, and turquoise water—but be aware that riptides are treacherous here. The beach gets its name from a strawberry-colored poison frog that inhabits the surrounding forest. The frog is the size of a fingernail and can be difficult to spot; focus your search near trees and around loose leaves, and you'll find one. Standard tours include Red Frog Beach as part of their day tour, but a water taxi can get you here for about $8 (20 min. from Bocas Town). Visitors get off in Magic Bay, pay a $1 entrance fee, and continue along an easy path for 5 minutes. There is a rustic bar with soft drinks, beer, and snacks. Continue west along the shore (if you can) to arrive at **Wizard Beach,** sometimes referred to as First Beach. A trail leads from Wizard Beach to Bastimentos Town.

CRAWL CAY

Crawl Cay, alternatively called Coral Cay, is located on the southern tip of Isla Bastimentos, about 30 minutes from Bocas Town. The area is known for shallow, translucent waters and an enormous garden of soft and hard coral, offering excellent snorkeling and diving. The **Crawl Cay Restaurant** is here too, making this one of the most popular excursions in Bocas del Toro. The restaurant, a collection of thatched huts over water, serves Panamanian-style seafood including crab, snapper, and shrimp ($8–$15 for a main course). Orders must be placed a full 1 to 2 hours ahead of time, so don't come hungry, or at least bring a snack to tide you over. Some unscrupulous tour companies save on gas by dumping guests here to snorkel around the restaurant—insist that they take you out to the actual reef and then back for lunch.

BAHIA HONDA COMMUNITY & NIVIDA BAT CAVES ★★

A visit to the Nivida Bat Cave in the Bahía Honda ranks as one of the most enjoyable—even spooky, but in a fun way—half-day tours in Bocas. After a 20-minute ride to Bahía Honda, visitors travel by motorized boat up a jungle-shrouded channel that provides excellent opportunities to see sloths hanging from tree branches and the occasional caiman silently resting in shallow water. Visitors walk through an old cacao farm, then don hard hats and rubber boots and enter a subterranean river cave that is home to hundreds of tiny fruit bats. The journey is an impressive, Indiana Jones–style adventure, though not for the ultra-squeamish; tours normally end with a visit to the Bahía Honda Ngöbe-Buglé indigenous community for a typical—and quite delicious—lunch. The community comprises 20 indigenous families living in homesteads around the bay, with a small "village" center located on the lee side of Bastimentos Island. Here Ngöbe-Buglé women demonstrate their process of weaving traditional bags, and have many on hand for sale. These tours are run by local operators; contact the **Jungle Lodge** (see "Where to Stay & Dine," below), which can plan a trip. Spanish-speaking **Rutilio Milton** (© **6669-6269**) offers tours, or try **Oscar's Bat Cave Tours** (© **6515-9276**). Tours cost about $25 per person, and you'll need to make a reservation at least a day in advance for lunch.

Where to Stay & Dine

If you're the kind of traveler who'd rather get away from it all, consider basing yourself out of Isla Bastimentos. The region's best lodges are concentrated here, and a few (Casa Cayuco, El Limbo on the Beach, and Au Natural) front the tranquil waters of the island's eastern shores, providing good swimming conditions year-round and a safe place for families with kids. Because of the distance from Bocas

Town, meals are included as part of a package. It can take from 45 minutes to an hour by boat to reach lodges here on Bastimentos. There are no stores here, so bring along any necessities. Aside from the options listed below, **Hotel El Limbo on the Beach** (✆ 757-9062; www.ellimbo.com) is situated on the best beach on Isla Bastimentos with clear water (not much sea grass), and a bit of reef for swimming and snorkeling, but I find it to be a bit overpriced for what you get.

Al Natural ★ The setting is lovely and remote, and the concept is well conceived; however, the price is a little steep for a such rustic accommodations, all of which could use a new coat of shellac. This is not to say that the rooms are uncomfortable— on the contrary, there are hot showers, comfortable mattresses on platforms, and mosquito nets, as well as custom-made furniture and woodwork. Showers are inside each room, and flush toilets are just outside. The resort fronts a beach with a tranquil sea year-round, and there is a short trail leading through the jungle and to another beach. The food is mostly seafood, and usually the owners receive kudos for their innovative cuisine. Honeymooners, young adults who are just past their backpacking prime, and easygoing travelers will be happiest here. The difference between the Natural House and the Natural House Deluxe is an additional bed and a ceiling fan; the deluxe is by far the nicest of the bungalows here. Note that Al Natural is closed from May until July 15.

The Al Natural Package includes three meals per day (and wine with dinner), lodging, round-trip transportation, and use of sports equipment; or book their "All Inclusive" package that includes 1 full-day excursion per day to Zapatilla Cay, fishing, snorkeling, and more. If you stay 7 nights, the final night is free. High-season rates (Dec 1–Apr 30) are shown below; for low-season rates subtract $10 per person for the Deluxe bungalow, and $5 for the Al Natural. Bring beach towels and a flashlight, and any other goodies you can't live without.

Isla Bastimentos. ✆ **757-9004** or 6576-8605. www.bocas.com/alnatura.htm. 5 units. Packages are per person, based on double occupancy: Al Natural Package $95–$120 1st night, $70–$95 thereafter; All-Inclusive Package $120 Al Natural, and $145 Deluxe. No credit cards. **Amenities:** Meals; sports equipment; tours. *In room:* Ceiling fan (deluxe only), no phone.

Casa Cayuco ★ ☺ This is the most kid-friendly hotel on Isla Bastimentos due to its tranquil beach, its fun jungle-style lodge, and other features such as a forest trail that meanders past a small lagoon with a "pet" caiman. The lodge has found a fine balance between hosting groups and retreats, while providing independent travelers with fond memories. Their two-story lodge feels very "Swiss Family Robinson," with high ceilings supported by log beams and not much else. The entire lodge is open-air, including the showers, but there are canvas drapes for shutting out the rain, and they also offer four cabins that are entirely enclosed (two fit four guests, one fits six, and the newest beachfront cabin is perfect for a couple). This is best called an "adventure lodge," not a luxury villa, yet special courses such as yoga retreats, excellent meals, and elegant craftsmanship render the lodge far beyond "rustic."

A trail leads from the lodge to the other side of the peninsula and another beach, but the waves are stronger there, and better swimming can be found right in front of the lodge. The American owners of Casa Cayuco are outdoor enthusiasts and certified guides and they plan unique excursions in the area such as surfing, whitewater kayaking, and trips to beaches on Isla Escudo de Veraguas. Rates are all-inclusive, with meals, transportation to and from Isla Colon Airport, lodging, and free use of kayak and snorkeling equipment. Due to its remote location, the resort has a 3-night minimum stay.

Isla Bastimentos. ☎ **509/996-4178.** www.casacayuco.com. Packages based on double occupancy $295–$305 per person; additional person $85–$95; single guest rate $245–$255. AE, MC, V. Closed Nov. Amenities: Restaurant; bar; sports equipment; tours; Wi-Fi. *In room:* Cellphone.

Eclypse de Mar Acqua Lodge ★★   This small ecolodge is situated on 6½ acres of rainforest in the center of the Bocas del Toro archipelago and consists of two honeymoon bungalows, four standard bungalows, and two rooms; bungalows are built on stilts over the water and the two rooms are in the main building. Rooms are not as private as bungalows, but are also thoughtfully decorated. Bungalows are painted warm colors and decorated in a classic Caribbean style; the lodge is just a 15-minute boat ride from the Bocas del Toro airport but is far enough away to feel secluded and appeal to couples seeking a romantic atmosphere. This ecolodge is solar-powered; the staff can customize excursions to nearby islands and beaches and kayaks and snorkeling gear are available to rent free of charge. There is also a nature reserve on-site where guests can spot caimans, birds, iguanas, sloths, and butterflies, as well as hiking trails.

Isla Bastimentos. ☎ **6611-4581.** www.eclypsedemar.com. $90 double room; $180 standard bungalow; $250 honeymoon bungalow. MC, V. **Amenities:** Restaurant, watersports, excursions. *In room:* No phone.

La Loma Jungle Lodge ★★★ 🎁   La Loma Jungle Lodge, an idyllic hideaway nestled in thick, tropical forest, is an intimate retreat for travelers who love and are comfortable with nature. It is hands-down one of my favorite lodges in Panama—but I must stress that it is not for everyone. The Jungle Lodge is located on the shore of Bahía Honda, and a short boat ride from the closest beach. The aesthetic is spare yet very stylish, and their 23-hectare (57-acre) property has a chocolate farm and a creek with natural bathing pools. There are just four thatched-roof ranchos. Three of the ranchos have a double and a twin bed in each; the fourth has a queen-size bed and two twins and sleeps four. All ranchos have hammocks and beds draped in voluminous mosquito nets. The open-air ranchos provide a sense of harmony and oneness with the surrounding jungle. At sunset and sunrise, the primal, animated chorus of wildlife that emanates from the jungle canopy is exciting to hear, and if you're lucky you might catch sight of a group of monkeys swinging through the trees. Cabin nos. 2 and 3 are higher up the slope, providing gorgeous, sweeping views, but it's a vigorous hike to reach both. Two cabins had no electricity at press time, but solar panels will be installed in October.

The young hosts, Henry and Margaret, provide a friendly, relaxed environment and are well versed in the flora, fauna, and culture of Bocas. Their motto is sustainable tourism: buying products from Ngöbe-Buglé Indians and employing them as local guides, and growing their own ingredients on an organic farm for their delicious, gourmet meals (included in the price). There are free activities, but most excursions cost extra.

Isla Bastimentos. ☎ **6619-5364** or 6592-5162. www.thejunglelodge.com. $100 per person based on double. Rates include all meals. MC, V. Amenities: Restaurant; tours; dugout canoe; surfboard rentals. In room: No phone.

La Popa Paradise Beach Resort ★★ Built in 2007, La Popa Paradise Resort offers some of the nicest accommodations in Bocas. The hotel offers 10 individual "casitas," all spacious and airy and decorated with Balinesian furniture, all with a breezy shaded veranda. The resort's motto is "barefoot luxury," and this can be seen in everything from the infinity pool to the 5,000-foot clubhouse to the on-site restaurant. There are also four economic rooms available that are particularly apt for families on a tighter budget; these were undergoing a renovation at press time, but should be ready to book by the time you read this. The Popa Resort fronts an attractive, privately owned white sand beach and guests can swim out and snorkel at an impressive coral reef just 300m from the hotel. The hotel caters to honeymooners and couples looking for a romantic getaway but takes on more of a family atmosphere in the summer months (June–Aug). La Popa tries to reduce its environmental impact by using solar panels and preparing meals with ingredients from its garden.

Isla Bastimentos. © **832-1498** or 6550-2505. www.popaparadisebeachresort.com. 16 units. $265–$320 oceanview casitas; $295–$350 oceanfront casitas; $335–$400 executive suite; $400–$500 penthouse; $120 economic rooms. AE, MC, V. **Amenities:** Restaurant; bar; infinity pool. *In room:* A/C, cable TV, minifridge, Wi-Fi.

Tranquilo Bay ★★★ 🏠 Tranquilo Bay is the best option for travelers seeking upscale accommodations on the Bocas Archipelago. Embraced by lush, vibrant jungle and fronted by a thicket of mangrove, this resort is a haven for adventurers who don't believe in giving up creature comforts for a chance to mingle with natural surroundings. The cabin exteriors are pared down, but inside are very comfortable accommodations in a handsome tropical decor, with orthopedic beds and large bathrooms with ample counter space and hot showers. As for excursions, the mantra here is to go where no one else goes, and the owners busy themselves exploring new areas to take guests in the region, including river kayaking on the mainland, snorkeling at remote areas, jungle hikes, and visits to isolated beaches. There is no beach here on the property, but beaches at Zapatillas Cays are a short hop away, and guests can kayak around the mangroves near the resort. Packages include all transportation (in Bocas and in Panama City), meals, drinks, and use of their equipment.

Isla Bastimentos. © **620-4179.** www.tranquilobay.com. 6 cabins. Packages are, per person, based on double occupancy: $1,690–$3,365 7 nights; $1,150–$1,990 4 nights; $945–$1,500 3 nights. Rates include all meals. MC, V. **Amenities:** Restaurant; bar; lounge; sports equipment; tours; Wi-Fi. *In room:* A/C, hair dryer, no phone.

ISLA SOLARTE

2km (1¼ miles) E of Isla Colón

Isla Solarte, also known as **Nancy's Cay,** is an 1.3-sq.-km (½-sq.-mile) island known for **Hospital Point,** one of the best areas for snorkeling and close to Isla Colón. Hospital Point is named for an old hospital built by the United Fruit Company to treat plantation workers suffering from yellow fever and malaria. Today an upscale residential community is spreading across the island, attracting foreigners seeking to a slice of paradise that is protected by a gate and security services.

ISLA CRISTÓBAL & LAGUNA BOCATORITO

10km (6¼ miles) S of Isla Colón

Isla Cristóbal is a 37-sq.-km (14-sq.-mile), mostly deforested island south of Isla Colón. The island and a peninsula that juts from the mainland form a nearly enclosed bay called **Laguna Bocatorito,** or Dolphin Bay—so-called for the bottlenose dolphin breeding site found here. It is one of the region's most enjoyable attractions because dolphins swim up close to visiting boats and prance about. The best time to come is from June to September, when dozens of dolphins meet in the bay to create a wild version of Sea World. For the rest of the year, here's a tip: Try to visit the bay after the morning tour boats do their thing (which amounts to disturbing the dolphins by speeding around in circles in an effort to stir things up and draw the dolphins to the surface), and find a tour or book a custom trip going at a quieter pace. More dolphins show themselves when the bay isn't being churned up. Or better yet, arrange to head out on a kayak rented from the island's only lodge, Hacienda del Toro, which can even provide you with hydrophones to hear what's going on underwater. For tours, see "What to See & Do" under "Isla Colón: Bocas Town," earlier in this chapter.

Where to Stay & Dine

GARDEN OF EDEN

Hacienda del Toro ★★ ☺   Situated on an old cattle ranch on the verdant shore of Laguna Bocatorito, this newer lodge is a self-styled "Caribbean Dude Ranch," and the only lodge to offer horseback riding among other unique activities. The cabins are spacious and fresh, in pastel-colored hues and decorated with local art, and they come with feather-soft beds. Each room has a deck that overlooks the bay, and comes with a wide hammock; one cabin has a full kitchen. The main building is an open-air, thatched-roof structure used as a dining room and lounge. Much of the neighboring land is pockmarked with areas of deforestation; however, the owners are letting the area revert to forest, and encouraging their neighbors to do so as well. On a half-day horseback ride, guests will still be able to lope through thick secondary jungle. Rates include breakfast, round-trip transportation from Bocas, and use of kayaks.

Isla Cristóbal.📞 **832-0860.** www.haciendadeltoro.com. $150 double; extra person $30; free for kids 9 and under. MC, V. **Amenities:** Restaurant; bar; outdoor pool; horseback riding tours and lessons; kayaks. *In room:* No phone , Wi-Fi.

COMARCA KUNA YALA

The Comarca Kuna Yala is a fascinating and primitive region that fulfills every tourist's, yachter's, and cruiser's island fantasy. There are more than 350 picture-postcard islands and islets ringed by powdery white sand, a coral reef, and piercing turquoise water—and most islands are populated with no more than a cluster of coconut palms. Given the pristine beauty of the region, it is *the* premier beach destination in Panama, but what really sets it apart is that it provides you with the opportunity to spend time with the Kuna indigenous group that lives here. The region was formerly known as the San Blas Archipelago, and although many Panamanians continue to use this moniker, it is now officially the Comarca Kuna Yala. The "Kuna Yala" means "Land of the Kuna," and a *comarca* is a semiautonomous province that is governed by three tribal chiefs, or *caciques,* with the input of dozens of regional representatives. As a semiautonomous province, the Kuna have maintained their cultural identity and integrity, and have complete control of economic matters such as tourism. (See "Special Considerations in the San Blas," below.) For example, it is considered improper to travel with an "outside" tour company that has not requested permission from tribal chiefs. Since the colonial period, the Kuna have successfully resisted invasions by pirates, colonists, missionaries, and adventurers—even scientists from the Smithsonian based in the comarca were given the boot after the Kuna couldn't establish what their purpose was.

There are an estimated 50,000 Kuna spread across 49 communities in the region, and scattered in areas as far away as Panama City and farther east in the Darién. Of the seven indigenous tribes in Panama, the Kuna Yala are the most visible, not only for their ubiquity but for the kaleidoscopic-colored costumes worn by the women in the tribe. Men wear western clothing, but Kuna women wear skirts and *mola*-appliquéd shirts in yellows and reds, head scarves, a gold ring in their septum, and usually a single black line drawn down the crest of their nose; their arms and legs are bound with tiny beads. The Kuna's livelihood depends on coconut harvesting, fishing, and subsistence farming, and on a very small scale, tourism.

The comarca extends well beyond the island region, incorporating the coastal forest on the northern slope of the San Blas Mountain Range. Because it has been allowed to remain untouched, the virgin forest is home to a species diversity not found anywhere else in Panama; if visiting the mainland jungle interests you, you'll need a local guide (your lodge can provide you with one), or you can book a trip with a company such as Xtrop. (See "Adventure-Tour Outfitters & Activities," below.)

LODGING IN THE SAN BLAS ARCHIPELAGO   There are no megaresorts or five-star hotels in the Kuna Yala Islands. Do not expect to find satellite TV, Internet, widespread telephone service, 24-hour electricity, or even laundry service at lodges and hostels here. This is Panama "unplugged," although there are two lodges in the eastern side of the comarca that provide a few creature comforts to satisfy travelers who do not relish "roughing it." If you're a particularly fussy traveler, you'll want to book with San Blas Sailing Adventures, which has luxury sailboats, or you might want to consider a different beach destination in Panama. Just outside the comarca's border, in the Colón Province, is the newly opened **Coral Lodge,** an elegant resort that uses El Porvenir as an arrival base and provides tours to islands within the comarca. Some hostels and lodges mentioned in this chapter now have an e-mail address, and some even have websites. E-mails are checked within 2 days; however, you might find it far more convenient to have a travel agency or tour operator book your stay, as most lodge owners speak little or no English. (See "Adventure-Tour Outfitters & Activities," below.) Also, because credit cards are not accepted in the region, you can charge your stay if booking with a tour operator or agency. It is highly recommended that you book ahead of time to secure a room or *cabaña,* and also to verify that a boat will be waiting at the airport dock to get you there. Spontaneous travelers who just show up will have better luck finding lodging in the El Porvenir area. All prices shown are per person, per night, and are **all-inclusive,** meaning three meals a day and local tours and transportation. Most hostels have Spanish-only guides, or you can go with a tour operator who will provide a bilingual guide during your trip.

One of the things that makes the Kuna Islands unique compared to other regions of Panama is that the Kuna Indians have not allowed foreign (or even Panamanian) investment on their lands, which accounts for the lack of resorts and high-end hotels favored by foreign investors. While some argue that this strictly enforced Kuna law has slowed possible economic development on the comarca, others believe it is the main reason the Kuna's culture has been able to survive and flourish. There has been recent talk of possibly changing this law in the future, but as of now, all hotels and lodging options must be Kuna owned and run. Personally, I think that the Kuna's determination to keep their land autonomous and free of foreign investments is what makes it so special; unlike Boquete, the Pacific Coast, and Bocas del Toro, which feel somewhat like tropical American/Canadian colonies, the San Blas Islands feel

Comarca Kuna Yala

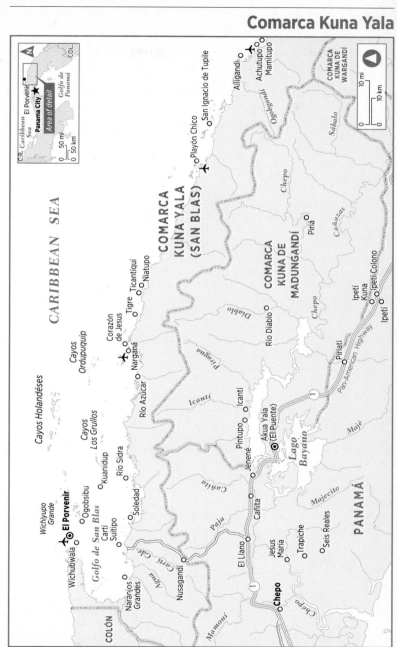

refreshingly free of overdevelopment and foreign encroachment, and as the islands become more and more popular with visitors, the tourism infrastructure will likely slowly catch up.

EL PORVENIR & WESTERN COMARCA KUNA YALA

El Porvenir is the governmental seat of the Comarca Kuna Yala and the principal gateway for most travelers. There isn't much marine life in the immediate area for snorkeling; what you come for here is to swing in a hammock, swim, and get some sun. With this in mind, 2 or 3 nights is about the maximum travelers stay here. There is one hotel on El Porvenir Island, but most travelers head straight to the dock for the short boat ride to hostels on the islands of Wichubwala, Nalunega, Ukutupu, and Ogobsibudsup. The cheapest lodging in San Blas can be found in this area, making it a popular destination with backpackers. Porvenir is a service-based island—but that isn't saying much, as all you'll find is an administrative center for governmental offices, a police station, a tiny museum that's usually closed, and public telephones. For a **map** of the region, stop at the police station to get the *Mapa de Comunidades, Recursos Turísticos y Servicios del Golfo de Kuna Yala* (cost $5).

Essentials

GETTING THERE & DEPARTING

BY PLANE   Both **Aeroperlas** (© **351-7500;** www.aeroperlas.com) and **Air Panama** (© **316-9000;** www.flyairpanama.com) have daily flights to El Porvenir, with less frequent routes to other islands and destinations on the comarca (call or check their websites for schedule information). Because of the new road from Los Llanos to Cartí, many previously regularly scheduled flights must now be chartered. The 20-minute flight to El Porvenir from Panama City costs about $130 on either airline, taxes included. The worst aspect of traveling to the comarca is that flights leave at the crack of dawn (6am), although large groups may charter a flight at a later hour. Return flights leave at 7am. *Tip:* If you do not have a return ticket or are unsure of your departure date, Mrs. Oti at the Hotel El Porvenir sells plane tickets for Air Panama. If there is space on Aeroperlas flights, you may simply pay when you arrive at the Albrook Airport. For **charter flights,** contact Air Panama (© **315-0439;** charter@flyairpanama.com). Be sure to call ahead to confirm flight times, as these are subject to changes by season.

BY ROAD & BOAT   There is no public ground transportation to the comarca, meaning almost all travelers arrive by boat or plane. Boat transportation to the island of Cartí from the Port of Cartí costs $1.50 each way; if you're heading out to other islands, expect to pay at least $10.

The road to the Comarca Kuna Yala is paved until El Llano, but from there it's a rough dirt road all the way to Cartí. The government has plans to pave the entire road, but how long that will take is anyone's guess. From Cartí, *cayucos,* which are large dugout canoes with outboard motors, transport travelers to the islands in the insular region. Do not attempt this road with a regular car—you *will* get stuck if you try, as this road is as rough as they get. Also, note that you'll have to cross a small river, so road travel to the comarca during rainy season is complicated at best and

SPECIAL considerations IN THE SAN BLAS

All islands here are owned by Kuna families, no matter how isolated or even if they're totally uninhabited. It is not, therefore, permitted to **camp** overnight on an uninhabited island without an owner's permission. Though you will not receive anything as serious as jail time or a fine, it is considered by the Kuna to be a tremendous breach of respect. The **cost to visit an island** is $1 per person; you'll be expected to pay for every island you visit, no matter how close they are to each other. Of course, if an island is uninhabited, the owner might or might not show up to charge you.

Unfortunately, **scuba diving is prohibited** within the Comarca Kuna Yala. However, snorkeling is not. Snorkeling is better in the eastern part of the region, not near El Porvenir. If you are interested in diving just outside the San Blas, you'll need to stay at the nearby **Coral Lodge** in the Colón Province, or contact **Panama Divers.** (See p. 161 and 156 for information about both.)

Kuna people are extremely sensitive to having their pictures taken. *Always* ask permission before taking a photo of a Kuna Indian, especially if it is a Kuna chief (recognizable by a felt hat and short jacket). Most Kunas, especially

those in areas frequented by tourists, will charge $1 to have their photo taken.

At press time, Movistar cellular phones do not have coverage in the comarca, but Cable & Wireless does, though there is only service in the Cartí-Rio Sidra sector. There are **public telephones** on the islands of El Porvenir, Wichubwala, and Gardi Sugdup, and there are telephones at the Sapibenega Kuna Lodge. Most hostels and lodges on islands have cellphones for emergencies. There are also satellite phones in areas where there's no cellphone coverage. There are basic **medical facilities** in Gardi Sugdup and Río Sidra; for more serious medical issues you'll need to fly to Panama City.

There is only one **bank** in the entire region, in the Nargana community, so come with enough cash plus a little extra just in case. Also, bring enough small bills for purchases.

The **food** served in the comarca is almost always fish and shellfish—usually cooked the same way every day. If you are allergic to fish, are a vegetarian, or simply do not fancy dining on seafood day in and day out, advise your hosts well ahead of time so that they can be prepared when you arrive. Bring snacks and sunscreen because there are no stores.

out of the question at worst, depending on rainfall. That said, the El Llano–Cartí road offers great mountain and rainforest scenery that, in my opinion, makes the bumpy ride worth it. However, it's important to note that this road is best for adventurous types who aren't daunted by an extremely bumpy ride, the possibility of getting stuck in mudholes, and crossing a (possibly) high river. Note that a flight from Panama City to El Porvenir takes about 20 minutes, while the last 45km (72 miles) of the El Llano–Cartí road alone can take upwards of 3 hours.

If you'd like to go by road but find driving a bit overwhelming, the following drivers can drop you off and pick you up at the Port of Cartí: Felix, ✆ **6668-6099;** Carlos, ✆ **6737-2103;** Sr. Ramos, ✆ **6695-3229;** Rigoberto, ✆ **6527-3367.** Though not bilingual, these drivers have experience driving the Llanos-Cartí road. Call to negotiate price, but expect to pay about $50 to $100 each way depending on road conditions and number of passengers.

ADVENTURE-TOUR OUTFITTERS & activities

Before embarking on a tour to Kuna Yala, be sure that your outfitter is actually permitted to give tours in the comarca; Kuna Yala is an autonomous region of Panama and tourism rules and regulations are set by the Kuna Council.

KAYAKING There is no outfitter with more experience operating in the comarca, or one that is more dedicated to preserving the Kuna Yala culture, than **Xtrop ★★★** (⟨☎ 317-1279; http.xtrop.com), which is short for Expediciones Tropicales. The Panama City–based company is highly respected, specializing in sea-kayak tours with an emphasis on nature and culture, and employing only local Kuna guides. Xtrop, which works with companies like Mountain Travel Sobek in the U.S., has received permission from Kuna chiefs to operate in some of the areas that are richest in marine life (they call them "aquatic trails"), and they have access to areas no one else can go, including forested coastal areas. Best of all, Xtrop is very active in developing programs in the region for sustainable tourism, so you can feel good about how your money is spent. Xtrop has over 15 years of experience in the comarca and is one of the few companies officially allowed to take tours and excursions to Kuna Yala. Trips are from 3 nights to a week long, and lodging is in tents or huts. Xtrop can also book just lodging for you, if that's the only service you need.

HIKING & GENERAL TOURS Ecocircuitos ★★ (⟨☎ 314-0068 or 314-0698; www.ecocircuitos.com) has guided walks through PEMASKY (Project for the Study and Management of Wilderness Areas of Kuna Yala), a protected coastal jungle in the comarca around the road to Cartí Suitupo, that is ranked as one of the best trails in the world for spotting birds and diverse flora. Ecocircuitos also offers multiday trips around Panama that include a couple of days visiting

BY CRUISE SHIP The Comarca Kuna Yala is a popular cruise-ship destination for its shimmering white-sand beaches. Ships dock and tender guests usually to Ikodue, which has bathrooms. Depending on the circumstances, it can, unfortunately, be an uncomfortable experience as some cruises are approached by poor Kuna women in *cayucos* begging for coins. Kuna women also cart over their handicrafts to sell.

GETTING AROUND Transportation around the islands is by motorboat (sometimes called a *panga*), or a *cayuco*. All lodging options listed in this chapter provide boat transportation as part of their all-inclusive price; day excursions by boat are included except for faraway destinations such as the Cayos Holandéses. Travel to and from the western comarca's gulf to the east (to the Dolphin Lodge or the Sapibenega Lodge) by boat is nearly impossible, due to choppy sea conditions, time (up to 4 hr.), and reluctance by boat owners to undergo the distance. The only air service between the two regions is a thrice-weekly flight from El Porvenir to Corazón de Jesús. You can also hire a cayuco to get you around the different islands if you're camping or you want to see the region on your own. Because gas is expensive on the Kuna Islands, boat transportation can get expensive fast. However, island hopping and searching for the perfect, secluded beach among 350+

islands in the comarca. **Adventures in Panama** (☏ **877/726-6222** in the U.S.; www.adventuresinpanama.com) can also book lodges for travelers having a hard time doing it on their own.

For a truly custom tour of the Kuna Yala Islands (or for that matter, anywhere in Panama) contact freelance guide **Gilberto Alemancia,** who oversees the Indigenous and Local Communities Department at the ATP (☏ **6948-0525;** gilbert04@yahoo.com). Gilberto has coordinated expeditions for National Geographic, Photo Safari, PhotoAdventure, Discovery Channel Adventure, and BBC, and is the go-to guy for all things Kuna. Fully bilingual and U.S.-educated, Gilberto is himself a Kuna, and extremely knowledgeable about that culture's history and customs. With advance notice, he can organize specialized tours, set up boat transportation and camping trips, or even accompany visitors to the different islands, which

can even include a stay at a traditional Kuna hut.

SAILING San Blas Sailing ★ (☏ **314-1800;** www.sanblassailing.com) is a French-owned company that has a fleet of monohull and multihull sailboats; their largest boat can hold eight passengers. They've been based in the comarca since 1997 and know the area intimately. Trips, which run from 3 to 14 nights and include meals, drinks, tours, and onboard accommodations, involve sailing around the islands, snorkeling, kayaking, and visiting Kuna villages. If you are looking for fine accommodations in the comarca, this is your best bet, but of course you'll spend all your nights on board. There have been customer complaints about poor communication and dangerous road conditions on the Llanos-Cartí road, however, which is something you may want to keep in mind.

islands is part of the fun, and if you have a big enough group and can split the cost, this option is well worth it.

What to See & Do

BEACHES & SNORKELING   Local tours are included in the price of lodging, but to neighboring islands and attractions only. The beaches at **Isla Hierba** are the closest to El Porvenir, and visitors to lodges near that island normally head here when they want to loll in the sun. A popular snorkeling site nearby is **Isla Perro ★★**, which has a sunken ship just off the coast. A stone's throw away is the **Isla Pelicano ★**, with fine white-sand beaches. For the best snorkeling, you'll need to head out to **Cayos Holandéses ★★★**, a chain of utterly perfect islands ringed with blue water and coral, and home to more marine life than you'd find closer to the heavily fished area around El Porvenir. There is also a wreck reef that has sunk many drug-running boats from Colombia. There are no tourism facilities. Private sailboats and yachts like to hang out around the Cayos; getting here requires extra time (2–3 hr. round-trip by boat from El Porvenir), and extra money ($150–$200) depending on the price of gas and number of people. The Cayos are roughly equidistant from El Porvenir and Río Sidra, about 20km (13 miles).

KUNA VILLAGES   Visits to Kuna communities can be custom-arranged with your lodge. Arranging visits is not complicated; however, there are a few villages that are more conservative and have not embraced the idea of tourism. Check your options with your tour/boat guide. The most common village, and really worth a visit because it seems like a metropolis when compared with surrounding island villages, is **Gardi Sugdup.** This island is part of the community of **Cartí,** which consists of several island villages and a stretch of coastline. It's a heavily populated island with a warren of passageways that fan out spiderlike around squashed-together wooden huts and cement public buildings and stores. There's a lot of trash floating around the place, but once you get past the dock, you'll find that putting yourself in the middle of this thriving Kuna community is a truly fascinating experience. In terms of tourism, this is probably the most visited Kuna village in the comarca, and it has a landing strip, a store, and a **museum** (daily 8am–4pm; admission $2). It's a humble museum, located in a thatched-roof hut, but there's enough here to keep a visitor's interest. You'll see displays of Kuna culture and rituals, and often a "docent" is available who speaks enough English to convey the meaning behind the artifacts on display.

Where to Stay & Dine

Aside from the lodging options listed below, another option in the Kuna Islands is camping, or my favorite, sleeping in a hammock under a couple of palm trees. Despite its tropical location, there are few mosquitoes or other biting insects on the islands, and nights are breezy and cool, making for comfortable sleeping conditions; in fact, you may want to pack a light sweater or blanket. Just ask your boatman to take you to an empty island, and you'll have your own private tropical paradise. You can arrange to have your meals brought to you by boat for an additional price. Remember, however, that there is no electricity or bathrooms, so this option is best for 1 or 2 nights. Be sure to get permission from the owner. The most popular islands for camping are Icotupu, 🕾 **299-9074;** Isla Pelicano, 🕾 **299-9000;** Isla Achutupu, 🕾 **299-9000;** and Isla Porvenir, 🕾 **299-9056.** Camping can also be set up through your hotel or by contacting Gilberto Alemancia (see "Adventure-Tour Outfitters & Activities" above). All hotel options below include three meals a day.

AROUND EL PORVENIR

Cabañas Ukuptupu   There are two sand-floor *cabañas* here, but the majority of lodging consists of connecting guest rooms on stilts over water, so you'll hear the sound of the lapping sea. There is a speck of a beach with hammocks and lounge chairs, a cement-floor dining area, and a holding tank for the fresh jumbo shrimp and lobsters that are often on the menu; the food here is simple, but very good. The Smithsonian Research Institute built these wooden structures before moving operations in 1998. Though this is the best hostel option in the Porvenir area, the complex is still very rustic. There are electrical outlets and power for a total of 8 hours a day (10am–2pm and 6–10pm). The best accommodations here, the Casablanc rooms, are spacious and have good views. The Kuna family who run Ukuptupu are very service oriented, and have an extensive selection of jewelry and crafts on sale. The *cabañas* are located on Ukuptupu Island, about 5 minutes from El Porvenir.

Isla Ukuptupu. 🕾 **6746-5088** or 6744-7511. www.ukuptupu.com. 17 units. $45 per person. No credit cards. **Amenities:** Restaurant; pool table.

THE KUNA revolution

The Kuna are the only indigenous group in Panama to gain their autonomy through violent rebellion. After Panama gained its independence from Colombia, the Kuna felt that the new Panamanian state was attempting to suppress their culture, customs, and lands. A determined people, they believed the only way they could protect their culture and guarantee their survival was through violence.

On February 21, 1925, the Kuna took advantage of the February *Carnavales* and attacked the national Panamanian police. The police had been drinking heavily, and the Kuna caught them off guard. An armed battle ensued through February 27, resulting in 27 casualties between the two sides.

On March 4, 1925, a peace act was signed between the Kuna and the Panamanian government that resulted in the creation of the Autonomous Kuna Comarca, encompassing the Caribbean Coastal region and over 350 islands near the Colombian Border. The government also promised to respect the customs of the Kuna, to establish schools in their lands, and to guarantee them the same rights and privileges enjoyed by other Panamanians. In return, the Kunas agreed to disarm, renounce their call for independence, and obey Panamanian law.

Today, the Comarca Kuna Yala is, for the most part, autonomous from the Panamanian government, and they consider themselves their own country. The Kuna continue to abide by their own rules and laws, and in fact, the only time the National Police is allowed to make decisions in the Comarca is when narco-trafficking is involved; otherwise, police only enter the comarca if they are called upon to do so by the *caciques* (policymakers) of the comarca.

Every year, on February 25, the Kuna reenact the events that lead to their autonomy. This is an interesting time to visit the islands, as you'll have the opportunity to see reenactments as well as enjoy the accompanying festivities.

Cabañas Wailidup ★   These cabins are owned by the friendly and knowledgeable Juan Antonio, who also owns the Kuna Niskua (below). The island is dotted with slender palms and requires all of 10 minutes to circumnavigate; what I like is that it's fronted by a mangrove-lined island and an uninhabited island, which make it feel protected. The simple restaurant and bar here is popular with yachters who stop off for a cocktail. These are the only cabins in the area that are over sand but on stilts, with wooden floors, and they have private bathrooms but no electricity.

Isla Wailidup. ✆ **259-3471.** kuna-niskua@hotmail.com. 6 units. $75 per person. No credit cards. **Amenities:** Restaurant; bar.

Hotel El Porvenir   This hotel is smack-dab next to the airstrip—but flight activity is limited to the early morning, and perhaps some travelers find it convenient to catch a few extra minutes of sleep before boarding their flight out of San Blas. The rooms are very drab, with tiled floors and semi-orthopedic beds, though all have private bathroom. There are public telephones on the island. There is electricity until 11pm, after which solar power is turned on. There is also a strip of beach with lounge chairs. The restaurant serves decent—but mostly fried—food with rice.

Isla El Porvenir. ✆ **221-1397,** 292-4543, or 6553-7766. hotelelporvenir@hotmail.com. 14 units. $45 per person. No credit cards. **Amenities:** Restaurant; bar; pool table.

THE KUNA society

The Kuna are a tightly knit indigenous group who live much as they have for centuries. Although three male *caciques* reign as policy deciders, it is a matriarchal society in which inheritance is passed down through women. Women are also primary breadwinners, considering the income they earn from selling *mola* panels and other handicrafts to tourists. Still, such modern delving into economics is new for the Kuna, who not very long ago had no word for money, and used coconuts as a "monetary" unit. (As proof of the effects of tourism on society, Kunas use the word "money" instead of *dinero*.)

When a Kuna girl is born, she is given a nickname but does not receive her official Kuna name until she reaches puberty. Of course, the nickname is what everyone goes back to calling her soon after her traditional puberty ceremony. During this ceremony, a girl is expected to cut her hair short and keep it this way her entire adult life. Kuna women, with their colorful dress, gold jewelry, and *mola*-making talent, are guardians of Kuna culture. Men, on the other hand, wear western clothing and rely on coconut-collecting and fishing to make a living. Kunas are monogamous and consider adultery a crime.

Squat with broad shoulders and disproportionately large heads, the Kuna are the second-smallest people in the world (African pygmies are the smallest). Although scientists still have no idea why, the rate of albinism here is the highest in the world. Albinos are called "Moon Children" and are considered to hold special powers and possess a high intelligence.

Molas are brightly colored reverse-appliqué panels and the principal artistic expression of the Kuna. Molas are made by sewing together layers of fabric and cutting down through the layers to form imaginative designs and figures. Kuna women wear *molas* sewn onto their blouses. *Molas* average $20 per panel, but often the price can be negotiated, especially when buying several.

Kuna Niskua Lodge ★   This friendly hostel sits back from the water and does not have sea views or a beach. The rooms are clean and attractive, with stylishly thatched walls, comfortable beds, and private bathrooms; electricity is available from 6 to 10pm. The best thing about the Kuna Niskua is its owner, Juan Antonio, who is Kuna and surely the most informative and hospitable guide in the region. The food served here is the same every night—fish and rice. There is a breezy covered area with hammocks for relaxing. The island here has about 200 people, but it seems more like 50 or so, with narrow passageways and a village center, allowing you to interact with local Kunas, most of whom are more than keen to sell you their handicrafts. Juan Antonio can put together specialized full-day cultural tours for an additional $50; otherwise local tours are included.

Isla Wichubwala.© **259-3471** or 6686-1086. 9 units. $65 single; $60 double per person; $55 triple per person. No credit cards. **Amenities:** Restaurant.

AROUND RIO SIDRA

Cabañas Kuanidup ★★ ◙   For those who really want to get away from it all, this remote island is the best in the western comarca. It's utterly rustic, but it's such a utopian, castaway-style isle that most visitors actually prefer the Robinson Crusoe–type lodging. Call the hotel for the best way to get here. About as large as a soccer field, Isla Kuanidup is fringed with palms strung with hammocks that look picture-perfect in their symmetry. The island is ringed in coral here but there also is a deeper, sandy spot by their dock that makes for an ideal swimming area (many islands have shallow-water beaches). Cabins are small, with a little foyer, sand floors, and okay foam mattresses. Choose a south-facing cabin—the north-facing ones take the brunt of the wind. Miguel, the owner, and his motley crew each morning rake the white sand in Zen-like perfection, and they have a well-stocked supply of beverages and booze. Kuanidup serves seafood only. (Prearrange meat or vegetarian dishes beforehand.) Cabins are lined in a row, and do not provide maximum privacy; however the owner has an uninhabited island if you want to get away from your neighbors for the day. There are also a volleyball net, a spacious eating area, and a set of covered picnic tables. Bathrooms (both showers and toilets) are shared, and there is no electricity here; at night guests must use kerosene lamps.

Isla Kuanidup. ⓒ **6656-4673** or 6742-7656. www.kuanidup.pa.kz. 8 units. Per person $60 Dec–Apr; $50 May–Nov. No credit cards. **Amenities:** Restaurant; bar.

EASTERN COMARCA KUNA YALA

The eastern region of the comarca is visited less frequently by tourists than the El Porvenir area. Travelers can expect to find here a higher level of biodiversity and wilder natural surroundings; according to Smithsonian scientists, the islands that dot the coast feature the highest diversity of coral species in Panama, yet this region, too, has suffered from overfishing. If you're lucky, however, you might see dolphins, manta rays, and manatees. Kuna villages in this region, especially **Corazón de Jesús,** are significantly more westernized, and the people who live here don less traditional clothing, live in modern buildings, and participate in modern pastimes like watching TV. If you'd like to visit a traditional village in this region, your best bet is the tidy **Isla Tigre,** which was the site of the violent overthrow of Panamanian forces in 1925, when the Kuna first asserted their independent authority over the region. Isla Tigre is a little less than 5km (3 miles) east of Corazón de Jesús. This village, along with Playón Chico and Mamitupo, has landing strips with flights from Panama City; Aeroperlas has flights from El Porvenir to Corazón de Jesús three times a week. Otherwise, it is difficult to access this region from the western side of the comarca.

You'll find the Comarca Kuna Yala's most **deluxe lodging** in this region, at the Dolphin Lodge and the Sapibenega Lodge, or you can tour the region in kayaks with the outfitter **Xtrop** (p. 292), which has a special license to visit the area's pristine regions. Lodges mentioned in this section include tours in the immediate area in the price; note that there is nowhere to stay on Corazón de Jesús.

Essentials

GETTING HERE & DEPARTING

BY PLANE **Aeroperlas** (ⓒ **351-7500;** www.aeroperlas.com) and **Air Panama** (ⓒ **316-9000;** www.flyairpanama.com) offer daily connecting flights from Panama City to Corazón de Jesús. You'll have to fly to El Porvenir, and from there take a short flight to Corazón de Jesús. Flights on both airlines cost about $132 round-trip. The flight between Panama City and Playón Chico costs about $140. There are also several flights a week between Panama City and Mamitupu, though you'll have to connect in Playón Chico. This flight costs about $145 round-trip on both airlines. Call the airlines to verify the days when flights leave for Corazón de Jesús, Playón Chico, and Mamitupu, as this information is subject to change.

Where to Stay

Dad Ibe Lodge ★★   This family-owned hotel is one of the better lodging options on the comarca. Popular with French and Americans looking for privacy, the lodge is located on a lovely uninhabited island, so you'll have to fly into Achutup or Mamitupo to get here. There's a very nice beach, but if you start feeling a bit claustrophobic, there are also two more uninhabited islands close enough for guests to swim to, and the staff will be happy to arrange tours to farther away islands. Like most accommodations in Kuna Yala, it's a pretty bare-bones operation, but every cabin offers a private bathroom and a hammock. Ask for a sea-facing cabin; these have a small balcony and spectacular views of the Caribbean Sea and mountains. Guest rooms are far from elegant, but decorated in warm, Caribbean tones and cool enough at night thanks to the constant Caribbean breeze. Best of all, the hotel restaurant is a bit more creative than most restaurants in this area.

Isla Ailigandi.© **6612-5448** or 293-8795. www.dadibelodge.com. 3 units. Single $120; double $95 per person; triple $80 per person. No credit cards. **Amenities:** Restaurant.

The Dolphin Lodge ★★   Also known as the Uaguinega Ecoresort, this "lodge" (and I use that term loosely) is run by a friendly Kuna family who have outfitted their property with a couple of extra amenities and a roster of tours that take visitors to beaches, on snorkeling trips, on bird-watching tours on the mainland, and on visits to Kuna villages such as the overpopulated, handicrafts-heavy Ustupu; they'll also take you to watch traditional dances on the island of Ogobsucun. Dolphin Lodge comprises 11 cabins, three of which are "junior suites"—these units have hardwood floors, ocean views, stylish bamboo-thatched walls, and terraces. Standard cabins have cement floors, some have ocean views, and interior walls are made of wood, not bamboo. Another difference is that standard units have electricity from 6 to 11pm only, while junior suites have 24-hour solar-powered electricity. All cabins are comfortable and clean, with quality mattresses and private bathrooms. This is the only lodge in the comarca with Internet service. There is an open-air dining area with simple but decent cuisine. They'll usually light a bonfire at night. The island of Uaguitupu has no village, and there is only a thin strip of beach; to get here you'll need to fly into Mamitupo.

Isla Uaguitupu.© **832-5144** or 315-1576. www.uaguinega.com. 11 units. Rates are per person, based on double occupancy. $125–$150 1st night double, $116–$135 2nd night double. MC, V. **Amenities:** Restaurant; bar.

Sapibenega Kuna Lodge ★★ 📷   The Sapibenega is not luxurious, but it does offer the highest quality accommodations in the entire comarca. The lodge is located on the gorgeous island of Iskardup, near a group of uninhabited islands; to get here you'll need to fly into Playón Chico and take a 5-minute motorboat ride to the island. Iskardup is ringed with lodging units, including ground-level individual cabins and two new cabins propped up on stilts over the water. These newer units have two rooms per cabin (note that walls are thin and you can hear you neighbors), are more spacious and comfortable, and come with balconies. All cabins have private bathrooms with tiled showers, hardwood floors, cane walls, thatched roofs, fans, and 24-hour electricity. There's not much on the island except an open-air *bohio* bar/restaurant on stilts over the water, hammocks, and that's about it. Daily tours take guests to uninhabited nearby islands, which are great for snorkeling, and cultural tours to Playón Chico and Kolebir, the latter of which is a traditional mainland Kuna village. The lodge can also arrange sailing, bird-watching, and jungle hikes to a waterfall.

Isla Iskardup. ⓒ **215-1406** or 6676-5548. www.spaibenega.com. 13 units. Rates are per person, based on double occupancy. $125 low season (June 2–Nov 30); $140 high season 1st night, $126 2nd night. **Note:** *There is a one-time $20 tax per adult.* Kids 1 and under free, kids ages 2–5 35% discount, kids ages 6–10 25% discount. MC, V. **Amenities:** 2 restaurants; bar.

THE DARIÉN PROVINCE

12

The Darién Province, a remote, sparsely populated expanse of tropical rainforest and swampland along Panama's eastern boundary with Colombia, is considered Central America's last grand, untamed wilderness. Home to nearly .8 million hectares (2 million acres) of protected land, the Darién includes **La Reserva Natural Privada Punta Patiño** and the **Parque Nacional del Darién,** the largest national park in Central America and a UNESCO Biosphere Reserve. This entire wilderness is commonly called the "Darién Gap," which refers to the roadless swath of forest that is the "missing link" in the Pan American Highway from Alaska to Chile. Colombia would like to extend the road, but Panamanians fear widespread environmental destruction and an increase in drug trafficking. For now at least, a road seems unlikely.

Given the Darién's inaccessibility, there are few places a traveler can actually visit within the boundaries of the province. The national park measures a staggering 15,000 hectares (1.5 million acres), yet only the **Pirre** and **Cana** stations offer trails and basic services. On the southern coast at Piñas Bay is the famous Tropic Star Lodge, and there are trails and dugout canoe trips on rivers around Punta Patiño.

Travelers can drive to the end of the Pan American Highway to Yaviza, but it's unlikely that you'd want to. The road is flanked by mostly deforested land with nothing of interest except for a few blink-and-you-miss-it hamlets providing truly grim lodging and mediocre services. The road is mostly unpaved and requires a 4WD during the rainy season. Some tours use the Pan American Highway to reach their final destination in the Darién.

The Darién is just not developed for do-it-yourself travelers, and tales abound of travelers getting lost for days in the jungle or having run-ins with terrorist groups along the northern Colombia border. Therefore, I strongly recommend that you let someone else do the planning for you. Destinations such as the Cana Field Station actually require booking a

tour that includes a charter flight to get there. Considering the lack of roads and the inexpensive flights aboard small planes that exist, most travelers fly here anyway, which can be an adventure in itself, soaring above the treetops, viewing Emberá villages below, and holding on tight for a landing on a dirt or grassy landing strip. If booking a tour, you will be put on a charter flight organized by your outfitter, or at the very least they will be able to book you on a regularly scheduled flight.

WESTERN DARIÉN ★

The Pan American Highway from Panama City is a relatively featureless road that is paved until Lago Bayano; from here it's a rocky ride to the endpoint at Yaviza. Given the poor condition of the road, it can take nearly a full day to drive this stretch—and when you're done, the only thing to do is turn around and head back. The exception is the turnoff to Metetí, which leads to Puerto Quimbo and to boats to La Palma, near the Punta Patiño reserve. **Ancon Expeditions** is now offering custom itineraries to the upper tributaries of the Sambú River in the southwestern

A Word of Caution for Visitors to the Darién

Travelers to the Darién should not be cavalier. The jungle is dense and can easily disorient hikers, and any kind of walking trip here should always be undertaken with a guide. In the Darién, you'll find a lot more creepy-crawlies than you will in the rest of Panama; snakes, some of them poisonous, will surprise you if you're not scanning the trail ahead. Hikers should also protect themselves from ticks and skin-burrowing chiggers; tuck your pants into your socks and bring lots of repellent with DEET. The May-to-December rainy season is wetter than in most parts of Panama, shrouding your vision and turning trails and roads into slick and gloppy mud. Unless you're fishing at the Tropic Star Lodge, it is not recommended that you visit the Darién during the rainy season. Also, if you're heading to higher altitudes like the Cerro Pirre, bring a jacket.

Although danger levels have been exaggerated greatly, the border with Colombia near the Caribbean Sea is unsafe due to narco-terrorist activity that spills over into Panama. The destinations mentioned in this chapter, however, are perfectly safe.

Darién, where you can explore deep rainforest seldom visited and stay in indigenous villages still practicing their traditional way of life. Contact Ancon for more information. **Ecocircuitos** (✆ **314-0068** or 314-0698; www.ecocircuitos.com) also offers 3-day tours of the Darién.

The **Chucanti Field Station** (✆ **6676-2466;** www.advantagepanama.com), in the western Darién, was opened recently by Advantage Tours. The biological research station for visiting scientists is also open to nature enthusiasts. Chucanti is a good spot for budget bird-watchers and hikers seeking to visit the Darién. The lodge provides access to the lower primary forests and cloud forests of the region, and visits are accompanied by a guide who provides information about flora and fauna, with additional input from whichever scientist is staying at the station that week. The station is just 135km (85 miles) from Panama City via the Pan American Highway. At the turnoff near the Cerro Chucanti hill, guides load gear onto mules and guests travel to the station by horse or by walking trail for 3 hours. The station is a simple wood-and-zinc-roof structure surrounded by leafy green forest. There are four guest rooms with private bathrooms, and though they are comfortable, this is a research station with simple amenities. Meals are hearty and typically Panamanian. Prices are $350 for 3 nights/4 days, and include round-trip transportation from Panama City, bilingual guide, lodging, and meals.

Advantage Tours has also recently built a small lodge in the small Emberá village of **La Marea.** Accommodations are basic but comfortable, and all rooms have their own bathrooms (no electricity). Like most of Advantage's tours, the Marea program is primarily for bird-watchers, though the best part of this trip is the opportunity to stay among the Emberá Indians and learn about their customs and traditions. The village is close to a harpy eagle nesting site, and harpy sightings have been reported. La Marea, which means "tide" in Spanish, can only be reached easily when the river tide is high, so if you arrive during low tide, expect a long adventure getting there. Before Advantage set up their lodge in this tiny community, La Marea was an economically and culturally depressed village that had lost many of its traditions and customs and had little hope for the future. However, since the advent of tourism, the small village has begun to prosper and regain its cultural traditions, relearning Emberá arts such as Jagua carving and basket weaving. In a sense, Advantage Tours and the people of La Marea have shown that eco-tourism can be a win-win situation for local communities, travelers, and tour companies alike. How "authentic" this newly discovered culture identity is remains to be seen, but it is an interesting idea.

PUNTA PATIÑO ★★★

Punta Patiño was the first private nature preserve to be established in Panama, and at 30,351 hectares (75,000 acres) it is the country's largest. The preserve is bordered by the Gulf of San Miguel and is characterized by a coastal web of mangrove swamps and the mighty Tiura River, which ribbons through undulating and endangered dry tropical forest. The preserve is also home to Emberá Indian communities and a concentration of harpy eagles, Panama's national bird. Owned and managed by the nonprofit Asociación Nacional Para la Conservación de la Naturaleza (ANCON), the preserve is tangible proof of the ability of nature to recover from human intervention, considering that a large swath of land here was once a cattle ranch and small farming community and now is a thriving forest. It's all here thanks to the hard work and perseverance of ANCON and Panama City mayor Juan Carlos Navarro, an environmentalist who was leading director when the preserve was created. Punta Patiño can be reached by road and boat, or by small plane and boat.

There are several reasons to visit the preserve. The region gives visitors a chance not only to explore dense primary and secondary forest that's home to peccaries, coatimundis, and capybaras that feed near the shore; it also provides for an adventurous ride aboard a *piragua,* or motorized dugout canoe, up the Tiura River. Along this river's shores three species of ancient mangroves thrive and provide refuge for bottlenose dolphins and marine birds such as kingfishers, herons, spoonbills, and ibises. For bird-watchers, the prize sighting here is the harpy eagle, one of the largest predators in the world. Harpy eagles like this region for its concentration of trees like the Quipo, whose chubby trunk and height make for ideal nesting conditions. Another reason to visit Punta Patiño is the **Mogue Emberá Indian community,** which gives travelers a cultural introduction to native peoples and their traditional arts like tagua carvings and basket-making. Through tourism, the Emberá tribes in this area have found a way to make a living that is based on protecting wildlife—instead of killing it—to draw more tourism dollars.

Adventure Tours & Where to Stay

Visits to the Punta Patiño preserve must be planned as part of an expedition. Two companies currently offer trips to Punta Patiño (which can be as short as 2 nights) that are part of a longer itinerary covering other destinations in the Darién.

Ancon Expeditions (✆ **269-9415;** www.anconexpeditions.com), affiliated with ANCON, is the Darién's foremost tour operator. The company also manages Punta Patiño Lodge; it sits high on a bluff overlooking the Pacific Ocean, and is a simple, two-story building with 10 air-conditioned cabins with private bathrooms. Ancon Expeditions uses this lodge as a base for all three of their expeditions to Punta Patiño. The quick, in-and-out tour is the 3-night/4-day "Coastal Darién Explorer" (from $695), which includes light hiking through forest and a day visit by canoe to an Emberá village. Worth highlighting is Ancon's "Darién Explorer Trek" (from $2,750) the company's signature Darién expedition. This 13-night/14-day adventure begins with an overnight in their Punta Patiño Lodge, followed by a night in an Emberá village. But rather than return to Punta Patiño, the trip continues upstream until reaching El Real, the jumping-off point for the Darién National Park and the trail head to the Pirre ranger station. There is a 2-day hike through virgin rainforest until you reach Cana (see below), eventually returning to Panama City via small plane. This is an adventure for travelers really seeking to experience remote wilderness far off the beaten track from most tours. Ancon Expeditions' Punta Patiño tours begin with a flight aboard a small plane or overland with a ride along the Pan American Highway and both options followed by a spectacular dugout boat ride to the private reserve.

Ecocircuitos (© **314-1586;** www.ecocircuitos.com) is another excellent tour operator offering a Punta Patiño expedition. The major difference between this tour and Ancon's is that Punta Patiño is reached by road along the Pan American Highway to Puerto Quimba, where travelers board a dugout canoe to go to the Mogue Emberá Indian community. Base camp is set up in the community, with lodging in tents, giving visitors more exposure to the Emberá (the reason why they've dubbed their tour the "Darién Ethnic Expedition"). The trip lasts 2 days/3 nights or 3 nights/4 days, and includes transportation, guided excursions, meals, and lodging. Prices for a 3-night/4-day trip are (approximately) $795 per person, based on two travelers; and $655 per person, based on four travelers. They also offer a "Rural Community Development in the Darién" volunteer experience, where participants can help the local community market soap and organic teas, as well as assist in local development. This program is based in the village of Santa Fe, a conservative Emberá community.

DARIÉN NATIONAL PARK & CANA FIELD STATION ★★★

The .6-million-hectare (1.5-million-acre) Darién National Park is not only the largest park in Panama—it is the largest in Central America. The park extends along 90% of the entire length of the border with Colombia, incorporating a dazzling rainforest rich in biodiversity, coastal lagoons and mangrove swamps, serrated peaks, and toffee-colored rivers that snake down to the Pacific Ocean. The vast size and pristine state of the park mean that populations of endemic and endangered species—jaguars, tapirs, ocelots, and pumas—are allowed to flourish. But what visitors see most, and with surprising frequency, are spider, howler, and white-faced capuchin monkeys, as well as sloths. The Darién is considered one of the last pristine wildernesses in the Americas, and it therefore has been designated a UNESCO Biosphere Site. It is an extraordinary, *Jurassic Park*–like wilderness, ideal for adventurous travelers who seek absolutely primeval surroundings and the sense of being far from civilization and the modern world.

What visitors also come to see here are **birds,** and indeed the Darién forest has been rated as one of the top 10 bird-watching sites in the world. Even non-birders can't help getting caught up in the excitement of so many colorful "showcase" species like macaws and toucans fluttering about. Dozens of tanager species in a kaleidoscopic range of colors are here, too, not to mention rare and endemic species such as red-throated caracaras, peregrine falcons, golden-headed quetzals, and the Pirre warbler. There are so many birds and in such abundance that sighting them doesn't take much effort—while swinging in a hammock, for example, you can eye parrots and macaws zipping through the air.

But as vast as the Darién National Park is, the majority of it is largely inaccessible. The only two access points are the ANAM park ranger's **Pirre Station** on the north side of the Cerro Pirre peak, and Ancon Expedition's **Cana Field Station** on the southeast side of the peak (reached by small plane). Cana is owned and operated by **Ancon Expeditions** (© 269-9415; www.anconexpeditions.com), and trips here must be booked as a tour through that company, unless you are traveling with a tour operator such as Field Guides, Wildland Adventures, or Victor Emanuel Nature Tours (see chapter 5) among others, which subcontract the lodge. Check out Ancon's "Darién Explorer Trek" (under "Punta Patiño," above) for a 14-day tour that arrives at Cana on foot and departs via small plane.

The Darién is one of the few places in Panama where it is recommended that you **do not travel independently and without a guide.** The reasons are plentiful: Hardly a soul here speaks English, there exists a considerable risk of becoming lost on any trail, and you're exposing yourself to a variety of potential pitfalls such as a twisted ankle or snakebites—the nearest medical clinic is hundreds of miles away. Also, with such a diversity of flora and fauna, it pays to have a guide to enhance your experience with interpretive information, cultural information about the Emberá and Wounaan communities, and history of the area.

The ranger station at Pirre (© 299-6965) offers basic shelter with bunk-style beds, a kitchen, and shared bathrooms. There is no electricity, and you must bring all supplies with you like food, water (or a water purifier), flashlights, towels, and so forth. The cost to spend the night is $10, with a park entrance fee of $3. There are several trails from easy to difficult that lead from the ranger station, but as stated earlier, it is unwise to walk these trails without a guide.

The Pirre Station is about a 3-hour walk during the dry season from the village of El Real; or you can get there in 2 hours in a dugout canoe from El Real, followed by a 1-hour hike to the station. Call **Aeroperlas** (© 315-7500; www.aeroperlas.com) to ask about flights between Panama City and El Real.

CANA FIELD STATION ★★★

Most travelers to Darién National Park are bird-watchers who visit the Cana Field Station on Ancon's 4-night, 5-day "Ultimate Darién Experience" expedition. Of course, you don't need to be a bird-watcher to visit, but it certainly helps, considering that there are plenty of hiking trails for soaking up the fabulous jungle ambien... The lodge is located a short walk from the old Cana mines, one of the most pr... tive gold mines in the history of the Americas, founded in the early 17th ce... the Spaniards. In the late 1800s, the mines drew nearly 20,000 people b... British operation, given how empty and remote the area now is. The... the 18th century, but reopened in the late 1800s complete with tra... de Cupe to ship gold, people, and equipment from Cana. Antig... and remnants of the train remain, and part of the fascinat... oughly they've been swallowed up by jungle.

With the Cana Field Station, it's all about locati... surely one of the most stunning sites in Panama...

trees drip with vines and sprout spiky bromeliads, and are interspersed with a riot of flowering trees. Because the lodge faces an open expanse, it provides a spectacular amphitheater for bird-watching, allowing guests to spy many species from a reclining chair or hammock on the front porch. The lodge is research-station rustic, but with comfortable beds with a sheet, shared bathrooms with hot water, a separate dining hall, and a roofed area strung with hammocks for hanging out. It's the kind of place where easygoing nature lovers will be happiest, those who do not mind queuing up for a shower, getting dressed by flashlight, or sharing simply prepared communal meals. Days begin at the crack of dawn, usually around 6:30am, to take advantage of early birding activity. Expeditions are led by Ancon's bilingual guides, who are some of the best in their field, and the staff are a convivial group of local Dariénites. From the lodge, there are several short trails around the property, and a longer, half-day hike up through thick, species-rich jungle to the top of Cerro Pierre peak, where guests sleep overnight at Ancon's tent-camping site. From here there is a sweeping view of the Darién National Park, and the option to walk higher into the cloud forest in search of the elusive golden-headed quetzal.

Trips to Cana include guides, excursions, meals, and a round-trip charter flight. Itineraries are for set dates but have some flexibility, or can be undertaken with a minimum of four travelers. Price per person for the 4-night trip, based on at least four travelers, starts at $1,450.

BAHÍA PIÑAS & THE TROPIC STAR LODGE ★★★

Visitors to Bahía Piñas come for the legendary sport fishing. Beyond the Tropic Star Lodge, there are two villages near Bahía Piñas, but both hold little interest to travelers. If the cost of the Tropic Star is too rich for your blood, you'd be better off setting up a fishing trip elsewhere along the Pacific Coast rather than eking out a local tour in Jacqué. Call **Aeroperlas** (✆ **315-7500;** www.aeroperlas.com) or **Air Panama** (✆ **315-0439;** www.flyairpanama.com) for information about flights between Panama City and Bahía Piñas.

WHERE TO STAY & DINE

remier wilderness fishing lodge is revered
d for record-breaking sailfish and black
:ies. It's one of Panama's earliest ecolodge
exan oil tycoon as a private getaway but
lodge in 1968. The American Kittredge
. Tropic Star enjoys a gorgeous location
ess tangle of wild jungle that stretches for
it attracts international VIPs, sports stars,
lusivity owes more to its remoteness and
to its luxuriousness. Any sport-fishing
he owners are family-friendly in order to
ng. The lodge's secret asset is the **Zane**
it attracts a rich supply of baitfish and the
lost of the fishing is done within 9.7 to

19km (6–12 miles) of the shore aboard one of their dozen 9.4m (31-ft.) Bertram boats. Since the lodge's inception, fishermen here have broken more than 200 world records, 40 of which are still valid today. Given this, the lodge can book a full 1 to 2 years ahead of time during high season.

The lodge has a maximum capacity of 36 guests who are personally attended to by 80 employees wearing Hawaiian shirts and big smiles. Guest rooms are individual air-conditioned cabins spread across a hilly slope, and feature outdoor decks that look out onto scenic Piñas Bay. Rooms come with two twins or a king-size bed, and are spacious and comfortably appointed but not as plush as those of a five-star hotel. The lodge has been impeccably maintained and updated throughout the years without forfeiting its original, retro-1960s design. There is also the "palacio" for a group of six, which used to be the original owner's home and is reached by cable car or 122 steps up the hill. The palacio has three bedrooms and a sunken living room.

The four-course meals are excellent; everything is baked, homemade, and fresh, especially the fish, of course. Rates include fishing excursions, lodging, meals, and all drinks except cocktails. Beyond fishing, there are plenty of other activities available such as scuba diving, kayaking the Río Piñas, hiking the lodge's wilderness trail that connects the white-sand Playa Blanca beach, or taking a cruise upriver to visit a Wounaan village. Packages below show price ranges from low season (Apr–Sept) and high season (Dec–Mar); the lodge closes October to November. To get here, you take a regularly scheduled flight or a small charter plane from Panama City (see above) to Piñas Bay, where they'll pick you up for the 10-minute boat ride to the lodge.

Piñas Bay. ✆ **800/682-3424.** www.tropicstar.com. 16 units. Packages per person, based on double occupancy: 7 nights $4,850–$5,495; 4 nights $2,895–$3,250. AE, MC, V. **Amenities:** Restaurant; bar; outdoor pool; sport-fishing excursions; kayaks; cultural excursions. *In room:* A/C, no phone.

FAST FACTS: PANAMA

FAST FACTS

American Express   American Express Travel Services has emergency card pickup at Agencia de Viajes Fidanque in Centro Comercial La Galeria on Avenida Ricard J. Alfaro in Panama City (& 265-2444), but you're better off calling their U.S.-based 24-hour number at 800/528-4800.

ATM Networks   See "Money & Costs," p. 37.

Business Hours   Hours for service-oriented businesses in Panama are generally 8am to 1pm and 2 to 5pm on weekdays, and 8am to noon on Saturdays. Businesses in Panama City usually don't close for lunch. Shops open at 9 or 10am and close at 6 or 7pm; shopping malls close around 8pm. Grocery stores are open 24 hours or 8am to 8pm.

Car Rentals   See "Getting Around," p. 35.

Drinking Laws   Panama's legal drinking age is 18, though it is rarely enforced. Beer, wine, and liquor can be purchased at any supermarket or liquor store, although only until 11pm. If you're in Panama during an election, liquor sales are prohibited for a 72-hour period until voting is over.

Electricity   Electrical plugs are the same as in the U.S., as is Panama's voltage, 110 AC.

Embassies & Consulates   The **United States Embassy** is located in Panama City on Demetrio Basilio Lakas Avenue in Clayton (✆ **207-7000**). The **Canadian Embassy** is at Torres de las Americas Tower A, 11th floor, in Punta Pacifica (✆ **294-2500**). The **British Embassy** is at Calle 53 Este and Nicanor de Obarrio in Panama City (✆ **269-0866**). **Australia** and **New Zealand** do not have embassies or consulates in Panama; however, the British Embassy can provide consular assistance to citizens of those countries.

Emergencies   For fire or an ambulance, dial ✆ **103;** for police, dial ✆ **104.**

Etiquette & Customs   Panama City professionals dress well in spite of the heat, meaning no flip-flops, shorts, or tank tops—so bring at least one nice outfit with you. Many better restaurants will not serve patrons in shorts, women included. In resort or beach areas, and in smaller towns with a large expat presence such as Boquete, casual wear is okay.

Panamanians usually greet each other with a light kiss on the right cheek, but they are accustomed to North American habits and most likely will greet you with a handshake if they know you're a gringo or if you are in a business environment. Punctuality is appreciated in business settings, but don't be surprised if your Panamanian guest shows up 30 or 45 minutes late for a dinner party. Many Panamanians do not like to be bothered on Sunday, so reconsider if calling on this day. In business settings, always begin a conversation with light talk before getting to the point. In contrast to North America, the do-it-yourself spirit is not very esteemed in Panama; rather, your ability to hire help to do it for you is what people value. Live-in and daily maids are very common in Panama, meaning as a guest you are not expected to make your bed or help out around the house. When entering a room, you are expected to greet everyone either individually or as a group.

In the San Blas Islands, Kuna Indians frequently request money to have their photo taken.

Gasoline (Petrol)   Because Panama has no petroleum distilleries, gas is usually slightly more expensive than in the U.S. At press time, 1 gallon of gas in Panama cost about $3. In more remote locations, such as Bocas del Toro and the Kuna Yala Islands, gas is can cost almost twice as much. Taxes are already included in the printed price. One Panama gallon equals 3.8 liters or .85 imperial gallons.

Holidays   For more information on holidays, see "Panama Calendar of Events & Festivals," p. 32.

Insurance   For travel overseas, most U.S. health plans (including Medicare and Medic-aid) do not provide coverage, and the ones that do often require you to pay for services upfront and reimburse you only after you return home.

As a safety net, you may want to buy travel medical insurance, particularly if you're traveling to a remote or high-risk area where emergency evacuation might be necessary. If you require additional medical insurance, try **MEDEX Assistance** (© **410/453-6300;** www.medexassist.com) or **Travel Assistance International** (© **800/821-2828** or 410/987-6233; www.travelassistance.com).

Canadians should check with their provincial health plan offices or contact **Health Canada** (www.hc-sc.gc.ca) to find out the extent of their coverage and what documentation and receipts they must take home in case they are treated overseas.

Travelers from the **U.K.** should carry their European Health Insurance Card (EHIC), which replaced the E111 form as proof of entitlement to free/reduced cost medical treatment abroad (www.ehic.org.uk). Note, however, that the EHIC only covers "necessary medical treatment," and for repatriation costs, lost money, baggage, or cancellation, travel insurance from a reputable company should always be sought (www.travelinsuranceweb.com).

For information on traveler's insurance, trip cancellation insurance, and medical insurance while traveling, please visit www.frommers.com/tips.

Internet Access   Internet access is plentiful in Panama, except in more remote areas. Nearly every hotel has at least one computer with Internet access; some have dataports or Wi-Fi (usually in the hotel lobby or business center). Most Internet cafes charge between $2 and $3 per hour. See "Fast Facts: Panama City," in chapter 6 for more information on Internet access in Panama City.

Language   Spanish is the official language in Panama, though English is widely spoken in the tourism industry, and many hotel owners are native English-speakers themselves. Panama's seven indigenous groups speak their own languages in their communities, and in some isolated areas indigenous groups do not speak Spanish fluently. On the Caribbean coast, creoles speak a patois called Guari-Guari or Wari-Wari, a mix of English, Spanish, and Ngöbe-Buglé.

Lost & Found   Be sure to tell all of your credit card companies the minute you discover your wallet has been lost or stolen, and file a report at the nearest police precinct. Your credit card company or insurer may require a police-report number or record of the loss. Most credit card companies have an emergency toll-free number to call if your card is lost or stolen; they may be able to wire you a cash advance immediately or deliver an emergency credit card in a day or two. **Visa**'s emergency number is © **800/847-2911** toll-free in the U.S., or call 800/111-0016 in Panama. **American Express** cardholders and traveler's check holders should call their 24-hour service in the United States at 800/528-4800. **MasterCard** holders should call $\mathcal{C}$ **800/307-7309** in Panama, or 800/627-8372 in the U.S. You can also call collect to 636/722-7111.

If you need emergency cash over the weekend when all banks and American Express offices are closed, you can have money wired to you via **Western Union** ($\mathcal{C}$ **800/325-6000;** www.westernunion.com).

Mail   Panama has no stamp vending machines or post boxes, so you'll have to head to the post office to send a postcard, or ask your hotel if they can do it for you. A letter sent regular mail to the U.S. will arrive in 5 to 10 days; the cost, at press time, is 35¢ for a letter and 25¢ for a postcard. For quick service, send a package via a courier; see "Fast Facts: Panama City," in chapter 6.

Measurements   See the chart on the inside front cover of this book for details on converting metric measurements to nonmetric equivalents.

Newspapers & Magazines   Panama's principal daily newspaper is *La Prensa;* the five other dailies include *La Panamá América, Crítica Libre, El Universal,* and *La Estrella. La Prensa* publishes a weekend guide supplement on Thursdays, and is the best paper for event listings. The English-language *Panama News,* once available in print, is available online at www.thepanamanews.com. *The Panama Visitor* is in Spanish and English and is a free bimonthly publication for tourists. You can find copies of the *Miami Herald* in English at supermarkets and at the Gran Morrison chain.

Passports   The websites listed provide downloadable passport applications as well as the current fees for processing applications. For an up-to-date, country-by-country listing of passport requirements around the world, go to the "International Travel" tab of the U.S. State Department at **http://travel.state.gov**.

Allow plenty of time before your trip to apply for a passport; processing normally takes 3 weeks but can take longer during busy periods (especially spring). And keep in mind that if you need a passport in a hurry, you'll pay a higher processing fee.

For Residents of Australia   Contact the **Australian Passport Information Service** at $\mathcal{C}$ **131-232,** or visit www.passports.gov.au.

For Residents of Canada   Contact the central **Passport Office,** Department of Foreign Affairs and International Trade, Ottawa, ON K1A 0G3 ($\mathcal{C}$ **800/567-6868;** www.ppt.gc.ca).

For Residents of Ireland   Contact the **Passport Office,** Setanta Centre, Molesworth Street, Dublin 2 ($\mathcal{C}$ **01/671-1633;** www.foreignaffairs.gov.ie).

For Residents of New Zealand   Contact the **Passports Office,** Department of Internal Affairs, 47 Boulcott St., Wellington, 6011 ($\mathcal{C}$ **0800/225-050** in New Zealand or 04/474-8100; www.passports.govt.nz).

For Residents of the United Kingdom   Visit your nearest passport office, major post office, or travel agency or contact the **Identity and Passport Service (IPS),** 89 Eccleston Square, London, SW1V 1PN ($\mathcal{C}$ **0300/222-0000;** www.ips.gov.uk).

For Residents of the United States   To find your regional passport office, check the U.S. State Department website (travel.state.gov/passport) or call the **National Passport Information Center** ($\mathcal{C}$ **877/487-2778**) for automated information.

Police   For police, dial $\mathcal{C}$ **104.**

Restrooms   It's rare to find a public restroom in Panama—you'll generally have to rely on hotel lobbies or restaurants. For the most part, they are clean, with modern septic systems. In some remote areas or beach locations, an outhouse-style restroom or a toilet that requires flushing with a bucket of water is more the norm. Restrooms are called *baños,* and are marked *hombres* or *caballeros* for men, and *damas* or *mujeres* for women.

Smoking All restaurants, bars, and dance clubs have recently gone nonsmoking, so smokers will have to take it outside. Smoking isn't even allowed in outside dining areas or balconies.

Taxes All hotels charge 10% tax. Restaurants charge 5% on the total cost of the bill, and often sneak in an automatic 10% for service—check your bill carefully to avoid overtipping.

Telephones Panama has a seven-digit phone numbering system, and there are no city or area codes. The country code for Panama is 507, which you use only when dialing from outside the country. Cellphones are prefixed by 6; in this book, telephone numbers include this prefix because most businesses' published phone numbers include the prefix.

The cheapest way to phone is to use a prepaid phone card, available in kiosks, supermarkets, and pharmacies in quantities of $5, $10, and $20—however, these cards have a life span of 15 to 30 days. **ClaroCOM** has the best rates with 5¢ per minute for national and international calls to the U.S. and the U.K., and 35¢ per minute to cellular phones. Cable and wireless **Telechip** cards are less value at 15¢ per minute for national calls and 25¢ per minute for international calls. The cards have an access phone number and a scratch-off code, as well as bilingual service. Remember that hotels charge a connection fee even if the connection number is a toll-free number.

If you need operator assistance when making a call, dial © **106.** For an international operator in the U.S., dial © **109** (AT&T), **108** (MCI), or **115** (Sprint).

Time Zone Panama is 5 hours behind Greenwich Mean Time (GMT), and 1 hour ahead of Costa Rica. Panama does not observe daylight saving, so from the first Sunday in November to the second Sunday in March, the time in Panama is the same as that in the U.S. Eastern Time Zone (New York, Miami, and others); from mid-March to early November, it's the same as that in the U.S. Central Time Zone (Chicago, Houston, and others).

Tipping Tipping in Panama at restaurants is 10% (see "Taxes," above). Taxi drivers do not expect tips, but you might consider it if you've rented a taxi for the day. Porters and bellhops should be tipped $2 to $5 depending on the caliber of the hotel.

Useful Phone Numbers U.S. Dept. of State Travel Advisory: © 202/647-5225 (staffed 24 hr.); U.S. Passport Agency: © 202/647-0518; U.S. Centers for Disease Control International Traveler's Hot Line: © 404/332-4559.

Water The water in most of Panama's major cities and tourist destinations is safe to drink, except in Bocas del Toro. Many travelers' stomachs react adversely to water in foreign countries, however, so it might be a good idea to drink bottled water outside of major hotels and restaurants.

TOLL-FREE NUMBERS & WEBSITES

MAJOR INTERNATIONAL AIRLINES

Aeroméxico
© 800/237-6639 (in U.S.)
www.aeromexico.com

Aero Perlas
© 378-6000 (in Panama)
www.aeroperlas.com

Air New Zealand
© 800/262-1234 (in U.S.)
© 800/663-5494 (in Canada)
© 0800/028-4149 (in U.K.)
www.airnewzealand.com

Air Panama
© 316-9000 (in Panama)
www.flyairpanama.com

American Airlines
© 800/433-7300 (in U.S. and Canada)
© 0844/4997-3000 (in U.K.)
www.aa.com

British Airways
© 800/247-9297 (in U.S. and Canada)
© 0844/493-0787 (in U.K.)
www.britishairways.com

Continental Airlines
© 800/523-3273 (in U.S. and Canada)
© 084/5607-6760 (in U.K.)
www.continental.com

Copa
© 800/359-2672 (in U.S. and Canada)
© 0871/1744-0335 (in U.K.)
www.copaair.com

Delta Air Lines
© 800/221-1212 (in U.S. and Canada)
© 084/5600-0950 (in U.K.)
www.delta.com

Iberia Airlines
© 800/722-4642 (in U.S. and Canada)
© 087/0609-0500 (in U.K.)
www.iberia.com

Qantas Airways
© 800/227-4500 (in U.S. and Canada)
© 084/5774-7767 (in U.K.)
© 13-13-13 (in Australia)
www.qantas.com

Spirit Airlines
© 800/772-7117 (in U.S.)
www.spiritair.com

TACA
© 800/535-8780 (in U.S.)
© 800/722-TACA (8222; in Canada)
© 087/1744-0337 (in U.K.)

United Airlines
© 800/864-8331 (in U.S. and Canada)
© 084/5844-4777 (in U.K.)
www.united.com

Virgin Atlantic Airways
© 800/821-5438 (in U.S. and Canada)
© 084/420-977 (in U.K.)
www.virgin-atlantic.com

CAR RENTAL AGENCIES

Alamo
© 800/462-5266 (in U.S. and Canada)
www.alamo.com

Avis
© 800/331-1212 (in U.S. and Canada)
© 084/4581-8181 (in U.K.)
www.avis.com

Budget
© 800/527-0700 (in U.S.)
© 800/268-8900 (in Canada)
© 084/4544-4444 (in U.K.)
www.budget.com

Dollar
© 800/800-4000 (in U.S.)
© 800/848-8268 (in Canada)
© 080/823-42474 (in U.K.)
www.dollar.com

Hertz
© 800/645-3131 (in U.S. and Canada)
© 800/654-3001 (for international
reservations)
www.hertz.com

National
© 800/CAR-RENT (227-7368; in U.S.
and Canada)
www.nationalcar.com

Thrifty
© 800/367-2277 (in U.S. and Canada)
© 918/669-2168 (international)
www.thrifty.com

MAJOR HOTEL & MOTEL CHAINS

Courtyard by Marriott
© 888/236-2427 (in U.S.)
© 0800/221-222 (in U.K.)
www.marriott.com/courtyard

Crowne Plaza Hotels
© 888/303-1746 (in U.S. and Canada)
www.ichotelsgroup.com/
crowneplaza

Holiday Inn
© 800/315-2621 (in U.S. and Canada)
© 0800/405-060 (in U.K.)
www.holidayinn.com

InterContinental Hotels & Resorts
© 800/424-6835 (in U.S. and Canada)
© 0800/1800-1800 (in U.K.)
www.ichotelsgroup.com

Marriott
© 888/236-2427 (in U.S. and Canada)
© 0800/221-222 (in U.K.)
www.marriott.com

Radisson Hotels & Resorts
☎ 888/201-1718 (in U.S. and Canada)
☎ 0800/374-411 (in U.K.)
www.radisson.com

Sheraton Hotels & Resorts
☎ 800/325-3535 (in U.S.)
☎ 800/543-4300 (in Canada)
☎ 0800/3253-5353 (in U.K.)
www.starwoodhotels.com/sheraton

Westin Hotels & Resorts
☎ 800/937-8461 (in U.S. and Canada)
www.starwoodhotels.com/westin

Wyndham Hotels & Resorts
☎ 877/999-3223 (in U.S. and Canada)
www.wyndham.com

GLOSSARY OF SPANISH TERMS & PHRASES

14

The official language of Panama is Spanish. However, with so many new hotel owners hailing from the U.S. and Canada, English is widely spoken in the tour industry. But this doesn't get you off the hook—taxi drivers, waiters, local tour guides, and everyday Panamanians speak little or no English. Arm yourself with basic words and phrases in Spanish and your trip won't be a constant battle to make yourself understood. Panamanians appreciate the effort, and really, part of the fun of traveling is learning the local lingo. Due to the long U.S. presence in Panama, you'll hear a few expressions that have been adapted from English, such as "parkear," meaning to park, or "watchiman," for security guard (watchman).

Panamanians speak at a relatively relaxed speed, and they have a more neutral accent when compared with their Latin American neighbors. Panamanians speaking in a slangy manner have a tendency to drop the "d" from words that end in *–ido* or *–ado,* as in *pelao,* instead of *pelado.* Like most Latin Americans, Panamanians are more conscious of salutations. Before launching into conversation or asking a question, do not forget a greeting such as "Buenos días" or "Buenas tardes," or as most Panamanians say, simply "Buenas."

BASIC WORDS & PHRASES

English	Spanish	Pronunciation
Hello	Buenos días	*bweh*-nohss *dee*-ahss
How are you?	¿Cómo está usted?	*koh*-moh ehss-*tah* oo-*stehd*
Very well	Muy bien	**mwee byehn**
Thank you	Gracias	*grah*-syahss
Good-bye	Adiós	**ad-***dyohss*
Please	Por favor	**pohr fah-***vohr*
Yes	Sí	**see**
No	No	**noh**
Excuse me (to get by someone)	Perdóneme	**pehr-***doh*-neh-meh
Excuse me (to begin a question)	Disculpe	**dees-***kool*-peh

English	Spanish	Pronunciation
Give me	Deme	*deh*-meh
Where is . . . ?	¿Dónde está . . . ?	*dohn*-deh ehss-*tah*
the station	la estación	la ehss-*tah*-syohn
the bus stop	la parada	la pah-*rah*-dah
a hotel	un hotel	oon oh-*tehl*
a restaurant	un restaurante	oon res-tow-*rahn*-teh
the toilet	el baño	el *bah*-nyo
To the right	A la derecha	ah lah deh-*reh*-chah
To the left	A la izquierda	ah lah ees-*kyehr*-dah
Straight ahead	Adelante	ah-deh-*lahn*-teh
I would like . . .	Quiero . . .	*kyeh*-roh
to eat	comer	ko-*mehr*
a room	una habitación	oo-nah ah-bee-tah-*syohn*
How much is it?	¿Cuánto?	*kwahn*-toh
The check	La cuenta	la *kwen*-tah
When?	¿Cuándo?	*kwan*-doh
What?	¿Qué?	keh
Yesterday	Ayer	ah-*yehr*
Today	Hoy	oy
Tomorrow	Mañana	mah-*nyah*-nah
Breakfast	Desayuno	deh-sah-*yoo*-noh
Lunch	Comida	coh-*mee*-dah
Dinner	Cena	*seh*-nah
Do you speak English?	¿Habla usted inglés?	*ah*-blah oo-*stehd* een-*glehss*
I don't understand Spanish very well.	No (lo) entiendo muy bien el español.	noh (loh) ehn-*tyehn*-do mwee byehn el ehss-pah-*nyohl*

NUMBERS

English	Spanish	Pronunciation
1	**Uno**	(*oo*-noh)
2	**Dos**	(dohss)
3	**Tres**	(trehss)
4	**Cuatro**	(*kwah*-troh)
5	**Cinco**	(*seen*-koh)
6	**Seis**	(sayss)
7	**Siete**	(*syeh*-teh)
8	**Ocho**	(*oh*-choh)
9	**Nueve**	(*nweh*-beh)
10	**Diez**	(dyehss)

DAYS OF THE WEEK

English	Spanish	Pronunciation
Monday	**Lunes**	(*loo*-nehss)
Tuesday	**Martes**	(*mahr*-tehss)
Wednesday	**Miércoles**	(*myehr*-koh-lehss)
Thursday	**Jueves**	(*wheh*-behss)
Friday	**Viernes**	(*byehr*-nehss)
Saturday	**Sábado**	(*sah*-bah-doh)
Sunday	**Domingo**	(doh-*meen*-goh)

SOME TYPICAL PANAMANIAN WORDS & PHRASES

A la orden   You're welcome.

Bien cuidado   A homeless person or beggar. Means "well taken care of," and refers to what such a person says when seeking a tip for having watched a parked car.

Blanco   Cigarette.

Bomba   Gas station.

Buay   Boy, adapted from English.

Buco   A lot, from the French "beaucoup."

Buenón/buenote   A handsome man.

Casa bruja   Cheap home made of scraps and usually built illegally on taken land.

Chinito   Corner store or small market, so-called because they are usually owned by Chinese descendants.

Cholo   Villager or country bumpkin.

¡Chuleta!   Interjection, akin to "Oh my God!" or "Shoot!"

Con mucho gusto   With pleasure.

Diablo Rojo   Red Devil, name for the old school buses used for public transportation.

Fría   Slang for beer.

Fulo/a   Blonde.

Gallo   Distasteful, tacky, awful.

Goma   Hangover.

Guaro   Hard alcohol.

Guial   Girl, adapted from English.

Ir por fuera   To leave. "*Voy por fuera*" means "I'm leaving."

La "U"   University.

Maleante   Gang member or low-class male.

Mami/Papi   Commonly used to address a stranger with friendly affection, or used to describe an attractive woman or man.

Palo   One dollar or one balboa, as in "It costs 10 *palos*."

Pebre   Food.

Pelado   Young boy, usually pronounced *pelao*.

Policia muerto   Speed bump, means "dead policeman."

Push-button   A pay-by-the-hour motel, adapted from motels that attracted U.S. military personnel and had signs saying "push the button to shut the door."

Priti   Pretty, but can also be used to describe something nice.

Rabiblanco/a   Term for a member of the elite, usually Caucasian. Translated, the term means "white tailed."

Racataca   A low-class, tacky woman.

Refresco   Soft drink.

Tongo   Slang for police officer.

Vaina   Thing or object.

Washington   A dollar.

Yeye   Wealthy show-off.

MENU TERMS

FISH

Almejas   Clams
Atún   Tuna
Bacalao   Cod
Calamares   Squid
Camarones   Shrimp
Cangrejo   Crab
Ceviche   Marinated seafood salad
Corvina   Sea bass

Dorado   Dolphin or mahimahi
Langosta   Lobster
Langostina   Jumbo shrimp
Lenguado   Sole
Ostras   Oysters
Pargo   Red Snapper
Pulpo   Octopus
Trucha   Trout

MEATS

Bistec   Beefsteak
Cordero   Lamb
Costillas   Ribs
Jamón   Ham

Pavo   Turkey
Pollo   Chicken
Puerco   Pork
Tasajo   Gooey smoked beef

VEGETABLES

Aceitunas   Olives
Ensalada   Salad
Lechuga   Lettuce
Ñamé   Starchy root vegetable

Papa   Potato
Tomate   Tomato
Yuca   Cassava or manioc

FRUIT

Fresa   Strawberry
Guayaba   Guava
Manzana   Apple
Maracuyá   Passion fruit
Marañyón   Cashew nut fruit

Naranja   Orange
Piña   Pineapple
Plátano   Plantain
Sandía   Watermelon

BASICS

Aceite Oil
Ajo Garlic
Azúcar Sugar
Bollos Corn patties filled with chicken or coconut
Chicha Fruit juice
Chicheme Sweet and hearty corn drink
Empanada Crunchy cornmeal pastry filled with meat
Emparedado Sandwich
Frito Fried
Gallo Corn tortilla topped with meat or chicken
Gallo pinto Rice and bean soup

Hielo Ice
Limón Lemon
Mantequilla Butter
Miel Honey
Mostaza Mustard
Pan Bread
Patacones Pounded and fried green plantains
Pimienta Pepper
Queso Cheese
Sal Salt
Sancocho Chicken stew
Tamale Filled cornmeal pastry
Tortilla Flat corn pancake

PANAMANIAN WILDLIFE

For such a tiny country, Panama is incredibly rich in biodiversity—some scientists call the country "hyperdiverse" given that flora and fauna from both North and South America meet here on this land bridge. Panama is home to a greater number of bird species than found in the U.S. and Canada combined, and there are more species of plants in the Canal Basin than found in all of Europe. Whether you come to Panama to check 100 or so species off your birding list, or just to check out of the rat race for a week or so, you'll be surrounded by a rich and varied collection of flora and fauna. The information below is meant to be a selective introduction to some of what you might see.

In many instances, the prime viewing recommendations should be taken with a firm dose of reality. Most casual visitors and even many dedicated naturalists will never see a jaguar or kinkajou. However, anyone traveling with a sharp, knowledgeable guide should be able to see a broad selection of Panama's impressive flora and fauna.

FAUNA
Mammals

Panama is home to more than 225 species of mammals. While it is very unlikely that you will spot a puma, you have good odds of catching a glimpse of a monkey, coatimundi, agouti, or sloth.

Jaguar *(Panthera onca)* This cat measures from 1 to 1.8m (3½–6 ft.) plus tail and is distinguished by its tan/yellowish fur with black spots. The name comes from yaguar, a Guaraní (indigenous group from Paraguay) word. **Prime Viewing:** Jaguars exist in major tracts of primary and secondary forest in Panama, as well as savannas and swamps. Jaguars are endangered and are extremely difficult to see in the wild. The largest concentrations of jaguars can be found in La Amistad International Park and Darién National Park.

Jaguar

Ocelot *(Leopardus pardalis)* Commonly mistaken for a margay, ocelots are larger and were once highly valued for their fur. Known for their fierce territorial disputes, ocelots are mostly nocturnal and sleep in trees. **Prime Viewing:** Ocelots are found in forests throughout Panama, especially in La Amistad and Darién parks, and they are occasionally spotted on walks in Soberanía National Park.

Ocelot

Baird's Tapir *(Tapirus bairdii)* Also known as the danta or macho de monte, Baird's tapir is the largest land mammal in Panama, growing to 2m (6½ ft.) in length and 1.2m (4 ft.) in height. Tapirs are active both day and night, foraging along riverbanks, streams, and forest clearings. **Prime Viewing:** An endangered species, tapirs can be found in wet forested areas, particularly on the Caribbean and south Pacific slopes. They are occasionally seen in the Darién wilderness.

Baird's Tapir

Kinkajou *(Potos flavus)* The nocturnal, tree-dwelling **kinkajou** has large eyes that give it a childlike appearance. **Prime Viewing:** Kinkajous are found in forests throughout Panama, but you really need to do a night trip to see one.

Kinkajou

Red Brocket Deer *(Mazama Americana)* These small animals measure 1 to 1.4m (3½–4½ ft.). Their size allows them to slip through dense vegetation. Small, straight antlers distinguish the male. **Prime Viewing:** The **red brocket deer** is easily spotted on Isla Contadora, but is also found in Soberanía National Park and on Isla Coiba.

Red Brocket Deer

Margay *(Leopardus wiedii)* An endangered species, the margay is one of the smaller wild cats of the region, and is often found in trees like its cousin, the ocelot. **Prime Viewing:** Forests in all regions of Panama.

Puma *(Puma concolor)* Nearly 1.5m (5 ft.) long when fully grown, these feline predators are the largest unspotted cats in the region. Also known as a mountain lion, the **puma** is brownish, reddish-brown, or tawny in

Margay

color with a white throat. **Prime Viewing:** Puma prowl in lowland forests, and semi-open areas.

Coatimundi (*Nasua narica*) Known as *gato solo* in Panama, the raccoonlike coatimundi can adapt to habitat disturbances and is often spotted near hotels and nature lodges. Active both day

Puma

and night, it is equally comfortable on the ground and in trees. **Prime Viewing:** Found throughout Panama in lowland rainforest and cloud forests. They are social animals, and are sometimes found in groups of 10 to 20.

Agouti Paca (*Dasyprocta*) The agouti paca is a rabbit-size rodent with glossy orange-brown fur that is easy to see, but they flee in panic when they realize they have been spotted. Agoutis live in rainforest and savanna areas. The agouti is sometimes confused with its larger cousin, the paca. In Panama, they're commonly referred to as *ñeque*, or *conejo pintado*: "painted rabbit." **Prime Viewing:** Agoutis like river valleys, swamps, and dense tropical forest, and they are commonly seen in the Metropolitan Park, on Cerro Ancón, in the Canal Zone, and on Isla Coiba.

Coatimundi

Collared Peccary (*Tayassu tajacu*) Called *saino* in Panama, the collared peccary is a black or brown piglike animal that travels in small groups (larger where populations are still numerous) and has a strong musk odor. **Prime Viewing:** Tropical dry forest and rainforest in most of Panama. Note that peccaries can be aggressive and it's best to keep your distance if you see one.

Agouti Paca

Anteater (*Cyclopes didactylus*) Also known as the pygmy or silky anteater, this nocturnal creature grows up to 18 centimeters (7 in.), not counting its thick tail (which is as long or longer than its body). **Prime Viewing:** The anteater lives in wet tropical forests in all regions of Panama, but

Collared Peccary

can be difficult to spot because it is nocturnal and lives high in trees.

Armadillo (*Dasypus novemcinctus*) The prehistoric-looking armadillo is nocturnal and terrestrial. **Prime Viewing:** Throughout Panama, usually poking around leafy understory.

Three-Toed Sloth (*Bradypus variegates*) The larger and more commonly sighted of Panama's two sloth species, the three-toed sloth has long, coarse brown to gray fur and a distinctive eye band. They have three long and sharp claws on each foreleg. Except for brief periods used for defecation, these slow-moving creatures are entirely arboreal. **Prime Viewing:** Low- and middle-elevation forests in all of Panama. This is one of the most commonly seen animals; look for them hanging on to tree branches.

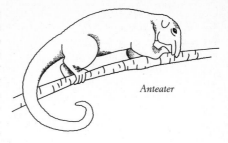

Anteater

Mantled Howler Monkey (*Alouatta palliate*) The highly social mantled howler monkey grows to 56 centimeters (22 in.) in size and often travels in groups of 10 to 30. The characteristic loud roar of the male can be heard as far as 1.6km (1 mile) away. **Prime Viewing:** Wet and dry forests across Panama. Almost entirely arboreal, they tend to favor the higher reaches of the canopy.

Armadillo

Spider Monkey (*Ateles geoffroyi*) Spider monkeys are extremely agile in trees, rarely touching down on the forest floor. They are large monkeys (64cm/25 in.) with brown or silvery fur, and they often sport a worried look. **Prime Viewing:** Throughout the Canal Basin and in the Darién forest.

Three-Toed Sloth

Hairy-Legged Bat (*Myotis keaysi*) The hairy-legged bat grows to a whopping 5.1 centimeters (2 in.) in length, not including the length of its tail. **Prime Viewing:** In caves, forests, rock crevices, gardens, and buildings throughout Panama.

Birds

Panama has more than 940 identified species of resident and migrant birds. The variety of habitats and compact nature of the country make it a major bird-watching destination.

Keel-Billed Toucan (*Ramphastos sulfuratus*) The rainbow-colored canoe-shape bill and brightly colored feathers make the keel-billed toucan a

Mantled Howler Monkey

Spider Monkey

favorite of bird-watching tours. The toucan can grow to about 51 centimeters (20 in.) in length. It's similar in size and shape to the chestnut mandibled toucan. Panama also is home to several smaller toucanet and aracari species. **Prime Viewing:** Lowland forests on the Caribbean and north Pacific slopes. The keel-billed toucan is often spotted around the Canal Zone and in the Darién.

Hairy-Legged Bat

Scarlet Macaw *(Ara macao)* Known as *guacamaya* in Panama, the scarlet macaw is a long-tailed member of the parrot family. It can reach 89 centimeters (35 in.) in length. The bird is endangered over most of its range, particularly because it is so coveted as a pet. Its loud squawk and rainbow-colored feathers are quite distinctive. **Prime Viewing:** Given the declining numbers of scarlet macaws in the wild, Isla Coiba National Park is the only region where these magnificent birds exist in numbers.

Keel-Billed Toucan

Resplendent Quetzal *(Pharomchrus mocinno)* Perhaps the most distinctive and spectacular bird in Central America, the resplendent quetzal, of the trogon family, can grow to 37 centimeters (15 in.). The males are distinctive, with bright red chests, iridescent blue-green coats, a yellow bill, and tail feathers that can reach another 76 centimeters (30 in.) in length. The females lack the long tail feathers and have a duller beak and less pronounced red chest. **Prime Viewing:** High-elevation wet and cloud forests, particularly in Volcán Barú National Park and the Finca Lérida estate near Boquete.

Scarlet Macaw

Magnificent Frigate Bird *(Fregata magnificens)* The magnificent frigate bird is a naturally agile flier and it swoops (unlike other seabirds, it doesn't dive or swim) to pluck food from the water's surface or—more commonly—it steals catch from the mouths of other birds. **Prime Viewing:** Along the shores and coastal islands of both coasts. Often seen soaring high overhead.

Montezuma's Oropendola *(Psarocolius Montezuma)* Montezuma's oropendola has a black head, brown body, a yellow-edged tail, a large black bill with an orange tip, and a blue patch under the eye. These birds build long, teardrop-shape hanging nests, often found in large groups. They have several distinct loud calls,

Resplendent Quetzal

including one that they make while briefly hanging upside down. **Prime Viewing:** Low and middle elevations along the Caribbean slope, especially around Bocas del Toro. The black oropendola lives east of the Canal Zone.

Amphibians

Frogs, toads, and salamanders are actually some of the most beguiling, beautiful, and easy-to-spot residents of tropical forests.

Red-Eyed Tree Frog (*Agalychnis callidryas*) The colorful 7.6-centimeter (3-in.) red-eyed tree frog usually has a pale or dark green back, sometimes with white or yellow spots, with blue-purple patches and vertical bars on the body, orange hands and feet, and deep red eyes. Also known as the gaudy leaf frog. Nocturnal. **Prime Viewing:** Low- and middle-elevation wet forests throughout Panama. This is a very beautiful and distinctive-looking frog that you will often see on T-shirts and postcards if not in the wild.

Reptiles

Panama's reptile species range from the frightening and justly feared fer-de-lance pit viper and massive American crocodile to a wide variety of turtles and lizards. **Note:** Sea turtles are included in "Sea Life," below.

Boa Constrictor (*Boa constrictor*) Adult boa constrictors average about 1.8 to 3m (6–10 ft.) in length and weigh over 27 kilograms (60 lb.). Their coloration camouflages them, but look for patterns of cream, brown, gray, and black ovals and diamonds. **Prime Viewing:** Low- and middle-elevation wet and dry forests, countrywide. They often live in rafters and eaves of homes in rural areas.

Fer-de-Lance (*Bothrops atrox*) The aggressive fer-de-lance is a pit viper that can grow to 2.4m (8 ft.) in length, and it is considered the most dangerous snake of Central and South America. Beige, brown, or black triangles flank either side of the head, while the area under the head is a vivid yellow. These snakes begin life as arboreal but become increasingly terrestrial as they grow older and larger. **Prime Viewing:** All regions, but especially the Darién.

Green Iguana (*Iguana iguana*) Green iguanas can vary in shades ranging from bright green to a

Magnificent Frigate Bird

Montezuma's Oropendola

Red-Eyed Tree Frog

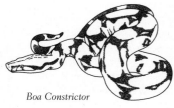

Boa Constrictor

Fer-de-Lance

dull grayish-green, with quite a bit of orange mixed in. The iguana will often perch on a branch overhanging a river and plunge into the water when threatened. **Prime Viewing:** All lowland regions of the country, living near rivers and streams, along both coasts.

Green Iguana

Basilisk (*Basiliscus vittatus*) The basilisk can run across the surface of water for short distances by using its hind legs and holding its body almost upright; thus, the reptile is also known as "the Jesus Christ lizard." **Prime Viewing:** In trees and on rocks located near water in wet forests throughout the country.

Basilisk

American Crocodile (*Crocodylus acutus*) Although an endangered species, environmental awareness and protection policies have allowed the massive American crocodile to mount an impressive

American Crocodile

comeback in recent years. While these reptiles can reach lengths of 6.4m (21 ft.), most are much smaller, usually less than 4m (13 ft.). **Prime Viewing:** Near swamps, mangrove swamps, estuaries, large rivers, and coastal lowlands, country-wide. You'll see these beasts in the canal and the Chagres River.

Sea Life

With 2,490km (1,547 miles) of shoreline on both the Pacific and Caribbean coasts, Panama has a rich diversity of underwater flora and fauna.

Whale Shark (*Rhincodon typus*) Although the whale shark grows to lengths of 14m (45 ft.) or more, its gentle nature makes swimming with them a special treat for divers and snorkelers. **Prime Viewing:** Whale sharks can be seen in the Pacific, off Coiba Island and around the Pearl Islands.

Whale Shark

Leatherback Sea Turtle (*Dermochelys coriacea*) The world's largest sea turtle (reaching nearly 2.4m/8 ft. in length and weighing more than 544kg/1,200 lb.), the leatherback sea turtle is now an endangered species. **Prime Viewing:** These large reptiles nest in the Caribbean around Bocas del Toro on beaches on Isla Bastimentos and in the San San Pond Sak Wetlands; in the Pacific, they are known to nest on Isla Cañas.

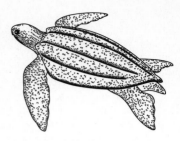

Leatherback Sea Turtle

Olive Ridley Sea Turtle (*Lepidochelys olivacea*) Also known as tortuga mulata, the olive ridley sea turtle is the smallest of the turtles that visit Panama, and they are famous for their massive group nestings, or *arribadas*. **Prime Viewing:** There is no guaranteed date for viewing an *arribada,* but you definitely won't see one during the dry season from December to March. The best site to view these turtles is at Isla Cañas.

Olive Ridley Sea Turtle

Manatee (*Trichechus manatus*) Manatees in Panama are Antillean manatees, a subspecies of the West Indian manatee. These "sea cows" can reach lengths of 3 to 4m (10–13 ft.) and weigh 499 to 1,588 kilograms (1,100–3,500 lb.).

Manatee

Prime Viewing: Coastal mangroves, especially in the San San Pond Sak Wetlands, and along the coast of the Comarca Kuna Yala.

Manta Ray (*Manta birostris*) **Manta rays** are the largest type of rays, with a wingspan that can reach 6m (20 ft.) and a body weight known to exceed 1,361 kilograms (3,000 lb.). Despite their daunting appearance, manta rays are quite gentle. If you are snorkeling or diving, watch for one of these extraordinary and graceful creatures. **Prime Viewing:** In mangrove swamps and coral reef, especially alongside steep walls and drop-offs, in the Caribbean and Pacific.

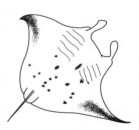

Manta Ray

Stingray (*Dasyatis Americana*) True to their name, stingrays can give you a painful shock if you touch the venomous spine at the base of their tails. Be careful when wading in sandy areas, where they prefer to bury themselves. **Prime Viewing:** Along both coasts and around islands, especially in shallow sand or grassy areas.

Stingray

Nurse Shark *(Ginglymostoma cirratum)* The most frequently spotted shark in Panamanian waters, the nurse shark spends most of its time resting on the ocean floor. Reaching lengths of 4.3m (14 ft.), their heads are larger than those of most sharks, and they appear to be missing the bottom half of their tail. **Prime Viewing:** Along the coast and especially around offshore islands.

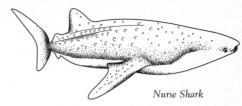

Nurse Shark

Barracuda *(Sphyraena barracuda)* The barracuda is a slender fish with two dorsal fins and a large mouth. Juvenile barracudas often swim near the shore, so exercise caution, as attacks on humans occasionally occur. **Prime Viewing:** Found in both the Caribbean and Pacific oceans.

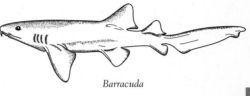

Barracuda

Moray Eel *(Gymnothorax mordax)* Distinguished by a swaying serpent-head and teeth-filled jaw that continually opens and closes, the moray eel is most commonly seen with only its head appearing from behind rocks. At night, however, it leaves its home along the reef to hunt for small fish, crustaceans, shrimp, and octopus. **Prime Viewing:** Rocky areas and reefs off both coasts.

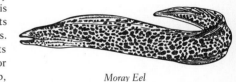

Moray Eel

Humpbacked Whale *(Megaptera novaeangliae)* The migratory humpbacked whale spends the winters in the Southern Hemisphere and migrates north along the Pacific Coast from June to September. These mammals have black backs and whitish throat and chest areas. Whales breed when spending time off the coast of Panama. **Prime Viewing:** Humpback whales can be spotted off the shore of the Pacific Coast, around Coiba Island, the Pearl Islands, and the Azuero Peninsula.

Humpbacked Whale

Bottle-Nosed Dolphin *(Tursiops truncates)* Their wide tail fin, dark gray back, and light gray sides identify bottle-nosed dolphins. Dolphins grow to lengths of 3.7m (12 ft.) and weigh up to 635 kilograms (1,400 lb.). **Prime Viewing:** Along both coasts, especially in Dolphin Bay in Bocas del Toro, the Gulf of Chiriquí, and around Punta Patiño.

Brain Coral *(Diploria strigosa)* The distinctive brain coral is named for its striking physical similarity to a human brain. **Prime Viewing:** Reefs off both coasts.

Bottle-Nosed Dolphin

Invertebrates

Creepy-crawlies, biting bugs, spiders, and the like give most folks chills. But this group, which includes moths, butterflies, ants, beetles, and even crabs, includes some of the most fascinating and easily viewed fauna in Panama.

Blue Morpho *(Morpho peleides)* The large blue morpho butterfly, with a wingspan of up to 15 centimeters (6 in.), has brilliantly iridescent blue wings when opened. Fast and erratic fliers, they are often glimpsed flitting across your peripheral vision in dense forest. **Prime Viewing:** Countrywide, particularly in moist environments.

Brain Coral

Blue Morpho

Leafcutter Ants *(Atta cephalote)* You can't miss the miniature rainforest highways formed by these industrious little red leafcutter ants carrying their freshly cut payload. The ants do not actually eat the leaves, but instead feed off a fungus that grows on the decomposing leaves in their massive underground nests. **Prime Viewing:** Can be found in most forests countrywide.

Golden Silk Spider *(Nephila clavipes)* The common Neotropical golden silk spider weaves meticulous webs that can be as much as .5m (2 ft.) across. The adult female of this species can reach 7.6 centimeters (3 in.) in length, including the legs, although the males are tiny. The silk of this spider is extremely strong and is being studied for industrial purposes. **Prime Viewing:** Lowland forests on both coasts.

Mouthless Crab *(Gecarcinus quadratus)* The nocturnal mouthless crab is a distinctively colored land crab with bright orange legs, purple claws, and a deep black shell or carapace. **Prime Viewing:** All along the Pacific Coast.

Leafcutter Ants

Golden Silk Spider

FLORA

Trees

It's often a good thing to be able to identify specific trees within a forest. We've included illustrations to get you started.

Mouthless Crab

Ceiba *(Ceiba pentandra)* Also known as the kapok tree, ceiba trees are typically emergent (their large umbrella-shape canopies emerge above the forest canopy), making the species among the tallest trees

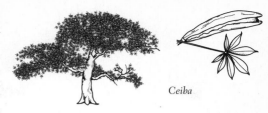

Ceiba

in the tropical forest. Reaching as high as 60m (197 ft.), their thick columnar trunks often have large buttresses. Ceiba trees may flower as little as once every 5 years, especially in wetter forests. **Prime Viewing:** Countrywide.

Guanacaste *(Enterolobium cyclocarpum)* The guanacaste tree is one of the largest trees found in Central America, and is called *corotu* in Panama. It can reach a total elevation of over 39m (130 ft.); its

Guanacaste

straight trunk composes 9 to 12m (30–40 ft.) of the height (the trunk's diameter measures more than 1.8m/6 ft.). **Prime Viewing:** Countrywide.

Strangler Fig *(Ficus aurea)* This parasitic tree gets its name from the fact that it envelops and eventually strangles its host tree. The *matapalo,* or **strangler fig,** begins as an epiphyte, whose seeds are deposited high in a tree's canopy by bats, birds, or monkeys. The young strangler then sends long roots down to the earth. The sap is used to relieve burns. **Prime Viewing:** Primary and secondary forests countrywide.

Strangler Fig

Cecropia *(Cecropia obtusifolia)* Several cecropia (trumpet tree) species are found in Panama. Most are characterized by large, hand-like clusters of broad leaves, and a hollow, bamboolike trunk. They are "gap specialists," fast-growing opportunists that can fill in a gap caused by a tree fall or landslide. Their trunks are usually home to Aztec ants. **Prime Viewing:** Primary and secondary forests, rivers, and roadsides, countrywide.

Cecropia

Gumbo Limbo *(Bursera simaruba)* The bark of the gumbo limbo is its most distinguishing feature: A paper-thin red outer layer, when peeled off the tree, reveals a bright green bark. In Panama the tree is called *carate,* and the peeling bark is a defense against invasive vegetation like the strangler fig. The bark is used as a remedy for gum disease; gumbo limbo–bark tea allegedly alleviates hypertension. Another remarkable property is the tree's ability to root from its cut branches, which when planted right end up, develop roots and leaves, forming a new tree within a few years. **Prime Viewing:** Primary and secondary forests, countrywide.

Gumbo Limbo

Flowers & Other Plants

Panama's biodiversity is exemplified by its 10,000 species of plants.

Heliconia (*Heliconia collinsiana*) Heliconias are closely related to bananas and birds of paradise, and their beautiful, crab claw–shaped pink flowers are commonly used as ornamental decoration. **Prime Viewing:** Low to middle elevations countrywide, usually found along streams and lakes.

Heliconia

Hotlips (*Psychotria poeppigiana*) Related to coffee, hotlips is a forest flower that boasts thick red "lips" that resemble the Rolling Stones logo. The small white flowers (found inside the red "lips") attract a variety of butterflies and hummingbirds. **Prime Viewing:** In the undergrowth of dense forests countrywide.

Poor Man's Umbrella (*Gunnera insignis*) The poor man's umbrella, a broad-leafed rainforest ground plant, is a member of the rhubarb family. The massive leaves are often used, as the colloquial name suggests, for protection during rainstorms. **Prime Viewing:** Low- to middle-elevation moist forests countrywide. Commonly seen in the Chiriquí Highlands.

Hotlips

Poor Man's Umbrella

Index

See also Accommodations and Restaurant indexes, below.

General Index

A

Abercrombie & Kent, 60
Accommodations. *See also* Accommodations Index
  best
    ecolodges and wilderness resorts, 11–13
    luxury hotels and resorts, 10–11
    small hotels and B&Bs, 13–14
  gay-friendly, 43
  green-friendly, 45
  price categories, 47
  tips on, 47–48
  tour operators and, 63
Achiote, 153
Achiote Road, 8, 152–153
Achotines Laboratory (Playa Venado), 210
ACS Motorcycle Tours, 71
Advantage Tours Panama, 5, 7, 9, 64, 67, 121, 125, 143–145, 148, 153, 302, 303
Adventure Life Journeys, 62
Adventures in Panama, 64, 65, 143, 151, 293
Adventures Panama Canal, 143, 145
Adventure travel, 59–78. *See also specific activities and destinations*
  activities, 64–74
  best, 4–6
  ecologically oriented volunteer and study programs, 78
  etiquette and safety tips, 77–78
  organized adventure trips (tour operators), 60–64
    Boquete, 232–233
    Comarca Kuna Yala, 292–293
    El Valle, 187
    Volcán, 220–221
  parks and reserves, 74–77
  suggested itinerary, 56–58
Aero Perlas, 36
Aeroperlas, 262
Afro-Caribbeans (creoles), 17
Agouti paca, 321
Air Panama, 36
Air travel, 35, 36, 80–81
Aizpurua, Nariño, 233

Alamo, 36
Albrook Airport (Panama City), 35, 81
Albrook Mall (Panama City), 126
Albrook (Panama City), 85
Alemancia, Gilberto, 293
Alhambra (David), 217
Al Tambor a la Alegría (Panama City), 131
Altos de Campana National Park, 75, 183–184
Amador Causeway (Panama City), 85, 122
  biking, 123
  restaurants, 110–112
American Airlines, 35
American Express, 308
  emergency number, 309–310
  Panama City, 88
Amphibians, 324
Ancla Sport Bar (Panama City), 132
Ancon Expeditions, 5, 7–9, 12, 54, 63, 64, 67, 113, 121, 125, 138, 143–145, 151, 153, 269, 271, 281, 301, 303–305
Ancón Theater Guild (Panama City), 130
Anemos (Panama City), 133
Anteaters, 321
Aparthotels, 48
Aprovaca Orquídeas (El Valle), 187
Archipiélago de las Perlas (Pearl Islands), 135, 164–171
Area Bancaria (Financial District, Panama City)
  accommodations, 93–97
  restaurants, 102–104
Armadillo, 321
Artesanía Bri-Bri Emanuel (Bocas Town), 278
Artesanías Cruz Volcán, 222
Art galleries, Panama City, 128–129
Arts & Antiques (Panama City), 128
Asociación Agroecoturística La Amistad (ASAELA), 226
Atlapa Convention Center (Panama City), 131
ATMs (automated-teller machines), 38
ATP (Autoridad de Turismo de Panama), 32, 81
Australia
  consular assistance, 308
  customs regulations, 34
  passports, 310
Avenida Central (Panama City), 127
Aventuras Panama, 71, 146, 147
Aventuras 2000, 151
Aventurist (Boquete), 232, 236
Avis, 36

Azuero Peninsula, 4, 197–214
  festivals and special events, 198

B

Bahía Damas, 252
Bahía Honda, 280, 282
Bahía Piñas, 306–307
Baird's tapir, 320
Bajareque, 230
Bajo Mono Loop, 232
Bambito, 224
Bar Baviera (Panama City), 132
Barco Hundido (Bocas Town), 278
Bar Platea (Panama City), 131
Barracuda, 327
Barrio Bolívar (David), 216
Barro Colorado National Monument, 76, 146
Barú Volcano National Park, 2, 7, 76, 224–225
  exploring, 233–236
Basilica Menor Santiago Apostal de Natá, 197
Basilisk, 325
Bastimentos Day (Bocas Town), 270
Bastimentos Town, 280
Batería Santiago (Portobelo), 155
Beaches. *See also specific beaches*
  best, 3–4
  Isla Bastimentos, 281–282
  Isla Colón, 265
  Isla Contadora, 166
  Pacific Coast, 173–183
  Pedasí, 207
  riptides, 42
Bed & breakfasts (B&Bs), best, 13–14
Beer, 29
Bella Vista (Panama City), 86
  restaurants, 102–104
Bennigan's Irish Grill (Panama City), 132
Best of Both Adventures for Women (Bocas Town), 269, 270
Beverages, 29
Bike Hike Adventures, 62, 65
Bikes & More (Panama City), 123
Bikes Moses (Panama City), 123
Biking and mountain biking, 65
  Bocas Town, 263
  Boquete, 236
  El Valle, 185
  Panama City and environs, 123, 143
Birds and bird-watching, 6, 65–67
  Altos de Campana National Park, 183–184
  best, 7–8
  Boquete, 232–233
  Chiriquí Highlands, 212

GENERAL INDEX

Birds and bird-watching (cont.)
Darién National Park,
304–305
El Valle, 186
field guides, 26
Finca Hartmann, 222
Finca Lérida (Boquete), 238
lodges and tour operators,
65–66
Panama City, 125
species of birds, 322–324
tips for, 25
Blackberry wine, 220
**Black Christ Festival (Festival
del Cristo Negro; Portobelo),
33, 154**
Blades, Ruben, 26
BLG (Panama City), 134
Blue cotingas, 8, 66, 153
Blue morpho butterfly, 328
**Blue Nasty Mermaid (Bocas
Town), 278**
Bluff Beach, 265
**Blu Room Martini Lounge
(Panama City), 133**
Boa constrictor, 324
Boat trips and cruises
Bocas del Toro, 262, 268–269
Bocas Town, 278
Comarca Kuna Yala, 292
Isla Grande, 160
Lake Gatún, 144
Panama Canal, 138–139
Portobelo, 157
Boca Brava Divers, 249
Boca Chica, 4
Boca del Drago, 264
Boca del Drago Beach, 265
**Bocas del Toro Archipelago, 9,
50, 52, 258–286**
climate, 260, 267
healthcare, 266
money matters, 263
riptides, 260
surfing, 73
wildlife, 24
Bocas Marine & Tours, 262
**Bocas Surf School (Bocas Town),
73, 269–270**
Bocas Town, 258, 260, 264–277
accommodations, 270–274
bookstore, 264
emergencies, 264
nightlife, 278
post office, 264
restaurants, 274–277
shopping, 278
sights and attractions,
264–270
Bocas Water Sports, 267, 268
Bocas Yoga (Bocas Town), 270
Books, recommended, 25–26
Boquete, 65, 229–248
accommodations, 240–244
ATMs, 230
getting around, 229–230

nightlife, 247
orientation, 230
restaurants, 244–247
shopping, 240
sights and attractions,
230–239
traveling to and from, 229
**Boquete Mountain Safari Tours,
232, 240**
**Boquete Outdoor Adventures,
10, 71, 236, 254**
Boquete Tree Trek, 236
**Boteros Bocatoreños (Bocas
Town), 268**
**Boteros Nuestra Senora del
Carmen (Bocas Town),
268–269**
Bottle-nosed dolphin, 327
Brain coral, 328
Breakfast, 27
Breebaart (Panama City), 129
Bri Bri Indians, 17
**Bridge of Life Biodiversity
Museum (Panama City), 122**
British Airways, 35
Budget, 36
Buenaventura Bristol, 72
Buena Vista (Bocas Town), 278
Bugs and bites, 40–41
**Buoy Line (near Isla Solarte),
267**
Business hours, 308
Bus travel, 37
Buzios (Panama City), 132–133
Buzos de Azuero (Pedasí), 207

C
**Caballero, Santiago "Chago,"
7, 233**
Cable & Wireless, 46
Café Havana (Panama City), 133
**Café Kotowa (Boquete),
237–238, 240**
Café Ruiz (Boquete), 237
Cahill Fishing, 68
**Caldera Hot Springs (Boquete),
236–237**
**Calendar of events and festivals,
32–33**
Calidonia (Panama City), 85
Caligo Ventures, 66
**Calzada de Amador (Amador
Causeway; Panama City),
85, 122**
biking, 123
restaurants, 110–112
Camino de Cruces, 143
**Camino de Oleoducto (Pipeline
Road), 142–143**
Camping
Kuna Islands, 294
Sierra Llorona, 149
Canada
customs regulations, 34
embassy, 308

health plan, 309
passports, 310
**Cana Field Station, 7, 12, 66, 67,
305–306**
**Canal Administration Building
(Panama City), 120–121**
Canal & Bay Tours, 138
The Canal Zone, 9, 50, 139–149
Caño, Eduardo, 236
Canopy Adventure, 4, 56, 186
Canopy tours (zip-lining), 4–5
Boquete, 236
El Valle, 186
Canopy Tower, 186
Carnaval (Carnival), 31, 32
Azuero Peninsula, 197, 198
Las Tablas, 203, 204
Car rentals, 36–37
Cartí, 294
Car travel, 36–37
Casa Blanca (Panama City), 132
**Casa de la Cultura y del Artista
Panameño (Panama City), 119**
Casa de Lourdes (El Valle), 188
**Casa Fuerte Santiago
(Portobelo), 155**
Casa Góngora (Panama City), 119
Casa Ruiz, S.A., 237
Casaya Island, 167
Casco Viejo (Panama City), 85
accommodations, 99
restaurants, 104–106
sights and attractions, 115–119
Casinos
David, 217
Panama City, 134
**Castillo Santiago de la Gloria
(Portobelo), 155**
**Catamaran Sailing Adventures
(Bocas Town), 268**
**Catedral de San Juan Bautista
(Chitré), 200**
**Catedral Metropolitana
(Metropolitan Cathedral;
Panama City), 116**
**Cathedral Tower (Panama City),
114–115**
Cayos Holandéses, 293
Cayos Zapatillas, 265, 267, 281
Cecropia, 329
Ceiba, 329
Cellphones, 45–46
**Centers for Disease Control and
Prevention, 39**
Central Panama, 50, 172–211
**Centro de Conservación de
Anfibios de El Valle (EVACC),
188**
Centro El Tucán (Achiote), 153
**Centro Médico Paitilla (Panama
City), 89**
**Cerámica Calderón (La Arena),
200**
Cerro Ancón (Panama City), 85
accommodations, 97–98
sights and attractions,
120–123

Cerro Gaital National Monument, 186
Cerro Punta, 224
Chagres River, 70, 145
Changuinola, 262
Chestnut-mandible toucans, 8, 153
Chiggers, 41
Chiriquí Gulf National Marine Park, 75, 248–252
Chiriquí Highlands, 10, 212
Chiriquí Mall (David), 217
Chiriquí River, 70, 235
Chiriquí River Rafting, 4, 10, 57, 71, 221, 235
Chiriquí Viejo River, 70, 235
Chitré, 199–202
Chucanti Field Station, 302
Church and Convent of St. Francis of Assisi (Panama City), 118
Cienequita Trail (Panama City), 121
Cigarros de Panamá (La Pintada), 195
ClaroCOM, 89, 311
Climate, 23, 31
Clínica Hospital San Fernando (Panama City), 89
Cloud forests, 24
Coatimundi, 321
Coba, Abelardo, 220
Coclé Province, western, 194–197
Coffee Adventures, 8, 232, 233, 237
Coffee farms and estates
  Boquete, 240
  Boquete area, 237–238
  Boquete Mountain Safari Tours, 232
  Finca Hartmann (near Volcán), 222–223
  La Torcaza Estate (Volcán), 221–222
Coiba Adventure, 253
Coiba National Park, 75
Collared peccary, 321
Colón, 42, 139, 149–153
Colón Free Zone, 151
Colón 2000, 149, 151
Comarca Kuna Yala (San Blas Archipelago), 2–3, 52, 287–299
  eastern, 297–299
  getting around, 292–293
  Kuna revolution, 295
  Kuna villages, 294
  special considerations in, 291
  western, 290–297
Congos, 17
Continental Airlines, 35
Coral Cay (Crawl Cay), 267, 282
Coral Dreams (Isla Contadora), 167
Coral Lodge, 67
Corazón de Jesús, 297

Coronado Golf & Beach Resort, 69
Corotu Bookstore (Panama City), 25, 88
Corpus Christi (La Villa de Los Santos), 32, 198
Costa Blanca Golf & Villas, 69–70
Country Inn & Suites Causeway, 8
Country Walkers, 62
Crater Valley Adventure Spa (El Valle), 188
Crawl Cay (Coral Cay), 267, 282
Credit cards, 38
Cruises. See Boat trips and cruises
Currency and currency exchange, 37–38
Customs House (Real Aduana de Portobelo), 155
Customs regulations, 34

D
Danuta's Holistic Therapy (Bocas Town), 270
Darién National Park, 7, 76, 304–306
Darién Province, 23–24, 42, 52, 300–307
  western, 301–303
The Darién Wilderness, 2
David, 214–219
David's (El Valle), 189
Decapolis Radisson, 72
Decapolis Radisson Sushi Bar & Martini Lounge (Panama City), 133
Deli Barú (Boquete), 245
Delta, 35
Delta Airlines, 35
Del Toro Surf (Bocas Town), 269
Dengue fever, 40
Desserts, 28
Diablo Ross Gallery (Panama City), 128
Día de la Virgen del Carmen (Bocas Town), 270
Diarrhea, traveler's, 40
Dietary distress, 40
Dining. See also Restaurants Index
  best, 14–15
  Central Panama road stops and hole in the walls, 174
  menu terms, 317–318
Disabilities, travelers with, 42
Diving, 5, 67–68
  Bocas del Toro, 267–269
  Chiriquí Gulf, 248–249
  Isla Coiba, 252, 254
  Isla Contadora, 167
  Isla Grande, 160
  Pedasí, 207
  Portobelo, 156–157
  Santa Catalina, 255–256

Dollar, 36
Donde Daniel (El Valle), 185
Drinking laws, 308
Dry season, 31

E
Eagles, harpy, 6–8, 52, 76, 147, 225, 302, 303
Easy Travel Panama, 80
Eating and drinking, 27–29
Ecocircuitos, 9, 63–64, 151, 232, 236, 292, 302, 304
Ecolodges and wilderness resorts, 47–48. See also Accommodations
  best, 11–13
  for bird-watching, 65–66
Ecologically oriented volunteer and study programs, 78
Economy, 17–18
Ecosystems, 23–25
Eco-tourism, 44
Ecotravel.com, 44
Ego & Narciso (Panama City), 132
El Cangrejo (Panama City), 86
  accommodations, 93–97
  restaurants, 106–110
El Caño Archaeological Park, 196
Electricity, 308
El Explorador gardens (Boquete), 238–239
El Hombre de la Mancha (Panama City), 88
El Nispero Zoo (El Valle), 187–188
El Pavo Real (Panama City), 133
El Porvenir, 290–297
El Rey supermarket chain (Panama City), 89, 102
El Rincón de la Biodiversidad (El Valle), 188
El Valle de Antón, 9, 65, 184–194
  accommodations, 189–192
  getting around, 185
  outdoor activities, 185–187
  restaurants, 192–194
  shopping, 189
  spas, 188–189
  traveling to/from, 184–185
  visitor information, 185
  zoos and museums, 187–188
Embassies and consulates, 308
The Emberá, 17
Emberá Indians, 189, 302, 303
  villages, 9, 145–146
Emergencies, 308
Entry requirements, 33–34
Environmentally Friendly Hotels, 45
EPA! (Panama City), 113
Escribano Island, 156
Esti River, 70, 235
Ethical tourism, 44
Etiquette and customs, 308–309
Etiquette and safety in the wilderness, 77–78

European Health Insurance Card (EHIC), 309
Evac Americas, 266
EVACC (Centro de Conservación de Anfibios de El Valle), 188
Exedra Books (Panama City), 88

F

Families with children, 43
best destinations for, 8–10
suggested itinerary, 55–56
Farallón, 4, 181–183
Farmacias Arrocha (Panama City), 89
Fauna, 23, 319–328
Felipe Motta (Panama City), 102
Fer-de-lance, 324
Feria de David, 32
Feria de las Flores y del Café (Flower and Coffee Festival; Boquete), 32, 239
Feria de las Tierras Altas (Volcán), 33
Feria de Orquídeas (Orchid Festival; Boquete), 32, 239
Feria Internacional del Azuero (La Villa de Los Santos), 32, 198
Fería Internacional del Mar (Bocas Town), 33, 270
Feria Internacional de San José de David, 216
Festival Corpus Christi (La Villa de Los Santos), 32
Festival de la Mejorana (Guararé), 33, 198
Festival de la Pollera (Las Tablas), 32, 198
Festival del Cristo Negro (Black Christ Festival; Portobelo), 33
Festival Patronales de La Virgen de Santa Librada (Las Tablas), 32, 198
Festivals and special events, 32–33
Field Guides, 66
Field guides, 26
Fiesta Casino (David), 217
Figali Convention Center (Panama City), 131
Finca Dracula, 226
Finca Fresas Pariente (Cerro Punta), 225
Finca Hartmann (near Volcán), 222–223
Finca Lérida (Boquete), 7, 238
Finca Suiza (near David), 6, 232, 247–248
First Beach (Wizard Beach), 280
Fishing, 5, 68–69
Chiriquí Gulf, 249
Gatún Lake, 144–145
Isla Coiba, 253–254
Pearl Islands, 167
Truchas Bambito, 226

Flamenco Shopping Plaza (Panama City), 128
Flamingo Center (Panama City), 126
Flora, 23, 328–330
Flory Saltzman Molas (Panama City), 128
Flow (Bocas Town), 269
Flower and Coffee Festival (Feria de las Flores y del Café; Boquete), 32, 239
Flowers, 330
Aprovaca Orquídeas (El Valle), 187
Finca Dracula, 226
Orchid Festival (Feria de Orquídeas; Boquete), 32
Panaflores (Cerro Punta), 225
Food and cuisine, 27–29
menu terms, 317–318
Foodie (Panama City), 102
Fort San Lorenzo, 135, 152–153
Frank Gehry Biodiversity Museum, 8
Fruit, 28
Fuerte San Fernando (Portobelo), 155
Fuerte San Jerónimo (Portobelo), 156
Fundación de la Provincia de Bocas del Toro (Bocas Town), 270
Fundación del Distrito de Chitré, 198
Futura Tours, 64

G

Galeria de Arte (Boquete), 240
Galería de Arte Indígena (Panama City), 129
Galería y Enmarcado Habitante (Panama City), 128
Gamboa, 139–149
accommodations, 147–149
sights and attractions, 140
tour operators, 141
traveling to, 140
Gamboa Rainforest Resort, 9, 68, 72, 136
jungle cruise, 144
Gamboa Tours, 145
Gardi Sugdup, 294
Gariche River, 235
Gasoline, 309
Gatún Dam, 152
Gatún Lake, 144–145
Gatún Locks, 152
Gays and lesbians, 42–43
Panama City, 134
Glam: The Club (Panama City), 134
Global Works, 78
Gloria Mendez Tours (Panama City), 113
Golden frog, 189
Golden silk spider, 328

Golf, 69–70
Mantaray Golf Course (Playa Blanca), 183
Golfo de Chiriquí, 75, 248–252
Gone Fishing, 69
González, Feliciano, 232
Granclement (Panama City), 105
Granito de Oro, 252
Gran Morrison chain (Panama City), 88, 129
Green iguana, 324–325
Grito de la Villa (Villa de Los Santos), 198
Guadalupe, 224
Guanacaste tree, 329
Guararé, 203
Gulf of Chiriquí, 52
Gulf of Chiriquí National Marine Park, 75, 248–252
Gumbo limbo, 329–330

H

Habana Panama (Panama City), 131
Habla Ya Spanish School (Boquete), 238
Hacienda del Toro, 70
Hairy-legged bat, 322
Handicrafts and gifts
Bocas Town, 278
Boquete, 240
El Valle, 189
La Arena, 200
Mercado de Artesanías La Arena, 200
La Pintada, 195
Penonomé, 194
Panama City, 128–129
Tolé, 255
Volcán, 222
Harmony Gift Shop (Boquete), 240
Harpy eagles, 6–8, 52, 76, 147, 225, 302, 303
Haven Spa (Boquete), 72, 233
Health concerns, 38–41
Heatstroke, 41
Heliconias, 330
Hepatitis A, 40
Hertz, 36
Highlands—Adventures/Turismo Ecologico (Volcán), 221
High season, 31, 48
Hikes and nature walks. See also specific destinations
Altos de Campana National Park, 183–184
best, 6–7
Boquete, 232
El Valle, 186
Finca Suiza, 247
Isla Coiba, 253
Parque Internacional La Amistad, 225–226
Volcán Barú National Park, 224–225, 234–235

Hipódromo Presidente Remón (Panama City), 125
History of Panama, 16–22
books on, 25–26
Holidays, 31–32
Holistic Alternative Therapy (Bocas Town), 270
Holy Week, 32
Horseback riding, 70
Boquete, 236
El Valle, 187
Santa Clara, 179
Horse racing, Panama City, 125
Hospital Nacional (Panama City), 89
Hospital Point, 267, 285
Hospital Punta Pacífica (Panama City), 89
Hotel Central (Panama City), 116
Hotels. See also Accommodations Index
best
ecolodges and wilderness resorts, 11–13
luxury hotels and resorts, 10–11
small hotels and B&Bs, 13–14
gay-friendly, 43
green-friendly, 45
price categories, 47
tips on, 47–48
tour operators and, 63
Hotlips, 330
Hot springs
Boquete, 236–237
El Valle, 187
Los Pozos Termales (Volcán), 222
Howler monkey, 322
Humpbacked whale, 327

I

IAMAT (International Association for Medical Assistance to Travelers), 39
Iglesia de la Merced (Panama City), 119
Iglesia de San Atanacio (La Villa de los Santos), 202
Iglesia de San Felipe (Portobelo), 156
Iglesia de San José (Panama City), 119
Iglesia de San Juan (Portobelo), 156
Iglesia de Santo Domingo de Guzmán (Parita), 198
Iglesia de Santo Domingo (Panama City), 119
Iglesia San Felipe de Neri (Panama City), 118
Iglesia San Pedro (Isla Taboga), 163

Iglesia y Convento de San Francisco de Asís (Panama City), 118
Iguana Bar and Surf Club (Bocas Town), 278
Illnesses, 39–40
Imagen Galería de Arte (Panama City), 128
Independence Days, 33
Indigenous groups, 17, 280. See also specific groups
Ingana Art Shop (Boquete), 240
Insect repellent, 41
Insurance, 309
InterContinental Playa Bonita Resort & Spa, 72
International Association for Medical Assistance to Travelers (IAMAT), 39
The International Ecotourism Society (TIES), 44
International Expeditions, 62
International Festival of the Sea (Bocas Town), 33, 270
International Society of Travel Medicine, 39
International Specimen Salon (Panama City), 124
Internet access, 46, 309
Ireland, passports, 310
Isla Bastimentos, 264–265, 280–285
Isla Bastimentos National Marine Park, 3, 75, 280
Isla Bolaños, 248
Isla Carenero (Careening Cay), 278–280
Isla Cebaco, 255
Isla Chapera, 166–167
Isla Coiba National Park, 2, 3, 67, 252–255
Isla Colón, 260–278. See also Bocas Town
accommodations and restaurants around, 277
getting around, 263
orientation, 264
traveling to and from, 261–263
visitor information, 263
Isla Contadora, 165–170
Isla Cristóbal, 286
Isla de Coiba, 24
Isla Escudo de Veraguas, 267
Isla Gámez, 248
Isla Grande, 73, 159–162
Isla Hierba, 293
Isla Iguana Wildlife Refuge, 75
Islands, 50
Isla Pelicano, 293
Isla Perro, 293
Isla San José, 170–171
Isla Solarte (Nancy's Cay), 285
Islas Secas, 67, 69, 251
Isla Taboga, 135, 162–164

Isla Tigre, 297
Itineraries, suggested, 52–58

J

Jaguars, 142, 147, 225, 239, 304, 319
J & J Transparente Boat Tours, 268
Java Juice (Boquete), 245
Jazz Festival (Panama City), 32
Jewelry, Panama City, 129
Journey Latin America, 62
Jungle Land Explorers, 144

K

Karnak (Panama City), 132
Kayaking, 5, 70–71
Comarca Kuna Yala, 292
Panama City and vicinity, 146–147
Keel-billed toucan, 322–323
Kinkajou, 320
Kuna Cooperative (Panama City), 127
Kuna Indians, 17, 26, 287–288
society and culture, 296
Kuna Islands. See Comarca Kuna Yala

L

La Amistad International Park, 2, 7, 76
La Arena, 200
La Barqueta, 4
La Buga Dive & Surf (Bocas Town), 5, 268, 269
La Casona de las Brujas (Panama City), 133
La Exposición (Panama City), 85
Lago Gatún, 144–145
La Guaira, 159
Laguna Bocatorito, 286
Lagunas de Volcán, 221
La India Dormida, 186
La Marea, 302
La Mejorana festival (Guararé), 203
Land formations, 23
Languages, 22, 309
Languages in Action (Panama City), 113
La Península de Azuero, 4, 197–214
festivals and special events, 198
La Pintada, 195
La Represa (Panama City), 129
La Ronda (Panama City), 129
Las Cabanas Lounge (Boquete), 247
Las Cruces Trail, 143
Las Lajas, 219
Las Lajas, Chiriquí Province, 3–4
Las Pencas (Panama City), 132

Las Perlas Archipelago, 3,
  164–171
Las Tablas, 203–206
Las Tinajas (Panama City), 131
La Torcaza Estate (Volcán),
  221–222
Lavandería Diamond Dry
  Cleaners Plus (Panama City),
  89
Lavandería Flash (Panama City),
  89
La Villa de los Santos, 202–203
Lay of the land, 23–25
Leafcutter ants, 328
Leatherback sea turtle, 326
Leptospirosis, 40
Lips (Panama City), 134
Liquid (Panama City), 131
The Londoner (Panama City),
  133–134
Los Destiladores, 206, 207,
  209–210
Los Mandarinos Boutique Spa
  and Hotel, 72
Los Momótides (Panama City),
  121
Los Pozos Termales (Volcán),
  222
Los Quetzales Lodge & Spa, 72
Lost and found, 309–310
Lowland rainforests, 23

M

Magnificent frigate bird, 323
Mail, 310
Malaria, 39–40
Mamey Island, 160
Manatees, 326
Mantaray Golf Course (Playa
  Blanca), 183
Manta rays, 326
Mantled howler monkey, 322
Marcos A. Gelabert Airport
  (Albrook Airport), 35, 81
Margay, 320
Margo Tours, 64, 113, 139, 145
Markets. See also Handicrafts
  and gifts
  Bocas Town, 278
  Panama City, 126–128
MasterCard emergency number,
  310
Meals and dining customs, 27
MEDEX Assistance, 309
Medical requirements for entry,
  34
Mercado de Artesanías
  La Arena, 200
  La Pintada, 195
  Penonomé, 194
Mercado de Mariscos (Panama
  City), 126
Mercado Nacional de Artesanías
  (Panama City), 126

Mercado Público (Panama City),
  126
Metro Mall (Panama City), 126
Metropolitan Cathedral (Catedral
  Metropolitana; Panama City),
  116
Metropolitan Nature Park
  (Panama City), 8, 121–122
Mi Jardín es Su Jardín
  (Boquete), 238
Ministerio de Gobierno y Justicia
  (Panama City), 118
Mi Pueblito (Panama City), 120,
  129
Mirador el Perú (Portobelo), 155
Miraflores locks, 137–138
Mogue Emberá Indian
  community, 303
Mogue River, 6
Mondo Taitu (Bocas Town), 278
Monkeys, 77
Mono Tití Road (Panama City),
  121
Montezuma's oropendola,
  323–324
Moods (Panama City), 131–132
Moray eel, 327
Morro Negrito, 73
Morro Negrito Surf Camp (Isla
  Ensenada), 73, 219
Mosquitoes, 40
Motorcycling, 71
Mountain ranges, 50
Mouthless crab, 328
Movistar, 46
Multicentro (Panama City), 126
Multiplaza Pacific (Panama City),
  126
Museo Afroantillano (Panama
  City), 123
Museo Antropológico Reina
  Torres de Araúz (Panama
  City), 123–124
Museo de Arte Contemporáneo
  (Panama City), 124
Museo de Arte Religioso
  Colonial (Panama City), 119,
  124
Museo de Belisario Porras (Las
  Tablas), 203–204
Museo de Ciencias Naturales
  (Panama City), 124
Museo de Herrera (Chitré), 200
Museo de Historia y de Arte José
  de Obaldía (David), 216
Museo de la Historia de Panamá
  (Panama City), 116
Museo de la Nacionalidad (La
  Villa de los Santos), 202
Museo del Canal Interoceánico
  de Panamá (Panama City), 116,
  124–125
Museo del Valle (El Valle), 188
Museo de Penonomé, 194

Museo Manuel F. Zarate
  (Guararé), 203
Music, 26

N

Nancy's Cay (Isla Solarte), 285
Natá, 197
National car rentals, 36
National Theater (Panama City),
  118, 130
Natural history, books on, 26
Natural Metropolitan Park, 1
Nature Air, 262
Nature walks. See also specific
  destinations
  Altos de Campana National
    Park, 183–184
  best, 6–7
  Boquete, 232
  El Valle, 186
  Finca Suiza, 247
  Isla Coiba, 253
  Parque Internacional La
    Amistad, 225–226
  Volcán Barú National Park,
    224–225, 234–235
Newspapers and magazines, 310
New Zealand
  consular assistance, 308
  customs regulations, 34
  passports, 310
Next (Panama City), 132
Ngöbe-Buglé Indians (Guaymí),
  17, 189, 194, 222, 230, 232,
  237, 240, 247, 255, 280
Nívida Bat Cave, 282
Noriega, Manuel Antonio, 21–22,
  26, 80, 153, 188
Nuevo Centro Artesanal de
  David, 216
Nurse shark, 327

O

Ocean Pulse, 268
Ocelots, 320
Oficina Casco Antiguo (Panama
  City), 118
Olive ridley sea turtle, 326
Orchid Festival (Feria de
  Orquídeas; Boquete), 32, 239
Orgánica (Panama City), 102
Oscar's Bat Cave Tours (Bahía
  Honda), 282
Outdoors (Panama City), 129
Oz Bar and Lounge (Panama
  City), 132

P

Pachamana (Bocas Town), 278
Pacific Coast beaches, 173
Palacio Bolívar (Panama City),
  117–118

Palacio Presidencial (Panama City), 116
Palmar Surfcamp, 178
Palo de Mayo (Bocas Town), 270
Panaflores (Cerro Punta), 225
Panama Audubon Society, 67, 125
Panama Big Game Sportfishing Club, 69
The Panama Canal, 20–21, 135, 136–139
  books about, 26
Panama Canal Fishing, 145
Panama Canal Murals (Panama City), 120–121
Panama Canal Railway, 139
Panama City, 50, 79–134
  accommodations, 90–100
    aparthotels, 92–93
    inexpensive, 91
    neighborhoods, 90–91
  American Express, 88
  average monthly temperatures and rainfall in, 31
  biking, 65
  bookstores, 88
  crime and safety, 42
  doctors and dentists, 88–89
  drugstores, 89
  emergencies, 89
  express mail services, 89
  eyeglasses, 89
  finding addresses in, 84
  gays and lesbians, 134
  getting around, 86–88
  getting there and departing, 80–81
  grocery and specialty stores, 102
  hospitals, 89
  laundry and dry cleaning, 89
  layout of, 84–85
  neighborhoods in brief, 85–86
  nightlife, 130–134
  post office, 89–90
  restaurants, 101–112
    hotel restaurants, 101
  safety, 90
  shopping, 126–129
  sights and attractions, 112–125
  spectator sports and recreation, 125
  suggested itinerary, 58
  taxis, 86
  visitor information, 81, 84
  walking, 86–87
The Panama Deception (film), 27
Panama Dive, 68
Panama Divers, 67, 156, 254, 291
Panama Explorer Club, 187, 191
Panama Fishing & Catching, 68
Panama hats, 128

Panama Marine Adventures, 138
Panama Pete Adventures, 143, 145, 147
Panama Rafters, 4, 71, 221, 235, 236, 245
Panama Rainforest Discovery Center (near Panama City), 6
Panama Sailing, 74
Panama Surf Tours, 5, 73, 256
Panama Travel Experts (Panama City), 113
Panama Viejo (Panama City), 86
  sights and attractions, 114–115
Panama Viejo Visitors' Center & Museum (Panama City), 114
Panamax ships, 137
Panama Yacht Adventures, 73
Panama Yacht Club, 74
Paradise Gardens (Boquete), 78, 239
Parita, 198–199
Parks and reserves, 74–77
Parque Arqueológico El Caño, 196
Parque Internacional La Amistad, 225–226
Parque Miguel de Cervantes (David), 216
Parque Nacional del Darién, 7, 76, 304–306
Parque Nacional Marino Golfo de Chiriquí, 75, 248–252
Parque Nacional Marino Isla Bastimentos, 3, 75, 280
Parque Nacional Sarigua (Sarigua National Park), 200
Parque Nacional Volcán Barú, 2, 7, 76, 224–225
  exploring, 233–236
Parque Natural Metropolitano (Panama City), 121
Paseo Esteban Huertas (Panama City), 118
Passports, 33, 310
Peace Corps, 78
Pearl Islands (Archipiélago de las Perlas), 135, 164–171
Pearls, Casaya Island, 167
Pedasí, 206–210
Pedasi Sports Club, 68
PEMASKY (Project for the Study and Management of Wilderness Areas of Kuna Yala), 292
Península de Azuero, 4, 197–214
  festivals and special events, 198
Penonomé, 194
Pesantez Tours, 64, 113, 175, 182
Pesca Panama (Isla Coiba), 68, 253
Petrol, 309

Pipeline Road (Camino de Oleoducto; Soberanía National Park), 6, 7, 142–143
Pirre Mountain, 6
Pirre Station, 305
Planning your trip, 30–48
  calendar of events and festivals, 32–33
  customs regulations, 34
  entry requirements, 33–34
  getting around, 35–37
  health concerns, 38–41
  holidays, 31
  money and costs, 37–38
  safety, 42
  specialized travel resources, 42–44
  staying connected, 45–46
  traveling to Panama, 35
  when to go, 31
Plantation Trail, 142
Playa Arenal, 207
Playa Barqueta, 216
Playa Blanca, 157
Playa Cacique, 166
Playa Coronado, 176–178
Playa del Toro, 207
Playa Ejecutiva, 166
Playa El Palmar, 178–179
Playa Galeón, 166
Playa Gorgona, 176
Playa Kobbe (Playa Bonita), 175–176
Playa Larga, 166, 281
Playa Los Destiladores, 4
Playa Restinga, 163
Playa Segunda (Second Beach), 280
Playa Suecas (Swedish Beach), 166
Playa Venado, 4, 73, 206, 210–211
Plaza Bolívar (Panama City), 117
Plaza de Francia (Panama City), 118
Plaza de la Independencia (Panama City), 116
Plaza Herrera (Panama City), 119
Police, 310
Polleras, 203
Polo Beach, 267
Pond Trail, 142
Poor man's umbrella, 330
Portobelo, 135, 154–159
Pozos Termales
  El Valle, 187
  Volcán, 222
Prescription medications, 39
Presidential Palace (Panama City), 116
Prostitution, 130
Puma, 320–321
Punta Culebra Marine Exhibition Center (Panama City), 8, 122

Punta Galeón Resort, 9
Punta G (Panama City), 134
Punta Patiño, 303–304
**Punta Patiño Nature Reserve,
8, 76–77**

Q
Quantum of Solace (film), 27
Quetzal, resplendent, 7, 323
Volcán Barú National Park,
233
Quetzal Trail, 6, 10, 224, 229

R
**Rainforest Discovery Center
(near Panama City), 148**
Rainforests, lowland, 23
**Real Aduana de Portobelo
(Customs House), 155**
Red brocket deer, 320
Red-eyed tree frog, 324
Red Frog Beach, 260, 282
**Red Frog Beach Club
(Bastimentos), 280**
Reef and Rainforest Tours, 62
**Refugio de Vida Silvestre
(David), 216–217**
**Refugio de Vida Silvestre Isla de
Cañas (near Playa Venado),
210**
Regions in brief, 49–52
RELIC (Panama City), 134
Reprosa (Panama City), 129
Reptiles, 324
Resplendent quetzal, 7, 323
Volcán Barú National Park,
233
Responsible tourism, 44–45, 78
Restaurant La Torre, 159
Restaurants. *See also*
Restaurants Index
best, 14–15
Central Panama road stops
and hole in the walls, 174
menu terms, 317–318
Restrooms, 310
Río Mar Surf Camp, 73
Riptides, 42
**Riva-Smith grocery store
(Panama City), 102**
River rafting. *See* White-water
rafting

S
Safety, 42
in the wilderness, 77–78
Sailing (yachting), 73–74
Comarca Kuna Yala, 293
**St. Francis of Assisi, Church and
Convent of (Panama City), 118**
**Salón Bolívar (Panama City),
117–118**
Salt Creek, 281
Salt Creek Village, 280

**San Benito Crafts School
(Volcán), 222**
San Blas Archipelago, 287. *See
also* Comarca Kuna Yala
San Blas Sailing, 74, 293
San San Pond Sak Wetlands, 266
Santa Catalina, 73, 254–260
Santa Clara, 4, 179–181
**Sarigua National Park (Parque
Nacional Sarigua), 77, 200**
Scarlet macaw, 323
Scuba Charters, 255–256
Scuba Coiba, 256
Scuba diving, 5, 67–68
Bocas del Toro, 267–269
Chiriquí Gulf, 248–249
Isla Coiba, 252, 254
Isla Contadora, 167
Isla Grande, 160
Pedasí, 207
Portobelo, 156–157
Santa Catalina, 255–256
Scuba Panama, 68
Scubaportobelo, 156
Seafood, 28
Seakunga Adventures, 71
Sea life, 325–328
Seasons, 31
Seco, 29
**Second Beach (Playa Segunda),
280**
Selvaventuras (Portobelo), 157
Semana Santa, 32
Azuero Peninsula, 198
Sendero Cerro Picacho, 225–226
Sendero Charco (Pond Trail), 142
Sendero de los Monos, 253
Sendero El Plantación, 142
Sendero El Retoño, 225
Sendero La Cascada, 225
Sendero La Cruz, 183–184
Sendero Los Quetzales, 234
Sendero Puma Verde, 225
Senior travel, 43
Serpentario (El Valle), 188
Sierra Llorona, 149
Sitio Barriles (near Volcán), 221
Sloth, three-toed, 322
**Smithsonian Rainforest Canopy
Crane (Panama City), 121–122**
**Smithsonian Tropical Research
Institute (Bocas Town), 270**
Smoking, 311
Snacks, 27–28
Snakes, 41
Serpentario (El Valle), 188
Snorkeling, 67–68
Bocas del Toro, 267–268
Chiriquí Gulf, 248–249
Hospital Point, 285
Isla Coiba, 252, 254
Isla Contadora, 167
Portobelo, 156–157
**Soberanía National Park, 1–2, 7,
74, 135, 142–144, 266**
Soposo Rainforest, 266

**Soposo Rainforest Adventures,
266**
**Souvenir El Cacique (Boquete),
240**
**Spa Flora Bella (Bocas Town),
270**
**Spanish Abroad, Inc. (Panama
City), 113**
Spanish-language classes
Bocas Town, 269
Boquete, 238
Panama City, 112–113
**Spanish Panama (Panama City),
112–113**
Spas, 71–72
Bocas Town, 270
Boquete, 233
El Valle, 188–189
Panama City, 125
**Special events and festivals,
32–33**
Spider monkey, 322
Spirit Airlines, 35
Sport fishing. *See* Fishing
Sportline (Panama City), 129
Starfish Beach, 264, 265
**Starfleet Scuba (Bocas Town),
266, 267–268, 270**
Stingrays, 326
Strangler fig, 329
Sugar & Spice (Boquete), 245
**Summit Gardens Park & Zoo
(near Panama City), 9, 78, 147**
Summit Golf & Resort, 69
Sunday Market (El Valle), 189
Sun exposure, 41
Sunset Cruise (Bocas Town), 278
Sunstroke, 41
SUPERCKLIN (Panama City), 89
Super Gourmet
Bocas Town, 274
Panama City, 102
Surfing, 5, 72–73
Bocas del Toro, 269
Morro Negrito Surf Camp
(Isla Ensenada), 219
Santa Catalina, 256
Sustainable tourism, 44–45
Swan's Cay, 265, 267

T
Taboga Island, 162–164
Taboga Wildlife Refuge, 163
The Tailor of Panama (film), 27
Taxes, 311
Teatro ABA (Panama City), 130
**Teatro Anita Villalaz (Panama
City), 131**
**Teatro en Círculo (Panama City),
130–131**
**Teatro la Quadra (Panama City),
130**
**Teatro Nacional (Panama City),
118, 130**
Telechip, 311

Telephones, 45, 311
Teribe (Naso) Indians, 17
Three-toed sloth, 322
Thrifty, 36
Ticks, 40
Tienda Artesanía (El Valle), 189
TIES (The International
    Ecotourism Society), 44
Tiger Rock, 267
Time zone, 311
Tipping, 311
Tocumen International Airport,
    35, 80
Torre de la Catedral (Panama
    City), 114–115
Tour operators and outfitters
    North American, 60, 62
    Panamanian, 63–64
    U.K.-based, 62
Traffic Island (Panama City), 132
Travel Assistance International,
    309
Traveler's checks, 38
Traveler's diarrhea, 40
Traveling to Panama, 35
Trees, 328–330
Trekking the Camino Real, 5
Trogons, 8, 66, 75, 143, 153, 184,
    212, 221, 323
Tropical illnesses, 39–40
Tropic Star Lodge, 5, 69
Tropix (Bocas Town), 269
Truchas Bambito, 226

U

United Kingdom
    customs regulations, 34
    embassy, 308
    health insurance, 309
    passports, 310
United States
    customs regulations, 34
    embassy, 308
    passports, 310
Urriola, Mario, 187

V

Vegetables, 28
Veneto Hotel & Casino, 72
Vía España (Panama City), 126
Victor Emanuel Nature Tours, 66
Violet hummingbirds, 184
Visa emergency number, 309
Visas, 33–34
Vita Luxury Spa & Holistic
    Wellness Center (Panama
    City), 125
Voice-Over Internet Protocol
    (VoIP), 46
Volcán, 219–224
Volcán Barú National Park, 2, 7,
    76, 224–225
    exploring, 233–236
Volcancito Loop, 232

Volunteer travel, 44–45
    ecologically oriented
    volunteer and study
    programs, 78

W

Wasabi Sushi Lounge (Panama
    City), 132
Water, drinking, 311
The Western Highlands, 52,
    212–257. See also Chiriquí
    Highlands
Western Union, 310
Western Wind Nature (Volcán),
    220–221
Whale shark, 325
White-tipped sicklebills, 184
White-water rafting, 4, 70–71
    Chiriquí Highlands, 235–236
Wi-Fi access, 46
Wildland Adventures, 62
Wildlife, 319–330. See also
    Adventure travel; Birds and
    bird-watching; Zoos
    products made from
    endangered, 127
    tips for seeing, 25
Wine Bar (Panama City), 134
Wizard Beach (First Beach),
    280, 282
Women travelers, 43–44
The Wounaan, 17

X

Xtrop, 5, 71, 292, 297

Y

Yachting and sailing, 73–74
Yellow fever, 39
YMCA Handicrafts Market
    (Panama City), 127
Yogini Spa (El Valle), 72, 188

Z

Zane Grey Reef, 306–307
Zanzíbar (Boquete), 247
Zapatilla Cays, 265, 267
Zoos
    El Nispero Zoo (El Valle),
    187–188
    Summit Gardens Park & Zoo
    (near Panama City), 9, 78,
    147

Accommodations

Albrook Inn (Panama City), 98
Al Natural (Isla Bastimentos),
    283
Anton Valley Hotel (El Valle), 192
Arco Properties (Panama City),
    99

Bananas Resort (Isla Grande),
    161
Bay View Resort (Playa El
    Palmar), 178–179
Best Western (David), 217
Best Western Las Huacas Hotel
    and Suites (Panama City), 96
Bocas Inn (Bocas Town), 271
Bocas Paradise Hotel (near
    Bocas Town), 272
Boquete Garden Inn, 240
Boquete Paradise Suites, 241
Breezes Resort & Spa (Farallón),
    181
Bristol Buenaventura (Farallón),
    181–182
The Bristol Panama (Panama
    City), 93
Burbayar Lodge (El Llano), 171
Cabañas de Playa Gorgona, 176
Cabanas Fistonich (Nueva
    Suiza), 226
Cabañas Kuanidup, 296–297
Cabañas Kucikas (Bambito), 226
Cabanas La Cholita (Isla
    Grande), 160
Cabanas Momentum B&B
    (Boquete), 243
Cabañas Ukuptupu, 294
Cabañas Villanita (Playa
    Gorgona), 176
Cabañas Wailidup, 295
Cala Mia (Isla Brava), 249–250
The Canal House (Panama City),
    99
Canopy Lodge (El Valle), 190
Canopy Tower (road to
    Gamboa), 147–148
Careening Cay (Isla Carenero),
    279
Casa Acuario (Isla Carenero),
    279
Casa Cayuco (Isla Bastimentos),
    283–284
Casa del Sol (Isla Contadora),
    168
Casa Grande (Bambito), 227
Casa Margarita (Pedasí),
    207–208
Central Hotel (Panama City), 99
Cerrito Tropical (Isla Taboga),
    163–164
Cerro La Vieja (Caimito),
    195–196
Cielito Sur (Nueva Suiza), 227
Club Gaviota (Playa Coronado),
    177
Cocomo-on-the-Sea (near Bocas
    Town), 272
Coco Plum Cabañas (near
    Portobelo), 157
The Coffee Estate Inn (Boquete),
    241
Contadora Island Inn, 168

Coral Lodge (near Isla Grande), 161–162, 288
Coral Suites Aparthotel (Panama City), 92
Coronado Golf & Beach Resort, 177
Corowalk Inn (Playa Coronado), 177–178
Country Inn & Suites-Panama Canal, 97
Courtyard Marriott (Panama City), 93
Crater Valley Adventure Spa (El Valle), 190–191
Crowne Plaza (Panama City), 93
Dad Ibe Lodge (Isla Ailigandi), 298
Davis Suites (Colón), 151
Dim's Hostal (Pedasí), 208
The Dolphin Lodge (Isla Uaguitupu), 298
Dos Palmitos Bed & Breakfast (Panama City), 98
Eclypse de Mar Acqua Lodge (Isla Bastimentos), 284
Eco Venao (Playa Venado), 210
Executive Hotel (Panama City), 96
Finca Don Flor de Café (Portobelo), 157
Finca Lérida (Boquete), 240
Finca Suiza Lodge (near David), 247–248
Four Points by Sheraton (Panama City), 93
Gamboa Rainforest Resort, 148
The Golden Frog Inn (El Valle), 191
Gone Fishing (Boca Chica), 250
Gran Hotel Bahía (near Bocas Town), 272
Gran Hotel Nacional (David), 217–218
Hacienda del Mar (Isla San José), 170–171
Hacienda del Toro (Isla Cristóbal), 286
Harbor Inn B&B (Colón), 151
Hostal Amador Familiar, 91
Hostal Cariguana (El Valle), 189–190
Hostal La Casa de Carmen (Panama City), 91
Hotel & Restaurante Los Capitanes (El Valle), 191
Hotel Bambito (Bambito), 227
Hotel Bocas del Toro (near Bocas Town), 272–273
Hotel California (Panama City), 100
Hotel Canadian (Chame), 176
Hotel Casa Max (near Bocas Town), 273–274
Hotel Castilla (David), 217

Hotel Cerro Punta, 227–228
Hotel Costa Inn (Panama City), 100
Hotel DeVille (Panama City), 94
Hotel Doña Mara (Isla Carenero), 279
Hotel Don Pepe (El Valle), 189
Hotel Dos Ríos (Volcán), 223
Hotel El Limbo on the Beach (Isla Bastimentos), 283
Hotel El Limbo on the Sea (near Bocas Town), 273
Hotel El Parador (Panama City), 96–97
Hotel El Porvenir, 295
Hotel Guayacanes (Chitré), 201
Hotel Hibiscus Garden (Santa Catalina), 256
Hotel Hong Kong (Chitré), 201
Hotel Isla Grande (Isla Grande), 160
Hotel Laguna (near Bocas Town), 273
Hotel La Pradera (Penonomé), 195
Hotel la Villa (La Villa de los Santos), 202–203
Hotel Marbella (Panama City), 97
Hotel Milan (Panama City), 97
Hotel Oasis (Boquete), 244
Hotel Petit Mozart (Boquete), 244
Hotel Piamonte y Restaurante (Las Tablas), 204–205
Hotel Puerta del Sol (David), 217
Hotel Rex (Chitré), 201
Hotel Rincón Vallero (El Valle), 191–192
Hotel Sereia do Mar (Playa Venado), 210
Hotel Versalles (Chitré), 202
Hotel y Restaurante Don Tavo (Volcán), 223
InterContinental Miramar (Panama City), 100
InterContinental Playa Bonita Resort & Spa (Playa Kobbe), 175–176
Isla Contadora Villa Romántica, 169
Islas Secas, 251–252
Isla Verde Hotel (Boquete), 243
Kalima Suites (Boquete), 240
Kuna Niskua Lodge (Isla Wichubwala), 296
La Buena Vida (Santa Catalina), 256
La Estancia (Panama City), 98
La Iguana Eco-Resort (Churuquita Grande), 196
La Loma Jungle Lodge (Isla Bastimentos), 284
La Playita (Playa Venado), 211

La Popa Paradise Beach Resort (Isla Bastimentos), 285
Las Brisas del Mar (Playa Barqueta), 218
Las Clementinas Hotelito (Panama City), 99
Las Olas Resort (Playa Barqueta), 218
Las Plumas (between Volcán and Cerro Punta), 228
Las Sirenas (Santa Clara), 179–180
Las Vegas Hotel Suites (Panama City), 92
Las Veraneras (Santa Clara), 180
La Veranda (near Bocas Town), 274
Le Meridien Hotel (Panama City), 100
Los Cuatro Tulipanes (Panama City), 99
Los Establos (near Boquete), 241–242
Los Mandarinos Hotel and Spa (El Valle), 190
Los Quetzales Lodge & Spa (Guadalupe), 228
Lula's Bed & Breakfast (near Bocas Town), 274
Luna Castle Hostel (Panama City), 99
Meliá Panama Canal (Colón), 153
Mountain River Lake Inn (Volcán), 223
New Washington Hotel (Colón), 151–152
Oasis Surf Camp (Santa Catalina), 256–257
Octopus Garden Hotel (Portobelo), 157–158
Pacific Bay Resort (Boca Chica), 250
Panama Big Game Sportfishing Club (Boca Brava Island), 250–251
The Panama Marriott Hotel (Panama City), 94
Panamonte Inn & Spa (Boquete), 242
Park Eden Bed & Breakfast (El Valle), 192
Pedasí Sports Club, 208
Perla Real Inn (Isla Contadora), 168
Pipa's (Playa Blanca), 183
Playa Blanca Resort (Farallón), 182
Playa Mango Resort (near Bocas Town), 277
Playa Tortuga Resort (Bocas Town), 270–271
Plaza Paitilla Inn (Panama City), 100
Posada los Destiladores, 209

Punta Caracol (near Bocas Town), 277
Punta Galeón Resort & Restaurant (Isla Contadora), 169
Purple House Hostel (David), 217
Radisson Colón 2000, 152
Radisson Decapolis Hotel (Panama City), 94–95
Rancho de Caldera (near Boquete), 248
Residencial el Valle (El Valle), 189
Residencial Moscoso (Pedasí), 208
Residencial Pedasí, 208
Residencial Piamonte (Las Tablas), 205
Restaurante El Palacio Oriental (David), 218
Riande Continental Hotel (Panama City), 95
Riverside Inn (Boquete), 242
Royal Decameron Beach Resort, Golf, Spa & Casino (Farallón), 182–183
Sapibenega Kuna Lodge (Isla Iskardup), 298–299
Seagull Cove Lodge (Boca Chica), 251
Sevilla Suites (Panama City), 92
Sheraton Panama Hotel and Convention Center (Panama City), 95
Sierra Llorona Panama Lodge (near Sabanitas), 149
Sister Moon Hotel (Isla Grande), 161
Soberanía Lodge (Gamboa), 148–149
Suites Ambassador (Panama City), 92–93
Sunset Cabins (Portobelo), 158
Swan's Cay Hotel (near Bocas Town), 273
Taverna Libanesa (David), 218
Tierra Verde (Isla Carenero), 279–280
Tinamou Cottage Jungle Lodge (Boquete), 242
Torres del Alba (Panama City), 93
Tranquilo Bay (Isla Bastimentos), 285
Tropical Suites (near Bocas Town), 271–272
Tropic Star Lodge (Piñas Bay), 306–307
Valle del Rio Inn (Boquete), 240
Valle Escondido (Boquete), 242–243
Veneto Hotel & Casino (Panama City), 95–96

Vereda Tropical Hotel (Isla Taboga), 164
Villa Camilla (Los Destiladores), 209–210
Villa Marina (Playa Venado), 211
Villa Marita (Boquete), 243–244
XS Memories (Santa Clara), 180

Restaurants

Alberto's Pizza & Pasta (Panama City), 111
Al Tambor de la Alegría (Panama City), 111
Anton Valley Hotel (El Valle), 192
Art Café La Crepe (Boquete), 246
Bambusillo (El Valle), 192
Beirut (Panama City), 108
Blanca's (Santa Catalina), 257
Blue Garden Restaurant (Bambito), 227
Bollos Chorreranos (near Chorrera), 174
Bucanero (Panama City), 110
Buena Vista Grill (Bocas Town), 276
Café Punto de Encuentro (Boquete), 245
Café Rene (Panama City), 105
Cafetería Manolo's (Panama City), 109
Caffè Pomodoro (Panama City), 109
Candy Rose (Isla Grande), 160
Can Oliver (Panama City), 103
Casa Vegeteriana (David), 217
Casa Vegeteriana (Panama City), 101
Club Punta Proa (Isla Grande), 160
Costa Azul (Panama City), 106–107
Crawl Cay Restaurant, 282
Crepes & Waffles (Panama City), 104
Cumana (El Valle), 192–193
Doña Mara Restaurant (Isla Carenero), 279
Donde Pope Si Hay (Isla Taboga), 163
Don Pepe (El Valle), 194
Dulcerías Yely (Pedasí), 209
Ego y Narcisco (Panama City), 106
El Aquario (Isla Taboga), 163
El Callejon del Gato (Panama City), 106
El Mesón (Chitré), 201
El Nido del Postre (Isla Grande), 160
El Pecado (Bocas Town), 275

El Rincón Vallero (El Valle), 193
El Trapiche (Panama City), 109–110
El Ultimo Refugio (Bocas Town), 275
El Valle Gourmet & Coffee Shop, 192
Estrella Volcanera Restaurant (Volcán), 223
Eurasia (Panama City), 102
Fresas Mary (Boquete), 244
Greenhouse (Panama City), 103
Guari Guari (Bocas Town), 275
Hotel y Restaurante Don Tavo (Volcán), 223
Il Forno Restaurant (Volcán), 224
Il Pianista (Boquete), 245
Jamming (Santa Catalina), 257
Juice Bar (El Valle), 192
Kiosco El Ciruelo (La Villa de los Santos), 203La Casa de Lourdes (El Valle), 193
La Casona Mexicana (Boquete), 246
La Popa (Isla Contadora), 169
La Posta (Panama City), 103
Las Barandas (Panama City), 107
Las Tinajas (Panama City), 110
Lemongrass (Bocas Town), 276
Leños y Carbón (Panama City), 110–111
Lima Limon (Panama City), 102
Los Capitanes (El Valle), 193–194
Macarena (Panama City), 106
Machu Picchu (Boquete), 245
Machu Picchu (Panama City), 107
Madame Chang (Panama City), 108
Manolo Caracol (Panama City), 105
Market (Panama City), 103–104
Martín Fierro (Panama City), 109
Masala (Panama City), 102
Matsui (Panama City), 107
McDouglas' Golden Grill (Bocas Town), 274
Miraflores Visitors Center Restaurant (Panama Canal), 137
Mi Ranchito (Panama City), 111–112
Mostaza (Panama City), 105
Napoli (Panama City), 104
New York Bagel (Panama City), 107
Niko's Café (Panama City), 101
9° Restaurant and Market (Bocas Town), 275
Om Café (Bocas Town), 276
Palms (Panama City), 102
Panamonte Inn Restaurant (Boquete), 245–246

Parrilla Argentina (Santa Catalina), 257
Parus (Panama City), 112
Pelicano's (Isla Contadora), 169
Penquino's (Santa Catalina), 257
Pizzería Pinocchio's (El Valle), 194
Pizzeria Portofino (Las Tablas), 205
Polineth (Volcán), 223
Pony Rosso Café (Panama City), 105
Puerta de la Tierra (Panama City), 105
Queso Chela (kilometer 57 west of Panama City), 174
Reef (Bocas Town), 276
Restaurant & Pizzería El Caserón (Las Tablas), 205
Restaurante Balneario Santa Clara, 180

Restaurante Caballo Loco (Portobelo), 158
Restaurante Cerro Brujo (Volcán), 224
Restaurante Geralds (Isla Contadora), 169-170
Restaurante Los Camisones (Santa Clara), 181
Restaurante Los Cañones (Portobelo), 158
Restaurante Los Faroles (Las Tablas), 205-206
Restaurante Lourdes (Boquete), 245
Restaurante Mary (Volcán), 223
Restaurante 1985 (Panama City), 107-108
Restaurante Romántico (Isla Contadora), 169
Restaurante Sagitario (Isla Contadora), 170

Restaurant Las Anclas (Portobelo), 158-159
Restaurant Mercado del Marisco (Panama City), 107
Restaurant Terrazas del Mar (near Vista Mar), 178
Restaurant Yasinori (Bocas del Drago), 277
Rincón Catracho (Playa Gorgona), 176
Rincon del Chef (Coronado), 178
Rincón Suizo (Panama City), 108
Roots (Bastimentos Town), 280
Sabrosón (Boquete), 246-247
Santa Librada (El Valle), 192
S'cena (Panama City), 105-106
Shelley's BBQ (Bocas Town), 276-277
Sushi Itto (Panama City), 104
Tammy's (Boquete), 245
Villa En Sueño (Isla Grande), 160